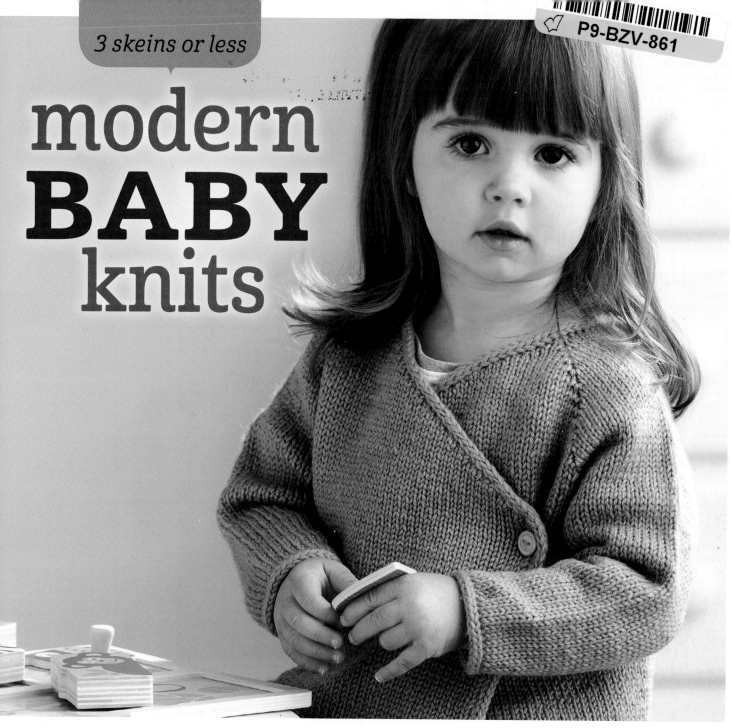

3 skeins or less

modern BABY knits

23 knitted baby garments, blankets, toys, and more! ✳ **TANIS GRAY**

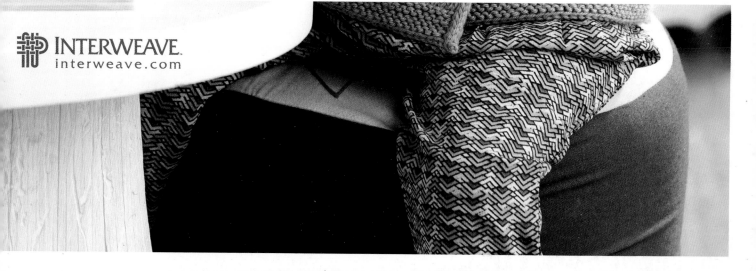

⊞ INTERWEAVE
interweave.com

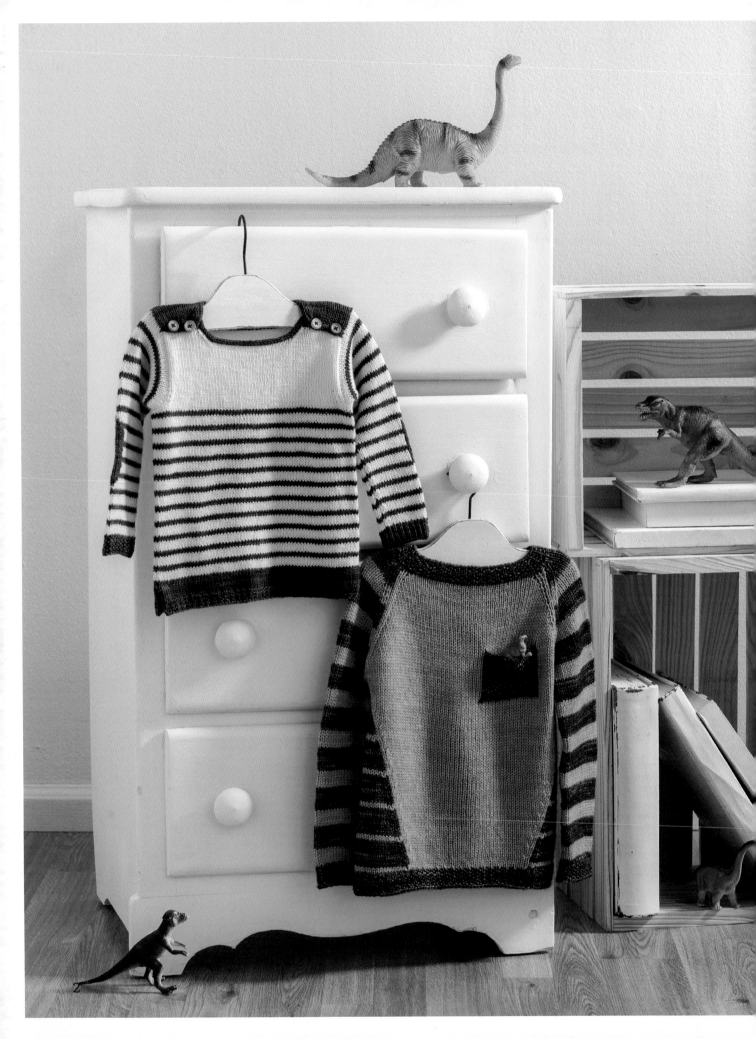

Contents

4 INTRODUCTION

THE PROJECTS

6 Fox Hat and Vest
Ekaterina Blanchard

12 Nature Blocks
Elizabeth Murphy

18 Rainbow Bonnet and Mitten Set
Lisa Chemery

22 Polka-Dot Pocket Pullover
Suvi Simola

28 Modern Filigree Baby Blanket
Tanis Gray

32 New Leaf Bonnet
Melissa LaBarre

36 Nuage Pullover
Nadia Crétin-Léchenne

42 Stripy Romper
Kate Oates

48 Diamond Pullover
Suvi Simola

54 Elizabeth Tunic
Taiga Hilliard

60 Wallie and Carter:
A Pair of Curious Bears
Rebecca Danger

66 Kimono
Karen Borrel

70 Chevron Pants
Justine Turner

74 Baby Tunic
Terri Kruse

78 Wee Ones Fair Isle Hats
Tanis Gray

82 Modern Chevron Dress
Raya Budrevich

86 Striped Jersey
Julie Partie

92 Reston Blanket
Kelly Herdrich

96 Zigzag Vest
Helen Rose

100 Camaro Pullover
Svetlana Volkova

104 Geometric Baby Blanket
Shannon Cook

108 Eyelet Dress
Megan Grewal

114 Bunny
Melissa Schaschwary

119 GLOSSARY

124 CONTRIBUTORS

125 ABOUT THE AUTHOR

126 SOURCES FOR YARNS

126 ABBREVIATIONS

127 DEDICATION AND
ACKNOWLEDGMENTS

Introduction

I am a firm believer that babies and children should live their lives in comfortable handknits. The label "handmade" regarding knits for children is often confused with "fussy" and "finicky" and implies tiny gauge and a pastel palette, when that doesn't have to be the case.

This book is designed with both the knitter and the wearer in mind, chock-full of designs that are easy to knit and have fuss-free finishing, bright colors, easy-care fibers, and modern silhouettes that little ones will want to wear. Having a young son myself, the thought of him staying still and perfectly clean in a garment that took ages to knit is nothing short of impossible! Children should be able to move, wiggle, dance, pretend, and play, all while wearing beautiful handmade garments, knit by those who love them. Don't tuck those kid knits away after a family photo session— let them live their life in them and wear them daily!

Designed by knitters around the world with a limited quantity of skeins and multiple yarn weights represented, these garments are fresh, modern, colorful, and—most important—practical and fun to knit with no fuss.

Featuring twenty-four patterns including pullovers, pants, rompers, accessories, dresses, blankets, and toys, whether you're knitting for your children or someone else's, these designs will not only stand the test of time, but they also can be knit with just a few special skeins of yarn you've been waiting to use.

From one mama to another, may your child's life be filled with love, knowledge, play, laughter, and handknits!

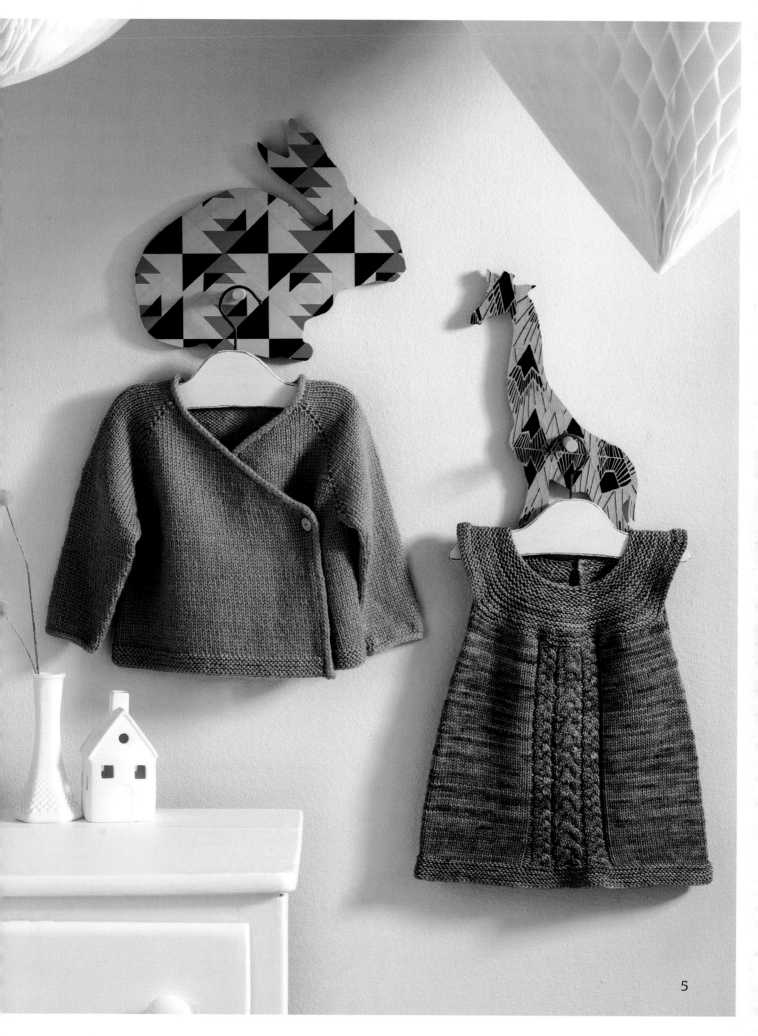

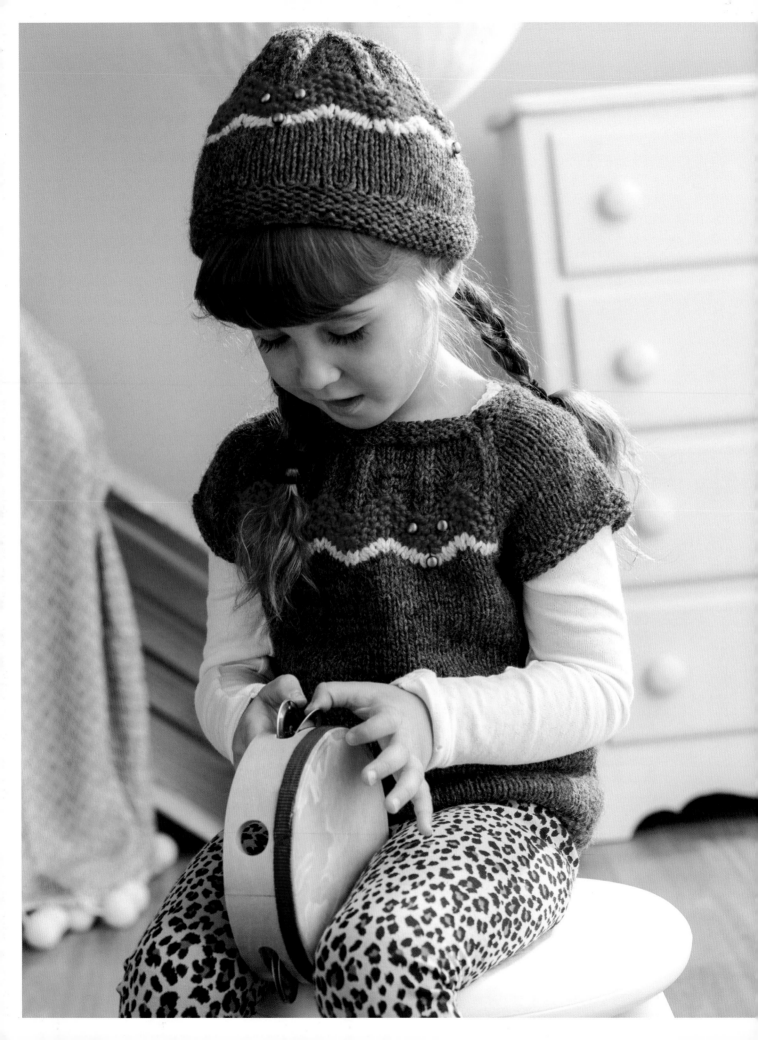

Fox
HAT AND VEST

EKATERINA BLANCHARD

The little one in your life will fall head over heels with this matching set. Foxes are an adorable unisex motif that will recall your favorite characters, from Aesop's Fables to Richard Scarry.

FINISHED SIZE

Hat

Preemie (3 months, 9 months, 18 months).

About 10 (12, 14, 16)" (25.5 [30.5, 35.5, 40.5] cm) circumference at brim and 4¼ (5¼, 6, 7¼)" (11 [13.5, 15, 18.5] cm) tall.

Hat shown measures 16" (40.5 cm).

Vest

6 months (9 months, 18 months, 24 months, 3T).

About 18¾ (19½, 20½, 22¼, 24)" (47.5 [49.5, 52, 56.5, 61] cm) chest circumference.
Vest shown measures 24" (61 cm).

YARN

Chunky weight (#5 Bulky).

Shown here: Cascade Yarns Eco+ (100% wool; 478 yd (437 m)/250 g): #8400 Charcoal Grey (gray; A), and #0958 Cinnamon (orange; B), 1 skein each, and Cascade Yarns Ecological Wool (100% Peruvian Highland wool; 478 yd (437 m)/250 g): #8010 Ecru (white; C), 1 skein.

NEEDLES

Hat ribbing: Size U.S. 6 (4 mm): 16" (40.5 cm) circular (cir).

Hat body: Size U.S. 7 (4.5 mm): 16" (40.5 cm) cir and set of 4 or 5 double-pointed (dpn).

Vest: Size U.S. 7 (4.5 mm): 16" (40.5 cm) cir, 32" (81.5 cm) cir, and set of dpn.

Adjust needle size if necessary to obtain the correct gauge.

NOTIONS

Markers (m); stitch holders or waste yarn; tapestry needle; sewing needle and matching thread; round shank buttons: 6 (9, 9, 12) for hat and 3 for vest.

GAUGE

18 sts and 24 rnds = 4" (10 cm) in St st on larger needles after blocking.

NOTES

The beanie features a colored chevron motif that is easy on the hand. It is worked entirely in the round from the bottom up and has a snug fit.

The vest follows a raglan construction and is worked in one piece from the bottom up. The lower body is worked in the round from the lower edge to the underarms. After completing the lower body, the sleeve cuffs are worked in the round, then joined to the body stitches. The yoke is worked in rows to the shoulders and neck. A small chevron motif is placed on the front and turned into a delicate fox muzzle using small round buttons.

Fox Hat

Brim

Using the long-tail method (see Glossary) CO 40 (48, 56, 64) sts onto smaller cir. Knit 1 row.

Place marker (pm) for beg of rnd and join for working in rnds, being careful not to twist sts. Work in garter st for 5 (5, 7, 9) rnds.

Next rnd: (inc) *K3, k1f&b; rep from * to end—50 (60, 70, 80) sts.

Body

With larger cir, work in St st for 5 (7, 9, 11) rnds.

Work Rnds 1–10 of Chevron chart once, working 10-st rep 5 (6, 7, 8) times.

Work Rnds 9 and 10 of Chevron chart 0 (1, 2, 4) more time(s).

Crown

Change to dpn when there are too few sts to work comfortably on cir.

Rnd 1: With A, *ssk, k6, k2tog; rep from * to end—40 (48, 56, 64) sts.

Rnd 2: Knit.

Rnd 3: *Ssk, k4, k2tog; rep from * to end—30 (36, 42, 48) sts.

Rnd 4: Knit.

Rnd 5: *Ssk, k2, k2tog; rep from * to end—20 (24, 28, 32) sts.

Rnd 6: Knit.

Rnd 7: *Ssk, k2tog; rep from * to end—10 (12, 14, 16) sts.

Rnd 8: Knit.

For smallest size:
Skip to Finishing section.

For all other sizes:
Rnd 9: *K2tog; rep from * to end—(6, 7, 8) sts.

Rnd 10: Knit.

Finishing

Cut yarn, leaving a 7" (18 cm) tail. Thread tail on tapestry needle, draw through rem sts, and pull tight to close hole.

Using sewing needle and matching thread, sew buttons to Chevron patt as shown in photograph.

Weave in loose ends. Wet-block (see Glossary) hat to measurements.

Fox Vest

Body

With A and longer cir, use the long-tail method (see Glossary) to CO 68 (74, 78, 86, 94) sts. Knit 1 row.

Place marker (pm) for beg of rnd and join for working in rnds, being careful not to twist sts.

Work in garter st for 3 rnds.

Next rnd: (inc) *K3 (4, 4, 5, 5) sts, k1f&b; rep from * to last 4 (4, 8, 2, 10) sts, knit to end—84 (88, 92, 100, 108) sts.

Work even in St st until piece measures 7¾ (8, 8¾, 9, 10)" (19.5 [20.5, 22, 23, 25.5] cm) from CO edge.

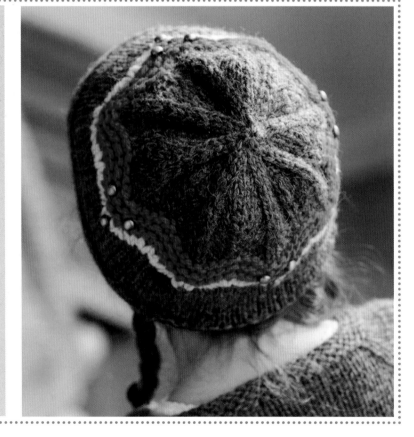

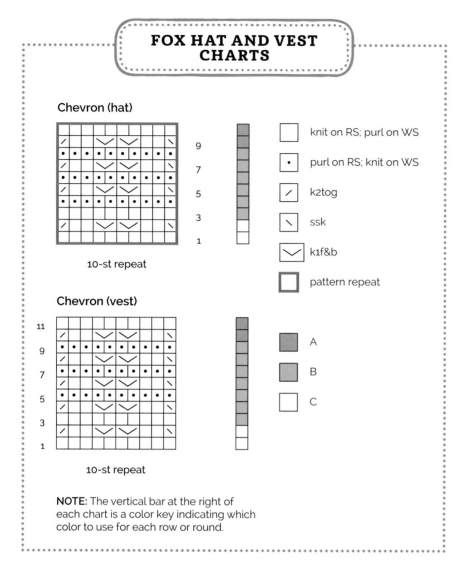

FOX HAT AND VEST CHARTS

Chevron (hat)

9
7
5
3
1

10-st repeat

Chevron (vest)

11
9
7
5
3
1

10-st repeat

□ knit on RS; purl on WS

• purl on RS; knit on WS

╱ k2tog

╲ ssk

⌄ k1f&b

□ pattern repeat

▨ A

▨ B

□ C

NOTE: The vertical bar at the right of each chart is a color key indicating which color to use for each row or round.

Sleeves

With dpn, CO 30 (32, 34, 34, 40) sts. Arrange sts as evenly as possible on dpn. Knit 1 row. Pm for beg of rnd and join for working in rnds, being careful not to twist sts.

Work in garter st for 3 rnds.

Next rnd: Knit to 4 (3, 3, 4, 5) sts before end of rnd, place next 8 (6, 6, 8, 10) sts on stitch holder or waste yarn for underarm. Place rem 22 (26, 28, 26, 30) sleeve sts on second holder. Cut yarn, leaving a long tail.

Rep for other sleeve.

Yoke

JOIN SLEEVES AND BODY

The body sts held on the longer cir are now joined to the sleeve sts. The yoke is then worked flat using the longer cir to accommodate the large number of sts.

Set-up row: (RS) Place first 4 (3, 3, 4, 5) body sts on holder for left under-arm, use the backward-loop method (see Glossary) to CO 1 st, knit next 34 (38, 40, 42, 44) body sts, place next 8 (6, 8, 8, 10) body sts on holder for right underarm, pm, knit 22 (26, 28, 26, 30) held sts from first sleeve, pm, knit next 34 (38, 40, 42, 44) body sts

and place next 4 (3, 3, 4, 5) body sts on holder for left underarm, pm, knit 22 (26, 28, 26, 30) held sts from second sleeve, then use the backward-loop method to CO 1 st.

The sleeves are now attached to the body—114 (130, 138, 138, 150) yoke sts; 1 st at each edge, 34 (38, 40, 42, 44) sts each for front and back, and 22 (26, 28, 26, 30) sts for each sleeve. The live underarm sts from sleeves and body are on holders and will be grafted together later.

Next row: (WS) Purl.

SHAPE YOKE
Set-Up
Work dec according to chosen size as foll:

Sizes 18¾ (24)"
Next row: (RS—dec) K1, sssk (see Abbreviations), knit to 3 sts before m, k3tog, sl m, knit to m, sl m, ssk, knit to 2 sts before m, k2tog, sl m, knit to end—108 (144) sts.

Size 19½"
Row 1: (RS—dec) K1, sssk, knit to 3 sts before m, k3tog, sl m, knit to m, sl m, ssk, knit to 2 sts before m, k2tog, sl m, knit to end—124 sts.

Row 2: Purl.

Rep dec row once more—118 sts.

Size 20½"
Next row: (RS—dec) K1, ssk, knit to 2 sts before m, k2tog, sl m, knit to m, sl m, ssk, knit to 2 sts before m, k2tog, sl m, knit to end—136 sts.

Size 22¼"
Next row: (RS—dec) Knit to m, sl m, knit to m, sl m, ssk, knit to 2 sts before m, k2tog, sl m, knit to end—134 sts.

Chevron

All Sizes:
When changing colors for the Chevron patt, twist the yarns on the WS to avoid holes, by bringing the new color over the color you have just finished using.

Row 1: (WS) Purl to last m, sl m, work Row 1 of Chevron chart over next 30 (30, 40, 40, 40, 40) front sts, p1.

Row 2: (RS) K1, work Row 2 of Chevron chart over next 30 (30, 40, 40, 40, 40) front sts, *sl m, ssk, knit to 2 sts before m, k2tog; rep from * once more, sl m, ssk, knit to last 3 sts, k2tog, k1—6 sts dec'd.

Rows 3–11: Cont as established until Rows 3–11 of Chevron chart have been worked once—78 (88, 106, 104, 114) sts.

SHAPE NECK
Shape neck according to chosen size as foll:

Size 18¾"
Row 1: (RS—dec) K1, (ssk, k6, k2tog) 3 times, *sl m, ssk, knit to 2 sts before m, k2tog; rep from * once more, sl m, ssk, knit to last 3 sts, k2tog, k1—66 sts.

Row 2: Purl.

Rep Row 1 once more—54 sts.

Size 19½"
Row 1: (RS) K1, knit to m, *sl m, ssk, knit to 2 sts before m, k2tog; rep from * once more, sl m, ssk, knit to last 3 sts, k2tog, k1—82 sts.

Row 2: Purl.

Row 3: K1, (ssk, k6, k2tog) 3 times, *sl m, ssk, knit to 2 sts before m, k2tog; rep from * once more, sl m, ssk, knit to last 3 sts, k2tog, k1—70 sts.

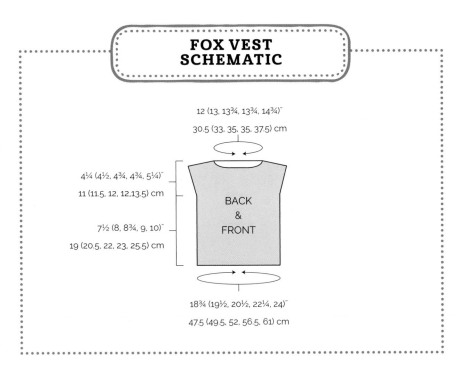

FOX VEST SCHEMATIC

12 (13, 13¾, 13¾, 14¾)"
30.5 (33, 35, 35, 37.5) cm

4¼ (4½, 4¾, 4¾, 5¼)"
11 (11.5, 12, 12, 13.5) cm

7½ (8, 8¾, 9, 10)"
19 (20.5, 22, 23, 25.5) cm

BACK & FRONT

18¾ (19½, 20½, 22¼, 24)"
47.5 (49.5, 52, 56.5, 61) cm

Row 4: Purl.

Rep Row 3 once more—58 sts.

Size 20½"
Row 1: K1, (ssk, k6, k2tog) 4 times, *sl m, ssk, knit to 2 sts before m, k2tog; rep from * once more, sl m, ssk, knit to last 3 sts, k2tog, k1—92 sts.

Row 2: Purl.

Row 3: K1, (ssk, k4, k2tog) 4 times, *sl m, ssk, knit to 2 sts before m, k2tog; rep from * once more, sl m, ssk, knit to last 3 sts, k2tog, k1—78 sts.

Row 4: Purl.

Row 5: K1, *ssk, knit to 2 sts before m, k2tog, sl m; rep from * once more, sl m, ssk, knit to last 3 sts, k2tog, k1—70 sts.

Row 6: Purl.

Rep Row 5 once more—62 sts.

Size 22¼"
Row 1: (RS) K1, knit to m, *sl m, ssk, knit to 2 sts before m, k2tog; rep

from * once more, sl m, ssk, knit to last 3 sts, k2tog, k1—98 sts.

Row 2: Purl.

Row 3: K1, (ssk, k6, k2tog) 4 times, *sl m, ssk, knit to 2 sts before m, k2tog; rep from * once more, sl m, ssk, knit to last 3 sts, k2tog, k1—84 sts.

Row 4: Purl.

Row 5: K1, (ssk, k4, k2tog) 4 times, *sl m, ssk, knit to 2 sts before m, k2tog; rep from * once more, sl m, ssk, knit to last 3 sts, k2tog, k1—70 sts.

Row 6: Purl.

Row 7: K1, *ssk, knit to 2 sts before m, k2tog, sl m; rep from * once more, sl m, ssk, knit to last 3 sts, k2tog, k1—62 sts.

Size 24"
Row 1: (RS) K1, knit to m, *sl m, ssk, knit to 2 sts before m, k2tog; rep from * once more, sl m, ssk, knit to last 3 sts, k2tog, k1—108 sts.

Row 2: Purl.

Rep Rows 1 and 2 once more—102 sts.

Row 3: K1, (ssk, k6, k2tog) 4 times, *sl m, ssk, knit to 2 sts before m, k2tog; rep from * once more, sl m, ssk, knit to last 3 sts, k2tog, k1—88 sts.

Row 4: Purl.

Row 5: K1, (ssk, k4, k2tog) 4 times, *sl m, ssk, knit to 2 sts before m, k2tog; rep from * once more, sl m, ssk, knit to last 3 sts, k2tog, k1—74 sts.

Row 6: Purl.

Row 7: K1, *ssk, knit to 2 sts before m, k2tog, sl m; rep from * once more, sl m, ssk, knit to last 3 sts, k2tog, k1—66 sts.

NECK EDGING
Work in garter st over remaining 54 (58, 58, 62, 66) sts for 4 rows. BO all sts.

Finishing
With yarn threaded on tapestry needle, sew left front seam using mattress stitch (see Glossary).

Place each set of held left underarm sts onto dpn and use Kitchener st (see Glossary) to join sts. Rep for right underarm sts.

Using sewing needle and matching thread, sew buttons to Chevron patt as shown in photograph. Close up any remaining hole and weave in loose ends. Wet-block (see Glossary) vest to measurements.

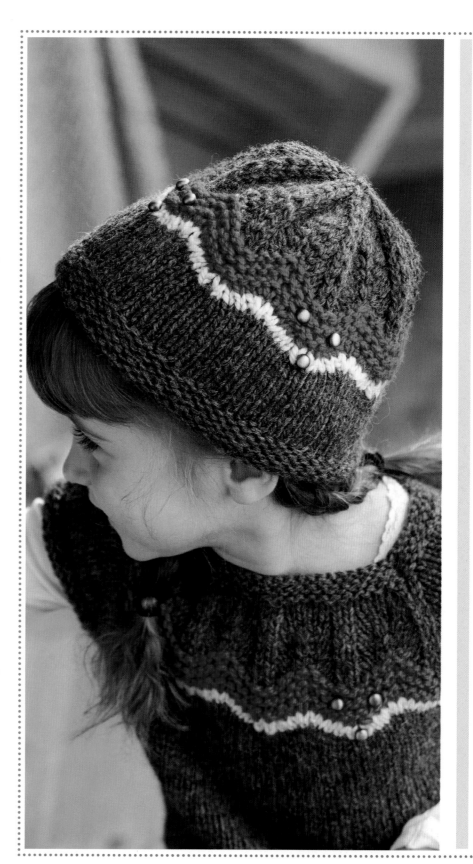

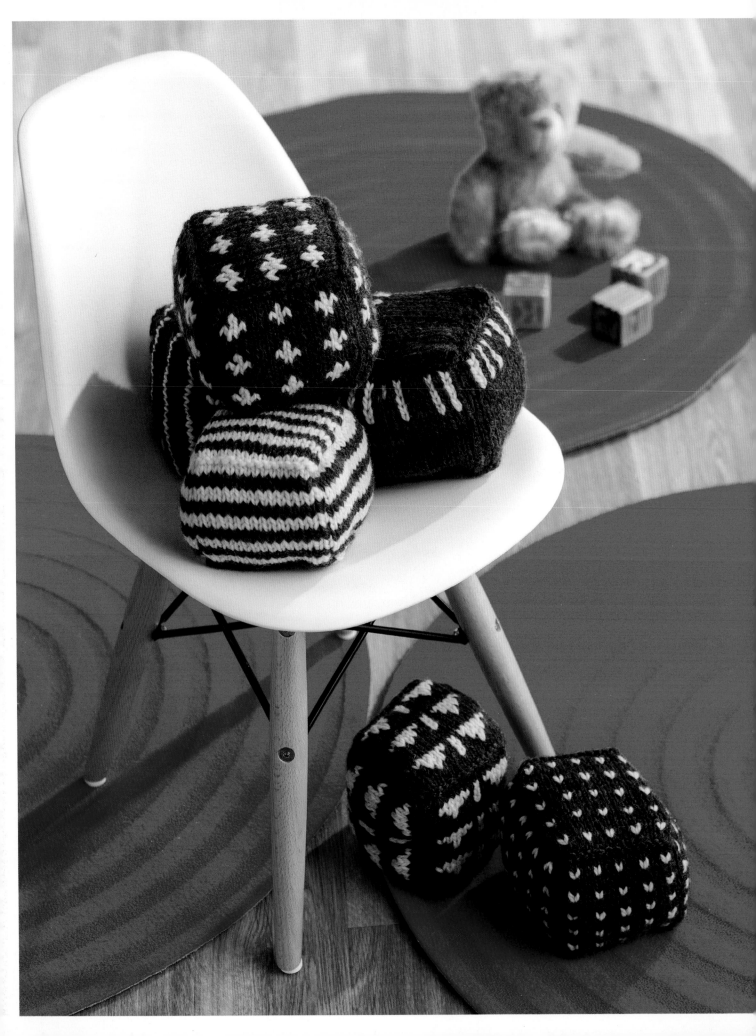

Nature

BLOCKS

ELIZABETH MURPHY

Inspired by the clean, simple lines of nature, these toy blocks are soft and stackable for babies and toddlers. The set of six blocks incorporates a few of children's favorite parts of nature: grass, mountains, stars, water, birds, and forest. The contrasting color patterns are perfect for beginners who want to step into colorwork.

FINISHED SIZE
Each block measures about 4" (10 cm) wide, 4" (10 cm) tall, and 4" (10 cm) deep.

YARN
Chunky weight (#5 Bulky).

Shown here: Cascade Yarns Ecological Wool (100% Peruvian Highland wool; 478 yd [437 m]/250 g): #8025 Night Vision (charcoal; A) and #8010 Ecru (white; B), 1 skein each.

NEEDLES
Size U.S. 10 (6 mm): straight.

Adjust needle size if necessary to obtain the correct gauge.

NOTIONS
Tapestry needle; 20 g of wool fleece or polyester stuffing per block.

GAUGE
17 sts and 22 rows = 4" (10 cm) in St st.

NOTES
Charts are read such that Row 1 is either read from right to left as RS row or from left to right as WS row depending on where you are in the pattern.

For blocks with a corresponding chart, sections 1–4 are worked over 17 sts (use the 17-st pattern outlined on the chart) whereas the sides are worked over 21 sts. The nature blocks are knit flat, then sewn up using the mattress stitch.

Mountain Block

With A, CO 17 sts.

SECTION 1

Row 1: (WS) Purl with A.

Row 2: Knit with A.

Rows 3–5: Work Rows 1–3 of Mountain chart (work center 17-st patt only).

Row 6: Knit with A.

Row 7: Purl with A.

Row 8: Knit.

Rows 9–20: Rep Rows 3–8 twice more.

Row 21: (ridge) Knit with A.

SECTION 2

Row 22: (RS) Knit with A.

Row 23: Purl with A.

Rows 24–26: Work Rows 1–3 of Mountain chart.

Row 27: Purl with A.

Row 28: Knit with A.

Row 29: Purl with A.

Rows 30–41: Rep Rows 24–29 twice more.

Row 42: (ridge) Purl with A.

SECTION 3

Rows 43–63: Rep Rows 1–21.

SECTION 4

Row 64–83: Rep Rows 22–41.

BO loosely.

SIDES

Row 1: (RS) With A and RS facing, pick up 21 sts along selvedge of section 3 (see schematic).

Row 2: Purl with A.

Rows 3–5: Work Rows 1–3 of Mountain chart.

Row 6: Purl with A.

Row 7: Knit with A.

Row 8: Purl with A.

Rows 9–20: Rep Rows 3–8 twice more.

BO loosely.

Repeat for second side by picking sts along other selvedge of section 3.

Weave in loose ends.

Water Block

With A, CO 17 sts.

SECTION 1

Row 1: (WS) Purl with A.

Row 2: Knit with A.

Row 3: Purl with A.

Row 4: Knit with B.

Rows 5–8: Rep Rows 1 and 2 twice.

Rows 9–20: Rep Rows 3–8 twice more.

Row 21: (ridge) Knit with A.

SECTION 2

Row 22: (RS) Knit with A.

Row 23: Purl with A.

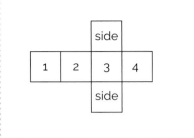

Row 24: Knit with A

Row 25: Purl with B.

Rows 26–29: Rep Rows 22 and 23 twice.

Rows 30–41: Rep Rows 24–29 twice more.

Row 42: (ridge) Purl with A.

SECTION 3

Row 43–63: Rep Rows 1–21.

SECTION 4

Row 64–83: Rep Rows 22–41.

BO loosely.

SIDES

Row 1: (RS) With A and RS facing, pick up 21 sts along selvedge of section 3 (see schematic).

Row 2: Purl with A.

Row 3: Knit with A.

Row 4: Purl with A.

Row 5: Knit with B.

Rows 6–9: Rep Rows 2 and 3 twice.

Rows 10–21: Rep Rows 4–9 twice more.

BO loosely.

Repeat for second side by picking up sts along other selvedge of section 3.

Weave in loose ends.

Star Block

With A, CO 17 sts.

SECTION 1
Row 1: (WS) Purl with A.

Rows 2–20: Work Rows 1–4 of Star chart 4 times (work center 17-st patt only).

Rows 18–20: Work Rows 1–3 of Star chart.

Row 21: (ridge) Knit with A.

SECTION 2
Row 22: (RS) Knit with A.

Rows 23–38: Work Rows 1–4 of Star chart 4 times.

Rows 39–41: Work Rows 1–3 of Star chart.

Row 42: (Ridge) Purl with A.

SECTION 3
Rows 43–63: Rep Rows 1–21.

SECTION 4
Rows 64–83: Rep Rows 22–41.

BO loosely.

SIDES
Row 1: (RS) With A and RS facing, pick up 21 sts along selvedge of section 3 (see schematic).

Row 2: Purl with A.

Rows 3–18: Work Rows 1–4 of Star chart 4 times.

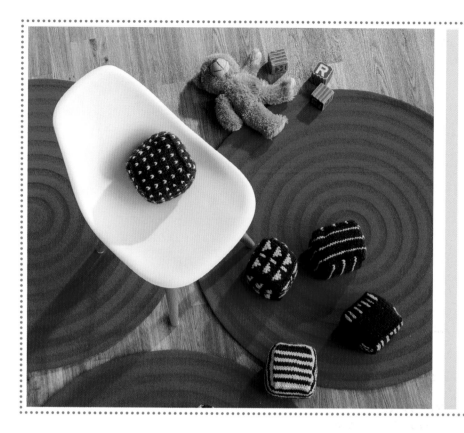

Rows 19–21: Work Rows 1–3 of Star chart.

BO loosely.

Repeat for second side by picking up sts along other selvedge of section 3.

Weave in loose ends.

Forest Block

Note: Do not cut yarns at color changes. Carry unused color loosely up wrong side of work until it is needed again.

With A, CO 17 sts.

SECTION 1
Row 1: (WS) Purl with A.

Row 2: Knit with A.

Row 3: Purl with B.

Row 4: Knit with B.

Rows 5–20: Rep Rows 1–4 four times.

Row 21: (ridge) Knit with B.

SECTION 2
Row 22: (RS) Knit with B.

Row 23: Purl with A.

Row 24: Knit with A.

Row 25: Purl with B.

Row 26: Knit with B.

Rows 27–38: Rep Rows 23–26 three times.

Rows 39 and 40: Rep Rows 23 and 24.

Row 41: (ridge) Knit with A.

NATURE BLOCKS CHARTS

Mountain

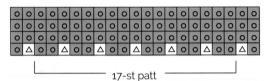

17-st patt

Star

17-st patt

Grass

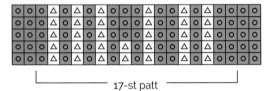

17-st patt

Bird

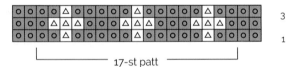

17-st patt

| ○ | knit with A on RS; purl with A on WS |
| △ | knit with B on RS; purl with B on WS |

SECTION 3
Rows 42–62: Rep Rows 1–21.

SECTION 4
Rows 63–82: Rep Rows 22–41.

BO loosely.

SIDES
Row 1: (RS) With B and RS facing, pick up 21 sts along selvedge of section 3 (see schematic).

Row 2: Purl with B.

Row 3: Knit with A.

Row 4: Purl with A.

Row 5: Knit with B.

Row 6: Purl with B.

Rows 7–18: Rep Rows 3–6 three times.

Rows 19 and 20: Rep Rows 3 and 4.

BO loosely.

Repeat for second side by picking up sts along other selvedge of section 3.

Weave in loose ends.

Grass Block
With A, CO 17 sts.

SECTION 1
Row 1: (WS) Purl with A.

Rows 2–6: Work Rows 1–5 of Grass chart (work center 17-st patt only).

Row 7: Purl with A.

Row 8: Knit with A.

Rows 9–20: Rep Rows 7 and 8.

Row 21: (ridge) Knit with A.

SECTION 2
Row 22: (RS) Knit with A.

Rows 23–27: Work Rows 1–5 of Grass chart.

Row 28: Knit with A.

Row 29: Purl with A.

Rows 30–41: Rep Rows 28 and 29.

Row 42: (ridge) Purl with A.

SECTION 3
Rows 43–63: Rep Rows 1–21.

SECTION 4
Rows 64–83: Rep Rows 22–41.

BO loosely.

SIDES
Row 1: (RS) With A and RS facing, pick up 21 sts along selvedge of section 3 (see schematic).

Row 2: Purl with A.

Rows 3–7: Work Rows 1–5 of Grass chart.

Row 6: Purl with A.

Row 7: Knit with A.

Rows 8–21: Rep Rows 6 and 7 seven times.

BO loosely.

Repeat for second side by picking up sts along other selvedge of section 3.

Weave in loose ends.

Bird Block
With A, CO 17 sts.

SECTION 1
Row 1: (WS) Purl with A.

Row 2: Knit with A.

Rows 3–5: Work Rows 1–3 of Bird chart (work center 17-st patt only).

Row 6: Knit with A.

Row 7: Purl with A.

Row 8: Knit with A.

Rows 9–20: Rep Rows 3–8 twice more.

Row 21: (ridge) Knit with A.

SECTION 2
Row 22: (RS) Knit with A.

Row 23: Purl with A.

Rows 24–26: Work Rows 1–3 of Bird chart.

Row 27: Purl with A.

Row 28: Knit with A.

Row 29: Purl with A.

Rows 30–41: Rep Rows 24–29 twice more.

Row 42: (ridge) Purl with A.

SECTION 3
Rows 43–63: Rep Rows 1–21.

SECTION 4
Rows 64–83: Rep Rows 22–41.

BO loosely.

SIDES
Row 1: (RS) With A and RS facing, pick up 21 sts along selvedge of section 3 (see schematic).

Row 2: Purl with A.

Rows 3–5: Work Rows 1–3 of Bird chart.

Row 6: Purl with A.

Row 7: Knit with A.

Row 8: Purl with A.

Rows 9–20: Rep Rows 3–8 twice more.

BO loosely.

Repeat for second side by picking sts along other selvedge of section 3.

Weave in loose ends.

Finishing
Note: Sections 1–4 and the sides are slightly different sizes, which is not noticeable after blocking, seaming the edges, and stuffing the blocks.

Block each piece before seaming.

Fold the sides up so that they touch sections 2 and 4, then fold over the top flap (section 1)—see schematic.

Cut a length of yarn A or B (depending on color on either side of the seams) measuring about 25" (63.5 cm) and thread on tapestry needle.

With WS together, sew each seam using mattress stitch (see Glossary), leaving one side open for stuffing.

Stuff with wool fleece or polyester stuffing until desired shape.

Sew final opening shut using whipstitch (see Glossary).

Weave in loose ends.

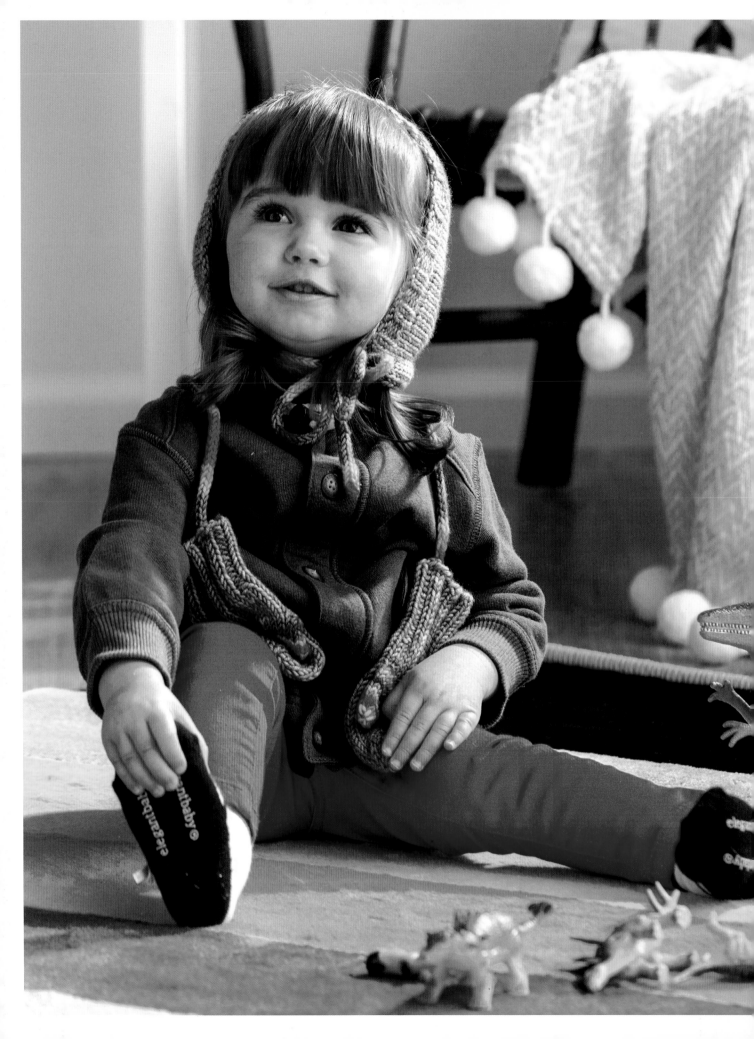

Rainbow
BONNET AND MITTEN SET

LISA CHEMERY

Two thumbs up! The use of self-striping rainbow yarn provides a touch of whimsy to a very practical set of accessories. The bonnet will stay on the head of the squirmiest of babies, while the mittens will not stray far from each other, thanks to the cord that connects them.

FINISHED SIZE

Bonnet:

Newborn (6 months, 12 months, 24 months).

About 12½ (14¼, 16, 17½)" (31.5 [36, 40.5, 44.5] cm) wide at neck and 5 (5½, 6, 7)" (12.5 [14, 15, 18] cm) tall.

Bonnet shown is 16" (40.5 cm) wide and 6" (15 cm) tall.

Mittens:

Newborn (6 months, 12 months, 24 months).

About 4½ (5¼, 5½, 6)" (11.5 [13.5, 14, 15] cm) in length and 5 (5¾, 5¾, 6¾)" (12.5 [14.5, 14.5, 17] cm) in circumference.

Mittens shown measure 5½" (14 cm) in length and 5¾" (14.5 cm) in circumference.

YARN

DK weight (#3 Light).

Shown here: Blue Moon Fiber Arts Socks That Rock Heavyweight (100% superwash merino; 350 yd [320 m]/198 g): Everyday Grey (A) and Pride (B), 1 skein each.

NEEDLES

Bonnet: Size U.S. 6 (4 mm): straight or circular (cir) for section worked in rows; set of 4 or 5 double-pointed (dpn).

Mittens: Size U.S. 6 (4 mm): set of dpn.

Adjust needle size if necessary to obtain the correct gauge.

NOTIONS

Markers (m); tapestry needle; pom-pom maker (optional).

GAUGE

19 sts and 30 rows/rnds = 4" (10 cm) in St st.

NOTES

The front of the bonnet is knit back and forth in rows, while the crown is knit in the round. An attached I-cord edging is worked between two I-cord ties along the bonnet's opening.

The mittens are worked in the round from the cuff to the tip. For the two largest sizes, a thumb is worked in the round (other sizes are worked without a thumb). An I-cord connects the two mittens together.

Bonnet

Body

CO 60 (68, 76, 84) sts with A on straight or cir.

Row 1: (RS) K1, *p2, k2; rep from * to last 3 sts, p2, k1.

Row 2: (WS) P1, *k2, p2; rep from * to last 3 sts, k2, p1.

Rows 3–6: Rep Rows 1 and 2 twice.

Row 7: (RS) Knit.

Row 8: Purl.

Rep Rows 7 and 8 until work measures 3½ (3¾, 4, 4¾)" (9 [9.5, 10, 12] cm) from CO edge.

Crown

Transferring sts to dpn, join for working in rnds. Place marker (pm) at beg of rnd and knit 1 rnd. Work crown decreases according to chosen size as foll:

For size 17½", work Rnds 1–18.

For size 16", work Rnds 3–18.

For size 14¼", work Rnds 5–18.

For size 12½", work Rnds 7–18.

Rnd 1: Slip marker (sl m), k2, [k8, k2tog] 8 times, k2—76 sts.

Rnd 2 and all even-numbered rnds: Knit.

Rnd 3: K2, [k7, k2tog] 8 times, k2—68 sts.

Rnd 5: K2, [k6, k2tog] 8 times, k2—60 sts.

Rnd 7: K2, [k5, k2tog] 8 times, k2—52 sts.

Rnd 9: K2, [k4, k2tog] 8 times, k2—44 sts.

Rnd 11: K2, [k3, k2tog] 8 times, k2—36 sts.

Rnd 13: K2, [k2, k2tog] 8 times, k2—28 sts.

Rnd 15: K2, [k1, k2tog] 8 times, k2—20 sts.

Rnd 17: K2, [k2tog] 8 times, k2—12 sts.

Top

All Sizes:

Cut yarn and thread tail on tapestry needle. Draw through rem sts, pull tight to close hole, and fasten off on WS. Make a 2½" (6.5 cm) diameter pom-pom (see Glossary) with B and fasten it securely to top of bonnet.

Ties

With dpn and B, CO 3 sts. Work standard I-cord (see Glossary) until piece measures about 9" (23 cm). With RS facing, bonnet upright, and opening in the middle, transition to working an attached I-cord along the bonnet's opening, from left side to right side as foll:

*K2, sl 1, yo, pick up and knit 1 st at left neck edge with RS facing. Pass slipped st and yo over picked-up st—3 sts on needle. Slide sts to other end of needle. Rep from * (making sure to keep pulling on working yarn as you work I-cord) until all edge sts have been picked up and you are at right neck edge.

Work standard I-cord until second tie is 9" (23 cm) long. K3tog, cut yarn, and thread tail on tapestry needle to weave in loose end inside the I-cord.

Finishing

Weave in loose ends. Block to finished measurements.

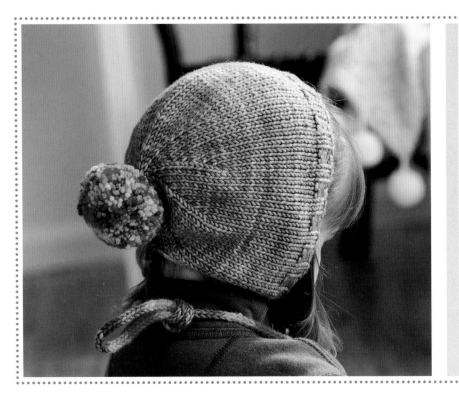

Mittens (make 2)

Cuff

CO 24 (28, 28, 32) sts with A and divide equally onto dpn.

Place marker (pm) and join for working in rnds, being careful not to twist sts.

Work in k2, p2 rib for 14 rnds.

Hand

Work in St st for 7 rnds.

For Sizes 5½" and 6" only:

Mark thumb gusset as foll (for other sizes, skip to All Sizes section):

Slip marker (sl m), k4 using piece of B scrap yarn about 5" (12.5 cm) long; slip these 4 sts back to left needle and knit them again with A working yarn, knit to end of rnd.

All Sizes:

Work in St st for 8 (12, 14, 16) more rnds or about 4 (4½, 4¾, 5)" (10 [11.5, 12, 12.5] cm) from CO edge.

Upper Hand

Work hand decreases according to chosen size as foll:

For size 6", work Rnds 1–10.

For sizes 5¼" and 5½", work Rnds 3–10.

For size 4½", work Rnds 5–10.

Rnd 1: *K6, k2tog; rep from * to end—28 sts.

Rnds 2, 4, and 6: Knit.

Rnd 3: *K5, k2tog; rep from * to end—24 sts.

Rnd 5: *K4, k2tog; rep from * to end—20 sts.

Rnd 7: *K3, k2tog; rep from * to end—16 sts.

Rnd 8: *K2, k2tog; rep from * to end—12 sts.

Rnd 9: *K1, k2tog; rep from * to end—8 sts.

Rnd 10: *K2tog; rep from * to end—4 sts.

Cut yarn, leaving a 10" (25.5 cm) tail. Thread tail on tapestry needle, draw through rem sts, pull tight to close hole, and fasten off on WS.

Thumb

Sizes 5½" and 6" only

Carefully remove B scrap yarn marking thumb gusset to expose live stitches; you should have 4 sts at the bottom and 3 sts at the top.

Place these sts onto 2 dpn. With B yarn, knit 4 bottom sts, then using a third dpn, pick up and knit 2 sts at side of thumb opening, knit 3 top sts, then pick up and knit 2 sts at other side of thumb opening—11 sts total.

Join for working in rnds, pm to indicate beg of rnd.

Work in St st for 8 (12) rnds tightly (alternatively, use a smaller size needle).

Next rnd: (dec) [K2tog] 5 times, k1—6 sts.

Cut yarn and thread tail on tapestry needle. Draw through rem sts, pull tight to close hole, and fasten off on WS. Use yarn tail at base of thumb to close up any remaining holes.

I-Cord

With dpn and B, pick up and knit 3 sts from WS of ribbing of 1 mitten, close to

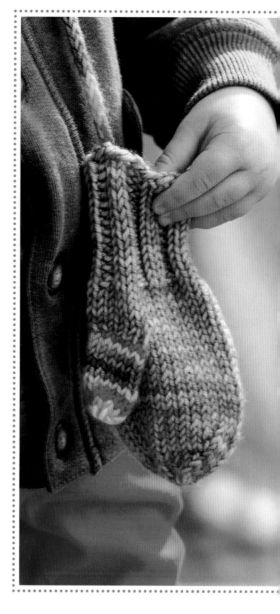

CO edge and on the thumb side. Work standard I-cord (see Glossary) until piece measures about 20 (25, 30, 35)" (51 [63.5, 76, 89] cm). To close I-cord, k3tog and cut yarn. Thread tail on tapestry needle, draw through rem st, pull tight, and fasten off to WS of second mitten's ribbing.

Finishing

Weave in loose ends on both mittens. Block to finished measurements.

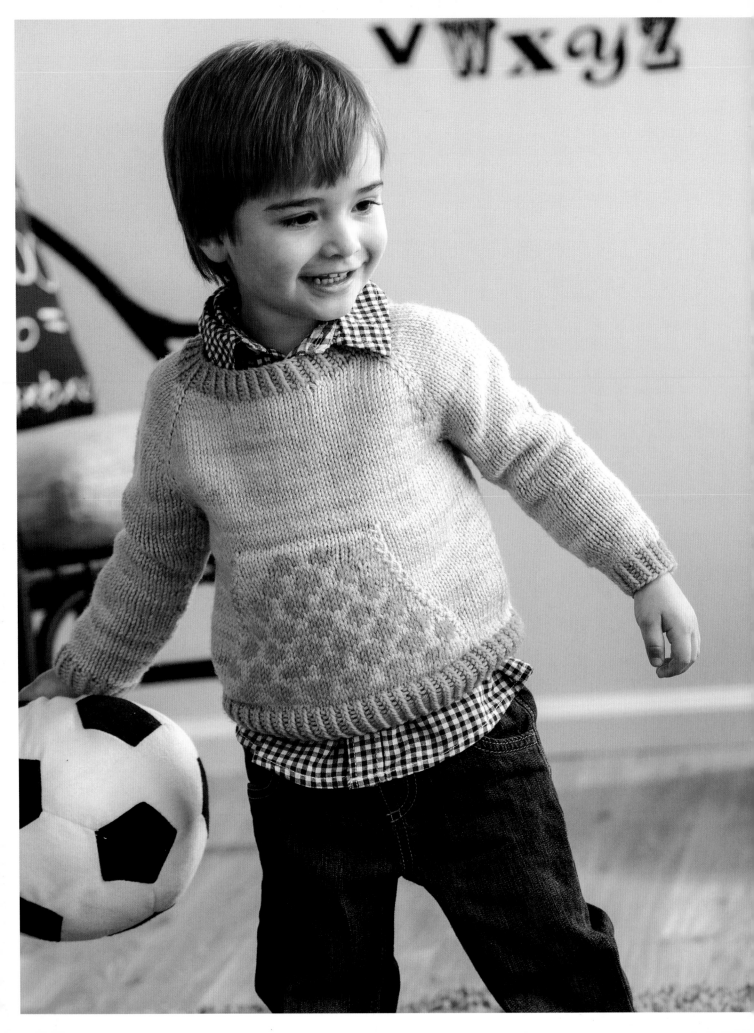

Polka-Dot Pocket
PULLOVER

SUVI SIMOLA

This cute pullover has a polka-dot patterned kangaroo pocket. The garment is worked from the top down, and the neck is shaped with short-rows for a more comfortable fit. The neck, hem, and cuffs are finished with a twisted rib. The pocket is worked back and forth in rows and sewn in place.

FINISHED SIZE

3 months (6 months, 12 months, 18 months, 24 months).

About 18½ (19¼, 20¾, 21½, 23¼)" (47 [49, 52.5, 54.5, 59] cm) chest circumference.

Sweater shown measures 23¼" (59 cm).

YARN

Worsted weight (#4 Medium).

Shown here: SweetGeorgia Superwash Worsted (100% superwash merino wool; 200 yd [182 m]/115 g): Birch (beige; A), 1 (1, 2, 2, 2) skein(s); Saffron (yellow; B), 1 skein.

NEEDLES
Sizes 18½ (19¼, 20¾, 21½)"

Size U.S. 7 (4.5 mm): 16" (40.5 cm) circular (cir) and set of 4 or 5 double-pointed (dpn).

Size 23¼"

Size U.S. 7 (4.5 mm): 16" (40.5 cm) cir, 24" (61 cm) cir, and set of dpn.

Adjust needle size if necessary to obtain the correct gauge.

NOTIONS

Markers (m); stitch holders or waste yarn; tapestry needle.

GAUGE

20 sts and 29 rnds = 4" (10 cm) in St st.

**K1TBL, P1 RIB
(WORKED IN RNDS ON EVEN
NUMBER OF STS)**
Rnd 1: *K1 through back loop
(k1tbl), p1; rep from * to end.

Rep Rnd 1 for patt.

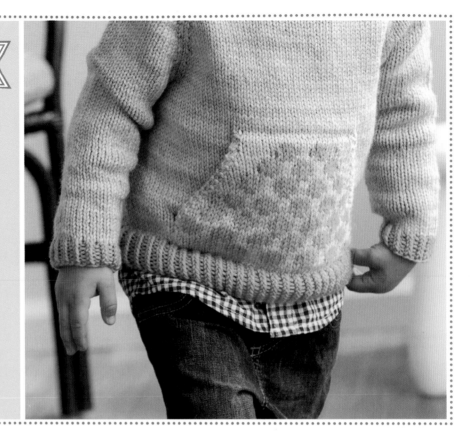

Body

With B, CO 64 (68, 76, 76, 80) sts using
dpn for first four sizes or shorter cir
for last size.

Place marker (pm) for beg of rnd and
join for working in rnds, being careful
not to twist sts.

Work in k1tbl, p1 rib (see Stitch Guide)
for 5 rnds.

Set-up rnd: With A, slip marker (sl
m), k22 (24, 26, 26, 28) sts for back,
pm, k10 (10, 12, 12, 12) sts for right
sleeve, pm, k22 (24, 26, 26, 28) sts for
front, pm, k10 (10, 12, 12, 12) sts for left
sleeve.

SHAPE YOKE AND NECK

The back neck is shaped with short-
rows at the same time as the yoke is
shaped with raglan increases.

Work short-rows (see Glossary)
as foll:

Short-Row 1: (RS) *K1, M1L (see
Glossary), knit to 1 st before m, M1R
(see Glossary), k1, sl m; rep from *
once more, k1, M1L, k1, wrap next st,
turn work.

Short-Row 2: (WS) *Purl to next m,
sl m; rep from * 3 more times, p2,
wrap next st, turn work.

Short-Row 3: *Knit to 1 st before
m, M1R, k1, sl m, k1, M1L; rep from *
3 more times, knit to previously
wrapped st, knit wrapped st tog with
its wrap, k1, wrap next st, turn work.

Short-Row 4: *Purl to next m, sl m;
rep from * 3 more times, purl to
previously wrapped st and purl

wrapped st tog with its wrap, p1,
wrap next st, turn work.

Short-Row 5: *Knit to 1 st before m,
M1R, k1, sl m, k1, M1L; rep from *
3 more times, knit to previously
wrapped st and knit wrapped st tog
with its wrap, k1 (1, 2, 2, 2), wrap next
st, turn work.

Short-Row 6: *Purl to next m, sl m;
rep from * 3 more times, purl to
previously wrapped st and purl
wrapped st tog with its wrap, p1 (1,
2, 2, 2), wrap next st very loosely,
turn work.

Short-Row 7: Knit to 1 st before m,
M1R, k1, sl m, k1, M1L, knit to 1 st
before beg of rnd marker, M1R, k1,
sl m.

Polka Dot 1

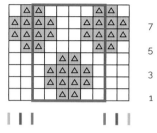

7

5

3

1

6-st repeat

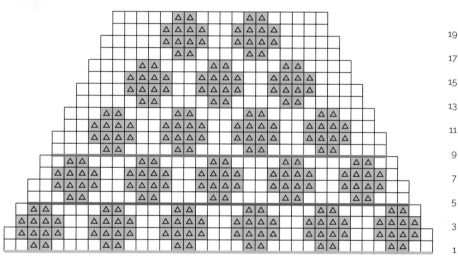

□ knit with A on RS; purl with MC on WS

△ knit with B on RS; purl with CC on WS

‖ sizes 18½″ and 19¼″

‖ size 20¾″

‖ sizes 21½″ and 23¼″

Polka Dot 2

19

17

15

13

11

9

7

5

3

1

36 sts dec'd to 18

When neck shaping has been completed, there are 28 (30, 32, 32, 34) sts each for front and back and 16 (16, 18, 18, 18) sts for each sleeve—88 (92, 100, 100, 104) sts.

SHAPE YOKE

Cont working raglan increases in rnds in foll section. Due to neck shaping, raglan increases on first rnd succeed raglan increases worked on short-rows, and rem wrapped sts should be knitted tog with their wraps. Change to longer cir needle when there are too many sts to fit around the shorter cir or dpn.

Next rnd: (inc) * K1, M1L, knit to 1 st before m, M1R, k1, sl m; rep from * 3 more times—8 sts inc'd.

Rep inc rnd every other rnd 2 (1, 2, 3, 4) more time(s), then every 4th rnd 3 (4, 4, 4, 4) times.

When raglan increases have been completed, there are 40 (42, 46, 48, 52) sts each for front and back and 28 (28, 32, 34, 36) sts for each sleeve—136 (140, 156, 164, 176) sts.

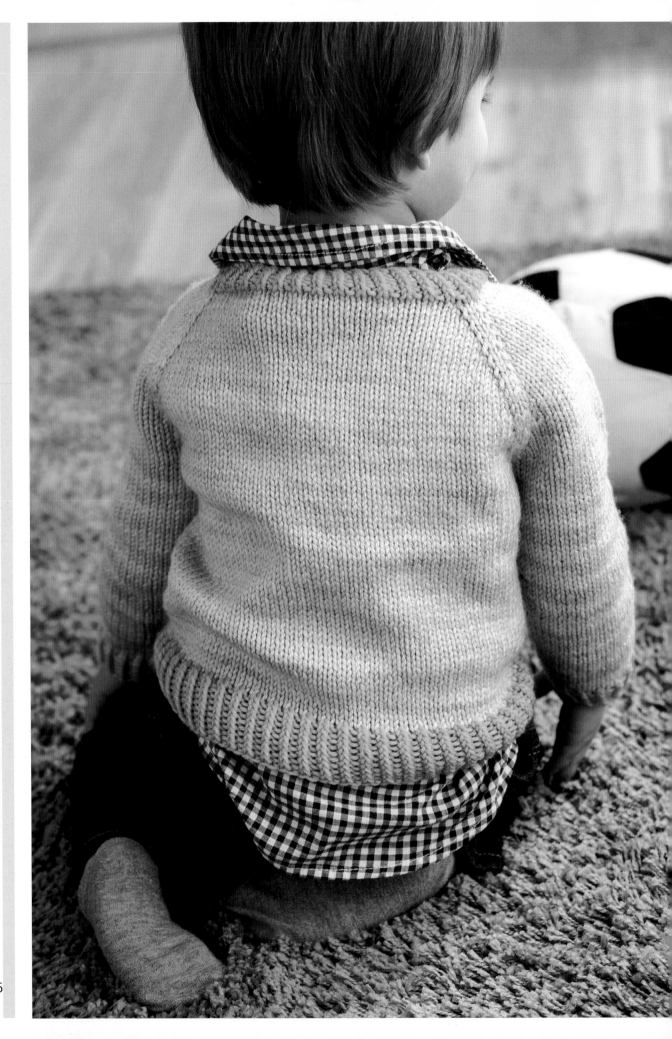

DIVIDE FOR BODY AND SLEEVES

Next rnd: Removing raglan markers when you come to them, knit 40 (42, 46, 48, 52) back sts, place 28 (28, 32, 34, 36) right sleeve sts on waste yarn or stitch holder, CO 6 sts for right underarm, knit 40 (42, 46, 48, 52) front sts, place 28 (28, 32, 34, 36) left sleeve sts on holder, CO 6 sts for left underarm and pm in center of these CO sts to denote beg of rnd—92 (96, 104, 108, 116) sts for body.

Work even in St st until body measures 5 (5, 5½, 5½, 6½)" (12.5 [12.5, 14, 14, 16.5] cm) from underarm.

EDGING

With B, knit 1 rnd, then work in k1tbl, p1 rib for 6 (9, 9, 9, 9) rnds. BO all sts.

Sleeves

Place 28 (28, 32, 34, 36) held sleeve sts on dpn.

With RS facing, join A in center of sts at base of underarm CO. Pick up and knit 3 sts across half of underarm CO, knit sleeve sts, pick up and knit 3 sts from other half of underarm CO. Pm for end of rnd—34 (34, 38, 40, 42) sts.

Work 5 rnds even.

Next rnd: (dec) K1, k2tog, knit to last 3 sts, ssk, k1—2 sts dec'd.

Rep dec rnd every 14 (16, 10, 11, 9th rnd 2 (1, 2, 1, 4) more time(s), then every 0 (15, 9, 10, 8)th rnd 0 (1, 2, 3, 1) time(s)—28 (28, 28, 30, 30) sts.

Cont working even in St st until sleeve measures 6 (6½, 7½, 8, 8½)" (15 [16.5, 19, 20.5, 21.5] cm) from joining rnd.

EDGING

With B and dpn, knit 1 rnd, then work in k1tbl, p1 rib for 5 rnds. BO all sts.

Rep for other sleeve.

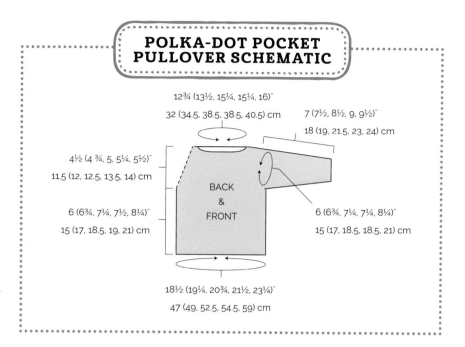

POLKA-DOT POCKET PULLOVER SCHEMATIC

12¾ (13½, 15¼, 15¼, 16)"
32 (34.5, 38.5, 38.5, 40.5) cm

7 (7½, 8½, 9, 9½)"
18 (19, 21.5, 23, 24) cm

4½ (4 ¾, 5, 5¼, 5½)"
11.5 (12, 12.5, 13.5, 14) cm

BACK & FRONT

6 (6¾, 7¼, 7½, 8¼)"
15 (17, 18.5, 19, 21) cm

6 (6¾, 7¼, 7¼, 8¼)"
15 (17, 18.5, 18.5, 21) cm

18½ (19¼, 20¾, 21½, 23¼)"
47 (49, 52.5, 54.5, 59) cm

Pocket

The pocket is worked in rows from the bottom up with A and B, following the Polka-Dot charts for middle sts and working edge sts in A.

With A, CO 36 (36, 40, 44, 44) sts, leaving a long tail for seaming later.

Set-up row: (WS) Purl.

Row 1: (RS) K2 with B, work Row 1 of Polka-Dot chart 1 according to chosen size [i.e., start at stitch 3 (3, 2, 1, 1) of Row 1, work 6-st rep 5 (5, 6, 6, 6) times, then work last 0 (0, 1, 2, 2) st(s)], k2 with A.

Row 2: (WS) K2 with A, work Row 2 of Polka-Dot chart 1 as established, k2 with A.

Cont as established until Rows 3–8 of Polka-Dot chart 1 have been worked once.

Next row: (RS—dec) [K1, ssk, k1] with A, work Polka-Dot chart 2 according to chosen size [i.e., start at Row 9 (9, 5, 1, 1)], [k1, k2tog, k1] with A.

Next row: (WS) [K2, p1] with A, work Polka-Dot chart 2 as established, [p1, k2] with A.

Cont as established until Rows 11–24 (11–24, 7–20, 3–20, 3–20) of Polka-Dot chart 2 have been worked once—20 (20, 24, 24, 24) sts.

Next row: (RS) Knit with A.

Next row: (WS) K2, purl to last 2 sts, k2.

BO all sts, leaving a long tail for seaming later.

Finishing

Weave in loose ends. Wet-block (see Glossary) pullover and pocket separately. Lay on a flat surface and let pieces dry completely.

Center pocket on front of pullover, aligning bottom of pocket with upper edge of bottom rib. Using mattress stitch (see Glossary), sew pocket onto front along bottom of pocket, straight sections of sides, and top of pocket, leaving sides open.

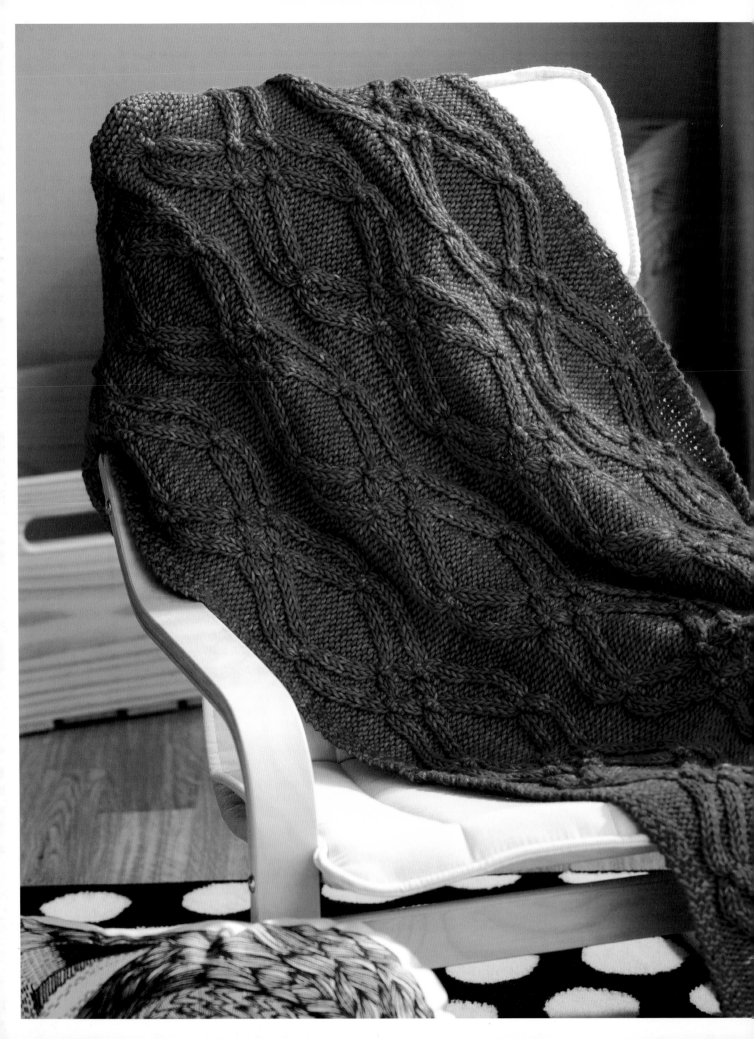

Modern Filigree
BABY BLANKET

TANIS GRAY

Swaddle yourself in cabled comfort! This luscious blanket is not only soft to the touch but also exquisitely warm. The superwash yarn ensures that the blanket will breeze through life's little accidents and stains.

FINISHED SIZE

About 21" (53.5 cm) wide and 37" (94 cm) high.

YARN

Chunky weight (#5 Bulky).

Shown here: Neighborhood Fiber Co. Studio Chunky (100% superwash merino; 300 yd [274 m]/227 g): Clintonville, 3 skeins.

NEEDLES

Size U.S. 10½ (6.5 mm): 32" (81.5 cm) circular (cir).

Adjust needle size if necessary to obtain the correct gauge.

NOTIONS

Two cable needles (cn); tapestry needle.

GAUGE

18½ sts and 20½ rows = 4" (10 cm) in Cable patt after blocking.

Slip (Sl) all sts purlwise (pwise) unless indicated otherwise.

2/2/2 LC
Sl 4 sts onto cn and hold in front, k2, sl 2 leftmost sts from cn to left needle, hold 2 sts on cn in back, p2, k2 from cn.

2/2/2 RC
Sl 2 sts onto first cn and hold in back, sl 2 sts onto second cn and hold in front, k2 from left needle, p2 from second cn, k2 from first cn.

2/1 LCP
Sl 2 sts onto cn, hold in front, p1, k2 from cn.

2/1 RCP
Sl 1 st onto cn, hold in back, k2, p1 from cn.

CABLE (MULTIPLE OF 44 STS + 8)
Row 1: (RS) K3, p2, *p3, 2/2/2 LC, p2, 2/2/2 LC, p5, k2, p2, k2, p8, (k2, p2) twice; rep from * to last 3 sts, k3.

Rows 2, 26, 28, and 30: (WS) K3, *(k2, p2) twice, k8, p2, k2, p2, k5, (p2, k2) 3 times, p2, k3; rep from * to last 5 sts, k5.

Row 3: K3, p2, *p3, (k2, p2) 3 times, k2, p5, k2, p2, 2/1 LCP, p6, 2/1 RCP, p2, k2, p2; rep from * to last 3 sts, k3.

Row 4: K3, *k2, p2, k3, p2, k6, p2, k3, p2, k5, (p2, k2) 3 times, p2, k3; rep from * to last 5 sts, k5.

Row 5: K3, p2, *p2, 2/1 RCP, p2, 2/2/2 RC, p2, 2/1 LCP, p4, 2/1 LCP, p2, 2/1 LCP, p4, 2/1 RCP, p2, 2/1 RCP, p2; rep from * to last 3 sts, k3.

Row 6: K3, *(k3, p2) twice, k4, p2, k3, p2, k5, p2, k3, p2, k2, p2, k3, p2, k2; rep from * to last 5 sts, k5.

Row 7: K3, p2, *p1, (2/1 RCP, p2) twice, 2/1 LCP, p2, 2/1 LCP, p4, (2/1 LCP, p2) twice, 2/1 RCP, p2, 2/1 RCP, p3; rep from * to last 3 sts, k3.

Row 8: K3, *k4, p2, k3, p2, k2, p2, k3, p2, k5, p2, k3, p2, k4, p2, k3, p2, k1; rep from * to last 5 sts, k5.

Row 9: K3, p2, *2/1 RCP, p2, 2/1 RCP, p4, 2/1 LCP, p2, 2/1 LCP, p4, 2/1 LCP, (p2, k2) twice, p2, 2/1 RCP, p4; rep from * to last 3 sts, k3.

Row 10: K3, *k5, (p2, k2) 3 times, p2, k5, p2, k3, p2, k6, p2, k3, p2; rep from * to last 5 sts, k5.

Row 11: K3, p2, *k2, p2, 2/1 RCP, p6, 2/1 LCP, p2, k2, p5, k2, p2, 2/2/2 RC, p2, k2, p5; rep from * to last 3 sts, k3.

Rows 12, 14, 16, and 18: K3, *k5, (p2, k2) 3 times, p2, k5, p2, k2, p2, k8, p2, k2, p2; rep from * to last 5 sts, k5.

Rows 13 and 17: K3, p2, *k2, p2, k2, p8, k2, p2, k2, p5, (k2, p2) 3 times, k2, p5; rep from * to last 3 sts, k3.

Row 15: K3, p2, *2/2/2 LC, p8, 2/2/2 LC, p5, 2/2/2 LC, p2, 2/2/2 LC, p5; rep from * to last 3 sts, k3.

Row 19: K3, p2, *k2, p2, 2/1 LCP, p6, 2/1 RCP, p2, k2, p4, 2/1 RCP, p2, 2/2/2 RC, p2, 2/1 LCP, p4; rep from * to last 3 sts, k3.

Row 20: K3, *k4, p2, k3, p2, k2, p2, k3, p2, k4, p2, k3, p2, k6, p2, k3, p2; rep from * to last 5 sts, k5.

Row 21: k3, p2, *2/1 LCP, p2, 2/1 LCP, p4, 2/1 RCP, p2, 2/1 RCP, p3, (2/1 RCP, p2) twice, 2/1 LCP, p2, 2/1 LCP, p3; rep from * to last 3 sts, k3.

Row 22: K3, *(k3, p2) twice, (k4, p2, k3, p2) 3 times, k1; rep from * to last 5 sts, k5.

Row 23: K3, p2, *p1, (2/1 LCP, p2) twice, 2/1 RCP, p2, 2/1 RCP, p3, 2/1 RCP, p2, 2/1 RCP, p4, (2/1 LCP, p2) twice; rep from * to last 3 sts, k3.

Row 24: K3, *k2, p2, k3, p2, k6, p2, k3, p2, k4, (p2, k3, p2, k2) twice; rep from * to last 5 sts, k5.

Row 25: K3, p2, *p2, 2/1 LCP, (p2, k2) twice, p2, 2/1 RCP, p4, k2, p2, 2/1 RCP, p6, 2/1 LCP, p2, k2, p2; rep from * to last 3 sts, k3.

Row 27: K3, p2, *p3, k2, p2, 2/2/2 RC, p2, k2, p5, k2, p2, k2, p8, (k2, p2) twice; rep from * to last 3 sts, k3.

Row 29: K3, p2, *p3, (k2, p2) 3 times, k2, p5, 2/2/2 LC, p8, 2/2/2 LC, p2; rep from * to last 3 sts, k3.

Rep Rows 1–30 for patt.

Blanket
CO 96 sts.

BOTTOM BORDER
Work in garter st (knit every row) for 6 rows.

MAIN SECTION
Work Rows 1–30 of Cable patt (from Stitch Guide or chart) 6 times, working 44-st rep twice.

TOP BORDER
Work in garter st for 6 rows.

BO loosely knitwise (kwise).

Finishing
Weave in loose ends. Block to measurements.

Cable Pattern

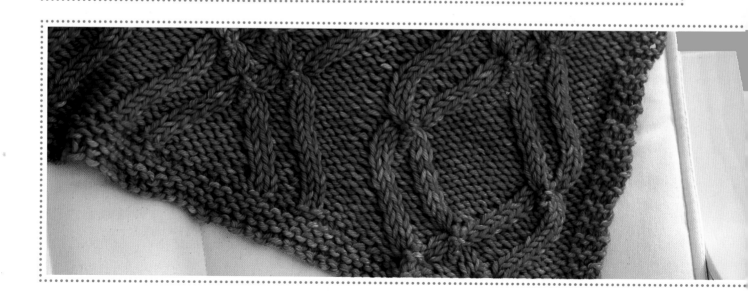

work twice (44-st repeat)

	knit on RS; purl on WS
•	purl on RS; knit on WS

2/1 RCP (see Stitch Guide)

2/1 LCP (see Stitch Guide)

2/2/2 RC (see Stitch Guide)

2/2/2 LC (see Stitch Guide)

pattern repeat

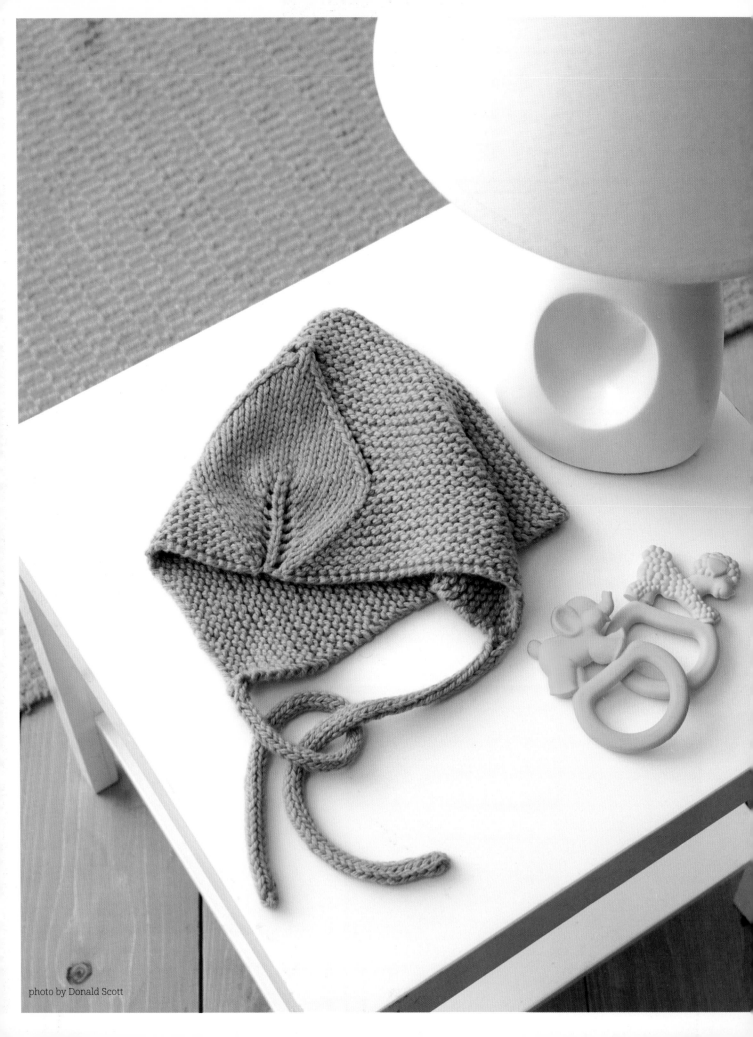

New Leaf
BONNET

MELISSA LABARRE

This sweet little bonnet is a great fall or winter accessory. It covers the ears, and the I-cord ties help keep it on restless little boys and girls. The leaf motif pops against a garter-stitch background. Worked in a worsted-weight yarn, it flies off the needles.

FINISHED SIZE

Newborn (3 months, 9 months, 12 months).

About 12¼ (13, 14½, 15¾)" (31 [33, 37, 40] cm) wide at neck and 5 (5½, 6¼, 7)" (12.5 [14, 16, 18] cm) tall.

Bonnet shown is 14½" (37 cm) wide at neck and 6¼" (16 cm) tall.

YARN

Worsted weight (#4 Medium).

Shown here: Spud & Chloë Sweater (55% superwash wool, 45% organic cotton; 160 yd [146 m]/100 g): #7502 Grass, 1 skein.

NEEDLES

Size U.S. 7 (4.5 mm): straight and set of 4 or 5 double-pointed (dpn).

Adjust needle size if necessary to obtain the correct gauge.

NOTIONS

Markers (m); tapestry needle.

GAUGE

18 sts and 36 rows = 4" (10 cm) in garter st.

NOTES

This bonnet is worked back and forth in rows, then closed using a three-needle bind-off. Stitches are then picked up at each corner to work I-cord ties.

Body

Using straight needles, CO 55 (59, 65, 71) sts. Do not join.

Row 1: (RS) K18 (20, 23, 26), place marker (pm), work Row 1 of New Leaf chart over next 19 sts, pm, k18 (20, 23, 26).

Row 2: (WS) K18 (20, 23, 26), slip marker (sl m), work Row 2 of New Leaf chart over next 19 sts, sl m, k18 (20, 23, 26).

Rows 3–37: Cont in patt as established, working the first and last 18 (20, 23, 26) sts in garter st and working New Leaf chart between markers.

Row 38: (WS) Knit all sts, removing markers as you encounter them.

Work in garter st for 0 (6, 12, 20) row(s), ending after a WS row.

Crown

Row 1: (RS—dec) K25 (27, 30, 33), k3tog, pm, ssk, k25 (27, 30, 33); 3 sts dec'd—52 (56, 62, 68) sts.

Rows 2 and 4: Knit.

Row 3: K24 (26, 29, 32), k2tog, sl m, ssk, k24 (26, 29, 32) sts; 2 sts dec'd—50 (54, 60, 66) sts rem.

Row 5: K23 (25, 28, 31), k2tog, sl m, ssk, k23 (25, 28, 31) sts; 2 sts dec'd—48 (52, 58, 64) sts rem.

Row 6: Knit.

Top

Turn bonnet inside out and place 24 (26, 29, 32) sts up to first marker on first dpn. Remove marker and place rem 24 (26, 29, 32) sts on second dpn. With a third dpn and using the three-needle method (see Glossary), BO all sts.

Ties

Place bonnet flat with RS facing, seam at top and leaf motif on the left. With dpn, pick up and knit 4 sts from lower right corner. Work standard I-cord (see Glossary) over 4 sts until piece measures 10" (25.5 cm). Cut yarn and thread tail on tapestry needle; draw needle through rem sts and pull firmly. Weave in loose ends. Rep for I-cord tie on left side.

Finishing

Weave in loose ends. Block bonnet using water or steam and lay flat to dry.

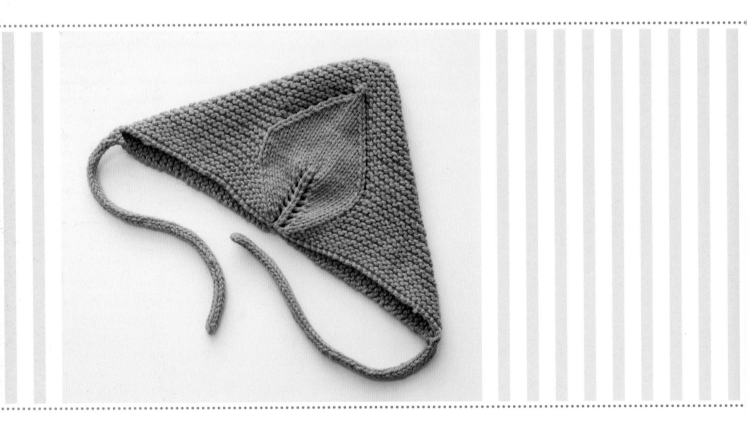

NEW LEAF BONNET CHART

New Leaf

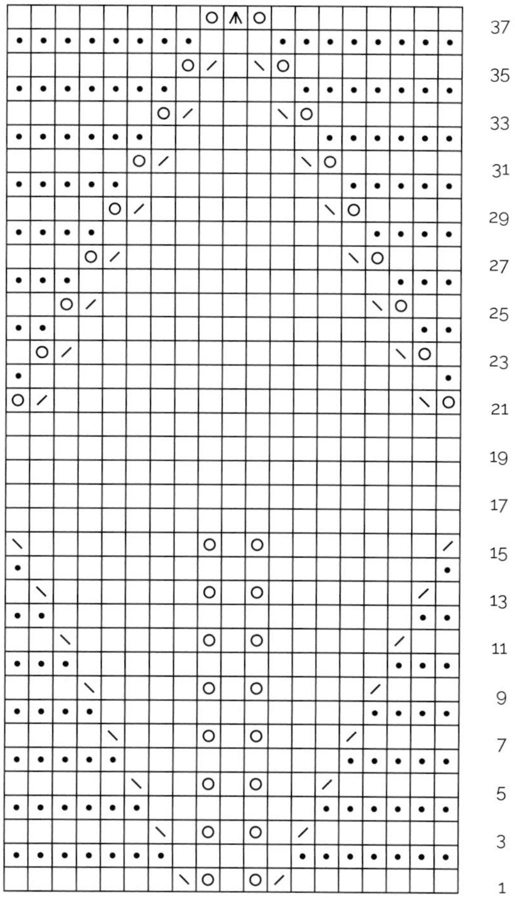

19 sts

- ☐ k on RS; p on WS
- • p on RS; k on WS
- O yo
- / k2tog on RS; p2tog on WS
- \ ssk on RS; p2tog tbl on WS
- ∧ sl 2 as if to k2tog, k1, p2sso

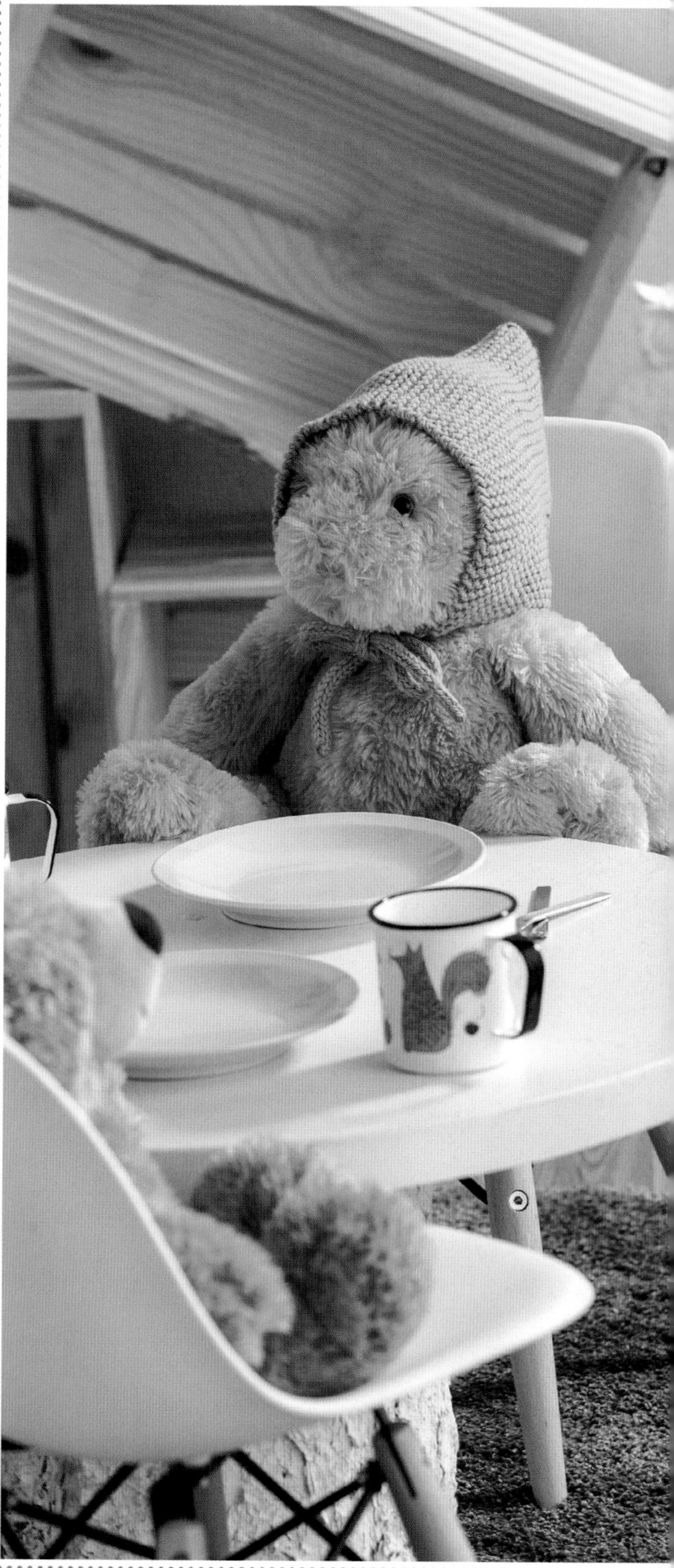

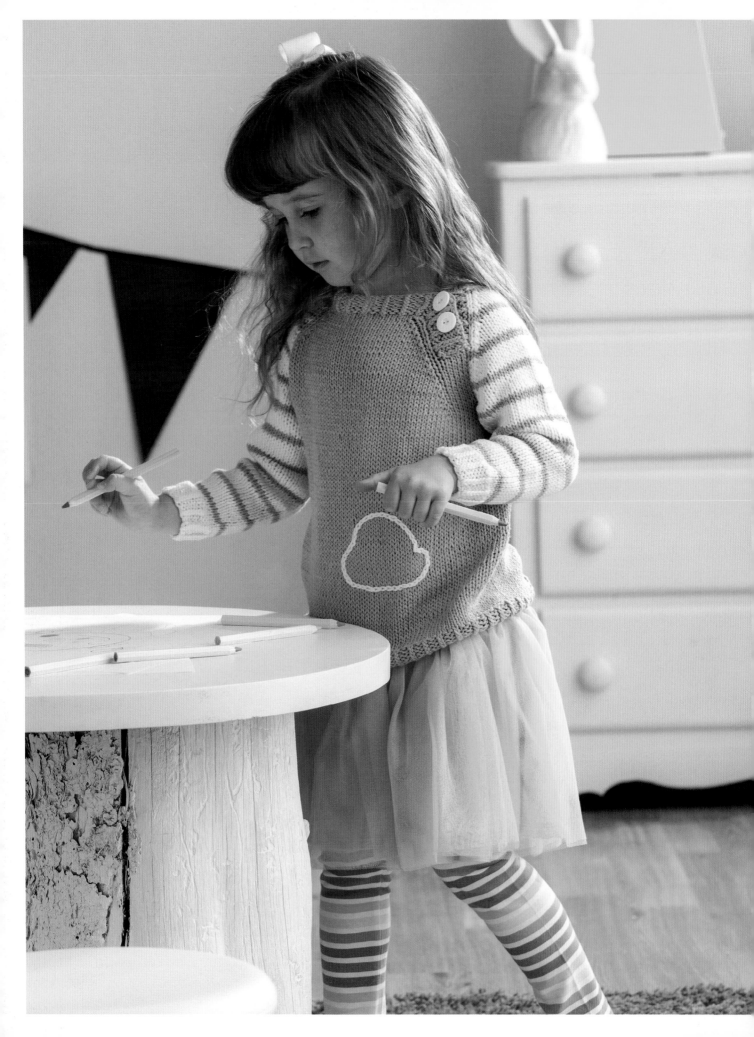

Nuage
PULLOVER

NADIA CRÉTIN-LÉCHENNE

This clever pullover is knit in a lightweight cotton for year-round comfort. The light-as-a-cloud garment is cleverly accentuated by a delicate embroidered cloud! Buttons at the raglan seams give an additional touch of whimsy.

FINISHED SIZE

6 months (18 months, 24 months, 3T, 4T, 5T).

About 19¼ (21¼, 22¾, 25¼, 26½, 28½)" (49 [54, 58, 64, 67.5, 72.5] cm) chest circumference.

Pullover shown measures 25¼" (67.5 cm).

YARN

DK weight (#3 Light).

Shown here: Berroco Weekend DK (75% acrylic, 25% Peruvian cotton; 268 yd [247 m]/100 g): #2904 Pebble (beige; A), 2 skeins; #2902 Vanilla (white; B), 1 skein.

NEEDLES

Size U.S. 6 (4 mm): 24" (61 cm) circular (cir) and set of 4 or 5 double-pointed (dpn).

Adjust needle size if necessary to obtain the correct gauge.

NOTIONS

Markers (m); stitch holders or waste yarn; size G/6 (4 mm) crochet hook; tapestry needle; sewing needle and matching thread; two ¾" (2 cm) buttons.

GAUGE

20 sts and 27 rows/rnds = 4" (10 cm) in St st after blocking.

SLEEVE STRIPE

Rnds 1 and 2: Knit with A.

Rnds 3–8: Knit with B.

Rep Rnds 1–8 for patt.

Do not cut yarn between stripes, carry unused yarn loosely on WS.

P2, K1TBL RIB IN THE ROUND (MULTIPLE OF 3 STS)
Rnd 1: *P2, k1 through back loop (k1tbl); rep from * to end.

Rep Rnd 1 for patt.

P2, K1TBL RIB IN ROWS (MULTIPLE OF 3 STS)
Row 1: (RS) *P2, k1 through back loop (k1tbl); rep from * to end.

Row 2: *P1 through back loop (p1tbl), k2; rep from * to end.

Rep Rows 1 and 2 for patt.

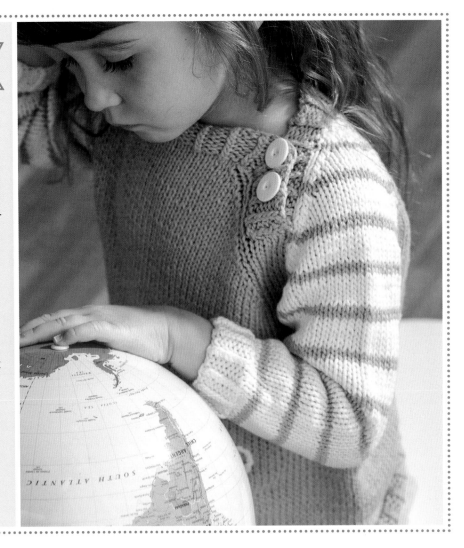

Body

With A, loosely CO 96 (105, 114, 126, 132, 141) sts on cir. Place marker (pm) and join for knitting in rnds, being careful not to twist sts. Work in p2, k1tbl rib (see Stitch Guide) for 1¼" (3.2 cm).

Next rnd: (inc) K1, M1L (see Glossary) 0 (1, 0, 0, 0, 1) time(s), knit to end—96 (106, 114, 126, 132, 142) sts.

Work even in St st until piece measures 7 (8, 9, 9¾, 10½, 11½)" (18 [20.5, 23, 25, 26.5, 29] cm) from CO.

DIVIDE FOR BODY AND SLEEVES

Next rnd: Knit and place next 4 (4, 4, 6, 6, 6) sts on holder for right underarm, knit and place next 44 (49, 53, 57, 60, 65) sts on holder for front, knit and place next 4 (4, 4, 6, 6, 6) sts on holder for left underarm, knit 44 (49, 53, 57, 60, 65) sts for back.

BACK

Next row: (WS) Purl with A.

Row 1: (RS—dec) K2, k2tog, knit to last 4 sts, ssk, k2; 2 sts dec'd—42 (47, 51, 55, 58, 63) sts.

Rows 2–4: Work in St st.

Rep last 4 rows 1 (1, 1, 2, 2, 3) more time(s)—40 (45, 49, 51, 54, 57) sts.

Work dec row every other row 10 (11, 12, 13, 13, 14) times—20 (23, 25, 25, 28, 29) sts.

Cut yarn and place rem sts on holder.

FRONT

Place 44 (49, 53, 57, 60, 65) held front sts on cir.

Next row: (WS) Purl with A.

Row 1: (RS—dec) K7, k2tog, knit to last 4 sts, ssk, k2; 2 sts dec'd—42 (47, 51, 55, 58, 63) sts.

Row 2: (WS) Purl.

Rep last 2 rows 3 (4, 5, 6, 6, 7) more times and then Row 1 once more—34 (37, 39, 41, 44, 47) sts.

Next row: (WS) BO 5 sts, purl to end.

Next row: (RS—dec) K2, k2tog, knit to last 4 sts, ssk, k2; 2 sts dec'd—27 (30, 32, 34, 37, 40) sts.

Next row: (WS) Purl.

Rep last 2 rows 5 (5, 5, 6, 6, 7) more times—17 (20, 22, 22, 25, 26) sts.

Cut yarn and place rem sts on holder.

Sleeves
LEFT SLEEVE

With B, loosely CO 30 (30, 33, 33, 36, 39) sts. Pm for beg of rnd and join for working in rnds, being careful not to twist sts. Knit in p2, k1tbl rib for 1¼" (3.2 cm).

Next rnd: (inc) K1, M1L 0 (0, 1, 1, 0, 1) time(s), knit to end—30 (30, 34, 34, 36, 40) sts.

Next rnd: Knit.

Change to A and work in Sleeve Stripe patt from Stitch Guide. *At the same time,* work sleeve shaping as foll:

Knit 5 rnds.

Next rnd: (inc) K1, M1L, knit to last st, M1R, k1—2 sts inc'd.

Rep inc rnd every 7 (8, 9, 10, 11, 12)th rnd 2 (2, 2, 3, 3, 3) more times while maintaining Sleeve Stripe patt—36 (36, 40, 42, 44, 48) sts.

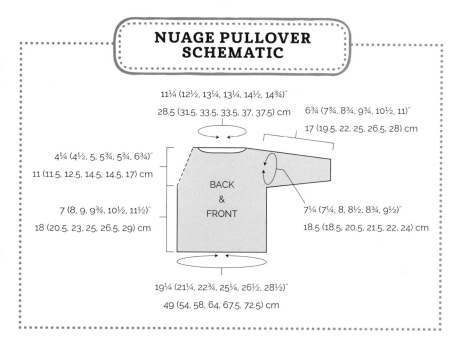

NUAGE PULLOVER SCHEMATIC

11¼ (12½, 13¼, 13¼, 14½, 14¾)"
28.5 (31.5, 33.5, 33.5, 37, 37.5) cm

6¾ (7¾, 8¾, 9¾, 10½, 11)"
17 (19.5, 22, 25, 26.5, 28) cm

4¼ (4½, 5, 5¾, 5¾, 6¾)"
11 (11.5, 12.5, 14.5, 14.5, 17) cm

7 (8, 9, 9¾, 10½, 11½)"
18 (20.5, 23, 25, 26.5, 29) cm

BACK & FRONT

7¼ (7¼, 8, 8½, 8¾, 9½)"
18.5 (18.5, 20.5, 21.5, 22, 24) cm

19¼ (21¼, 22¾, 25¼, 26½, 28½)"
49 (54, 58, 64, 67.5, 72.5) cm

Work even in St st while maintaining Sleeve Stripe patt until sleeve measures 6¾ (7¾, 8¾, 9¾, 10½, 11)" (17 [19.5, 22, 25, 26.5, 28] cm) from CO.

Next rnd: Knit to last 2 (2, 2, 3, 3, 3) sts, knit and place next 4 (4, 4, 6, 6, 6) sts on holder for left underarm.

(*)The rest of the sleeve will be knit back and forth in rows. Purl 1 row.

Row 1: (RS—dec) K2, k2tog, knit to last 4 sts, ssk, k2—2 sts dec'd.

Row 2: (WS) Purl.

Row 3: (RS—dec) Knit to last 4 sts, ssk, k2—1 st dec'd.

Row 4: (WS) Purl.

Rep last 4 rows 1 (1, 1, 2, 2, 3) more time(s), then work Rows 1 and 2 a total of 9 (9, 11, 10, 11, 12) times—10 sts.

Work short-rows (see Glossary) as foll to shape top of sleeve:

Short-Row 1: (RS) K2, k2tog, k3, wrap next st, turn work.

Short-Row 2: (WS) Purl to end.

Short-Row 3: (RS) K2, k2tog, k1, wrap next st, turn work.

Short-Row 4: (WS) Purl to end.

Short-Row 5: (RS) Knit to end of row, working wrapped sts tog with their wraps—8 sts.

Place rem sts on holder.

RIGHT SLEEVE
Work as for left sleeve until beg of section worked in rows marked with (*).

The rest of the sleeve will be knit back and forth in rows. Purl 1 row.

Row 1: (RS—dec) K2, k2tog, knit to last 4 sts, ssk, k2—2 sts dec'd.

Row 2: (WS) Purl.

Row 3: (RS—dec) K2, k2tog, knit to end—1 st dec'd.

Row 4: (WS) Purl.

Rep last 4 rows 1 (1, 1, 2, 2, 3) more time(s), then work Rows 1 and 2 a total of 8 (8, 10, 9, 10, 11) times—12 sts.

Work short-rows as foll to shape top of sleeve:

Short-Row 1: (RS) K2, k2tog, knit to last 4 sts, ssk, k2.

Short-Row 2: (WS) Purl to last 3 sts, wrap next st, turn work.

Short-Row 3: (RS) Knit to last 4 sts, ssk, k2.

Short-Row 4: (WS) Purl to last 5 sts, wrap next st, turn work.

Short-Row 5: (RS) Knit to last 4 sts, ssk, k2.

Short-Row 6: (WS) Purl to end of row, working wrapped sts tog with their wraps—8 sts.

Place rem sts on holder.

Neckband

Using mattress stitch (see Glossary), sew raglan seams.

With A, starting at bottom corner of the left front raglan, pick up and knit 13 (13, 15, 15, 15, 16) sts along left raglan edge of front up to neck, knit 17 (20, 22, 22, 25, 26) held front sts, knit 8 right sleeve sts, knit 20 (23, 25, 25, 28, 29) held back sts, knit 8 left sleeve sts, pick up and knit 12 (12, 15, 15, 15, 15) sts along left raglan edge of sleeve— 78 (84, 93, 93, 99, 102) sts.

Work in p2, k1tbl rib for 3 rows.

Next row: (RS—buttonholes) (P2, k1tbl) twice, yo, p2tog, k1tbl, p2, k1tbl, yo, p2tog, k1tbl, *(p2, k1tbl); rep from * to end.

Work in p2, k1tbl rib for 3 rows. Loosely BO all sts knitwise.

Finishing

Using B and crochet hook, embroider a little cloud on front as shown in photograph, using the chain stitch (see Glossary).

LEFT ARMHOLE

Place each set of 4 (4, 4, 6, 6, 6) left underarm sts on a dpn. With RS facing each other and using three-needle method (see Glossary), BO all sts.

RIGHT ARMHOLE

Rep as for left armhole.

If necessary, use yarn tail to close any hole under the arms.

Weave in loose ends. Block pullover to measurements. Sew buttons opposite buttonholes.

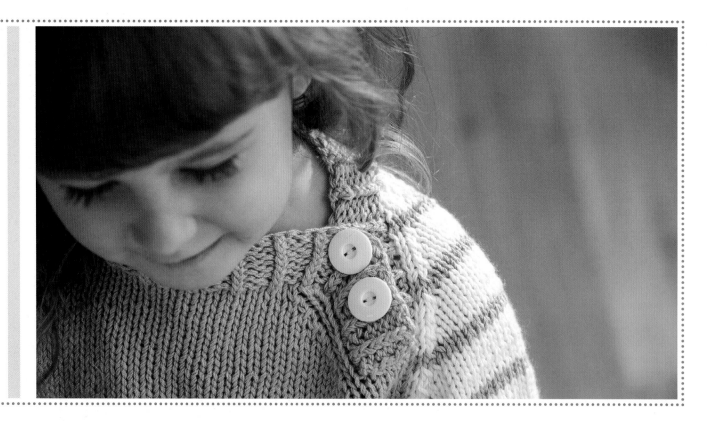

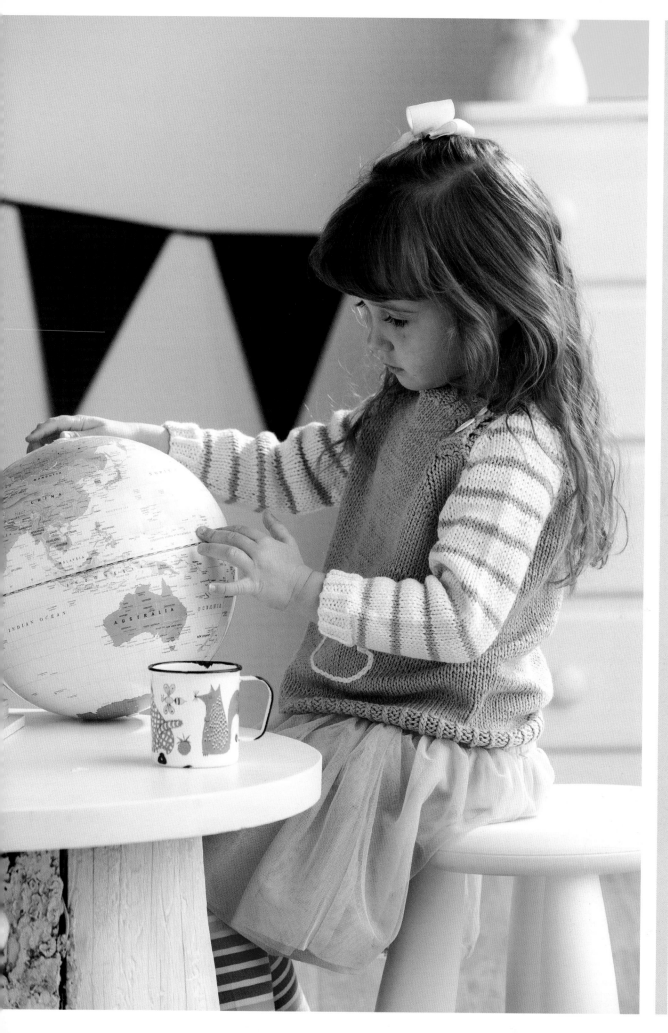

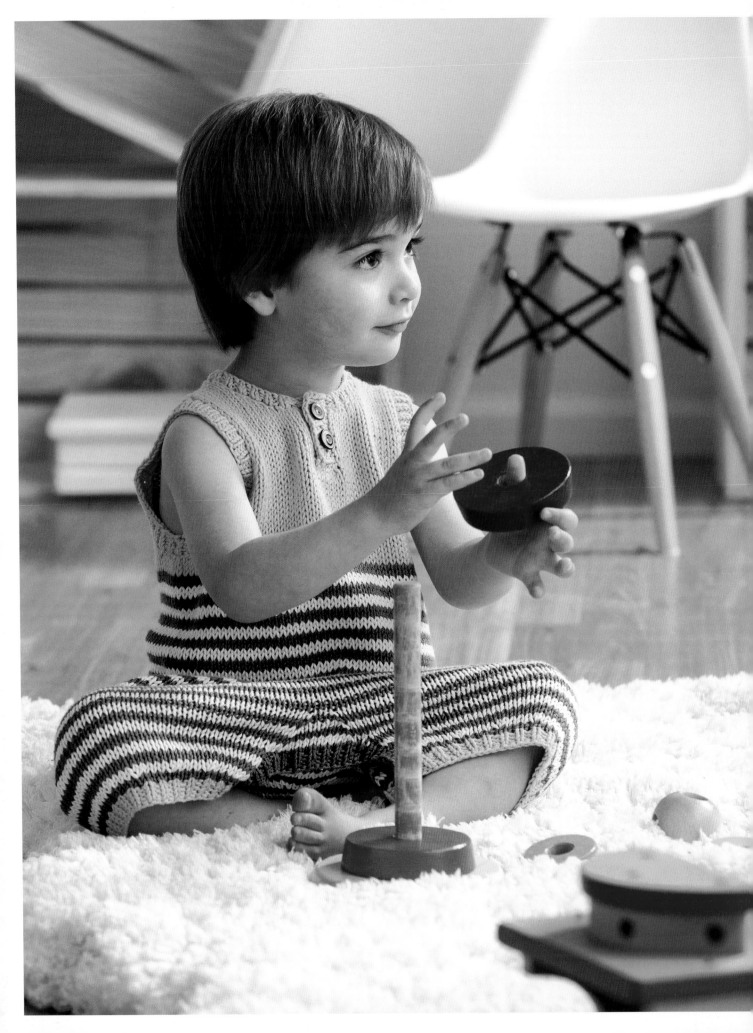

Stripy
ROMPER

KATE OATES

This colorful sleeveless romper keeps baby breezy and free to move comfortably. It features a placketed henley neckline to allow for easy on/off over the head, snaps at the bottom for easy diaper changes, and some optional short-row shaping at the bum to accommodate bulkier cloth diapers. It is worked from the top down, so you can easily knit to fit.

FINISHED SIZE
Newborn (6 months, 12 months, 18 months, 24 months, 3T).

About 16¾ (18½, 20, 20¾, 23¼, 24)" (42.5 [47, 51, 52.5, 59, 61] cm) chest circumference.

Romper shown measures 23¼" (59 cm).

YARN
Worsted weight (#4 Medium).

Shown here: Berroco Modern Cotton (60% cotton, 40% rayon/viscose; 209 yd [191 m]/100 g): #1654 Bluebird (blue; A), #1601 Sandy Point (white; B), and #1636 Meadow Lark (yellow; C), 1 skein each.

NEEDLES
Main body: Size U.S. 7 (4.5 mm): 16" (40.5 cm) circular (cir) and set of 4 or 5 double-pointed (dpn).

Edging: Size U.S. 6 (4 mm): 16" (40.5 cm) cir and set of dpn.

Adjust needle size if necessary to obtain the correct gauge.

NOTIONS
Markers (m); stitch holders or waste yarn; smooth waste yarn for provisional cast-on; tapestry needle; sewing needle and matching thread; 1 (1, 1, 2, 2, 2)½" (1.3 cm) button(s); 4 pairs of 5/16" (0.8 cm) snaps.

GAUGE
20 sts and 26 rnds = 4" (10 cm) in St st on larger needles.

STITCH GUIDE

STRIPY PATTERN IN THE ROUND
Rnds 1 and 2: Knit with A.

Rnds 3 and 4: Knit with B.

Rep Rnds 1–4 for patt.

STRIPY PATTERN IN ROWS
Row 1: Knit with A.

Row 2: Purl with A.

Row 3: Knit with B.

Row 4: Purl with B.

Rep Rows 1–4 for patt.

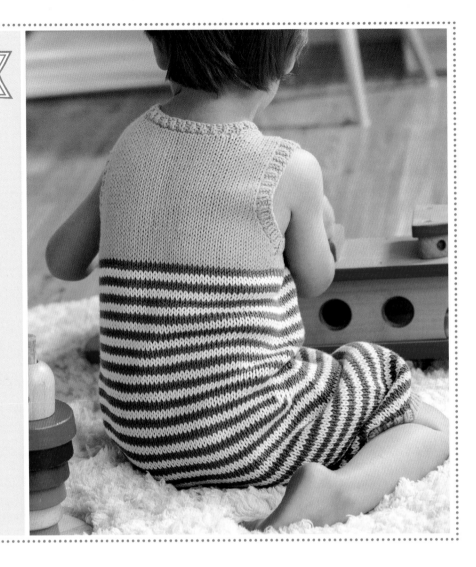

Back

This section is knit entirely with C.

RIGHT BACK

Using waste yarn and a provisional method (see Glossary), CO 4 (5, 6, 6, 7, 8) sts on larger dpn. Do not join. Beg with WS, work in St st with C for 2 rows.

Row 1: (WS) Purl.

Row 2: (RS—inc) K1, M1R (see Glossary), knit to end—5 (6, 7, 7, 8, 9) sts.

Rep Rows 1 and 2 once more and then work Row 1 once more—6 (7, 8, 8, 9, 10)

sts. Cut yarn and place sts on stitch holder or waste yarn.

LEFT BACK

Using waste yarn and a provisional method, CO 4 (5, 6, 6, 7, 8) sts on larger dpn. Do not join. Beg with WS, work in St st with C for 2 rows.

Row 1: (WS) Purl.

Row 2: (RS—inc) Knit to last st, M1L (see Glossary), k1—5 (6, 7, 7, 8, 9) sts.

Rep Rows 1 and 2 once more and then work Row 1 once more—6 (7, 8, 8, 9, 10) sts.

JOIN LEFT AND RIGHT BACK

Next row: (RS) Knit 6 (7, 8, 8, 9, 10) left back sts; using cable method (see Glossary) CO 16 (16, 16, 18, 18, 18) sts for back neck, knit 6 (7, 8, 8, 9, 10) held right back sts—28 (30, 32, 34, 36, 38) sts.

Work even in St st until piece measures 3 (3¼, 3¼, 3½, 3¾, 3¾)" (7.5 [8.5, 8.5, 9, 9.5, 9.5] cm) ending after a WS row.

Row 1: (RS—inc) K1, M1R, knit to last st, M1L, k1; 2 sts inc'd—30 (32, 34, 36, 38, 40) sts.

Row 2: Purl.

Rep the last 2 rows 3 (3, 4, 4, 5, 5) more times—36 (38, 42, 44, 48, 50) sts.

Next row: (RS) Using cable method, CO 3 (4, 4, 4, 5, 5) sts, knit to end.

Next row: CO 3 (4, 4, 4, 5, 5) sts, knit to end—42 (46, 50, 52, 58, 60) sts. Cut yarn and place sts on holder.

Front

This section is knit entirely with C.

RIGHT FRONT

Carefully remove waste yarn from provisional CO for right back and place 4 (5, 6, 6, 7, 8) exposed sts on larger dpn, ready to work RS. Work 4 rows even in St st.

Next row: (RS—inc) Knit to last st, M1L, k1.

Next row: Purl.

Rep the last 2 rows twice more.

Next row: (RS) Knit to last st, M1L, k1. Do not turn. Using cable method, CO 4 (4, 4, 5, 5, 5) sts for front neck—12 (13, 14, 15, 16, 17) sts.

Work even in St st until piece measures 3 (3¼, 3¼, 3½, 3¾, 3¾)" (7.5 [8.5, 8.5, 9, 9.5, 9.5] cm) ending after a WS row. Cut yarn and place sts on holder.

LEFT FRONT

Carefully remove waste yarn from provisional CO for left back and place 4 (5, 6, 6, 7, 8) exposed sts on larger dpn, ready to work RS. Work 4 rows even in St st.

Next row: (RS—inc) K1, M1R, knit to end.

Next row: Purl.

Rep the last 2 rows twice more.

Next row: (RS) K1, M1R, knit to end.

Next row: Purl to end. Using cable method, CO 4 (4, 5, 5, 5, 5) sts for neck edge—12 (13, 14, 15, 16, 17) sts.

Work even in St st until piece measures 3 (3¼, 3¼, 3½, 3¾, 3¾)" (7.5 [8.5, 8.5, 9, 9.5, 9.5] cm) ending after a WS row.

JOIN LEFT AND RIGHT FRONT

With larger cir, knit 12 (13, 14, 15, 16, 17) held right front sts; using cable method, CO 4 sts, then knit 12 (13, 14, 15, 16, 17) left front sts—28 (30, 32, 34, 36, 38) sts.

Row 1: (RS—inc) K1, M1R, knit to last st, M1L, k1; 2 sts inc'd—30 (32, 34, 36, 38, 40) sts.

Row 2: Purl.

Rep the last 2 rows 3 (3, 4, 4, 5, 5) more times—36 (38, 42, 44, 48, 50) sts.

Next row: (RS) Using cable method, CO 3 (4, 4, 4, 5, 5) sts, knit to end.

Next row: CO 3 (4, 4, 4, 5, 5) sts, knit to end—42 (46, 50, 52, 58, 60) sts.

Join Front and Back

Set-up rnd: With C, knit 42 (46, 50, 52, 58, 60) front sts, place marker (pm) for beg of rnd at left side, knit 42 (46, 50, 52, 58, 60) held back sts, pm at right side, then knit front sts again—84 (92, 100, 104, 116, 120) sts.

Work 3 rnds even with C. Cut yarn.

Lower Body

The rest of the romper is worked in Stripy patt (see Stitch Guide). Work Rnds 1–4 of Stripy patt a total of 2 (3, 4, 5, 6, 7) times.

Then shape lower body as foll:

Rnd 1: (inc) With A, [K1, M1L, knit to 1 st before m, M1R, k1, slip marker (sl m)] twice; 4 sts inc'd.

Rnds 2–7: Work even in Stripy patt.

STRIPY ROMPER SCHEMATIC

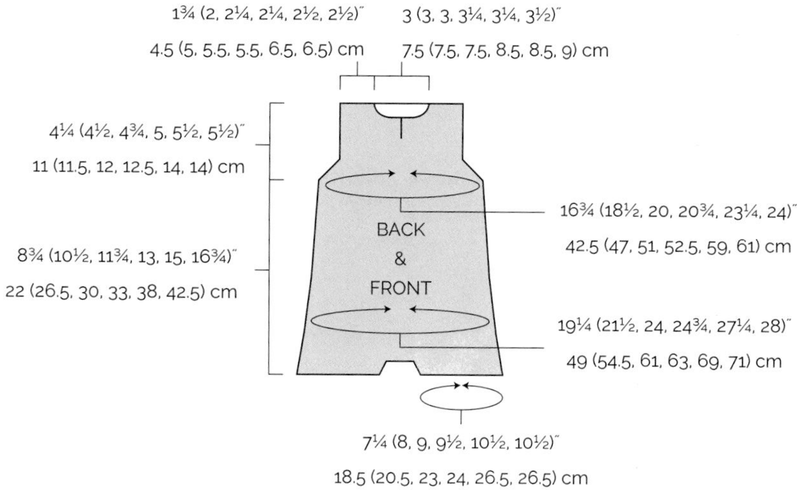

1¾ (2, 2¼, 2¼, 2½, 2½)"
4.5 (5, 5.5, 5.5, 6.5, 6.5) cm

3 (3, 3, 3¼, 3¼, 3½)"
7.5 (7.5, 7.5, 8.5, 8.5, 9) cm

4¼ (4½, 4¾, 5, 5½, 5½)"
11 (11.5, 12, 12.5, 14, 14) cm

8¾ (10½, 11¾, 13, 15, 16¾)"
22 (26.5, 30, 33, 38, 42.5) cm

BACK & FRONT

16¾ (18½, 20, 20¾, 23¼, 24)"
42.5 (47, 51, 52.5, 59, 61) cm

19¼ (21½, 24, 24¾, 27¼, 28)"
49 (54.5, 61, 63, 69, 71) cm

7¼ (8, 9, 9½, 10½, 10½)"
18.5 (20.5, 23, 24, 26.5, 26.5) cm

Rnd 8: (inc) With B, [K1, M1L, knit to 1 st before m, M1R, k1, sl m)] twice; 4 sts inc'd.

Rnds 9–12: Work even in Stripy patt.

Rnd 13: (inc) With A, [k1, M1L, knit to 1 st before m, M1R, k1, sl m] twice; 4 sts inc'd—96 (104, 112, 116, 128, 132) sts.

Rnds 14 and 15: Work even in Stripy patt.

Work back shaping in next section or skip ahead to Both Styles section.

OPTIONAL BACK SHAPING

Note: If child wears cloth diapers and thus requires a little extra room in the tush, these short-rows are suggested (shown). Otherwise, the romper should be plenty roomy even without them.

Work short-rows (see Glossary) as foll:

Short-Row 1: (RS) With B, k5, pm, k38 (42, 46, 48, 54, 56), wrap next st, turn work.

Short-Row 2: (WS) With A, p38 (42, 46, 48, 54, 56) sts, wrap next st, turn work.

Short-Row 3: With A, knit to wrapped st, knit st tog with its wrap, wrap next st, turn work.

Short-Row 4: With B, purl to wrapped st, purl st tog with its wrap, wrap next st, turn work.

For smallest size:
Skip to Both Styles section.

For all other sizes:
Short-Row 5: With B, knit to wrapped st, knit st tog with its wrap, wrap next st, turn work.

Short-Row 6: With A, purl to wrapped st, purl st tog with its wrap, wrap next st, turn work.

Short-Rows 7 and 8: Rep Short-Rows 3 and 4.

BOTH STYLES

Next rnd: With B, knit (if Back Shaping section was completed, knit any rem wrapped st tog with its wrap).

Work foll Rnds 1–4 a total of 0 (1, 2, 2, 2, 2) time(s):

Rnd 1: (inc) With A, [k1, M1L, knit to 1 st before m, M1R, k1, sl m] twice; 4 sts inc'd.

Rnds 2–4: Work even in Stripy patt.

You have 96 (108, 120, 124, 136, 140) sts.

Work even in Stripy patt until piece measures 10¼ (12¼, 12¾, 14½, 16¼, 18)" (26 [31, 32, 37, 41.5, 45.5] cm) from front shoulder seam.

Next rnd: Maintaining Stripy patt, knit 23 (26, 29, 30, 33, 34) sts for left back, pm, k2, pm, knit 46 (52, 58, 60, 66, 68) sts for right back and front, pm, k2, pm, knit to end.

CROTCH

Next rnd: (inc) Maintaining Stripy patt, *knit to marker, sl m, M1R, knit to m, sl m, M1L, rep from * to end; 4 sts inc'd.

Work inc rnd every other round a total of 3 (3, 4, 4, 5, 5) times—108 (120, 136, 140, 156, 160) sts. Work even ending after Rnd 4 of Stripy patt.

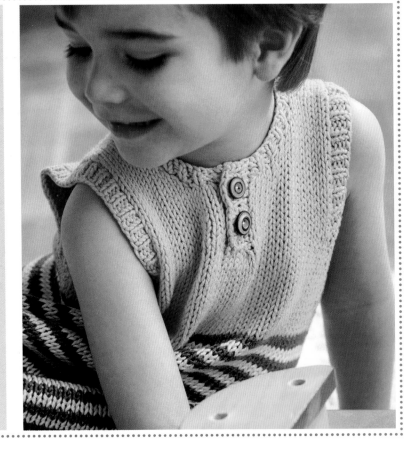

Next rnd: Removing markers as you come to them, knit to 1 st before m, place next 10 (10, 12, 12, 14, 14) sts on holder for back crotch, place next 44 (50, 56, 58, 64, 66) sts on holder for right leg, place next 10 (10, 12, 12, 14, 14) sts on holder for front crotch—44 (50, 56, 58, 64, 68) sts rem for left leg.

LEFT LEG

Maintaining Stripy patt, work in St st for 2 (2, 6, 6, 6, 6) rows.

Row 1: (RS—dec) *K3, k2tog; rep from * to last 4 (0, 1, 3, 4, 1) st(s), knit to end—36 (40, 45, 47, 52, 53) sts.

Row 2: Purl.

Row 3: With C and using smaller cir, knit.

Row 4: *P1, k1; rep from * to last 0 (0, 1, 1, 0, 1) st, purl to end.

Work in k1, p1 rib as established for 4 more rows. BO all sts in rib.

RIGHT LEG

Place 44 (50, 56, 58, 64, 68) held right leg sts on larger cir. With RS facing, work in St st for 4 (4, 8, 8, 8, 8) rows.

Row 1: (RS—dec) *K3, k2tog; rep from * to last 4 (0, 1, 3, 4, 1) st(s), knit to end—36 (40, 45, 47, 52, 53) sts.

Row 2: Purl.

Row 3: With C and using smaller cir, knit.

Row 4: *P1, k1; rep from * to last 0 (0, 1, 1, 0, 1) st, purl to end.

Work in k1, p1 rib as established for 4 more rows. BO all sts in rib.

Finishing
NECK EDGING

Neck edging is worked with C only.

With smaller cir, RS facing, and beg at center right front along neckline, pick up and knit 4 (4, 4, 5, 5, 5) sts along center front, 6 sts along diagonal neckline, 26 (26, 26, 28, 28, 28) neck sts, 6 sts along diagonal neckline and 4 (4, 4, 5, 5, 5) sts along center front—46 (46, 46, 50, 50, 50) sts.

Next row: (WS) *P1, k1; rep from * to last 2 sts, p2.

Work in k1, p1 rib as established for 3 more rows. BO all sts in rib.

PLACKET

Placket is worked with C only.

Right Front

With smaller cir, RS facing, and beg at bottom of placket, pick up and knit 9 (11, 11, 13, 13, 13) sts along center right front (along vertical edge), including neck edging.

Next row: (WS) *P1, k1; rep from * to last st, p1.

Work in k1, p1 rib as established for 3 more rows. BO all sts in rib.

Left Front

With smaller cir, RS facing, and beg at top of placket, pick up and knit 9 (11, 11, 13, 13, 13) sts along center left front (along vertical edge), including neck edging.

Next row: (WS) *P1, k1; rep from * to last st, p1.

Work in k1, p1 rib as established for 1 more row.

Next row: (WS—buttonhole) *Work 4 (4, 4, 3, 3, 3) sts in Rib patt, work 2-st one-row buttonhole (see Glossary); rep from * another 0 (0, 0, 1, 1, 1) time, work in k1, p1 rib as established to end.

Work in k1, p1 rib for 1 more row. BO all sts in rib.

ARMHOLE EDGING

Armhole edging is worked with C only.

With smaller cir, RS facing, and beg at center underarm, pick up and knit 54 (54, 60, 60, 66, 66) sts evenly spaced around opening. Pm and join for working in rnds. Work in k1, p1 rib for 4 rnds. BO all sts in rib.

Rep for other armhole.

BOTTOM EDGING

Bottom edging is worked with A only.

Place 10 (10, 12, 12, 14, 14) held front crotch sts on smaller dpn.

With smaller cir, RS facing, and beg at front right leg, pick up and knit 10 (10, 12, 12, 12, 12) sts along inside right leg, knit 10 (10, 12, 12, 14, 14) front crotch sts, pick up and knit 11 (11, 13, 13, 13, 13) sts along inside left leg—31 (31, 37, 37, 39, 39) sts.

Next row: (WS) *P1, k1; rep from * to last st, p1.

Work in k1, p1 rib as established for 3 more rows. BO all sts in rib.

Rep for held back crotch sts.

SNAP PLACEMENT

Sew 4 evenly spaced snaps to WS of front bottom edging. Sew corresponding snaps to RS of back bottom edging (bottom edgings will overlap so that front edging stays on top).

Sew button(s) to button placket opposite buttonholes. Weave in loose ends. Block to measurements.

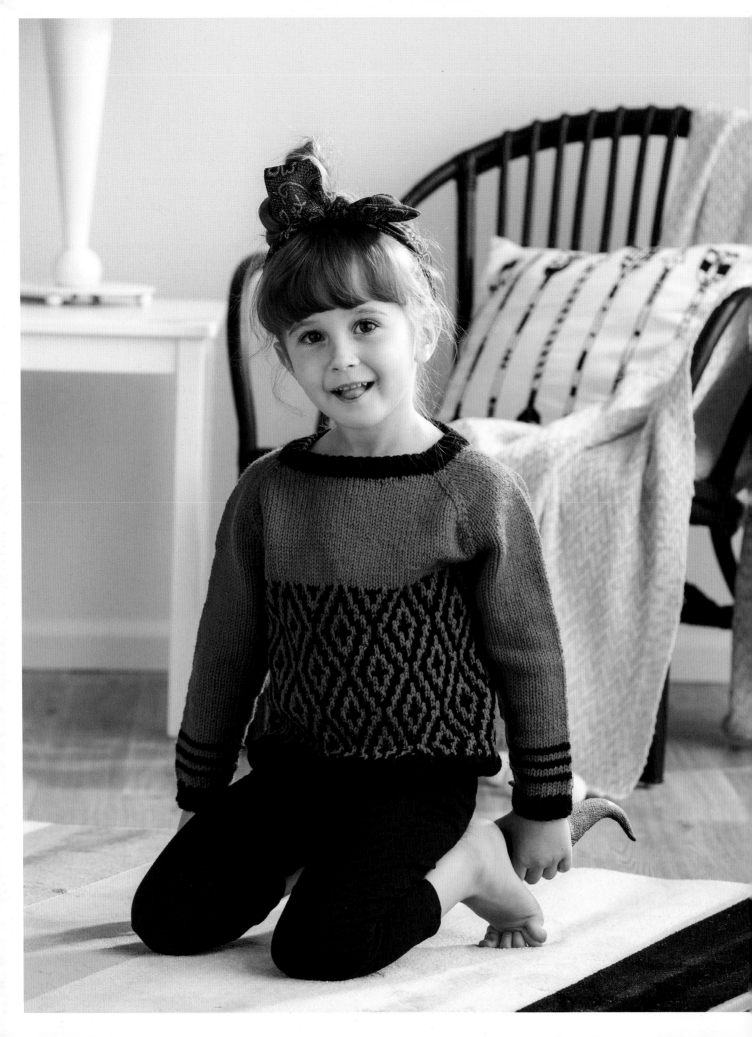

Diamond
PULLOVER

SUVI SIMOLA

This smart sweater for the little one is worked seamlessly from the top down in two colors. The neck is shaped with short-rows for a more comfortable fit. The Diamond pattern is worked in slip stitch, using only one color at a time. The Neck, hem, and cuffs are finished with a twisted rib.

FINISHED SIZE

3 months (6 months, 12 months, 18 months, 24 months, 4T).

About 18½ (19¼, 20¾, 21½, 23¼, 25½)" (47 [49, 52.5, 54.5, 59, 65] cm) chest circumference.

Pullover shown measures 25½" (65 cm).

YARN

Worsted weight (#4 Medium).

Shown here: Cascade Yarns 220 Superwash (100% superwash wool; 220 yd [200 m]/100 g): #810 Teal (A), 1 (1, 2, 2, 2, 2) skein(s); #815 Black (B), 1 skein.

NEEDLES

Sizes 18½ (19¼, 20¾, 21½)"
Size U.S. 7 (4.5 mm): 16" (40.5 cm) circular (cir) and set of 4 or 5 double-pointed (dpn).

Sizes 23¼ (25½)"
Size U.S. 7 (4.5 mm): 16" (40.5 cm) cir, 24" (61 cm) cir, and set of dpn.

Adjust needle size if necessary to obtain the correct gauge.

NOTIONS

Markers (m); stitch holders or waste yarn; tapestry needle.

GAUGE

20 sts and 26 rnds = 4" (10 cm) in St st.

20 sts and 38½ rnds = 4" (10 cm) in Diamond patt.

**K1TBL, P1 RIB
(WORKED IN RNDS ON EVEN
NUMBER OF STS)**
Rnd 1: *K1 through back loop
(k1tbl), p1; rep from * to end.

Rep Rnd 1 for patt.

SLEEVE STRIPE
Work in St st.

Rnds 1 and 2: Color B

Rnds 3 and 4: Color A

Rnds 5–8: Rep Rnds 1–4.

Rnds 9 and 10: Color B

Rnds 11–14: Color A

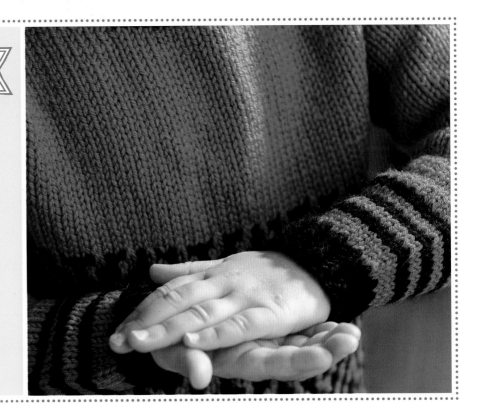

Upper Body

With B, CO 64 (68, 76, 76, 80, 84)
sts using dpn for first four sizes or
shorter cir for last two sizes.

Place marker (pm) for beg of rnd and
join for working in rnds, being careful
not to twist sts.

Work in k1tbl, p1 rib (see Stitch Guide)
for 5 rnds.

Set-up rnd: With A, sl m, k22 (24,
26, 26, 28, 30) sts for back, pm, k10
(10, 12, 12, 12, 12) sts for right sleeve,
pm, k22 (24, 26, 26, 28, 30) sts for
front, pm, k10 (10, 12, 12, 12, 12) sts for
left sleeve.

SHAPE YOKE AND NECK

The back neck is shaped with short-
rows at the same time as the yoke is
shaped with raglan increases. Work
short-rows (see Glossary) as foll:

Short-Row 1: (RS) *K1, M1L (see Glossary), knit to 1 st before m, M1R (see
Glossary), k1, sl m; rep from * once
more, k1, M1L, k1, wrap next st, turn
work.

Short-Row 2: (WS) *Purl to next m, sl
m; rep from * 3 more times, p2, wrap
next st, turn work.

Short-Row 3: *Knit to 1 st before
m, M1R, k1, sl m, k1, M1L; rep from *
3 more times, knit to previously
wrapped st, knit wrapped st tog with
its wrap, k1 (1, 1, 1, 1, 2), wrap next st,
turn work.

Short-Row 4: *Purl to next m, sl
m; rep from * 3 more times, purl
to previously wrapped st and purl
wrapped st tog with its wrap, p1 (1, 1,
1, 1, 2), wrap next st, turn work.

Short-Row 5: *Knit to 1 st before
m, M1R, k1, sl m, k1, M1L; rep from *
3 more times, knit to previously

wrapped st and knit wrapped st tog
with its wrap, k1 (1, 2, 2, 2, 2), wrap
next st, turn work.

Short-Row 6: *Purl to next m, sl
m; rep from * 3 more times, purl
to previously wrapped st and purl
wrapped st tog with its wrap, p1 (1,
2, 2, 2, 2), wrap next st very loosely,
turn work.

Short-Row 7: Knit to 1 st before m,
M1R, k1, sl m, k1, M1L, knit to 1 st
before beg of rnd marker, M1R, k1,
sl m.

When neck shaping has been completed, there are 28 (30, 32, 32, 34, 36)
sts each for front and back and 16 (16,
18, 18, 18, 18) sts for each sleeve—88
(92, 100, 100, 104, 108) sts.

SHAPE YOKE

Cont working raglan increases in
rnds in foll section. Due to neck shaping, raglan increases on first rnd

succeed raglan increases worked on short-rows, and rem wrapped sts should be knitted tog with their wraps. Change to longer cir when there are too many sts to fit around the shorter cir or dpn.

Next rnd: (inc) * K1, M1L, knit to 1 st before m, M1R, k1, sl m; rep from * 3 more times—8 sts inc'd.

Rep inc rnd every other rnd 2 (1, 2, 3, 4, 5) more time(s), then every 4th rnd 3 (4, 4, 4, 4, 4) times.

When raglan increases have been completed, there are 40 (42, 46, 48, 52, 56) sts each for front and back and 28 (28, 32, 34, 36, 38) sts for each sleeve—136 (140, 156, 164, 176, 188) sts.

DIVIDE FOR BODY AND SLEEVES

Next rnd: Removing raglan markers when you come to them, k40 (42, 46, 48, 52, 56) sts for back, place 28 (28, 32, 34, 36, 38) right sleeve sts on waste yarn or stitch holder, CO 6 (6, 6, 6, 6, 8) sts for right underarm, k40 (42, 46, 48, 52, 56) front sts, place 28 (28, 32, 34, 36, 38) left sleeve sts on holder, CO 6 (6, 6, 6, 6, 8) sts for left underarm and pm in center of these CO sts to denote beg of rnd—92 (96, 104, 108, 116, 128) sts for body.

Knit 2 rnds with A.

Lower Body

Note: The rest of the body is worked with A and B following the Diamond chart in 2-rnd sequences. The vertical bar at the right of the chart indicates which color to use for each 2-rnd sequence. The Diamond patt is worked over a multiple of 12 sts + 1 and any extra sts on either side of the Diamond patt will be worked in garter stitch.

DIAMOND PULLOVER SCHEMATIC

12¾ (13½, 15¼, 15¼, 16, 16¾)"
32 (34.5, 38.5, 38.5, 40.5, 42.5) cm

7 (7½, 8½, 9, 9½, 10¾)"
18 (19, 21.5, 23, 24, 27.5) cm

4½ (5, 5, 5½, 5¾, 6)"
11.5 (12.5, 12.5, 14, 14.5, 15) cm

BACK & FRONT

5½ (6, 6¾, 6¾, 7½, 9½)"
14 (15, 17, 17, 19, 24) cm

6¾ (6¾, 7½, 8, 8½, 9¼)"
17 (17, 19, 20.5, 21.5, 23.5) cm

18½ (19¼, 20¾, 21½, 23¼, 25½)"
47 (49, 52.5, 54.5, 59, 65) cm

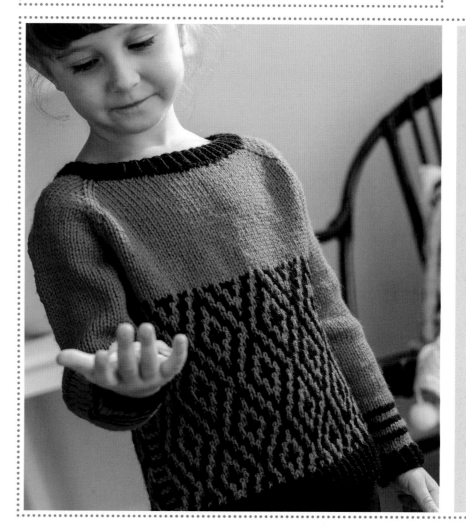

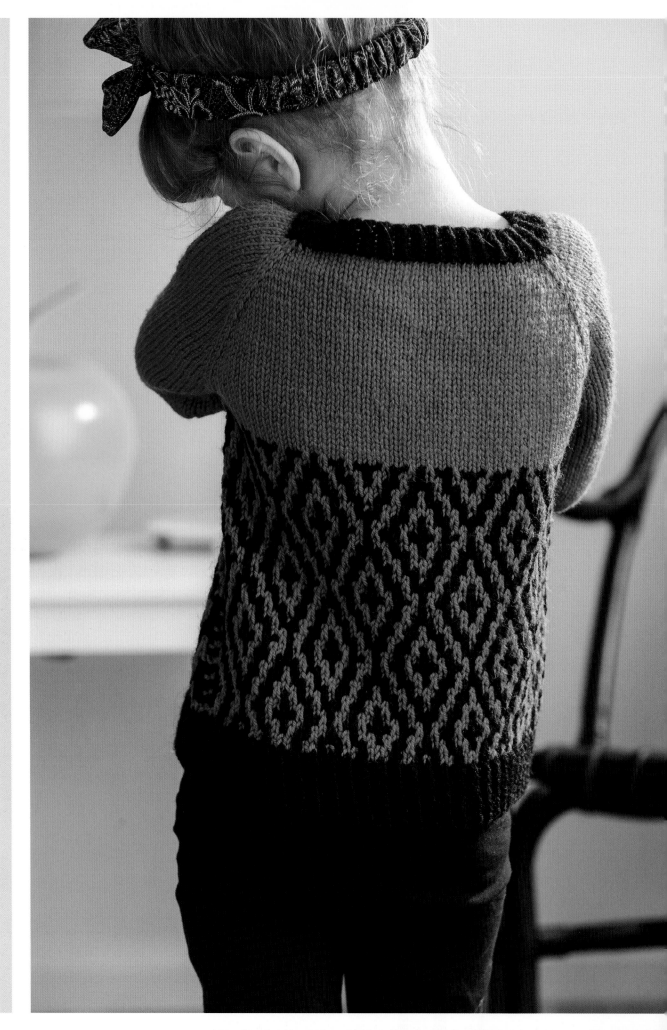

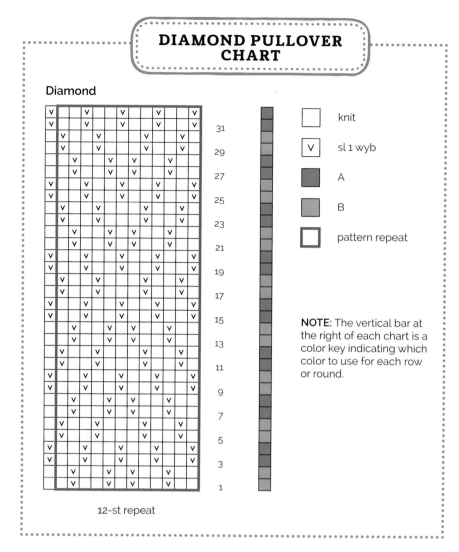

DIAMOND PULLOVER CHART

Diamond

31
29
27
25
23
21
19
17
15
13
11
9
7
5
3
1

12-st repeat

- ☐ knit
- ☑ sl 1 wyb
- ■ A
- ■ B
- ☐ pattern repeat

NOTE: The vertical bar at the right of each chart is a color key indicating which color to use for each row or round.

Size 19¼" only:
With B, work Rnds 1–32 of Diamond chart, working the 12-st patt rep 8 times. Work Rnds 1–8 once more.

Size 21½" only:
With B, work Rnds 1–32 of Diamond chart, working the 12-st patt rep 9 times. Work Rnds 1–14 once more.

All Other Sizes:
Rnd 1: With B, *k5 (–, 2, –, 5, 2) sts, pm, work Rnd 1 of Diamond chart, working the 12-st patt rep 3 (–, 4, –, 4, 5) times, work last st of Diamond chart, pm, k4 (–, 1, –, 4, 1) st(s); rep from * once more.

Rnd 2: With B, *p5 (–, 2, –, 5, 2) sts, pm, work Rnd 2 of Diamond chart, working the 12-st patt rep 3 (–, 4, –, 4, 5) times, work last st of Diamond chart, pm, p4 (–, 1, –, 4, 1) st(s); rep from * once more.

Cont as established until Rnds 3–32 of Diamond chart have been completed.

Work first 8 (–, 14, –, 22, 32) rnds once more, then work first 0 (–, 0, –, 0, 8) rnds again.

EDGING
With B, knit 1 rnd, then work in k1tbl, p1 rib for 6 (9, 9, 9, 9, 9) rnds. BO all sts.

Sleeves
Place 28 (28, 32, 34, 36, 38) held sleeve sts on dpn.

With RS facing, join A in center of sts at base of underarm CO. Pick up and knit 3 (3, 3, 3, 3, 4) sts across half of underarm CO, knit sleeve sts, pick up and knit 3 (3, 3, 3, 3, 4) sts from other half of underarm CO. Pm for end of rnd—34 (34, 38, 40, 42, 46) sts.

Work 5 rnds even.

Next rnd: (dec) K1, k2tog, knit to last 3 sts, ssk, k1—2 sts dec'd.

Rep dec rnd every 14 (16, 10, 11, 9, 9) th rnd 2 (1, 2, 1, 4, 1) more time(s), then every 0 (15, 9, 10, 8, 8)th rnd 0 (1, 2, 3, 1, 6) time(s)—28 (28, 28, 30, 30, 30) sts.

At the same time, when sleeve measures 4 (4½, 5½, 6, 6½, 7¾)" (10 [11.5, 14, 15, 16.5, 19.5] cm) from joining rnd, work Sleeve Stripe patt from Stitch Guide.

Cont working even in St st until sleeve measures 6 (6½, 7½, 8, 8½, 9¾)" (15 [16.5, 19, 20.5, 21.5, 25] cm) from joining rnd.

EDGING
With B and dpn, knit 1 rnd, then work in k1tbl, p1 rib for 5 rnds. BO all sts.

Rep for other sleeve.

Finishing
Weave in loose ends and wet-block (see Glossary) garment to measurements.

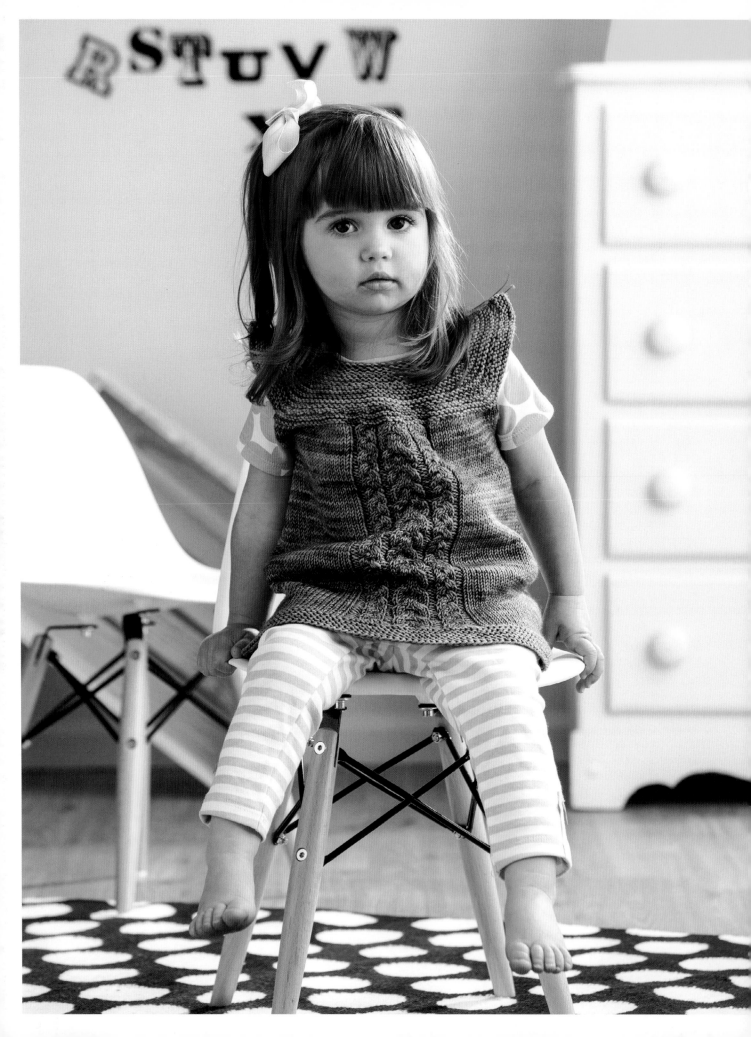

Elizabeth

TUNIC

TAIGA HILLIARD

Elizabeth is a sweet and graceful tunic top. This is knit from the top down, mostly in the round, with a slight A-line. Built with positive ease, it looks great as a tank in the summer and over a long-sleeve shirt in the winter.

FINISHED SIZE
Newborn (3 months, 12 months, 18 months, 24 months, 3T, 4T).

13¼ (16¼, 17¾, 18¾, 20¼, 21¼, 22)" (33.5 [41.5, 45, 47.5, 51.5, 54, 56] cm) chest circumference.

Tunic shown measures 22" (56 cm).

YARN
DK weight (#3 Light).

Shown here: Dream in Color Everlasting DK (100% superwash merino wool; 275 yd [251 m]/100 g): #711 Surf, 1 (1, 1, 2, 2, 2) skein(s).

NEEDLES
Size U.S. 6 (4 mm): 24" (61 cm) circular (cir).

Adjust needle size if necessary to obtain the correct gauge.

NOTIONS
Markers (m); stitch holder or waste yarn; cable needle (cn); tapestry needle; sewing needle and matching thread; one ⅝" (1.5 cm) button.

GAUGE
22 sts and 33 rnds = 4" (10 cm) in St st.

28 sts and 24 rnds of Cable patt measure 3½" (9 cm) wide and 2¾" (7 cm) high.

NOTE
When working Cable chart in the round, read all chart rows from right to left as RS rounds. When working back and forth in rows, read the odd-numbered chart rows from right to left as RS rows and read the even-numbered chart rows from left to right as WS rows.

C4B
Slip 2 stitches onto cable needle and hold in back, knit 2, knit 2 from cable needle.

C4F
Slip 2 stitches onto cable needle and hold in front, knit 2, knit 2 from cable needle.

CABLE IN ROWS (MULTIPLE OF 28 STS)
Row 1: P2, C4B, k2, p2, k8, p2, k2, C4F, p2.

Row 2 and all even-numbered rows: K2, p6, k2, p8, k2, p6, k2.

Row 3: P2, k2, C4F, p2, C4B, C4F, p2, C4B, k2, p2.

Row 5: P2, C4B, k2, p2, k8, p2, k2, C4F, p2.

Row 7: P2, k2, C4F, p2, k8, p2, C4B, k2, p2.

Row 9: P2, C4B, k2, p2, C4B, C4F, p2, k2, C4F, p2.

Row 11: P2, k2, C4F, p2, k8, p2, C4B, k2, p2.

Rows 1–12 form Cable patt.

CABLE IN THE ROUND (MULTIPLE OF 28 STS)
Rnd 1: P2, C4B, k2, p2, k8, p2, k2, C4F, p2.

Rnd 2 and all even-numbered rnds: P2, k6, p2, k8, p2, k6, p2.

Rnd 3: P2, k2, C4F, p2, C4B, C4F, p2, C4B, k2, p2.

Rnd 5: P2, C4B, k2, p2, k8, p2, k2, C4F, p2.

Rnd 7: P2, k2, C4F, p2, k8, p2, C4B, k2, p2.

Rnd 9: P2, C4B, k2, p2, C4B, C4F, p2, k2, C4F, p2.

Rnd 11: P2, k2, C4F, p2, k8, p2, C4B, k2, p2.

Rnds 1–12 form Cable patt.

Neck
Using the long-tail method (see Glossary), CO 40 (48, 54, 58, 60, 62, 64) sts.

Row 1: (WS) Knit.

Row 2: (RS—buttonhole) K2, yo, k2tog, knit to end.

Row 3: Knit.

Row 4: BO 3 sts purlwise (pwise), k1f&b (see Glossary), knit to end— 38 (46, 52, 56, 58, 60, 62) sts.

Row 5: Knit.

Row 6: K2,*k1, k1f&b; rep from * to last 2 sts, k2—55 (67, 76, 82, 85, 88, 91) sts.

Knit 5 (5, 5, 5, 5, 7, 7) rows.

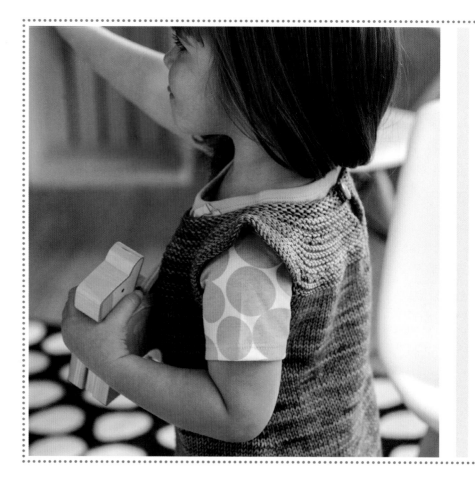

Next row: (RS) K3 (3, 2, 2, 3, 2, 3), *k1, k1f&b; rep from * to last 2 sts, k2—80 (98, 112, 121, 125, 130, 134) sts.

Knit 5 (5, 5, 5, 5, 7, 7) rows.

Next row: (RS) K2 (2, 2, 3, 3, 2, 2), *k1, k1f&b; rep from * to last 2 sts, k2—118 (145, 166, 179, 185, 193, 199) sts.

Knit 2 (2, 2, 4, 4, 4, 4) rows.

Divide for Body

Next row: (WS) Knit 19 (23, 25, 26, 28, 29, 30) sts for right back, BO next 22 (26, 33, 37, 37, 38, 39) sts knitwise (kwise), knit 36 (47, 50, 53, 55, 59, 61) sts for front, BO next 22 (26, 33, 37, 37, 38, 39) sts kwise, knit 19 (23, 25, 26, 28, 29, 30) sts for left back—74 (93, 100, 105, 111, 117, 121) sts; 36 (47, 50, 53, 55, 59, 61) sts for front and 38 (46, 50, 52, 56, 58, 60) sts for back.

Place front sts on waste yarn or stitch holder. Cut yarn and with RS facing, join working yarn at rightmost st of right back.

BACK

Row 1: (RS) Sl 1, knit to end.

Row 2: Sl 1, purl to end.

Rep the last 2 rows, until piece measures ¾ (1, 1¼, 1½, 2, 2¼, 2½)" (2 [2.5, 3.2, 3.8, 5, 5.5, 6.5] cm) from dividing row. Cut yarn and place back sts on waste yarn.

FRONT

Place 36 (47, 50, 53, 55, 59, 61) held front sts on working needle. With RS facing, join yarn to rightmost st.

Row 1: (RS) Sl 1, k1 (0, 0, 2, 0, 2, 3), *k1 (4, 3, 3, 2, 2, 2), k1f&b, k2 (4, 4, 3, 3, 3, 3); rep from * 7 (4, 5, 6, 8, 8, 8) more times, k2 (1, 1, 1, 0, 2, 3)—44 (52, 56, 60, 64, 68, 70) sts.

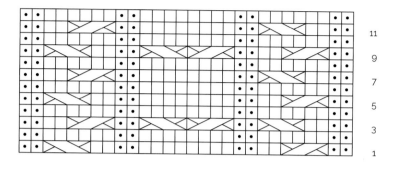

ELIZABETH TUNIC CHART

11
9
7
5
3
1

☐ knit on RS; purl on WS

• purl on RS; knit on WS

⬂ sl 2 sts onto cn, hold in front, k2, k2 from cn

⬀ sl 2 sts onto cn, hold in back, k2, k2 from cn

ELIZABETH TUNIC SCHEMATIC

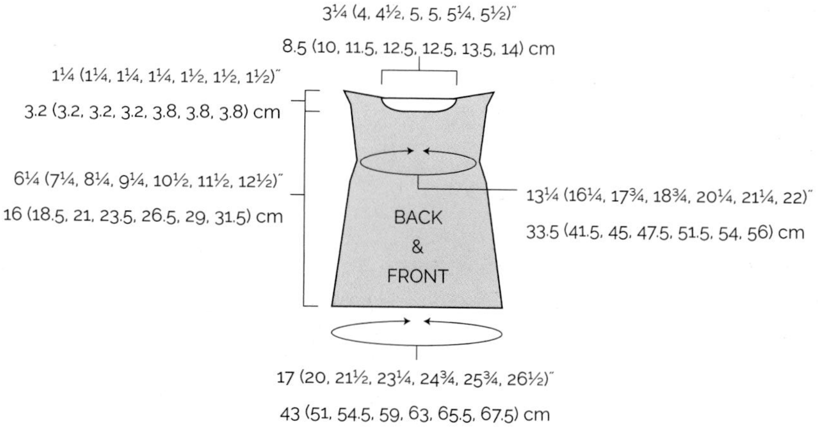

3¼ (4, 4½, 5, 5, 5¼, 5½)"
8.5 (10, 11.5, 12.5, 12.5, 13.5, 14) cm

1¼ (1¼, 1¼, 1¼, 1½, 1½, 1½)"
3.2 (3.2, 3.2, 3.2, 3.8, 3.8, 3.8) cm

6¼ (7¼, 8¼, 9¼, 10½, 11½, 12½)"
16 (18.5, 21, 23.5, 26.5, 29, 31.5) cm

BACK & FRONT

13¼ (16¼, 17¾, 18¾, 20¼, 21¼, 22)"
33.5 (41.5, 45, 47.5, 51.5, 54, 56) cm

17 (20, 21½, 23¼, 24¾, 25¾, 26½)"
43 (51, 54.5, 59, 63, 65.5, 67.5) cm

Row 2: Sl 1, p7 (11, 13, 15, 17, 19, 20), place marker (pm), k2, p6, k2, p8, k2, p6, k2, pm, purl to end.

Row 3: Sl 1, knit to m, slip marker (sl m), work Row 1 of Cable patt (from Stitch Guide or chart) over next 28 sts, sl m, knit to end.

Row 4: Sl 1, purl to m, sl m, work Row 2 of Cable patt, sl m, purl to end.

Cont in patt as established, working in St st outside of markers and working in Cable patt between markers, until piece measures ½ (¾, 1, 1¼, 1½, 1¾, 2)" (1.3 [2, 2.5, 3.2, 3.8, 4.5, 5] cm) from dividing row and ending with a WS row. Do not cut yarn.

Join Front and Back

Note: The back is longer than the front to create neck drop. The Cable patt will be maintained over the 28 center front sts until bottom edging.

Set-up rnd: Pm for beg of rnd, k8 (12, 14, 16, 18, 20, 21), sl m [cable marker], work Cable patt over next 28 sts, sl m [cable marker], k8 (12, 14, 16, 18, 20, 21), pm [side marker to divide front and back], knit 38 (46, 50, 52, 56, 58, 60) held back sts—82 (98, 106, 112, 120, 126, 130) sts total.

**Rnd 1: Knit to cable marker, work Cable patt over 28 center front sts, knit to end.

Rep last rnd 4 (4, 5, 5, 6, 6, 6) more times.

Rnd 2: (inc) *K1, M1L (see Glossary), knit to cable marker, work Cable patt over 28 center front sts, knit to last st before side marker, M1R (see Glossary), k1, sl m, rep from * to end—4 sts inc'd.

Rep from ** 2 (2, 2, 3, 3, 3, 3) more times—94 (110, 118, 128, 136, 142, 146) sts.

Rnd 3: Knit to cable marker, work Cable patt over 28 center front sts, knit to end.

Rep Rnd 3 until piece measures 5½ (6½, 7½, 8½, 9½, 10½, 11½)" (14 [16.5, 19, 21.5, 24, 26.5, 29] cm) from center front CO edge or about 1" (2.5 cm) less than desired length.

Edging

Rnd 1: Purl.

Rnd 2: Knit.

Rep the last 2 rnds 2 (2, 2, 3, 3, 3) more times.

BO all sts pwise loosely.

Finishing

Weave in all ends and sew button opposite buttonhole. Block and enjoy!

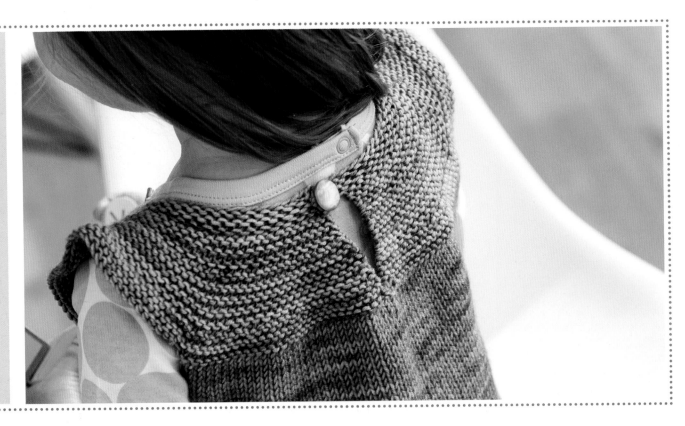

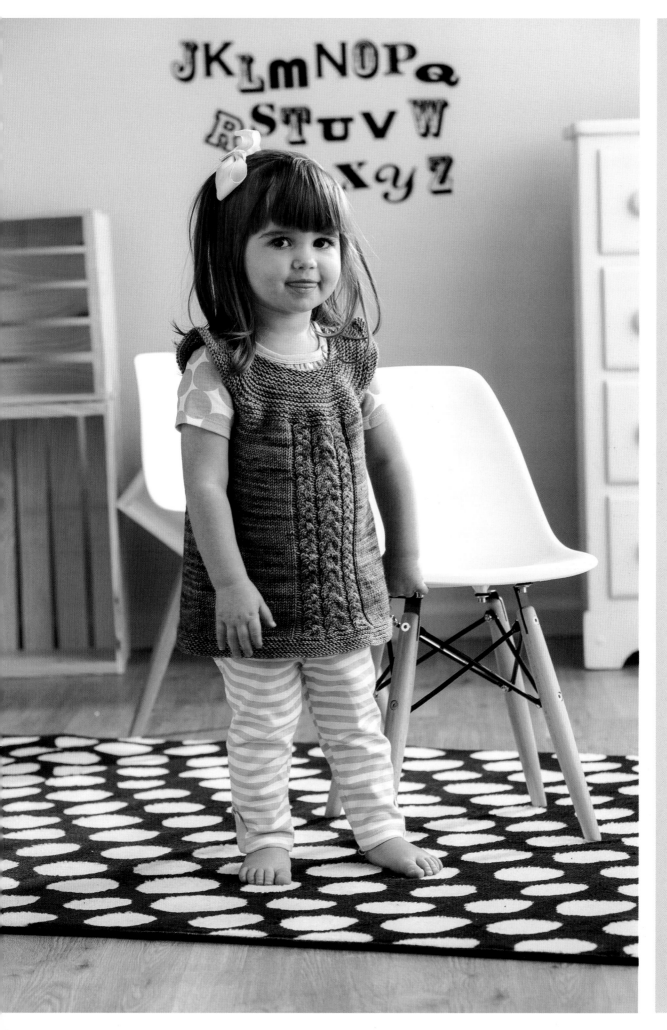

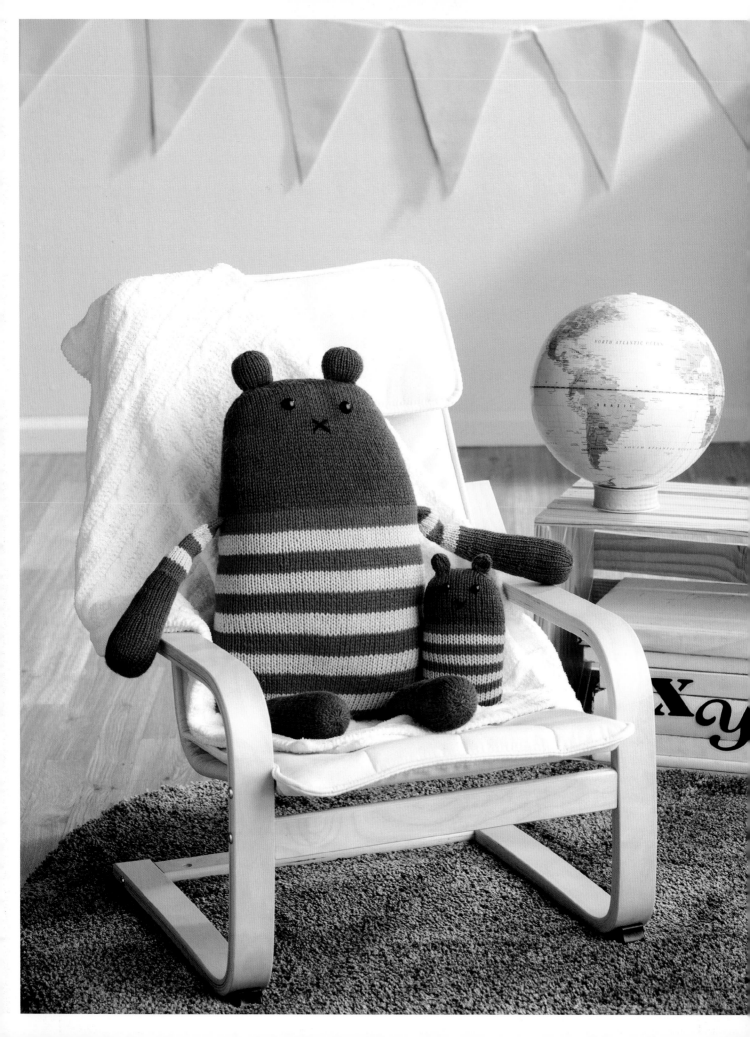

Wallie and Carter
A PAIR OF CURIOUS BEARS

REBECCA DANGER

Wallie and Carter are all about adventures! They love to go out exploring, especially on nature walks. Sometimes, Wallie (the big bear) gets tired, though, and likes to stay home and snuggle in a chair or in bed with a good book. Carter doesn't mind at all: he is the right size to fit in a pocket or baby's hands, so he is always ready to go!

FINISHED SIZE
Wallie: About 25" (63.5 cm) tall and 11" (28 cm) wide.

Carter: About 7" (18 cm) tall and 4½" (11.5 cm) wide.

YARN
Worsted weight (#4 Medium).

Shown here: Rowan Pure Wool Superwash Worsted (100% superwash wool; 219 yd [200 m]/100 g): #105 Cocoa Bean (brown; A), #139 Peacock (aqua; B), and #137 Oxygen (light blue; C), 1 skein each.

NEEDLES
Size U.S. 5 (3.75 mm): 40" (101.5 cm) circular (cir) for working magic-loop method.

Adjust needle size if necessary to obtain the correct gauge.

NOTIONS
Removable markers (m); tapestry needle; small amount of black yarn to embroider face; 1 set of ⅝" (1.5 cm) black safety eyes for Wallie (optional—see notes); 1 set of ⅜" (1 cm) black safety eyes for Carter (optional—see notes); polyester stuffing.

GAUGE
28 sts and 40 rnds = 4" (10 cm) in St st before stuffing.

Wallie and Carter are knit in one piece in the round using the magic-loop method (see Glossary). Stitch markers are placed so that limbs and ears can be picked up from the body and knit in one piece.

Instructions are included to knit all pieces separately as well. If so, markers can still be placed to indicate where to sew limbs to body.

Safety eyes should not be given to anyone under the age of three, as they can be chewed off and ingested. To make your bears safe for baby, use black yarn to embroider eyes and nose.

Wallie and Carter can easily be knit on other needle/yarn combinations. Gauge is not important. Simply use needles two or three sizes smaller than those recommended for your yarn to make a tight knit fabric your stuffing doesn't show through.

Finished size and yardage needed will vary depending on needles used: larger finished bears and more yardage for larger needles, smaller finished bears and less yardage for smaller needles.

Add a rattle insert, jingle bell, or even crinkle plastic into Carter for a perfect baby toy that makes noise when moved or squeezed!

Use Meg Swansen's Jogless Jog technique (see Glossary) when working stripes in the round.

Wallie

Body

With B and using Turkish/Eastern method (see Glossary), CO 92 sts (46 loops on each needle tip). Place marker (pm) to indicate beg of rnd and beg knitting in rnds using magic-loop method.

Rnd 1: With B, knit loops from CO—92 sts.

Place removable markers in sts #4, 11, 36, and 43 to mark leg placement.

Rnd 2: With B, (k1f&b, k44, k1f&b) twice—96 sts.

Rnds 3–6: Knit with B.

Rnds 7–12: Knit with C.

Rnds 13–18: Knit with B.

Rnds 19–66: Rep Rnds 7–18 four more times—there are 11 stripes in total, 6 with B and 5 with C.

Place removable markers in sts #3, 46, 51, and 94 on Rnd 65 to mark arm placement.

Head

The rest of the head will be knit with A only as foll:

Rnds 67–90: Knit with A.

Rnd 91: (Ssk, k46) twice—94 sts.

Rnds 92, 94, 96, 98, 100, and 102: Knit.

Rnd 93: (K45, k2tog) twice—92 sts.

Rnd 95: (Ssk, k44) twice—90 sts.

Rnd 97: (K43, k2tog) twice—88 sts.

Rnd 99: (Ssk, k42) twice—86 sts.

Rnd 101: (K41, k2tog) twice—84 sts.

Rnd 103: (K1, ssk, k36, k2tog, k1) twice—80 sts.

Rnd 104: (K1, ssk, k34, k2tog, k1) twice—76 sts.

Rnd 105: (K1, ssk, k32, k2tog, k1) twice—72 sts.

Rnd 106: (K1, ssk, k30, k2tog, k1) twice—68 sts.

Rnd 107: (K1, ssk, k28, k2tog, k1) twice—64 sts.

Rnd 108: (K1, ssk, k26, k2tog, k1) twice—60 sts.

Rnd 109: (K1, ssk 3 times, k16, k2tog 3 times, k1) twice—48 sts.

Place removable markers in sts #1, 17, 25, and 40 to mark ear placement.

Cut yarn, leaving a 10" (25.5 cm) tail. Stuff body with polyester stuffing. Add safety eyes (or embroider eyes) and embroider nose using photo as a guide. Once body is stuffed, thread tail on tapestry needle and use Kitchener stitch (see Glossary) to graft set of 24 live front head sts to corresponding set of 24 back head sts and close top of head. Add stuffing as you finish closing up the head.

Left Ear

Ears are knit with A only.

Note: To knit as a separate piece, CO 16 sts and knit sts in the rnd (counts as Rnd 1). Work rest of pattern as written.

Rnd 1: With A and starting from marker in st #1 on top of head, pick up and knit 8 sts along top of head toward center top of the head. Then starting from marker in st #40 on top of head, pick up and knit 8 sts along top of head toward edge of head—16 sts.

Rnd begins at lower edge of ear (i.e., first st picked up is first st of rnd). Pm to indicate beg of rnd and beg to work in rnds as foll:

Rnd 2: (K1f&b, k6, k1f&b) twice—20 sts.

Rnds 3–14: Knit.

Rnd 15: K2tog 10 times—10 sts.

Lightly stuff ear. Cut yarn and thread tail on tapestry needle, pull it through rem sts to close ear.

Right Ear

Work as for left ear, starting from marker in st #17 on top of head toward edge of head, then picking up sts from marker in st #25 toward center top of head.

Left Arm

Note: To knit as a separate piece, CO 12 sts and knit sts in the rnd (counts as Rnd 1). Work rest of pattern as written.

Rnd 1: With B and starting from marker in st #94 from Rnd 65, pick up and knit 6 sts along waist toward marker in st #3. Then, going in opposite direction, pick up and knit 6 sts 1 rnd above just picked-up sts—12 sts.

Pm to indicate beg of rnd and beg to work in rnds as foll:

Rnds 2–6: Knit with B.

Rnds 7–9: Knit with C.

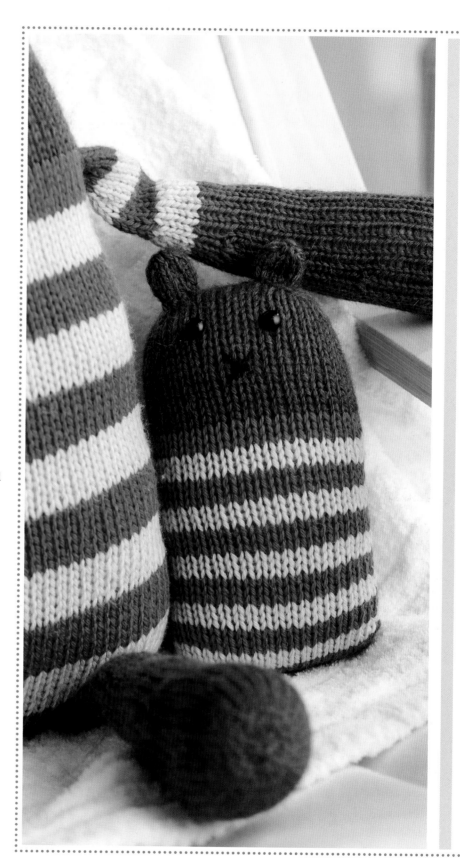

Rnd 10: With C, (k1f&b, k5) twice—14 sts.

Rnds 11 and 12: Knit with C.

Rnds 13–18: Knit with B.

Rnd 19: Knit with C.

Rnd 20: With C, (k6, k1f&b) twice—16 sts.

Rnds 21–24: Knit with C.

Rnd 25–29: Knit with B.

Rnd 30: With B, (k1f&b, k7) twice—18 sts.

Knit with A only to end of arm as foll:

Rnds 31–39: Knit.

Rnd 40: (K8, k1f&b) twice—20 sts.

Rnds 41–49: Knit.

Rnd 50: (K1f&b, K9) twice—22 sts.

Rnds 51–59: Knit.

Rnd 60: (K10, k1f&b) twice—24 sts.

Rnds 61–69: Knit.

Rnd 70: K2tog 12 times—12 sts.

Stuff arm with polyester stuffing. Cut yarn and thread tail on tapestry needle, pull it through rem sts to close arm.

Right Arm

Work as for left arm, starting from marker in st #51 from Rnd 65 toward marker in st #46. Be sure to place beg of rnd at back of body to avoid color changes showing on front of bear.

Left Leg

Legs are knit in A only.

Note: To knit as a separate piece, CO 16 sts and knit sts in the rnd (counts as Rnd 1). Work rest of pattern as written.

Rnd 1: With A and starting from marker in st #4 from Rnd 1, pick up and knit 8 sts toward marker in st #11. Then, going in opposite direction, turn bear, pick up and knit 8 sts 1 rnd behind just picked-up sts—16 sts.

Pm to indicate beg of rnd and beg to work in rnds as foll:

Rnds 2–9: Knit.

Rnd 10: (K1f&b, k7) twice—18 sts.

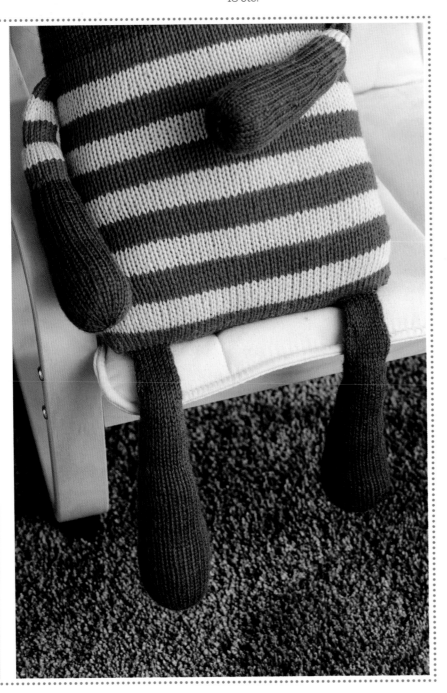

Rnds 11–19: Knit.

Rnd 20: (K8, k1f&b) twice—20 sts.

Rnds 21–29: Knit.

Rnd 30: (K1f&b, k9) twice—22 sts.

Rnds 31–39: Knit.

Rnd 40: (K10, k1f&b) twice—24 sts.

Rnds 41–49: Knit.

Rnd 50: (K1f&b, k11) twice—26 sts.

Rnds 51–59: Knit.

Rnd 60: (K12, k1f&b) twice—28 sts.

Rnds 61–69: Knit.

Rnd 70: K2tog 14 times around—14 sts.

Stuff leg with polyester stuffing. Cut yarn and thread tail on tapestry needle, pull it through rem sts to close foot.

Right Leg
Work as for left leg, starting from marker in st #36 from Rnd 1 toward marker in st #43.

Carter

Body
With B and using Turkish/Eastern method, CO 36 sts (18 loops on each needle tip). Pm to indicate beg of rnd and beg knitting in rnds using magic-loop method:

Rnd 1: With B, knit loops from CO—36 sts.

Rnd 2: With B, (k1f&b, k16, k1f&b) twice—40 sts.

Rnd 3: Knit with B.

Rnds 4–6: Knit with C.

Rnds 7–9: Knit with B.

Rnds 10–33: Rep Rnds 4–9 four more times—there are 11 stripes in total, 6 with B and 5 with C.

Head
The rest of the head will be knit with A only as foll:

Rnds 34–41: Knit with A.

Rnd 42: (Ssk, k18) twice—38 sts.

Rnds 43, 45, 47, and 49: Knit.

Rnd 44: (K17, k2tog) twice—36 sts.

Rnd 46: (Ssk, k16) twice—34 sts.

Rnd 48: (K15, k2tog) twice—32 sts.

Rnd 50: (K1, ssk, k10, k2tog, k1) twice—28 sts.

Rnd 51: (K1, ssk, k8, k2tog, k1) twice—24 sts.

Place removable markers in sts #1 and 13 to mark ear placement.

Rnd 52: (K1, ssk, k6, k2tog, k1) twice—20 sts.

Cut yarn, leaving a 10" (25.5 cm) tail. Stuff body with polyester stuffing. Add safety eyes (or embroider eyes) and embroider nose as shown. Once body is stuffed, thread tail on tapestry needle and use Kitchener stitch to graft set of 10 live front head sts to corresponding set of 10 back head sts and close top of head. Add stuffing as you finish closing up the head.

Left Ear
Ears are knit with A only.

Note: To knit as a separate piece, CO 8 sts and knit sts in the rnd (counts as Rnd 1). Work rest of pattern as written.

Rnd 1: With A and starting from marker in st #1 from Rnd 51, pick up and knit 4 sts (2 sts from dec rnds, then 2 from top of head). Then, going in opposite direction, turn bear, pick up and knit 4 sts 1 rnd behind just picked-up sts—8 sts.

Pm to indicate beg of rnd and beg to work in rnds as foll:

Rnd 2: (K1f&b, k2, k1f&b) twice—12 sts.

Rnds 3–6: Knit.

Rnd 7: K2tog 6 times—6 sts.

Stuff left ear as desired (the sample's ears are unstuffed).

Cut yarn and thread tail on tapestry needle, pull it tight through rem sts to close ear.

Right Ear
Work as for left ear, starting from marker in st #13 from Rnd 51 and picking up 2 sts from dec rnds and 2 sts from top of head. Be sure to move toward back of bear when picking up final 4 sts.

Finishing
If knit in one piece, weave in loose ends. If knit in pieces, stuff limbs and whipstitch (see Glossary) them to the body, using removable markers as a guide for placement. Tah-dah, how "bear-y" cute!

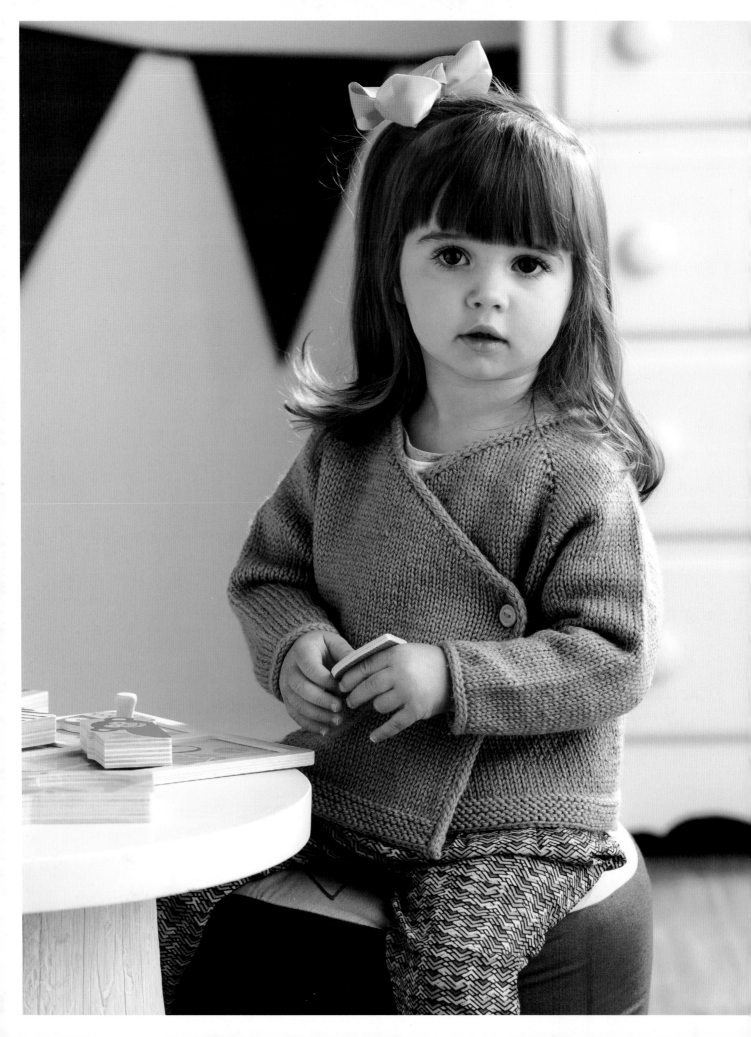

Kimono

KAREN BORREL

This wrapped cardigan is very easy and quick to knit in top-down construction, and the kimono shape is ideal for gentle on-and-off. A touch of color on the I-cord border keeps it light and bright!

FINISHED SIZE

3 months (12 months, 18 months, 24 months).

17½ (19½, 21, 23¼)" (44.5 [49.5, 53.5, 59] cm) chest circumference.

Kimono shown measures 21" (53.5 cm).

YARN

Worsted weight (#4 Medium).

Shown here: Ella Rae Superwash Classic (100% superwash wool; 219 yd [220 m]/100 g): #22 Light Grey (A), 2 skeins; #49 Cactus (B), 1 skein.

NEEDLES

Size U.S. 4 (3.5 mm): 24" (61 cm) or 32" (81.5 cm) circular (cir) and set of 4 or 5 double-pointed (dpn).

Adjust needle size if necessary to obtain the correct gauge.

NOTIONS

Markers (m); stitch holders or waste yarn; tapestry needle; sewing needle and matching thread; two ⅝" (1.5 cm) buttons.

GAUGE

22 sts and 28 rows/rnds = 4" (10 cm) in St st.

NOTES

The cardigan is worked from the top down to the underarms, the sleeves are left on hold while the lower body is worked flat. The sleeves are then worked in the round to minimize seaming. The I-cord border is worked at the end by picking up sts all around.

STITCH GUIDE

3-IN-1 INCREASE (3-IN-1 INC)
Work (k1, yo, k1) all in the same st—2 sts inc'd.

Raglan increases will be worked with 3-in-1 increases. There is therefore no need to use markers for the raglan increases, a raglan section is the group of 3 sts above the "hole" formed by the yarnover on the previous increase row.

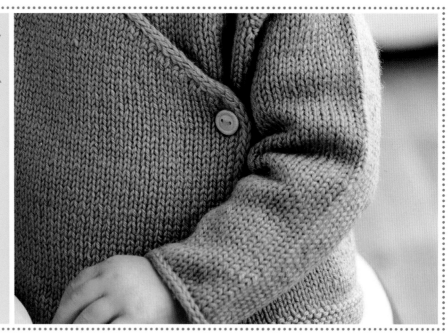

Body

Using the long-tail method (see Glossary), CO 44 (46, 48, 50) sts on cir—do not join.

Row 1 and all odd-numbered rows: (WS) Purl.

Row 2: (RS) K2 for left front, 3-in-1 inc, k8 for left sleeve, 3-in-1 inc, k20 (22, 24, 26) for back, 3-in-1 inc, k8 for right sleeve, 3-in-1 inc, k2 for right front—52 (54, 56, 58) sts.

Row 4: Using the backward-loop method (see Glossary), CO 2 sts, *knit to raglan section (see Stitch Guide), 3-in-1 inc; rep from * 3 more times, knit to end, CO 2 sts—64 (66, 68, 70) sts; 5 sts each front, 22 (24, 26, 28) back sts, 10 sts each sleeve, and four 3-st raglan sections.

Rep Rows 3 and 4 for yoke shaping 12 (14, 15, 17) more times—208 (234, 248, 274) sts; 41 (47, 50, 56) sts each front, 46 (52, 56, 62) back sts, 34 (38, 40, 44) sts each sleeve, and four 3-st raglan sections.

Next row: (WS) Purl.

DIVIDE FOR BODY AND SLEEVES

Next row: (RS—buttonhole) K1, k2tog, yo, *knit to raglan section, place 3 sts of raglan section, next 34 (38, 40, 44) sts and 3 sts of next raglan section on stitch holder for left sleeve; using backward-loop method, CO 2 sts for underarm; rep from * once more, knit to last 3 sts, yo, k2tog, k1.

Work even in St st until piece measures 4½ (5, 5½, 6)" (11.5 [12.5, 14, 15] cm) from dividing row.

Knit in garter st for ¾" (2 cm) ending after a WS row. BO all sts on RS.

Sleeves

Place 40 (44, 46, 50) held sleeve sts on dpn. With RS facing, join yarn in center of sts at base of underarm CO. Pick up and knit 2 sts across half of underarm CO, knit 40 (44, 46, 50) sleeve sts, pick up and knit 2 sts across half of underarm CO, place marker (pm)

for beg of rnd and join for working in rnds—44 (48, 50, 54) sts.

Work even in St st for 4 rnds.

Next rnd: (dec) K1, k2tog, knit to last 3 sts, ssk, k1—2 sts dec'd.

Rep last 5 rnds 4 (6, 6, 7) more times—34 (34, 36, 38) sts.

Work even in St st until sleeve measures 6½ (7, 7½, 8)" (16.5 [18, 19, 20.5] cm) from underarm.

With CC, knit 1 rnd.

Work I-cord bind-off as foll: Using backward-loop method, CO 3 sts and slip these 3 sts on left needle, *K2, ssk, slip these 3 sts on left needle; rep from * to end until 3 sts rem, sl 1, k2tog, pass slipped st over. Thread tail on tapestry needle and fasten off.

Rep for other sleeve.

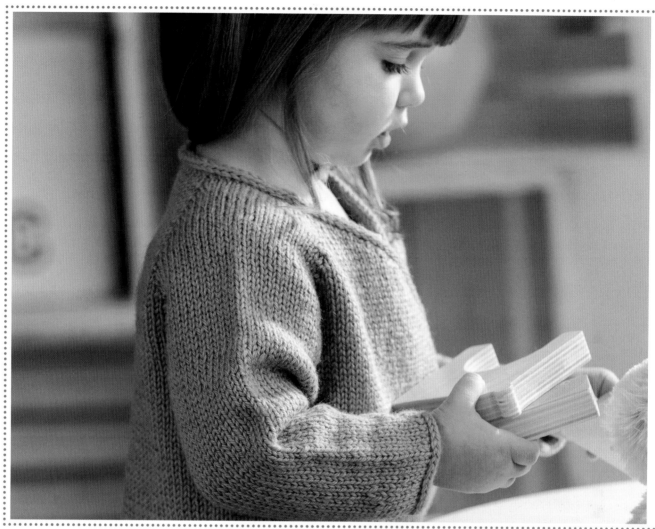

Edging

With RS facing, join B at lower corner of right front. Pick up and knit 4 sts along garter edge, 25 (27, 29, 31) sts along each front edge, 29 (33, 35, 39) sts along neckline edge and 44 (46, 48, 50) sts along CO row until you reach lower corner of left front.

Next row: (WS) Work I-cord bind-off as for sleeve.

Finishing

Weave in loose ends. Wet-block (see Glossary) garment to measurements. Sew buttons opposite buttonholes.

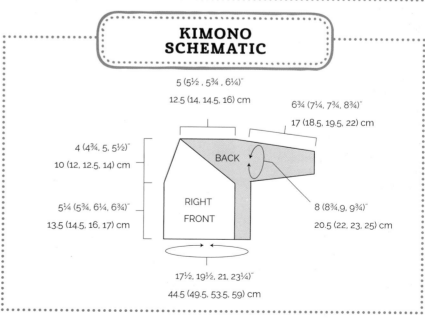

KIMONO SCHEMATIC

5 (5½ , 5¾ , 6¼)"
12.5 (14, 14.5, 16) cm

6¾ (7¼, 7¾, 8¾)"
17 (18.5, 19.5, 22) cm

4 (4¾, 5, 5½)"
10 (12, 12.5, 14) cm

BACK

5¼ (5¾, 6¼, 6¾)"
13.5 (14.5, 16, 17) cm

RIGHT FRONT

8 (8¾, 9, 9¾)"
20.5 (22, 23, 25) cm

17½, 19½, 21, 23¼)"
44.5 (49.5, 53.5, 59) cm

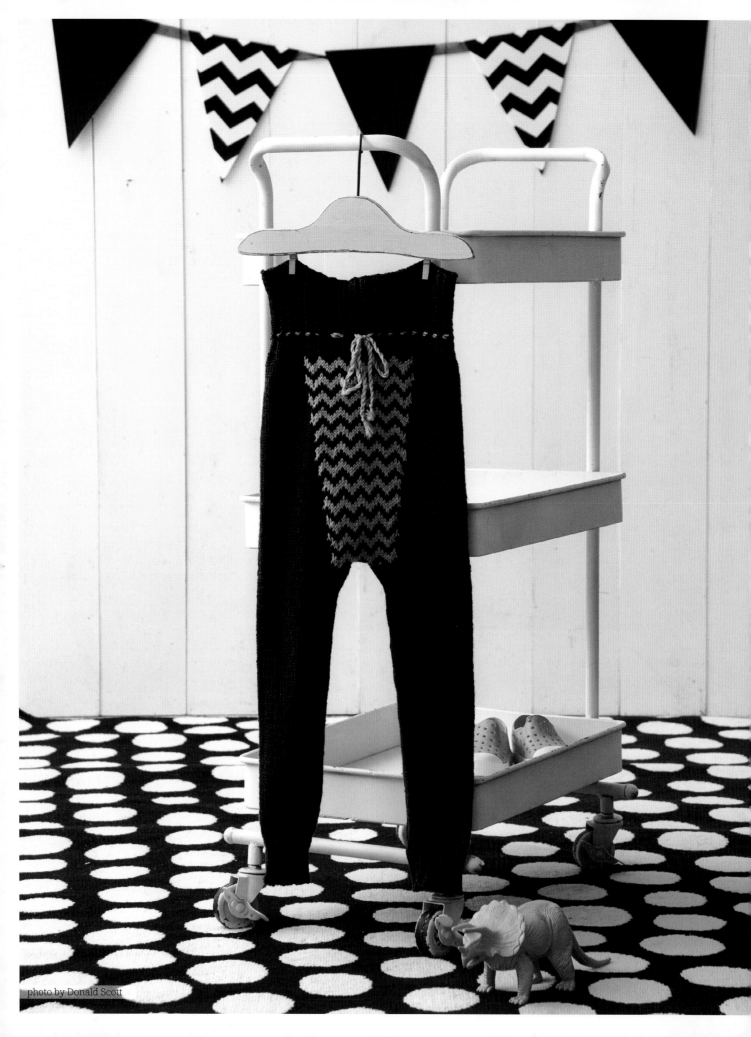

Chevron Pants

JUSTINE TURNER

How cute are these pants? Perfectly proportioned for the diaper-wearing set, these tough trousers feature a comfortable fold-over waist and drawstring tie for security.

FINISHED SIZE

3 months (6 months, 12 months, 18 months, 24 months, 4T).

18¼ (19¼, 20, 20½, 20¾, 21½)" (46.5 [49, 51, 52, 52.5, 54.5] cm) waist circumference, 9¼ (9¾, 10¾, 11½, 12¼, 12½)" (23.5 [25, 27.5, 29, 31, 31.5] cm) body length, and 8 (10¼, 12¼, 13¾, 14½, 15)" (20.5 [26, 31, 35, 37, 38] cm) leg length.

Pants shown measure 20¾" (52.5 cm) waist circumference.

YARN

Fingering weight (#1 Super Fine).

Shown here: Spud & Chloë Fine (80% superwash wool, 20% silk; 248 yd [227 m]/65 g): #7809 Snorkel (dark blue; A), 1 (2, 2, 2, 2, 2) skein(s); #7806 Calypso (aqua; B), 1 skein.

NEEDLES

Body and legs: Size U.S. 3 (3.25 mm): 32" (81.5 cm) circular (cir) and set of 4 or 5 double-pointed (dpn).

Bottom edging and waistband: Size U.S. 2 (2.75 mm): 32" (81.5 cm) cir.

Adjust needle size if necessary to obtain the correct gauge.

NOTIONS

Markers (m); stitch holder; smooth waste yarn for provisional cast-on; safety pins; tapestry needle.

GAUGE

24 sts and 34 rows/rnds = 4" (10 cm) in St st on larger needles after blocking.

30 sts and 34 rnds = 4" (10 cm) in Chevron patt on larger needles.

Back

Using waste yarn and a provisional method (see Glossary), CO 61 (65, 67, 69, 71, 73) sts.

Row 1: (RS) With A and larger cir, knit.

Row 2: Purl.

Row 3: Knit 12 (11, 12, 13, 11, 12) sts with A, place marker (pm), work Row 1 of Chevron chart over next 37 (43, 43, 43, 49, 49) sts, pm, knit 12 (11, 12, 13, 11, 12) sts with A. There are 6 (7, 7, 7, 8, 8) repeats of the 6-st Chevron pattern, use additional markers if necessary to separate pattern repeats.

Cont in patt as established, working in St st outside of markers and working in Chevron patt between markers, for 9 (5, 9, 9, 9, 11) more rows.

Next row: (RS—reset markers) Knit to m with A, remove m, k1 with A, pm, work Chevron patt (maintaining pattern by starting with second st on chart) over next 35 (41, 41, 41, 47, 47) sts, sl 1 st to right needle, remove m, sl

st back to left needle, pm, knit 13 (12, 13, 14, 12, 13) sts with A.

The number of sts remains constant with 1 additional stitch in A on either side of the Chevron patt and 2 fewer stitches worked in Chevron patt.

*Cont in patt as established, working in St st outside of markers and working in Chevron patt between markers, for 3 (3, 4, 5, 4, 3) more rows.

Next row: (reset markers) Work to m in St st with A, remove m, k1 with A, pm, work Chevron patt to 1 st before m, sl 1 st to right needle, remove m, sl st back to left needle, pm, work in St st with A to end.

Rep from * 9 (11, 9, 8, 11, 14) more times until there are 15 (17, 21, 23, 23, 17) sts in Chevron patt in the center and 23 (24, 23, 23, 24, 28) A sts on either side.

Work even in patt as established until piece measures 6½ (7, 7½, 8, 8¾, 9)" (16.5 [18, 119, 20.5, 22, 23] cm) from CO edge, ending with a WS row.

With RS facing, place 28 (30, 31, 32, 33, 34) sts on stitch holder for back left leg, 5 sts on safety pin for crotch, and 28 (30, 31, 32, 33, 34) sts on second holder for back right leg.

Front

Using waste yarn and a provisional method, CO 61 (65, 67, 69, 71, 73) sts.

Row 1: (RS) With A and larger cir, knit.

Row 2: Purl.

Row 3: Knit 18 (17, 18, 19, 17, 18) sts with A, pm, work Row 1 of Chevron chart over next 25 (31, 31, 31, 37, 37) sts, pm, knit 18 (17, 18, 19, 17, 18) sts with A. There are 4 (5, 5, 5, 6, 6) repeats of the 6-st Chevron pattern, use additional markers if necessary to separate pattern repeats.

Cont in patt as established, working in St st outside of markers and working in Chevron patt between markers, for 9 (5, 11, 15, 9, 8) more rows.

Next row: (reset markers) Work to m in St st with A, remove m, k1 with A, pm, work Chevron patt to 1 st before

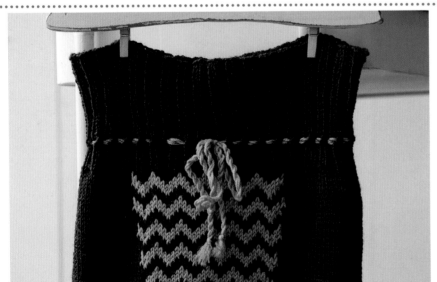
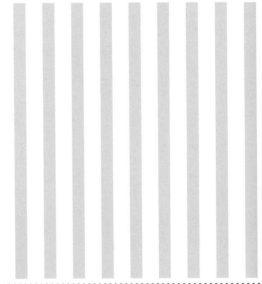

m, sl 1 st to right needle, remove m, sl st back to left needle, pm, work in St st with A to end.

*Cont in patt as established, working in St st outside of markers and working in Chevron patt between markers, for 8 (6, 10, 14, 8, 5) more rows. Work reset markers row once.

Rep from * 3 (5, 3, 2, 5, 8) more times until there are 15 (17, 21, 23, 23, 17) sts in Chevron patt in the center and 23 (24, 23, 23, 24, 28) A sts on either side.

Work even in patt as established until piece measures 6½ (7, 7½, 8, 8¾, 9)" (16.5 [18, 119, 20.5, 22, 23] cm) from CO edge, ending with a WS row.

With RS facing, place 28 (30, 31, 32, 33, 34) sts on holder for front right leg, 5 sts on safety pin for crotch, and 28 (30, 31, 32, 33, 34) sts on second holder for front left leg. Pin a safety pin to this piece to designate it as the front.

Join Front and Back
Sew side seams using mattress stitch (see Glossary), but do not join provisional CO row or final row of live sts.

Left Leg
The left leg is knit with A only.

With RS facing and front piece in front, pm for beg of rnd, slip front left leg sts onto larger cir, then slip back left leg sts onto needle—56 (60, 62, 64, 66, 68) sts. Beg of rnd is on inside of leg.

Rnd 1: Knit.

Rnd 2: (dec) K1, k2tog, knit to last 3 sts, ssk, k1—2 sts dec'd.

Rep the last 2 rnds 2 (3, 3, 3, 4, 4) more times—50 (52, 54, 56, 56, 58) sts.

*Knit 5 (7, 8, 9, 10, 10) rounds.

CHEVRON PANTS CHART

Chevron

5
3
1

6-st repeat

☐ (shaded with o) knit with CC on RS; purl with CC on WS

☐ knit with MC on RS; purl with MC on WS

☐ pattern repeat

Next rnd: (dec) K1, k2tog, knit to last 3 sts, ssk, k1—2 sts dec'd.

Rep from * 6 (7, 8, 7, 7, 8) more times—36 (36, 36, 40, 40, 40) sts.

Work even in St st until leg measures 6½ (8¾, 10¾, 12, 12¾, 13¼)" (16.5 [22, 27.5, 30.5, 32, 33.5] cm).

LEG EDGING
Change to smaller cir.

Next rnd: *K2, p2; rep from * to end.

Rep last rnd 13 (15, 15, 17, 17, 17) more times. Use larger cir to BO loosely in rib.

CROTCH
Slip front crotch sts onto a dpn, slip back crotch sts onto another dpn. With WS facing, use a three-needle method (see Glossary) to BO all sts. Alternatively, use the Kitchener st (see Glossary) to graft the two sets of live sts together.

Right Leg
The right leg is knit with A only.

With RS facing and back piece in front, pm for beg of rnd, slip back right leg sts onto larger cir, then slip front right leg sts onto needle—56 (60, 62, 64, 66, 68) sts. Beg of rnd is on inside of leg.

Work as for left leg.

Waistband
Carefully remove waste yarn from provisional CO and place 122 (130, 134, 138, 142, 146) live sts on smaller cir. Pm for beg of rnd and join for working in rnds.

Rnd 1: *K1f&b, k60 (64, 66, 68, 70, 72) sts; rep from * to end—124 (130, 136, 140, 144, 148) sts.

Rnd 2: *K2, p2; rep from * to end.

Rep last rnd 7 (7, 9, 9, 9, 9) more times.

Next rnd: (waistband holes) *K2tog, yo; rep from * to end.

Next rnd: *K2, p2; rep from * to end.

Rep last rnd 23 (23, 27, 29, 29, 29) more times.

Use larger cir to BO loosely in rib.

Finishing
Weave in loose ends and use yarn tails to close any holes at crotch. Block pants to measurements.

With B, make a twisted cord (see Glossary) about 35" (89 cm) long and thread it through waistband holes.

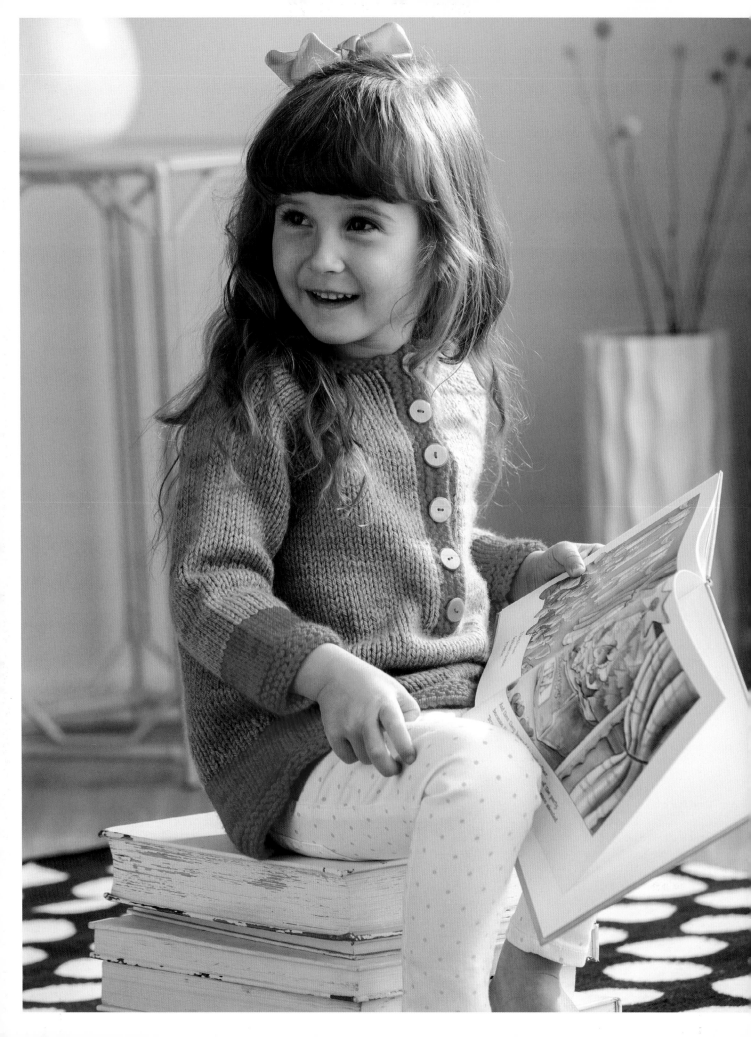

Baby Tunic

TERRI KRUSE

Not only cute, tunics are also very functional baby and toddler wardrobe items. They can be worn as a dress and then, as your child grows, as a sweater. The contrasting colors on the hem, cuffs, and buttonband will make this your kid's favorite item!

FINISHED SIZE

3 months (6 months, 12 months, 24 months, 3T).

About 18 (19¼, 20¼, 22, 24½)" (45.5 [49, 51.5, 56, 62] cm) chest circumference.

Tunic shown measures 24½" (62 cm).

YARN

Worsted (#4 Medium).

Shown here: Blue Moon Fiber Arts Gaea (100% certified organic 2.1 micron merino; 305 yd [278 m]/226 g): Everyday Grey (gray; A), 1 (1, 1, 2, 2) skein(s); Psychobarbie (pink; B), 1 skein.

NEEDLES

Size U.S. 8 (5 mm): 16" (40.5 cm) circular (cir) for sizes 18 (19¼, 20¼, 22)" or 24" (61 cm) circular (cir) for size 24½"; set of 4 or 5 double-pointed (dpn) for all sizes.

Adjust needle size if necessary to obtain the correct gauge.

NOTIONS

Removable markers (m); tapestry needle; sewing needle and matching thread; six ¾" (2 cm) buttons.

GAUGE

15 sts and 22 rows/rnds = 4" (10 cm) in St st.

Upper Body

With B, CO 32 (32, 34, 38, 40) sts.

Set-up row: (RS) K5 (5, 5, 5, 6) sts for left front, place marker (pm), k4 (4, 5, 6, 6) for left sleeve, pm, k14 (14, 14, 16, 16) sts for back, pm, k 4 (4, 5, 6, 6) sts for right sleeve, pm, k5 (5, 5, 5, 6) sts for right front.

Next row: (WS) Knit.

SHAPE YOKE

Row 1: (RS—inc) With A, *knit to m, M1L (see Glossary), slip marker (sl m), k1, M1R (see Glossary); rep from * 3 more times, knit to end.

Row 2: Purl.

Rep last 2 rows 9 (10, 11, 11, 13) more times—112 (120, 130, 134, 152) sts.

DIVIDE FOR BODY AND SLEEVES

Removing markers when you come to them, knit 15 (16, 17, 17, 20) left front sts, place 24 (26, 29, 20, 34) left sleeve sts on waste yarn holder, CO 2 (2, 2, 4, 4) sts, pm in center of these CO sts (left side marker), knit 34 (36, 38, 40, 44) back sts, place 24 (26, 29, 30, 34) right sleeve sts on waste yarn holder, CO 2 (2, 2, 4, 4) sts, pm in center of these CO sts (right side marker), knit 15 (16, 17, 17, 20) right front sts—68 (72, 76, 82, 92) sts

Next row: (WS) Purl.

UPPER BODY

Row 1: (RS—inc) *Knit to 2 sts before m, M1R, k1, sl m, k1, M1L; rep from * once more; 4 sts inc'd—72 (76, 80, 86, 96) sts.

Rows 2–4: Work even in St st.

Rep last 4 rows 0 (0, 0, 1, 1) more time(s) and Row 1 once more—76 (80, 84, 94, 104) sts.

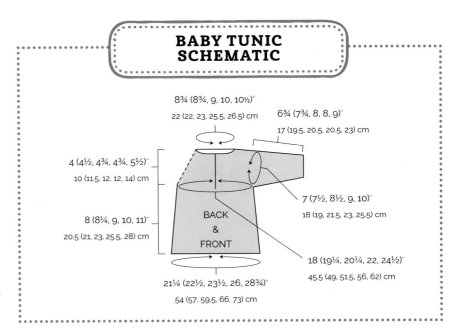

BABY TUNIC SCHEMATIC

8¾ (8¾, 9, 10, 10½)"
22 (22, 23, 25.5, 26.5) cm

6¾ (7¾, 8, 8, 9)"
17 (19.5, 20.5, 20.5, 23) cm

4 (4½, 4¾, 4¾, 5½)"
10 (11.5, 12, 12, 14) cm

8 (8¼, 9, 10, 11)"
20.5 (21, 23, 25.5, 28) cm

BACK & FRONT

7 (7½, 8½, 9, 10)"
18 (19, 21.5, 23, 25.5) cm

18 (19¼, 20¼, 22, 24½)"
45.5 (49, 51.5, 56, 62) cm

21¼ (22½, 23½, 26, 28¾)"
54 (57, 59.5, 66, 73) cm

Work even in St st for 5 rows.

Lower Body

Next row/rnd: (WS) Purl, CO 4 sts at end of row for front placket.

Pm for end of rnd and join for working in rnds—80 (84, 88, 98, 108) sts.

Work even in St st for 12 (12, 15, 18, 22) rnds.

SHAPE FRONT

Work in short-rows (see Glossary) as foll:

Short-Row 1: Knit to 1 st before left side marker, wrap next st, turn work.

Short-Row 2: Purl to 1 st before right side marker, wrap next st, turn work.

Short-Row 3: Knit to 5 sts before last wrapped st, wrap next st, turn work.

Short-Row 4: Purl to 5 sts before last wrapped st, wrap next st, turn work.

Rep last 2 short-rows 2 (2, 2, 3, 3) more times.

SHAPE BACK

Knit to left side marker.

Short-Row 1: Knit to 1 st before right side marker, wrap next st, turn work.

Short-Row 2: Purl to 1 st before left side marker, wrap next st, turn work.

Short-Row 3: Knit to 5 sts before last wrapped st, wrap next st, turn work.

Short-Row 4: Purl to 5 sts before last wrapped st, wrap next st, turn work.

Rep last 2 short-rows 2 (2, 2, 3, 3) more times. Knit to end.

Next rnd: Knit, working wrapped sts and their wraps tog as you come to them.

EDGING

With B, knit 8 (9, 10, 10, 12) rnds in St st, then work 6 rnds of garter st. BO all sts in patt.

Placket

With RS facing and B, starting at top of left front, pick up and knit 26 (28, 30, 32, 34) sts along left front edge until joining rnd. CO 1 st. Work 6 rows in garter st. BO all sts in patt.

With RS facing and B, starting at bottom of right front edge (above joining rnd), pick up and knit 26 (28, 30, 32, 34) sts. Using removable markers, mark positions for 6 buttons on right front edge, the lowest ½" (1.3 cm) up from base of placket and the highest ½" (1.3 cm) down from neck edge, and the rem buttons evenly spaced in between.

Knit 2 rows.

Next row: (WS—buttonholes) *Knit to m, yo, k2tog; rep from * to last m, knit to end.

Knit 3 rows. BO all sts in patt.

With tail threaded on tapestry needle, sew down placket above joining rnd making sure to place buttonband behind buttonhole band.

Sleeves

Place 24 (26, 29, 20, 34) held sleeve sts on dpn. Join A, pick up and knit 2 (2, 2, 4, 4) sts across CO sts at base of armhole. Pm in the center of these CO sts to denote end of rnd and join for working in rnds.

Work 4 (4, 5, 5, 5) rnds in St st.

Next rnd: (dec) K1, ssk, knit to last 3 sts, k2tog, k1.

Rep dec rnd every 7 (9, 9, 7, 8)th rnd 3 (3, 3, 4, 4) more times.

At the same time, change to CC when sleeve measures 4¼ (5, 5¼, 5¼, 5¾)" (11 [12.5, 13.5, 13.5, 14.5] cm) from joining rnd.

Work 6 rnds in garter st. BO all sts in patt.

Rep for other sleeve.

Finishing

Weave in loose ends. Block tunic to finished measurements. Sew buttons to buttonband opposite buttonholes.

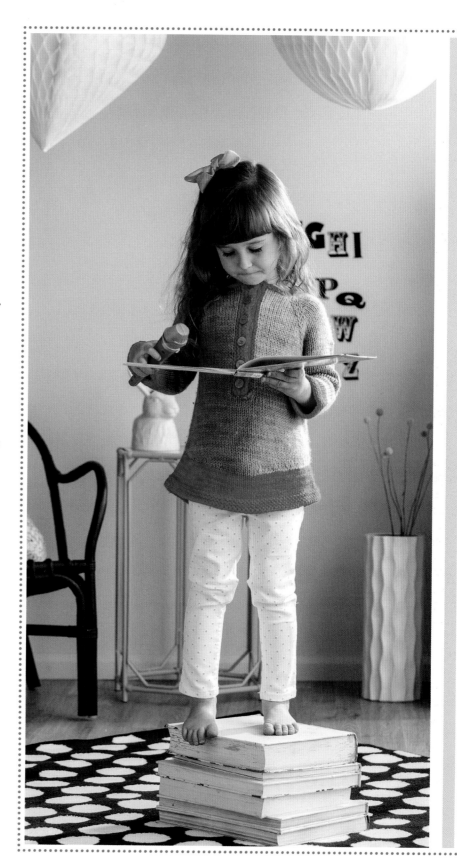

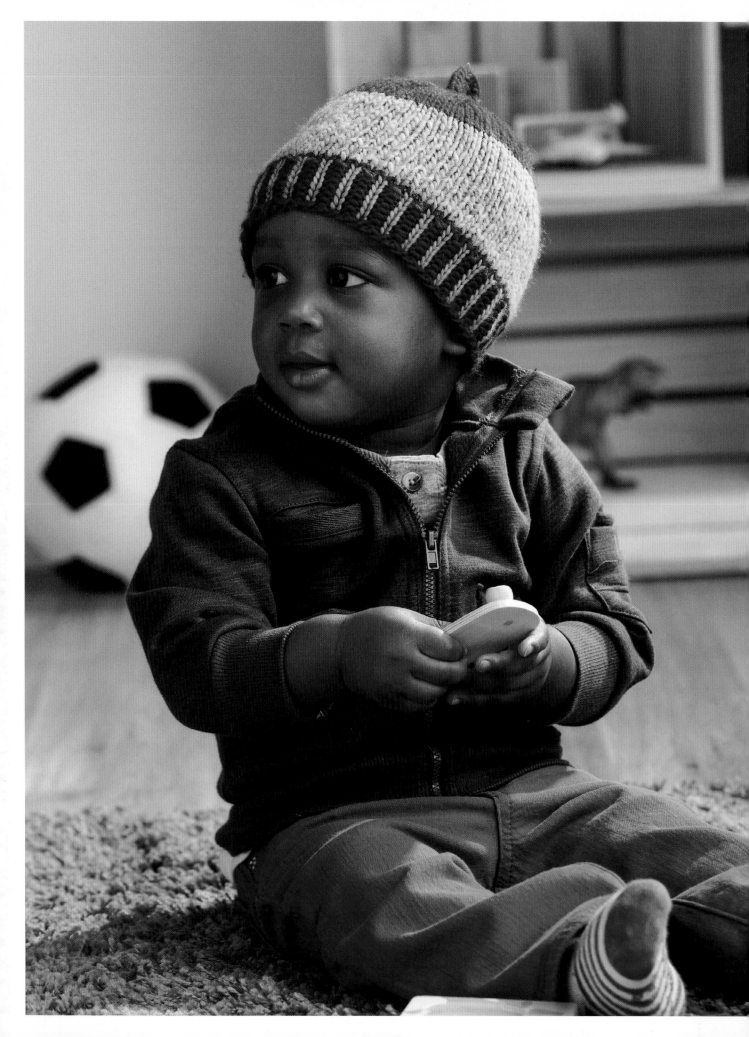

Wee Ones
FAIR ISLE HATS

TANIS GRAY

Even the grayest of days deserves a pop of color! These riotously cheerful hats will satisfy your inner Fair Isle geek and spark a conversation wherever you go.

FINISHED SIZE
9 months.

About 14½" (37 cm) circumference and 7" (18 cm) tall.

YARN
Worsted weight (#4 Medium).

Shown here: Jil Eaton/Classic Elite Yarns MinnowMerino (100% extrafine superwash merino; 77 yd [70 m]/50 g).

For navy version: #4724 Midnight (navy; A), #4755 Cerise (pink; B), and #4750 Goldie (yellow; C), 1 skein each.

For maroon version: #4717 Claret (maroon; A), #4720 Aqua (blue; B), and #4735 Chartreuse (green; C), 1 skein each.

NEEDLES
Size U.S. 8 (5 mm): 16" (40.5 cm) circular (cir) and set of 4 or 5 double-pointed (dpn).

Adjust needle size if necessary to obtain the correct gauge.

NOTIONS
Marker (m); tapestry needle.

GAUGE
18 sts and 22 rnds = 4" (10 cm) in Fair Isle patt (either version) after blocking.

Brim

With A and using cable cast-on method (see Glossary), CO 66 sts. Place marker (pm) for beg of rnd and join for working in rnds, being careful not to twist sts.

Work in [k1 with B, p1 with A] rib for 3 rnds.

Work in [k1 with C, p1 with A] rib for 2 rnds.

Work in [k1 with B, p1 with A] rib for 3 rnds.

Knit 1 rnd with A.

Body

Navy version only: Work Rnds 1–16 of Fair Isle chart working 6-st repeat 11 times. Knit 6 rnds with A.

Maroon version only: Work Rnds 1–17 of Fair Isle chart working 6-st repeat 11 times. Knit 5 rnds with A.

Crown

Change to dpn when there are too few sts to work comfortably on cir needle.

With A, dec for crown as foll:

Rnd 1: *K4, k2tog; rep from * to end—55 sts.

Rnds 2, 4, 6, 8, and 10: Knit.

Rnd 3: *K3, k2tog; rep from * to end—44 sts.

Rnd 5: *K2, k2tog; rep from * to end—33 sts.

Rnd 7: *K1, k2tog; rep from * to end—22 sts.

Rnd 9: *K2tog; rep from * to end—11 sts.

Rnd 11: *K2tog; rep from * to last st, k1—6 sts.

Rnd 12: *K2tog; rep from * to end—3 sts. Do not cut yarn.

Finishing

Work standard I-cord (see Glossary) over 3 sts until piece measures 3" (7.5 cm). Cut yarn and thread tail on tapestry needle; draw needle through end sts of I-cord and pull firmly. With I-cord, create loop ending at center top of hat and fasten off on WS.

Weave in loose ends. Block to measurements.

WEE ONES CHARTS

Fair Isle – Maroon version

17 15 13 11 9 7 5 3 1

6-st repeat

Fair Isle – Navy version

15 13 11 9 7 5 3 1

6-st repeat

○ knit with B

△ knit with C

□ pattern repeat

○ knit with B

△ knit with C

□ pattern repeat

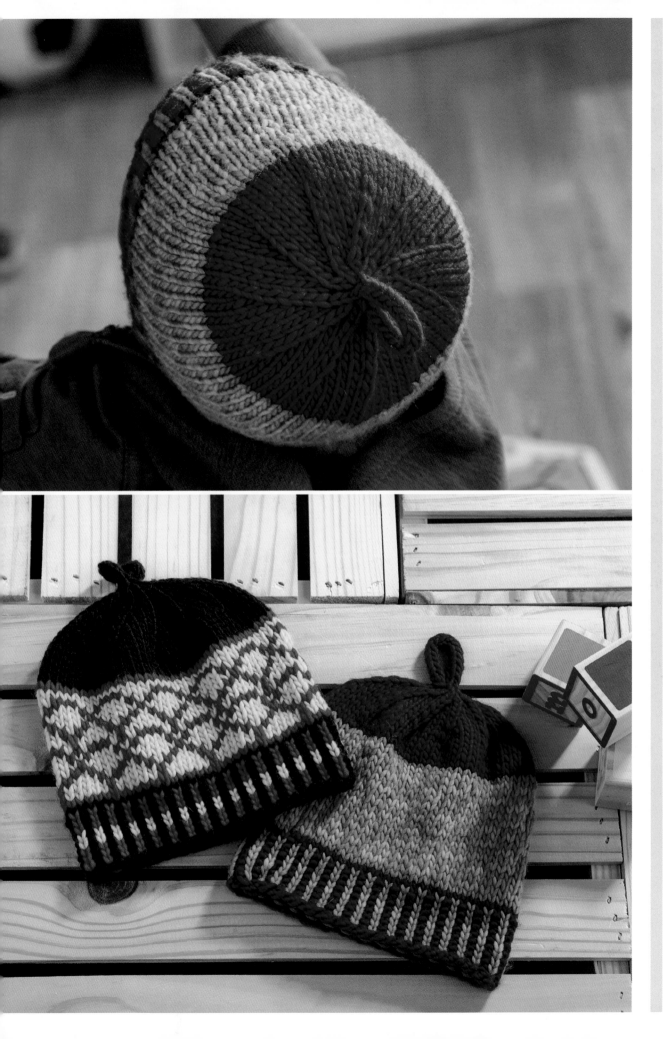

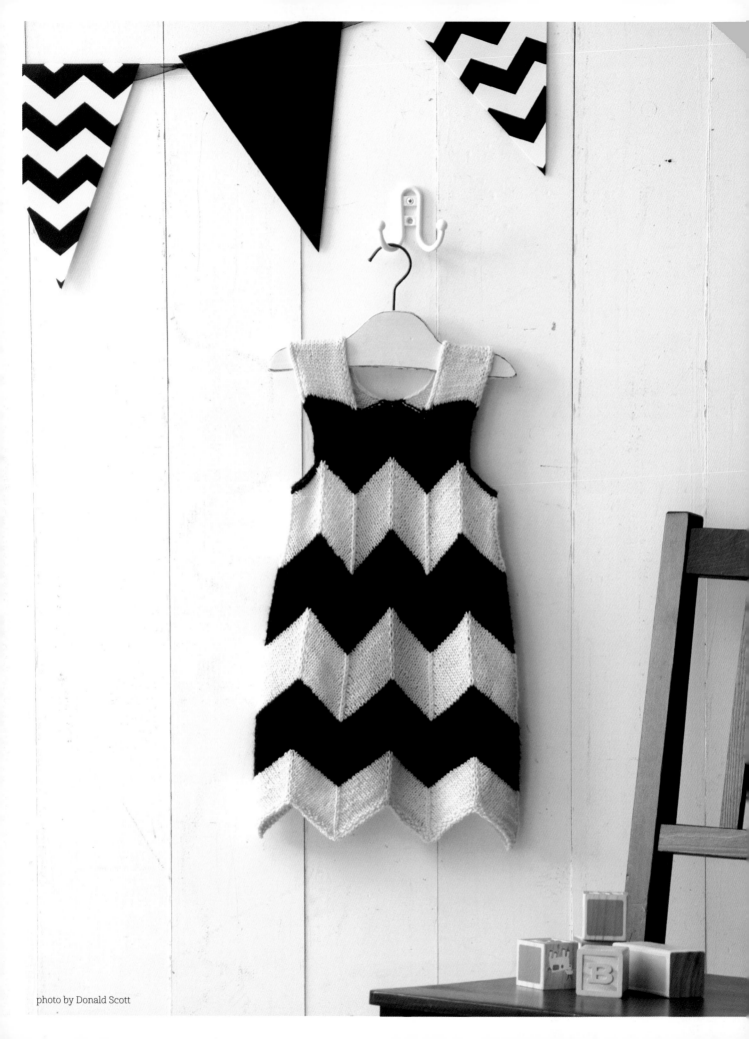

photo by Donald Scott

Modern Chevron
DRESS

RAYA BUDREVICH

Behold this ultramodern design for the fashionable little girl! A series of wide zigzags in bold contrasting colors are created using stacked columns of increases and decreases that flow seamlessly throughout the entire garment. The dress is knit from the bottom up with a minimal amount of seaming required.

FINISHED SIZE
3 months (6 months, 12 months).

About 15 (16½, 18)" (38 [42, 45.5] cm) chest circumference.

Dress shown measures 18" (45.5 cm).

YARN
Sportweight (#2).

Shown here: Lorna's Laces Shepherd Sport (100% superwash merino wool; 200 yd (183 m]/70 g), Natural (A) and Charcoal (B), 1 skein each.

NEEDLES
Size U.S. 4 (3.5 mm): 40" (101.5 cm) circular (cir) for working magic-loop method and set of 4 or 5 double-pointed (dpn).

Adjust needle size if necessary to obtain the correct gauge.

NOTIONS
Markers (m; 1 in a unique color for beg of rnd); stitch holders or waste yarn; tapestry needle.

GAUGE
24 sts and 32 rnds = 4" (10 cm) in St st.

24 sts and 18 rnds of 24-st Chevron patt measure 3¼" (8.5 cm) wide and 2¾" (7 cm) high.

NOTE
To extend length of skirt, work additional chevron color blocks.

Dress

Set-up rnd: With A, CO 132 (156, 180) sts. Place marker (pm) for beg of rnd (marker 1) and join for working in rnds, being careful not to twist sts. Pm every 22 (26, 30) sts to separate future chevron repeats.

Rnd 1: *K1, p1; rep from * to end.

Rnd 2: *P1, k1; rep from * to end.

LOWER SKIRT

*Rnd 1:** With A, work Rnd 1 of 22 (26, 30)-st Chevron patt (see Stitch Guide) 6 times.

Rnd 2: With A, work Rnd 2 of 22 (26, 30)-st Chevron patt 6 times.

Rnds 3–18: Rep Rnds 1 and 2 eight more times.

Rep from * twice (once, once) more, changing to alternate color for each block of 18 rnds.

SHAPE SKIRT

**Change to alternate color.

Rnd 1: (dec) *K1, k9 (11, 13), CDD, k9 (11, 13); rep from * to end; 12 sts dec'd—120 (144, 168) sts.

Rnd 2: Knit.

Rnd 3: Work Rnd 1 of 20 (24, 28)-st Chevron patt 6 times.

Rnd 4: Work Rnd 2 of 20 (24, 28)-st Chevron patt 6 times.

Rep last 2 rnds 7 more times.

Rep from ** 0 (1, 2) more time(s), working Chevron patt over 2 fewer sts each time—120 (132, 144) sts.

DIVIDE FOR UNDERARM
Change to alternate color.

Next rnd: Remove marker 1 (beg of rnd m), k3, BO to 2 sts before marker 2 (right underarm), k2, knit to marker 4, k3, BO to 2 sts before marker 5 (left underarm), k2, knit to end.

There are two sets of 45 (49, 53) live sts. Place one set on waste yarn or stitch holder for back to be worked later.

Front

With RS facing, join working yarn to set of 45 (49, 53) live sts and work front as foll:

Row 1: (RS) Ssk, M1R, work Row 1 of 20 (22, 24)-st Chevron patt twice, k1, M1L, k2tog—45 (49, 53) sts.

Row 2: (WS) Purl.

Rep last 2 rows 4 (3, 2) more times.

DIVIDE FOR SHOULDERS
Row 1: (RS) Ssk, M1R, work Row 1 of 20 (22, 24)-st Chevron patt, k1f&b, place center marker between loops of k1f&b after st #23 (25, 27), M1L, k8

(9, 10), CDD, k8 (9, 10), M1R, k1, M1L, k2tog; 1 st inc'd—46 (50, 54) sts.

Row 2: (WS) Purl.

LEFT SHOULDER
Row 1: (RS) Ssk, M1R, k1, M1L, k8 (9, 10), CDD, k6 (7, 8), k2tog, k1; 2 sts dec'd—21 (23, 25) sts. Remove center marker and place rem 23 (25, 27) sts on waste yarn for right front shoulder.

Row 2: (WS) Purl.

Rep last 2 rows 3 (3, 4) more times—15 (17, 17) sts.

Change to alternate color.

Next row: (RS) Ssk, M1R, knit to last 3 sts, k2tog, k1; 1 st dec'd—14 (16, 16) sts.

Next row: (WS) Purl.

Next row: Ssk, M1R, knit to last 3 sts, M1L, k2tog, k1.

Next row: Purl.

Rep last 2 rows 4 (5, 6) more times. Place rem 14 (16, 16) sts on waste yarn.

RIGHT SHOULDER
With RS facing, place 23 (25, 27) held right front shoulder sts on working needle and join working yarn in color corresponding to chevron block.

Row 1: (RS) K1, ssk, k6 (7, 8), CDD, k8 (9, 10), M1R, k1, M1L, k2tog; 2 sts dec'd—21 (23, 25) sts.

Row 2: (WS) Purl.

Rep last 2 rows 3 (3, 4) more times—15 (17, 17) sts.

Change to alternate color.

Next row: (RS) K1, ssk, knit to last 2 sts, M1L, k2tog; 1 st dec'd—14 (16, 16) sts.

Next row: (WS) Purl.

Next row: K1, ssk, M1R, knit to last 2 sts, M1L, k2tog.

Next row: Purl.

Rep last 2 rows 4 (5, 6) more times. Place rem 14 (16, 16) sts on waste yarn.

Back

With RS facing, place 45 (49, 53) held back sts on working needle and join working yarn in color corresponding to chevron block.

Row 1: (RS) Ssk, M1R, work Row 1 of 20 (22, 24)-st Chevron patt twice, k1, M1L, k2tog.

Row 2: (WS) Purl.

Rep last 2 rows 7 more times.

DIVIDE FOR SHOULDERS

Row 1: (RS) Ssk, M1R, work Row 1 of 20 (22, 24)-st Chevron patt, k1f&b, place center marker between loops of k1f&b after st #23 (25, 27), M1L, k8 (9, 10), CDD, k8 (9, 10), M1R, k1, M1L, k2tog—46 (50, 54) sts.

Row 2: (WS) Purl.

RIGHT SHOULDER

Change to alternate color.

Row 1: (RS) Ssk, M1R, k1, M1L, k8 (9, 10), CDD, k6 (7, 8), k2tog, k1; 2 sts dec'd—21 (23, 25) sts. Remove marker and place rem 23 (25, 27) sts on waste yarn for left back shoulder.

Row 2: (WS) Purl.

Rep last 2 rows 3 (3, 4) more times—15 (17, 17) sts.

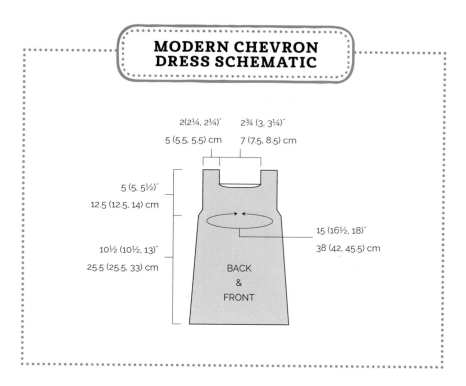

MODERN CHEVRON DRESS SCHEMATIC

2 (2¼, 2¼)˝
5 (5.5, 5.5) cm

2¾ (3, 3¼)˝
7 (7.5, 8.5) cm

5 (5, 5½)˝
12.5 (12.5, 14) cm

10½ (10½, 13)˝
25.5 (25.5, 33) cm

15 (16½, 18)˝
38 (42, 45.5) cm

BACK & FRONT

Next row: (RS) Ssk, M1R, knit to last 3 sts, k2tog, k1; 1 st dec'd—14 (16, 16) sts.

Next row: (WS) Purl.

Next row: Ssk, M1R, knit to last 3 sts, M1L, k2tog, k1.

Next row: Purl.

Rep last 2 rows 4 (5, 6) more times. Place rem 14 (16, 16) sts on waste yarn.

LEFT SHOULDER

With RS facing, place 23 (25, 27) held left back shoulder sts on working needle and join working yarn in color corresponding to chevron block.

Row 1: (RS) K1, ssk, k6 (7, 8), CDD, k8 (9, 10), M1R, k1, M1L, k2tog; 2 sts dec'd—21 (23, 25) sts.

Row 2: (WS) Purl.

Rep last 2 rows 3 (3, 4) more times—15 (17, 17) sts.

Next row: (RS) K1, ssk, knit to last 2 sts, M1L, k2tog; 1 st dec'd—14 (16, 16) sts.

Next row: (WS) Purl.

Next row: K1, ssk, M1R, knit to last 2 sts, M1L, k2tog.

Next row: Purl.

Rep last 2 rows 4 (5, 6) more times. Place rem 14 (16, 16) sts on holder.

Finishing

With dpn and tapestry needle, use Kitchener st (see Glossary) to graft each set of front shoulder sts to corresponding set of back shoulder sts to create shoulder straps.

Weave in loose ends. Block dress to accentuate the pointed chevrons.

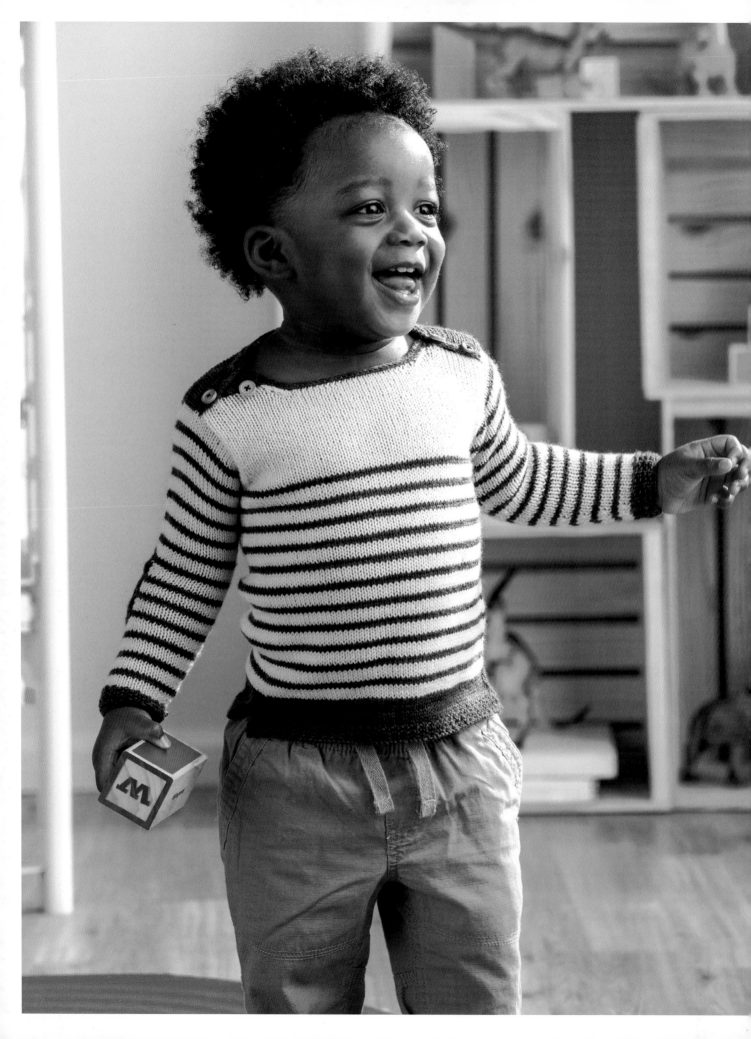

Striped
JERSEY

JULIE PARTIE

This striped jersey is inspired by the all-time classic French sailor shirt, but a modern twist is given by some precious details: contrasting elbows and shoulders, side slits, nice edgings, and a lovely buttoned I-cord neckline. Use a classic color combination to make it the timeless item of your baby's wardrobe or rock it with a zingy color for a modern pop version!

FINISHED SIZE
Newborn (3 months, 6 months, 18 months, 24 months).

About 15½ (16½, 17¾, 19½, 21)" (39.5 [42, 45, 49.5, 53.5] cm) chest circumference.

Jersey shown measures 19½" (49.5 cm).

YARN
Fingering weight (#1 Super Fine).

Shown here: Lorna's Laces Shepherd Sock (80% superwash merino wool, 20% nylon; 430 yd [393 m]/100 g): Natural (white; A) and China Blue (blue; B), 1 skein each.

NEEDLES
Size U.S. 4 (3.5 mm): 16" (40.5 cm) circular (cir).

Adjust needle size if necessary to obtain the correct gauge.

NOTIONS
Markers (m); stitch holders or waste yarn; tapestry needle; safety pins; sewing needle and matching thread; four ½" (1.3 cm) buttons.

GAUGE
28½ sts and 39 rnds = 4" (10 cm) in St st.

28½ sts and 36 rows = 4" (10 cm) in St st.

NOTES
This sweater is worked from the bottom up in rows up to the side slits, then the lower body is worked in the round up to the armholes. The front and back upper body pieces are worked flat; stitches are then picked up around the armholes for the sleeves so that the elbow patch can be worked in rows. The only seaming needed is at the underarms.

Work the Elbow chart in the intarsia method (see Glossary) using a separate small ball or bobbin in B and twisting yarns around each other at color changes to prevent holes from forming.

STITCH GUIDE

STRIPED PATT (IN THE ROUND)
Rnds 1–4: Knit with A.

Rnds 5 and 6: Knit with B.

Rep Rnds 1–6 for patt.

STRIPED PATT (IN ROWS)
Row 1: (RS) Knit with A.

Row 2: (WS) Purl with A.

Rows 3 and 4: Rep Rows 1 and 2.

Row 5: (RS) Knit with B.

Row 6: (WS) Purl with B.

Rep Rows 1–6 for patt.

RIB (WORKED OVER AN ODD NUMBER OF STS)
Row 1: (RS) Knit.

Row 2: (WS) *K1, p1; rep from * to last st, k1.

Rep Rows 1 and 2 for patt.

I-CORD BIND-OFF (I-CORD BO)
*K2, k2tog tbl, slip these 3 sts back to left needle; rep from * to end.

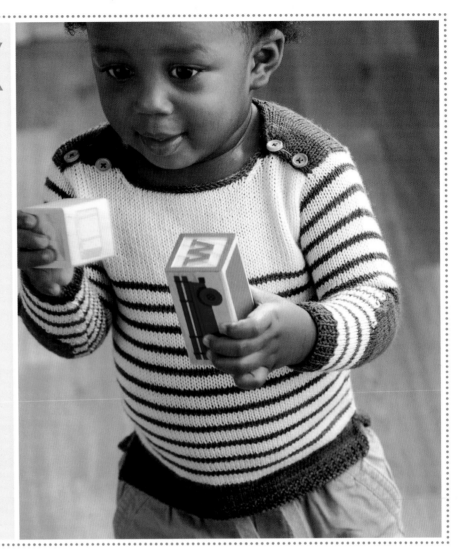

Lower Body

BACK

With B, CO 59 (63, 67, 73, 79) sts. Work 8 rows in Rib patt from Stitch Guide, then work 6 (6, 8, 8, 8) rows in St st. Place back sts on waste yarn.

FRONT

With B, CO 59 (63, 67, 73, 79) sts. Work 8 rows in Rib patt, then work 6 (6, 8, 8, 8) rows in St st.

JOIN FRONT AND BACK

Next row/rnd: (RS) Knit front sts to last 4 sts; with RS facing, place back

piece behind front piece, knit next front st and first held back st tog; rep for rem 3 front sts and 3 back sts—right side slit completed. Knit rem back sts to last 4 sts; with RS facing, place front piece behind back piece, knit next back st and first front st tog, rep for next back and front sts. Place marker (pm) for beg of rnd and join for working in rnds, then work rem 2 back sts and 2 front sts tog; left side slit completed—110 (118, 126, 138, 150) sts.

Next rnd: Knit with B.

Change to A and work in Striped patt from Stitch Guide until body measures about 6¼ (7, 7¾, 8¼, 9)" (16 [18, 19.5, 21, 23] cm) from CO edge, ending after 2 rnds with A.

DIVIDE FOR BODY AND SLEEVES

Next rnd: With A, k52 (56, 60, 65, 71), BO next 6 (6, 6, 8, 8) sts, knit to 3 (3, 3, 4, 4) sts before m, BO next 6 (6, 6, 8, 8) sts—49 (53, 57, 61, 67) sts each for front and back.

STRIPED JERSEY SCHEMATIC

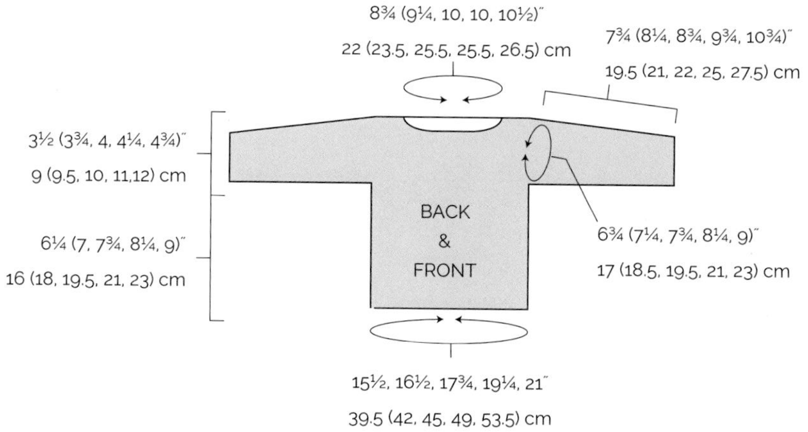

8¾ (9¼, 10, 10, 10½)"
22 (23.5, 25.5, 25.5, 26.5) cm

7¾ (8¼, 8¾, 9¾, 10¾)"
19.5 (21, 22, 25, 27.5) cm

3½ (3¾, 4, 4¼, 4¾)"
9 (9.5, 10, 11,12) cm

6¼ (7, 7¾, 8¼, 9)"
16 (18, 19.5, 21, 23) cm

BACK
&
FRONT

6¾ (7¼, 7¾, 8¼, 9)"
17 (18.5, 19.5, 21, 23) cm

15½, 16½, 17¾, 19¼, 21"
39.5 (42, 45, 49, 53.5) cm

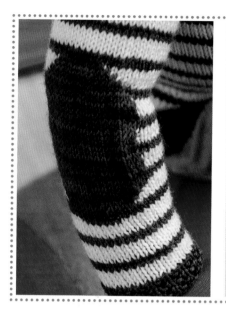

Front and back are now worked as separate pieces back and forth in rows up to the shoulders using only A.

Front
SHAPE NECK
Row 1: (RS) With A, K2, ssk, knit to last 4 sts, k2tog, k2; 2 sts dec'd—47 (51, 55, 59, 65) sts.

Row 2: (WS) Purl.

Rep last 2 rows 1 (1, 1, 2, 2) more time(s)—45 (49, 53, 55, 61) sts.

With A, work even in St st ending with a WS row until front measures 2 (2¼, 2¼, 2½, 2¾)" (5 [5.5, 5.5, 6.5, 7] cm) from dividing rnd.

Row 1: (RS—dec) K11 (12, 13, 14, 16), k2tog, k1, turn work leaving rem center and right front sts on hold on cir.

Row 2: (WS) Purl.

Row 3: (RS—dec) Knit to last 3 sts, k2tog, k1, turn work.

Row 4: (WS) Purl.

Rep last 2 rows once more—11 (12, 13, 14, 16) sts rem.

With B, work even in St st for 9 (9, 11, 11, 13) rows. Place 11 (12, 13, 14, 16) left front shoulder sts on holder.

Place next 17 (19, 21, 21, 23) center sts on second holder and join A to work on the 14 (15, 16, 17, 19) right front shoulder sts.

Row 1: (RS—dec) K1, ssk, knit to end.

Row 2: (WS) Purl.

Rep last 2 rows twice more—11 (12, 13, 14, 16) sts.

With B, work even in St st for 9 (9, 11, 11, 13) rows.

EDGING
With B and WS facing, purl 11 (12, 13, 14, 16) held right front shoulder sts, pick up and purl 11 (11, 12, 12, 14) sts along right neckline, purl 17 (19, 21, 21, 23) held center sts, pick up and purl 11 (11, 12, 12, 14) sts along left neckline, and purl 11 (12, 13, 14, 16) sts held left front shoulder sts—61 (65, 71, 73, 83) sts. With RS facing, work I-cord bind-off

(see Stitch Guide) to last 3 sts, k3tog. Cut yarn and draw tail through rem st.

Back
SHAPE NECK
With RS facing, place 49 (53, 57, 61, 67) held back sts on cir and work with A as foll:

Row 1: (RS) K2, ssk, k to last 4 sts, k2tog, k2; 2 sts dec'd—47 (51, 55, 59, 65) sts.

Row 2: (WS) Purl.

Rep last 2 rows 1 (1, 1, 2, 2) more time(s)—45 (49, 53, 55, 61) sts.

With A, work even in St st ending with a WS row until back measures 3 (3¼, 3¼, 3½, 3¾)" (7.5 [8.5, 8.5, 9, 9.5] cm) from dividing rnd.

With B, work even in St st for 6 (6, 8, 8, 10) rows.

Row 1: (RS—dec) K11 (12, 13, 14, 16), k2tog, k1, turn work leaving rem center and left back sts on hold on cir.

Row 2: (WS) Purl.

89

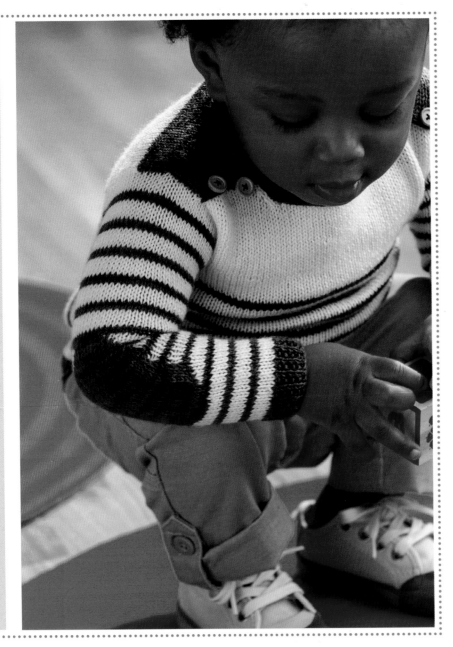

work Rows 1 and 2 once more—11 (12, 13, 14, 16) sts.

EDGING
With B and WS facing, purl 11 (12, 13, 14, 16) held left back shoulder sts, pick up and purl 11 (11, 12, 12, 14) sts along left neckline, purl 17 (19, 21, 21, 23) held center sts, pick up and purl 11 (11, 12, 12, 14) sts along right neckline and purl 11 (12, 13, 14, 16) held right back sts—61 (65, 71, 73, 83) sts.

With RS facing, work I-cord BO and buttonholes at the same time as foll:

K3, [sl 2 sts purlwise, pass right slipped st over left slipped st, sl next st and pass second st over slipped st and slip last st on right needle back to left needle, (sl last 3 sts from right needle back to left needle, k3) twice]—first buttonhole completed; sl last 3 sts back to left needle, work I-cord BO 2 (3, 4, 5, 7) times, work second buttonhole (i.e., rep section in [ ]), work I-cord BO to last 9 (10, 11, 12, 14) sts, work third buttonhole, work I-cord BO to last 5 sts, work fourth buttonhole, work I-cord BO to last 3 sts, k3tog. Cut yarn and draw tail through rem st.

Sleeves
Overlap front and back shoulders; place safety pins to mark button placement (buttons will be sewn on front shoulders on color-change row) and to keep shoulders in place.

SHAPE SLEEVE
With A, RS facing, and beg at center of underarm, pick up and knit 49 (53, 55, 59, 65) sts around armhole. When reaching the shoulders and picking up sts, be sure to insert your needle tip through overlapped shoulder layers to close shoulder hole without having to seam it.

Next row: (WS) Purl with A.

Row 3: (RS—dec) Knit to last 3 sts, k2tog, k1, turn work—12 (13, 14, 15, 17) sts.

Row 4: (WS) Purl.

Knit even in St st for 8 (8, 10, 10, 12) rows, then work Rows 3 and 4 once more—11 (12, 13, 14, 16) sts. Place 11 (12, 13, 14, 16) right back shoulder sts on holder.

Place next 17 (19, 21, 21, 23) center sts on second holder and join B to work on the 14 (15, 16, 17, 19) left back shoulder sts.

Row 1: (RS—dec) K1, ssk, knit to end.

Row 2: (WS) Purl.

Rep Rows 1 and 2 once more, knit even in St st for 8 (8, 10, 10, 12) rows, then

Elbow Patch (smallest 3 sizes)

Elbow Patch (largest 2 sizes)

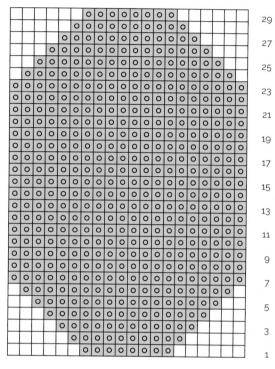

☐ knit with A on RS; purl with A on WS

⊙ knit with B on RS; purl with B on WS

Work 8 rows even in Striped patt.

Next row: (RS—dec) With A, k2, ssk, knit to last 4 sts, k2tog, k2—2 sts dec'd.

Rep dec row every 6th row 6 (8, 8, 10, 11) more times maintaining Striped patt—35 (35, 37, 37, 41) sts.

At the same time, when sleeve measures at least 2 (2½, 2½, 3¼, 4)" (5 [6.5, 6.5, 8.5, 10] cm) from pick-up row and ending after a WS row with B, start working the elbow patch in intarsia.

ELBOW PATCH
Right Sleeve
Next row: (RS) Knit 8 (9, 10, 10, 12) sts with A, work Row 1 of Elbow Patch chart over next 18 (18, 18, 20, 20) sts in intarsia, knit with A to end.

Cont as established, working Elbow Patch chart over 23 (23, 23, 29, 29) rows and maintaining Striped patt and decreases at the same time.

Left Sleeve
Next row: (RS) Knit 19 (20, 21, 21, 23) sts with A, work Row 1 of Elbow Patch chart over next 18 (18, 18, 20, 20) sts in intarsia, knit with A to end.

Cont as established, working Elbow Patch chart over 23 (23, 23, 29, 29) rows and maintaining Striped patt and decreases at the same time.

EDGING
Cont working in Striped patt (still working the decreases if necessary) until sleeve measures 7 (7½, 7¾, 8¾, 9¾)" (18 [19, 19.5, 22, 25] cm) from pick-up row and ending after 4 rows with A.

With B, work in Rib patt for 7 (7, 9, 9, 9) rows. Loosely BO all sts in patt on WS.

Finishing
Sew sleeve seams using mattress stitch (see Glossary).

Weave in loose ends. Block to measurements. Sew buttons opposite buttonholes.

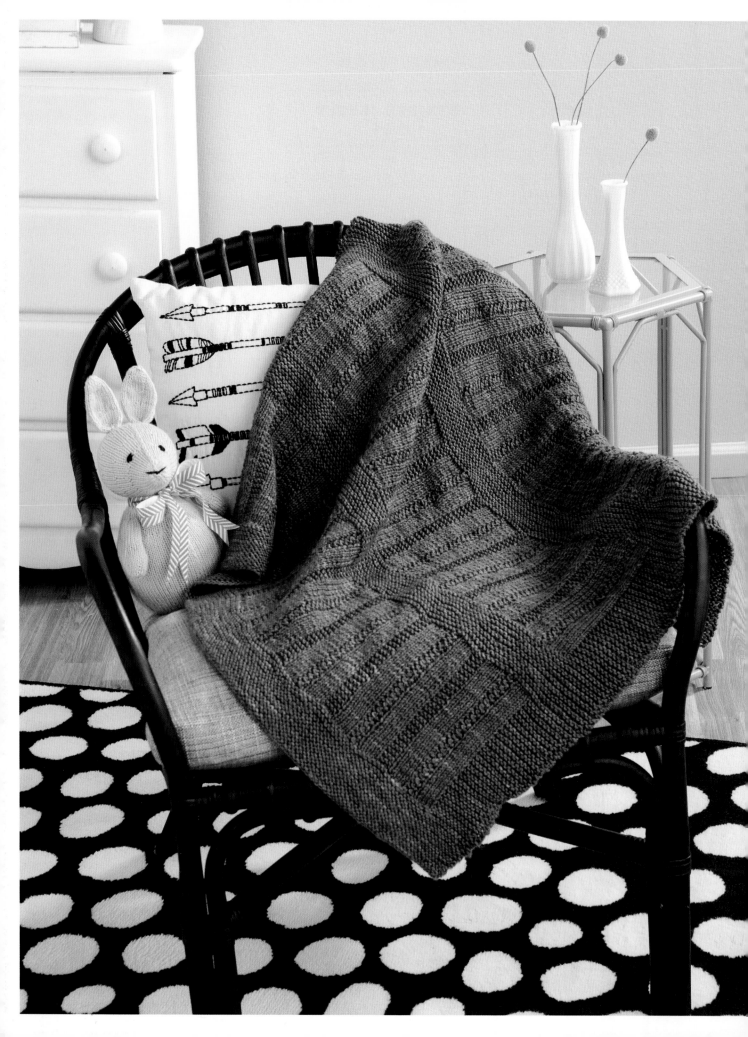

Reston

BLANKET

KELLY HERDRICH

With its interesting stitch pattern bookended by stockinette and garter-stitch stripes and rows, the Reston blanket will simply fly off the needles. This is ideal for beginning knitters looking to try a new technique, as well as seasoned knitters who want a quick, modern baby knit with an easy-to-memorize pattern.

FINISHED SIZE
28" (71 cm) high and 31½" (80 cm) wide.

YARN
Worsted weight (#4 Medium).
Shown here: Miss Babs Yowza! Whatta Skein! (100% superwash merino; 560 yd [512 m]/227 g): Light Clematis, 2 skeins.

NEEDLES
Size U.S. 8 (5 mm): straight or at least 24" (61 cm) circular (cir).
Adjust needle size if necessary to obtain the correct gauge.

NOTIONS
Markers (m); tapestry needle.

GAUGE
18½ sts and 29½ rows = 4" (10 cm) in Reston stitch patt.

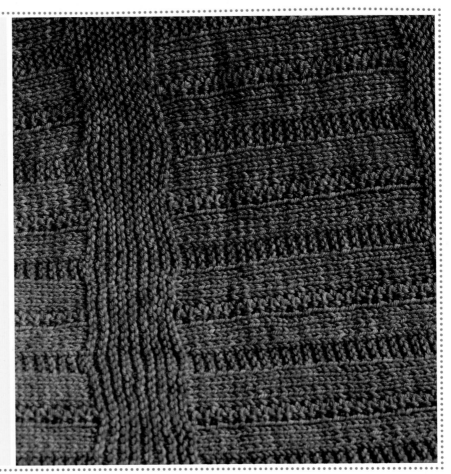

STITCH GUIDE

SL 1, K2TOG, PSSO
Sl 1 st as if to purl, k2tog, pass slipped st over—2 sts dec'd.

CO 1
Using the backward-loop method (see Glossary), CO 1 st.

RESTON STITCH (MULTIPLE OF 14 STS)
Row 1: (RS) K4, CO 1, sl 1, k2tog, psso, CO 1, k4, p3.
Row 2: (WS) Purl.

Rep Rows 1 and 2 for patt.

Bottom Border
Loosely CO 147 sts.

Work 22 rows in garter st.

Set-up row: (WS) K12, place marker (pm), purl to the last 12 sts, pm, k12.

Main Section
*Row 1:** (RS) K12, slip marker (sl m), work Row 1 of Reston stitch patt (see Stitch Guide) 8 times, k4, CO 1, sl 1, k2tog, psso, CO 1, k4, sl m, k12.

Row 2: K12, sl m, purl to last 12 sts, sl m, k12.

Rows 3–48: Rep Rows 1 and 2.

Work 18 rows in garter st.

Rep from * twice more.

Top Border
Work 4 rows in garter st. BO loosely.

FINISHING
Weave in loose ends. Block lightly to measurements.

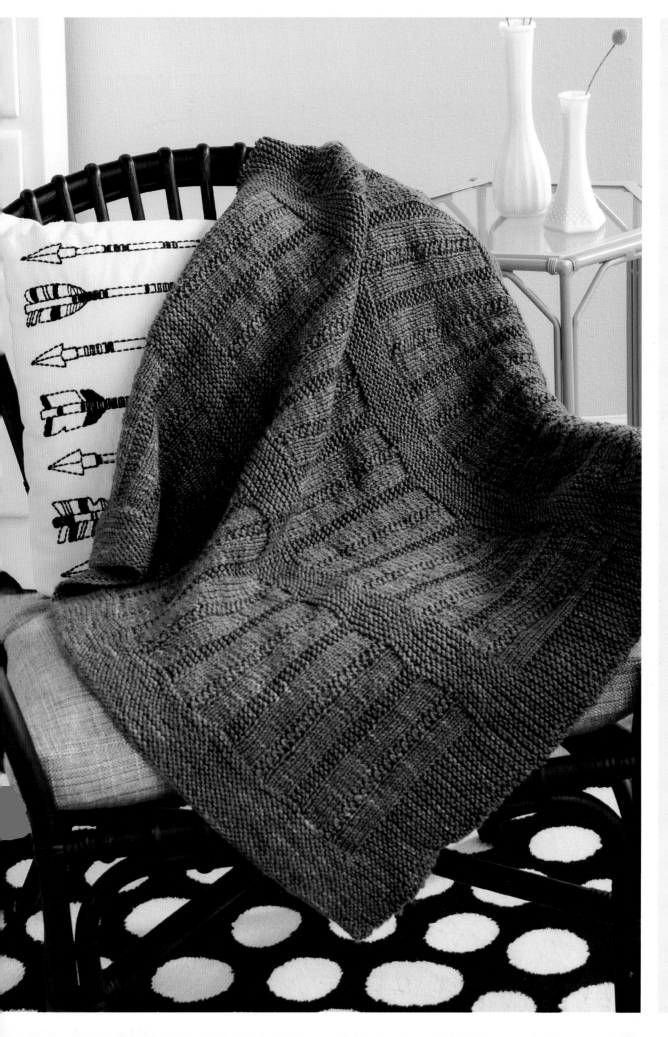

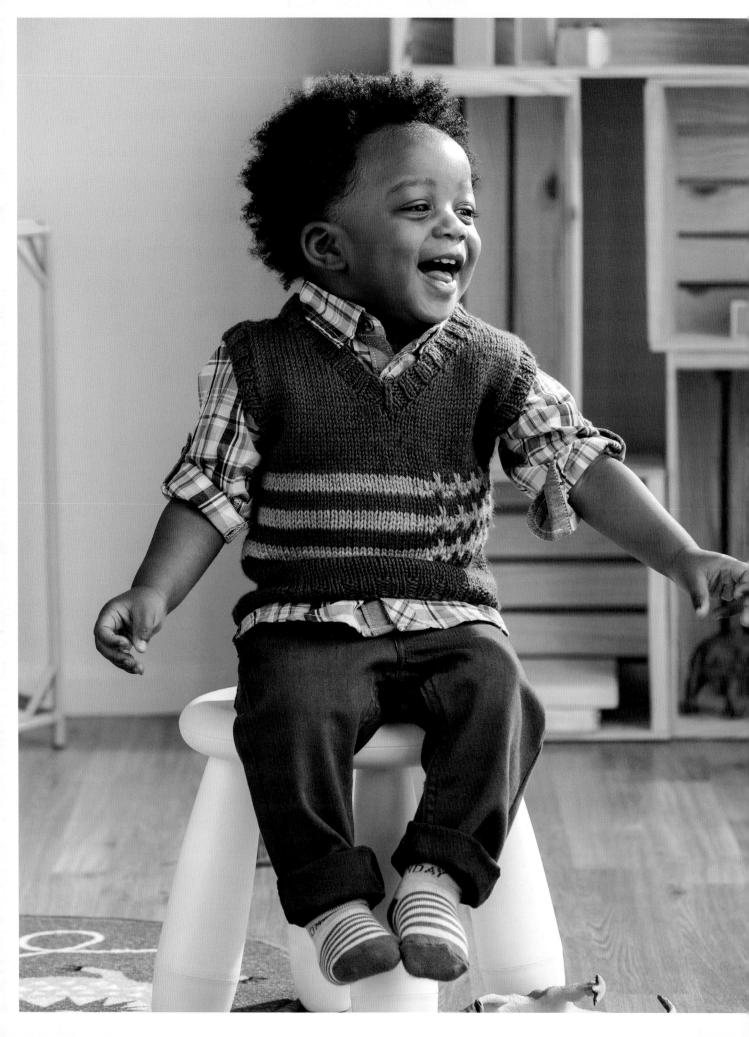

Zigzag

VEST

HELEN ROSE

Easy, wearable, and fun, this vest is
the perfect project to make for your child. The
color changes are smooth as can be, thanks
to the jogless stripes technique.

FINISHED SIZE

3 months (6 months, 12 months, 18 months, 24 months, 4T).

17½ (18½, 20, 20¾, 21½, 25½)" (44.5 [47, 51, 52.5, 54.5, 65] cm) chest circumference.

Vest shown measures 20" (51 cm).

YARN

Worsted weight (#4 Medium).

Shown here: Classic Elite Yarns Liberty Wool (100% superwash wool; 122 yd [112 m]/50 g): #7878 Mouse Brown (brown; A), 2 (2, 2, 3, 3 0) skeins; #7806 Reflecting Pond (variegated; B), 1 skein.

NEEDLES

Main body: Size U.S. 7 (4.5 mm): 16" (40.5 cm) circular (cir).

Edging: Size U.S. 6 (4 mm): set of 4 or 5 double-pointed (dpn).

Adjust needle size if necessary to obtain the correct gauge.

NOTIONS

Markers (m); waste yarn or stitch holders; tapestry needle.

GAUGE

20 sts and 24½ rnds = 4" (10 cm) in St st on larger needle.

NOTES

The vertical bar at the right of the Zigzag chart is a color key indicating which color to use for each rnd.

Use the jogless stripes technique (see Glossary) when changing colors at beg of rnd.

Body

LOWER BODY

With A and dpn, CO 88 (92, 100, 104, 108, 128) sts. Place marker (pm) for beg of rnd and join for knitting in rnds, being careful not to twist sts.

Rnds 1–5: *K2, p2; rep from * to end.

Change to cir.

Rnd 6: (inc) K1f&b, k43 (45, 49, 51, 53, 63) sts, k1f&b, knit to end of rnd—90 (94, 102, 106, 110, 130) sts.

Work even in St st until piece measures 1¼ (2, 3, 3½, 4, 4)" (3.2 [5, 7.5, 9, 10, 10] cm) from CO edge.

ZIGZAG SECTION

Set-up rnd: K13 (14, 16, 17, 18, 23), pm, k20, pm, k14 (16, 19, 20, 21, 29), pm (side marker), k20, pm, knit to end.

Next rnd: With CC (as indicated by color key), knit to m, slip marker (sl m), work Rnd 1 of Zigzag chart 5 times, sl m, knit to m, sl m, work rnd 1 of Zigzag chart 5 times, sl m, knit to end.

Cont as established until Rnds 2–23 of Zigzag chart have been worked once.

With A, work even in St st until piece measures 6 (6¾, 7, 7¼, 8½, 8½)" (15 [17, 18, 18.5, 21.5, 21.5] cm) from CO edge.

Divide Back and Front

Next row: (RS—dividing row) K44 (46, 50, 52, 54, 64), turn.

Next row: (WS) P44 (46, 50, 52, 54, 64), turn—44 (46, 50, 52, 54, 64) back sts. Front sts rem on cir are unworked or can be placed on waste yarn or stitch holder.
Back is worked back and forth in rows as foll:

Row 1: (RS) BO 1 (1, 1, 1, 1, 2) st(s), knit to end—43 (45, 49, 51, 53, 62) sts.

Row 2: BO 1 (1, 1, 1, 1, 2) st(s), purl to end—42 (44, 48, 50, 52, 60) sts.

Row 3: BO 1 st, knit to end—41 (43, 47, 49, 51, 59) sts.

Row 4: BO 1 st, purl to end—40 (42, 46, 48, 50, 58) sts.

Row 5: K2tog, knit to last 2 sts, k2tog—38 (40, 44, 46, 48, 56) sts.

Work even in St st until piece measures 5 (5¼, 5½, 5¾, 6, 7¼)" (12.5 [13.5, 14, 14.5, 15, 18.5] cm) from dividing row, ending with a WS row.

BO 1 (1, 2, 2, 2, 3) st(s) at beg of next 4 rows—34 (36, 36, 38, 38, 44) sts. BO all sts.

Front

With RS facing and cir, knit 46 (48, 52, 54, 56, 66) front sts.

Row 1: (WS) Purl.

Row 2: (RS) BO 1 (1, 1, 1, 1, 2) st(s), knit to end—45 (47, 51, 53, 55, 64) sts.

Row 3: BO 1 (1, 1, 1, 1, 2) st(s), purl to end—44 (46, 50, 52, 54, 62) sts.

Row 4: BO 2 sts, knit to end—42 (44, 48, 50, 52, 60) sts.

Row 5: BO 2 sts, purl to end—40 (42, 46, 48, 50, 58) sts.

Row 6: K2tog, knit to last 2 sts, k2tog—38 (40, 44, 46, 48, 56) sts.

Work even in St st until piece measures about ¾ (¾, ¾, ¾, ¾, 1)" (2 [2, 2, 2, 2, 2.5] cm) from dividing row, ending with a WS row.

LEFT FRONT

Row 1: (RS) K19 (20, 22, 23, 24, 28), turn. Right front sts rem on cir are unworked.

Row 2: P18 (19, 21, 23, 24, 28).

Row 3: Knit to last 2 sts, k2tog; 1 st dec'd.

Row 4: Purl.

Rep the last 2 rows until 7 (8, 8, 10, 10, 12) sts rem.

Work even in St st until piece measures 5 ½ (5 ¾, 6, 6 ¼, 6 ½, 7 ¾)" (14 [14.5, 15, 16, 16.5, 19.5] cm) from dividing row.

Next row: BO 4 (4, 4, 5, 5, 6) sts, knit to end.

Next row: BO 3 (4, 4, 5, 5, 6) sts. Cut yarn, leaving a long tail to seam shoulder later.

RIGHT FRONT

With RS facing and cir, knit 19 (20, 22, 23, 24, 28) right front sts.

Row 1: (WS) Purl.

Row 2: Ssk, knit to end; 1 st dec'd.

Row 3: Purl.

Rep the last 2 rows until 7 (8, 8, 10, 10, 12) sts rem.

Work even in St st until piece measures 5½ (5¾, 6, 6¼, 6½, 7¾)" (14 [14.5, 15, 16, 16.5, 19.5] cm) from dividing row.

Next row: BO 4 (4, 4, 5, 5, 6) sts, knit to end.

Next row: BO 3 (4, 4, 5, 5, 6) sts. Cut yarn, leaving a long tail to seam shoulder later.

Finishing
Block vest to measurements. With A tail threaded on tapestry needle, sew shoulder seams. Weave in loose ends.

NECK EDGING
Neck edging is worked with A and dpn.

With RS facing and beg at left shoulder seam, pick up and knit 26 (30, 30, 34, 34, 38) sts along back neck, pick up and knit 24 (24, 28, 28, 32, 32) sts along right side of neck until 2 rows before center front, pm, pick up and knit 2 sts on one side of center front,

M1L (see Glossary) to create center stitch at the base of the V-neck, pick up and knit 2 sts on other side of center front, pm, pick up and knit 24 (24, 28, 28, 32, 32) sts. Pm for beg of rnd and join for working in rnds.

Rnd 1: Work in p2, k2 rib until m, sl m, k5, sl m, then work in p2, k2 rib to end of rnd.

Rnd 2: Work in rib as established to m, sl m, k1, (sl 2, k1, p2sso) (see Stitch Guide), k1, sl m, then work rib as established to end of rnd.

Rnd 3: Work in rib to m, sl m, knit to m, sl m, then work in rib to end of rnd.

Rnd 4: Work in rib to m, sl m, (sl 2, k1, p2sso), sl m, then work in rib to end of rnd.

Rnd 5: Rep Rnd 3.

BO in patt and weave in loose ends.

ARMHOLE EDGING
Armhole edging is worked with A and dpn.

With RS facing and beg at right underarm seam, pick up and knit 64 (68, 68, 72, 72, 84) sts evenly spaced around opening. Pm and join for working in rnds. Work in k2, p2 rib for 5 rnds. BO all sts in patt and weave in loose ends. Rep for other armhole.

ZIGZAG VEST CHART

Zig Zag

4-st repeat

NOTE: The vertical bar at the right of each chart is a color key indicating which color to use for each row or round.

☐	knit
⊚	wrap yarn around needle twice and knit
v	sl 1 wyb
⦁v	sl 1 wyb dropping extra wrap
▨	A
▨	B
☐	pattern repeat
⩔	dr (see Stitch Guide)

ZIGZAG VEST SCHEMATIC

8¾ (9¼, 10, 10½, 10¾, 12½)"
22 (23.5, 25.5, 26.5, 27.5, 31.5) cm

5½ (5¾, 6, 6¼, 6½, 7¾)"
14 (14.5, 15, 16, 16.5, 19.5) cm

6 (6¾, 7, 7¼, 8½, 8½)"
15 (17, 18, 18.5, 21.5, 21.5) cm

BACK & FRONT

17½ (18½, 20, 20¾, 21½, 25½)"
44.5 (47, 51, 52.5, 54.5, 65) cm

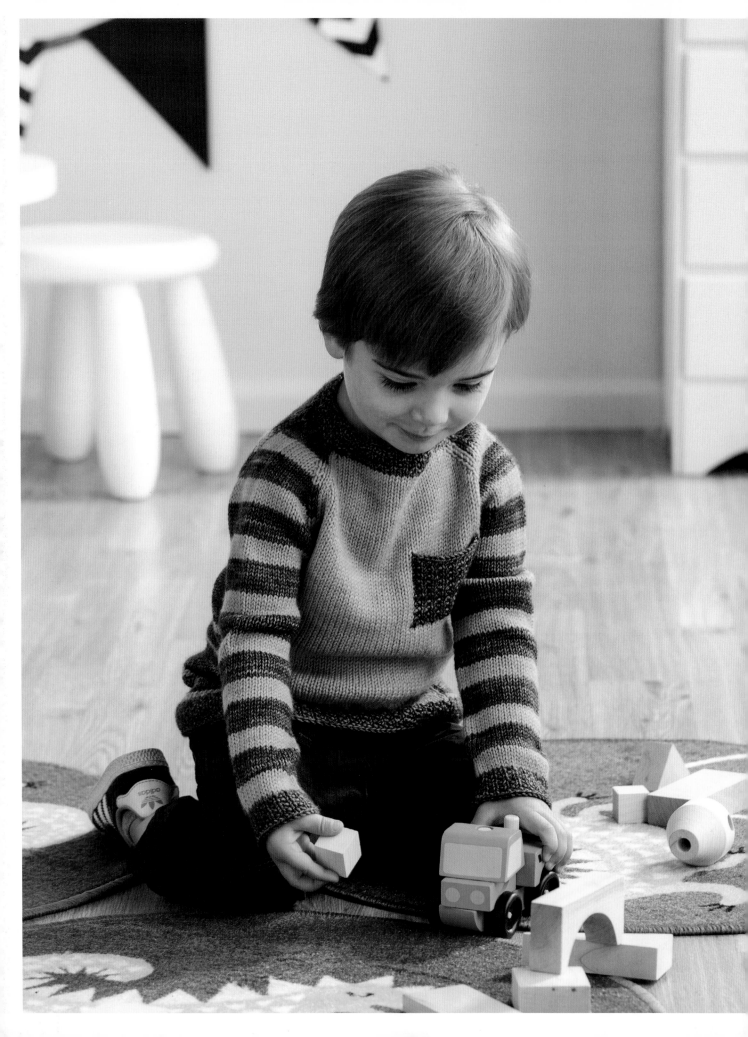

Camaro
PULLOVER

SVETLANA VOLKOVA

Camaro is an easy-to-wear raglan pullover knit in a fun and trendy color-block style. It features modern geometric lines, a ribbed pocket, and different stripes on the back and sleeves. You may use two colors as in the sample or play with more combinations, as color options are endless. The sweater is knit from the neck down in pieces and then sewn together with mattress stitch. Fast and easy to knit, it could be an ideal first project for the new knitter.

FINISHED SIZE
Newborn (3 months, 12 months, 24 months).

About 15½ (17¼, 19, 22)" (39.5 [44, 48.5, 56] cm) chest circumference.

Pullover shown measures 22" (56 cm).

YARN
Sportweight (#2 Fine).

Shown here: The Verdant Gryphon Bugga! Sport Weight (70% merino, 20% cashmere, 10% nylon; 412 yd [377 m]/121 g): November Moonlight (gray; A), 1 (1, 1, 2) skein(s); Midnight After You're Wasted (green; B), 1 skein.

NEEDLES
Edging: Size U.S. 3 (3.25 mm): 32" (81.5 cm) circular (cir).

Body and sleeves: Size U.S. 4 (3.5 mm): 32" (81.5 cm) cir for working magic-loop method.

NOTIONS
Removable markers (m); stitch holders or waste yarn; tapestry needle; sewing pins.

GAUGE
22 sts and 34 rows = 4" (10 cm) in St st on larger needle.

STITCH GUIDE

Rib (worked on even number of sts)

Row/Rnd 1: (RS) Knit.

Row/Rnd 2: (WS) *K1, p1; rep from * to end.

Rep Rows/Rnds 1 and 2 for patt.

BACK STRIPE

Work in St st, odd-numbered rows are RS.

Rows 1–10: Color A

Rows 11 and 12: Color B

Rep Rows 1–12 for patt.

SLEEVE STRIPE

Work in St st, odd-numbered rows are RS.

Rows 1–8: Color A

Rows 9–14: Color B

Rep Rows 1–14 for patt.

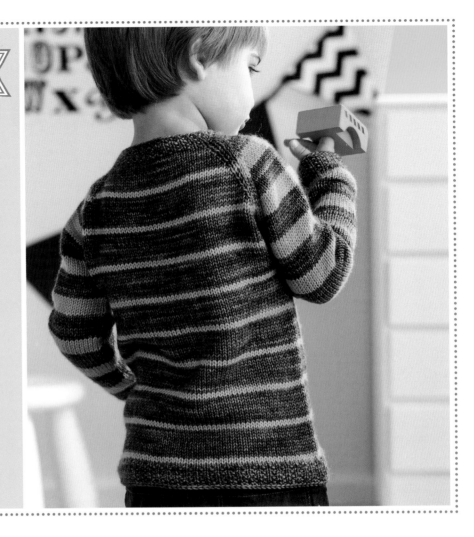

Neck

With A and smaller cir, CO 66 (68, 74, 78) sts. Place marker (pm) and join for working in rnds using the magic-loop method (see Glossary), being careful not to twist sts. Work in Rib patt from Stitch Guide for 8 rnds.

Set-up rnd: *K23 (24, 27, 31) for back, pm, k10 (10, 10, 8) sts for right sleeve, pm; rep from * once.

Back

With A and larger cir, knit 23 (24, 27, 31) sts and place rem sts on waste yarn or stitch holder for front and sleeves.

Change to Back Stripe patt from Stitch Guide. At the same time, work raglan increases as foll:

Set-up row: (WS) Yo, purl to end, yo.

Row 1: (RS—inc) K3, LLI (see Glossary), knit to last 3 sts, RLI (see Glossary), k3—2 sts inc'd.

Row 2: Purl.

Rep the last 2 rows 11 (13, 14, 16) more times—49 (54, 59, 67) sts.

Work 6 rows even, place removable marker to mark underarm placement, then work another 0 (2, 4, 6) row(s) even.

Beg to increase for diagonal front lines as foll: *[work 2 rows even, work inc row, work 1 row even]; rep from * until piece measures 6 (7, 7 ½, 8 ½)" (15 [18, 19, 21.5] cm) from under-

arm. Cut yarn and place back sts on holder.

Sleeves

Place 10 (10, 10, 8) held right sleeve sts on larger cir. With A and WS facing, work Sleeve Stripe patt from Stitch Guide. *At the same time*, work raglan increases as foll:

Set-up row: (WS) Yo, purl to end, yo.

Row 1: (RS—inc) K3, LLI, knit to last 3 sts, RLI, k3—2 sts inc'd.

Row 2: Purl.

Rep the last 2 rows 11 (13, 14, 16) more times—36 (40, 42, 44) sts.

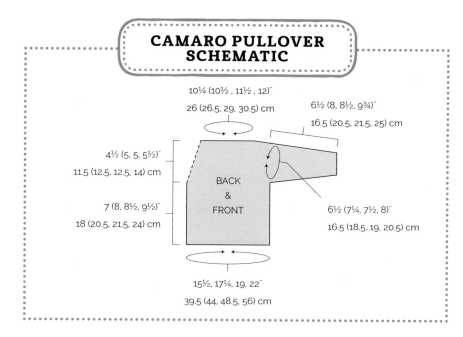

CAMARO PULLOVER SCHEMATIC

10¼ (10½ , 11½ , 12)˝
26 (26.5, 29, 30.5) cm

6½ (8, 8½, 9¾)˝
16.5 (20.5, 21.5, 25) cm

4½ (5, 5, 5½)˝
11.5 (12.5, 12.5, 14) cm

7 (8, 8½, 9½)˝
18 (20.5, 21.5, 24) cm

BACK & FRONT

6½ (7¼, 7½, 8)˝
16.5 (18.5, 19, 20.5) cm

15½, 17¼, 19, 22˝
39.5 (44, 48.5, 56) cm

Work 6 rows even, place removable marker to mark underarm placement, then work another 18 (20, 22, 24) rows even.

Next row: (RS—dec) K2, k2tog, knit to last 4 sts, ssk, k2—2 sts dec'd.

Rep dec row every 18th row 1 (2, 2, 3) more time(s), then work even until piece measures 5½ (7, 7½, 8¾)" (14 [18, 19, 22] cm) from underarm.

With A and smaller cir, work in Rib patt for 10 rows. BO all sts knitwise (kwise) on RS.

Rep for other sleeve.

Front
Place 23 (24, 27, 31) held front sts on larger cir. With B and WS facing, work raglan increases as foll:

Set-up row: (WS) Yo, purl to end, yo.

Row 1: (RS—inc) K3, LLI, knit to last 3 sts, RLI, k3—2 sts inc'd.

Row 2: Purl.

Rep the last 2 rows 11 (13, 14, 16) more times—49 (54, 59, 67) sts.

Work 6 rows even, place removable marker to mark underarm placement, then work another 0 (2, 4, 6) row(s) even.

Beg to decrease for diagonal front lines as foll:

Row 1: (RS) Knit.

Row 2: (WS) Purl.

Row 3: (dec) K2, k2tog, knit to last 4 sts, ssk, k2—2 sts dec'd.

Row 4: Purl.

Rep Rows 1–4 until piece measures 6 (7, 7½, 8½)" (15 [18, 19, 21.5] cm) from underarm. Cut yarn.

Bottom Edging
With RS facing, place held front sts on smaller cir, then place held back sts on needle. Pm for beg of rnd and join to work in rnds. Work in Rib patt for 10 rnds. BO all sts kwise on RS.

Pocket
Mark desired placement of the pocket on the front with sewing pins. Bottom pocket edge on sample is 6" (15 cm) from neck edge and 2" (5 cm) from left underarm.

With A and smaller cir, pick up and knit 13 (15, 15, 17) front sts at desired bottom pocket edge and knit 16 (18, 18, 20) rows in Rib patt. BO all sts kwise on RS.

Finishing
Using mattress stitch (see Glossary), sew sleeves to body along raglan increase lines, sew back to front along diagonal front lines, and sew sleeve seams.(see Glossary): front raglans from top down, flowing into side seams; and then back raglans flowing into sleeve seams .

Sew sides of pocket to front using whipstitch (see Glossary).

Weave in loose ends. Wet-block (see Glossary) pullover to measurements.

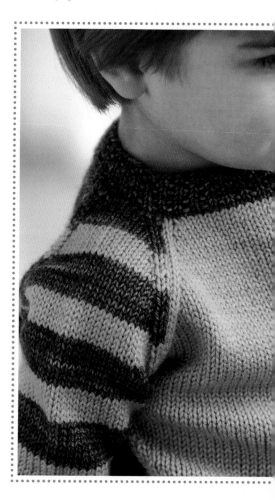

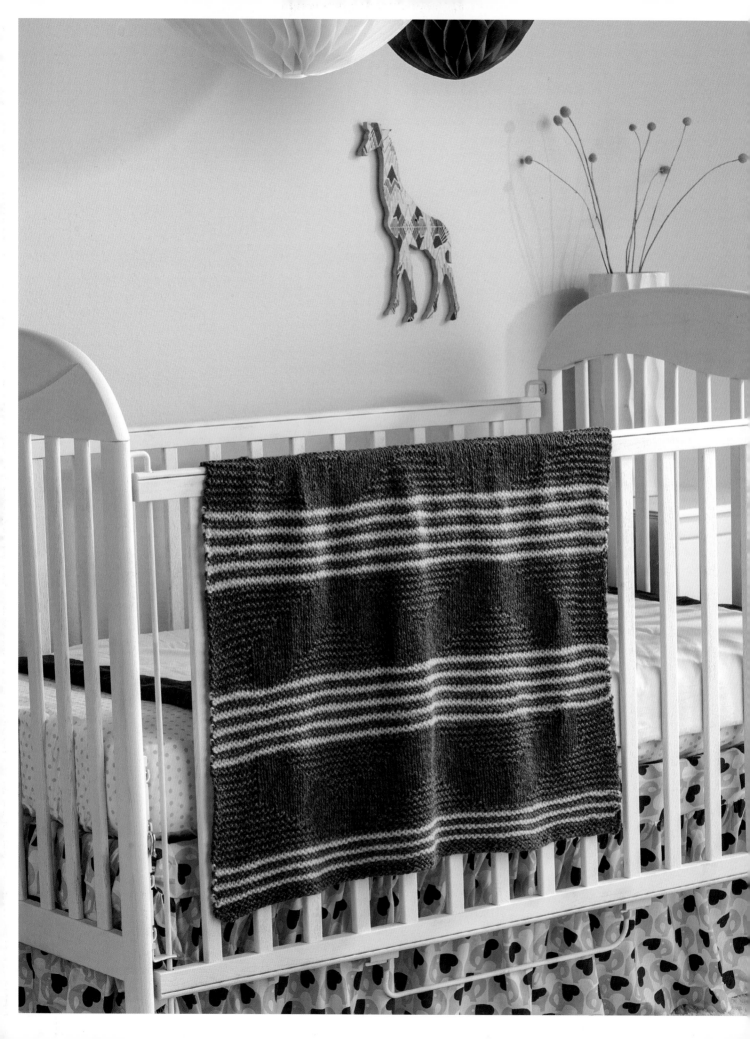

Geometric
BABY BLANKET

SHANNON COOK

This modern geometric baby blanket makes for a stylish addition to any room in your home. This cozy blanket is sure to be a standout piece that is both addicting and fun to knit up in a chunky yarn with large needles for a nice drape!

FINISHED SIZE
About 29" (73.5 cm) wide and 36" (91.5 cm) high.

YARN
Chunky weight (#5 Bulky).

Shown here: Cascade Yarns Eco+ (100% Peruvian Highland wool; 478 yd [437 m]/250 g): #8400 Charcoal Grey (A) and #4176 Goldenrod (B), 1 skein each.

NEEDLES
Size U.S. 11 (8 mm): 32" (81.5 cm) circular (cir).

Adjust needle size if necessary to obtain the correct gauge.

NOTIONS
Tapestry needle.

GAUGE
13 sts and 18 rows = 4" (10 cm) in St st.

12 sts and 20 ½ rows = 4" (10 cm) in garter st.

NOTES
In short striping sequences (such as the two-row pattern of this blanket), the unused color yarns can be carried up the side. Rather than cutting the yarn, simply drop the last yarn worked, pick up the next yarn under the old color, and begin knitting with the new color. Make sure not to pull the yarn too tightly.

GEOMETRIC PANEL 1 (MULTIPLE OF 36 STS)

Row 1 and all odd-numbered rows: (RS) Knit.

Row 2: (WS) K13, p9, k14.

Row 4: K11, p13, k12.

Row 6: K9, p17, k10.

Row 8: K7, p21, k8.

Row 10: K5, p12, k1, p12, k6.

Row 12: K3, p12, k5, p12, k4.

Row 14: K1, p12, k9, p12, k2.

Row 16: P11, k13, p12.

Row 18: P9, k17, p10.

Row 20: P7, k21, p8.

Row 22: P5, k25, p6.

Row 24: P3, k29, p4.

GEOMETRIC PANEL 2 (MULTIPLE OF 36 STS)

Row 1 and all odd-numbered rows: (RS) Knit.

Row 2: (WS) P4, k27, p5.

Row 4: P6, k23, p7.

Row 6: P8, k19, p9.

Row 8: P10, k15, k11.

Row 10: P12, k11, p12, k1.

Row 12: K2, p12, k7, p12, k3.

Row 14: K4, p12, k3, p12, k5.

Row 16: K6, p23, k7.

Row 18: K8, p19, k9.

Row 20: K10, p15, k11.

Row 22: K12, p11, k13.

Row 24: K14, p7, k15.

Bottom Border

With A and using the long-tail method (see Glossary), CO 92 sts.

Row 1: (WS) Knit with A.

Rows 2–5: Knit with A.

Rows 6 and 7: Knit with B.

Rows 8 and 9: Knit with A.

Rows 10–17: Rep Rows 6–9 twice, ending with A and a WS row.

Panel 1

Row 1: (RS) With A, k10, work Row 1 of Geometric Panel 1 twice (from Stitch Guide or chart), k10.

Row 2: K10, work Row 2 of Geometric Panel 1 twice, k10.

Rows 3–24: Cont in patt as established, working the first and last 10 sts in garter st and working Geometric Panel 1 twice in the center section.

Border 1

Rows 1 and 2: Knit with B.

Rows 3 and 4: Knit with A.

Rows 5–16: Rep Rows 1–4 three times.

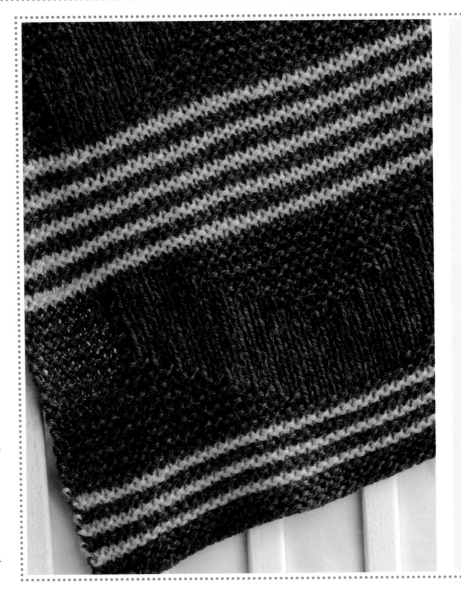

Rows 17 and 18: Knit with B.

Panel 2

Row 1: (RS) With A, k10, work Row 1 of Geometric Panel 2 twice (from Stitch Guide or chart), k10.

Row 2: K10, work Row 2 of Geometric Panel 2 twice, k10.

Rows 3–24: Cont in patt as established, working the first and last 10 sts in garter st and working Geometric Panel 2 twice in the center section.

Border 2

Rep Rows 1–18 of Border 1.

Panel 3

Rep Rows 1–24 of Panel 1.

Border 3

Rep Rows 1–18 of Border 1.

Panel 4

Rep Rows 1–24 of Panel 2.

Top Border

Rows 1 and 2: Knit with B.

Rows 3 and 4: Knit with A.

Rows 5–12: Rep Rows 1–4 twice, ending with A and a WS row.

Rows 13–17: Knit with A.

BO all sts loosely.

Finishing

Block the blanket lightly to finished measurements. Weave in loose ends.

Geometric Panel 1

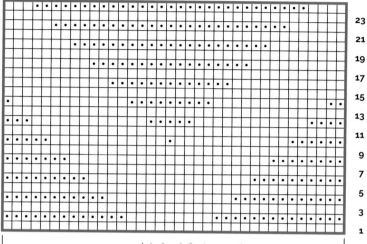

work twice (36-st repeat)

Geometric Panel 2

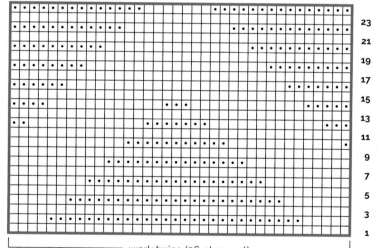

work twice (36-st repeat)

knit on RS; purl on WS

· purl on RS; knit on WS

pattern repeat

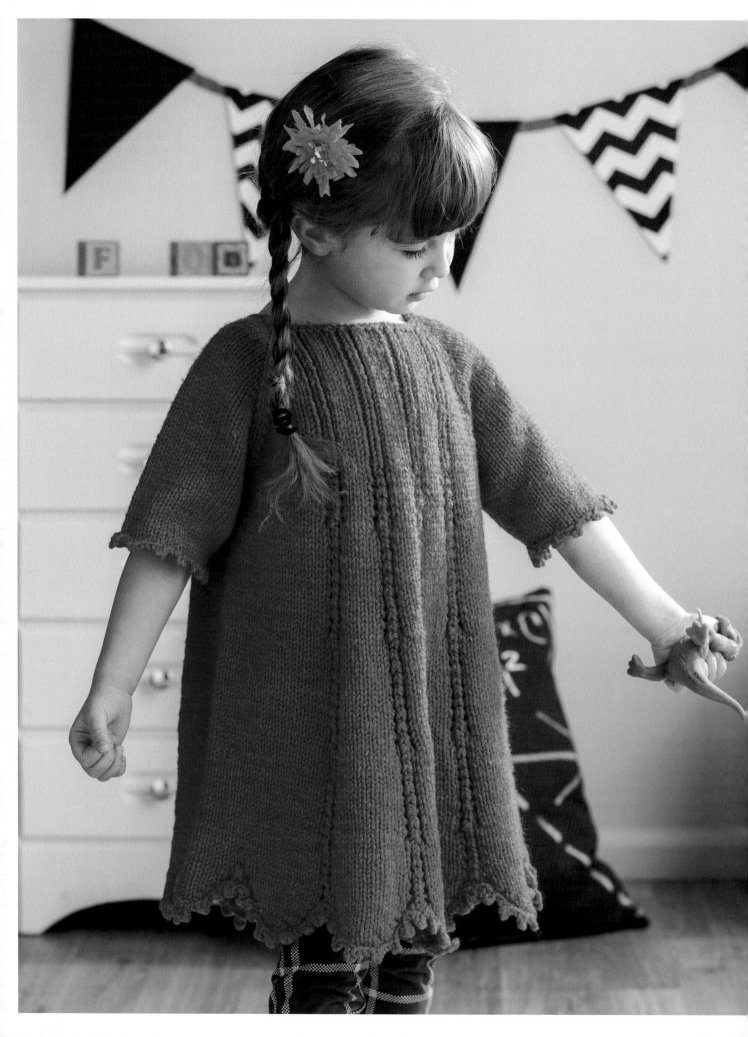

Eyelet
DRESS

MEGAN GREWAL

This eyelet dress is a simple and contemporary garment that is meant to grow with the child into a tunic. It's perfect for wearing over leggings or skinny jeans!

FINISHED SIZE
Newborn (3 months, 6 months, 12 months, 24 months, 4T).

About 17½ (18¼, 19, 20, 24, 26)" (44.5 [46.5, 48.5, 51, 61, 66] cm) chest circumference.

Dress shown measures 26" (66 cm).

YARN
Worsted weight (#4 Medium).

Shown here: Brown Sheep Lamb's Pride Superwash (100% wool; 200 yd [183 m]/100 g): SW145 Blaze (orange), 2 (2, 2, 3, 3, 3) skeins.

NEEDLES
Neck edging and buttonband: Size U.S. 6 (4 mm): 16" (40.5 cm) circular (cir).

Body: Size U.S. 8 (5 mm): 32" (81.5 cm) cir for working magic-loop method.

Sleeves: Size U.S. 8 (5 mm): set of 4 or 5 double-pointed (dpn).

Adjust needle size if necessary to obtain the correct gauge.

NOTIONS
Markers (m; 1 in a unique color for beg-of-rnd); stitch holders or waste yarn; tapestry needle; sewing needle and matching thread; one ⅝" (1.5 cm) button.

GAUGE
16 sts and 23 rnds = 4" (10 cm) in St st on larger needles.

18 sts and 24 rows/rnds = 4" (10 cm) in Rib patt on larger needles.

7 sts and 23 rnds of Eyelet patt on larger needles measure 1⅝" (4.1 cm) wide and 4" (10 cm) high.

NOTES
This eyelet dress is worked from the neck down in rows with an opening at the back neck edge, then joined to be worked in the round. The upper body features raglan shaping and a rib pattern, while the lower body features an eyelet pattern with increases worked into the pattern. Scallops are worked all around the bottom edge, finishing with a picot hem. Sleeves are half length and also have a picot hem.

CENTERED DOUBLE DECREASE (CDD)
Sl 2 sts as if to k2tog, k1, pass slipped sts over.

RIB IN ROWS (MULTIPLE OF 7 STS)
Row 1: K2, p1, k1, p1, k2.

Row 2: P2, k1, p1, k1, p2.

Rep Rows 1 and 2 for patt.

RIB IN THE ROUND (MULTIPLE OF 7 STS)
Every rnd: K2, p1, k1, p1, k2.

7 (9, 11, 13)–ST EYELET
Rnd 1: K2 (3, 4, 5), yo, CDD, yo, k2 (3, 4, 5).

Rnd 2: Knit.

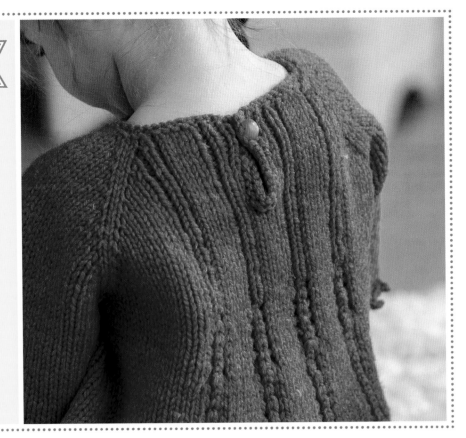

Yoke

With smaller cir and using the long-tail method (see Glossary), CO 44 (46, 50, 52, 56, 60) sts. Do not join. Knit 1 row.

Set-up row: (WS) K8 (8, 9, 9, 10, 11) for right back, place marker (pm) for raglan, k6 (7, 7, 8, 8, 8) for right sleeve, pm, k16 (16, 18, 18, 20, 22) for front, pm, k6 (7, 7, 8, 8, 8) for left sleeve, pm, k8 (8, 9, 9, 10, 11) for left back.

SHAPE YOKE

Change to larger cir.

Note: The yoke is shaped with raglan increases at the same time as the opening in the back is worked; read all the way through the following section before proceeding.

Row 1: (RS—raglan inc set-up) Work Row 1 of Rib patt from Stitch Guide once, k0 (0, 1, 1, 2, 2), p0 (0, 0, 0, 0, 1), M1R (see Glossary), k1, slip marker (sl m), k1, M1L (see Glossary), knit to 1 st before m, M1R, k1, sl m, k1, M1L, p0 (0, 0, 0, 0, 1), k0 (0, 1, 1, 2, 2), work Row 1 of Rib patt twice, k0 (0, 1, 1, 2, 2), p0 (0, 0, 0, 0, 1), M1R, k1, sl m, k1, M1L, knit to 1 st before m, M1R, k1, sl m, k1, M1L, p0 (0, 0, 0, 0, 1), k0 (0, 1, 1, 2, 2), work Row 1 of Rib patt once—52 (54, 58, 60, 64, 68) sts.

Row 2: (WS) Work sts as they appear (knit the knits and purl the purls), working new sts for front and back in Rib patt and new sleeve sts in St st.

Row 3: (raglan inc row) *Work in patt to 1 st before m, M1R, k1, sl m, k1, M1L; rep from * 3 more times, work in patt to end.

Row 4: Rep Row 2.

Work raglan inc row every other row 3 (3, 3, 4, 3, 2) more times, working new sts for front and back in Rib patt and new sleeve sts in St st and ending after a WS row—84 (86, 90, 100, 96, 92) sts.

Sizes 17 ½ (18 ¼, 19)" only:

Rnd 1: (RS—raglan inc rnd) *Work in patt to 1 st before raglan m, M1R, k1, sl m, k1, M1L; rep from * 3 more times, work in patt to end.

Pm for beg of rnd (marker is at center back) and join for working in rnds—92 (94, 98) sts.

Rnd 2: Work sts as they appear, working new sts for front and back in Rib patt and new sleeve sts in St st.

Rep last 2 rnds 1 (1, 0) more time(s); 4 rep of Rib patt completed each on back and front—100 (102, 98) sts.

Work raglan inc rnd every other rnd 3 (4, 5) times, working all new sts in St st—124 (134, 138) sts.

There are 2 rep of Rib patt on each back section and 4 rep of Rib patt on front. Work raglan inc row every other row 1 (2, 3) time(s), working all new sts in St st and ending after a WS row—108 (112, 116) sts.

Rnd 1: (RS—raglan inc rnd) *Work in patt to 1 st before raglan m, M1R, k1, sl m, k1, M1L; rep from * 3 more times, work in patt to end.

Pm for beg of rnd (marker is at center back) and, using the magic-loop method (see Glossary), join for working in rnds—116 (120, 124) sts.

Rnd 2: Work sts as they appear, working new sts in St st.

Rep last 2 rnds 4 (5, 6) more times—148 (160, 172) sts.

DIVIDE FOR BODY AND SLEEVES

Next rnd: *Work in patt to raglan m, remove m, place next 26 (29, 29, 32, 34, 36) sts on waste yarn or holder

for right sleeve, remove m, CO 5 (5, 5, 5, 8, 8) for underarm; rep from * once more, work in patt to end of rnd—82 (86, 90, 94, 108, 116) sts.

Shape Lower Body

Next rnd: (eyelet) Work Rnd 1 of 7-st Eyelet patt from Stitch Guide twice, pm, k13 (15, 17, 19, 26, 30), pm, work Rnd 1 of 7-st Eyelet patt four times, pm, k13 (15, 17, 19, 26, 30), pm, work Rnd 1 of 7-st Eyelet patt twice.

Next rnd: Knit.

Rep last 2 rnds 2 (3, 3, 3, 4, 4) more times.

INCREASES

Rnd 1: (Eyelet Inc 1) [K3, yo, k1, yo, k3] twice, sl m, knit to m, sl m, [k3, yo, k1, yo, k3] 4 times, sl m, knit to m, sl m, [k3, yo, k1, yo, k3] twice—98 (102, 106, 110, 124, 132) sts.

Cont as established without increasing for 9 (11, 13, 15, 17, 19) more rnds, working 9-st Eyelet patt in center back and center front sections.

Rnd 2: (Eyelet Inc 2) [K4, yo, k1, yo, k4] twice, sl m, knit to m, sl m, [k4, yo, k1, yo, k4] 4 times, sl m, knit to m, sl m, [k4, yo, k1, yo, k4] twice—114 (118, 122, 126, 140, 148) sts.

Cont as established without increasing for 9 (11, 13, 15, 17, 19) more rnds, working 11-st Eyelet patt in center back and center front sections.

Rnd 3: (Eyelet Inc 3) [K5, yo, k1, yo, k5] twice, sl m, knit to m, sl m, [k5, yo, k1, yo, k5] 4 times, sl m, knit to m, sl m, [k5, yo, k1, yo, k5] twice—130 (134, 138, 142, 156, 164) sts.

Cont as established without increasing for 7 (9, 11, 13, 15, 17) rnds, working 13-st Eyelet patt in center back and center front sections.

Rnd 3: (Eyelet Inc 3) [K5, yo, k1, yo, k5] twice, sl m, knit to m, sl m, [k5, yo, k1, yo, k5] 4 times, sl m, knit to m, sl m, [k5, yo, k1, yo, k5] twice—130 (134, 138, 142, 156, 164) sts.

Cont as established without increasing for 7 (9, 11, 13, 15, 17) rnds, working 13-st Eyelet patt in center and back front sections.

Sizes 18 ¼ (19, 20, 24, 26)" only:
Rnd 4: (Eyelet Inc 4) [K6, yo, k1, yo, k6] twice, sl m, knit to m, sl m, [k6, yo, k1, yo, k6] 4 times, sl m, knit to m, sl m, [k6, yo, k1, yo, k6] twice—(150, 154, 158, 172, 180) sts.

Cont as established without increasing for— (3, 3, 5, 3, 7) rnds, working 15-st Eyelet patt in center back and center front sections.

SCALLOP HEM SET-UP
Sizes 19 (20)"

Rnd 1: [K6, yo, CDD, yo, k6] twice, sl m, k2tog, knit to 2 sts before m, ssk, sl m, [k6, yo, CDD, yo, k6] 4 times, sl m, k2tog, knit to 2 sts before m, ssk,

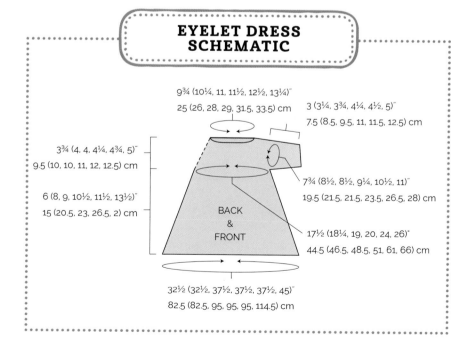

EYELET DRESS SCHEMATIC

9¾ (10¼, 11, 11½, 12½, 13¼)"
25 (26, 28, 29, 31.5, 33.5) cm

3 (3¼, 3¾, 4¼, 4½, 5)"
7.5 (8.5, 9.5, 11, 11.5, 12.5) cm

3¾ (4, 4, 4¼, 4¾, 5)"
9.5 (10, 10, 11, 12, 12.5) cm

6 (8, 9, 10½, 11½, 13½)"
15 (20.5, 23, 26.5, 2) cm

7¾ (8½, 8½, 9¼, 10½, 11)"
19.5 (21.5, 21.5, 23.5, 26.5, 28) cm

BACK & FRONT

17½ (18¼, 19, 20, 24, 26)"
44.5 (46.5, 48.5, 51, 61, 66) cm

32½ (32½, 37½, 37½, 37½, 45)"
82.5 (82.5, 95, 95, 95, 114.5) cm

sl m, [k6, yo, CDD, yo, k6] twice; 4 sts dec'd—150 (154) sts.

Rnd 2: Knit.

Rep last 2 rnds 0 (1) more time—150 (150) sts.

Size 24"
Rnd 1: [K6, yo, CDD, yo, k6] twice, sl m, M1R, knit to m, M1L, sl m, [k6, yo, k1, yo, k6] 4 times, sl m, M1R, knit to m, M1L, sl m, [k6, yo, k1, yo, k6] twice; 4 sts inc'd—176 sts.

Rnd 2: Knit.

Rep last 2 rnds once more—180 sts.

All Sizes:
Cont as established without shaping until lower body measures 6 (8, 9, 10 ½, 11 ½, 13 ½)" (15 [20.5, 23, 26.5, 29, 34.5] cm) from dividing rnd—130 (150, 150, 150, 180, 180) sts.

Last rnd: Removing markers as you come to them (except for beg-of-rnd marker at center back), *k5 (6, 6, 6, 6, 6), yo, CDD, yo, k5 (6, 6, 6, 6, 6); rep from * to end.

SCALLOP HEM
Scallop hem is worked in 1 continuous rnd, with short-rows on each scallop.

Size 17½" (scallop worked over 13 sts)
Set-up: K7, turn.

*Short-Row 1:** Sl 1, p12, turn.

Short-Row 2: Sl 1, k10, turn.

Short-Row 3: Sl 1, p9, turn.

Short-Row 4: Sl 1, k8, turn.

Short-Row 5: Sl 1, p7, turn.

Short-Row 6: Sl 1, k5, turn.

Short-Row 7: Sl 1, p3, turn.

Short-Row 8: Sl 1, k14, turn.

Rep from * 9 more times, working Short-Row 8 of last rep as sl 1, k8.

Sizes 18 ¼ (19, 20, 24, 26)" (scallop worked over 15 sts)
Set-up: K8, turn.

*Short-Row 1:** Sl 1, p14, turn.

Short-Row 2: Sl 1, k12, turn.

Short-Row 3: Sl 1, p11, turn.

Short-Row 4: Sl 1, k10, turn.

Short-Row 5: Sl 1, p9, turn.

Short-Row 6: Sl 1, k8, turn.

Short-Row 7: Sl 1, p7, turn.

Short-Row 8: Sl 1, k5, turn.

Short-Row 9: Sl 1, p3, turn.

Short-Row 10: Sl 1, k16, turn.

Rep from *—(9, 9, 9, 11, 11) more times, working Short-Row 10 of last rep as sl 1, k9.

PICOT BIND-OFF
BO 2 sts, *slip st from right needle to left needle, CO 2 sts, BO 4 sts; rep from * to end of rnd.

Sleeves
Place 26 (29, 29, 32, 34, 36) held sleeve sts on dpn. With RS facing, join yarn in center of sts at base of underarm CO. Pick up and knit 3 (3, 3, 3, 4, 4) sts across half of underarm CO, knit held sleeve sts, pick up and knit 2 (2, 2, 2, 3, 3) sts from other half of underarm CO. Pm for end of rnd—31 (34, 34, 37, 42, 44) sts.

Next rnd: K2 (2, 2, 2, 4, 4), ssk, knit to last 3 (3, 3, 3, 4, 4) sts, k2tog, knit to end—29 (32, 32, 35, 40, 42) sts.

Work 6 (6, 8, 6, 6, 8) rnds even.

Next rnd: (dec) Ssk, knit to last 2 sts, k2tog—27 (30, 30, 33, 38, 40) sts.

Rep dec rnd every 7 (7, 9, 7, 7, 9)th rnd 1 (1, 1, 2, 2, 2) more time(s)—25 (28, 28, 29, 34, 36) sts.

Cont working even in St st until sleeve measures 3 (3 ¼, 3 ¾, 4 ¼, 4 ½, 5 ¼)" (7.5 [8.5, 9.5, 11, 11.5, 13.5] cm) from joining rnd.

PICOT BIND-OFF
BO 2 sts, *slip st from right needle to left needle, CO 2 sts, BO 4 sts; rep from * to end of rnd.

Rep for other sleeve.

Finishing
Weave in loose ends.

BACK BUTTONBAND
With RS facing and smaller cir, join yarn at top corner of right back. Pick up and knit 9 (9, 9, 11, 11, 11) sts along right back edge, then pick up and knit 9 (9, 9, 11, 11, 11) sts along left back edge—18 (18, 18, 22, 22, 22) sts. Knit 1 row.

Buttonhole row: K1, k2tog, yo, knit to end of row.

BO all sts kwise.

Sew button opposite buttonhole. Block to measurements.

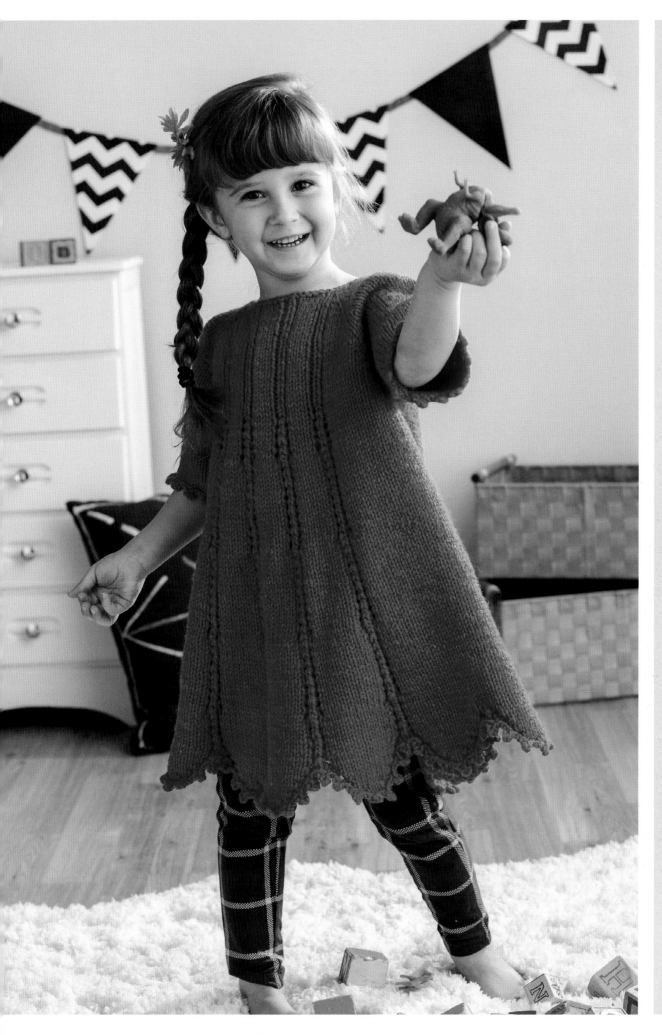

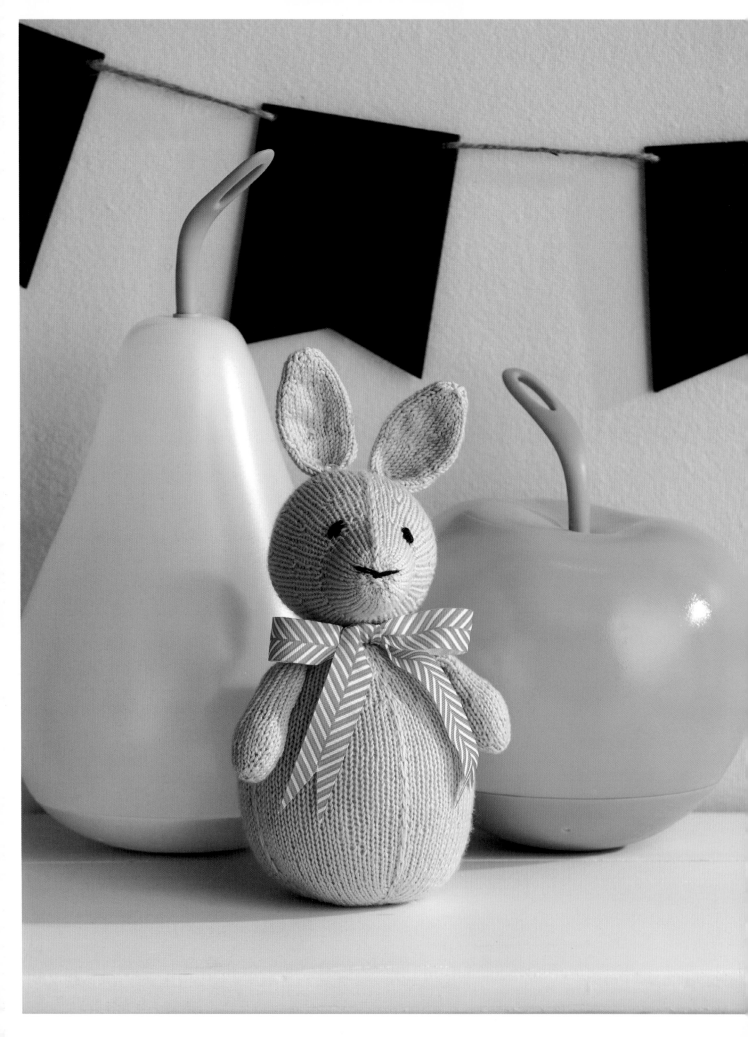

Bunny

MELISSA SCHASCHWARY

Every child adores a bunny, and you can bet that this is the best bunny you could bargain for. Sweet and simple, it stands up tall (owing to a gentle beanbag weight) and wears a gentle expression.

FINISHED SIZE

8½" (21.5 cm) tall without the ears, 11" (28 cm) tall in total.

YARN

Sportweight (#2 Fine).

Shown here: Debbie Bliss Cashmerino Baby (55% merino wool, 33% microfiber acrylic, 12% silver; 137 yd [125 m]/50 g): #012 light gray, 2 skeins.

NEEDLES

Size U.S. 1 (2.25 mm): 40" (101.5 cm) circular (cir) for working magic-loop method and set of 4 or 5 double-pointed (dpn).

Adjust needle size if necessary to obtain the correct gauge.

NOTIONS

Markers (m); tapestry needle; 12" (30.5 cm) square piece of fabric; poly-pellets to fill beanbag; embroidery thread for facial features; sewing scissors; sewing needle and matching thread; polyester stuffing; 12" (30.5 cm) of decorative ribbon.

GAUGE

28 sts and 36 rnds = 4" (10 cm) in St st.

NOTES

Bunny is knit in 6 separate pieces: head, body, ears (2), and arms (2). All pieces are knit in the round.

A beanbag is sewn, filled, and placed into the base of the body to add extra weight and help the bunny to stand. Facial features are stitched in once all pieces are completed and seamed together.

Beanbag

Using sewing scissors and fabric, cut 2 discs with a diameter of 5" (12.5 cm) each. Lay 1 disc on top of the other and, using a sewing needle and thread or a sewing machine, sew along outer circumference through both discs, leaving a 2" (5 cm) opening. Fill the beanbag with poly-pellets being careful not to overfill. Sew opening closed and set aside.

Head

Set-up: (nose end) CO 7 sts, place marker (pm) for beg of rnd, and join for working in rnds, being careful not to twist sts.

Rnd 1: Knit.

Rnd 2: (inc) [M1L (see Glossary), k1] 3 times, sl 1, [M1L, k1] 3 times—13 sts.

Rnd 3: K6, sl 1, knit to end.

Rnd 4: (inc) [M1L, k1] 6 times, k1, [M1L, k1] 6 times—25 sts.

Rnds 5 and 6: K12, sl 1, knit to end.

Rnd 7: Knit.

Rnds 8–16: Rep Rnds 5–7 three times.

Rnd 17: (inc) [M1L, k2] 6 times, sl 1, [M1L, k2] 6 times—37 sts.

Rnd 18: K19, sl 1, knit to end.

Rnd 19: Knit.

Rnd 20: K19, sl 1, knit to end.

Thread tail from CO sts on tapestry needle, draw through CO sts, and pull tight to close. Weave in end.

Rnds 21–25: Work Rnds 18–21 once, then work Rnds 18 and 19 once more.

Rnd 26: (inc) [M1L, k3] 6 times, sl 1, [M1L, k3] 6 times—49 sts.

Rnd 27: K24, sl 1, knit to end.

Rnd 28: Knit.

Rnd 29: K24, sl 1, knit to end.

Rnds 30–34: Work Rnds 27–29 once, then work Rnds 27 and 28 once more.

Rnd 35: (inc) [M1L, k4] 6 times, sl 1, [M1L, k4] 6 times—61 sts.

Rnd 36: K30, sl 1, knit to end.

Rnd 37: Knit.

Rnd 38: K30, sl 1, knit to end.

Rnds 39–43: Work Rnds 36–38 once, then work Rnds 36 and 37 once more.

Rnd 44: (dec) [K4, k2tog] 5 times, sl 1, [k4, k2tog] 5 times—51 sts.

Rnd 45: K25, sl 1, knit to end.

Rnd 46: (dec) [K3, k2tog] 5 times, k1, [k3, k2tog] 5 times—41 sts.

Rnd 47: K20, sl 1, knit to end.

Rnd 48: (dec) [K2, k2tog] 5 times, sl 1, [k2, k2tog] 5 times—31 sts.

Start stuffing head with polyester stuffing.

Rnd 49: Knit.

Rnds 50 and 51: K15, sl 1, knit to end.

Rnd 52: Knit.

Rnd 53: (dec) [K1, k2tog] 5 times, sl 1, [k1, k2tog] 5 times—21 sts.

Rnd 54: K10, sl 1, k10.

Rnd 55: *K2tog; rep from * to last st, k1—11 sts.

Finish stuffing head. Cut yarn, thread tail on tapestry needle, draw through rem sts, and pull tight to close. Weave in loose ends.

Body
SHAPE LOWER BODY

With cir CO 12 sts, pm for beg of rnd, and use magic-loop method (see Glossary) to join for working in rnds, being careful not to twist sts.

Rnds 1 and 2: Knit.

Rnd 3: (inc) [Sl 1, M1L, k2, M1L] 4 times—20 sts.

Rnd 4: Knit.

Rnd 5: (inc) [Sl 1, M1L, k4, M1L] 4 times—28 sts.

Rnd 6: [Sl 1, k6] 4 times.

Rnd 7: (inc) [K1, M1L, k6, M1L] 4 times—36 sts.

Rnd 8: [Sl 1, k8] 4 times.

Rnd 9: (inc) [Sl 1, M1L, k8, M1L] 4 times—44 sts.

Rnd 10: Knit.

Rnd 11: (inc) [Sl 1, M1L, k10, M1L] 4 times—52 sts.

Rnd 12: [Sl 1, k12] 4 times.

Rnd 13: (inc) [K1, M1L, k12, M1L] 4 times—60 sts.

Rnd 14: [Sl 1, k14] 4 times.

Rnd 15 (inc): [Sl 1, M1L, k14, M1L] 4 times—68 sts.

Rnd 16: Knit.

Rnd 17: (inc) [Sl 1, M1L, k16, M1L] 4 times—76 sts (18 sts between each pair of slipped sts).

Rnd 18: [Sl 1, k18] 4 times.

Rnd 19: Knit.

Rnds 20 and 21: [Sl 1, k18] 4 times.

Rep Rnds 19–21 ten more times.

SHAPE UPPER BODY

Rnd 1: (dec) *K1, [k2tog, k2] 4 times, ssk; rep from * to end—56 sts.

Rnds 2 and 3: [Sl 1, k13] 4 times.

Rnd 4: Knit.

Rnds 5 and 6: [Sl 1, k13] 4 times.

Rnd 7: (dec) [K1, k2tog, k9, ssk] 4 times—48 sts.

Rnds 8 and 9: [Sl 1, k11] 4 times.

Rnd 10: (dec) [K1, k2tog, k7, ssk] 4 times—40 sts.

Rnds 11 and 12: [Sl 1, k9] 4 times.

Rnd 13: (dec) [K1, k2tog, k5, ssk] 4 times—32 sts.

Rnds 14 and 15: [Sl 1, k7] 4 times.

Place beanbag into base of body and begin stuffing body.

Rnd 16: (dec) [K1, k2tog, k3, ssk] 4 times—24 sts.

Rnds 17 and 18: [Sl 1, k5] 4 times.

Rnd 19: (dec) [K1, k2tog, k1, ssk] 4 times—16 sts.

Rnds 20 and 21: [Sl 1, k3] 4 times.

Finish stuffing the body being careful not to overstuff.

Rnd 22: (dec) [K1, k2tog, k1] 4 times—12 sts.

Cut yarn, leaving a 12" (30.5 cm) tail to attach head to neck later. Thread tail on tapestry needle and draw through rem sts.

Arms (make 2)

CO 6 sts, pm for beg of rnd, and join for working in rnds, being careful not to twist sts.

Rnd 1: Knit.

Rnd 2: *M1L, k1; rep from * to end—12 sts.

Rnds 3 and 4: Knit.

Rnd 5: [K1, M1L, k2] 4 times—16 sts.

Rnds 6 and 7: Knit.

Rnd 8: [K1, M1L, k3] 4 times—20 sts.

Rnds 9–13: Knit. Thread tail from CO sts on tapestry needle, draw through CO sts, and pull tight to close. Weave in end.

Rnd 14: (dec) [K2, k2tog] 5 times—15 sts.

Rnds 15–29: Knit.

Stuff lower arm being careful not to overstuff.

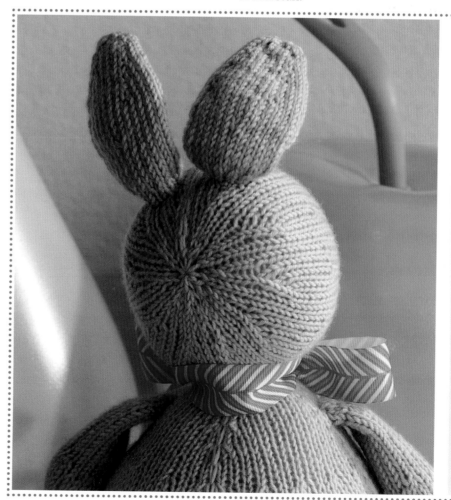

Rnd 30: (dec) *K2tog; rep from * to last st, k1—8 sts.

Rnd 31: Knit.

Rnd 32: [K2tog] 4 times—4 sts.

Cut yarn, thread tail on tapestry needle, and draw through rem sts. Cut yarn, leaving a 10" (25.5 cm) tail to attach arm to body later.

Ears (make 2)

CO 6 sts, pm for beg of rnd, and join for working in the rnd, being careful not to twist sts.

Rnd 1: Knit.

Rnd 2: *M1L, k1; rep from * to end— 12 sts.

Rnds 3 and 4: Knit.

Rnd 5: [K1, M1L, k2] 4 times—16 sts.

Rnds 6 and 7: Knit.

Rnd 8: [K1, M1L, k3] 4 times—20 sts.

Rnds 9 and 10: Knit.

Rnd 11: [K1, M1L, k4] 4 times—24 sts.

Rnds 12 and 13: Knit.

Rnd 14: [K1, M1L, k5] 4 times—28 sts.

Rnds 15–19: Knit.

Rnd 20: (dec) K2tog, k2, ssk, k2, k2tog, k2, [k2tog, k6] twice—23 sts.

Rnds 21–26: Knit.

Rnd 27: (dec) K2, ssk, k2, k2tog, k2, [k2tog] 6 times, k1—15 sts.

Rnd 28: Knit.

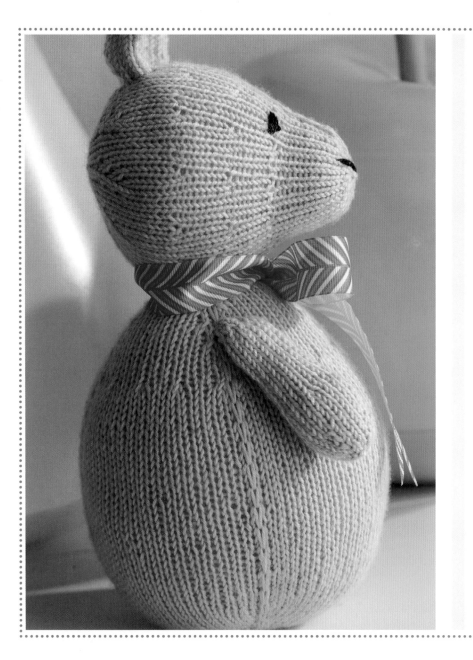

Rnd 29: (dec) K3, k2tog, knit to end—14 sts.

Divide sts evenly between 2 dpn and using a third dpn and the three-needle method (see Glossary), BO all sts. Cut yarn, leaving a 10" (25.5 cm) tail to attach ear to head later.

Finishing

Pinch ears slightly at the bottom and bring the yarn tail through the ear to maintain the "pucker." Seam the ears to the head using mattress stitch (see Glossary) and the existing yarn tail.

Use the mattress stitch to seam the head to the body, then the arms to the body. Following photo and using scrap yarn, embroider nose and eyes.

Cast-Ons

BACKWARD-LOOP CAST-ON

*Loop working yarn and place it on needle backward so that it doesn't unwind. Repeat from *.

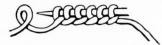

CABLE CAST-ON

If there are no stitches on the needles, make a slipknot of working yarn and place it on the needle, then use the knitted method to cast on one more stitch— two stitches on needle. Hold needle with working yarn in your left hand. *Insert right needle between the first two stitches on left needle (Figure 1), wrap yarn around needle as if to knit, draw yarn through (Figure 2), and place new loop on left needle (Figure 3) to form a new stitch. Repeat from * for the desired number of stitches, always working between the first two stitches on the left needle.

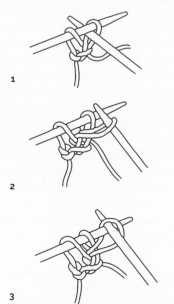

LONG-TAIL CAST-ON

Leaving a long tail (about ½" [1.3 cm] for each stitch to be cast on), make a slipknot and place on right needle. Place thumb and index finger of your left hand between the yarn ends so that working yarn is around your index finger and tail end is around your thumb and secure the yarn ends with your other fingers.

Hold your palm upward, making a V of yarn (Figure 1). *Bring needle up through loop on thumb (Figure 2), catch first strand around index finger, and go back down through loop on thumb (Figure 3). Drop loop off thumb and, placing thumb back in V configuration, tighten resulting stitch on needle (Figure 4). Repeat from * for the desired number of stitches

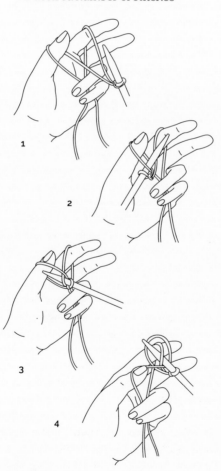

MAGIC-LOOP CAST-ON

For a full tutorial, see http://www .knittingdaily.com/how-to-knit/ knitting-in-the-round/the-magical-magic-loop.

PROVISIONAL CAST-ON

With waste yarn and crochet hook, make a loose crochet chain about four stitches more than you need to cast on. With knitting needle, working yarn, and beginning two stitches from end of chain, pick up and knit one stitch through the back loop of each crochet chain (Figure 1) for desired number of stitches. When you're ready to work in the opposite direction, pull out the crochet chain to expose live stitches (Figure 2).

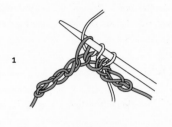

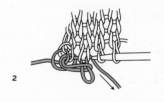

TURKISH/EASTERN CAST-ON

This method is worked by first wrapping the yarn around two parallel needles, then using a third needle to knit the loops on each of the two needles. The loops on one needle are the foundation for the instep, and the loops on the other needle are the foundation for the sole.

Hold two double-pointed needles parallel to each other. Leaving a 4" (10 cm) tail hanging to the front between the two needles, wrap the yarn around both needles from back to front half the number of times as desired stitches (four wraps shown here for eight stitches total), then bring the yarn forward between the needles (Figure 1).

Use a third needle to knit across the loops on the top needle, keeping the third needle on top of both the other needles when knitting the first stitch (*Figure 2*).

With the right side facing, rotate the two cast-on needles like the hands of a clock so that the bottom needle is on the top (*Figure 3*).

Knit across the loops on the new top needle (*Figure 4*).

Rotate the needles again and use a third needle to knit the first two stitches of the new top needle. There will now be two stitches each on two needles and four stitches on another needle (*Figure 5*).

1
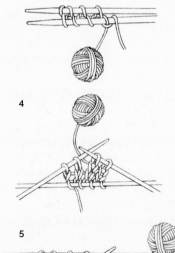

2

3

4

5

Bind-Offs
THREE-NEEDLE BIND-OFF

Place the stitches to be joined onto two separate needles and hold the needles parallel so that the right sides of knitting face together. Insert a third needle into the first stitch on each of two needles (*Figure 1*) and knit them together as one stitch (*Figure 2*), *knit the next stitch on each needle the same way, then use the left needle tip to lift the first stitch over the second and off the needle (*Figure 3*). Repeat from * until no stitches remain on first two needles. Cut yarn and pull tail through last stitch to secure.

1
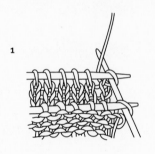

2
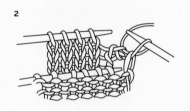

3
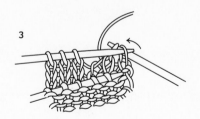

Increases
RAISED (M1) INCREASES
Left Slant (M1L) and Standard M1

With left needle tip, lift strand between needles from front to back (*Figure 1*). Knit lifted loop through the back (*Figure 2*).

1
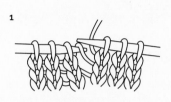

2
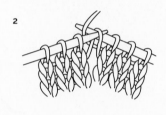

Right Slant (M1R)

With left needle tip, lift strand between needles from back to front (*Figure 1*). Knit lifted loop through the front (*Figure 2*).

1
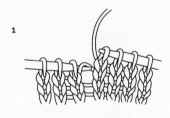

2
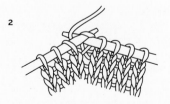

BAR INCREASE

This type of increase forms a small bar similar to a purl stitch at the left-hand side of the increased stitch. Depending on the yarn and stitch pattern, this bar may or may not be noticeable.

Knitwise (K1F&B)

Knit into a stitch but leave the stitch on the left needle (*Figure 1*), then knit through the back loop.

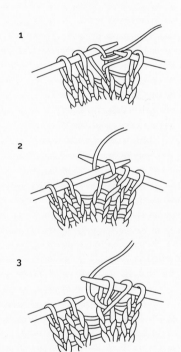

Purlwise (P1F&B)

You can work this increase purlwise by purling into the front and back of the same stitch.

LIFTED INCREASE (LI)

This type of increase is nearly invisible in the knitting. It can be worked to slant to the right or to the left, which can be used as a design element along raglan shaping. You can separate the increases by the desired number of stitches to form a prominent ridge.

Right Slant (RLI): Knit into the back of the stitch (in the "purl bump") in the row directly below the first stitch on the left needle (*Figure 1*), then knit the stitch on the needle (*Figure 2*) and slip the original stitch off the needle.

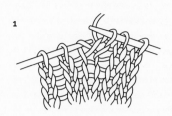

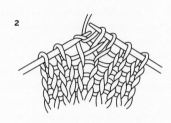

Left Slant (LLI): Knit the first stitch on the left needle, insert left needle tip into the back of the stitch (in the "purl bump") below the stitch just knitted (*Figure 1*), then knit this stitch (*Figure 2*).

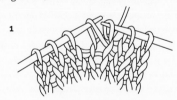

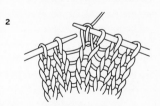

Short-Rows
KNIT SIDE

Work to turning point, slip next stitch purlwise (*Figure 1*), bring the yarn to the front, then slip the same stitch back to the left needle (*Figure 2*), turn the work around and bring the yarn in position for the next stitch—one

stitch has been wrapped, and the yarn is correctly positioned to work the next stitch. When you come to a wrapped stitch on a subsequent row, hide the wrap by working it together with the wrapped stitch as follows: Insert right needle tip under the wrap from the front (*Figure 3*), then into the stitch on the needle, and work the stitch and its wrap together as a single stitch.

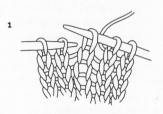

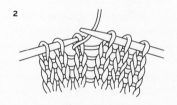

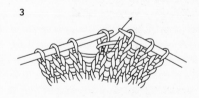

PURL SIDE

Work to the turning point, slip the next stitch purlwise to the right needle, bring the yarn to the back of the work (*Figure 1*), return the slipped stitch to the left needle, bring the yarn to the front between the needles (*Figure 2*), and turn the work so that the knit side is facing—one stitch has been wrapped, and the yarn is correctly positioned to knit the next stitch. To hide the wrap on a subsequent purl row, work to the wrapped stitch, use the tip of the right needle to pick up the wrap from the back, place it on the left needle (*Figure 3*), then purl it together with the wrapped stitch.

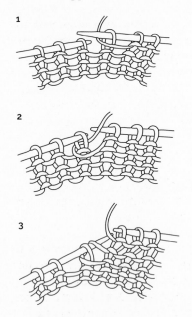

I-Cord

Using two double-pointed needles, cast on the desired number of stitches (usually three to five). *Without turning the needle, slide stitches to other end of needle, pull the yarn around the back, and knit the stitches as usual. Repeat from * for desired length.

Twisted Cord

Cut several lengths of yarn about five times the desired finished cord length. Fold the strands in half to form two equal groups. Anchor the strands at the fold by looping them over a doorknob. Holding one group in each hand, twist each group tightly in a clockwise direction until they begin

to kink. Put both groups in one hand, then release them, allowing them to twist around each other counter-clockwise. Smooth out the twists so that they are uniform along the length of the cord. Knot the ends.

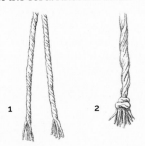

Seams
MATTRESS STITCH SEAM

With RS of knitting facing, use threaded needle to pick up one bar between first two stitches on one piece (*Figure 1*), then corresponding bar plus the bar above it on other piece (*Figure 2*). *Pick up next two bars on first piece, then next two bars on other (*Figure 3*). Repeat from * to end of seam, finishing by picking up last bar (or pair of bars) at the top of first piece.

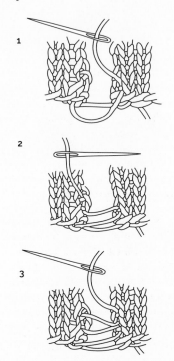

WHIPSTITCH

With right side of work facing and working one stitch in from the edge, bring threaded needle out from back to front along edge of knitted piece.

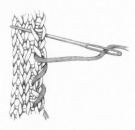

Wet-Towel Blocking

Run a large bath or beach towel (or two towels for larger projects) through the rinse/spin cycle of a washing machine. Roll the knitted pieces in the wet towel(s), place the roll in a plastic bag, and leave overnight so that the knitted pieces become uniformly damp. Pin the damp pieces to a blocking surface and let air-dry thoroughly.

Pom-Poms

Create your pom-pom template: Trace the circumference of a glass or other round object onto cardboard two times. Cut out these two circles. Trace smaller circles inside the larger circles and cut them out as well. Cut wedge openings in both discs (*Figure 1*).

Cut a piece of yarn about 12" (30.5 cm) and place the end between the two pieces of cardboard. Hold the two pieces of cardboard together and begin wrapping yarn around the cardboard template. The more yarn you wrap around, then the denser your pom-pom will be. Make a loose slipknot with the tie yarn that is sandwiched between the cardboard. Slip your scissors in between the two pieces of cardboard and begin cutting around the circle (*Figure 2*). Tighten the slipknot and slide out the cardboard.

Trim your pom-pom: Create two more cardboard templates the same diameter as what you want your pom-pom to be. Sandwich your pom-pom between them and pierce the center with a tapestry needle to secure. Trim around the edges of the template (*Figure 3*). Remove templates and needle to reveal your pom-pom!

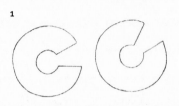

1

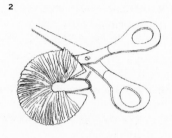

2

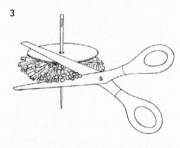

3

Embroidery
CHAIN STITCH
Bring threaded needle out from back to front at center of a knitted stitch. Form a short loop and insert needle back where it came out. Keeping the loop under the needle, bring needle back out in center of next stitch to the right.

BUTTONHOLES
Two-stitch One-row Buttonhole
Work to where you want the buttonhole to begin, bring yarn to front, sl 1 pwise, bring yarn to back (*Figure 1*).

*Sl 1 pwise, pass first slipped st over second; rep from * one more time.

Place last st back on left needle (*Figure 2*), turn. Cast on three stitches as follows: *Insert right needle between the first and second stitches on left needle, draw up a loop, and place it on the left needle (*Figure 3*); rep from * two more times, turn.

Bring yarn to back, slip first stitch of left needle onto right needle and pass last cast-on stitch over it (*Figure 4*).

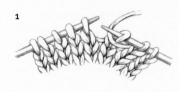

1

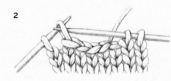

2

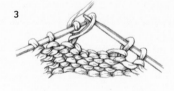

3

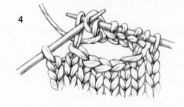

4

Meg Swansen's Jogless Jog
Knitting color stripes in the round can result in jogs at the "seam" line where each new round begins. In *Meg Swansen's Knitting* (Interweave, 1999), Meg offers an ingenious technique for eliminating these jogs when working solid-color stripes of two or more rounds.

Work the first stripe (let's call that color A) for the desired number of rounds, change colors (color B) and knit one round.

Work the first stitch of the second round with color B as follows: Pick up the right side of the stitch in the row below the stitch on the needle (it will be color A), put it on the left needle and knit it together with the first stitch on the needle. You will have worked the first stitch of the round twice, but because you work into the stitch below the one on the needle the second time, you have only worked it for one round, and it appears as if it were worked just once.

The jog between the two colors disappears, and the beginning of the round for color changes only is shifted one stitch to the left. Note: Do not change the position of markers required for the placement of any shaping decreases or increases (such as ones used for waist shaping).

Continue working as many rounds as you want with color B.

To change to another color, simply repeat the process, working the first stitch of the round a second time by picking up the stitch in the row below the stitch on the needle and knitting it together with the first stitch on the needle, thereby shifting the beginning of the round one more stitch to the left for color changes.

EKATERINA BLANCHARD focuses on making designs that have a playful, modern style and are easy to wear and knit, but not without a bit of interest. Originally from Russia, she lives in France with her husband and two children.

KAREN BORREL lives and designs in Canada. She loves simple knits with enough details to make them different. She tries to include garter stitch, her favorite stitch, or a pop of color in a lot of her designs. Most of her work is self-published on Ravelry and has been available through magazines and books in France.

RAYA BUDREVICH is the founder of Blissful Knits, a dyeworks company based in Portland, Oregon. As a stay-at-home mom of two boys, she is grateful for the opportunity to reinvent herself by integrating her love of color, texture, and style with a longtime passion for knitting.

LISA CHEMERY is the designer behind Frogginette Knitting Patterns. Originally from France, Lisa lives in Germany with her physicist husband and her two young children. She started designing knitwear in 2008, with a particular love for children's knits that are fun to knit and easy to wear, with a European flair. Ravelry.com/designers/lisa-chemery

SHANNON COOK of VeryShannon.com is a knitting and sewing pattern designer, blogger, author/publisher, wife, and mom to two daughters. She is happily living a handmade life near the ocean on Vancouver Island. She is also the recent coauthor and copublisher of *Seasonless* (Marian Rae Publications, 2014) and *Journey* (Marian Rae Publications, 2013).

NADIA CRÉTIN-LÉCHENNE loves nothing more than having wool between her fingers. She learned to knit as a child and soon became a compulsive knitter. Her daily routine is mostly made of quiet hours, spent dreaming about yarn and designs, always with a cup of coffee nearby. She lives in Switzerland, in a very tiny village, with her husband and six children.

REBECCA DANGER is a craft pattern designer who lives in Lake Stevens, Washington, with her husband, Mr. Danger, their sons, Presley and Maverick, and their two pugs, Abbey and Lucy, plus a whole menagerie of knitted and sewn toys. She's got a great blog at rebeccadanger.typepad.com and a monster of a website at dangercrafts.com.

MEGAN GREWAL is a simple Canadian girl living in a snowbelt, which provides many opportunities to wear warm cardigans and cozy caps. With a background in quilting and garment construction, Megan tries to design garments that are comfortable and fun, by incorporating whimsical and creative design elements into classic knitwear. With a troop of nine children, there are plenty of opportunities to get creative! Visit her on her blog: littlelambyknits.blogspot.com.

KELLY HERDRICH learned to knit while living in England, where she currently resides with her husband and three (not-yet-knitting) daughters. A former educator and a published author, she formed *kelly without a net* designs in 2008 and is the designer of the popular "in threes: a baby cardigan."

TAIGA HILLIARD loves designs that have a classic feel to them, but with a twist , and especially enjoys working with cashmere or other luxury yarns. When she does not have needles in her hands, she enjoys photography and reading.

TERRI KRUSE lives in North Dakota with her children. She has self-published over fifty patterns and has had designs in *Knitty, Interweave Knits, Knitscene*, and several book publications. When she isn't knitting and designing, she's probably trying to find a football or hockey game to watch.

MELISSA LABARRE is coauthor of the Interweave books *New England Knits* and *Weekend Hats* and has contributed designs to several books, magazines, and yarn company design collections. Her self-published designs can be found on her blog, knittingschooldropout.com. Melissa lives in western Massachusetts with her husband and two young daughters.

ELIZABETH MURPHY is a fiber artist, designer, and photographer. Nestled into a tiny cabin in the northwoods of Wisconsin, she lives on an off-grid homestead with her husband, Mike, and their three unschooled boys. thesittingtree.net

KATE OATES is the designer for Tot Toppers and When I Grow Up and the author of a new book, *Knits for Boys*. She enjoys designing hats and garments for babies and children in particular; these projects often reflect a whimsical spirit. She lives with her family in South Carolina.

JULIE PARTIE (Lili Comme Tout Designs) is a happy mama of twins, living in France. She loves to work fun constructions and nice details to spice up timeless knits and give them a graphic and modern twist. lilicommetout.canalblog.com

As a busy mom of four and a pediatrician, **HELEN ROSE** fondly remembers opening up the handmade gifts that her oldest received as an infant and now smiles as she stores them for future grandbabies. Her goal at Rosebud is to help knitters at every skill level create lovely wearable heirlooms. Go to her website at rosebud knitting.com or see her Ravelry page (helenmrose) to discover her other patterns.

MELISSA SCHASCHWARY lives in the Midwest with her husband, two daughters and a small herd of family pets. Many of Melissa's designs are inspired by her favorite children's book illustrations, classic movies, and the wild things growing in her flower garden (when it isn't covered in snow).

SUVI SIMOLA lives with her husband and three children in Finland. She's been self-publishing patterns since 2008, and her designs have also been published in several knitting magazines and books. ravelry.com/designers/suvi-simola

JUSTINE TURNER has a qualification in Knitwear Technology and Design and has been publishing her patterns for the past seven years. She lives in beautiful New Zealand, where wool is part of the heritage and culture with which she wrapped each of her babies from day one. You can find Justine on Ravelry or Facebook as Just Jussi (rhymes with "fussy") or at her website www.justjussi.com.

SVETLANA VOLKOVA grew up in Ukraine, where she learned to knit from her grandmother. She lives in Moscow with her Russian husband, son, and cat: a full-time mum by day and knitwear designer when she gets a free minute.

ABOUT THE AUTHOR

Tanis Gray has worked in the creative field since graduating from RISD in 2002. Having worked at Vogue Knitting and Martha Stewart, she prefers being tangled up in yarn and knitting whenever possible. Gray is the author of *Knit Local, Capitol Knits, Knitting Architecture, Cozy Knits, Wanderlust,* and *Three Skeins or Less: Fresh Knitted Accessories* and is a regular guest on *Knitting Daily TV*. She lives outside of Washington, D.C.

INDEX

backward-loop cast-on *119*
bar increase *121*
bind-offs *120*
buttonholes *123*

cable cast-on *119*
cast-ons *119–120*
chain stitch *123*
color stripes, knitting *123*

I-cord *122*
increases *120-121*

left-slant lifted increase (LLI) *121*
left-slant raised increase (M1L)
lifted increase (LI) *121*
long-tail cast-on *119*

knitwise bar increase (k1f&b) *121*

magic-loop cast-on *119*
make one raised increase (M1) *120*

mattress stitch *122*
Meg Swansen's jogless-jog color stripes *123*

pom-poms *122–123*
provisional cast-on *119*
purlwise bar increase (p1f&b) *121*

right-slant lifted increase (RLI) *121*
right-slant raised increase (M1R) *120*

seams *122*
short-rows *121–122*

three-needle bind-off *120*
Turkish/Eastern cast-on *119*
twisted cord *122*

wet-blocking *122*
whipstitch *122*

SOURCES FOR YARNS

Berroco, Inc.
1 Tupperware Drive, Suite 4
North Smithfield, RI 02896
berroco.com

Blue Moon Fiber Arts , Inc.
56587 Mollenhour Road
Scappoose, OR 97056
bluemoonfiberarts.com

Brown Sheep Company, Inc.
100662 County Road 16
Mitchell, NE 69357
brownsheep.com

Cascade Yarns
cascadeyarns.com

Classic Elite Yarns
16 Esquire Road, Unit 2
North Billerica, MA 01862
classiceliteyarns.com

Debbie Bliss/Knitting Fever, Inc.
PO Box 336
315 Bayview Avenue
Amityville, NY 11701
knittingfever.com

Ella Rae/Knitting Fever, Inc.
PO Box 336
315 Bayview Avenue
Amityville, NY 11701
knittingfever.com

Dream In Color, Inc.
dreamincoloryarn.com

Jil Eaton/Classic Elite Yarns
16 Esquire Road, Unit 2
North Billerica, MA 01862
classiceliteyarns.com

Lorna's Laces
4229 North Honore Street
Chicago, IL 60613
lornaslaces.net

Miss Babs Hand-Dyed Yarns & Fibers, Inc.
PO Box 78
Mountain City, TN 37683
missbabs.com

Neighborhood Fiber Co.
neighborhoodfiberco.com

Rowan/Westminster Fibers
165 Ledge Street
Nashua, NH 03060
Knitrowan.com
westminsterfibers.com

Spud & Chloë/Blue Sky Alpacas
PO Box 88
Cedar, MN 55011
spudandchloe.com

SweetGeorgia Yarns, Inc.
110-408 East Kent Avenue South
Vancouver, BC
Canada V5X 2X7
sweetgeorgiayarns.com

The Verdant Gryphon
verdantgryphon.com

ABBREVIATIONS

approx: approximately
beg: begin(ning)
BO: bind off
CC: contrast color
cir: circular
cm: centimeters
CO: cast on
cont: continue(ing)
dec('d): decrease(d)
dpn: double-pointed needle(s)
g: gram(s)
inc('d): increase(d)
k: knit
k1f&b: knit into front and back of next stitch (1 st increased)
k2tog: knit 2 together

kwise: knitwise
k2tog: knit 2 together
k3tog: knit 3 together (2 stitches decreased)
m: marker
mm: millemeters
p: purl
p1f&b: purl into back and front of next stitch (1 st increased)
patt: pattern
pwise: purlwise
patt: pattern(s)
pm: place marker
rem: remain
rep: repeat
RS: right side

sk2p: slip 1, knit 2 together, pass slipped stitch over
sl: slip
sm: slip marker
ssk: slip, slip, knit
sssk: slip, slip, slip, knit
st(s): stitch(es)
St st: stockinette stitch
tbl: through back loop
WS: wrong side
wyb: with yarn in back
wyf: with yarn in front
WS: wrong side
yd(s): yard(s)
yo: yarn over

DEDICATION

For Debbie Marchetti. Knit on in heaven, dear friend.

ACKNOWLEDGMENTS

As always, books come together with the help of many talented people. Much appreciation goes out to Vanessa Lyman and Kerry Bogert, who kept things rolling; to the fabulous trio Bekah Thrasher, Joe Hancock, and Tina Gill, for their artistic eyes and for taking my storyboards and turning them into a reality; to Erica Smith, my editor—together again, my friend; to Minh-Huygen Nguyen, I appreciate your eagle eyes; and to Allison Korleski, who agreed with me that there needed to be a book like this out there. My deepest and warmest thanks to the imaginative designers in this book who were a pleasure to work with, who met the challenge of limited skeins and a modern look and came from all across the globe to take part in this adventure. Most especially, thank you to my husband, Roger, and our son, Callum. Our family may be crazy, but it's ours—I love you both.

ACQUISITIONS EDITOR
Kerry Bogert

EDITOR
Erica Smith

TECHNICAL EDITOR
Minh-Huyen Nguyen

COVER & INTERIOR DESIGNER
Bekah Thrasher

PHOTOGRAPHER
Joe Hancock

STYLIST
Tina Gill

STYLIST ASSISTANT
Jeff Erwine

Metric Conversion Chart

To convert:	to:	multiply by:
Inches	Centimeters	2.54
Centimeters	Inches	0.4
Feet	Centimeters	30.5
Centimeters	Feet	0.03
Yards	Meters	0.9
Meters	Yards	1.1

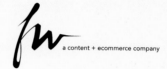

www.fwcommunity.com

19 18 17 16 15   5 4 3 2 1

Distributed in Canada by
Fraser Direct
100 Armstrong Avenue
Georgetown, ON, Canada L7G 5S4
Tel: (905) 877-4411

Distributed in the U.K. and Europe by
F&W MEDIA INTERNATIONAL
Brunel House, Newton Abbot, Devon,
TQ12 4PU, England
Tel: (+44) 1626 323200,
Fax: (+44) 1626 323319
Email: enquiries@fwmedia.com

Distributed in Australia by
Capricorn Link
P.O. Box 704, S. Windsor NSW,
2756 Australia
Tel: (02) 4560 1600
Fax: (02) 4577 5288
Email: books@capricornlink.com.au

SRN: 16CR01
ISBN-13: 978-1-63250-152-3

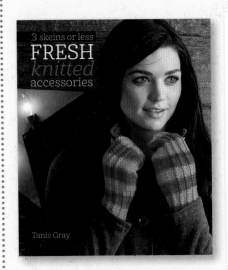

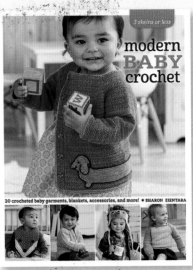

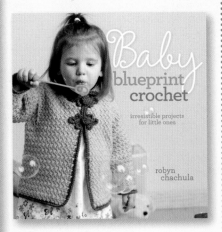

3 SKEINS OR LESS: FRESH KNITTED ACCESSORIES
Tanis Gray
978-1-62033-673-1
$24.99

3 SKEINS OR LESS: MODERN BABY CROCHET
20 Crocheted Baby Garments, Blankets, Accessories, and More!
Sharon Zientara
978-1-63250-217-9
$22.99

BABY BLUEPRINT CROCHET
Irresistible Projects for Little Ones
Robyn Chachula
978-1-59668-201-6
$21.95

INTERWEAVE KNITS

knittingdaily

Interweave Knits

Interweave Knits inspires and informs the modern knitter with projects and articles that celebrate the handmade life. Each issue features lush projects from your favorite designers, in-depth technique articles to further your knitting knowledge, information on the latest must-have yarns, designer profiles, and much more.

www.interweave.com/magazines

Knitting Daily

Knitting Daily is a community for knitters who want inspiration, innovation, motivation, knitting content and patterns for all levels and interests.

www.knittingdaily.com

www.wadsworth.com

www.wadsworth.com is the World Wide Web site for Thomson Wadsworth and is your direct source to dozens of online resources.

At *www.wadsworth.com* you can find out about supplements, demonstration software, and student resources. You can also send e-mail to many of our authors and preview new publications and exciting new technologies.

www.wadsworth.com
Changing the way the world learns®

The Interplay of Influence

NEWS, ADVERTISING, POLITICS, AND THE INTERNET

SIXTH EDITION

KATHLEEN HALL JAMIESON
University of Pennsylvania

KARLYN KOHRS CAMPBELL
University of Minnesota

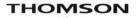

THOMSON
WADSWORTH

Australia ■ Brazil ■ Canada ■ Mexico ■ Singapore
Spain ■ United Kingdom ■ United States

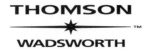

The Interplay of Influence:
News, Advertising, Politics, and the Internet, Sixth Edition
Kathleen Hall Jamieson and Karlyn Kohrs Campbell

Publisher: *Holly J. Allen*
Assistant Editor: *Darlene Amidon-Brent*
Editorial Assistant: *Sarah Allen*
Technology Project Manager: *Jeanette Wiseman*
Marketing Manager: *Mark Orr*
Marketing Assistant: *Alexandra Tran*
Marketing Communications Manager: *Shemika Britt*
Project Manager, Editorial Production: *Christine Sosa*
Creative Director: *Rob Hugel*
Art Director: *Maria Epes*

Print Buyer: *Lisa Claudeanos*
Permissions Editor: *Stephanie Lee*
Production Service: *Scratchgravel Publishing Services*
Photo Researcher: *Robin Sterling*
Copy Editor: *Linda Purrington*
Cover Designer: *Harold Burch*
Cover Image: *Fotosearch (photos 1–5) and Harold Burch (photo 6)*
Cover Printer: *Webcom*
Compositor: *Stratford Publishing Services, Inc.*
Printer: *Webcom*

Printed in Canada
1 2 3 4 5 6 7 09 08 07 06 05

Library of Congress Control Number: 2005923118

ISBN 0-534-55938-7

Thomson Higher Education
10 Davis Drive
Belmont, CA 94002-3098
USA

For more information about our products, contact us at:
Thomson Learning Academic Resource Center
1-800-423-0563

For permission to use material from this text or product, submit a request online at
http://www.thomsonrights.com.
Any additional questions about permissions can be submitted by e-mail to
thomsonrights@thomson.com.

To our grandmothers,
Myra Moore Hall Zabel and Hinke Douma Kohrs,
who loved us, indulged our eccentricities, and nurtured our dreams.

Brief Contents

1 The Media: An Introduction   1

2 What Is News?   40

3 News as Persuasion   84

4 Influencing the News Media   119

5 How Corporate Power Influences What We See   156

6 What Is Advertising?   171

7 Persuasion through Advertising   198

8 Influencing Advertisers   234

9 How to Influence the Media   261

10 Political versus Product Campaigns   282

11 How Has the Internet Changed Politics?   305

12 News and Advertising in the Political Campaign   317

Notes   353

Index   369

Contents

1 THE MEDIA: AN INTRODUCTION   **1**

A Brief History of the Mass Media   4

The Mass Media: Social Systems   5

The Role of Mass Media Advertising   5

The Audience   6

Media and Measurement   6

Television   7
     The Rise of Cable   8
     The Changing Modes of Delivering Images through Television   12
     Ratings   15
Radio   22
     Arbitron Ratings   23
     Talk Radio   24
Newspapers   25
Magazines   27
The Internet   29
     The Internet as a Transnational Communicator   30
     The New Programmers   30
     Expanded Interactivity   32

The New Media Environment   33

Twenty-Four-Hour News   33

Changing Influence of the Press   33

To Sum Up   37

Selected Readings   39

2 WHAT IS NEWS?   **40**

Hard News Defined   41

1. Hard News Is Personalized, about Individuals   42
2. Hard News Is Dramatic, Conflict-Filled, and Violent   45
3. Hard News Is Action, an Event, an Identifiable Occurrence   48
4. Hard News Is Novel, Deviant, Out of the Ordinary   49
5. Hard News Reports Events Linked to Issues Prevalent in the News at the Time   50

What Is Covered and Reported   54

Audience Interest   54

External Constraints   54

    Access   54

    Cost   57

    The Impact of Technology: Lower Costs, Direct Video-streaming,
and the Tethered Reporter   59

    Time and Space   59

Internal Constraints   61

    Use of Available Footage   61

    Covering Visual Events   61

    Covering Newsworthy People   63

    Avoiding Stories That Give Offense   64

    Becoming the News   65

Changing News Norms   66

Relevance to Governance or Abuse of Power   67

Public Display   67

Hypocrisy Forecast   68

Hypocrisy Added   68

Statute of Limitations   68

Lying and Recency   69

Hypocrisy Broadly Construed   71

How the Story Is Presented   72

Reporter Expertise   72

Fairness and Balance   73

Story Length   74

Story Structure   76

Objectivity   78

To Sum Up   79

Selected Readings   82

3   NEWS AS PERSUASION   84

Dramatizing and Sensationalizing Content   84

The Screen   84

The Camera   85

Special Effects   87

Editing   88

Filmed and Taped Coverage   90

Anchors and On-Air Reporters   92

Inaccurate and Incomplete Reporting   94

Deadlines and Competition   94

Breaking News   95

Exclusive Breaking News   96

Story Structure   96

Anonymous and Composite Sources, Misrepresented Tape   97
Readers' Advocates   99
News Analysis   101
Media Convergence   102

Unbalanced Interpretation   103
Insinuation through Selection of Language   103
Ideological Bias   104
Self-Censorship   107
    The Fairness Doctrine   107
    Beats   107
    Government Support   107
    Audience Taste   109

Direct Intervention   110
Breaches of Neutrality   110
Producing Social Change   111
Journalists as Direct Participants   111
The Civic Journalism Movement   113

To Sum Up   113

Analysis: Analyzing a News Item   114
Newsworthiness   114
Reporter   114
The News Story   115
Constraints   115
Framing   115
Inclusion/Exclusion   116
Setting   116
Timing   116
Placement   116
Patterns   117
Manipulation   118
Impact   118

Selected Readings   118

4 INFLUENCING THE NEWS MEDIA   119
Influencing Journalistic Norms and Routines   119
Manipulating Deadlines   119
Manipulating Access   123
Setting Up a Controlled Channel   126
Manipulating News Assignments   127
Media Competition   128
Using Access to Media to Manipulate the Agenda   129
Expanded Opportunities for Direct Address   129
    Satellites   129
    The Internet   129

Language and Symbols   129

The Perils of Live Coverage   134

Prepackaged News   135

  Pseudo-Events   136

  News Feeds   137

  Prepared Editorials   140

Commercial Pressures   140

Costs of Preempting Programming   141

Pressures from Advertisers   143

Threat of Lawsuits   144

Political Pressure   145

Presidential Newsworthiness   146

National Security   147

Government Manipulation   147

To Sum Up   155

Selected Readings   155

**5   HOW CORPORATE POWER INFLUENCES
      WHAT WE SEE   156**

A Brief History of Media Consolidation   156

A Focus on Profits   158

Staff Cuts   158

Reduction in Serious Political Content That Draws Low Audiences   162

To Attract Audiences, Definition of News Shifts toward Human Interest   165

Loss of News That Is of Local but Not Regional or National Interest   165

Magnified Pro-Business Message While Minimizing Scrutiny
     of Parent Corporations   166

Cross-Promotion: Synergy   167

Fewer Voices Providing News   168

To Sum Up   169

Selected Readings   170

6   WHAT IS ADVERTISING?   171

Defining Advertising   172

Shifting Ad Placement   173

Product Placement   173

Blurring Program and Ad Content   174

Incentives to View Ads   174

Mediated Advertising   178

Kinds of Traditional Mass Media Advertising   180

Product Ads   180

The Product as Ad   181

Service Ads   181
Goodwill Ads   182
Advocacy Ads   183
Direct-Response Ads (Infomercials)   184
Public Service Announcements   185
Political Ads   186
Issue Advocacy Ads   186

Nontraditional Advertising   186
In-Store Advertising   187
Digital Billboards   187
Search Advertising   187
   Sponsored Links   188
   Spam   188

How to Determine Whether It's an Ad   189
How Ads Reveal the Advertiser   189
How Ads Reveal the Intended Audience   189

Advertising and Reality: Stereotypes   192

Advertising Values   193
The World According to Commercials   193
Seeing the Other Side   196

The Interplay of News and Advertising   196

To Sum Up   197

Selected Reading   197

7   PERSUASION THROUGH ADVERTISING   198
The Advertiser's Aims   198

Creating Product Recognition   198
Trademarks   198
Naming   200
Packaging   201
Slogans   201

Differentiation   203
Unique Selling Proposition   203
Association   204

Participation   205
Disentangling Meaning   206
Identification with Ad Characters   206
Significant Experiences   207
Making the Audience an Accomplice   208

Redundancy   212
Repeated Claims   212
Repeated Exposure   214

Advertisers' Strategies for Persuasion   214

Naming the Product   217
Differentiating Products   218
  Pseudo-Claims   218
  Comparison with an Unidentified Other Ad   218
  Comparing Their Product with an Unnamed Other Product   219
  Comparison of the Product with Its Earlier Form   219
  Irrelevant Comparisons   219
  The Pseudo-Survey   220
  Use It: It's Been Tested by Disinterested Experts   220

Creating Associations   221

Associations with Celebrities and Authorities   221
  Use It: Be Like Me   221
  Use It: I'm an Authority   221
Cannibalizing the Past for Associations   222
  Appropriating Historical People and Events   223
  Trading on Someone's Good Name   224
  Appropriating a Famous Phrase   224
  Creating a Memorable Phrase   225
  Exploiting Social Movements   225
  Nationalistic Associations   227
Associating Media Outlets to Products   228
Exploiting Argumentative Forms to Create Associations and Participation   228
  Implying Causality   228
  Juxtaposition   229
  Exploiting Coincidental Relationships   229
  Implying "If . . . Then"   230
  Implying "If Not . . . Then Not"   231

But Does Advertising Work?   232

To Sum Up   232

Selected Readings   233

8 INFLUENCING ADVERTISERS   234

Regulation and Self-Regulation   234

The Federal Trade Commission   234
The Powers of Other State and Federal Agencies   238
The National Advertising Division   240
The National Association of Broadcasters   242
Network Standards   243

Obstacles to Regulation   244

Problems Faced by Regulators   245
Determining Deception   245
Effects of Stricter Regulation   246

What Advertisers May Not Say and Do   247
Limitations on Distortion   247
   Product Characteristics   248
   Product Performance   248
   Puffery   249
   Fantasy   250
Limitations Imposed by the Audience   251
   Children in Audiences   251
   Taboos   252

To Sum Up   255

Analysis: Analyzing an Ad   255
What Type of Ad Is It?   255
If the Ad Is a PSA   255
If the Ad Is an Idea Ad (pro-life or pro-choice, for example)   256
If the Ad Advertises a Service Rather Than a Product (for example, travel
   on a certain airline)   256
If the Ad Is a Goodwill Ad   256
If the Ad Is a Political Ad   256
If the Ad Is a Product Ad   257
Audience   257
Ad Content (not all points apply to PSAs)   257
Assumptions (values presumed in the ad)   258
Programming or Content Sponsored by an Ad   259
Content Surrounding (Contextualizing) an Ad   259
Media Mix   259
Pressure on Advertiser   259
Effect   259

Selected Readings   260

9   HOW TO INFLUENCE THE MEDIA   **261**
Individual Complaints   261

Group Pressure   266
Boycotts   266
Legal Actions   270
Promoting Self-Regulation   272

Pressure from an Established Organization   274

Pressure from a Social Movement   276

Creating Legislative Pressure   278
State Level   278
Federal Level   278

To Sum Up   279

Analysis: Constructing a Strategy for Message Distribution   279
Step 1: Isolating the Message   280
Step 2: Defining the Intended Audience   280
Step 3: Determining the Newsworthiness of the Message   280
Step 4: Determining Factors Constraining Release   280
Step 5: Selecting Appropriate Channels   280
Step 6: Adapting the Message to the Channel   281
Step 7: Monitoring Your Success or Failure   281
Selected Readings   281

10   POLITICAL VERSUS PRODUCT CAMPAIGNS   282
Defining Ads   282
Candidate Access: Free Time   283
What Protects Voters: Responsibility of Journalists   283
Products versus Candidates   284
Using the Media   284
Creating an Image   285
Targeting the Audience   285
Economic versus Political Values   287
Regulation   288
Censorship   288
Equal Opportunity   292
Right to Access   292
Cost and Access   293
Campaign Spending Limits   293
McCain-Feingold: Campaign Finance Reform   294
527s   295
Issue Advocacy   296
Campaign Objectives   298
Voting versus Buying   299
Criteria for Victory   302
Unpaid Coverage   303
Quality   303
Endorsements   304
Financing   304
To Sum Up   304
Selected Readings   304

11 HOW HAS THE INTERNET CHANGED POLITICS?   **305**

How the Interactivity of the Internet Is Changing Politics   305
Increasing Citizen Access to Information   306
    Mobilizing and Raising Money through the Web   307
    Feedback   308
    New Forms of Attack   308
    The Reader as Writer and Critic   310
The Downside   310
    Lurkers and Trolls   310
    Spreading Inaccurate Information   311

Mainstream as Monitor of the New Medium   312

Democratizing the Production of Content: The Citizen as Content Producer   312

Web Ads   314

To Sum Up   315

Selected Readings   316

12 NEWS AND ADVERTISING IN THE POLITICAL CAMPAIGN   **317**

Controlling News Coverage   317
Controlling Media Access   318
Setting the Media's Agenda   318
Creating Credible Pseudo-Events   319
Using Ads to Contextualize News   320
Blurring the Distinction between News and Commercials   321
Exploiting Media Concepts of the Political Process   322
    The Campaign   322
    The Candidates   323
Responding to or Preventing Attack   328
Backlash   329
Last-Minute Attacks   330

Adwatches   331
Responding to Last-Minute Attacks   334
Exploiting Blunders   338
Attacks Legitimized by the Media   339
Enlisting the Help of Journalists   341
Tests of Credibility Applied by Journalists   341

How Has Television Changed Politics?   342
Image versus Issues; Character versus Positions   344
The Comparative Relevance of Character and Stands on Issues   344
    Determining Which Issues Are the Likely Focus of a Campaign   345
    Determining Which Facets of Character Are the Likely Focus in a Campaign   346

The Interplay of Influence: Issues and Character in Ads,
    News, and Debates   346

Ads   347
    Limitations   347
News   347
    Limitations   348
Debates   348
    Limitations   348

To Sum Up   350

Analysis: Political Ads and News   351
Determining Who Is Newsworthy   351
Determining What Is Covered   351
Relationship of Candidates and Reporters   351
The Image of the Candidate   351
Candidates' Ads   352

Selected Readings   352

NOTES   353

INDEX   369

Preface

Since we wrote the first edition (in 432 BCE), the media world has been turned upside down and inside out. Very little of that first edition survives. What does survive is the structure we developed in that book for making sense of media. An interplay of influence remains. The patterns of deception in advertising we described have proved remarkably durable as have the strategies politicians use to influence voters through news coverage and advertising.

But the economics and structure of media have changed with the rise of consolidation and deregulation. Technological changes from satellites to satellite phones mean instant access to news-as-it-happens. Twenty-four-hour cable and the Internet have upended traditional assumptions about when, how, and where the public gets the news. Talk radio has become a force with which politicians must reckon. Fox News has emerged as a bastion of conservative assumptions and gained a substantial cable audience in the process. People meters are replacing diaries as a means of assessing audience size. And the Internet has made it possible for those who once were simply part of the consuming audience not only to talk back to the powers that control the dissemination of news and ads but also to take on those roles themselves.

Edition by edition we have chronicled these changes, but this sixth edition of *The Interplay of Influence* is the first to include two entirely new chapters as well as significant revised material. A section on the Internet from Chapter 11 of the previous edition has been greatly expanded and now constitutes its own chapter, "How Has the Internet Changed Politics?" The role of the Internet in the 2004 presidential campaign is a major focus of that chapter. Chapter 5, "How Corporate Power Influences What We See," is also new to this edition, discussing how the corporate nature of mass media affects news, advertising, and politics. Other chapters include updated topic coverage, statistics, and examples to ensure that this edition covers the most current material pertinent to the study of mass media. For example, we have added substantial material on the role and regulation of money in politics and fact in political ads, which takes into account all new campaign finance rules. In this new edition, we have recorded the most recent changes taking place in the world of mass media.

Here is a summary of the changes in this edition:

- A new chapter on politics and the Internet
- A new chapter on how the corporate nature of mass media affects news, advertising, and politics
- Updated coverage of political advertising to accommodate all the new campaign finance rules

- Thoroughly updated topic coverage, statistics, and examples throughout, including government regulations relating to mass media and political and social events covered by and affected by the media

We continue to believe that a rhetorical perspective on media is a powerful means of helping audiences understand how the media work, on whom, and why. We also continue to believe that an understanding of rhetoric is a powerful tool for those seeking to influence news, advertising, and the political process.

Kathleen Hall Jamieson
Karlyn Kohrs Campbell

The Interplay of Influence

1

The Media: An Introduction

Many Americans wake up to the sounds of music and news on a clock radio, wash and dress to the *Today* show or *Good Morning America,* breakfast with a morning paper, commute to the patter of a favorite disc jockey, check their e-mail on the computer at home or work, relax with prime-time television, and doze to the strains of music on a CD. The mass media are undeniably a central part of life in the United States.

This book is about the influence of the mass media, specifically television, radio, newspapers, magazines, and the Internet. Many books on this subject already exist, but this book considers not only how the media influence all of us, but also how the media are in turn influenced by others—individuals, groups, government agencies, politicians, and other mass media. We hope to show that media persuasion works two ways: the media persuade us, but we and others can and do influence the media. This book is neither a history of nor an attack on media; it is a study of the communication and persuasion that take place through them.

Our perspective is rhetorical, focusing on how news, advertising, and politics in the Internet age shape conceptions of reality and influence attitudes and behaviors. We examine the ways that consumer choices, individual and group protest, and regulatory mechanisms influence the media. As students of rhetoric, we know that any choice has an influence; whatever decisions newspeople, advertisers, or programmers make, the result will be a worldview shaped by those decisions.

We are not, then, looking for evidence that media personnel make choices—that is an inevitable part of using symbols. Rather, we examine patterns of choice. The decisions of newspeople, advertisers, and programmers are significant, as they fall into systematic patterns that consistently present a particular view of "reality." We hope to make explicit the assumptions underlying their choices. A rhetorical perspective is controversial in regard to news, because we are used to thinking of the news as "objective," as a report of what occurs. But a rhetorical perspective is natural and common for political and product advertising and for analyzing politicians' efforts to influence the public by manipulating news coverage; these efforts are obviously and intentionally persuasive.

Because of our rhetorical perspective, we focus our attention on mediated messages that are most significant in terms of audience beliefs and attitudes: news, editorials and commentary, and advertising. Because these messages are all part of political communication, this book ends with a discussion of news and advertising in political campaigns. The primary news channels in our society are television, newspapers, magazines, and

---

BOX 1-1   How Much Americans Say They Watch

According to the General Social Survey produced in 2005, more than 96 percent of Americans say that they watch television for at least 1 hour on an average day. About half claim to watch more than 3 hours of television a day.[a] Heavy users of television tend to be less well educated and working in occupations of lower prestige; however, people who are more well off financially are increasing the amount of time they spend watching television, probably because they have access to diverse programs through cable and satellite transmissions.[b] For example, in spring 2000, 90 percent of television homes with incomes over $75,000 had pay cable.[c] More than 95 million, or 98 percent, of U.S. homes have at least one television set;[d] an average television household has 2.8 sets;[e] and 41 percent of U.S. households with television have three or more sets.[f] Of U.S. homes with television, 84 percent use cable services.[g] As of 1999, approximately 91 percent of U.S. households owned a VCR. Again, income influences the rate of ownership of media technology. Nearly all people with incomes over $75,000 own a VCR in comparison with 60 percent of people with incomes under $20,000.[h]

[a]General Social Surveys, 1972–2002: Cumulative Code Book, conducted for the National Data Program for the Social Sciences at the National Opinion Research Center, University of Chicago.
[b]Xiaoming Hao, "Trend: Television Viewing among American Adults in the 1990s," *Journal of Broadcasting & Electronic Media* 38 (Summer 1994): 359.
[c]"Morph and Merge," *Advertising Age,* 10 April 2000, p. 530.
[d]Brian Lowry, "Company Town," *Los Angeles Times,* 9 August 2001, p. 6.
[e]Data from Nielsen/NetRatings Shows Broadband Market Opportunity," *ISP Business,* No. 5, Vol. 4, 1 May 2001, p. 11.
[f]Steve Sternberg, "Family Viewing Alive, If Not Thriving," *Television Week,* 26 May 2003, p. 17.
[g]"Fall Cable Preview," *New York Times Magazine,* 28 September 2003.
[h]Joel Brinkley, "Downtime: A Step toward a Versatile High-Definition VCR," *New York Times,* 16 September 1999, p. B13.

---

the Internet, so most of our illustrations are drawn from them. We pay particular attention to television, which is still the most influential mass medium, and to the Internet, which is new technology that has most decisively shaped the mediated world.

The ideas developed here are based on three fundamental assumptions. First, we assume that all communication is reciprocal, jointly created by the source and the audience. No one can commit an act of communication alone. Communication is an *inter*action (*inter* = between) or a *trans*action (*trans* = through, across) that comes into being because the participants cooperate in creating meaning and sharing experience. For this reason, participation and identification are key concepts in our analysis.

Second, we assume that each medium has unique resources for communicating and influencing, because of the characteristic ways in which we receive, perceive, and interact with it. Each is a special kind of channel with distinctive capacities for inducing and shaping our participation. As a result, we contrast the communicative and persuasive potential of the various media.

Third, we assume that the nature and impact of mediated messages cannot be separated from the economic and political system in which the media function. The media reflect certain cultural values and assumptions precisely because media outlets are large corporations supported by advertising and constrained by governmental and internal

BOX 1-2   Rhetoric

That art or talent by which discourse is adapted to its end.

—George Campbell

The use of language as a symbolic means of inducing cooperation in beings that by nature respond to symbols.

—Kenneth Burke

BOX 1-3   Rhetoric Is Unavoidable

Even if a given terminology is a *reflection* of reality, by its very nature as a terminology it must be a *selection* of reality; and to this extent it must also function as a *deflection* of reality.[a]

[a]Kenneth Burke, *Language as Symbolic Action* (Berkeley: University of California Press, 1966), p. 45.

regulation and public pressure. For this reason, we explore the commercial bases of the media and detail the forms of regulation and the influences bearing on them.

This book is organized to examine news, advertising, and political communication, in that order. In each instance, we examine the media, first as persuaders who influence their audiences, then as entities influenced and regulated by citizens, groups, and government. We begin by exploring the commercial character of the mass media and the different methods by which audiences are measured, which determines economic viability and advertising revenues. We look first at what news is, then examine its influence, and finally consider how the news media are influenced.

We then explore the nature and types of commercial messages. We study the ways in which advertising persuades us as well as the ways in which advertisers can be influenced. The final sections on political communication synthesize material from news and advertising because both are involved in political communication.

Continuing our earlier format, however, we look first at how people are influenced politically through and by the media, then at how the media in turn are influenced by politicians and their supporters.

The media are so familiar, so much a part of our everyday lives, that we all feel we know and understand them, but it is precisely because they are so familiar that we need to study them. Familiarity, for example, may blind us to the distinctive communication that takes place through the media, and especially to the processes by which media influence us.

Although all are mass media, a distinction must be made between media that reach masses of people simultaneously, such as radio or television, and media that reach large numbers of people one person at a time, such as the Internet. The phrase "mass media" can be understood to refer to an audience that is amassed by the medium or, alternatively, that a medium is intended to reach very large numbers of people, one at a time, and does. The first is true of television; the second, of the Internet.

One important distinction between mass communication and other forms of communication in the United States is their commercial basis: *the primary function of the mass media is to attract and hold large audiences for advertisers.* They also inform and entertain, of course, but informing and entertaining are only means to the end

---

BOX 1-4   Participation/Identification

To *participate* is to take part, to join in, or to share with others. To participate is to be actively involved. *Participation* refers to the active role of the audience in creating meaning and sharing experience. When participation occurs, source and audience jointly create the message.

To *identify* is to associate or affiliate yourself closely with a person or group or with their values. In this process you see yourself as like someone else, imagine yourself in another's position, or empathize with others' problems and rejoice in their successes.

---

of providing mass audiences for advertisers. Mass communication is defined by its context—industrial, affluent, mass society—and mass communication differs from other forms of communication because it is commercial.

A BRIEF HISTORY OF THE MASS MEDIA

The development of the mass media coincided with U.S. growth into an industrial, mass, affluent society, and virtually all of us now depend on a system called "the market" for producing, distributing, and selling goods to satisfy our needs. We do not produce what we consume; instead, we sell our labor for wages and buy goods produced by others.

If such a marketing system is to work well, we need to gain information about available goods and services, their location, price, and comparative advantages. Making that information known is advertising's central function.

Even this brief description shows that an industrial society is highly organized. In addition to market dependence, such a society fosters and depends on a division of labor so that goods can be produced more cheaply and efficiently. Carried to its obvious conclusion, this division of labor created the assembly lines that transformed cars from rare, luxury items for the wealthy into Model T Fords most Americans could afford to buy.

Such a society also depends on technology. As the cost of labor and raw materials rises, items such as ready-to-wear clothes can be kept within the price ranges of most citizens only when machines speed up and simplify the processes of production, enabling industries to mass-produce the items. The elements of mass media systems reflect this division of labor and reliance on technology.

Industrial societies are mass societies. If an industrial system is to work, there must be a large market for goods, because the savings that come from machines and assembly lines can only be realized if many cars or dresses can be produced and sold to many people. Industrial societies also tend to be affluent societies. Industries require large amounts of capital, and successful industries must sell their goods to many individuals who must have the money to buy them. Like other industries, the media reach large audiences who must be able to afford newspapers, magazines, radios, television sets, and access to computers, as well as the products they advertise.

THE MASS MEDIA: SOCIAL SYSTEMS

Wherever they exist, the mass media are complex systems composed of interrelated elements or parts. Because mass media in the United States are wholly or predominantly commercial, measures of audience behavior (what audiences watch, hear, or read and what they buy) and revenues (the results of audience behaviors) are central to the system.

Audiences, as measured by ratings, determine the success or failure of *programming* or content. Content reaches the audience through distributors—outlets such as the networks, individual stations, wire services, theaters, magazines, newspapers, and websites. *Producers* of content (including subsystems of reporters, actors, camera crews, labor unions, and publishers) are financed by *advertisers* or backers who in turn depend on profits from consumer purchases for their money.

Advertising agencies connect advertisers with distributors (outlets), with content producers, and with *audience-* and *market-research organizations* such as Nielsen and Arbitron, which measure the audiences for all forms of programming and gather data on audience behavior, such as viewing and purchasing patterns.

Government regulators include the Federal Communications Commission (FCC), which licenses distributors, and the Federal Trade Commission (FTC) and the courts, which set limits on advertising, news, and program content.

Citizen regulators generate political pressure and include watchdog groups such as the Coalition for Better Television. *Self-regulatory mechanisms* arise to forestall government or legal regulation or to defuse political pressure; some of these are newspaper readers' advocates, the National Association of Broadcasters, the Electronic Media Ratings Council, the National Advertising Division of the Better Business Bureau, and the National Advertising Review Board.

As social systems, the mass media are part of the larger social system of our society. U.S. social norms are expressed in laws, moral codes, conventions (what we find entertaining, appropriate, or offensive), and values (what we believe in, such as the efficacy of free enterprise, the legitimacy of the profit motive, and the importance of freedom of speech). These norms influence audience behavior and underlie all forms of regulation.

All social systems seek to survive, to maintain their stability and equilibrium. In the United States, the chief requirement is commercial: to survive, mass media must generate profits or adequate financing, which requires attracting substantial audiences. Ratings and other measures assess how well the media do this, and revenues depend on such measurements. Audience behavior (what is listened to, watched, read, and bought) and audience norms (what entertains, what offends) are fundamental to mass media systems. These in turn reflect how the mass media have developed in the history of this society.

THE ROLE OF MASS MEDIA ADVERTISING

Mass media are central to industrial, mass, affluent societies. We depend on them to know what jobs are available, what goods we can buy, where, and for how much. The essential role of mass media advertising under such conditions is described by David Potter:

It is when potential supply outstrips demand—that is, when abundance prevails—that advertising begins to fulfill a really essential economic function. In this situation the producer knows that the limitation upon his growth no longer lies, as it lay historically, in his productive capacity, for he can always produce as much as the market will absorb; the limitation has shifted to the market, and its selling capacity which controls his growth.[1]

The advertising that Potter describes is done through the mass media, whose primary function is to attract and hold large audiences for advertisers. Mass media in the United States are commercial media; their job is to gather audiences for persuaders. They also inform and entertain, of course, but informing and entertaining are only means to the end of delivering mass audiences to advertisers.

THE AUDIENCE

As central elements in mass media systems and the mass society, advertisers have two related purposes: to reach the largest possible audience and to reach the ideal (target) audience for their products. An "efficient advertising buy" (reaching the largest number of the ideal or target audience at the lowest price) is measured in cost per thousand (CPT) people reached and in audience desirability—the age, sex, income, education, occupation, region, location (urban, suburban, rural), and ethnic background of audience members reached.

Advertisers speak of "upscale" and "downscale" audiences. An audience is upscale if its members are above average in education and disposable income and in the prime age group. An audience is downscale if it is older, less affluent, less well educated, rural, and blue-collar. The size of the audience, in other words, is not as important as its composition. Thus, for example, the CNN show that charges the highest rates for advertising time is *Moneyline,* which "gets higher advertising rates than any other show on the network, although its actual viewership is half that of, say, *Larry King Live.* The reason is that the viewers of the money shows tend to be those with money. So money shows get high-end advertising—brokerages, expensive cars, luxury items—that generally don't appear on prime time television."[2]

MEDIA AND MEASUREMENT

There are five major media: television, radio, newspapers, magazines, and the Internet. In what follows, we describe each of these media, including the ways in which each has been affected by their interaction and by technological changes, emphasizing their role in providing news. In addition, because all of them are wholly or partly funded by advertising, we explore the ways in which each medium is measured, that is, what kind of rating systems are used to enable advertisers to know who views or reads their content and whether those people are the audiences they wish to reach.

Television

According to the Federal Communication Commission, in 2003 there were 760 VHF (very high frequency; Channels 2 to 13) and 585 UHF (ultra high frequency; Channels 14 and up) television stations in the United States. In early 2004, the three major broadcast networks (ABC, CBS, NBC) had a combined audience of 30 million for their nightly newscasts, with their morning news shows attracting about half that number. A June 9, 2002, Survey of Americans by the Pew Center for the People and the Press found that roughly one third (32%) regularly watch one of the nightly network news broadcasts, compared with 30% in 2000,which is comparable to the overall cable news audience of 33%.[3]

Most commercial television stations are affiliated with a network. Until 1986, when people said "the networks" they were referring to ABC, NBC, CBS, and, occasionally, CNN, but in that year the Fox Broadcasting Company began developing the Fox network. Owned by Media Corporation president Rupert Murdoch, the Fox network expanded its number of affiliate stations from 130 to 200 when it purchased the rights to broadcast NFL football games.

Fox News Channel (FNC), which began operating October 7, 1996, "is a 24-hour general news service devoted to delivering fair and balanced coverage of the day's news events." Launched with an ability to reach audiences in 17 million homes in l996, by 2000 Fox was available in more than 54 million households. In 2003, that number exceeded 80 million. The network, reported its parent company, carries 18 hours of live programming weekdays, more daily news daily "than any other channel."[4]

In fall 2003, *Fox News Sunday* attracted 1.6 million viewers compared to 0.5 million for ABC's *This Week,* 2.7 million for CBS's *Face the Nation,* and 4.2 million for NBC's *Meet the Press.*[5] Because FNC is available only on cable and satellite, this viewership is noteworthy. Equally important, in June 2003, the Fox news audience was greater than the combined total of MSNBC, CNN, and CNN Headline News.[6] Of note is that "during the war in Iraq in March 2003, Fox consistently bested CNN in the ratings."[7] Moreover, by fall 2003, "the seven-year-old network ha[d] displaced CNN as the No. 1 cable news network. On an average, non-crisis night, Fox News attracts more viewers than CNN ever did. Initially driven by the combative style of *The O'Reilly Factor,* Fox News this year started beating CNN in every daypart, be it talk or straight news. And in recent months, Fox News has even started beating CNN's rating for major, breaking news."[8]

Still another news network is emerging. In 2002 the Sinclair Broadcasting Group (SBG), the eighth largest in revenue, which owns 62 stations in 39 markets that reach 25 percent of the nation's television audience, began distributing a 17-minute daily news report to its stations and affiliates. Fourteen of the SBG stations integrate the feed into their local news. SBG follows Fox in casting itself as a counterweight to the liberal bent of mainstream news.

Public Broadcasting Service (PBS), headquartered in Alexandria, Virginia, is a private, non-profit media enterprise owned and operated by the nation's 349 public television stations. Nonetheless, ratings and revenues are important to public (educational, nonprofit) television, which is heavily dependent for support on the same U.S. corporations that advertise on commercial television. The funding for public television comes

---

BOX 1-5   PBS's *NewsHour*

New York, NY—On Friday, October 20, 1995, *The MacNeil/Lehrer NewsHour* became *The NewsHour with Jim Lehrer* when Robert MacNeil, who announced his retirement late last year, stepped down as co-anchor of the nightly newscast. . . .

The *NewsHour with Jim Lehrer* remains the nation's only hourlong newscast, seen week-nightly on more than 300 PBS stations.

As executive editor and sole anchor, Lehrer will guide the program. . . . The *NewsHour with Jim Lehrer* will originate from Washington DC. . . .

The *NewsHour with Jim Lehrer* is funded by the Archer Daniels Midland company, New York Life Insurance company, public television stations and the Corporation for Public Broadcasting. It is produced by MacNeil/Lehrer Productions and WETA/26 Washington DC, in association with Thirteen/WNET New York.[a]

[a]Press release from *The MacNeil/Lehrer NewsHour.*

---

from three sources: government appropriations, contributions from viewers, and corporate sponsorship of programming.

Corporations often transform sponsorship of public television programming into image ads to demonstrate that they are good citizens. Such promotion not only ensures that large audiences in the commercial media are made aware of corporate good deeds, such advertising also increases the size of the upscale audience reached by the program.

Reaching this upscale audience is a second reason for corporate largess. One of public television's main selling points is the quality of its audience. The director of development at KCET-TV describes the audience to prospective corporate clients as being "made up largely of well-educated, affluent adults who are often in a position to influence your business." Thus, although the cost per thousand viewers is very high, supporting public television is a good investment, as illustrated, for example, by Mobil Oil Company's former underwriting of the Public Broadcasting Service's *Masterpiece Theater*.

When advertising agencies and corporations argued successfully that corporate funding for PBS programming could be maintained or increased only if the FCC were persuaded to change its rule prohibiting institutional advertising and corporate logos on public television, new regulations were adopted permitting PBS to use corporate logos and to identify the products that underwriters produce.[9] In other words, public television was compelled to become much more commercial. Some limitations exist, because two thirds of all public television stations are licensed to educational institutions that are prohibited from running advertisements, but some stations currently sell advertising in their program guides—an action that has aroused controversy.[10] In March of 2004, PBS loosened its guidelines on the content of credits, which now allow sponsors to speak on camera and display a product. The result is that program credits can mimic the 15-second commercials that appear on commercial stations.[11]

The Rise of Cable   The rise of cable television has altered all these relationships. In 1982, cable television had 27 million subscribers, more than one quarter of all U.S. television households; by mid-1986, 42 percent of all television households subscribed.

BOX 1-6   A&E, the Arts and Entertainment Channel, Competition for PBS

Jointly owned by Capital Cities/ABC, NBC, and the Hearst Corporation, A&E went on the air on February 1, 1984, the result of a merger of the ARTS Channel (owned by ABC and Hearst) and the Entertainment Channel (a venture of Rockefeller Center and RCA). It had 9 million subscribers and a solitary advertiser, Ford. By May l995, A&E was the fifth most viewed cable network,[a] with 64 million subscribers via more than 9,300 cable systems in the United States and Canada.[b]

To persuade cable systems around the country to carry the channel, an effort was made to make A&E part of the fabric of every community in which it operated. A National Cable Library project was initiated, and working through local cable systems, A&E offered to set up video libraries, composed of tapes of its programming, in local libraries.

The A&E network succeeded by being relent-lessly frugal. It produced little original programming, instead acquiring programs, mainly from the BBC. In 1984, 60 percent of its shows came from the BBC; in 1989, less than 40 percent did. By combining dance and opera with slapstick comedy and historical documentaries and programs about war, A&E attracts the viewers advertisers seek. A&E claims to offer advertisers desirable demographics: people 35 to 45 years old, with four years of college, and average annual incomes of $40,000 to $50,000.[c]

[a]N. R. Kleinfield, "A&E: A Cable Success Story," *New York Times*, 16 April 1989, p. 31H; "A&E Television Network," *Advertising Age*, 8 May l995, p. C6.
[b]"1995 Guide to National Cable TV Networks," *Advertising Age*, 5 May 1995, p. C43.
[c]*Advertising Age*, 5 May 1995, p. C6.

By 1997, cable television penetration was 69.6 percent, and in 1998 the number of homes receiving cable television increased to more than 65 million.[12] Just over half of all cable households subscribed to a pay cable channel, such as Home Box Office,[13] and in April 1999 HBO had 28.7 million subscribers.[14] By 2003, 84 percent of U.S. homes had cable, with 55 million of them having access to high-definition television, which has ten times the resolution of ordinary television.[15] In January 2004, with 70.5 million households, cable had roughly three quarters of the paid television market. The remainder was controlled by satellite. Moreover, by 1996 there were three 24-hour-a-day cable news stations: CNN, now owned by Time Warner, with 66 million households; MSNBC, with 25 million households; and Fox News.

Cable systems with many channels offer the possibility of diversified programming. Whereas in the early 1950s the typical home received only CBS/NBC/ABC, in the early years of the 21st century, according to Media Dynamics Inc., that number had risen to over 69 channels. Channels now present exclusively children's programs, news, sports, comedy, and first-run movies. A sports network, ESPN, gained viewers in 1989, but ratings for National Football League (NFL) broadcasts on the other networks remained virtually unchanged. ESPN's contract with the NFL permitted the network to televise one game per week during the second half of the regular football season. Nine percent more viewers watched the games on ESPN in 1989 than had watched in 1988. In 1993, ESPN started a second sports channel targeted at a younger audience. By 1995, ESPN was the most frequently watched basic cable channel.[16] MTV has spun off MTV Country, MTV Classic, MTV Rock, and MTV Latino. The Arts and Entertainment Channel has spawned the Biography Channel and the History Channel.

BOX 1-7   Public Access Television: Deep Dish TV Network

There are some real alternatives to commercial television, but the story of the Deep Dish Television Network illustrates just what a struggle it is to create and maintain alternative programming. Originally, public, educational, and government (PEG) access channels were created to open up new outlets for local expression, promote added diversity in television programming, advance educational and instructional television, and increase information about the services and activities of local governments. Between 1979 and 1984, the federal government adopted a hands-off policy toward access, and many stations were threatened with elimination. The Cable Communications Act of 1984 saved public access cable television by asserting the basic right of all communities to have access to and representation on cable systems. In addition, in *Capital Cities, Inc. v. Crisp* (1984), the U.S. Supreme Court ruled that the government (both federal and state) could not place content restrictions on signals sent to local cable systems. This guaranteed freedom from censorship to access channels.

Beginning in 1986, the Deep Dish Television Network became the first public access satellite network. "The First National Public Access Satellite Project" was a ten-part series that aired in hour-long shows over a ten-week period starting in April. Compiled from over 20,000 hours of locally produced programming, the series incorporated almost half of the 360 tapes received from local access stations, and it aired on at least 186 cable stations in the United States, reaching viewers in all but eight states.[a] The first program was devoted to information about public access.

Those that followed each had a different subject, ranging from domestic labor and housing crises to international relations and issues of concern to women, minority groups, and children.

The 1988 season included programs about labor, Latino experiences and images, farming and agriculture, war and militarism, communication across national borders, perspectives on AIDS, the use of humor and theater to promote social change, understanding Central America, and videos produced by and about young people (mostly teenagers) and older people. Two hundred and fifty access stations in forty-three states ran the second season, and Deep Dish Television calculated that it had reached more than 12 million U.S. households.

Two series were aired in 1990. The first addressed the rise of "hate programming" on public access channels and included programs that detailed specific incidents of as well as community responses to programming by "hate groups." The second series addressed the relationships among environmental issues and racism, labor, and particular groups of socially, politically, or economically disadvantaged people. Other programming during that year aroused controversy, particularly programming concerned with U.S. propaganda illegally broadcast to Cuba, excerpts from Cuban television, and a live address by former Nicaraguan president Daniel Ortega after he lost his bid for reelection in February 1990.[b] Deep Dish programs are far from neutral; they are meant to raise awareness and generate questions in the minds of viewers. Accordingly, many are offensive to some audience members. In spite of the con-

---

The impulse of cable programmers to use multiple channels to target audiences is evident in the rise of financial news channels. CNN has launched CNNfn, for example, and FNN, the original financial news network, has merged with CNBC.

Some cable systems provide nonprofit or public access channels that give local and minority groups and individuals access to the airwaves. Some channels are free of advertising; others cluster ads at the end of a half hour of programming. In March 2004, C-SPAN, the cable public affairs channel that carries gavel-to-gavel coverage of

troversy aroused in 1990, Deep Dish received a National Endowment for the Arts (NEA) grant for its 1991 spring season for a series "Behind Censorship: The Assault on Civil Liberties."

In 1991 Deep Dish members produced the "Gulf Crisis TV Project," a series of programs exploring peaceful alternatives to the military agenda of war in the Persian Gulf. The first four programs aired on more than two dozen PBS stations and on almost 300 public access channels, and were taped by at least 40 other PBS stations for possible use. The series also was purchased by stations outside the country and aired in Britain, Japan, Australia, and Germany. More than 200 tapes from around the country were used to create these four programs.

The second series, "Behind Censorship," was sponsored by WYBE-Philadelphia public television for redistribution on the PBS satellite system in spring 1992. The fall 1992 season, "Rock the Boat," was advertised as alternative perspectives on the history of Native American survival in the 500 years since Columbus arrived in the Western Hemisphere. Because of technical difficulties and staff turnover, the 1993 season series, "Visions of Ourselves," did not air until the fall. Although originally planned for distribution in 1993, the series "Sick and Tired of Being Sick and Tired" did not air until spring 1994, long after the Clinton administration health care reform program had gone down to defeat. Technical, staff, and financial problems caused the delay, but what might have been an important contribution to the debate came too late.

Public access television relies on individuals and organizations to create the raw materials out of which programming is created. The quality of such programming is affected by the level of technical skills of those involved, which vary greatly. Compiling these videotapes into series to be distributed by satellite requires skilled and dedicated staff, who must also do all the other tasks related to disseminating information about programming. Financing for these projects usually comes from grants and other nonprofit sources, requiring the staff to find interested sources of support and to write applications. Finally, it is difficult to reach audiences. Many of you will never have heard of Deep Dish Television or have seen any of its programming. If it is familiar, it may well be because you were exposed to its programming on a PBS station. Viewership on public access cable channels is low, in part because it is difficult to find out about the programming offered and because the quality of the programming varies, with some of it painfully similar to home movies and videotapes. Nonetheless, Deep Dish Television produced high-quality, alternative programming that expressed the views of disadvantaged groups and presented positions on controversial subjects that tend to be overlooked or underemphasized on commercial television. However, the difficulties of Deep Dish Television suggest just how hard it is to produce alternative programming on a regular and predictable schedule.

For current information on Deep Dish programming, see deepdishtv.org

[a]*Deep Dish Directory*, 1986. Available from Deep Dish Television Network, 339 Lafayette St., New York, NY 10012.
[b]"Censored Air," *Nation*, vol. 253, no. 2, 1991, p. 40.

Congress as well as congressional hearings and political speeches by major party candidates, celebrated its 25th anniversary.

C-SPAN has been a 25-year experiment in direct communication. In a tribute to C-SPAN, *Wall Street Journal* columnist John Fund observed,

The network's cinéma-vérité cameras and wireless microphones convey a . . . sense of orderly detachment, even when the subject is heated campaigns. C-SPAN has captured everything from Republican officials dissecting polls to a charming scene in New Hampshire, where a French couple asked John Kerry a question in French, and he responded in their native tongue. Ruth Marcus of the *Washington Post* tells of a time when she went to a campaign chili feed and, after seeing the same event later on C-SPAN, decided "that its cameras actually captured more of the candidate's interaction with voters than I was able to see in person."[17]

Begun as a single channel, by 2004 C-SPAN had three 24-hour-a-day channels and 34 million weekly viewers. C-SPAN also operates a satellite radio service and ten websites. C-SPAN helped to pioneer political call-in television with daily morning programming in which viewers could express their opinions about events of the day or question C-SPAN guests.

Still other channels, such as in-house home shopping channels, offer two-way interactive systems, allowing viewers to purchase products by calling toll-free numbers. In 1995, interactive technology was an $11.1 billion industry that included a range of products and activities, such as video games, virtual reality, home shopping, CD-ROMs, Internet, interactive toll-free numbers, television programs, and commercial online services.[18] An example of such interactive products is Windows, a Microsoft computer operating system. Through this system, an individual can interact with a range of content providers, including American Greetings, C-SPAN, the New York Times Company, QVC, Hollywood Online, and ESP-Net SportsZone.[19] Interactive technology raises the threat of privacy invasion, because certain systems can be used to accumulate personal and otherwise inaccessible information about users.

Cable also has pioneered what some tout as the future in message delivery—pay-per-view (PPV). In 1990, between 13 and 18 million U.S. homes were capable of receiving pay-per-view events. By 1998, that number had climbed to more than 55 million. Pay-per-view occurs on channels that carry programs to subscribers. Movies and boxing events are the types of programming most frequently carried on a pay-per-view basis. Of all U.S. households, only 23 percent had used PPV in 1998. Those who use PPV do so on average once every two months.[20]

In 1984, Congress enacted legislation that specified that cable rate deregulation would occur in 1987. Subsequent complaints about rate increases and poor service led to calls for re-regulation. Congress responded with the 1992 Cable TV Consumer Protection Act, which rolled back cable rates in most areas and regulated future increases. Federal legislation passed in February 1996 deregulated rates for cable systems that reached fewer than 50,000 subscribers.[21]

The Changing Modes of Delivering Images through Television Factors affecting television's future include direct satellite transmission to homes without the use of cable, the costs of laying cable, the carrying capacity of fiber-optics cable, the potential for using existing telephone lines, and the sophistication of interactive systems for purchasing programs and products. Low-power (low-band, very-high-frequency) television offers such opportunities.

Direct Broadcast Satellite (DBS) transmits television programming via satellite directly to antennas at subscribers' homes. Three companies spearheaded efforts to develop DBS systems: Hughes's DirecTV, Hubbard Broadcasting USSB, and Prime-

---

BOX 1-8   Shopping Electronically—Home Shopping Network and Infomercials

In 1986, Home Shopping Network Inc., which captivated bargain-hungry consumers by offering discounted merchandise through cable television, expanded into broadcast television by agreeing to purchase nine UHF stations in major markets for an estimated $150 million. The stations Home Shopping acquired were in Newark (New Jersey), Smithtown (Long Island), Boston, Baltimore, Philadelphia, Cleveland, Houston, San Francisco, and Los Angeles. By the early 1990s, HSN had become a national network, rivaling the major commercial networks for the number of stations owned in markets across the country. In May 1995, HSN and America Online launched a new area on the online service for shopping. HSN Interactive now offers Global Plaza and Masterworks, another online store offering best-sellers and fine books, works of art, and music in addition to an array of jewelry and other gifts.[a]

To maximize their use of UHF stations, most of which have limited range and small viewerships, Home Shopping and Infomall cable network, owned by Paxson Communications, provide six to seven hours a day of public service and children's programming, which makes them eligible under current FCC rules to be carried by cable operators in their areas.[b]

Twelve of the nation's top cable networks now offer more than 20 hours per week of infomercial programming, according to the Cabletelevision Advertising Bureau. CAB says those with the most paid programming hours per week are Lifetime (52), Black Entertainment Television (48), and the Nashville Network and the Discovery Channel (42 each). Top multiple-system cable operators Cox Cable Communications and Jones Intercable recently formed a joint venture to combine their fledgling infomercial networks, Consumer Information Network and Product Information Network. "As you study the infomercial industry, it is the fastest growing advertising segment in America," says Greg Liptak, president of Jones Satellite Networks and program director of Product Information Network. In the past ten years, he says, the industry's annual revenue has skyrocketed from $30 million to $900 million.[c]

In l994, 29 percent of all adults watched one of the home shopping channels, but only 10 percent reported making a purchase. Home shopping viewers tend to be over age 30, are predominantly women, and are concentrated in the $30,000+ household income segments.[d] In comparison, 70 percent of all adults have seen infomercials, and 17 percent have bought infomercial products.

[a]Mark Berniker, "NBC Joins Microsoft's Multimedia Fold; Broadcaster Wants to Enter Online, CD-ROM, Interactive TV Markets," *Broadcasting & Cable,* 22 May 1995, p. 21.
[b]Julie A. Zier, "Paxson Building Infomercial Net," *Broadcasting & Cable,* 16 January 1995, p. 102.
[c]Rich Brown, "Infomercial Marketers Make Their Pitch," *Broadcasting & Cable,* 23 January 1995.
[d]"Exposure of Home Shopping/Infomercials among the U.S. Adult Population: January–February 1994," a Times Mirror survey published in *TV Dimensions '95,* ed. Ed Parazian (New York: Media Dynamics, Inc., 1995), p. 144.

---

star, a joint venture project of Time Warner Cable, TCI, and Cox Communications. Although customers had to purchase an 18-inch satellite dish and receiver, ranging in cost from $150 to $500, nearly 10 million U.S. homes had purchased the DBS service as of April 1999.[22] In January 2004 the FCC reported that 23.7 million Americans, or about one in five who pay for television, received television through a satellite service.

In March 2004 the FCC ruled that satellite providers such as DirecTV and the Dish Network must follow the same rules as cable and broadcast in the areas of political and children's advertising. This meant that commercial time on children's programs must be limited to 12 minutes per hour on weekdays and to 10½ minutes per hour on weekends. Satellite operators also were required to give political candidates the lowest ad rates offered to commercial buyers.

In the past, low-power television stations functioned almost exclusively as boosters or translators, making signals available to communities that could not receive regular transmissions. Low-power stations that originate programming are experimental. In Washington, DC, a low-power station beams Spanish-language programs to one particular area, an example of low-power television aiming a weak signal at a specific audience. In spring 1995, the FCC listed 1,591 licensed low-power television (LPTV) stations.[23] In the mid-1990s, LPTV stations could broadcast on more than one channel at a time. Although the new technology limited LPTVs to only 10 to 20 channels, in contrast with up to 180 on a DBS system, many communications companies continued to purchase LPTV licenses so they could offer affordable broadcasting services to rural customers who could not readily receive cable television.[24]

Over-the-air pay television systems also are beginning to compete with cable systems in urban areas. In 1982, the Microband Corporation of America urged the FCC to allow three such "wireless cable" systems in each of the nation's fifty largest television markets. (In fall 1989, Microband filed for bankruptcy.)

Wireless cable, also known as "multichannel, multipoint distribution service" (MMDS), sends multiple channels of video programming by microwave transmission rather than by cable. In its compressed, digital form, MMDS provides more than 100 channels within a radius of approximately 40 miles from the transmitter tower that receives the programs via satellite. The MMDS transmitter delivers video to homes that are in its "line of sight." The microwave signal is received by an antenna on the subscriber's home; then a box, usually set on top of the television, decodes and decompresses the digital signal. In 1999, approximately 250 systems serviced more than 1 million MMDS subscribers.[25] In its early years, wireless cable suffered from poor signal reception and limited offerings, often of only one channel. Today's MMDS digital technology delivers a clearer picture and CD-quality sound. The costs of MMDS and the time required to build the transmitters and antennas are far less than for laying cable. Because of its potential, large corporations are moving into this area.

Future development also depends on regulation and patterns of ownership. For example, the FCC formerly banned telephone companies from controlling cable systems in their service areas and television networks from controlling cable systems anywhere in the country. Legislation passed in 1996 permitted telephone companies to deliver video and long-distance cable and permitted other companies to offer local telephone service.[26]

In response to this prospect of deregulation, the GTE Corporation, owner of telephone companies around the nation, introduced video services. MCI Communications and Sprint Corporation, the second- and third-largest long-distance carriers in the country, also entered the video market—MCI by merging with WorldCom, and Sprint by joining with Telecommunications Inc. (TCI), Comcast Corporation, and Cox Cable to create a nationwide wireless personal communications service (PCS).[27]

By 1998, AT&T had acquired two of the biggest cable providers in the United States, Telecommunications Inc. and the MediaOne Group, making it among the nation's larger cable television companies. AT&T used its cable service to carry a variety of digital services to subscribers, including local phone calling and high-speed access to the Internet.[28] AT&T sold its cable services to Comcast in 2002.

Digital Television In 1996 the government required television stations to begin the process of changing from analog to digital transmission. As part of this process stations

---

BOX 1-9   Video on Demand

"Video-on-demand is starting to get to a tipping point, in that the total universe of video-on-demand homes in the United States is about 17 million," said Steve Schiffman, executive vice president for marketing and new media at the national Geographic Channel.[a]

[a]Nat Ives, "Advertising," *New York Times*, 22 November 2004, p. C5.

---

received at no cost an additional channel and with it the option of using it for high-definition television (HDTV), splitting it into multiple standard-definition channels (SD) or creating a combination of the two. In practice this meant that the analog—one-station-one-content-stream—model of television would be transformed into one in which a station could send content on as many as six separate channels at the same time. A station that opts for six channels will carry standard-resolution video; a high-definition channel will offer sharp wide-screen video and compact-disc–quality sound.

This allocation of the publicly owned spectrum, which many in the academic community argued should have been auctioned for a yield of up to $70 billion, came only with the voluntary commitment to emphasize local needs and include public affairs programming.

Digital television is a revolution in the making. By proliferating channels, it should fragment the audience even more and further erode a common popular culture. On the positive side, the proliferation of channels, like the proliferation of web activity, offers additional outlets for creative expression and increases the choices available to audiences. Digital access increases the likelihood that C-SPAN-like stations will carry state and local governmental deliberations. PBS's South Carolina affiliate is already providing gavel-to-gavel coverage of the South Carolina General Assembly. In Fresno, California, KFSN's multicasts include a news and public affairs channel.

Some digital channels will be reserved for high-speed cable modems, telephone service, video on demand, and interactive shopping. Others will carry premium services, such as additional channels of HBO, Starz, or Showtime.

An increase in channels and, thus, an increased ability to target specific audiences are both a boon and a bane for advertisers. Dollars to be spent on ads do not increase with the increase in channels. Instead, they shift; they have to be distributed differently. Reports one advertiser, "If advertisers can pinpoint the teen upstairs with the teen product and mother downstairs with the female-oriented channel—that is a ways away, but that is very, very key to the whole development."[29]

Ratings   Ratings measure who is watching or listening or reading, and they determine what we see and hear and read. All television programming is measured by the A.C. Nielsen Company. Nielsen ratings determine how much an advertiser will pay to air a commercial at various times and, thus, determine how large a network's or station's

---

BOX 1-10   Digital Television

"About 1,200 of the country's 1,600 television stations have made the expensive transition to the digital mode. Roughly 215 stations currently are multicasting, according to Decisionmark Corporation. . . . More than 130 are offering news on those collateral channels. High-definition (HDTV) television sets—those equipped to receive the new channels—so far have reached only about five million of the nation's 106 million households, but sales are zooming. The public will buy almost six million digital sets in 2004. . . , 8.3 million in 2005, 11.9 million in 2006, and 16.2 million in 2007."[a]

[a]Neil Hickey, "TV on Steroids," *Columbia Journalism Review,* March–April 2004, p. 45.

---

profits will be. Networks and stations base their charges for commercial time on ratings. Advertisers buy time according to ratings, total cost, and the number of target-audience members among viewers. Ratings are the only underpinning for all of these.

Nielsen Ratings The A.C. Nielsen Company is the biggest marketing research firm in the world, and it operates in the United States and in thirty other worldwide markets. Most of its income comes from research in checking supermarket and drugstore shelves to find out how well certain products, brands, and sizes are selling. The Media Research Division, which computes the ratings, is only a small part of the Nielsen Company.

In the United States, Nielsen Media Research "offers television audience estimates for broadcast and cable networks, television stations, national syndicators, regional cable television systems, satellite providers, advertisers and advertising agencies. . . . Through a network of affiliates, [its] coverage is extended to more than 70 countries, representing 85% of the world's advertising spending. In addition, Nielsen collects Internet usage and advertising information through Nielsen//NetRatings."[30]

Several hundred companies (advertising agencies, advertisers, program suppliers, and the networks) subscribe to the Nielsen ratings, but the networks are the largest customers, as judged by the prices they pay for the service. Networks rely on Nielsen for about 90 percent of their information, and each pays Nielsen roughly $10 million a year for its services.

The national Nielsen ratings, collected in the Nielsen National TV Ratings Report, statistically estimate the number of homes viewing a program by projecting from the viewing patterns of the homes in their sample, which are equipped with measuring devices called audimeters, combined with data from diaries that viewers fill out.

A national rating represents the percentage of sample homes tuned in to the same show. For instance, if a program scores a rating of 20 for the week, that means that 20 percent of the sample homes tuned in to that show for at least six minutes (about 199 sets out of the average 993 reporting). A rating is the estimated percentage of television homes (households with television sets) that watched a program, projected from the sample data. In September 2003, with roughly 108.4 million television households in the United States, a single national household rating point represented 1% of that total, which translated to 1,084,000 households.

BOX 1-11   Television Ratings and Shares

Both ratings and shares measure how many people watch a given program. Ratings measure the percentage of people viewing a program out of all U.S. households with television sets, whether turned on or not. Shares measure the percentage of people viewing a program out of those U.S. households watching television at any given time.

Rating = % of U.S. households with television tuned to Channel x.

Share = % of U.S. households watching television tuned to Channel x.

	Rating	Share
Channel A	40	66.6
Channel B	20	33.3

By 2000, the percentage agreeing to fill out Nielsen diaries had dropped to 30 in some cities.[a] Nielsen projected that by 2005 it would be using people meters to assess viewership in the top ten markets. Protests by the networks and advocacy groups concerned that the method may undercount Black and Latino viewership, prompted Nielsen in spring 2004 to delay implementing the plan in New York City and promise to study ways to improve the accuracy of numbers reflecting viewership by these groups. "The fear," noted Raymond Hernandez and Stuart Elliott writing in the *New York Times*, "was that such undercounts would lead not only to lower prices for commercials on shows watched by minority viewers but would also discourage stations and networks from scheduling such shows—or encourage them to cancel those now scheduled."[b]

[a]Bill Carter, "Who Needs the Sweeps?" *New York Times*, 24 April 2000, pp. C1, C17.
[b]Raymond Hernandez and Stuart Elliott, "Nielsen Delays New Method of Tracking in New York," *New York Times*, 7 April 2004, p. C1.

Nielsen also reports what percentage of households actually watching television is tuned in to a particular program; this number is called "share of audience." Ratings indicate the sorts of events capable of assembling a mass audience. The first night of the Persian Gulf War attracted an audience of 133 million; 95 million viewed O. J. Simpson's chase in the white Bronco; Clinton's admission that he had had a relationship with Monica Lewinsky drew 67.6 million viewers; and about 33 million viewers watched Princess Diana's funeral, which began airing at 6 A.M., eastern time.[31]

One weakness in the ratings is that they measure viewing demographically—by age, income, education, and family size—and demographics have little to do with interests, tastes, attitudes, or activities. The ratings also are distorted because they do not reflect viewing in hotels, hospitals, bars, prisons, clubs, summer camps, military bases, college dormitories, or homes for the elderly.

Audience measurement changed dramatically with the introduction of a device known as the "people meter," which instantly analyzes the age, sex, and income of viewers. These are the demographics of greatest interest to advertisers. The people meter resembles a handheld remote control and has buttons for each family member. Each viewer in the 4,000 homes that have agreed to participate in each two-year cycle punches in when starting to view a program and punches out when leaving. A central computer records who is watching what and when. The people meter not only indicates more accurately than diaries who is watching but also provides more accurate data on what is being watched. With the proliferation of cable channels and other independent stations, diary keepers found it increasingly difficult to record their viewing.

BOX 1-12   BET, Black Entertainment Television

Black Entertainment Television, a 24-hour-a-day, Washington-based operation, was the nation's first television network aimed at an African American audience. The network's founder and president, Robert L. Johnson, launched BET in 1980. In 1991, BET Holdings Inc. completed a $72.3 million initial public offering to become the first black-owned company traded on the New York Stock Exchange.[a] In 1989, BET was carried on just 1,825 of the nation's 7,500 cable systems and ranked twentieth out of forty-two basic services in terms of subscribers (with 23.8 million) and was fifteenth out of twenty networks in revenues, with a projected $22.4 million in 1989. Although by April 1995 BET provided programming such as news, public affairs, jazz, off-network sitcoms, gospel, music videos, and sports, for 42.3 million subscribers in the United States, the network no longer ranked among the top 20 basic services.[b] Now offered as part of the basic cable package, its revenues come from advertising and subscriber fees. In Spring 2004 Nielsen indicates that BET's audience in prime time averaged 560,000 viewers. Its most popular program, "Celebration of Gospel," averaged more than a million. Projections for 2004 suggested that the channel would take in more than $300 million in ad revenue. BET faces a challenge from other networks programming to reach African American viewers. So, for example, the *Wall Street Journal* notes that "MTV and Comedy Central, which like BET is owned by Viacom, boast shows that have strong black appeal. MTV relies heavily on hip-hop music and lifestyle shows aimed at minority viewers. And Comedy Central's 'Chappelle's Show,' starring black comedian Dave Chappelle, has become a hit."[c]

BET relies heavily on low-cost programming, although it produces more than 20 percent of the shows that it airs. Johnson explains: "Our strong cash flow is the basis of our ability to deliver a quality product at a low cost, mainly because our heavy concentration is in music videos—essentially given to us at no cost for promotional considerations—and in our ability to buy off-network product at a low cost because we are buying black-oriented sitcoms that didn't find their way out of network into any form of syndication."[d]

Company founder Johnson also has ventured into publishing with *YSB* and *Emerge* magazines, and has worked to develop home-shopping programs aimed at African Americans.[e] BET also acquired Action Pay Per View, broadcast in 7 million homes,[f] and has formed joint ventures to make family-oriented films with Blockbuster and action films with Encore[g]

[a]Alfred Edmond, Jr., "Milestones in Black Business," *Black Enterprise,* January 1995, p. 104.
[b]"Black Entertainment Television to Explore State of the Family," *Business Wire,* 13 June 1995.
[c]Joe Flint, "BET Reaches Out as Rivals Threaten, " *Wall Street Journal,* 13 April 2004, B3.
[d]Rich Brown and Don West, "Bob Johnson on the Information Revolution: All Ahead Slow," *Broadcasting & Cable,* 3 July 1995, p. 17.
[e]"Top 50 Black Powerbrokers in Entertainment," *Black Enterprise,* December 1994, p. 66.
[f]Brown and West, p. 19.
[g]Laura M. Litvan, "A Broadcaster's Vision," *Nation's Business,* February 1995, p. 14.

The meter eliminates that problem. Moreover, because it gives a minute-by-minute account of viewing, rather than the 15-minute report from a diary, the people meter is better able to tell individual advertisers who is watching their ads. Nielsen began using such meters in the fall of 1987. When Nielsen replaced other forms of monitoring with people meters, reported network viewership dropped by 6 percent in the first year; by 1990, the falloff had reached 10 percent. By summer 1997, the audience shares of the three major networks (NBC, ABC, CBS) had fallen to 47 percent. This meant that in early 1997, Fox, whose rise we noted earlier; United Paramount Network (UPN) and Warner Brothers (WB); independent stations; and cable commanded 53 percent of all the viewers.[32]

Facing a decline in advertising revenues in early 1988, the networks commissioned a 22-month study through the Committee on Nationwide Television Audience Measurement, a group created by the networks in 1963. The study, completed by Statistical Research Inc., cost $1 million and was reported in seven volumes. Just before the winter holidays in 1989, the report was released. It contained recommendations such as: Nielsen should appoint an ombudsman to monitor measurement.

Small sets and sets in unusual places such as garages and hotel rooms should be monitored.
People away from home should be monitored.
Households should be replaced more than once every two years (the report found that fatigue reduces the reliability of the reports after the first year).
The meters should be simplified to encourage use by children.
Techniques for encouraging participation should be found (only 55 percent of those asked agree to participate).
Multiple sets in the same home should be followed.[33]

ABC, NBC, and ESPN commissioned the Nielsen Company to study viewing outside homes, and a survey was conducted from November 2 to November 29, 1989. More than 4,000 people aged 12 and older participated, filling out diaries that logged all their viewing during this time, inside and outside the home. The results indicated than an average of 0.5 to 1.3 million people were watching television somewhere other than in their homes during some part of the day. Thirty-five percent reported viewing at work. Twenty-one percent viewed television in college residence halls, 16 percent in hotel rooms, 9 percent in bars and restaurants, and 4 percent in second homes; 15 percent fell into other categories. The overall increase in viewing averaged 2 to 3 percent, equivalent to three tenths to seven tenths of a rating point, as much as the average rating for most cable channels. Such an increase in audience would be worth almost $225 million in advertising revenues to network television.[34]

In summer 1995, Nielsen reported, "More than 23 million adult viewers watch in excess of five hours of television in out-of-home locations each week. . . . Settings include offices, college buildings, hotels, restaurants/bars and second homes, all of which are not counted in Nielsen's standard ratings."[35]

The very rich, the well educated, the poor, and minority groups—particularly poorer African American and Latino families—traditionally were underrepresented in Nielsen samples. Minorities and poorer Americans were underrepresented because Nielsen field representatives tended to be whites, who encountered hostility when they knocked on doors in ghettos or barrios. It was difficult to find African American and Latino families who would agree to fill out diaries, and Nielsen did not begin distributing Spanish-language diaries until 1978. The high level of literacy required and the tediousness of the task limited all diary participation to the better educated and the middle class; thus African Americans and Latinos who agreed to fill out diaries tended to be those whose viewing patterns resembled those of white middle-class audiences. The distribution of people meters faced similar problems.

The underrepresentation of African Americans and members of other minority groups created significant problems for television stations that appealed to such audiences. Because their primary viewership was underrepresented in the ratings sample, such outlets got lower ratings and therefore found it more difficult to attract advertisers. This situation in turn made it harder for minority programming or minority outlets to survive.

Starting in 1991, Nielsen expanded its monthly National Audience Demographic Report to include African American households and about twenty African American demographic categories. At the same time, a number of organizations, including Tribune Entertainment and Burrell Uniworld, pledged to launch educational campaigns designed to increase cooperation in the ratings process among African American and Latino households.

Some still felt that audience estimates remained skewed in favor of white viewers. In 1994, at the urging of African American television producers and advertising agencies, Nielsen once again announced revisions in its collecting and reporting methods. It would increase the representation of African Americans in its sample and consider the creation of a separate sample and report for African Americans.[36]

This attention was driven, in part, by demography. U.S. census figures show that "the African American population is expected to swell to 39 million by 2010, 50% faster growth than the rest of the population." The publisher of *Target Market News* reports that advertisers spent $1.2 billion to reach African Americans in 1997, double what was spent a decade before.[37]

In April 2004 Nielsen announced that it would delay implementing local people meters (LPMs) in New York. An ad in the *New York Times* of April 15, 2004, by a coalition of African American and Latino groups responded by saying, "Thank you for hearing our concerns. Now, it's time to address them." The ad asked, "Why did virtually all the top rated African American and Latino programs see drastic viewership declines under the LPM system, while shows geared toward predominantly white audiences see no decline or even an increase in ratings?"[38] In November 2004 Univision and Nielsen withdrew their lawsuits against each other. Nielsen switched to people meters in New York and Chicago in summer 2004.

Nielsen promised that by 2006, it would expand its sample, saying,

Nationwide, the number of African American television households in our sample will nearly double from 670 households to 1,200. That is approximately 12% of the sample. The number of Latino television households in the national sample will increase from 540 to 1,000 households when the expansion is completed in 2006. That is approximately 10% of the sample. According to Nielsen, these increases will produce more stable data and more representative demographic information about African American and Latino television audiences.[39]

BOX 1-14   Portable People Meters

Thousands of paid volunteers in Houston, Texas, have agreed to wear Portable People Meters (PPMs) that will, without any further action on their part, record all the media that they listen to and watch, even for small periods of time (Jon Gertner, "Watching What You Watch," *New York Times Magazine*, 10 April 2005, pp. 34, 36–41, 56, 58, 64, 67). This is a joint effort by Arbitron and Nielson to overcome all the problems of diaries, which often are inaccurate, and people meters, which record only what is viewed on a particular television set. This may be the beginning of a ratings revolution.

BOX 1-15   Republicans and Television

In 2004 the Bush-Cheney campaign learned through market research that Republicans were less likely to watch television than Democrats. Thus, buying ads on television was more cost efficient for the Democratic candidates. The Bush team responded in part by "placing advertisements on in-house networks at private gyms, guaranteeing a captive audience."[a]

[a]Adam Nagourney, "Bush Campaign Manager Views the Electoral Divide," *New York Times,* 19 November 2004, p. A23.

Although Nielsen ratings are only rough estimates of viewership and although they ignore some viewers and undercount others, they are the bases on which advertisers buy time to air commercials, which, in turn, determines the profitability of programs and television stations.

The assumption that viewing programming equals viewing advertising, of course, has always been suspect. The remote control increased the likelihood that viewers would turn to other channels during commercial breaks.

The equation changed with the arrival of devices that permitted viewers to skip through television ads. In 2004 there were about 3 million digital video recorders (DVRs) in U.S. homes, 1 million of them TiVos. The invention of TiVo increased the chances that viewers were skipping ads altogether. The advent of DVRs (which record preset programs to a hard drive) made it tougher for the television industry, in the words of Jack Loftus, a vice president with Nielsen Media Research, to assess "consumers' interaction with TiVo and DVR technology" and, hence, "their television viewing behavior." When Nielsen and TiVo reached an agreement by which TiVo would provide "a breakdown of how some of its customers are using their digital video recorders," Loftus applauded, saying, "This could affect future programming decisions and commercial placements."[40]

Television programming now has a commercially significant afterlife in DVD (digital video display) form. TV-DVDs of popular programs brought in more than $1 billion in 2003. (Some series producers are planning their productions with DVD sales in mind.)

Radio

Radio best illustrates media specialization and segmentation. It once was dominated by national networks comparable to those we now associate with television. Originally there were four national networks—ABC, CBS, NBC, and the Mutual Broadcasting System—but what remains of them are primarily news services. Today, radio has become a segmented medium. Thirty-four national radio networks are currently in existence, compared with twenty-three in 1990 and just nine in 1974.[41] Some of them provide 24-hour-a-day adult popular, Top 40, jazz, classical, or country and western music. Two factors have contributed to the proliferation of networks. One is an increase in the number of radio stations from about 4,000 in 1968 to 12,262 in 1998;[42] in 2001 there were 4,716 AM stations, 6000 FM, and 2,216 Educational FM stations. In 2003, there were 5,067 AM stations and 8,831 FM stations, including educational stations. The second is an effort by advertisers to reach specialized audiences. For example, only 30 of the 9,993 commercial radio stations in the country play classical music, yet most of them are profitable. There is a recognizable public demand for classical music, and advertisers are eager to reach the audience such programming attracts.[43]

Although music, news, and sports constitute the bulk of network fare, the radio dial is increasingly filled with daily, weekly, or monthly "long-form" programming, from music/variety series like NBC's *Live from the Hard Rock Cafe* to national talk/call-in shows, many inspired by the phenomenal success of the syndicated *Rush Limbaugh Show.*

As advertisers target messages to build brands, radio's share of the total advertising dollars spent on media is rising. To a greater extent than television, radio reaches its largest audiences outside the home. The times during which we drive to work (morning drive time), drive from work (afternoon drive time), and listen in the office while working are what attract advertisers.

One unusual network, National Public Radio (NPR), took to the air in October 1970. Beginning with 90 member stations, it had grown to 593 in 1997. NPR produces forty-six hours a week of original national programming from its Washington, DC, headquarters, and more than half of that is news and public affairs, including its well-known news program *All Things Considered,* which airs nationally during afternoon drive time and attracts 7.2 million listeners each week.[44] In the early 1990s, NPR started *Talk of the Nation,* a 2-hour radio call-in program, which addresses political, social, and scientific issues. Every week, nearly 19.3 million listeners tune their radios to hear NPR programming.[45]

A comparable public network, American Public Radio, was formed in 1982. Many stations carry programming from both NPR and APR. In July 1994, APR changed its name to Public Radio International. Based in Minneapolis, Minnesota, PRI has 530 affiliate stations that can subscribe to any mix of the more than 300 hours per week of programs that PRI transmits each week via satellite. PRI broadcasts the business news program *Marketplace,* the *Christian Science Monitor's Monitor Radio,* and variety programs such as the quiz show *Whad'Ya Know?* and the long-running *Prairie Home Companion.* Total listenership for PRI is about 18 million per week on 591 stations.[46]

Along with a small number of noncommercial radio stations, such as the Pacifica Radio Network, PRI and NPR are among the few sources of in-depth news on radio. Most news coverage on commercial radio is satellite-delivered headline services.

The ratings system for radio is very similar to the local market and demographics ratings systems for television. However, radio ratings measure individual, not household, listenership, and they include out-of-home listening.

Arbitron Ratings　The Arbitron Company is a research company specializing in measuring consumers' local media use and buying habits. Arbitron Radio, the company's largest division, compiles radio station rating reports, measuring audiences in 270 local markets and serving 2,300 radio stations and 3,500 agencies and advertisers. Detailed ratings data can be found at http://www.arbitron.com/downloads/radiotoday04.pdf.

Arbitron ratings dominate radio in the same way that Nielsen ratings dominate television. Radio stations charge advertisers on the basis of how many listeners Arbitron determines they have (measured in listening five minutes out of a quarter hour). Drive time (6 to 10 A.M. and 3 to 7 P.M.) is radio's equivalent of prime time for advertising, and during these peak periods, radio delivers an audience that cannot readily switch to television.

Advertisers want their commercials to reach particular consumers, and to compete with other stations for these consumers, stations need the resources of networks, particularly programming they could not afford to produce themselves. Some networks are regional, such as the New York Yankees baseball network. Others are national but aimed at a particular ethnic group, such as the Black Radio Network, a news source geared toward African Americans that has 168 affiliates. Although radio often is considered a local medium, this claim is open to dispute. About one fifth of all radio stations in the United States use one of the national networks for their music programming, and most stations rely on national services for their news programming.[47] As a result, although programs may be beamed from a local station, the programming can originate elsewhere.

Arbitron reports that AM/FM radio listening in 2004 is down 14 percent from 1994. Nonetheless, 228 million Americans 12 years old and older tune in to broadcast radio weekly. At the same time, driven by increasing broadband connections at home, 19 million are listening to online radio at least once a week; in 2000 that figure stood at 7 million. Total subscribers to XM Satellite Radio and its competitor, Sirius Satellite Radio, will probably surpass 8 million by the end of 2005. The pay model of satellite

---

BOX 1-17   Black Radio Today

Arbitron's *Black Radio Today* reports that of the 13,800 radio stations broadcasting in the United States, 1,100 are black-formatted and provides data to show that radio is a medium popular among African Americans ages 18+. Arbitron also provides commuter profiles for metropolitan areas, including profiles for Asians in such areas as New York City. This includes their average commuting time (39 minutes in NYC), when they commute, what transportation they use, their numbers in the population, and the percentages of full- and part-time workers, compared to all in the market (www.arbiton.com).

---

radio was originally marketed to people in cars; Sirius and XM are signing up car makers to offer it as a factory-installed option.[48] As families purchase portable tuners, satellite radio is increasingly found in homes.[49]

Talk Radio The National Association of Radio Talk Hosts was founded in 1988; 75 members attended its first meeting. At its peak, the group had more than 3,000 members. Although the association no longer exists, its cofounder Carol Nashe recently created the Carol Nashe Group of Radio Talk Show Hosts Consultants, offering radio placement services, consulting, and public relations for radio personalities.[50]

The importance of talk radio was clear in the 1992 presidential campaign, when both Vice President Dan Quayle and Democratic aspirant Bill Clinton addressed the National Association's convention. In the same year, Bush and Quayle appeared on Limbaugh's program, and Clinton staged his comeback in New York on *Imus in the Morning*. Although exit polls found that talk shows were second only to debates in the help they provided voters in reaching decisions, nearly one voter in five could not evaluate talk radio's role in the campaign. Politicians' belief in the influence of talk radio persisted after the election. In fall 1993, the day after Clinton's national address on health-care reform, more than sixty-five talk show hosts broadcast from the White House lawn. In the final week of the 2002 midterm election, talk radio hosts from around the country were invited to Washington, DC, for one-on-one interviews with top administration officials.

Although he was talking about a television, rather than a radio call-in show, Clinton's message in 1993 was clear: "You know why I can stiff you on the press conferences?" Clinton asked at a Radio and Television Correspondents Association dinner in March 1993. "Because Larry King has liberated me from you by giving me to the American people directly."

Without a doubt, the most influential individual political call-in host is Rush Limbaugh, who is credited by the Republican leadership with the Republican takeover of the House and Senate in 1994. Heard on more than 600 stations, Limbaugh's nationally syndicated 3-hour radio show reaches a cumulative weekly audience of more than 17 million. His 1992 book *The Way Things Ought to Be* was in the top spot on the *New York Times* best-seller list for seven straight weeks and has sold more than 2 million hardcover copies. "The Limbaugh Letter," a monthly publication with 170,000

BOX 1-18   Political Radio

"President Bush's campaign officials mostly avoid television programs like 'Hardball with Chris Matthews,' 'Inside Politics,' or 'Face the Nation.' . . . But on one recent Thursday, Terry Holt, Mr. Bush's campaign press secretary, called in to 'The Marc Bernier Show' [in Florida] . . . to talk extensively about how the president wanted to help orange growers and would not be satisfied until 'every American who wants a job can have a job.' It was one of several telephone visits Mr. Holt made to radio stations in the past few weeks, though he has not appeared on a national television program since he started his job in early November. . . . It is a network that Democrats do not have—though they are trying to cultivate one—that Mr. Bush's campaign strategists believe will give him an edge in an election that could go to whichever side best mobilizes its core voters.'"[a]

[a]Jim Rutenberg, "Bush's Campaign Finds a Platform on Local Radio," *New York Times*, 29 December 2003, p. A1. Copyright © 2003 by The New York Times Co. Reprinted with permission.

---

subscribers, is promoted on his radio and television show. His audience, he reports, is upscale and educated. The power of his message is increased as well by his invitations to supporters and opponents to communicate with him by telephone, fax, and e-mail.

An Annenberg Public Policy Center survey conducted in fall 2003 found that talk radio "is more popular among Republicans and Independents. A majority of Republicans (60%) and Independents (60%) listen to talk radio at least monthly, compared to fewer than half of Democrats (46%). More than a third of Republicans (39%) and Independents (36%) listen to talk radio every week. When it comes to specific programs, nearly a quarter of Republicans (22%) listen to Rush Limbaugh every week and more than a third (37%) at least once a month. Two in 10 Independents (20%) also listen to Limbaugh at least once a month. However, fewer than one in 10 Democrats (9%) ever listen to Rush Limbaugh's show. Party identification also shows up among NPR listeners. Independents (34%) are more likely to listen to NPR weekly than either Democrats (25%) or Republicans (22%). Four in 10 Republicans (40%) and Democrats (41%) and nearly half of Independents (47%) listen to NPR at least once a month."

Talk radio also can be a political springboard. New Jersey governor Christine Todd Whitman was a part-time radio call-in host before successfully running for governor, and Maryland's governor Donald Schaefer hosted a weekly show.

Since the Telecommunications Act of 1996 eased rules on ownership, there is increased concentration of ownership in radio. Clear Channel, for example, has grown from 43 stations to more than 1,200.[51]

Newspapers

In 1984, there were approximately 1,688 daily newspapers in the United States, with a combined circulation of 63,340,320. By 1997, that number had dropped to 1,520 dailies, with a combined circulation of 57,000,000. In 2003 there were 1,468 dailies. Competing with them for readers and advertising dollars were 7,214 weekly newspapers, some distributed free of charge, with a combined circulation of 70,434,299.[52] Almost all daily newspapers subscribe to a major wire service, with the result that much

---

BOX 1-19   Newspaper Websites

"Eight of the top 20 news Web sites or groups in the U.S. during March were affiliated with newspapers, according to audience statistics from Nielsen//NetRatings. The top sites in Nielsen//NetRatings' Current Events & Global News category were CNN, Yahoo! News, MSNBC, AOL News, and Gannett Newspapers. Three individual news-paper sites were in the top 20: NYTimes.com, USAToday.com, and washingtonpost.com. Newspaper chains on the list were Gannett Co. Inc., Knight Ridder, Tribune Co., Hearst Corp., and Advance Publications Inc."[a]

[a]*Editor and Publisher,* 20 April 2004.

---

of the news they print, especially on national and international events, originates with the wire services.

A Pew Center for the People and the Press survey of June 9, 2002, found that "Just 41% of respondents say they read a paper the previous day, compared with 47% in 2000 and 48% in 1998."[53] To attract more readers, newspaper editors are trying various tactics to appeal to diverse audiences, including Latinos, gays, and young people. The *Miami Herald* has added a weekly page of Brazilian news in Portuguese and a weekly page of Haitian news in Creole. Several newspapers are including special inserts targeted at younger readers. Newspaper chains are also interested in electronic publishing.

In response to what is perceived as a threat by computer companies and online services to the prominence of their role as providers of information, newspapers are joining the technological revolution. In April 1995, Gannett, Knight Ridder, Times Mirror, and five other corporations, representing 185 newspapers, announced the formation of New Century Network. With this network, not only would the news and classified advertising of the newspapers of one city be available to customers in another, but services such as ordering tickets for sports and entertainment events across the country would also be accessible. "We believe it will change the face of the newspaper industry," said Peter Winter, interim head of the network.[54]

By 1999, all the country's major newspapers were offering an online edition and were marketing to advertisers such features as the help-wanted pages online.

Circulation data are the ratings system for newspapers, data compiled by the Audit Bureau of Circulations, which releases circulation figures for about 1,000 daily newspapers based on unaudited reports provided by the newspapers themselves. Those figures have received especially careful scrutiny

since the Tribune Company announced in June that it had inflated the circulation of *Newsday* and the Spanish-language paper *Hoy.* The Belo Corporation and Hollinger International subsequently disclosed overstatements at the *Dallas Morning News* and the *Chicago Sun-Times,* respectively. The disclosures not only hurt the chains in question, forcing them to dedicate millions of dollars to overhauling their circulation departments and compensating advertisers who paid for phantom readers, but they have also prompted internal scrutiny by an industry struggling to stem losses in readership.[55]

TABLE 1.1   Top 150 Newspapers by Largest Reported Circulation

Publication Name	Publisher Name	City, ST	Frequency	Largest Reported Circulation
1. *USA Today*	Gannett Company Inc.	Washington, DC	Fri M (F–M)	2,612,946
2. *The Wall Street Journal*	Dow Jones & Co. Inc.	New York, NY	M (M–F)	2,070,498
3. *New York Times*	New York Times Company	New York, NY	Sun	1,680,582
4. *Los Angeles Times*	Tribune Publishing Company	Los Angeles, CA	Sun	1,253,849
5. *The Washington Post*	Washington Post Company	Washington, DC	Sun	1,000,565
6. *Chicago Tribune*	Tribune Publishing Company	Chicago, IL	Sun	953,814
7. *New York Daily News*	New York Daily News	New York, NY	Sun	835,121
8. *Philadelphia Inquirer*	Knight Ridder, Inc.	Philadelphia, PA	Sun	744,242
9. *Denver Post/Rocky Mountain News*	The E.W. Scripps Company/Media News Group, Inc.	Denver, CO	Sun	733,621
10. *Houston Chronicle*	Hearst Newspapers	Houston, TX	Sun	720,711

Gray screen indicates publication is participant in Reader Profile service. White indicates publication is participant in Subscriber Profile service.
Source: Audit Bureau of Circulations, 31 March 2005.

New rules requiring senior executives at each paper to sign their names to the circulation figures they report each quarter provide safeguards against such abuses. Some chains, such as McClatchy, which owns the *Minneapolis Star Tribune*, sent detailed questionnaires to its publishers, finance directors, and circulation managers to assess how susceptible their papers were to similar fraud.

The figures that have just been released indicate that newspaper circulation remains stagnant. Table 1.1 shows the December 2004 circulation figures for the top ten newspapers in the United States as released by the Audit Bureau of Circulations.

Magazines

Under the impact of television, radio and magazines became specialized or segmented media. Because advertisers could reach the same mass audience more cheaply and quickly via television, many well-known mass circulation magazines, such as *Look* and the *Saturday Evening Post,* went out of business. Recently, magazines targeted at special audiences—such as *Motorcyclist, Fantasy,* and *Science Fiction*—have sprung up. There are only a few national magazines, and three are newsweeklies: *Time, Newsweek,* and *U.S. News & World Report. Time* is owned by Time Inc., *Newsweek* by the Washington Post Company. They are typical; many magazines are owned by chains, large corpora-

---

BOX 1-20   Simmons Methodology

Simmons randomly selects households for participation using a single-state stratified probability sample. Households selected for participation are mailed a household survey booklet covering household usage/ownership of selected products and services. To obtain a more precise outcome, each adult (age 18+), teen (12–17), and child (6–11) is mailed a personal booklet.

Approximately 20,000 adults participate each year, providing extensive information on news-papers, magazines, yellow pages, online/interactive services, broadcast and cable television, radio and movies. Surveys also collect personal information on demographic, lifestyle, and psychodemographic descriptors; product/service usage; and retail shopping behavior.[a]

[a]Online at http://www.claritasuniversity.com/Knet/Simmons _FS.pdf, accessed 6 December 2004.

---

tions, and conglomerates, in part because it is very costly to start a magazine and because the survival rate for magazines is low. By contrast, *U.S. News & World Report* is employee-owned. On average, only 10 percent of new magazines survive beyond their first year; nevertheless, as of 1998, there were 2,724 consumer, farm, and international magazines.[56]

The degree of specialization in this medium is evident in the practices of some of the mass circulation magazines. Many publish special editions designed to permit advertisers to reach specific audiences. *Time*, for instance, publishes regional editions, editions aimed at special groups, and an international edition. One edition goes primarily to college students, another to the 1.3 million people living in the most affluent zip code areas within metropolitan markets, and still another to about 640,000 business and professional people. Similarly, *Sports Illustrated* publishes four regional editions and a special homeowners' edition, limited to slightly more than 500,000 subscribers located in zip code areas with the highest concentrations of home ownership. Other magazines, such as *Cosmopolitan* and *Good Housekeeping*, publish Spanish-language editions. In other words, although mass circulation magazines exist, many of them publish special editions with advertising aimed at distinct audiences.

Media follow demographics. With demographers projecting the largest cohort of adolescents since the baby boomers, publishers have spun off magazines for younger readers. *People* magazine created *Teen People*, *CosmoGirl*, *Elle Girl*, and *Teen Vogue*. Recognizing that tweens aspire to be teens and teens, adults, *Seventeen* and *YM* decided to focus on older teens; *CosmoGirl* writes for girls 13 to 15. The new niche magazines have drawn circulation from the traditional ones. According to the Magazine Publishers of America, *Seventeen* has a circulation of 2.1 million, down 11% from 2002.

Magazines have several advantages over television for advertisers. According to data collected by the Pew Center for the People and the Press, 20 percent of people who earn more than $75,000 or are over 50 years of age read a newsmagazine regularly, compared with an average 13 percent of all other age and income categories.[57] A magazine becomes a trusted and familiar source reflecting an image with which the subscriber can identify. In addition, some advertisers now banned from television, such as cigarette manufacturers, must rely on print outlets.

BOX 1-21   Magazine Advertising Revenues

New York, NY (November 8, 2004)—Total magazine rate-card-reported advertising revenue for the month of October 2004 closed at $2,156,283,915, an increase of +14.4% compared to October 2003, according to Publishers Information Bureau (PIB). Ad pages totaled 23,653.91, up +8.4% from last year. Year-to-date, rate-card-reported revenue closed at $17,067,428,173, an increase of +10.3%, with ad pages totaling 187,953.29, registering a +3.0% gain.[a]

[a]Reported by Magazine Publishers of America website, online athttp://www.magazine.org/Advertising_and_PIB/PIB_Revenue_and_Pages/Revenue___Pages_by_Ad_Category__monthly___YTD_/9550.cfm, accessed 7 December 2004.

Magazines are rated by Simmons Market Research Bureau and the Magazine Publishers of America. Surveys by Simmons determine the number of readers per magazine copy. A very high rating is 6, meaning that, on average, six people read one copy of the magazine, and 1.8 is a very low rating. Simmons gathers data through interviews and questionnaires. Such surveys provide advertisers with information about how long readers look at the ads in a particular magazine as well as how much it costs to reach the desired target audience.

The Internet

Three quarters of U.S. adults had Internet access in spring 2004.[58] In 2000, the Pew Center stated, "Fully one-in-three Americans now [go] online for news at least once a week, compared to 20% in 1998. And 15% say they receive daily reports from the Internet, up from 6% two years ago."[59] The numbers are impressive. In the month of February 2004, comScore Media Metrix reported that CNN sites attracted 13.3 million visitors at home and 8.4 million at work; MSNBC followed with 12.5 and 8.4 million respectively, and the New York Times Digital drew 6.1 and 4.4.[60] Among popular Internet news sites, a Pew poll released June 11, 2000, found that believability "ratings for the online sites of the major national news organizations are substantially higher than ratings for the news organizations themselves."[61]

In early July of 1994, the Magazine Publishers of America called for a standard means of measuring advertising on the World Wide Web. Each click of the computer mouse now registers as a hit. Of course, the same viewer may click the mouse many times.

One of the challenges of the Internet has been finding a way to make it commercially viable. The websites that have become profitable include the *Wall Street Journal*'s Online Journal, begun in 1996. At the end of 2003 paid circulation for this site was 689,000.[62] The secret of this is its accessibility.

Other news sites have done well by providing content not available elsewhere. "ABCNews.com, begun in 2002, turned a profit in 2003 by offering ABC News programming that either isn't available elsewhere or at times and places that television viewing isn't option." The outlet offers an "online politics show [and] . . . a round-the-clock news program that's available only on line."[63]

Access to high-speed connections (broadband) has increased dramatically in recent years and with it advertisers' capacities to deliver video ads on line. By the end of 2003, 49.5 million or 38 percent of U.S. households had broadband connections. "Of the 50 million people who surf the Web at work, 94 percent have broadband connections."[64]

In November 2004, Google announced that its search engine could now find more than 8 billion web pages.[65]

The Internet as a Transnational Communicator The Internet has transformed media that once reached only a local audience into international communicators. Audio-streaming on the Web carries radio to the United States from places as distant as Beijing. Audio-streaming compresses audio information to reduce the amount of data sent to the computer and then decodes and decompresses the same material. Online from either Philadelphia or Minneapolis, we can access one another's hometown newspapers as well as the newspapers from most other cities in the United States and many from elsewhere in the world. Want to read *USA Today*? Try www.usatoday.com. Futurist Alvin Toffler projects that in the future "You're going to turn on your TV and get Nigerian TV and Fijian TV in your own language."[66]

The Internet also can continue to function after other media channels have been knocked out. "During the bombing of Kosovo," for example, "the Serbian government's online Radio Yugoslavia broadcast to an international audience long after its television and radio stations were rubble."[67] The United Kingdom site www.live-radio.net carries more than 2,000 stations from more than 100 countries.

This capacity makes the Internet a natural medium for organizers. Elizabeth Economy, senior fellow at the Council on Foreign Relations, for example, noted in 1999 that "the China Democracy Party, whose leaders were arrested last year, was found to have used the Internet to organize across the country. The thing that was so threatening was certainly not the number of people, but rather that this was inter-provincial, that in over two-thirds of Chinese provinces, the China Democracy Party was able to establish branches. . . . The China Democracy Party still exists. It's still there, and it can emerge at any time because of the Internet."[68]

The New Programmers A major reason that traditional media were dominated by institutional programmers was the cost of access. The Internet has changed that. It has the capacity to reverse the traditional flow of information and entertainment from wealthier countries to poorer ones. A programmer in India has the same capacity to communicate on the Web as one in New York City. The democratization of production is evident as well in the advent of reviews of books by readers as well as by professional reviewers on www.amazon.com.

Creating information requires access to information. Proximity to a large library or to a storehouse of interpersonal influence was once a prerequisite for most research, which professionalized that activity. When the federal government provided access to MedLine and Healthfinder, comprehensive archives of scholarship about medicine, it increased the likelihood that a person would arrive at a doctor's office armed with information drawn from the most recent clinical trials. At the University of Pennsylvania, one of Jamieson's colleagues found answers on the Web that had eluded doctors. After being stung by an unidentified insect, his arm began to swell. His doctor didn't recog-

---

BOX 1-22   Internet Censorship

In November 2004, Iran began blocking pro-democracy websites and web logs. The *New York Times* reported, "The crackdown suggests that hard-liners are determined to curtail freedom in cyberspace. Many rights advocates had turned to the Internet after the judiciary shut down more than 100 pro-democracy newspapers and journals in recent years."[a]

Similarly, China has created what some have dubbed the "great firewall of China," with what the *Wall Street Journal* called a "phalanx of barri-ers" "to block access to dissenting views." Specifically, "China's Internet police are using a filtering technology to, in effect, disable a popular feature of the search engine Google" and outlaw searches for certain words such as "China's president," "overthrow," "Tiananmen," and "democracy."[b]

[a]Nazila Fathi, "Iran Jails More Journalists and Blocks Web Sites," *New York Times*, 8 November 2004, p. A10.
[b]Charles Hutzler, "China Finds New Ways to Restrict Access to the Internet," *Wall Street Journal,* 1 September 2004, p. B1.

---

nize the bite and was concerned about the associated symptoms. On a website about insect bites, the professor who had been bitten found pictures that looked much like his bite. This led to a diagnosis and an appropriate medical response.

Whereas the traditional media have always relied on institutional suppliers for their content, the Internet is proving to be fertile territory for people who want to originate news or images. Because the World Wide Web is unregulated, anyone who wants to start a news station on it requires only the technical expertise to do so. Those who wish to communicate their lives or favorite vistas to the world can just hook up a webcam, a video camera attached to their computer. In mid-1999, one directory of webcam sites (www.earthcam.com) listed more than 5,000 sites, a number that doubled annually for three years.[69] Want to learn about life in college? A number of students are transmitting their lives in the dorm 24 hours a day on their own webcams. Some of the results have been unanticipated. In 1998, "Ryan Scott, 21, had a seizure . . . in his dorm room at Southern Methodist University in Dallas." His webcam was on, making it possible for his girlfriend to see it happen. "She alerted Scott's mom, who called campus officials. Paramedics arrived in Scott's room just as he was coming to. He says the alert may have saved his life."[70] Webcams also can offer access to images that help us manage our day-to-day lives. Before heading off to work, don't wait for a traffic report from local broadcast news; instead, dial up a webcam showing traffic on the highway that worries you. Feel like getting away from the summer heat? Dial up the webcam that watches Mount Everest.

Other Web activities have redefined the notion that television is an intimate medium. As television and the computer converge, we may increasingly see them as the same medium. In August 1999, www.adoctorinyourhouse.com carried a live webcast of the gastric bypass surgery of popular singer Carnie Wilson.

Of course, not everyone welcomes this kind of intimacy. Whereas we might applaud the webcam that catches the burglar breaking into our apartment, most of us are probably less kindly disposed to one that catches us in a passionate embrace with a best friend's significant other or spies on us as we discreetly relieve ourselves in the bushes.

BOX 1-23   Collecting Information on Viewers

In spring 2004 there are about 3 million DVRs, a third of them TiVos. While people are watching TiVo'd content, TiVo is watching them. TiVo collects and aggregates information on its users, which many became aware of when TiVo announced that Janet Jackson's breast-revealing "wardrobe malfunction" at the 2004 Superbowl was the "most replayed moment in TiVo's history."[a] In spring 2004, TiVo reps said that "it will begin selling specific viewing data about some of its users to the TV industry through a partnership with Nielsen Media Research."[b]

[a]Lee Gomes, "Though a Trailblazer, Is TiVo Overreaching in Its Patent Claims?" *Wall Street Journal*, 9 February 2004, p. B1.
[b]Nick Wingfield and Jennifer Saranow, "TiVo Tunes in to Its Users' Viewing Habits," *Wall Street Journal*, 9 February 2004, p. B1.

Dave Banisar, of the Electronic Privacy Information Center, notes, "Just because you're walking down a public street doesn't mean that the government or any other person should have the right to follow you around wherever you go and take notes of who you see and what you do."[71]

One of the problems occasioned by the proliferation of new producers is an absence of quality control; a corresponding advantage is an explosion of speech and a multiplication of the outlets for creative expression. On the problem side of this equation are websites that promote flaky cures for serious illnesses. "There is a contaminated flood . . . of information on the Web of uncertain validity and parentage," says Jerome Kassirer, editor of the *New England Journal of Medicine.* "People have to be cautious about using any health information they find on the Web." Indeed, "[f]our companies already have been charged with making unsubstantiated claims about products that were supposed to 'cure' or 'effectively treat' serious illnesses such as arthritis, cancer, HIV/AIDS, and liver disease."[72] In response, the U.S. Federal Trade Commission (FTC) has begun Operation Cure.all to police health claims on the Internet. With the U.S. Department of Health and Human Services, the FTC is conducting a consumer education campaign to help viewers identify reliable health websites.

The Internet can also prove problematic when it is used to disseminate defamatory claims about someone. For example, in August 1999, singer Lauryn Hill received an apology from the controllers of the "bitter waitress" website, where it had been alleged that Hill had demanded to be served by a person of a certain race. An outlet for waitpeople who are undertipped, the website had spread a false and potentially defamatory claim in part because its organizers had not institutionalized a fact-checking process.

Expanded Interactivity Whereas the audience for traditional media was largely the passive recipient of whatever content was available and exercised control by choosing to watch or not, read or not, listen or not, the watchword of the Internet is interactivity.

With interactivity comes a dramatic change in the concept of the audience. "This new era," writes Ingrid Volkmer, "enables the news junkie-cybernauts of New York, Mexico City, Cape Town, Beijing, Moscow, and Berlin not only to watch breaking news on CNN International but also to interact with journalists covering these events (via sites such as Microsoft Network's political e-zine 'Slate') and exchange views with each other. This new communication level not only redefines Marshall McLuhan's vision of a global village by creating worldwide communities, but also creates new uses for the computer terminal, which has been transformed from a data-processing machine to a multifunctional tool for online interactivity."[73]

THE NEW MEDIA ENVIRONMENT

Twenty-Four-Hour News

Twenty-four-hour-a-day news on CNN, Fox, and MSNBC and 24-hour-a-day updates on the websites of the world's newspapers have created a changed media environment. Among other things, continuously airing news rather than news punctuated by the deadlines of going to press or going on air at a specified, predictable time also increases the likelihood that news outlets will carry inaccurate, incomplete, or false stories. "The problem nowadays," writes former White House correspondent James Naughton, "is that we're expected to make the right calls on the run. . . . Many journalists now spend valuable time scanning the Web and surfing cable channels to be sure they're not belated in disclosing what someone else just reported, breathlessly, using sources whose identity we'll never know."[74]

Changing Influence of the Press

In the era when three major television networks and a morning or evening paper were the primary sources for news, media elites such as Walter Cronkite had considerable sway with citizens and leaders. President Lyndon Johnson, for example, knew he had lost public support for the Vietnam War when Cronkite, anchor for the CBS network news, commented that "It is increasingly clear to this reporter that the only rational way out [of the conflict] . . . will be to negotiate, not as victors but as an honorable people who lived up to their pledge to defend democracy and did the best they could." After this declaration, Johnson continued to defend his policies but shifted his rhetoric to that of unification. Cronkite's message changed Johnson's stance toward the political offensive in Vietnam. "It was the first time in American history that a war had been declared over by an anchorman," wrote David Halberstam. "Lyndon Johnson watched and told his press secretary, George Christian, that it was a turning point, that if he had lost Walter Cronkite, he had lost Mr. Average Citizen."[75] Today, it is unclear who the media elites are, and none has the influence that Cronkite had in the 1960s.

In a bow to the influence that once belonged to the press and as a sign that that influence is a memory, on the weekend after his August 1998 confession that he had misled the public and his family about his relationship with Lewinsky, Clinton went for a widely publicized boating outing with Cronkite. The message was not lost on the press. "Not only did he choose to align himself with a figure of larger-than-life rectitude," noted Michael Wolff, "but he chose one who provided a marked contrast to the present-day faces who deliver the news. . . . Cronkite, the last and greatest figure of an all-powerful network–news media that offered not only information but temperament,

CASE STUDY 1-1   Altering News Norms: The Influence of CNN

Before the advent of CNN, if you or I wanted to learn what had happened in the world on a given day, we would either have to locate an all-news radio station or wait until early evening to tune in to a network news broadcast. People interested in world affairs adjusted their time to that of the networks. Meals and social activities were scheduled around network news time. The availability of 24-hour-a-day news changed all that. News is now available at our convenience.

The sheer quantity of news coverage dictated some other changes in the ways in which CNN news was programmed. Instead of a single "star" anchor, CNN developed a cast of anchors; focus on the personality of the anchor decreased. A second difference in patterns of anchoring and reporting emerged. Women and minorities were more likely to appear in those roles on CNN than on the other networks. This pluralization of the news also was reflected in the use of tape and reporters from around the world.

By broadcasting around the clock, CNN ensured that without disrupting "commercial" programming, it could "go live." At 2:32 P.M. EST, CNN led the other networks by four minutes with the report that shots had been fired at President Ronald Reagan. Moreover, it could stay on the air with a live report as long as the news producer wished. CNN, for example, aired 29 straight hours of coverage on the attempted assassination, Hinckley's motives, and Reagan's progress.

Live coverage makes us more aware of the extent to which most broadcast news is packaged by the conventions of editing discussed earlier. In the 29 hours of CNN coverage of the assassination attempt, "CNN's viewers got the story in the jumbled way that a journalist receives fragments of information before transforming them into an orderly, polished report. The 'process' of gathering news determined the form in which the news was delivered. With CNN's unlimited time, the story could unfold at its own pace. With all those 'ragged edges' exposed."[a]

As the tanks moved in on the demonstrators in Tiananmen Square in Beijing, the CNN reporters could no longer sustain the calm, controlled tone that ordinarily characterizes edited news. Neither we nor they could be certain what was happening. CNN audiences around the world were encircled by the tensions and tragedies of the moment. Those who received their information in the 2-minute, predigested packages of edited news could not experience this story in the same way.

In its first decade, CNN established the importance of the function it served. CNN was the only network on "live" on January 28, 1986, when the space shuttle *Challenger* exploded. For hours in 1987, audiences followed CNN's coverage of efforts to rescue Baby Jessica, the young Texas girl who had fallen into a well. That programming drew the highest rating CNN had received up to that time—a 6.6.

In summer 1989, CNN's coverage of Tiananmen Square riveted audience attention on the ongoing struggle of the Chinese students to democratize their country. In May 1989, those watching CNN's coverage of Tiananmen Square heard anchor Bernard Shaw confirm the extent to which live coverage had affected world affairs:

> I am being told that the Chinese government has closed the city of Beijing and no journalists are being allowed. . . . Unbelievably, we all came here to cover a summit, and we walked into a revolution. . . . Now we are being told that if we don't stop transmitting, the Chinese government will take our equipment. It will be interesting to see what happens. . . . President Bush is being quoted by reporters covering him in Maine, and it's being relayed to us. He is saying, "Word of the news blackout is very disturbing."

By 1990, we routinely expected to see "CNN LIVE" imprinted on newspaper photos of breaking news.

As noted earlier, CNN's *World Report* has modified the ideology underlying news as well. In the 2½-minute segments aired unedited from around the globe, we see the play of competing ideologies at work. The differences were evident in news stories following the invasion of Kuwait by Iraq. From the Palestinians came stories claiming that the U.N. sanctions against Iraq created a double standard; they pointed out that when U.N. resolutions had condemned Israeli actions, U.N. sanctions had been effectively blocked by a U.S. veto in the U.N. Security Council. Small countries dependent on Arab oil focused their stories primarily on the economic impact of the embargo; some declared they were being used as pawns in a U.S. game. One story from the Philippines emphasized the economic hardship imposed on that country by the inability of its nationals working in Kuwait to continue sending payments to their families at home. Only on CNN could audiences around the world hear the 76-minute speech that Iraq's leader Saddam Hussein sent to the United States to be broadcast to the public.

Because CNN broadcasts around the globe, it has become a vehicle for airing the competing claims of various nations and their leaders. Voices previously unlikely to be heard by U.S. audiences have received airplay. In September 1990, for example, CNN carried a speech by Jordan's King Hussein appealing for moderation by all sides in the Kuwait–Iraq crisis. King Hussein warned that the world was slipping into war in the Middle East just as it had slipped into World War I. Within days, the Saudi ambassador to the United States was on CNN delivering a rebuttal to Hussein's speech. The appropriate analogy, argued the ambassador, was the role Hitler's aggression played in starting World War II. One index of power is the ability to have one's message heard; by that measure, CNN has empowered countries and leaders that otherwise would play a smaller role on the international stage. In short, CNN has accelerated the emergence of a world with multiple foci.

At the same time, it has become a medium of information for world leaders themselves. Message after message from Saddam Hussein to the world indicated that he had been following world reaction. The presumed channel: CNN. And in August 1989, the *New York Times* reported a presidential aide noting that President Bush was considering ways to respond to the threat to U.S.

hostages in Lebanon while in his study "watching CNN." The president's press secretary, Marlin Fitzwater, told the reporter, "CNN has opened up a whole new communications system between governments in terms of immediacy and directness. In many cases, it's the first communication we have."[b]

Because of its on-the-spot coverage of the bombing of Baghdad as the war in the Persian Gulf began, scores of CBS, NBC, and ABC affiliates dumped their network coverage in favor of CNN. For example, WCCO, a CBS affiliate in Minneapolis, routinely interrupted the *CBS Evening News* to switch to CNN, and in a close three way ratings race for number 1, WCCO's ratings clobbered those of its NBC and ABC affiliate rivals during the opening week of the Persian Gulf War.

CNN's dominance of news coverage of the opening days of the war may have been a turning point in television news, shifting power from ABC, NBC, and CBS and toward CNN. "The gulf crisis is a defining event," said S. Robert Lichter of the Center for Media and Public Affairs in Washington, DC. "It's as if history is conspiring to help CNN." Larry Gerbrandt of Paul Kagan Associates, cable television analysts, agreed: "No one will ever doubt their advertising line again—that CNN is the most important network in the world. This is the greatest journalism story of the decade."[c]

EXERCISE: The rise of MSNBC and Fox News challenged CNN's place as the alternative to mainstream broadcast. Review the data on p. 7 on the audiences for CNN and Fox. How, if at all, would you expect competition from Fox to change CNN's coverage of domestic and world events?

[a]Hank Wittemore, *CNN: The Inside Story* (New York: Little, Brown, 1990), p. 192.
[b]Quoted in Wittemore, p. 302.
[c]Adapted from Bob Wisehart, "Amid the Chaos, CNN Establishes a New World Order," *Sacramento Bee,* 20 January 1991, pp. D1, D4.

CASE STUDY 1-2   Judging Newsworthiness

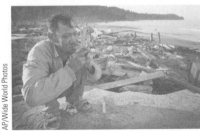

On the beach near Khao Lak, Thailand, Kusol Wetchakul offers prayers for the soul of his sister after she was killed by the devastating tsunami of December 26, 2004.

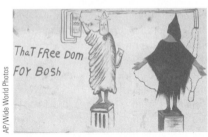

A mural in Sadr City, Iraq, depicts America's Statue of Liberty, at left, flipping the switch on electrical wires attached to a detainee in Abu Ghraib prison.

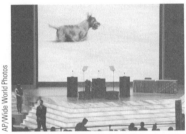

President Bush's dog, Barney, is seen in a Republican National Committee video presented at the Republican National Convention in New York.

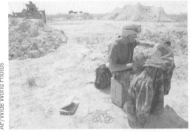

Time magazine photographer Robert Nickelsburg uses his jacket to protect his screen while filing pictures with a satellite phone near Ad Diwaniyah in central Iraq.

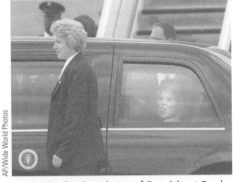

Jenna Bush, daughter of President Bush, sticks her tongue out at the media as she departs the airport in St. Louis.

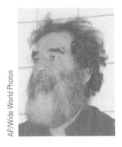

Former Iraqi President Saddam Hussein in custody after his arrest near his Tikrit home.

EXERCISE: What makes each of these pictures newsworthy? How are traditional news norms altered by the ability to transmit images from around the globe? What effect will such coverage have on politics? On the conduct of world leaders? On issues of concern?

credibility, heroism even, proffered a cheerful wave and a sage smile as his sloop moved out of the Vineyard harbor past the press jackals on the shore."[76]

In this changed environment, the press has lost the respect that enlarged its power to contest with the president over the national agenda. Forty-eight percent of the public believes that the media play a negative role in society; 46 percent trust the media less than they did 5 years ago; 79 percent think the media rearrange and distort the facts to make a better story; 71 percent believe legitimate news outlets are sinking to the level of tabloids with gossip and unsubstantiated stories; and 45 percent regard the press with indifference, 22 percent with respect, 20 percent with disgust, and 6 percent with admiration.[77] The Pew Research Center for the People and the Press released a survey report on June 8, 1998, that stated, "Public displeasure with the national news media is clear, but this sentiment has not eroded the credibility of major news organizations. . . . [T]he basic believability ratings have not changed since the Center's last survey in 1996."[78]

The effects were evident in the inability of the press to set the agenda on the Clinton-Lewinsky scandal or to establish it as a matter of importance in assessing Clinton's performance as president. From January 1998, when the scandal broke, through January 1999, in the wake of Clinton's impeachment by the House and trial in the Senate, public approval of Clinton's performance in office did not drop below 60 percent. That finding is remarkable in the face of a consistent assumption by reporters for much of that time that the affair with Lewinsky and Clinton's concealment of it would spell the end of the public's confidence in him as president.

TO SUM UP

We have presented some perspectives for examining the existing mass media in the United States. Increasingly the media are converging; however, their goal remains the same—attracting an audience for advertisers. Because some audiences are considered more desirable by advertisers, the sorts of programming those audiences prefer are likely to appear. As channels of communication proliferate, the mass media are increasingly shifting from a focus on large heterogeneous audiences with high disposable incomes, to smaller niche markets, but the underlying commercial dynamic remains largely the same.

Use InfoTrac® College Edition to access information on topics in this chapter from hundreds of periodicals and scholarly journals. Enter keyword and subject searches: *mass media, elite media, media ownership, media audience.*

CASE STUDY 1-3 · Twenty-Four-Hour News: The Clinton-Lewinsky Scandal

---

Coverage of the Clinton-Lewinsky scandal provides an example of the 24-hour phenomenon at work. The sexual harassment lawsuit filed against President Bill Clinton in 1997 by Paula Jones, a former Arkansas state aide, prompted *Newsweek* reporter Michael Isikoff to search for other alleged instances of sexual misconduct by the president. Isikoff received a tip on January 13, 1998, that Kenneth Starr, the Whitewater independent counsel, had begun investigating perjury and obstruction of justice charges in connection with the Jones sexual harassment lawsuit. Isikoff found that Starr had established a sting operation on a former White House intern who had indicated on tape to her friend and coworker, Linda Tripp, that she had had a sexual relationship with the president. When Isikoff informed his editors of this story, they decided to delay publishing the piece because they felt there was insufficient information on Monica Lewinsky and on the specifics of this new Starr investigation.

Matt Drudge, author of an online gossip column, *The Drudge Report,* found out about *Newsweek*'s decision and released the story himself on Sunday, January 18, on his website under the title "A White House Intern Carried on a Sexual Affair with the President of the United States!" Drudge, in effect, scooped *Newsweek*. The magazine responded by dispatching reporters to the 24-hour cable stations. The information flow after Drudge's report was a deluge. According to a journalist who wrote an analysis of coverage during the first weeks of the Clinton-Lewinsky crisis, "Americans found themselves besieged by an unprecedented rush of information. If the *Guinness Book of Records* recorded media stampedes, the Clinton crisis would be in first place, knocking out O. J. Simpson and the death of Princess Diana for massive, round-the-clock, soap-opera coverage."[a]

In the weeks that followed, several news venues ran stories with little corroboration, leading to corrections and retractions. On January 26, the *Dallas Morning News* reported that someone in the White House had witnessed the president and Lewinsky in a "compromising situation."[b] The story ran both on the newspaper's website and in the early edition of the paper. The Dallas report was re-reported in several media outlets around the country. The report was factually false. The anonymous source that originally provided the information retracted the statement. Two days after the story ran, the *News* explained that it now had another source who confirmed the story but that the original source "felt compelled to withdraw his confirmation of the initial story because of the time pressure and because those elements of the story he had initially outlined were incorrect."[c] The newspaper had failed to follow the standard rule of requiring two independent sources to corroborate the story. Even after gaining a second source, the *News* still reported information that never proved true.

In another example, a *New York Post* headline proclaimed, "The Big Creep Told Me to Lie," indicating that Lewinsky had made such a statement on Tripp's tape. No evidence surfaced to verify that remark.

In the 24-hour news cycle, journalists can release stories at any hour of the day. The newspaper or CNN reporter with the story wins the competition to get the story first. The *Wall Street Journal* ran a story on its website on February 4, 1998, saying that a White House steward had testified to the federal grand jury that he witnessed Clinton and Lewinsky alone in the study near the Oval Office. The newspaper did not check with the White House or the steward's lawyer before putting the story on the website. On February 9, the *Journal* retracted the story when it learned that the steward's testimony did not include those details.[d]

A second outcome of this 24-hour cycle is an expanded definition of who counts as a journalist. Matt Drudge played an important role in spreading unsubstantiated information. Because of the Internet's low cost and ease of use, it provides the opportunity for anyone with basic technical expertise to create a website. Drudge seized that opportunity to create his online column, *The Drudge Report.* Drudge, who has no formal journalism experience, devotes his website to political and social gossip. When he struck gold with Isikoff's story, he became famous overnight, and the national Fox network gave him his own television talk show. He also appeared on several political talk shows, including *Meet the Press.* There, NBC Washington bureau chief Tim Russert moderated the conversation between Drudge and *Newsweek*'s Isikoff. On the show, Drudge revealed that he knew that another White House staffer was going to come forward with her own story of sexual relations with the president. That claim, which went unchallenged by Russert, proved inaccurate.

Another novice, columnist Arianna Huffington, appeared on the 24-hour CNBC cable news show *Equal Time* to explain that she believed Clinton had had sex with the widow of an ambassador whose burial in Arlington National Cemetery had elicited controversy. She confessed, however, that she did not have proof. Nonetheless, the show carried the unsubstantiated rumor.

Source: Jennifer L. Stromer-Galley.
[a]Sherry Ricchiardi, "Standards Are the First Casualty," *American Journalism Review* (March 1998), p. 30.
[b]David Jackson, "Source Affirms Clinton Affair, Attorneys Say," *Dallas Morning News,* 26 January 1998, p. 1A.
[c]Carl P. Leubsdorf and David Jackson, "Intermediary Talks with Starr's Staff," *Dallas Morning News,* 28 January 1998, p. 1A.
[d]Ricchiardi, "Standards," p. 30.

SELECTED READINGS

Auletta, Ken. *Backstory: Inside the Business of News.* New York: Penguin Press, 2003.

Bagdikian, Ben H. *The New Media Monopoly.* Boston: Beacon Press, 2004.

Cappella, Joseph, and Kathleen Hall Jamieson. *Spiral of Cynicism.* Oxford: Oxford University Press, 1997.

Kimmel, Daniel M. *The Fourth Network: How Fox Broke the Rules and Reinvented Television.* Chicago: Ivar R. Dee, Publisher, 2004.

Kubey, Robert, and Mihaly Csikszentmihalyi. *Television and the Quality of Life: How Viewing Shapes Everyday Experience.* Hillsdale, NJ: Erlbaum, 1990.

Lichty, Lawrence W., and Malachi C. Topping. *American Broadcasting: A Source Book on the History of Radio and Television.* New York: Hastings House, 1975.

Mazzocco, Dennis. *Networks of Power: Corporate TV's Threat to Democracy.* Boston: South End Press, 1994.

McChesney, Robert W. *The Problem of the Media: U.S. Communication Politics in the 21st Century.* New York: Monthly Review Press, 2004.

Schudson, Michael. *Discovering the News: A Social History of American Newspapers.* New York: Basic Books, 1978.

———. *The Power of News.* Cambridge, MA: Harvard University Press, 1995.

Turow, Joseph. *Breaking Up America.* Chicago: University of Chicago Press, 1997.

———. *Media Systems in Society: Understanding Industries, Strategies, and Power.* New York: Longman, 1992.

———. *Media Today: An Introduction to Mass Communication.* Boston: Houghton Mifflin, 1999.

What Is News?

At 2:22 P.M. EST, December 16, 2004, the headlines on the web page of the *New York Times* read as follows:

"Britain's Highest Court Overturns Anti-Terrorism Law"
"Symantec Buys Veritas in 2nd Software Merger This Week"
"Hussein Meets His Defense Lawyer for First Time"
"Bush Says Social Security Overhaul Needed Now"

At the same time, LATimes.com featured five headlines, three of them similar to the ones on the *New York Times* page:

"Bush Says Now Is the Time to Overhaul Social Security"
"British Anti-Terror Law Suffers Blow"
"TV Portrayal of Religion Attacked"
"Symantec Closes Deal for Veritas"
"New Tape Attributed to Bin Laden"

Meanwhile the *Honolulu Star Bulletin* (Starbulletin.com) seemed more than half an ocean away from the preoccupations of the major West and East Coast dailies. Its headlines reported,

"Property Tax Values Soar"
"Elite Surfers Ride Waimea"
"Air Guard Volunteers Gear Up for Iraq"
"State Seals at Capitol to Get Safety Check"
"UH Lab Finds Shark 'Compass'"

None of the headlines that appeared in these U.S. papers made the top three of *Le Monde* (Le Monde.fr), which instead focused on the opening of the European Council in Brussels and the third-quarter economic indicators for the country.

Just what *is* news? Despite many efforts, no neat, satisfactory answer to that question can be given. Some deaths are news; many more are not. Some strikes draw headlines; others are ignored. Some protests become lead stories; others go unnoticed; still others are deliberately disregarded. The best answer seems to be that news is what reporters, editors, and producers decide is news.

For people on Oahu, the 20- to 30-foot waves at Waimea Bay and the pictures of surfers riding them were probably of more interest than they would be to a *New York Times* reader, unless of course that reader lives on Oahu and receives the national edition of the *Times* delivered daily. Because a person can drive to Waimea Bay from any place on that island in just over an hour, there is an immediacy to news about the waves that the striking down of the British antiterror law lacks.

The notion that what is news in New York may not be news in Los Angeles and what is news on both coasts might not be in Hawaii or Paris contradicts traditional notions that news is "out there," that reporters "just cover the story," that news is "what's happening." Instead, that answer says news is selected, even created, by newspeople. It claims that news is not just "the facts," but also rhetoric—messages influencing how readers and viewers perceive reality. We would be surprised if this were not the case.

News is gathered, written, edited, produced, and disseminated by human beings who are members of organizations and who have beliefs and values. Organizations such as networks have functions and goals as well as relationships to government, to regulatory agencies, to advertisers, to their parent companies, and to the vast audiences they seek to attract. These beliefs, values, functions, and interests are bound to influence the messages these networks publish and broadcast.

On a more complex level, this answer suggests that newsgatherers and news organizations are persuaders who shape our views of reality, who induce us to believe one thing rather than another. We examine this controversial argument in the next chapter. Here, however, we treat the simpler claim. We examine the concept of "hard news" or "spot news" (everyone concedes that "soft news," such as feature stories, is not objective) in order to set up a model of the news story. We explore the criteria governing what newspeople define as news, the constraints influencing what actually will be covered, and the conventions controlling how a news event will be presented.

We begin by identifying the norms that define what is newsworthy. Then we discuss the external and internal factors that influence what is actually covered and reported. Finally, we describe considerations that affect how the news is presented.

HARD NEWS DEFINED

Hard news is the report of an event that happened or that was disclosed within the previous 24 hours and treats an issue of ongoing concern. The crime story is the model for hard news.[1] A violent crime (murder, armed robbery, rape) is an event, a definable happening. It occurs between individuals (perpetrator and victim). It is dramatic, conflict-filled, and involves extreme physical action and emotional intensity. It disrupts legitimate order and threatens the community. Ordinarily, what happened can be told in a short, simple story, and information about the event can be verified by official sources such as the police or the district attorney. The crime scene (or its effects) is usually visual, is easily reduced to tape or photograph, and is part of the regular beat of a reporter.

A typical crime has all the qualities of a newsworthy event: it is (1) personalized—it happened to specific individuals; (2) dramatic, conflict-filled, controversial, violent;

(3) actual and concrete, not theoretical or abstract; (4) novel or deviant; and (5) linked to issues of ongoing concern to the news media. These characteristics reflect the qualities of mass media messages discussed in Chapter 1.

1. Hard News Is Personalized, about Individuals

Mass media news must be accessible to, and interesting for, a diverse mass audience. Consequently, news stories must be clear, simple, and attention-getting. Hard news is personalized and individualized because such stories create wide audience identification. We care more about the reactions of a hurricane victim than about statistics on the force of the wind, and we are eager to see the person who faced down the tank in Tiananmen Square. The human connection allows us to imagine ourselves in the situation or to create meaning out of what is puzzling and complex. Unlike stories about destruction of the ozone layer or the spread of nuclear weapons, stories about individuals have causes and consequences on a manageable scale. Individuals can act or speak in a time span that fits into a news story, and it is easier to visualize a person than an idea, a process, or a structure.

An interview can personify an abstract idea or clothe an idea in living flesh. So, for example, as former *MacNeil/Lehrer NewsHour* anchor Robert MacNeil noted, "In Somalia, it was not merely the pictures that wrung the hearts of the public. The pictures were made more eloquent by the words of Audrey Hepburn of UNICEF and Mary Robinson of Northern Ireland."[2] And when the Abu Ghraib stories broke in spring 2004, alleging that Iraqi prisoners had been abused at the hands of U.S. soldiers, it was the evocative pictures of prisoner humiliation that gave the story its emotional punch. (Note the use of the word "pictured" in the official report: "The pictured abuses, unacceptable even in wartime, were not part of authorized interrogations nor were they even directed at intelligence targets," noted the Final Report of the Independent Panel to Review Department of Defense Detention Operations.[3]) The personal and individual character of hard news, its ability to be captured in pictures and its capacity to evoke pictures in our minds, reflects the use of interviews and human sources as the bases for the research underlying most news stories.

Interviews not only personalize but also allow reporters to draw on the expertise of others, an important advantage for reporters, who are usually generalists, not specialists. The news is personalized and individualized by heavy coverage of the president; of congressional leaders; of the wealthy, powerful, and prestigious; and of sports, stage, screen, and fashion celebrities. These are the "stars" of the news who, like the star hired to lure us to a film, are intended to draw the mass audience to the news channel.

The emphasis on individuals can create distortion. In finding a spokesperson, the news media generally choose the more flamboyant, articulate, and theatrical characters who are willing to assume that role, not necessarily the most thoughtful or most central figures.

Defining hard news as personal, about individuals, means that it is not about processes or the exploration of ideas; it is the story of a group or a movement only to the extent that a group or movement can be personified by one member's testimony. The focus on individuals simplifies and clarifies. It creates audience identification; it reflects journalistic reliance on human sources and on the interview.

The tendency to focus on people rather than processes means that some important questions may go unanswered. Former *Washington Post* editor Ben Bagdikian recalls the

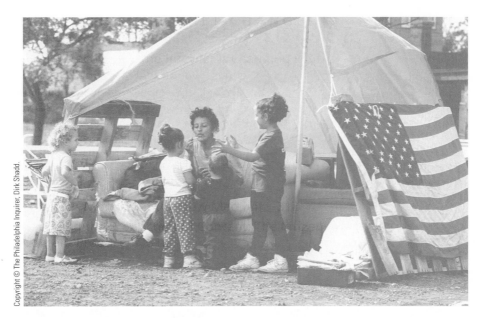

Elba Gonzalez shares the tent city with her children.

experience in the 1980s of seeing for the first time the homeless begging for money. "Newspapers and television had lots of stories about the homeless," he notes. "But I kept waiting year after year for our best newspaper or broadcast journalists to ask [the] . . . right question and highlight the answers: 'Why, in the midst of this wonderful prosperity of the 1980s do we have for the first time since the Great Depression, growing numbers of men, women, and children living in the streets?' "[4]

That pattern persisted in July 1995 when a tent city erected by the homeless in Philadelphia drew a front-page photo and story from the *Philadelphia Inquirer*. Under banners reading "Philadelphia, House Your People," "We Want Houses," and "*No Casas No Paz* (No Houses No Peace)," the approximately thirty homeless people—half of them children—had set up five donated tents in a vacant lot. When outdoor temperatures persisted in the 90-degree F range, concerns about children living outside in the heat were raised by welfare workers. "Being homeless is not grounds for taking away anyone's children," a housing official is quoted as saying. "But the impact of the heat is something we're concerned about."

Those concerns are the stuff of which drama is made. At the center of the drama is a young mother, shown in the picture seated on a torn couch under a small tent with her three children. At the side of the tent, the Kensington Welfare Rights Union has placed a U.S. flag, a symbol inviting readers to see irony in the plight of the destitute family.

Conflict was added to the mix with the visit of welfare workers to the site, coupled with the fire department turning off the hydrants and the police ticketing nearby residents who were assisting the protesters. Capturing conflict and drama and personalizing the issue by focusing on mothers and children camped in an otherwise vacant lot, the *Philadelphia Inquirer*'s story was headed "Camp Seeks, and Fears, City's Notice."

CASE STUDY 2-1   Focusing on the Individual to Make News

In spring 1990, newspaper readers read that *Outweek* had published gay rights activists' statements that a number of prominent and presumed heterosexual celebrities, newspeople, and politicians were gay. Gay rights activists Michael Petrelis and Carl Goodman held a news conference in Washington, DC, in May 1990, to read out the names of twelve individuals in public life whom they claimed were gay. Using the opportunity provided by live television, a gay author "outed" a gubernatorial candidate in a northeastern state on a talk show.

Billboards advocating the reelection of Republican Senator Mark Hatfield were altered to read "closeted gay . . . living a lie . . . voting to oppress." And immediately after his death, supermarket tabloids carried stories claiming that business tycoon Malcolm Forbes had been gay. *Outweek,* whose national circulation is 40,000, published a detailed account of what it reported to be Forbes's activities.

Outing is controversial within the gay community. The National Gay and Lesbian Task Force, the Human Rights Campaign Fund, and the Lambda Legal Defense and Education Fund oppose outing, calling it blackmail and psychological terror. Proponents of outing argue, "If I say someone is straight, I have not revealed anything private. But if I say he is gay, there is the impression that I have." Outing for such activists is a claiming of "role-models."[a]

By featuring supposed revelations about individuals who are of ongoing news interest, those favoring outing capitalize on news norms. "Revealing," "uncovering," and "exposing" are words of honor to most reporters. But other news norms argue against coverage. Those listed as gay—including television and film stars Richard Chamberlain and John Travolta—have denied it,

and those sources listing them have provided nothing that sustains the tests of proof. In addition, even in an age obsessed with the private lives of public figures, some find such publicizing an invasion of privacy.

In the column "Press Gallery" published in the weekly *Roll Call,* a publication focused on the actions of Congress, two reporters framed the issues raised by the Petrelis and Goodman press conference this way: "Reporters were skeptical, since, among other things, Petrelis and Goodman gave no proof of the listees' alleged sexual preference. Another problem for the reporters was trying to figure out why they should be reporting this exceedingly private information or misinformation." The reporters concluded: "PG [Press Gallery] contends that in almost every case, a politician's sexual preference, fidelity, bizarre boudoir behavior, or other personal peccadilloes are not fair game unless the politician is stupid enough to invite scrutiny. . . . We also agree . . . that rank hypocrisy also qualifies a Member for disclosure."[b]

But press behavior was not that clear-cut. The *Philadelphia Inquirer* and NPR among others named Mark Hatfield as the senator whose billboards were being defaced. Some sources, *Roll Call* and the *Washington Times* among them, covered the press conference but published no names. Some outlets, the *Washington Post* and the *New York Times,* remained silent.

[a]Michael Matza, "Outrage," *Philadelphia Inquirer*, 28 June 1990, pp. 1, 8E.
[b]"How the Media Should Deal with the 'Outing' of Alleged Homosexual Members," *Roll Call,* 4 June 1990, pp. 14, 16.

The subhead suggested conflict: "The homeless camp is, in part, a protest. So far, it's getting only unwanted attention."

The *Inquirer*'s article admits that the camp drew press attention only when the prospect of conflict with the city arose. "For a while—as flies buzzed around their donated food, as the heat hit record highs and the rain fell in torrents, as children bathed at fire hydrants and slept in stuffy tents staked in dusty gravel—it looked as if nobody would notice," said the article. "Then, for better or worse, the homeless camp at the corner of Fourth Street and Lehigh Avenue started getting attention. The fire department turned off the hydrants."[5]

With shelters overcrowded, the tent city was the welfare rights group's way of trying to impel city action, action predicated on the sympathetic coverage of local news outlets. The article answered the question "Why are the homeless there?" with two explanations: This was a protest to draw attention to the absence of adequate housing, and the shelters were overcrowded. Some questions went unasked: Why are the shelters overcrowded? Is there an increase in homelessness in summer? Has the city reduced the number of housing units? Cut shelter capacity? Is it significant that all of the homeless quoted in the article bear Latino surnames? Is that an indication that the problem is uniquely concentrated in this group? And because the family shown in the photo has recently moved from Puerto Rico, is this a problem occasioned by immigration? As important is the absence of a larger social context: Is this a problem unique to Philadelphia or common to other large urban areas as well? Is it local or national in scope? And, if national, what is being done or can be done about it?

As this example illustrates, personalizing issues is a problem both because it diverts attention from more substantive questions and because the choice of whom to cover frequently is skewed by their class, race, ethnicity, and gender—or the class, race, ethnicity, and gender of the chooser. For example, during the week of the highly publicized rape of a white investment banker in Central Park allegedly (but inaccurately, as it turned out) by a nonwhite gang, twenty-eight other women in New York also reported rapes. Nearly all of these were women of color, and their assaults, including at least one of comparable brutality, went largely unreported by the press.[6]

2. Hard News Is Dramatic, Conflict-Filled, and Violent

Mass media news must gain and hold audience attention. Presenting hard news as drama is a way to structure a story to do just that. Drama begins with what is called an "inciting action," an event that disrupts normal routines (this is the event that becomes the "news peg," discussed in the next section). Conflict escalates in rising action to a climax, the high point of tension, which is followed by an unraveling or resolution. Such structure, as illustrated by jokes, plays, novels, and the episodes of television series, is beloved by audiences and can evoke intense participation and identification.

The typical news story is organized dramatically to identify a problem, to describe it in a narrative of rising action, to locate the protagonists and set them against each other (usually in short interviews), and to create some sort of resolution. This format gives coherence to data, and it makes an item a "story" in the most literal sense, a story that is likely to gain and hold an audience. Hard news is exciting, and the essence of excitement is drama.

Conflict is an intrinsic element in drama; drama's rising action unfolds through increasingly intense conflict. Conflict disrupts routine and is thus novel and unusual (another criterion discussed in the next section). Conflicts are newsworthy events, and reporting conflict is a way to create interest. The presidential election campaign that runs for more than a year is treated as a horse race or a sports contest in part so that it can be divided into specific events: primary victories, caucus defeats, slugging it out in debates, or going one-on-one with hecklers during a speech. Such events are filled with the drama and conflict characteristic of hard news. News coverage emphasizes conflict by interviewing and quoting opposing sides on an issue; such interviews not only allow a reporter to remain detached, but they also create an impression of fair and balanced coverage.

BOX 2-1   Write a Story

In 1963, Reuven Frank, then president of NBC News, wrote a memo to his staff that read as follows: "Every news story should, without any sacrifice of probity or responsibility, display the attributes of fiction, of drama. It should have structure and conflict, problem and denouement, rising action and falling action—a beginning, a middle, and an end."[a]

[a]Cited by John Corry, "TV: The News Movie, New Form of Program," *New York Times*, 26 January 1988, p. 24Y.

CASE STUDY 2-2   The Role of the Media in the 1994 Health-Care Reform Debate

A comprehensive study of the news coverage of the 1994 health-care reform debate concluded that:

- Reporters tended not to cover the very real areas of agreement between Democrats and Republicans. Consensus, although necessary for the survival and passage of a health-care bill, seemed uninteresting to reporters. Republicans and Democrats did agree on certain key issues. Senate Minority Leader Bob Dole and President Clinton agreed that reform was needed. They also agreed that insurance purchasing pools of some sort were a good idea. (The reasons were straightforward. Such groups spread risks across large groups of consumers and have the marketplace clout to hold down costs.) Unresolved were the size, composition, and management of the groups. Clinton called them "alliances" and made them mandatory; Dole called them "voluntary purchasing cooperatives."

There was also bipartisan support for some insurance reform proposals. Each of the seven plans before Congress in February—three sponsored by Democrats, four by Republicans—would have barred insurance companies from denying policies to those with existing illnesses, and would have provided "portability" by allowing workers to keep their insurance when they switched jobs. However, these points of agreement did not receive much attention from journalists.

- Journalists focused on some plans more than others. The Clinton plan framed the debate. In print, the Clinton plan was about five times more likely to be mentioned, and in broadcast, it was about four times more likely to be mentioned than the second most-mentioned plan, which in both print and broadcast was a modification of the Clinton plan, backed by Senate Majority Leader George Mitchell. In the process, plans with substantial congressional support—

This focus on conflict creates imbalance in the reporting of both international and domestic affairs. Reporting of foreign affairs tends, for example, to stress conflict, whereas some in elected positions might instead be trying to reach accommodation on particular foreign policy questions. Thus, for example, early in 2000 when U.S. immigration officials ruled that a young Cuban boy, the lone survivor in an attempt by his mother to reach Florida by boat, should be returned to his father in Cuba, news coverage gravitated toward those who challenged that decision and as a result prolonged the confrontation with the Cuban government. When Republican Congressman Dan Burton issued a congressional subpoena that would require the boy to remain in the United States to testify, he received national news attention. Meanwhile, President Clinton, who repeatedly noted that he wanted to keep politics out of it and who supported the decision of the immigration officials, received less news play.

Violence is the most dramatic form of conflict, and it is nearly always treated as newsworthy. The attraction of violence explains the relatively heavy coverage of crime and its capacity to sell papers and attract viewers. So routine have some types of crime become, however, that they draw only perfunctory coverage. "Repeatedly bludgeoned with crime and violence by every medium," writes *Baltimore Sun* police reporter David Simon, our culture is now so bored with ordinary tragedy that we only become excited by those crimes that are larger, more unlikely and more bizarre. During the year I spent

---

Wellstone-McDermott to the Clinton plan's left, and Michel to the Clinton plan's right—were effectively denied the national stage.

- Reporters were interested in conflict, sometimes to the exclusion of covering other health plans. Media focus on the clash between Clinton and Cooper, both Democrats with separate health plans, shunted into the shadows the four Republican plans, eclipsing from public view some very real policy options. Senator John Chafee (R-RI) proposed a plan that provided universal coverage, but, unlike Clinton's, did not require that employers provide it. Other plans— including those by Senator Bob Michel of Illinois and Senator Phil Gramm of Texas—offered tax breaks to buy insurance and tax-sheltered savings accounts to pay for coverage, and other ideas.

- Viable policy options were prematurely judged "dead" by reporters and hence did not receive coverage. Early in the process, seven different pieces of legislation, each representing a different plan,

were simmered down to two—and in the process, important ideas slipped from public view. A world traveler who returned to the United States in mid-January would have surmised from the news coverage that only Clinton's plan and the Cooper-Breaux plan were before Congress.

When researchers queried reporters about the focus on Clinton and Cooper-Breaux rather than Michel or Wellstone-McDermott, they were told that neither the Wellstone-McDermott nor the Republican alternative (Michel) had any chance of passing. That prophecy proved false. One of the five bills that emerged from committee included a single-payer provision in the form of extension of Medicare, similar to the Wellstone-McDermott bill. And the compromise proposal being crafted as the legislative process drew to a close bore more than a passing resemblance to the Michel bill.[a]

[a]From "Media in the Middle: Fairness and Accuracy in the 1994 Health Care Reform Debate," a report by the Annenberg Public Policy Center of the University of Pennsylvania, funded by The Robert Wood Johnson Foundation (February 1995).

CASE STUDY 2-3   The Drama of School Violence

On Tuesday afternoon, April 20, 1999, images of children being rushed from their suburban school appeared first on cable and then on broadcast news. The story was filled with suspense. Initial news reports indicated that gunfire had been heard. There were hostages, said some reports. Then came reports of dead students and a dead teacher. Finally the news emerged of bombs in the schools, bodies that might have been booby-trapped. As the story unfolded, viewers learned that two white teenagers had killed twelve class-mates and a teacher. Analyst Andrew Tyndall found that the evening network newscasts gave the story of the killings at Littleton 144 minutes of air play during the four days following the event.

Why so much coverage? First, the news was dramatic, violent, and filled with involving visuals including those of children leaving the school, SWAT teams, and victims.

The story was also novel, a deviation from expectations and from routine. Whereas violence is expected in urban schools, this massacre—which produced more deaths than any previous school-related shooting—had happened in a peaceful suburban school. Although one might have ex-

pected the killers to be malcontents at the bottom of their class, these were kids from good homes who brought home good report cards.

The story focused on individuals, particularly on the two who did the killing, and on their home life, their parents, and their friends. "This was every parent's nightmare," observed CNN's Jeff Greenfield. Coverage also focused on the death of a young woman who had been asked by her would-be killer whether she believed in God. She answered that she did, and he pulled the trigger.

The story also fit into the pattern of past stories of school violence, including an incident in March 1998 when an 11-year-old and a 13-year-old killed four children and a teacher, as well as an incident in 1997 that resulted in three deaths. Paul Friedman, executive producer of *ABC News*, explained that the story raised "all the questions we all have about raising children and getting along with adolescents and understanding adolescents, as parents and authority figures trying to do the right thing."[a]

[a]Lawrie Mifflin, "Media," *New York Times*, 3 May 1999, p. C13.

---

in the Baltimore homicide unit, the only murders to make the *Baltimore Sun*'s front page involved two separate incidents of arson that claimed the lives of three and two young toddlers, respectively. The rape and murder of an 11-year-old girl, abducted as she walked home from a city library branch, made the front page of the metro section. The death of an 81-year-old woman, sodomized and then suffocated in her South Baltimore home, ran on an inside page, next to the weather chart.[7]

Still, a violent event is likely to be a matter of community concern, of great interest to many people. This is particularly true when the vulnerable have been the victims of violence.

3. Hard News Is Action, an Event, an Identifiable Occurrence

Hard news relates the details of a specific occurrence that is the occasion for a news report, the "peg" on which the news story is hung. An event is concrete and discrete; ordinarily it can be explained clearly in a limited time or space. A single event is more likely to be intelligible and to be a novel, dramatic event involving specific individuals. Many events can be photographed or taped, an important consideration for both print and television journalism. This norm, like the emphasis on individuals, works against coverage of processes or ideas.

Although hard news is believed to involve fast-breaking, unforeseen events, news organizations typically cover events that can be scheduled in advance, so reporters and camera crews can be present and record them. As a result, newspeople tend to cover news conferences and briefings, speeches, announcements, ceremonies, and other scheduled events. This is one reason that pseudo-events (events staged just for media coverage) and what are called "photo opportunities" are effective ways to manipulate news coverage.[8] The problem of needing to know in advance about the unexpected explains why reporters are tempted to ask participants to re-create what happened when faced with a situation such as a riot.

In his study of a California newspaper, Mark Fishman found that journalistic concepts of newsworthy events coincided with what he called "bureaucratic phase structures," the ways various bureaucracies punctuate processes in order to divide them into stages—for example, arrests, indictments, verdicts, and sentencings in crime news. He found that journalists depended on such definitions for the meaning and relevance of what they observed, for determining which events were newsworthy, which accounts were suspicious or reliable, what was controversial, and what constituted the sides and terms of a controversy.[9] These were the bases on which journalists decided what counted as an event.

Hard news is the story of an act or an occurrence. This single, isolated event is simpler to communicate and easier to understand than a process or an idea. It is likely to be dramatic and novel and to involve individuals. The emphasis on events, however, reveals a contradiction at the heart of newsgathering: the desire to cover events as they happen and the need to cover events that are scheduled in advance.

As coverage of homelessness illustrates, tying news stories to a specific event limits, even prevents, the treatment of processes, structures, patterns, and systems.

4. Hard News Is Novel, Deviant, Out of the Ordinary

Hard news reports what happened today, not what happens every day. Although novel events are more likely to be covered if they are part of a current theme in the news, hard news is the opposite of the routine and accepted. The syndicated column "News of the Weird" is a flagrant example of this norm.

One study concluded that all mass media content is entertainment in that it is conducted "outside the expected limits of routine behavior."[10] Even news stories are entertainment designed to attract and hold a mass audience. For example, during the times that surveys are conducted by television rating services, local television news programs air "lurid and titillating news features, most often those with a sex or violence angle that can be heavily promoted, ideally as a weeklong series."[11]

The problems with this entertainment requirement—related to the criterion of novelty that we describe—are suggested by Tom Wicker: "The dull, the routine, the unexciting, is seldom seen as news, although . . . the dull, routine, unexciting management of rates and routes for the railroads, truckers, and airlines may affect far more Americans in their daily lives than some relatively more glamorous presidential directive or congressional action."[12]

Reporters, chosen partly for their nose for what is new and unusual, have a low tolerance for the long haul of a complex story that may take years to develop. This well-known media emphasis on novelty also tempts protesters to invent ever more extreme ways to dramatize their cause in order to obtain coverage.

Those protesting the development and use of nuclear power illustrate this problem. Their concerns were dramatized in 1978 with the accident at Three Mile Island, and they received substantial press coverage. Since that time, however, press interest has been low, although protesters believe that their concerns continue to be legitimate, and work on nuclear plants continues. Even the disaster at Chernobyl in 1986 did not help them, once it was established that the Soviet plant had few similarities to plants in the United States. As a result, U.S. protesters become more desperate to attract journalistic attention. For example, one antinuclear protester, participating in a demonstration marking the thirty-sixth anniversary of the first nuclear test at the Nevada Test Site, knelt in front of a bus carrying workers to the test site and poured red fluid from a baby's bottle. As sheriff's deputies lifted her from the road, she screamed: "This is the blood of the future! This is the blood of our children!"[13]

Resource-poor groups often have to depend on deviance and disruption to receive media coverage. In her study of newspaper access, Edie Goldenberg concluded that "the more a group's political goals deviate from prevailing social norms, the more likely the group is to gain access to the press, other things being equal."[14] Elsewhere she writes that "the intensity of a conflict is a good predictor of coverage, . . . 'unruly groups,' those who initiate violence or strikes, are relatively successful compared with those that do not."[15] As these comments indicate, the emphasis on novelty in hard news is closely related to its focus on drama, conflict, and violence; the novelty of a large demonstration is likely to be overshadowed by the violent acts of a few.

Similarly, the news media are more likely to cover a protest group representative who is flamboyant and theatrical, regardless of who has the largest following.

5. Hard News Reports Events Linked to Issues Prevalent in the News at the Time

News coverage follows certain issues at various times, such as the issue of civil rights in the 1960s, women's liberation for a period in the 1970s, and gay rights in the 1980s and 1990s. For example, when the United States began its space program, each launch received detailed news coverage. Much of this coverage concerned whether or not NASA was ready to launch the rockets involved in the *Mercury, Gemini,* and *Apollo* programs and whether flights that included astronauts were safe. As years passed without disasters, however, the space program generally, as well as the shuttle launches begun in 1983, came to seem routine, and newspeople began to treat them perfunctorily.

Accordingly, reporters did not continue to probe questions of safety and were caught unawares by the *Challenger* disaster. Television and print reporters did not know of the imminent danger to the *Challenger* space shuttle due to the likelihood that the seals—called O-rings—in the solid-rocket boosters might malfunction because of the cold weather at launch time. They had grown accustomed to successful shuttle flights and relied on NASA's assurances that all was well.

BOX 2-2   Who's the News?

"[E]lection news now focuses more on the jour- nalists than on the candidates. In the 1960s, when presidential candidates appeared on television they were usually pictured speaking: 84 percent of the time, candidates' images on the screen were accompanied by their words. The average sound bite was 40 seconds in length. In contrast, the average sound bite in 1992 was less than 9 sec- onds, and pictures of the candidates were not usually accompanied by the sound of their voices. For every minute the candidates spoke on the net- work evening news in 1992, the reporters who were covering them talked 6 minutes."[a]

[a]Thomas E. Patterson, *Tomorrow's News, Project Vote Smart,* Center for National Independence in Politics (Sum- mer 1995): 1.

The assumption that shuttle flights were routine and safe produced a kind of report- ing that put pressure on NASA to launch the *Challenger* on January 28, 1986, despite unsafe conditions. Richard G. Smith, head of the Kennedy Space Center in Florida at the time of the *Challenger* explosion, argued that snide news stories about aborted launches had created "98 percent of the pressure" to go ahead with the ill-fated *Chal- lenger* flight.

What Smith was referring to included statements by newscasters, such as those by Dan Rather on the *CBS Evening News.* Rather referred to news about one delay as "the latest on today's high-tech low comedy" and later said that because of postponements, the launch was now known as "Mission Impossible."[16] What became newsworthy were delays—launches aborted for reasons of safety—and these delays became an ongoing story of implied incompetence, a news perspective that may have contributed to the disaster itself. Similar pressures to launch may have been implicated in the *Columbia* space shuttle disaster in February 2002, in which seven astronauts were killed.[17]

Stories about continuing issues generate audience identification and create the com- forting sense of a pattern in the complexity of modern life. The coverage of individuals who are certifiably newsworthy reflects this concern for continuity in the news. The newsworthy are those who have made news in the past, such as elected officials; athletic champions; and film, television, or rock stars. For example, a presidential candidate labeled a "front-runner"—a status conferred on those who win early caucus or primary votes—becomes more newsworthy and consequently gets more news coverage.

Some themes are woven into the very nature of newsgathering in the United States. These include the following:

1. *Appearance versus reality.* This reflects an emphasis on conflict and the "objective" role of skeptical newsgatherers who uncover hypocrisy. On the positive side this theme holds public officials to high standards; on the negative, it invites the cyn- ical assumption that those who aspire to lead are all corrupt.
2. *Little guys versus big guys.* This theme reflects an emphasis on the personal and individual by taking a particular interest in the underdog or outsider or exposing corrupt and self-interested actions by the powerful against the powerless.

BOX 2-3   How Do News Themes Operate in the News Accounts of the Nomination of Bernard Kerik to Serve as Homeland Security Secretary?

Bernard Kerik was corrections commissioner in New York City from 1998 to 2000 and then New York City police commissioner during the administration of Mayor Rudy Giuliani, a position he held at the time of the terrorist attacks of September 11. When the Bush administration announced that Kerik was the president's choice to serve as secretary for Homeland Security in the second Bush term, the initial press accounts cast him as the protagonist in a Horatio Alger story. "A Street Cop's Rise from High School Dropout to Cabinet Nominee," noted a headline in the *New York Times*.[a] "Homeland Security Nominee Goes from 'Lost Son' to Security Czar," said a headline filed by the Newhouse News Service.[b]

The accounts also highlighted Kerik's role in protecting the city on September 11 as a central biographical feature that burnished his qualifications for the new job. "When the second jet crashed into the World Trade Center on September 11, 2001," said that article in the *Times,* "Bernard B. Kerik, the New York Police Commissioner, was standing a block away, shouting evacuation orders through the torrent of debris. For the man in charge of protecting New York, he wrote later, that moment 'was unimaginable.'"[c]

Press investigations raised a counternarrative. "Spotlight on mixed legacy," said *Newsday.*[c] "Some view him as an underdog who beat the odds, as others say his rise was political and cite ex-aides scandal."[d] "Kerik's Surveillance Activity in Saudi Arabia Is Disputed;" said a headline in the *Washington Post*, "Cabinet Pick Is Accused of Carrying Out Hospital Chief's Agenda."[e]

On December 10, Kerik asked the Bush administration to withdraw his nomination. Again the headlines told the story. "New Yorker Bernard Kerik Withdraws over a Former Household Employee Who Might Have Entered the United States Illegally," said the *LA Times*. "Former New York Police Commissioner Bernard Kerik on Friday withdrew himself from consideration as the nation's next Homeland Security chief, saying he had determined that a former household employee might have been an illegal immigrant," noted the article. "Kerik was Bush's choice to head the department charged with enforcing the nation's immigration laws, including policing the borders to prevent foreign nationals from crossing illegally."[f]

Perhaps Kerik was *not* the little guy who had earned his way to the top but someone who abused power and violated the law. Again the headlines synopsized this second story line. "News Finds Kerik in Cash Conflict: Got Thousands, Didn't Report It."[g]

Perhaps appearance had not represented reality but instead camouflaged secrets. "One secret after another has tumbled out since the collapse of Bernard B. Kerik's nomination as homeland security secretary—an undisclosed marriage, clandestine love affairs, unsavory business ties and unreported gifts," noted the *New York Times*.[h]

News reports also raised a larger issue: What did missing this and other information about potential abuse of power say about the vetting process of Bush administration officials? "Issue of Kerik in '00 Puts Focus on Vetting Issue," noted a *New York Times* headline.[i]

[a]Kenin Flynn, William Rashbaum, Eric Lipton, and Christopher Drew, 3 December 2004, p. A1.
[b]4 December 2004.
[c]Ibid.
[d]Graham Rayman and Dan Janison, 5 December 2004, p. A3.
[e]John Mintz and Lucy Shackelford, 8 December 2004, p. A3.
[f]Warren Vieth and Edwin Chen, 11 December, p. A1.
[g]*New York Daily News,* 12 December 2004, p. 4.
[h]Nina Bernstein and Robin Stein, "Mystery Woman in Kerik Case: Nanny," 16 December 2004, p. A33.
[i]14 December 2004, p. A1.

BOX 2-4   Is the Press More Willing to Believe Those in Power at Some Times Than at Others?

"The executive editor of the *Washington Post*, Leonard Downie Jr, said in yesterday's newspaper that he and other top editors had erred before the war in Iraq by not giving front-page prominence to more articles that cast doubt on the Bush administration's claims that Saddam Hussein was hiding weapons of mass destruction.

"'We were so focused on trying to figure out what the administration was doing that we were not giving the same play to people who said it wouldn't be a good idea to go to war and were questioning the administration's rationale,' Mr. Downie said in a front-page article that assessed the newspaper's prewar coverage. . . . In May, The *New York Times* published a 1,220-word article in which the newspaper's editors acknowledged that in the run-up to war they had not been skeptical enough about articles that depended 'at least in passed on information from a circle of Iraqi informants, defectors and exiles bent on "regime change" in Iraq whose credibility has come under increasing public debate.'"[a]

The *New York Times'* mea culpa said, "Over the last year this newspaper has shone the bright light of hindsight on decisions that led the United States into Iraq. We have examined the failings of American and allied intelligence, especially on the issue of Iraq's weapons and possible Iraqi connections to international terrorists. We have studied the allegations of official gullibility and hype. It is past time we turned the same light on ourselves. . . . We have found a number of instances of coverage that was not as rigorous as it should have been. In some cases, information that was controversial then, and seems questionable now, was insufficiently qualified or allowed to stand unchallenged. Looking back, we wish we had been more aggressive in re-examining the claims as new evidence emerged—or failed to emerge."[b]

[a]Jacques Steinberg, "Washington Post Rethinks Its Coverage of War Debate," *New York Times,* 13 August 2004, p. A5. Copyright © 2004 by The New York Times Co. Reprinted with permission.
[b]The Editors, "The Times and Iraq," *New York Times,* 26 May 2004, p. A10. Copyright © 2004 by The New York Times Co. Reprinted with permission.

3. *Good against evil.* The essence of drama, this theme is related to crime as a news model and to investigative journalism as a norm for reporting and the reporter's role.

4. *Efficiency versus inefficiency.* This is usually an attempt to uncover waste and mismanagement, illustrating the emphasis on politics and government in the news.

5. *The unique versus the routine.* Reflecting a stress on novelty, this theme is illustrated by the human interest stories appearing at the end of most newscasts or in syndicated newspaper columns, such as "News of the Weird."

All these themes presume that there are identifiable forces at work in the world and that they usually are in conflict. News coverage influences us by defining what the sides are and what each side means.

Themes provide continuity in the news and help make sense out of a welter of happenings. They increase the potential for audience identification. Some themes reflect the journalist's role and the concept that reporters have of their function in this society.

These five criteria—a focus on individuals, drama-conflict-violence, discrete events, novelty or deviance, and ongoing issues or themes—define what newsgatherers consider newsworthy. As the coverage of the 1999 shootings in Littleton, Colorado, suggests, activities that meet these criteria are likely to obtain news coverage.

WHAT IS COVERED AND REPORTED

Newsgathering is affected by access, costs, and limitations of time and space. News stories must attract and hold an audience and avoid offending advertisers, audiences, and media owners.

These factors influence what choices newspeople make and ultimately determine which stories will be printed and aired.

Audience Interest

Audiences are interested in news that affects their lives. Until the terrorist attack of September 11, 2001, it was unlikely that news of a terrorist attack in Russia would invite much U.S. viewer attention. After September 11, its relevance to U.S. citizens is clearer. Because the war in Iraq is controversial and costing lives and large amounts of money, interest in it is high as well. But gas prices drew more audience attention in 2004 than either, and high on the list of closely watched stories were hurricanes and the flu vaccine shortage.

External Constraints

Some of the factors influencing news coverage lie outside the event or medium itself. These are external constraints. If an event is to be covered, reporters must know it is to happen; if it is to be videotaped, there must be enough advance notice to get a camera crew to the scene. The event must happen early enough to let reporters meet their deadlines, and the cost of the coverage must seem reasonable. In addition, coverage is affected by competition from other media and from other newsworthy events.

Access   News organizations struggle to impose order in the midst of chaos. Reporters often have little or no idea when or where the news will break: when or where a crime will be committed, a riot will break out, or one country will attack another. Thus reporters are assigned to beats so they can monitor the goings-on in places where newsworthy events often occur—the police station, city hall, the State Department, the House of Representatives, the Supreme Court, the White House. The chance that an event will be covered is increased if it is part of a reporter's regular beat, or if official sources that are regularly consulted call it to her or his attention. For instance, one study of 2,850 stories appearing in the *New York Times* and the *Washington Post* found that such routine channels accounted for 58.2 percent of the articles.[18]

Many newsworthy events fall between the cracks of assigned beats. Reporters may be assigned to substantive beats, such as energy or the environment, to overcome this problem. In addition, general assignment reporters are dispatched to cover breaking stories or to ferret out newsworthy events. The beat system is really a pattern of access for reporters. It is a method by which reporters survey the scene to learn what is happening and by which they develop "informed, reliable sources" of information. Modern news organizations rely heavily on officials in government bureaucracies. Events on regular beats or those confirmed by official sources tend to be covered and reported; events outside these beats or denied by official sources usually go unpublished.[19]

BOX 2-5   Foreign News Coverage by U.S. Media

Coverage of world affairs in U.S. media has been decreasing steadily. "Except in time of war or natural disaster, many news executives, particularly in television, concluded more than a decade ago that Americans had little interest in news beyond their borders.

"Media analyst Andrew Tyndall says the ABC, CBS and NBC evening newscasts plummeted from 4,032 minutes of coverage from other countries in 1989 to 1,382 minutes in 2000, before rebounding to 2,103 minutes last year. Tyndall attributes the steep decline to the end of the Cold War and network budget cuts that slashed the number of overseas bureaus.

"Newspapers stretched their limits during the war. At the *Chicago Tribune,* the space for foreign news increased by more than a quarter—and the paper made good use of a foreign staff that has grown from 10 to 15 reporters since 2001. 'After 9/11, there was a sense of vindication at this institution for spending the money on foreign coverage,' said foreign editor McMahon.

"Could the modest rebound in foreign coverage continue? History suggests otherwise. 'Within six months of the end of the first Gulf War, Iraq disappeared from the daily coverage,' Tyndall said. The Tyndall Report shows 1,177 minutes of network reporting on Iraq in January 1991, when the war started, but just 48 minutes in August 1991.

"The war in Afghanistan received 306 minutes of coverage on the newscasts in November 2001, but that dropped to 28 minutes by February 2002, and last month it was one minute."[a]

Network Newscasts versus Some Newspapers

A study by the Freedom Forum Media Studies Center analyzed the amount of coverage, in words printed or spoken, given to national and international events from January 3 to January 27, 1995.[b] The study compared the top three networks' evening newscasts with the national and international reports of three newspapers. The *Des Moines Register* (circulation 188,000) and the *Atlanta Constitution* (circulation 307,000) were chosen because they were typical of regional newspapers read by about 20 million Americans every day. The *New York Times* (circulation about 1.2 million) was chosen because it is a leading metropolitan newspaper that is distributed nationally.

The researchers found that the ABC, CBS, and NBC evening news provided a larger volume of reporting, measured in words, on the California floods than did some papers, and provided reports on the earthquake in Kobe, Japan, that were comparable to the newspapers' coverage. Perhaps most surprising, the researchers said, *ABC World News Tonight,* for example, offered more coverage on the complex welfare debate than any of the three newspapers whose coverage the researchers analyzed.

The volume of national and international news in the *New York Times* was more than six times that of all news on all subjects on the three networks. The amount of national and international news in the *New York Times* is more than three times that of the other two papers, the report found, adding that it provided about 25,000 words each day on national and international news. The *Atlanta Constitution* provided about 8,000 words, the *Des Moines Register* about 7,500. The network evening news broadcasts use about 4,000 words on an entire broadcast.

[a]Howard Kurtz, "For Media after Iraq, a Case of Shell Shock," *Washington Post,* 28 April 2003, A1.
[b]*New York Times,* 6 April 1995, p. A10.

Many news stories could not be written without the help of confidential sources. Jack Nelson, award-winning reporter at the *Los Angeles Times,* noted that such sources help uncover information others try to conceal from the public, and that some of the most important exposés have been developed this way, including stories about the Pentagon Papers and Watergate. Specifically, the Pulitzer Prize–winning My Lai stories of

BOX 2-6   What Inferences Can You Draw from the Stories That
           Attracted Audience Interest in 2004?

Top News Interest Stories of 2004

STORY	FOLLOWING VERY CLOSELY (%)
1. High gasoline prices* (October)	64
2. News about the situation in Iraq* (May)	54
3. Hurricanes Charley, Frances, and Ivan (September)	52
4. Killing of Russian school kids in Chechnya (September)	48
5. News about presidential candidates (October)	46
6. Flu vaccine shortage (October)	44
7. Ronald Reagan's death and memorial (June)	40
8. Condition of U.S. economy* (September)	39
9. Reports that no WMD were found in Iraq (February)	37
10. Mel Gibson's film *Passion of the Christ* (March)	37
11. Code Orange alerts about terrorism (January)	35
12. Iraqi prison abuse scandal (June)	34
13. Terrorist bombings in Madrid, Spain (March)	34
14. Mad cow disease in Washington State (January)	29
15. Iraq transfer of power (July)	29
16. Race for Democratic presidential nomination (February)	29
17. 9/11 Commission hearings (April)	29
18. Debate over gay marriage (March)	29
19. Richard Clarke criticism of Bush war on terror (April)	28
20. Saddam Hussein court appearance (July)	26

*Interest in these stories was tracked over many months; the highest reported interest shown here.

In late December 2004, the Pew Research Center for People and the Press issued its annual report on the news stories that drew the highest audience interest in that year. "News reports on high gasoline prices typically draw broad public attention, and that proved the case again this year. In October, 64% of Americans followed reports on gas prices very closely, making it the year's top story in terms of public interest," said the report.[a]

"The situation in Iraq, which dominated the news last year, was the second-rated story in 2004 (54% very closely in May). But several specific developments in Iraq including the failure to find weapons of mass destruction (37% very closely), and the prison abuse scandal (34% very closely) also drew significant attention.[b]

"The series of hurricanes that struck the U.S. in late summer attracted strong interest from about half of Americans (52%). About the same number (48%) closely followed the massacre of scores of Russian schoolchildren by Chechen rebels, making it the top international story aside from the war in Iraq. The shortage of flu vaccines garnered very close attention from 44%, and four in ten followed reports about Ronald Reagan's death and memorial services very closely."[c]

[a]Table and quotes from The Pew Research Center for the People and the Press, "Public Opinion Little Changed by Presidential Election," 20 December 2004. Reprinted with permission.
[b]Ibid.
[c]Ibid.

BOX 2-7   Appearing on Television—Necessary to Be Credible in Print?

Chris Matthews, former speechwriter and spokesman for House Speaker Tip O'Neill and author of *Hardball,* wanted to be a pundit—to be a regular on political television talk shows. Larry Kramer, executive editor of the *San Francisco Examiner,* agreed to make Matthews a columnist complete with the prestigious title of "Washington bureau chief." "He needed to be a journalist," Kramer explained, "to have the kind of respectability to be on TV." Matthews had the sorts of talents that work on television; Kramer needed visibility for his afternoon newspaper, which Matthews could provide by appearing on these shows "with our name under his picture."

Matthews became such a familiar face on television talk shows that *Washingtonian* magazine named him "one of the top 50 journalists" in the city.

Matthews's story is not an isolated case. The *Chicago Tribune* employs a media consultant to coach and promote its Washington correspondents for television. Other print media have followed suit. Television commentator David Gergen became an editor at *U.S. News & World Report. Newsweek,* which gives reporters cash bonuses for television appearances, hired Morton Kondracke as its Washington bureau chief after he became a regular on television.

Some observers fear the impact of television opinion journalism on basic journalistic values of reporting, neutrality, and objectivity as it reinforces the skills that get one and keep one on television—a knack for asserting opinions in concise, memorable, sound bites. "I need someone who is glib, colorful, whose thoughts can be condensed into a conversational style," said Karen Sughrue, when she was executive producer of *Face the Nation.*

Sue Ducat, former producer of PBS's *Washington Week in Review,* reports being inundated by requests from print reporters seeking to appear on the show. Although payment for an appearance on most talk shows is small, being on television is the surest way for print reporters to get rich—it leads to book contracts and, most lucrative of all, to the lecture circuit.

The journalist-as-Washington-insider, offering advice, is an essential part of these programs. Many of the shows, such as CNN's *Capital Gang,* mix journalists, partisans, and government officials together as equals—a process likely to distance journalists from the public they are supposed to represent and to make criticism of the government policies supported by their "guests" less likely.[a]

[a]Thomas B. Rosenstiel (*Los Angeles Times*), "Some Say TV Show Culture May Change Values of Journalists," *Minneapolis Star Tribune,* 23 May 1989, pp. 1, 2E.

Seymour Hersh were made possible by the confidential involvement of three army officers, a member of Congress, and two congressional aides.[20]

Although beats and official sources are efficient ways for reporters to obtain and check information, this system limits some kinds of coverage. For example, because early events in a developing social movement fall outside this system of beats and sources, they tend not to be noticed by the news media. Only as movements increase in size and scope and seek press coverage will reporters be assigned to cover them. Examples are the South African divestment movement, the antinuclear disarmament movement, feminism, and gay rights.

Cost It costs money to bring the news to the public. Because a notepad, pencil, and tape recorder cost far less than a camera crew, it is cheaper to gather news for a newspaper or magazine than for television. The more costly a story, the more important it must be before it will be covered and published. In the 1970s, Dan Rather, then a CBS reporter, wrote about this constraint and about how it affects investigative reporting: "A newspaper can commit a so-called 'investigative team' to a story and tie up the time and salaries of maybe a half dozen reporters. But that's all. If a television network commits to that kind of assignment, the cost can quickly run into six figures and above."[21] Such costs explain why investigative reporting is more common in the print media.

Until their websites gave newspapers a place to post them, stories that are written but not published ("overset") used to be more costly for newspapers than for television. An unused set of stories cost a newspaper its overhead plus the reporter's salary. An unused taped segment can cost thousands of dollars. Consequently, although a newspaper assignment editor stores overset for possible use on a slow news day or in Sunday's larger paper, a television producer must be more certain that what is assembled can be and probably will be aired. Yet more television stories are gathered for use on the evening news than are actually aired. To cover their costs, networks try to find other places for these segments. A segment that does not air on ABC's *World News Tonight* may air on tomorrow's *Good Morning America* or be fed to affiliates for use on their local news shows. When a network is on the air 24 hours a day, it faces the opposite problem. For example, MSNBC frequently re-airs material aired earlier on its sister broadcast network NBC, and much of the content found in half an hour of CNN's *Headline News* will reappear the next hour as well until it is displaced with "new" news.

The competitors to national network news mentioned in Chapter 1 have influenced newsgathering decisions. The video news services offered by CONUS, Associated Press TV, Reuters, CNN, and other similar organizations are comparable to the national and international news wire services. As a result, many independent (unaffiliated) stations are using material from various satellite services to report on world and national news. The networks have responded to such competition. In addition to establishing satellite links that allow their affiliates to share locally produced news stories with one another, the major networks have offered to help their affiliate stations pay for satellite vans that are like mobile television stations. But increasingly, as they have closed their own international bureaus, the networks too have come to rely on so-called independent sources. This is problematic, notes former network executive Tom Wolzien, because "There are far fewer cases now where the companies have their own people on the scene. There's a giant river of video running around the world, and news organizations take a ladle and dip out of the news river instead of sending their own people. So did what you're seeing really happen? Or perhaps was it skewed? There's no telling."[22]

In return for such subsidies, a network has the right to use its affiliate's van when a significant news event occurs in the affiliate's area. These vans, with their satellite dishes, enable local stations to cover national and international news; as affiliates' vans are used by the networks, they extend the real coverage of the networks as well.

Similar factors influence the coverage of foreign news. To cover and report foreign news, a newspaper or network must support a foreign correspondent and, for same-day coverage, incur the cost of transmitting videotape or photographs by satellite. Such costs are one explanation for the small amount of news we receive from Africa and Central and South America, despite the frequency of newsworthy events. Once an expenditure has been built into the system, however, it is more likely that the people and equipment will generate news stories, no matter how newsworthy the events. For example, a network or newspaper maintaining London correspondents is more likely to report news from Great Britain and to seek British reactions to events in the United States than is a network or newspaper without a London correspondent. As the heavy coverage of the Iraq war illustrates, however, the number of stories also is related to perceptions of relevance for the U.S. audience.

In addition, the declining cost of portable, lightweight cameras and portable satellite uplinks has not only contributed to their use but also increased the likelihood that CNN, MSNBC, and Fox will carry breaking news from around the world, live.

The Impact of Technology: Lower Costs, Direct Video-streaming, and the Tethered Reporter Technology has increased the capacity of reporters to transmit events as they happen. The power of technology was on display in the earliest days of the Iraq War in 2003. "Not only were CBS correspondents in Baghdad," recalled CBS's Bob Schieffer, "they were also reporting from specially equipped television stations on wheels that accompanied American ground troops as they made their way toward the Iraqi capital. Equipped with video phones and tiny satellite dishes, they were able to broadcast even during hair-raising nighttime rides through choking Iraqi dust at speeds of up to 40 miles per hour."[23]

In the 2004 primary season MSNBC married the idea to new technology to cut the cost of regular coverage of the Democratic contenders. It "picked young reporters who normally wouldn't get much airtime, and equipped them with technology tested on the Iraqi battlefields. Each gets a small video camera, a tripod, and a powerful laptop that allows him or her to edit footage and send it to MSNBC over any high-speed Internet connection, which means the closest Starbucks. . . . The network saves a bundle since there is no cameraman, no soundman, no high-priced satellite hookup."[24]

When events are carried live as they happen, the blessings of portable technology can carry a curse, however. Making sense of what is being shown is difficult when the reporter and viewer see it for the first time at the same time. "The gratuitous use of technology is particularly endemic with twenty-four-hour news outlets," notes former CNN correspondent Bonnie Anderson. "During a major breaking news story, the correspondent is literally tethered to a live microphone and camera nonstop in order to satisfy the news appetite of the programs that follow one after the other. As a result, the reporter has no time or way to report, to interview people on the scene, to make phone calls, to gather information, to even get close to the action."[25]

Time and Space Like a newspaper, a network evening newscast has a certain amount of space to fill. Television time can be increased by adding news bulletins or special reports, and newspaper space can be increased by adding extra pages, a special section, or even a special edition, but to do so is costly. On days filled with newsworthy events, some stories that might otherwise be printed or aired will be omitted.

Because a certain amount of time or space must be filled on a predictable basis, however, what is newsworthy on a day barren of interesting events will be different from what is newsworthy on an action-filled day. Yet because we receive a newspaper of a certain number of pages or a half-hour news telecast, we are likely to conclude that the events covered on the two days are of comparable importance. A publisher or producer has yet to announce, "There was no news today, so the next eighteen pages (or the next twenty-one minutes) are empty." As *Face the Nation* moderator Bob Schieffer observes,

---

BOX 2-8   Embedded Journalists

During the March 2003 Iraq War the Bush administration created a new relationship between the military and the press through a Pentagon program "embedding" 600 TV, radio, and print reporters with the U.S. and British troops. "But just as the war in Iraq divided the country, the nation's news organizations are being assailed from the left and the right. Some critics say they served as cheerleaders for the Pentagon propaganda machine. Other critics say they were too negative about a stunningly successful war effort. Still others say they glossed over Iraq's civilian casualties. And even some news executives say the real-time reports from the field provided misleading snapshots of how the war was going.

"Whatever its flaws, the war coverage was so close-up and relentless that there was no time for a credibility gap to develop, either for the Pentagon or the media. There was, instead, a comprehension gap, as viewers and readers drowned in information and struggled to make sense of the blur of events.

"When the Pentagon invited media outlets ranging from the New York Times to People magazine to MTV to accompany U.S. and British forces, it was nothing less than an attempt to bury the ghosts of Vietnam. That jungle war bred a generation of mistrust between the military, which felt that downbeat press reports had helped turn the country against the conflict, and the media, which felt misled by officials insisting that victory was around the corner."

Although "the military has launched an official review, Pentagon spokeswoman [Victoria] Clarke sees no reason to abandon the embedding process in a future war. 'You've got hundreds and hundreds of journalists who have now had a very real and enlightening experience with the U.S. military, and that's a good thing,' she said. 'I'm sure there are still some skeptics on the military side, but they're smaller in number.'"[a]

[a]Howard Kurtz, "For Media after Iraq, a Case of Shell Shock," *Washington Post*, 28 April 2003, p. A1.

"The quest for something to put on the air never stops. Television can't show a blank screen when nothing is happening, so the drive to find information never ends. When new information can't be found, old information is repeated."[26]

Twenty-four-hour-a-day news channels such as CNN, MSNBC, and Fox have not increased the amount of news but instead have increased the speed with which political information and changing events move into the nation's living rooms and onto citizens' computers. Wire services, of course, have provided an around-the-clock news stream for decades, but whereas editors had access to wires, instant news is available to anyone with cable, satellite, or a computer. Internet outlets have increased the speed with which news is disseminated, illustrated by the impact of Internet "blogs" during the 2004 election cycle.

For decades, network news occurred in half-hour units. Cable has conventionalized an alternative one-hour form. On CNN, *Newsnight with Aaron Brown* competes with MSNBC's *Countdown with Keith Olberman.*

What is covered and published is influenced by factors outside the story itself. These include access, cost, available time or space, and the number of newsworthy events to fill them.

Internal Constraints

The characteristics of the medium may influence whether or not an event is covered and, of more importance, whether a story is printed or aired. These characteristics of the medium are what we call "internal constraints." Some of these constraints are a necessary part of the medium; some are conventions.

Use of Available Footage Television news coverage is unique because television can replay its own past from tape and film archives, storehouses of the conventions and commonplaces that are television's memory. In the archives are televisual bits of the lives of famous people who engaged in dramatic events during television's lifetime. The information stored in television's memory is different from that in the morgues of the nation's newspapers. For example, when the senior advocacy group AARP endorsed legislation moving through Congress in November 2003, and Democrats attacked the organization for selling out seniors to insurers, broadcast news called up coverage of angry seniors protesting the last major piece of legislation supported by the elderly organization: catastrophic health insurance. In the 2004 campaign the audio recordings of John Kerry's 1971 antiwar testimony before the Senate Foreign Relations Committee made it possible for the so-called Swift Boat Veterans for Truth to use it against him in advertised attacks.

Covering Visual Events For print and television journalism, the ability to tape, photograph or in the case of 24-hour cable carry an event live is an important determinant of coverage and publication

Television has a strong preference for visual events, but newspapers also try to accompany stories with attention-getting photographs. The 1984 famine in Ethiopia was widely reported in U.S. newspapers beginning in late 1983 and early 1984. But not until late October and early November 1984, when pictures of the victims began appearing on network television news, were massive efforts mobilized to help the starving people of that country. On October 23, 15.5 million viewers of the *NBC Nightly News* saw televised coverage of the famine. In the seven weeks following the NBC broadcast, Catholic Relief Services, one of the two charities mentioned by name in the NBC broadcast, reported 91,000 pieces of mail offering help, including $13 million in contributions.[27]

The reason for the long delay in securing and transmitting the story to television news was that the Marxist government of Ethiopia had put up roadblocks to stop the reporters. Journalists were denied permission to enter the country to get the story. The photographer and reporter who brought back the dramatic tape aired by the BBC, and picked up by NBC and others, had cajoled their way into the country. An acting official had inadvertently given them access to the refugee camps.

Similarly, at the end of the first Persian Gulf War, President George Bush "was determined not to be drawn into Iraq's internal battles, confident that the blows he had dealt Saddam Hussein would prompt his overthrow. Instead, Saddam attacked the Kurds and pictures of their misery were so affecting that Bush felt forced to intervene to protect them."[28]

Politicians respond to this bias by feeding the media's appetite for compelling visual images. The results occasionally are comic. In August 1989, President George Bush's speechwriters conceived the idea of having Bush dramatize his antidrug speech to the nation by holding up a bag of crack purchased by narcotics agents near the White House. The attorney general asked drug enforcement officials to make the buy. The *Washington Post* reported the results:

> The first time, the alleged drug dealer never showed up. On the second try, the undercover Drug Enforcement Administration agent wore a body microphone that didn't work. Then the cameraman who was supposed to be videotaping the deal missed the action because he was assaulted by a homeless person. "This is like a Keystone Kops thing," U.S. District Judge Stanley Sporkin said to the witness, DEA special agent Sam Gaye.[29]

Television's repeated airing of certain visual moments imprint them in public memory and permit them to define the event from which they were abstracted. The pictures of the planes crashing into the World Trade Center on September 11, 2001, and the picture of the rescuers raising a U.S. flag above the smoldering rubble define that event. Similarly, the repeatedly aired moment in which President George W. Bush declared that the terrorists would hear from us soon can be recalled by simply showing a still image of it, because it has been shown so often first in news and then in Republican ads.

Because television is a visual medium, it deals well with issues that can be reduced to concrete, dramatic illustrations. Some important issues, such as the economy, are not easily reduced to tangible, dramatic, 2-minute-and-35-second bites of information.

The problems involved in news coverage of economic issues were exemplified by limited and delayed coverage of widespread failures of savings and loan (S&L) associations in the late 1980s and early 1990s. Former *Wall Street Journal* reporter Ellen Hume writes that when Michael Gartner, president of NBC News, was asked why television hadn't covered the crisis much even after it made headlines in 1988, he commented "that the story didn't lend itself to images, and without such images, 'television can't do facts.'"[30]

In 1990, the problem that had surfaced years earlier finally received wide coverage. There were several reasons for the increase in television attention to the S&L scandal: (1) it was estimated that the cost of a federal bailout might reach $500 billion; (2) respected members of Congress, including five prominent senators, were shown to have delayed measures to limit costs in response to lobbying and campaign contributions from the thrifts; and (3) President Bush's son Neil, a director of the Silverado Banking, Savings and Loan Association in Denver, was charged with a conflict of interest in its delayed closing and was sued by federal regulators, who charged that "'gross negligence' had led to a collapse that could cost taxpayers more than $1 billion."[31] News coverage had been delayed by the lack of economic expertise among reporters and by the complexity and geographic spread of the story.

Specialized media outlets, whose reporters had the expertise to interpret what was occurring, broke the story earlier. In 1983, the *American Banker* linked a New York City deposit broker (later convicted of fraud) to a criminal investigation of several midwestern banks that were short tens of millions of dollars. In 1985, the *National Mortgage News* began to detect that, in many cases, failing savings institutions had been defrauded. In 1989, two of its reporters, Stephen Pizzo and Paul Muolo, along with Mary Fricker, a financial reporter at the *Santa Rosa* (California) *Press Democrat*, published *Inside Job: The Looting of America's Savings and Loans.* The book appeared on the *New York Times* best-seller list.

BOX 2-9   Issues and Visuals

Think about the issues raised by the two major party presidential contenders in 2004. Which can be easily explained and pictured in news, and which can't? A plan to permit part of an individ- ual's Social Security payroll tax to be invested in the stock market? Reimportation of drugs from Canada? A plan to simplify the tax code? A pro- posal to raise the minimum wage?

Stan Strachan, editor and one of the founders of the *National Mortgage News,* commented that if the savings crisis had "reached the public consciousness a few years earlier, we could have saved a huge amount of money."[32]

Noting the difficulty in getting stories on this problem published, Tom Freedman, formerly legislative director to Representative Charles E. Schumer (D-NY), asserted, "The nuts and bolts of banking and housing legislation were not 'sexy' issues." He added, "In Washington, there is widespread acceptance of the idea that the public doesn't want complicated news."[33] In such cases, news norms affect political decision making. Only certain kinds of stories will attract coverage by journalists, and this coverage in turn creates the public concern that energizes lawmakers. When complex issues don't attract news coverage, politicians are likely to ignore them to focus on simpler, more dramatic issues whose coverage has aroused public concern.

The economy is complex. Economists speak in a language not readily intelligible to the general population. No single economic indicator, of itself, gives a complete and accurate picture of the country's economic condition. Because it is a construct, the economy cannot be televised in the same way a battle or a presidential inauguration can. Consequently, television seeks out the human interest angle in an economic story and focuses on the rate of inflation, translated into the increased cost of a basket of groceries in representative cities; on the Federal Housing Administration and Veterans Administration mortgage rates, translated into how much more it will cost some average citizen this month to buy an FHA- or VA-financed home; and on the unemployment rate, translated into a story of the impact of continued unemployment on a specific worker in South Succotash. Because these facets of the economy lend themselves to bar graphs plotting change from month to month and to representative illustrations, coverage of these aspects is the mainstay of the economic news that a viewer can expect to see on television, along with interviews of such national figures as Alan Greenspan, head of the Federal Reserve System.

Covering Newsworthy People   An event is more likely to be covered and published if it involves people in positions of authority or people who have been newsworthy in the past. Not only are such stories personal and about individuals, but they also satisfy a deep-seated curiosity of the mass audience about how the other half lives. Newsworthy people are leaders in their professions, celebrities of all kinds, and powerful people (world leaders, politicians, the very rich). It is axiomatic, for example, that the president is news. As the extensive coverage in 2004 of the daughters of both Democratic nominee John Kerry and incumbent President Bush suggest, the offspring of presidential candidates are newsworthy as well.

So are past presidents—and their families—as news stories about the births of Caroline Kennedy's children and about John Kennedy Jr.'s romances, marriage, and death indicate. Their association with a past president and a current senator (their uncle Edward M. Kennedy, D-Mass.) make such events newsworthy.

Whether the association with a past president and an influential family justified the hour-by-hour coverage of the search for the bodies of John Kennedy Jr., his wife, and his sister-in-law in summer 1999, after the three were killed in a plane crash off Martha's Vineyard, is another question. The relentless coverage of the grieving families prompted some people to call for voluntary agreement among broadcasters and writers that under such circumstances the family should not be approached for interviews, nor should camera crews be stationed outside their houses.

The rationale for the hours-on-end coverage of the deaths of pilot John Kennedy Jr. and his passengers is straightforward. At a time of year that usually produces big drops in ratings, coverage of the tragedy drove up viewership. A network representative reported, "The three networks devoted much of their airtime Saturday [the day after the plane was reported missing] to coverage of the story. NBC's coverage had a 5.8 rating and 14 share, ABC's had a 5.3 rating and 13 share, and CBS had a 3.6 rating and 10 share. That's about double the normal viewership on a summer Saturday at ABC."[34]

Similarly, as the coverage of rape charges against basketball star Kobe Bryant indicate, celebrities in trouble are a magnet for cable programming. And, as treatment of the deaths of singer Johnny Cash and entertainer Bob Hope attests, barring catastrophic world events, the death of a star can be counted on to lead the evening news. The celebrification of news extends to the point that one CNN network executive suggested that on the first anniversary of September 11, the network interview such celebrities as Britney Spears, Justin Timberlake, and Oprah Winfrey. "Would these stars have helped increase public understanding of the lasting impact of 9/11?" asked veteran CNN reporter Bonnie Anderson in her book *News Flash*. "Of course not. But that wasn't the point. They would have drawn many more viewers than normal. Fortunately, journalism won out, and these interviews were not conducted that day"[35]*

Avoiding Stories That Give Offense   An event is less likely to be covered and reported if it offends media owners, the government, advertisers, or the mass audience. For example, on November 30, 1989, NBC's *Today* show aired a piece by investigative reporter Peter Karl of NBC-owned WMAQ-TV in Chicago. The 3-minute piece summarized a five-part series that Karl had done for WMAQ on defective airplane bolts. The report did not mention that the defective bolts were produced by General Electric, the parent company of NBC. After a week of public criticism, *Today* broadcast a 4-minute follow-up that identified GE by name.[36]

The news media also avoid offending business. Lou Cannon accounts for the weakness of journalistic business reporting in part by the newspapers' desire to shield themselves against financial disclosure. He quotes Peter Silverman, business and financial news editor of the *Washington Post*, as saying that "newspapers themselves are among the most secretive and the most protective about the facts and figures of their own business. They are not likely to ask others to do what they are unwilling to do themselves."[37]

When the audience is offended, the media usually listen. For example, under pressure from individuals and government, all three networks adopted guidelines for the

---

CASE STUDY 2-4   The Death of Pat Tillman

A front-page article in the *Washington Post* titled "In the Kill Zone: Managing the Facts: Army Spun Tale around Ill-Fated Mission," reported on December 6, 2004, that the story the U.S. Army told the nation about the death of football star Pat Tillman in the war in Afghanistan in April 2004 had omitted a number of key facts. The story as told by the Army indicated that "He ordered his team to dismount and then maneuvered the Rangers up a hill near the enemy's location. . . . As they crested the hill, Tillman directed his team into firing positions and personally provided suppressive fire." The *Post*'s Steve Coll added, "It was a stirring tale and fitting eulogy for the Army's most famous volunteer in the war on terrorism, a charismatic former pro football star whose reticence, courage and handsome beret-draped face captured for many Americans the best aspects of the country's post-Sept. 11 character.

"It was also a distorted and incomplete narrative, according to dozens of internal Army documents obtained by the *Washington Post* that describe Tillman's death by fratricide after a chain of botched communications, a misguided order to divide his platoon over the objection of its leader, and undisciplined firing by fellow Rangers.

"The Army's public release made no mention of 'friendly fire,' even though at the time it was issued, investigators in Afghanistan had already taken at least 14 sworn statements from Tillman's platoon members that made clear the true causes of his death."

EXERCISE: What is the importance of Coll's reference to "dozens of internal Army documents" and "sworn statements"? Why would the public have been disposed to believe the Army's original story about Tillman's death?

---

coverage of riots. There are conventions for coverage of violence that exclude graphic presentations of blood and killing, because it is assumed that dinner-hour audiences would be offended.

A dramatic, newsworthy event, however, can disrupt the application of such norms. For example, on the morning of January 22, 1987, shortly after Pennsylvania state treasurer R. Budd Dwyer committed suicide at a televised news conference, Harrisburg television station WHTM broadcast a videotape of the event. The station did not first warn its viewers, who included children home from school because of a snowstorm. The station repeated the film on its two evening newscasts, although it added warnings. Similarly, television stations in Philadelphia and Pittsburgh also showed complete footage of the tragedy immediately after it happened, although they did not rebroadcast it on evening newscasts. Viewers protested the showings.

Newspapers that published only pictures of Dwyer waving or holding the revolver were praised. Newspapers that used a picture of Dwyer with the barrel of the gun in his mouth, such as the *Philadelphia Inquirer*, the *Kansas City Star, the Sacramento Bee,* and the *Washington Post*, received numerous complaints from readers.[38] In 2004 similar disputes arose over televised use of film showing the beheading of American Nick Berg and newspaper use of pictures of dead Americans whose bodies had been burned and suspended from bridge struts by Iraqi terrorists.

Becoming the News Television is a more intrusive medium than print. In most cases, a print reporter will alter the observed environment less than a television reporter accompanied by a camera crew. Does television coverage change the nature of the story? The question was answered dramatically in June 1981, when ABC's crew for the newsmagazine *20/20* was filming a story about the emergency care of infants in Arizona. The filming focused on the Air Evac Rescue Program, a service that airlifts patients to physicians or physicians to patients. On June 2, "several Air Evac officials delayed for an hour the departure of an emergency flight from Phoenix to Douglas, a mining town with a population of 12,000 near the Mexican border, so that a larger plane could be outfitted for the television producers and cameramen."[39] The infant waiting for the physician was suffering from "respiratory distress," but the child's life was not in danger.

The *Arizona Republic* covered the story on the front page. The director of the Air Evac service was suspended. ABC contended that it had not requested the delay; nonetheless, the delay would not have occurred if the film crew had not been covering the story. What if the infant had died as a result of the delay? Did the absence of a life-threatening situation justify delay in the name of televised coverage of the Air Evac unit? These are the sorts of troublesome questions posed by the intrusive nature of television.

In other words, news coverage and publication are influenced by the criteria of newsworthiness, the conventions of news coverage, and the characteristics of the medium itself. A story is more likely to be aired on television if there is footage available in the archive, if the event is visual, if the item concerns newsworthy people, if it is inoffensive to audience tastes, and if there is little chance that the sheer fact of coverage itself will become newsworthy.

CHANGING NEWS NORMS

Sex scandals are not a new phenomenon in the United States. In a biography ostensibly written to support President Warren G. Harding's illegitimate child, his mistress, Nan Britten, described how she and Harding had passionately embraced in the coat closet of the Oval Office. Nor was Warren and Nan's daughter the only illegitimate offspring of a prominent politician to make campaign history. "Ma, Ma, Where's My Pa? Gone to the White House, Ha! Ha! Ha!" was chanted in the presidential campaign of 1884, in which Pa, Grover Cleveland, emerged the victor. The way that Cleveland handled the charge that he had fathered an illegitimate child was instructive. When asked by his consultants how to blunt the attack, he simply told them to tell the truth.

As these stories of dalliances past are transmitted from generation to generation, they are not told as tales about the creation or questioning of press norms. The narratives that have preoccupied the American public recently are more likely to have that focus, however.

When is the private sexual behavior of a politician newsworthy? During the past 40 years in the United States, dissimilar norms have governed the answer to that question. In this section, we will chronicle the changes from the revelation of behaviors that affect the capacity to govern or reflect an abuse of power to the revelation of any public display of impropriety; and from an assumption of the public's right to know when a leader is lying about recent activities to the assumption that reporters should write about any evidence of hypocrisy, broadly construed, and any past behavior even tangentially related to a current controversy.

CASE STUDY 2-5   Saving Jessica Lynch

The *Washington Post* carried the dramatic story of a valiant young woman fighting for the U.S. Army in Iraq when she and her colleagues were ambushed in Nasiriyah. The screenwriter for the movie *Saving Jessica Lynch* recalls that the story was "all about how she emptied her rifle, emptied her handgun, went for her survival knife, stabbed three more guys, and then they brutalized her. And a week later, against all odds, we rescued her."[a]

Early accounts reported that she had been both shot and stabbed.[b] *New York Times* reporter Steve Young notes that "When it happened, Private Lynch's rescue seemed like the one thing all Americans, no matter their politics, could agree on: a shining example of 21st-century military pre-

cision that went off without a hitch. In the intervening months, however, questions have arisen as to how she was wounded, whether she shot her assailants, why a unit hunting for weapons of mass destruction was diverted for her rescue, and why the incident was filmed by a cameraman working for the Department of Defense, among other issues."[c]

---

[a]John Fasano, cited in "Saving Private Lynch from Misinformation," *New York Times,* 5 October 2003, sec. 2.
[b]Steve Young, "Saving Private Lynch from Misinformation," *New York Times,* 5 October 2003. Copyright © 2003 by The New York Times Co. Reprinted with permission.
[c]Ibid.

Relevance to Governance or Abuse of Power

The time was the early 1960s. Although the sexual escapades of candidate and President John F. Kennedy were known at least by some, reporters and editors alike assumed that they constituted private behavior and as such were his concern, not the public's. Former network anchor Walter Cronkite explains that "[t]he rule had it that, as long as his outside activities, alcoholic or sexual, did not interfere with or seriously endanger the discharge of his public duties, a man was entitled to his privacy."[39]

This norm held even in a circumstance in which the candidate prominently featured his wife and family in the campaign. Hypocrisy was not yet the test to determine whether private behavior should become public knowledge. Since reporters did not at the time know of Kennedy's relationship with Judith Campbell Exner, a friend of a mobster, they had no cause, under the standard articulated by Cronkite, to raise questions about the potential influence of the president's indiscretions on governance.

Public Display

In the 1970s, the downfall of two powerful members of Congress revealed the standards that justified press revelation at the time. When word got out that Wayne Hays had put his mistress, Elizabeth Ray, who proudly announced, "I can't type," on the taxpayer-funded payroll, the revelation made headlines. The standard cited was abuse of power. The reporting about an inebriated Wilbur Mills caught with stripper Fanne Foxe, "The Argentine Firecracker," after a car accident left them wading in the Washington Tidal Basin confirmed that public display could trigger press reports as well.

Hypocrisy Forecast

The nascent hypocrisy standard was forecast by the *New Republic*'s Michael Kinsley in a response to the suppression of a piece that had condemned the sexual exploits of Democratic presidential aspirant Senator Edward Kennedy of Massachusetts. The supposedly private sexual relations of candidates with people to whom they are not married is within the bounds of appropriate journalistic practice, argued Kinsley, because "great effort goes into arranging, or even fabricating, elaborate family tableaux for the benefit of the press and the public. . . . It's the hypocrisy that gripes me," wrote Kinsley. "If a politician ever truly attempted to keep his private life private, or, alternatively, if he announced to the world that he and his wife had decided the nuclear family is an outmoded social form, I would not be concerned about most of what is generally hidden under the veil of 'privacy.'"[40]

Hypocrisy Added

In 1987, hypocrisy was formally added to a journalistic pantheon that included public display and abuse of power. In the spring of that year, Democratic presidential hopeful and Colorado Senator Gary Hart countered rumors of sexual misconduct by daring reporters to "go ahead" and "put a tail on me." He predicted, "They'd be very bored."[41] His challenge established a test of personal credibility that reporters for the *Miami Herald* accepted. The married candidate's subsequent weekend with a young woman, Donna Rice, and his claims about the innocence of their time together quashed his presidential prospects.

As Jamieson wrote in *Eloquence in an Electronic Age,* comparing the situations of John Kennedy and Gary Hart, "The news stories confirmed two dramatic changes in the political climate. Where reporters' observations of President John Kennedy's trysts went unreported, Hart was 'staked out.' The barrier that once shielded the private lives of politicians from public view ha[d] crumbled."[42] At a press conference after the *Herald* revelations, *Washington Post* reporter Paul Taylor created a controversy by making the hypocrisy standard explicit. Taylor asked Hart directly, "Have you ever committed adultery?" Hart refused to answer. Hypocrisy had emerged as a test of political credibility. One function of the press was now unmasking it.

Statute of Limitations

Until 1992, the cases confronting the press had involved the current behaviors of politicians: Ray was on Hays's payroll; Foxe was with Mills at the Tidal Basin; pictures existed of Hart and Rice on a boat aptly named *Monkey Business.* In 1992, while Bill Clinton was running for the Democratic presidential nomination, allegations about an earlier extramarital affair raised the question, What is the statute of limitations for the press on investigating candidate behavior?

While governor of Arkansas, Bill Clinton had recommended Gennifer Flowers for a job in state government. On a tape of a telephone conversation between the two that Flowers made before the 1992 campaign, Clinton told her that if she were asked whether she had talked with him about the job, she should deny it. She was to say that she learned of the job from a newspaper ad.

Flowers's tapes also included disparaging remarks about New York governor Mario Cuomo, presumed at the time to be Clinton's rival for the nomination. Although the Clinton presidential campaign would argue that the tapes had been edited to sound incriminating, by apologizing for the remarks about Cuomo Clinton essentially authenticated at least some of them. If the tapes were genuine, the exchange of a state job for sex would constitute abuse of power. It was on that norm that reporters would pivot when pressed about the newsworthiness of the Flowers story.

Clinton preempted the use of hypocrisy as a justification for continued pursuit of the story when he admitted in a January 1992 interview with *60 Minutes* that he had "caused pain" in his marriage. The presence of his wife at his side testified that both believed it was inappropriate to say more. The audience for that interview was magnified by the fact that the program aired at the end of the Super Bowl. In the interview, Clinton in effect admitted to past indiscretions and implied strongly that that sort of behavior was in the past, apparently relying on the principle that if it's old, it should not be retold.

Lying and Recency

Not everyone in the pressroom thought the Flowers story merited the attention it received. Writing in the *Wall Street Journal* in January 1992, columnist Al Hunt defined the scandal over Democratic candidate Bill Clinton's alleged affair with Gennifer Flowers not as a sex scandal but as "a press scandal." A candidate's private life should become the focus of press and public attention, argued Hunt, under very few conditions, among them, if the candidate lies in "a contemporaneous situation," "if any extramarital sexual relationships directly affect a politician's public life or governing decisions," and "if there's blatant hypocrisy involved. Any candidate who's running on a platform of restoring morality in America had better be pretty pure—just as there's a greater burden on defense hawks to explain a lack of military service, or pro-busing liberals to explain sending their kids to private schools."[43]

The condition of recency was not met in the Clinton-Flowers situation. By Flowers's admission, the alleged affair was long over. Because the claimed behavior had occurred behind closed doors, whether Clinton was lying or not was almost impossible to ascertain. The situation involved no relevance to governance, no demonstrated abuse of power, and no blatant contradictions of the sort Hunt described between Clinton's rhetoric and the supposed affair.

Had Clinton lied? In the *60 Minutes* interview, he had responded to a question about his presumed 12-year affair with Flowers by saying that the allegation was "false." More than four years later, in his deposition before the trial in which Paula Jones accused him of sexual harassment, Clinton would admit to having had sexual intercourse with Flowers once. Presumably the denial in 1992 was not to an affair but to the notion that the "affair" had lasted 12 years.

The standard posited by Hunt carries a trap for politicians, and this trap was sprung on Bill Clinton in 1998. Once an allegation about one's private life has surfaced, as the charge that Clinton had engaged in a sexual relationship with a White House intern did in early 1998, the press ask the politician whether it is true or false and persist until an answer is elicited. If the politician denies the charges, then under the standard that makes lying newsworthy, reporters seek disconfirming evidence. In this scenario, leaders would be well advised to hang a picture of Grover Cleveland above their desks.

In 1992, the *60 Minutes* interview effectively dispatched interest in Gennifer Flowers back to the tabloids where the story had originated. When, in the fall 1992 issue of a men's magazine, Flowers alleged that she had aborted Clinton's child, the rest of the press ignored the story.

On January 18, 1998, online gossip columnist Matt Drudge posted a bulletin on his website, saying that editors at *Newsweek* had killed a story about President Clinton's having had an affair with a White House intern. By January 21, that story had migrated to the *Washington Post*. On January 26, at the end of a statement on after-hours school care for children, Clinton looked directly into the cameras and said insistently, "I want to say one thing to the American people. I want you to listen to me. I'm not going to say this again. I did not have sexual relations with that woman, Miss Lewinsky. I never told anybody to lie, not a single time—never. These allegations are false." The next morning, Hillary Rodham Clinton was asked by Matt Lauer, the co-anchor of NBC's *Today* show, "What is the exact relationship between your husband and Monica Lewinsky? Has he described the relationship in detail to you?" Later in the same interview, Lauer asked, "If an American president had an adulterous liaison in the White House and lied to cover it up, should the American people ask for his resignation?"

As the scandal and coverage of it proceeded, Clinton's approval ratings rose while those of the press dropped. A CBS poll on March 16, 1998, reported that by a margin of 62 to 31 percent, the public thought that Clinton's personal life was a private matter and not a public matter related to his job.

When they were not tracking titillating detail, reporters offered two justifications for the public inspection of Clinton's supposedly private behavior: the possibility that Clinton had lied under oath in a deposition in the Paula Jones case and had asked others to lie to cover up the Lewinsky affair as well, and the possibility that Clinton had asked his well-placed friend Vernon Jordan to secure a New York job for Lewinsky in exchange for her denials. These are standard justifications: lying and abuse of power.

If the press thought lying was newsworthy, the Republicans in Congress thought it was impeachable. One liberal commentator summarized the result by saying that "[c]onservative Republicans, accustomed to making no distinction between private and public morality, pressed on with their inquisition, oblivious to its effect on the country."[44]

The questions carried to the country when the videotape of Clinton's deposition before the grand jury was released and nationally aired were, in the words of the same reporter, "more alarming than the answers. The questions were invasive, intrusive, shockingly personal—an interrogation so personal as to make Freud blanch. In the end, we all know more about Bill Clinton's sex life than we know about our best friend's."[45] The House voted to impeach, but the Senate would not convict Clinton and remove him from office. On the first article of impeachment, which charged Clinton with committing perjury, the vote was 55 (not guilty) to 45 (guilty) in the Republican-controlled Senate. On the second article, the vote was 50–50, with 67 needed to convict.

Because the Republicans had made Clinton's lying about and covering up of his consensual sexual activity an impeachable offense, they implicitly licensed the press to apply the same standards to their own behavior. Hypocrisy was the norm that justified printing a series of revelations. Republican impeachment supporter Helen Chenoweth of Idaho had launched her bid for reelection in 1998 with an ad that said, "Our Founding Fathers knew that political leaders' personal conduct must be held to the highest standards. President Clinton's behavior has severely damaged his ability to lead our nation and the free world." The *Idaho Statesman* responded to the ads with information revealing that 14 years earlier, Chenoweth had had an extended affair with a married man.

Hypocrisy was also at issue in two other stories. According to the first, pro-life Georgia Republican and impeachment advocate Bob Barr had paid for an abortion for his first wife. The author of the Defense of Marriage Act, Barr has been married three times. The second story involved Dan Burton, an Indiana Republican, impeachment advocate, and chair of the House Government Reform and Oversight Committee, who had publicly called Clinton a "scumbag." When he learned that the fact was about to be revealed in a news report, Burton preemptively acknowledged that he was the father of an illegitimate child.

Those who thought this type of reporting was appropriate were given assistance by an offer made by *Hustler* publisher Larry Flynt, who paid for an ad in the *Washington Post* that ran on October 4, 1998. It asked, "Have you had an adulterous sexual encounter with a current member of the United States Congress or a high-ranking government official?" Flynt offered up to a $1 million if the information could be verified and if he decided to publish it.

Flynt's biggest catch was unexpected by those in the corridors of Washington power. Under a threat that *Hustler* would reveal that he had been unfaithful to his wife, Republican speaker-elect Robert Livingston announced in an emotional speech, delivered to the House in the opening hour of the impeachment debate, that he would not stand for the speakership. George Condon Jr. wrote, "Perhaps less shocking [than his decision], because it is becoming the norm, but nonetheless depressing is the reason for Livingston's demise—personal sexual behavior that has no discernible effect on public affairs."[46]

Hypocrisy Broadly Construed

Reports about the activities of Chenoweth, Barr, and Burton fell within the boundaries of the norm of hypocrisy. Each had publicly condemned behavior similar to the acts in which each had privately engaged. The case of Henry Hyde was different from these three. This time there was no public display, no abuse of power, no hypocrisy, and no lying, and the behavior had occurred more than three decades earlier. In the new climate, however, allegations about sexual indiscretions by a leading Republican constituted news.

On September 16, 1998, *Salon,* an electronic magazine, revealed that Hyde, the 74-year-old chair of the House Judiciary Committee, had had an extended affair with a married woman more than three decades earlier. The source of the story was the tennis partner of the woman's former husband, who had made the original allegations. Hyde confirmed the story.

In the wake of the Hyde disclosure in September 1998, representatives of both major parties condemned the public revelation of that information. The heads of the Democratic and Republican National Congressional Committees both announced that they would withhold campaign funds from any member of their party who engaged in personal attacks against an opponent.[47]

HOW THE STORY IS PRESENTED

When an event is covered and a decision is made to air or publish the story, the conventions governing news presentation come into play. These conventions are influenced by five factors: reporters' lack of specialized expertise, ideals of fairness and balance in publication of controversial material, story length, story structure, and the norm of objectivity in news presentations.

Reporter Expertise

Although every effort is made to enhance reporters' on-air credibility, reporters cannot be experts on all the topics they cover. For the most part, journalists are generalists who rely on the expertise of others for information.[48] Most reporters begin on general assignment beats that require coverage of a number of varied topics; many are assigned to more than one beat. Whatever the beat, they are likely to cover stories related to a number of subjects—thus communication to a mass audience works against specialization. Reporters sometimes argue that their lack of expertise is an advantage; it puts them in the same position as their audiences.

Such attitudes can lead to selective vision. For example, despite an enormous volume of commentary attempting to account for the rape of a white investment banker in New York City's Central Park by a nonwhite gang,[49] the most obvious gender-related explanations were notable for their absence. Almost all coverage focused on race and poverty; almost none surveyed the research on gang rape, which reveals that such crimes are frequently committed by white middle-class athletes and fraternity members. In Helen Benedict's survey, only one of some thirty reporters who routinely covered sex crimes had ever read a book on rape, and few had made any effort to consult experts. In explaining the *New York Times'* selective coverage of the Central Park rape, the metropolitan editor acknowledged, "I can't imagine the range of reaction to the sexual aspect of the crime would be very strong."[50]

News organizations are also wary of acculturation. For example, the *New York Times* rotates its foreign correspondents every three to five years in the belief that greater familiarity with a country may slant reporters' stories.

A major change in the last decade has been the enormous growth in the use of computer technology and, with it, increased access to computerized databases. Whereas most reporters used to have limited research facilities and research staff and depended in large part on materials drawn from the news outlet's archive, or morgue, this is no longer true. A reporter at a small newspaper in a rural area has access to the same "information superhighway" as a reporter at the *New York Times*. The explosion in the amount of information easily available may have led to an increase in research. In 1990, ABC News had four full-time researchers. In 1998, it had eight full-time, professional researchers in New York and three more in Washington.

Nonetheless, most journalists' research tool of choice is the interview rather than documents from the library or other sources. The interview frees newsworkers from determining facts by using the sophisticated, expensive, or time-consuming methods of other kinds of investigators. However, the principle that something is so because somebody says it is allows newsworkers to capitalize on the fruits of these more complex

---

BOX 2-10   The Interplay of Influence between Stations and Advertisers

"Boston's WHDH-TV made a gutsy call in airing what it knew was dynamite: a tv spot urging a boycott of Folger's coffee because purchases contribute to 'misery, destruction and death' in El Salvador by indirectly aiding its coffee growers and right-wing government. Now it's dealing with the bang that followed, Procter and Gamble's yanking of all its ads from the station."[a]

[a]Editorial, *Advertising Age,* 21 May 1990, p. 28.

---

techniques by talking with those who have already used them. The people interviewed must be those who are in a position to know, and entitled to know, what they say. Typically, people whom journalists consider competent experts are bureaucrats and agency officials.

Not only is an interview a research tool, but it also personalizes a story. When the interview format is used to present a story, the reporter can remain a detached observer; and if conflicting views are presented, the interview is a natural way of dramatizing an issue and reporting material in a balanced manner.

Lack of expertise can allow inaccuracies or bias to creep into a reporter's work. To compensate, reporters, particularly those writing for elite media, check their stories with informed sources. Problems can arise here too.

"Reporters are still uncomfortable about saying things on their own authority, so they turn to the experts," writes Stephen Hess. Hess was a speechwriter in the Eisenhower White House and an urban affairs adviser to President Richard Nixon, and he is now on the staff of the Brookings Institution and has written several books on the press. In 1989, the year Hess decided to count his own calls, he received 1,294 calls from 183 news organizations in 17 countries. Contacted on a July afternoon in 1995, he already had received calls that day from the BBC, Reuters, the AP, *Time,* and McClatchy.[51]

Jack Nelson, then head of the Washington bureau of the *Los Angeles Times,* agreed with Hess: "When you are going to make an opinionated kind of statement, particularly in the news columns, editors insist you attribute it to someone other than yourself—so you go shopping."[52]

Out of his experiences, Hess has come to surmise "that TV news is increasingly dishonest in that increasingly its stories gather quotes or other material to fit a hypothesis." With smaller budgets and staffs, reporters are under pressure to make every story usable and under pressure to do fewer interviews. "In other words," says Hess, "reporters tend to interview only those who fit a preconceived notion of what the story will be and a story's hypothesis becomes self-fulfilling." This phenomenon, he believes, is beginning to erode a strength of journalism—its capacity to see for itself.[53]

Fairness and Balance

Presenting opposing viewpoints has become a staple of news presentation. One commentator writes: "'Objectivity,' contrary to popular belief, does not refer to the truthfulness of media interpretation, but demands merely impartiality of coverage, which is stylistically supplied by quoting two opposing sources."[54] The interview, already an important journalistic technique, is therefore naturally extended to provide an impression of balance.

Many problems have more than two solutions, however, and many issues generate more than two opposing viewpoints. News stories almost never reflect such complexity; instead, they tend to present issues in terms of pros and cons, to look at social movements as made up of moderates and militants, to divide reaction into support for or resistance to administration policy. This tendency reflects the emphasis on conflict and drama in hard news; the distortions it creates are often criticized for treating electoral campaigns as horse races or athletic contests.

Preoccupation with winning and losing was evident in coverage of the 1984 debates between Reagan and Mondale. News coverage focused on Mondale's use of "There you go again," the phrase Reagan had used so effectively in 1980 in responding to Jimmy Carter. What was forgotten in the process was the issue Reagan and Mondale were discussing—Social Security. We would argue that such coverage is a natural outgrowth of the criteria for hard news and the conventions governing news presentation, which shape the resulting stories and influence the view of reality they present.

The emphasis on opposing points of view can create another kind of distortion. It is as if the media must find an opposition and, for purposes of balance, promote it as relatively equal in size and importance to its counterpart, even if the opposition is minuscule.

Story Length

The typical news story is short and simple. There are ordinarily fifteen to twenty stories on the evening network news, and each story averages slightly more than one minute in length. The "action news" approach to local newscasts, recommended by Frank N. Magid Associates of Marion, Iowa, the largest of the news consulting firms, consists of thirty to forty short, fast-paced items in the twenty-two minutes of a typical half-hour newscast.

The nature of the television medium means that listeners cannot skip items that bore them, and bored listeners may switch channels or turn off the set. Broadcasters sometimes say that their stories would be longer if the nightly network newscasts were extended to 45 minutes or an hour, but when in 1963 the networks moved from 15 minutes to 30 minutes of news, the length of the individual stories did not increase appreciably.

The constraints of time and space force reporters to simplify. Print reporters order their material into a pyramidal structure that opens with a lead (the first paragraph) identifying who, what, where, when, how, and why. Material is then developed in order of decreasing importance so it can be cut from the end if space runs short. The result is that a single, discrete event is reported, and such coverage tends to separate events from their context.

Special kinds of news stories have been developed to correct for this kind of distortion: feature articles that highlight human interest, interpretive and background stories that explain the more complex event or place events in a more meaningful frame of reference, news analysis and commentary, and editorials. These appear in all media, but they are most common in the elite media, although even here they are limited. Bob

---

BOX 2-11   Is Television More Cluttered Than Ever?

"Clutter" is the television industry's term for everything that is nonprogramming time—commercials, public service announcements (PSAs), promos, station IDs, and program credits. Commercials make up the greatest part of clutter.

2003 Prime-Time Clutter Watch (Minutes:Seconds)

	Network Commercial Minutes			Non-Program Minutes		
	2002	**2003**	**Index**	**2002**	**2003**	**Index**
ABC	10:15	10:15	100	15:16	15:31	102
CBS	9:03	9:19	103	14:06	14:18	101
Fox	9:04	9:11	101	14:47	15:13	103
NBC	9:41	9:19	96	14:49	15:07	102

Source: MindShare analysis of 2003 data from CMR, MediaPost Communications, online at http://www.mediapost.com. Accessed 11 March 2005.

Woodward and Carl Bernstein, the *Washington Post* reporters who became famous for their investigative work on the events of Watergate, remarked that during their investigative reporting they had no time or opportunity to write a synthetic piece integrating their findings into a coherent whole.[55] For the most part, this kind of news coverage appears in specialized media or programming, in newsweeklies, in weekly commentary magazines, or in documentaries. The result is that such stories are more likely to reach smaller, more specialized audiences.

Walter Cronkite, the former anchor of the *CBS Evening News* and a highly respected journalist, stated repeatedly that network news simply provides a headline service. In fact, a half-hour news program provides fewer total words than the front page of the *New York Times.* The success of such public television programs as *The NewsHour with Jim Lehrer,* however, attests to television's ability to discuss ideas in depth.

Until the inception of ABC's *Nightline,* a half-hour program devoted to one to three issues, no in-depth commercial news program had attracted an audience big enough to warrant regularly scheduled in-depth news. *Nightline,* created to provide detailed coverage of the Iranian hostage crisis, continues to defy conventional wisdom by drawing a high-income audience attractive to advertisers and challenging the ratings of its late-night rivals, the *Tonight Show* and the *David Letterman Show.*

To celebrate its fifteenth anniversary in 1995, *Nightline* dedicated one hour to a special on the political and economic crisis in Mexico, instead of a retrospective of the show's highlights. "We always do exceptionally well when we put on a serious show like that," said Ted Koppel. Executive producer Tom Bettag goes further: "When we do something light or frivolous, our ratings are always lower."[56]

The different ways in which space and time are organized in newspapers and on television affect news coverage. Television has a limited number of available commercial minutes and cannot expand the hours of the day or the time available for advertising. By contrast, as the amount of advertising sold increases, the amount of news published in a newspaper (the "news hole") also increases.

Story Structure

News stories are stories. News reports, particularly televised news reports, are likely to be shaped into a narrative-dramatic structure. This kind of structure not only gives coherence to various bits of data, but it is also ideal for emphasizing action, drama, and conflict. Even within the conventional structure of the print story—moving from more important to less important facts—a news item is likely to begin with an action identified as a problem, to develop through a narrative of increasing tension or conflict (including the identification of opposing forces, often interviewed and quoted), and to close with a suggested or predicted resolution. This structure dominates coverage in television news. It is ideally suited to reporting single, dramatic events, to presenting characters (spokespeople who are quoted), to focusing on action, and to covering novel, exciting events. Conversely, it is ill suited to coverage of an idea, concept, or process. Because journalists rely so heavily on narrative-dramatic structure, this more abstract content is not only harder to report but more likely to be distorted. An example of this technique is presented in the news account shown in Figure 2-1.

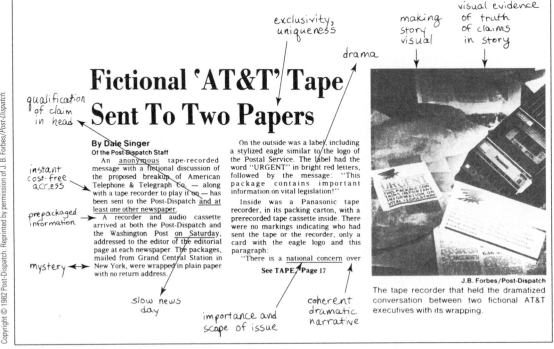

FIGURE 2-1   This article contains a fictional story within a nonfictional story within a news story. The story of Bill and Charlie is enveloped by the story containing its senders' purpose, which is contained within the news account.

Tape

■ FROM PAGE ONE

tied to ongoing issue

our nation''s telecommunications' policy, and rightly so. Here, ready to play, is a fictional and entertaining conversation between two executives involved in the changing of this policy. Although imaginary, the conversation is probably closer to truth than to fiction.''

novel way of communicating information

The tape recording begins with a telephone call from a man identifying himself as ''Charlie Brown,'' asking to speak with the president of Illinois Bell Telephone Co., who is identified only as ''Bill.'' The chairman of AT&T is Charles L. Brown. The president of Illinois Bell is William L. Weiss.

personalized

Included on the professionally produced 10-minute tape is a discussion between Charlie and Bill about the proposed settlement worked out by AT&T and Assistant Attorney General William Baxter. The settlement was announced in January as an end to a longstanding antitrust suit against AT&T.

Under the agreement, AT&T would divest itself of its regional operating companies, which would become free-standing companies. AT&T would retain its Western Electric, Bell Laboratories and Long Lines, or long distance, operations.

As the taped discussion continues, the man portraying the president of Illinois Bell becomes increasingly disturbed as ''Charlie'' spells out the working details of the settlement. He makes it appear as if the parent company would be keeping all of the money-making activities, leaving the regional operating companies with unprofitable local service.

''We'll really have some rate problems,'' Bill tells Charlie, in a voice that sounds close to tears. ''The state's going to get upset, the governor will get upset, the utility commission will get upset. Charlie, this is beginning to sound very difficult.''

drama

Later, Bill moans, ''How in the world am I going to get and keep the best people?'' Charlie replies, ''With what we're leaving you, you won't need the best people.''

The tape ridicules Baxter, saying that the assistant attorney general was in such a rush to arrange the settlement that ''he called from the ski slope, then he hurried back here and we settled.''

At the end, Bill pleads with Charlie not to leave him hanging, and Charlie, before hanging up, assures him he will help out, but only on an ''arm's length'' basis. At the beginning and the end of the tape is the famous recording by the Coasters of the song ''Charlie Brown,'' including the refrain:

''He's gonna get caught, just you wait and see.
''Why's everybody always picking on me?''

Officials with Southwestern Bell Telephone Co. in St. Louis and with AT&T in Washington said they had no idea who sent the recording. They criticized the tape as a poor way to try to influence editorial opinion.

balance

Pickard Wagner, an AT&T spokesman in Washington, said, ''The fact that it is completely anonymous and disparages the head of AT&T and Illinois Bell illustrates the depths that whoever is behind this is sinking to.''

Dana Campbell, division staff manager for media relations for Southwestern Bell, added, ''It sounds like someone is trying to play games. It makes me a little angry. I get a little perturbed with anyone who sends out something in the mail without identifying himself.''

because readers might assume paper has been manipulated, editor assures readers ploy will have no impact on editorial positions

The package sent to the Post-Dispatch was addressed personally to William F. Woo, head of the newspaper's editorial page since 1974. He called the tape recorder ''some press agent's concept of a swell idea. I'm not at all amused by it. Inasmuch as it's anonymous, we will pay as much attention to it as we do to unsigned letters, which is to say none at all.''

suggests that ploy is deviant

Woo said he could not recall ever receiving an anonymous press release before. He noted that, like the tape-recorded message, the newspaper's editorials have raised serious questions about the proposed AT&T settlement.

uniqueness

''This sort of anonymous attack is really disgusting,'' he said. ''I wish I knew where it came from, and when we do find out where it came from, the tape recorder and message will be returned with a sharp note.''

we don't accept bribes!

tied to ongoing issue

FIGURE 2-1 (continued)

Objectivity

Some of the roles that journalists play, such as the "detached observer," the "investigator," or the "objective" reporter of events, have already been mentioned. Social historian Michael Schudson points out that objectivity became an ideal in journalism rather recently and that it became an ideal "precisely when the impossibility of overcoming subjectivity in presenting the news was widely accepted and . . . precisely because subjectivity had come to be regarded as inevitable."[57] One communications researcher notes that in the role of reporter, the journalist no longer uses mainly "an intellectual skill as critic, interpreter and contemporary historian but a technical skill at writing, a capacity to translate the specialized language and purpose of government, science, art, medicine, finance into an idiom that can be understood by broader, more amorphous, less educated audiences."[58] This role detaches the journalist from the events reported and has a significant impact on the style of news coverage.

Reporters rarely speak in the first person, refer to their own actions in observing events and finding facts, or reveal their perceptions of the sources' motives; nor do they ordinarily indicate the validity of quoted statements. News coverage of Senator Joseph McCarthy's charges of subversion in high places illustrates the limitations of this conception of the journalistic role. Hillier Krieghbaum commented, "It was, in a way, a nose to nose confrontation with the realistic requirements of objectivity and fairness. [Now journalists] had to face up to the reality that a prominent individual, with senatorial privilege, could make virtually any statement that he wanted to. What did a reporter do if a senator's facts were in doubt—or obviously wrong?"[59] Daniel Patrick Moynihan, while a senator from New York, wrote, "McCarthy went on . . . making such charges, and the national press, which detested and disbelieved him throughout, went on printing them. The American style of objective journalism made McCarthy."[60] Reporter Lou Cannon pointed to still another dimension of the problem:

> As McCarthy well knew, objective reporting gives the accuser a powerful advantage over the accused. This is because the accusation usually becomes the lead and the lead becomes the headline. The denial might be carried in a sublead in newspapers that used it; otherwise the reader had to plow through the story to find the denial even though all newspaper editors are aware that many readers do not get beyond the first few paragraphs.[61]

Moreover, news stories are written in the limited vocabulary of ordinary language accessible to the mass audience; the standard style for modern newswriting removes all signs of the reporter's identity or consciousness. This is the counterpart, in newswriting, of the impersonal, organizational, virtually anonymous source characteristic of mass communication.

Whereas the ordinary reporting role requires detachment, the investigative reporter's role moves from detachment to an adversarial position that uses skepticism to uncover hypocrisy, corruption, or misuse of power. This role is epitomized by Mike Wallace's role on *60 Minutes*. Wallace enacts the probing investigator determined to expose evil, to protect the underdog, and to unearth the reality behind deceptive appearances.

Journalists who adopt this role tend to produce mildly skeptical stories, like the reporting done by CNN and NBC correspondents Bruce Morton and Lisa Myers.

BOX 2-12 Fox Challenge to Objectivity: News in Late-Night Comedy

---

Comedy Central's *The Daily Show with Jon Stewart* attracts over a million viewers a night Monday through Thursday. Jay Leno and David Letterman reach 4 to 6 million and Conan O'Brien attracts almost 3 million,[a]

The Daily Show is structured as a fake news show. Although social satire, the show imparts a great deal of political information. So, for example, when Stewart notes that the Pacific island of Palau was supporting the U.S. coalition in Iraq, he joked that Palau's chief had announced, "We will fight them on the beaches," and Stewart adds, "that's about it." The commentary implies that the U.S. "coalition of the willing" includes some very small countries and excludes some major ones such as Germany and France.

Elected officials and those aspiring to lead take the show seriously. Democratic hopeful John Edwards announced on The Daily Show that he was running for president After Edwards made his announcement, Stewart quipped, "I have to warn you we are a fake show, so you might have to do this again somewhere." Bush adviser Karen Hughes appeared on the show to tout her new book and praise the leadership of her boss. When she noted that she had enjoyed a Stewart piece that showed Democratic contender John Kerry snowboarding right and then left and then right and then left, Stewart responded, deadpan, that the segment employed irony.

[a]Bill Carter, "Comedy Central Sews Up Star for Four Years," *New York Times*, 19, March 2004, p. E3.

Both Morton and Myers tend to cast doubt on motives, to debunk, to use the conventions of balance to raise objections or to suggest internal contradictions. This treatment, frustrating or infuriating to even the most powerful newsmakers, is a familiar journalistic perspective and a logical extension of the role of detached observer.

The roles of print and television reporters differ because the media themselves differ. However impersonal the style of the television reporter, "it is, above all, a personal voice that tells the day's news on the tube. One actually hears the voice; one sees the face, body, and manner of the person who speaks. This individual is constantly on view, intruding his person and personality almost continuously into the narrative."[62] This important difference between audience experience of print and television news may be one factor accounting for greater trust in television news.

TO SUM UP

In this chapter we have explored how news organizations define what news is. We have set out five criteria defining hard news, we have explored the external and internal constraints affecting what will be covered and reported, and we have shown how conventions of news presentation influence the character of the story that emerges. The inescapable conclusion is that through their methods of newsgathering and reporting, the news media shape our views of reality.

Reporters influence us in many ways: by choosing what to write about, by deciding which sources to consult, by selecting a particular lead and structuring a story in a given way. All the decisions made by newsgatherers combine to create stories that are rhetorical and persuasive.

CASE STUDY 2-6   When Is a Hunger Strike Newsworthy?

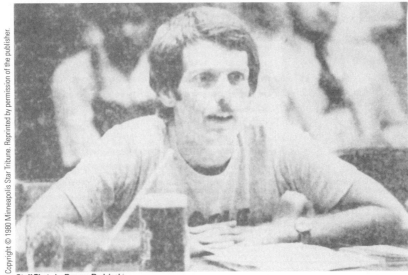

Staff Photo by Regene Radniecki

Hoye to end fast

Rick Hoye told a committee of the University of Minnesota regents Thursday that the university should be involved in ending world hunger by supporting a boycott of Nestlé Co. products. Hoye, 28, who began fasting June 6 after the regents voted against boycotting Nestlé products, plans to end the protest at 1 p.m. today. The university student, an international relations major, lost 40 pounds and will begin eating on the advice of his doctor to avoid permanent damage to his health. Hoye and other Nestlé critics object to the company's marketing of infant formula in underdeveloped countries.

The Minneapolis Tribune, July 11, 1980, p. 1B.

Rick Hoye, a 28-year-old junior majoring in international relations at the University of Minnesota, began a hunger strike June 6, 1980, to dramatize his contention that the university's Board of Regents ought to reverse its earlier vote and order a boycott of Nestlé products on the campus. Before the hunger strike, Hoye headed a campus chapter of the Infant Formula Action Coalition, a group that had worked unsuccessfully for over a year to pass the boycott. Fifty student groups supported the boycott. In February 1980, the university senate, a body composed of faculty and students, had passed a resolution advocating a boycott. In June 1980, the board of regents voted 8 to 3 against a boycott. That vote followed the recommendation of university president C. Peter Magrath, who con-

tended that it was inappropriate for a public university to become involved in such a boycott.

The proposed boycott was designed to protest Nestlé's manufacture and promotion of infant formulas in underdeveloped countries. Because these mothers used the formula in unsanitary conditions and diluted it with impure water, they increased the likelihood that their infants would suffer from malnutrition or contract diseases. By breastfeeding the infants instead, mothers could minimize these risks.

To dramatize the hunger strike, Hoye pitched a tent outside Morrill Hall, the building housing both the board of regents meeting room and the office of the university's president. A large sign at the side of the tent read:

UNIVERSITY OF MINNESOTA

NESTLÉ BOYCOTT

HUNGER STRIKE BY RICK HOYE

DAY ———— WEIGHT ————

After thirty-four days, Hoye ended his fast when a committee of the board of regents listened to his case. Although the university did not subsequently boycott Nestlé products, Hoye's strike was a qualified success. His dramatic "visualization" of the process of starvation drew more press coverage to his cause than had his two years of previous work. With press attention came attention from the university's board of regents. One of the regents, who had supported the boycott, learned of Hoye's hunger strike not through administration channels but by reading about it in a newspaper.

With press attention came access to university officials. The *Minneapolis Star* noted, for example, that "after a Star reporter called [President] Magrath's office Tuesday, he talked to Hoye for the first time since the fast started, and then returned the call."[a]

With press attention came the opportunity to address a committee of the board of regents.

With press attention came increased public awareness of the issue.

The media could have dismissed Hoye's strike as a stunt; instead, they treated it sympathetically. "He is not a nut, or a publicity-crazed radical out to topple the university administration—not even the Nestlé administration," wrote Joe Kimball of the *Minneapolis Tribune*.[b] And the *Star's* associate editor Harold Chucker wrote, "Despite their snorts and grunts, the cynics—some of them, anyway—have a grudging admiration for the idealist. They see themselves at a younger age when they, too, believed anything was possible with the right kind of protest or demonstration."[c]

Why Did Hoye Receive Media Attention?

The cause Hoye advocated had a following—a body of committed supporters. Groups on campus had endorsed the boycott. The campus senate, a representative body, had endorsed the boycott.

The proposed boycott had met opposition. The board of regents had voted it down; the president opposed it. This opposition gave the story conflict, and with the conflict came a recognizable cast of characters. The president would speak for those who opposed the boycott. By staging a dramatic hunger strike, Hoye invited the media to see the conflict as ongoing and to pit him against the regents and the president.

Because Hoye had headed the coalition, he was a credible spokesperson for those on campus advocating boycott.

Because Hoye was an international relations major, his interest in world hunger seemed consistent with his reason for being a student.

Because Hoye had seen mothers feeding their infants contaminated formula in Guatemala and Honduras in 1978, his concern about the issue could be grounded in his personal experience.

Because the hunger strike could be tied to the argument that the infant formula contributed to malnutrition and disease, the dramatic act could not be casually dismissed as a gimmick.

Because Hoye suffered the effects of the fast—nausea, vomiting, light-headedness—and because his doctor warned that he risked permanent damage to his health, the media could not report the story one time and then abandon it. Once covered, the story demanded a follow-up. Would he starve to death? Would his health be damaged? Would he give up? The nature of Hoye's protest involved reporters in a dramatic narrative. One story demanded another and another until the full drama was played out and Hoye either got what he wanted or abandoned the strike.

Hoye apparently had nothing to gain from the strike personally. He would not benefit personally if Nestlé products were boycotted. This was not a way to be elected to an office, for example. Thus, his action appeared disinterested and selfless. The tent, the sign, the physical evidence of weight loss, the sign's daily report of weight dramatized and made concrete an issue that was otherwise abstract. By making it concrete, Hoye made the issue attractive to and usable by the mass media.

(continued on next page)

CASE STUDY 2-6   *(continued)*

**What Were the Risks Involved
in This Dramatic Act?**

Hoye's hunger strike, rather than the reason for the strike, might have become the focus of media coverage. Because Hoye no longer headed the coalition, he might not have been seen as a representative of or a spokesperson for the boycott. The significance of Hoye's act would be reduced if he was not perceived to represent those favoring the boycott.

Perhaps the relation between the tent and the hunger strike or between the hunger strike and the boycott would not have been recognized clearly.

Follow-Up

Hoye's action was part of a national effort led by Boston-based INFACT (Infant Formula Action Coali-

tion). INFACT instigated a 7-year boycott of Nestlé products, which eventually prompted the large company to limit its marketing of possibly damaging infant formula in less-developed countries.

This case study illustrates one student's use of the principles governing what makes news. The next section of this chapter examines other factors that influence what will be covered.

[a]*Minneapolis Star,* 3 July 1980, p. 11A.
[b]Joe Kimball, "Student 'Sticks Neck Out' with Fast," *Minneapolis Tribune,* 4 July 1980, p. 5B.
[c]Harold Chucker, "Young Idealist Shouldn't Repeat Cynics' Mistakes," *Minneapolis Star,* 24 July 1980, p. 8A.

In words that paraphrase rhetorical theorist Kenneth Burke, journalism professor James Carey expresses our (the authors') point of view: "All journalism, including objective reporting, is a creative and imaginative work, a symbolic strategy; journalism sizes up situations, names their elements, structure, and outstanding ingredients, and names them in a way that contains an attitude toward them."[63] In short, all journalism is rhetorical.

 Use InfoTrac College Edition to access information on topics in this chapter from hundreds of periodicals and scholarly journals. Enter keyword and subject searches: *news programming, hard news, news censorship.*

SELECTED READINGS

Anderson, Bonnie M. *News Flash: Journalism, Infotainment, and the Bottom-Line Business of Broadcast News.* San Francisco: Jossey-Bass, 2004.

Dayan, Daniel, and Elihu Katz. *Media Events: The Live Broadcasting of History.* Cambridge, MA: Harvard University Press, 1992.

Ettema, James S., and Theodore L. Glasser. "Narrative Form and Moral Force: The Realization of Innocence and Guilt through Investigative Journalism." *Journal of Communication* 38 (Summer 1988): 8–26.

Hess, Stephen. *The Washington Reporters.* Washington, DC: Brookings Institution, 1981.

Jamieson, Kathleen Hall, and Paul Waldman. *The Press Effect: Politicians, Journalists, and the Stories That Shape the Political World.* New York: Oxford University Press, 2003.

Levy, Mark, and John P. Robinson. *The Main Source: Learning from Television News.* People and Communication Series, vol. 17. Beverly Hills, CA: Sage, 1986.

Manoff, Robert Carl, and Michael Schudson, eds. *Reading the News.* New York: Pantheon, 1987.

Meyrowitz, Joshua. *No Sense of Place: The Impact of the Electronic Media on Social Behavior.* New York: Oxford University Press, 1985.

Mindich, David T. Z. *Tuned Out: Why Americans under 40 Don't Follow the News.* New York: Oxford University Press, 2005.

Rosenberg, Howard. *Not So Prime Time: Chasing the Trivial on American Television.* Chicago. Ivan R. Dee, Publisher, 2004.

Schieffer, Bob. *Face the Nation*; *My Favorite Stories From the First 50 Years of the Award-Winning News Broadcast.* New York: Simon and Schuster, 2004.

Smith, Anthony. *Goodbye Gutenberg: The Newspaper Revolution of the 1980's.* New York: Oxford University Press, 1980.

Zelizer, Barbie, and Stuart Allan. *Journalism after September 11.* London: Routledge, 2002.

3

News as Persuasion

News is persuasive not simply in what it covers, a claim we made in Chapter 2, but also in the way it is presented. In this chapter we analyze the presentation of news, including dramatizing and sensationalizing coverage, inaccurate and incomplete reporting, unbalanced interpretations, and direct intervention in news events. Here we assume newspeople have decided something is newsworthy, and we examine how they present it.

In this chapter we consider the claim that media resources are used to influence our interpretations of events, to support certain perspectives and to reject others, and, in general, to function ideologically—that is, to promote "ideas which represent the interests of social groups and classes."[1] We examine this claim primarily as it relates to television news, particularly network news, because it is now the most trusted news source in our society.

DRAMATIZING AND SENSATIONALIZING CONTENT

The best-known statement about the mass media is probably Marshall McLuhan's "The medium is the message," later revised as "The medium is the massage." What these statements point to is the importance of technology in understanding how any medium can be persuasive. The impact of television news is, in part, a function of the screen, the camera, special effects, and the use of videotape.

The Screen

Although the size of screens has increased dramatically, the television screen is still small—very small indeed compared with a screen in a movie theater or to the size of people and objects in real life—and therefore it miniaturizes the things it depicts. Ballet dancers become tiny dolls; huge trucks are the size of toys. Within this frame, everything is tiny.

Even cataclysms are shrunk to the size of small rectangles. In a report for *Nightline* aired on July 26, 1994, ABC's Jim Wooten explained the inadequacy of television to capture the condition of refugees in Zaire. "Not with these pictures, or a million more" could he capture the extent of the crowd and the people's terror and desperation, he said. He told us what the camera could not capture by telling us what the situation was *not* like: "It is not like the famine in Somalia. It is not like the flight of the Iraqi Kurds into the mountains of Iran and Turkey. . . . It is not like anything I've ever seen in thirty years as a reporter."

The television screen also reduces everyone and everything to the same size. An anchor is as large (or as small) as the Empire State Building. As a result, television alters our perceptions of space and proportion. Some of what we now experience as television will change when high-definition television (HDTV) becomes the norm. HDTV will provide a larger viewing screen able to carry a higher level of detail and quality. Whereas existing sets are one quarter wider on the horizontal side than on the vertical, an HDTV set will be almost twice as wide as it is tall. From a distance, today's screens look square; HDTV will look rectangular. Among other changes in the viewing experience, more horizontal eye movement will be required. Some scholars predict that "[t]he combination of closer-viewing distance and wider screen will have the effect of putting the viewer 'in' the picture, because the screen will occupy a much greater proportion of the field of vision."[2] We now sit at some distance from the screen to dull the imperfections apparent at closer viewing.

The language of the television screen is the language of close-ups. Close-up shots compensate for the poor quality of the television picture. The most common camera shots used on television are illustrated in Figure 3-1. These typical close-up shots represent the personal and social contact that characterizes television as a medium. The dramatic close-up depicts close personal distance or touching distance, the chest shot or medium close-up represents far personal distance, and the medium shot depicts close social distance (just beyond touching distance)—the distance at which we carry on impersonal business, as with salespeople.

Distance is related to intimacy. Television simulates intimate relationships between total strangers by bringing viewers close to actors and reporters. They enter our living rooms and bedrooms; they talk to us while we eat. The reliance on close-ups creates new rules for our sense of interpersonal space. For example, when encountering newspeople face to face, viewers tend to treat them as friends although they have never met them in person. Because of the size of the screen and the use of close-ups, our experience of television, whether news or entertainment, involves personal and social contact and a sense of intimacy. As we noted in the last chapter, television news, unlike print, is personal in the sense that we see and hear a real person—an anchor or correspondent—presenting it. The television screen and the close-ups reinforce its personal character.

The Camera

The camera has a point of view; its lens becomes a viewer. Rules governing the shooting of news footage recognize the biases involved in camera angles and shots. For example, slow motion footage is considered tender, even romantic; jumpy images are considered dramatic; and extreme close-ups are considered intense.

Camera angles are important in our perceptions of the people and events depicted. According to one study of journalistic practices, "For a news cameraworker, facticity is produced by meeting an event 'head on,' with camera placement fixed to simulate the angle of a person of average height confronting another person eye to eye. All else is condemned as 'distortion.'" If an interview is shot head-on, at eye level, that camera position suggests equality between the interviewer and the interviewee; if the camera

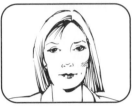
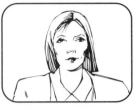
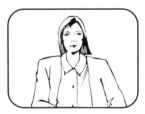

Dramatic close-up   Medium close-up   Medium shot

FIGURE 3-1   Common television camera shots

looks up (worm's-eye view) at the person being interviewed, it suggests that the interviewee is more powerful and has a psychological advantage. Conversely, if the camera looks down (bird's-eye view) at the person being interviewed, it belittles the interviewee. That is why interviews and press conferences are shot head-on and from a fixed perspective.[3]

Camera shots and angles are significant in television news. Reporters and anchors are shown in the medium close-up and medium shot, as are nearly all individuals in hard news stories. These distances are considered impartial and detached, the visual counterpart of journalistic objectivity. By contrast, more intimate shots are used for drama, to capture emotional reactions. Disaster victims, for example, may be shown in dramatic close-ups, but because this is an "emotional" and thus a nonobjective distance, reporters and anchors will not be shown in this way. Similarly, news programs rarely show individuals full length in longer shots at public distance. Such distances depersonalize the people depicted and decrease the emotional involvement of the viewer. They destroy the personal and social contact that is the hallmark of television news. Only crowds (such as audiences, rioters, or groups of soldiers) or individuals in establishing shots (used to identify where the event is taking place) are shown full length in longer shots.

The camera has particular limitations and strengths. Photographic meaning is usually not self-evident; some explanation of context is required.[4] The camera eye is myopic; it cannot distinguish between trivial and important details. But photographs are powerful and dramatic visualizations of emotion. Irving Kristol puts it this way: "What television *can* do, however—and do with extraordinary power—is to mobilize the audience's emotions around a vivid, simplified, essentially melodramatic vision of the political world, in which praise and blame are the magnetic poles. What television can do, in other words, is what demagogic rhetoric used to do less efficaciously."[5] The emotional power of television is a by-product of its visual resources and the size and intimacy of the television screen.

Ordinary news footage takes advantage of the power of the camera. Correspondents reporting stories are framed against easily recognizable locations filled with symbolic significance: the White House, Big Ben, Red Square. A story about New York may be framed against its skyline; a strike is identified by a line of pickets or a silent factory; a murder is indicated by a pool of blood or the outline of a corpse on a sidewalk or a drug bust by needles and a stack of plastic packets. In this way the topics of news stories are instantly identified for the viewer, and the authority of reporters is enhanced—they are there, on the spot.

BOX 3-1   Camera Angle as Point of View

Henry Hampton, producer of "Eyes on the Prize I" (1954–65) and "Eyes on the Prize II" (1965–80), documentaries on the history of the civil rights movement, advised those who reviewed thousands of feet of television news footage to look for those moments when the news cameras changed position, literally and figuratively, in reporting stories about the movement. These are the shifts he identifies.

In the beginning of the movement, in stories about the U.S. Supreme Court school desegregation decision, the cameras showed the black characters sympathetically and their white antagonists as villains. As the movement heated up, the cameras moved behind the march leaders and looked outward at the hostile sheriffs and their deputies.

Later, when "Black Power" became the cry of Stokely Carmichael and other activists, the cameras shifted away from the movement point of view. By the time of the 1967 riots (for the record, he notes, many African Americans still call them "rebellions"), the camera's point of view had shifted once again to look from behind the police lines aimed outward at the rioters. "Millions of viewers have taken their racial lessons from the position of the lens, for the full impact of television is as much a result of by-product as it is of intent."[a]

[a]This box has been adapted from Henry Hampton, "The Camera Lens as Two-Edged Sword," *New York Times*, 15 January 1989, p. 29H.

Special Effects

Technology changed the potential of the television camera and screen through Chyron machines, which superimpose text on pictures; Adda electronic graphics-storage units; and Quantel computers, which create visual excitement by manipulating television images. ABC News led in the use of such equipment. When Mike Buddy was a director of ABC's *World News Tonight,* he was described as spending much of his day "packaging" news stories through technological equipment that gives editorial content a visual "shampoo."

The heavy use of special effects is designed to attract viewers and increase ratings. News producers defend the use of special effects on the grounds that U.S. television viewers have been trained to absorb information via commercials, so news programs must apply the same techniques. The view is that, on television at least, action speaks louder than words, and that emotion-filled pictures speak loudest.

The persuasive impact of television news is directly related to the television screen, the use of close-ups, the power of the camera, and the resources of special effects. These effects are used not only to dramatize and sensationalize news content but also to enhance the authority and credibility of correspondents and anchors. Wrongly used, however, they can also undermine credibility. For example, in 1994, the versatility of digital imaging tempted an ABC News producer to broadcast a composite image, leading the watching public to believe that correspondent Cokie Roberts was reporting on the State of the Union Address from in front of the Capitol Building in Washington, DC, instead of from the ABC studio.[6]

Editing

Both print journalism and broadcast journalism compress time. Events that took days or hours to transpire are reduced to a few paragraphs or a few minutes of airtime. Shortening an event makes it difficult to maintain a sense of continuity. When continuous action is broken visually by the removal of a section of tape or film, the image seems to jump; this editing procedure is called a "jump cut." When an editor wants the viewer to know that segments have been lifted from different parts of a speech, for example, a jump cut is deliberately used to tell the viewer that editing has occurred.

Ordinarily, producers do not want to draw attention to such breaks in continuity. To avoid breaks, "cutaways"—shots that cut away from the main action—are used to show, for example, audience reaction. During a speech, the camera may cut away to the face of the candidate's spouse; during a football game, it may cut away to the scoreboard or the cheerleaders. Because the camera limits the visual field, viewers see what the camera sees and cut away from the action with it, even if they would prefer to keep watching the game.

Because of the capacity to edit tape and film, television can distort by reordering events. For example, a 1984 Ronald Reagan commercial intercut images of Reagan on a whistle-stop train tour with clips of Reagan ads that had aired earlier. As a result, some of the people in the second ad who appeared to be watching Reagan's train were in fact nowhere in sight of it; they were actors who had filmed their segments of the ads long before the train had pulled away from the station.

The ability to edit means that the character of an interview can be altered. Cutaway shots are often filmed at the beginning or end of a shooting session and later edited into the tape. At the end of a news segment, for instance, the camera will shift from the interviewee to the interviewer to shoot reaction shots that will be intercut into the interview. This is the procedure routinely followed on such newsmagazines as CBS's *60 Minutes*, and it includes not only reaction shots but also film of correspondents such as Mike Wallace repeating the questions. When such procedures are used, interviews can be subtly altered.

In late October 1989, television minister Pat Robertson was interviewed by Rebecca Chase of ABC News about his reaction to the sentencing of fellow televangelist Jim Bakker to 45 years in prison for fraud. Chase asked Robertson's reaction to "the rather stiff sentence received by Bakker." Robertson responded that although the sentence was stiff, he had expected it. After all, the judge was called "Maximum Bob" in the Carolinas. Then Chase asked whether Robertson felt that the sentence closed the era of church scandals. Robertson answered, "I am delighted to see it. I think that God really has done a job cleaning his church." When the interview aired, Robertson heard himself saying that he was delighted at the Bakker sentence. His answer to one question had been edited to follow a different question. Because Robertson had taped the complete interview, he was able to play it on his television show, *700 Club*. The night after the *700 Club* broadcast aired, ABC admitted that editing had distorted Robertson's original statement.[7]

Related charges have been made against CBS's *60 Minutes*, a Sunday night newsmagazine that has been described as "without question the most influential news program in the history of the medium."[8] The show is known for its hard-edged, often sensational investigative reporting, typified by the segments that feature correspondent Mike Wallace. Dramatic stories have kept the program among the top ten in the Nielsen ratings, but both the confrontational, or "ambush," interview (approaching the target of an investigation for an interview without warning or with a damning document or quotation) and program editing have raised journalistic and ethical questions. Bill Brown, one of the original producers of *60 Minutes*, describes the confrontational device as intrinsically unfair because it is so heavily weighted in favor of the reporter.

In May 1995, those confrontational tactics were turned against ABC reporter Sam Donaldson by a reporter for the tabloid-style show *Inside Edition*. Steve Wilson accused Donaldson of hypocrisy for investigating government waste on ABC while accepting a $97,000 federal subsidy for the mohair sheep raised on his New Mexico ranch. The *Washington Post* reported this exchange:

> "Steve, I'm a rancher. You wouldn't say to me I don't have a right to buy a ranch?"
>
> Wilson tried to regain the offensive. "Are you going to keep babbling here?" he demanded.
>
> "You asked me to talk to you, Steve."
>
> "And you haven't given me a straight answer yet."
>
> "Is that—the way you accuse me of babbling, is that fair? Is that really fair?"
>
> "What's fair, Sam, is I can get out a question and you give me an honest, direct answer. . . . You make a pretty good living. A little more than $2 million a year, I'm told."
>
> "So I don't have a right to buy ranch land? . . . You're not asking questions, you're making accusations. You're going to try to hold me up as somebody who is smelly. And Steve, it's not true, and you know it. Maybe you need to make a living this way, but I don't."[9]

Throughout, Donaldson crafted sound bites that would present him in the most positive light possible, and by refusing to run from Wilson, the ABC reporter denied his pursuer the footage that would make him look guilty or evasive. "The choices were to be seen to be running or to stand and answer his questions," Donaldson told the *Washington Post*.[10]

Still, evidence gathered by three North Texas State University professors challenges the assumption that confrontational coverage necessarily hurts its subjects. In fact, companies exposed on *60 Minutes* may have benefited from the publicity. After monitoring the stock prices of the thirteen companies featured on *60 Minutes* over a 5-year period, the researchers concluded that, for fifteen days after the show aired, the shares of these companies did 12 percent better on average than the rest of the market.[11]

As viewers, we are aware of the subtle manipulation possible through editing, but our awareness is rarely conscious. We test the accuracy and reliability of some material according to our perceptions of editing, however. For example, reporters who wanted to demonstrate incoherence in Reagan's extemporaneous speeches and answers had to air longer-than-usual segments to confirm that the segments they were showing had not been edited into incoherence.

As our examples illustrate, disputes over editing arise most frequently in connection with television newsmagazines and documentaries, although regular newscasts are also edited. The special effects we have described increase the possibilities for manipulation of filmed and taped material to make it more dramatic, more sensational, and hence more appealing to viewers.

Illustratively, in the early hours of April 22, 2000, an AP photographer captured a still photo of a federal immigration agent in riot gear confronting 6-year-old Elian Gonzalez and the fisherman who had rescued the Cuban youngster from the sea where his mother had died fleeing Cuba. The federal official was in the home of Elian's Cuban-born relatives in Miami to take the boy to a reunion with his father in Washington, DC. In the right hand of the agent was a gun, which appeared to be pointed at the fisherman clutching the boy. Early on the day of the event, CNN cropped the photo to eliminate the fisherman, inviting the inference that the gun was pointed at the boy.[12]

Filmed and Taped Coverage

Since 1961, most television programming has been taped or filmed. Although the electronic media, unlike print, are able to transmit news events as they occur, until the advent of CNN, live coverage was rare and noteworthy: the space shots; President Kennedy's funeral; the Kefauver, Army-McCarthy, and Watergate congressional hearings; presidential debates and major speeches; political party conventions; royal weddings; and some coverage of breaking news. Now we expect live coverage from events such as the Tiananmen Square protest, the 1989 San Francisco earthquake, O. J. Simpson's ride in the white Bronco, the search for the bodies of John F. Kennedy Jr. and his wife and sister-in-law, and the war in Iraq. CNN has built its reputation as a news organization in large part on its willingness to "go live" for important events. In the 1994–95 season, the decision to carry the O. J. Simpson trial boosted ratings for CNN.

The local anchors delivering news are generally broadcast live. The first feed of the network news is live, although segments presented within the newscast have been taped; subsequent replays of the network news are taped. Thus, *CBS Evening News* is fed live from New York at 6:30 P.M., eastern time, but a tape of that feed is played on Channel 9 in Washington, DC, at 7 P.M. The quality of the tape used to store and replay information is so good that viewers cannot distinguish taped from live coverage.

In the process of transforming live events into "taped, live, edited" events, verbal and visual errors are removed. As a result, the spontaneity that characterized early television has been lost. Until viewers contrast live and taped coverage, they are unaware of the subtle distortion created when errors are suppressed. Occasional moments in the presidency of Ronald Reagan created such awareness, as when he misread his note cards and announced in his second inaugural address that he wanted to fill the world with "sand" rather than the "sound" written on his cards. A similar awareness occurred in 1988, when the nightly news carried candidate George H. W. Bush's ad-libbed comment during a speech that September 7 was the anniversary of the bombing of Pearl Harbor.

The San Francisco earthquake that occurred on October 18, 1989, demonstrated how accustomed we have become to the controlled, polished presentations of evening news. The earthquake struck at 5:04 P.M. Because ABC was prepared to carry the World Series game, Candlestick Park appeared to be the epicenter of the quake. The Goodyear blimp, also at ABC's disposal, captured the first pictures of the damaged Oakland Bay Bridge. In the absence of fresh pictures, the networks violated the norm that news must

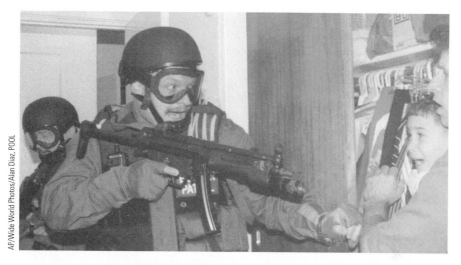

AP/Wide World Photos/Alan Diaz, POOL

This Associated Press photo was shown on network television throughout the world after immigration officials removed Elian Gonzalez from the home of his Miami relatives in April 2000.

be new, and they repeatedly aired the same pictures: a fire burning out of control and the damaged bridge. Sources that ordinarily are not newsworthy were interviewed simply because they were in San Francisco. Tom Brokaw of NBC interviewed an NBC reporter in a Bay Area traffic jam. Ted Koppel of ABC interviewed the pilot of the blimp. Neither interviewee had any information to add to the network coverage. Local reporters appeared with information about specific San Francisco locations. But the most important questions remained unanswered for hours. Where specifically was the epicenter? How many had been killed and injured? What was being done to rescue people trapped by falling buildings and collapsing bridges? How many buildings had been destroyed?

"The communications wonders that we all take for granted were out of service," noted Walter Goodman of the *New York Times*, "There were pictures without sound and sound without pictures, jumpy pictures and ill-defined ones. The vulnerability of these men and the medium on which the nation depends was unsettling: matters must really be out of control when the controllers of the news are unable to deliver it."[13]

If the improvisation that characterized network coverage of the earthquake is at one end of the news continuum, the staging of events is at the other end. For the past few years, reenactments have been a staple of the so-called tabloid news programs such as Fox's *America's Most Wanted* and NBC's *Unsolved Mysteries.*

The controversy over reenactments in network news arose in July 1989, when ABC's *World News Tonight* hired actors to depict a supposed meeting between U.S. diplomat Felix Bloch, accused of being a spy, and a foreign agent. The camera angle, the shot through crosshairs, the shadowy scene, and the black-and-white footage all suggested that ABC had scooped its competitors by being on the scene to document the transfer of a briefcase presumably containing state secrets. As controversy swirled around the

ABC re-creation, ABC formally reprimanded those who had aired the piece, instituted a policy on re-creations, and required that they be used only with the permission of Roone Arledge, ABC's president at the time.

In November 1989, NBC News announced that it was banning dramatic reenactments from all its programming.[14] CBS announced that it would not use re-creations on the *CBS Evening News with Dan Rather* but would continue their use on the now defunct *Saturday Night with Connie Chung*. Chung's program used re-creations to show such things as a day in the life of a teenage drug dealer.

On November 17, 1993, *Dateline NBC* aired a report, "Waiting to Explode," about the propensity of some General Motors pickup trucks to burst into flames in a collision. That report included film of a fiery crash that *Dateline NBC* staged to demonstrate what it said could happen in a side-impact crash involving a GM truck. Faced with a lawsuit by GM, NBC acknowledged that in the demonstration crash, conducted by a private testing company in Indiana, tiny toy rockets were attached to the underside of the truck, a 1977 Chevrolet pickup, and ignited by remote control to ensure that sparks would be present when a Chevrolet Citation struck the truck's side-mounted gas tank. The retraction was delivered to forestall a costly legal process for the network. Walter Goodman, television critic of the *New York Times*, commented, "Maybe in collaborating on the embarrassing test, the producers were carried away by the virtue of their case; it would not be the first time that journalists allowed themselves liberties in behalf of some higher good. But more likely, a crash-and-fire picture was just irresistible."[15] Goodman's comments highlight the visual bias of newsgatherers as well as their assumption that violations of journalistic norms are permissible when done for a good cause.

Editing allows television producers to exploit the potential of the screen, the camera, and special effects to dramatize and sensationalize coverage. Because nearly all television news is edited, even televised news that is not reenacted differs from the actual event in important and predictable ways.

Anchors and On-Air Reporters

Television legitimizes the carriers of news to a greater extent than print does. Walter Cronkite, until March 1981 the anchor of the *CBS Evening News*, was considered the most trusted man in the United States. Cronkite's nightly closing comment, "And that's the way it is," put him and his news team in the position of authenticators: If you saw it on the network news, it had to be important; it had to be true. In fact, some media analysts argue that the existence of a small group of individuals who regularly bring us word of newsworthy happenings in the world is reassuring.

In the process of reporting, newspeople legitimize certain stories and the ways in which they frame events. Being on the news is evidence of being important. Newspeople rarely raise questions that remain unanswered on the news; instead, they tend to speak in declarative sentences and present stories that fit neatly into problem–solution formats. Network and local newscasts legitimize an evidence-giving process that relies on their credibility as reporters and on the credibility of television as a medium; you are legitimate only if we say so and only if viewers can actually see you on the tube. Within the newscast, individuals of higher credibility legitimize less credible reporters. Cronkite, for example, invested CBS reporters with some of his credibility when he

---

BOX 3-2   News Producers Making News[a]

In February 1993, NBC News made the front page with its infamous *Dateline NBC* episode about General Motors trucks. The news division admitted that it had strapped "sparking devices" to the bottom of a truck to make sure it would explode in a test crash. NBC News president Michael Gartner resigned after the incident.

In October 1993, the executive producer of the *NBC Nightly News*, Jeff Bralnick, made headlines by referring to the Somali faction leader, General Mohammed Farah Aidid, as an "educated jungle bunny." He made the remark, first reported in the *Daily News*, at an NBC editorial meeting.

Also in October 1993, the executive producer of ABC's *World News Tonight*, Emily Rooney, found herself in the news when she said publicly that the "old stereotype" about the liberal bias of the news media "happens to be true," a comment reported in interviews in *Electronic Media* and *TV Guide*. Peter Jennings, *World News Tonight* anchor, made similar statements to *TV Guide*. Some staff members saw the comments as an attack on their journalistic standards.

"This is a continuation of what happens when journalists become public personalities," said Bob Lichter, director of the Center for Media and Public Affairs in Washington. "The news is part of pop culture now, so the people who bring you the news are pop culture figures."

[a]All quotes in this box are from Elizabeth Kolbert, "Television," *New York Times*, 18 October 1993, p. C7.

---

said, "Here with the story from _____ is _____." The presence of a reporter in a location near the event being reported is used to bolster credibility.

There is fierce competition for ratings dominance among the nation's local television outlets, a competition fueled by finances because stations earn a large share of their gross income (30 to 50 percent of it, usually) from their early- and late-evening local newscasts.[16] Because anchors seem to be an important factor in ratings and because they are relatively easy to change, there is widespread use of "skin-testing," or assessing the on-air appeal of someone for an audience, by national rating services to measure audience response to anchors. This form of testing may measure sex appeal or empathy, but it cannot measure journalistic competence or ability. An anchor who attracts the most appealing audience for advertisers—viewers 18 to 54 years old—will generate premium rates for advertising even if the ratings of the news program are lower than the competition's. Equally important, a popular early-evening local news program supplies a crucial lead-in to the prime-time lineup. An appealing anchor may also induce the audience to identify with a particular news program, one route to promoting loyal viewership. Despite all the competition they face, for example, between September 2003 and September 2004 the three network evening news programs anchored by three familiar faces attracted a combined average audience of 26.3 million.[17]

The pressure for ratings is felt by the networks. Those who have been anchors on network newscasts thus far have been journalists with impressive credentials as reporters, but the retirements of Dan Rather and Tom Brokaw have created new challenges. Roone Arledge, former president of ABC News, believes the function of the anchor is to provide the "excitement of a lead-in voice to mobilize the passion of the audience."[18] Like media technology, television anchors are important elements in the processes by which television news is made credible as well as the ways in which it is dramatized and sensationalized.

INACCURATE AND INCOMPLETE REPORTING

The race to be the first to report breaking news, the 24-hour news cycle created by cable news services, and the competition among news outlets all contribute to news coverage that is inaccurate or incomplete.

Deadlines and Competition

Newspapers, television programs, and radio shows are part of our scheduled lives. We expect our favorite programs to appear at their regular times; we expect the newspaper to be at the front door by a certain hour. If people in the news media are to meet our expectations, they must also meet the deadlines that make it possible for shows to air on time or for the newspaper to arrive on schedule. Events occurring too close to the deadline or after the deadline has passed strain the abilities of journalists, and they may be omitted or treated superficially. Events that occur after today's deadline must be particularly novel, dramatic, and personal if they are to be tomorrow's news.

To make the morning edition of most daily newspapers, copy must be filed by early evening. Deadlines for large Sunday papers are even earlier, often early Saturday afternoon. If meetings are scheduled for the evening or if conferences or other events take place on weekends, they are unlikely to receive coverage.

Technology has made the pressure of deadlines even greater. The press corps is now digital, and the result is, writes Katharine Q. Seelye, "A deadline every minute, once the preserve of the wire services, is now the motto for most of the press corps, from print reporters with newspaper websites to still photographers, cable producers, and bloggers. The news cycle has condensed into one endless loop, and with it has come an endless stream of technology to accommodate it, or fuel it, since it is hard to say which came first."[19]

The fact of deadlines would not in itself cause journalists to scramble for the latest, freshest, and most dramatic news, but in a competitive news environment deadlines create that kind of pressure. No producer or publisher wants to lose the audience to a competitor because the competitor has a scoop or a unique angle on an important story. The emphasis on being first with a story encourages superficial reporting and the publication and broadcast of inaccuracies. As *Washington Post* consultant Lou Cannon notes, speed "is a value which competes with the value of accuracy, and in competitive situations it is difficult for accuracy to gain the upper hand. We put half-baked stories that need further checking on the air or into the newspapers when the stories certainly could wait another day."[20] Competition also produces races among the networks to be the first to "call" the results of elections. During coverage of the Clinton-Lewinsky liaison, for example, the rush to air led to the broadcasting of erroneous reports that a secret service agent had observed the two in a compromising situation. With technological advances, that pressure has increased.

The desire to air material first sometimes causes complications. At 2 P.M. eastern time, one afternoon in midsummer 1990, for example, a federal judge presiding over the drug trial of Marion Barry, then mayor of Washington, DC, released a black-and-white surveillance tape showing the mayor smoking crack. The problem for broadcasters was deciding how to deal with the expletives on the tape and with the mayor's repeated attempts to seduce governmental informer Rasheeda Moore.

NBC-owned WRC-TV was on the air with the footage at 2:03 P.M. Because WRC had been given the tape by a source more than a month earlier, its staff had had the time to edit out the potentially offensive language and scenes. For fear of influencing the trial, the station had opted to withhold the tape, an instance of self-censorship, until the judge officially released it. Starting at 2:22 P.M., CBS affiliate WUSA-TV preempted network programming with the video only. At 11:30 that evening WUSA-TV aired the complete tape with the expletives included. At 9 P.M., C-SPAN aired the entire tape.[21]

Breaking News

Breaking news is unscheduled news, a happening no one could have foreseen—an assassination attempt or a disaster. Such occurrences strain journalistic resources and pose problems for television news, despite its special ability to bring us events as they occur. First, it is very costly for television to preempt regular programming for news coverage, because such preemption may affect ratings, and ordinarily, fewer commercials will be shown during breaking news. Imagine the alternative: news reports on assassination attempts against President Reagan and Pope John Paul II interrupted by commercials for soaps and soups! Roone Arledge explains the situation this way:

"Competitive factors militate against networks living up to their responsibilities. It's a major step for a network to preempt a prime-time entertainment program to do a news program, because the results are going to be that your ratings for the week or for that night are going to be lower. And huge things rise and fall on this."[22] When the networks preempted their schedules to cover the aftermath of the San Francisco earthquake in 1989, that decision cost between $1.5 and $2 million in lost advertising revenue per network.[23]

Inaccurate reporting of breaking news events is attributable to the difficulties of on-air editing, to the desire to beat the competition to the story, and to new angles on that story. These problems are illustrated by coverage of the assassination attempt on President Reagan in April 1981. *New York Times* television critic John J. O'Connor wrote that "ABC was the first to telephone my office about the attempt on Ronald Reagan's life, naturally anxious to announce that it had beat its network competitors to the air."[24] According to a report in *TV Guide*, ABC beat its competitors by four minutes.[25]

The desire to be first with new information, combined with on-air editing, produced major errors in the coverage of the Reagan shooting. The first error was the report that the president was unhurt when he actually had been shot in the chest. The second was the report that Press Secretary Jim Brady had died of his wounds. CBS first made this false report, and the other networks followed. The third error was the report that Reagan was undergoing open-heart surgery, an on-air mistake made by NBC reporter Chris Wallace and picked up by the other networks. Because of competition, each network monitored the others closely; consequently, errors spread within minutes. The fourth error was the report at 7:15 P.M. that the president was still in surgery after four hours; in fact, he had been out of surgery for more than an hour.

Similarly, during the opening days of the war against Iraq in 1991, CNN mistakenly reported that a SCUD missile that exploded in Tel Aviv had carried a warhead of nerve gas. Less than a half-hour later, CNN corrected the error.

Under deadline pressure or on-air live, reporters and commentators mistakenly attributed to foreign agents the April 19, 1995, bombing of the Murrah Federal Office Building in Oklahoma City. "The betting here is on Middle East terrorists," said CBS News's Jim Stewart. News broadcasters' reliance on unnamed sources was a clue that officials were unwilling to be associated with such speculative inferences. "The fact that it was such a powerful bomb in Oklahoma City immediately drew investigators to consider deadly parallels that all have roots in the Middle East," noted ABC's John McWethy the day of the bombing. The people arrested turned out to be young midwesterners.

These errors highlight the limitations of television news coverage. It is preeminent in fast transmission of videotape of recent events, as of an assassination attempt, but it is severely limited in covering stories that take place outside the range of the camera's eye, as inside a hospital. In such circumstances, television reporters are prone to make serious errors, such as substituting "open-heart" for "open-chest" surgery—errors that print reporters avoid because they usually have time to check such stories and do not face the pressure to put hearsay on the air immediately.

Coverage of breaking news illustrates the differences between traditional broadcast and traditional print reporting. Print reporting may allow time to check out a story and provide complete, accurate coverage. Television reporting permits the immediate transmission of tape, events, and rumors. Tom Wicker summarized the difference this way: "When information is speedily provided by impeccable sources, the advantage is all with TV." By contrast, a newspaper can sift out rumor, mistakes, and conflicting claims "to give its readers a reasonably accurate and comprehensive report—but well after the fact."[26]

The competition among the networks and the development of digital technology compounds the problems of coverage of breaking news. As these examples illustrate, such coverage is prone to be incomplete and inaccurate.

Exclusive Breaking News

At an October 1996 meeting of the Radio and Television News Directors Association, CBS News president Andrew Heyward castigated his colleagues for hyping the news. "Think about the ridiculous claims we make all the time," he said, "expecting them to be taken seriously. Can you remember the last 'story you'll never forget'? How about the one before that? I can't. Barbara Walters refuses to use the word 'shocking' in her copy anymore. . . . And how about 'exclusive'? Soon we'll be pasting the word 'exclusive' over Dan [Rather], Peter [Jennings], and Tom [Brokaw] as they read the news: No one has *him* after all. . . . Over the years . . . we've exaggerated so much that we've eroded our own ability to convey what's truly significant."[27]

Story Structure

Inaccurate reporting also results from inflexible attitudes about issues and about how a story should be written. For example, newspeople reject the notion that some things, such as the consequences of enacting a piece of legislation, cannot be calculated. Members of the press have a natural desire to know what the results of a newsworthy action will be for them and their audience. Consequently, because the audience wants to know what impact the legislation will have and what it will cost, and because the press knows that unforeseen effects often are significant and newsworthy, reporters are particularly interested in gathering information about the specific effects of proposed action.

Some data, however, simply are not available. During the 1978 debate over the bill extending protection from mandatory retirement to age 70, for example, reporters repeatedly pressed supporters of the bill for figures on the number of older workers who would be forcibly retired if the bill did not pass but who would opt to stay in the labor force if it did pass. The staff of the House Select Committee on Aging rebuffed press requests for such a figure on the grounds that it could not be calculated accurately, for a number of reasons, as follows.

Workers will stay on the job if inflation has been or is projected to remain high, since inflation erodes their pensions, but they will not stay on for financial reasons if their pension plans contain an escalator to compensate for inflation. The committee staff contended that accurate data on how workers behave in periods of high inflation when given a choice about retirement did not exist, nor did data correlating types of pension plans to income and to workers facing mandatory retirement who would be protected by the bill. In addition, workers stay on the job longer if their health is good; it would be difficult to predict the health of workers who faced mandatory retirement or would face it in the next 3 to 5 years. In fact, data on precisely how many workers faced mandatory retirement were not exact.

A similar problem confronted reporters covering congressional arguments over raising the minimum wage in 1995. Conservatives claimed that such a move costs jobs. Liberals disputed that assertion. The studies cited on each side were contradictory and inconclusive.

Anonymous and Composite Sources, Misrepresented Tape

Early in the 1980s, four cases focused attention on journalistic practices that lead to inaccurate reporting and on the processes by which print journalism corrects for such practices. Others followed in the 1990s and in the first decade of the 21st century.

In 1981, *Washington Post* reporter Janet Cooke won a Pulitzer Prize in the feature-writing category for a story, "Jimmy's World," that she later admitted was a fake. The story was a composite of fabricated quotations and events that never happened. In a series of stories written by *Washington Post* ombudsman Bill Green, some of the processes that produced Cooke's story were revealed. These included the pressure on reporters to write good stories to advance in their careers, the problem of anonymous sources, and the gaps in procedures for checking stories when reporters say that the identity of the main characters must be protected.[28]

The second case involved reporter Michael Daly of the *New York Daily News.* In a column reporting on violence in Northern Ireland, Daly told the story of a British army patrol through the eyes of gunner Christopher Spell, a name he later admitted was a pseudonym. A *Daily News* editorial said that "a number of key facts in the account proved to be erroneous, and others could not be corroborated." Like Cooke,

Daly resigned, but he said the column that cost him his job was not very different from some 300 others he had written over the previous 2 years, in which he had often used reconstructions and pseudonyms.[29]

The third case involved Teresa Carpenter, the *Village Voice* reporter who received the Pulitzer Prize (the one Cooke had returned) for an article about Dennis Sweeney, the killer of political activist Allard K. Lowenstein, published on May 12, 1980. By a 13 to 1 vote, the National News Council, a policing mechanism set up by journalists, decided that complaints about the story were warranted. The council wrote that it was "disturbed by a paragraph that reads as if Carpenter had interviewed Dennis Sweeney in his cell at Rikers Island, when in fact she had not," and said that the article was "marred by the overuse of unattributed sources, by a writing style so colored and imaginative as to blur precise meanings and by . . . reckless and speculative construction." The *Voice* stood by the article, however, and said that "Ms. Carpenter's principal sources corroborated to the National News Council's staff the material that was the subject of the complaint."[30]

The fourth case concerned a December 1981 *New York Times Magazine* article by Christopher Jones, who subsequently admitted that he had lifted quotations and an entire paragraph from *Time* magazine's dispatches and had plagiarized a passage from an André Malraux novel, *The Royal Way,* to fabricate a fictitious trip to southwestern Cambodia. The *Times'* then-executive editor, Abe Rosenthal, said, "The major mistake we made is in not following our customary procedures in showing an article in a specialized subject by any writer without outstanding credentials in the field to one of our own specialists."[31] Editorially, the *Times* commented, "When a newspaper uses precious front-page space, as the *Times* did yesterday, to expose a lie in its own columns, it is trying to do much more than confess a procedural lapse. The point is to reaffirm a compact with the reader: that what is printed has been honestly gathered and labeled; that any credible challenge will be rigorously examined, and that serious error will get prompt and conspicuous notice."[32]

In all these cases, the pressure to write a good story led reporters to rearrange details to meet literary requirements, to use colorful language, and to create dramatic composite characters. The praise of editors and the awarding of prizes attest to such values in journalism. Bob Woodward, the former investigative reporter who was Cooke's editorial superior at the *Post*, said simply, "This story was so well-written and tied together so well that my alarm bells simply didn't go off."[33]

Subsequently, Alastair Reid, a longtime staff writer at the *New Yorker*, described how in nonfiction articles over the years, he had invented characters, rearranged events, and composed conversations. Reid claimed that these techniques made his articles truthful in spirit, if not in detail.

Reid's views were sharply criticized by other journalists. Fred Friendly, former president of CBS News and senior program adviser at the Columbia University Graduate School of Journalism, said: "A composite is a euphemism for a lie. . . . It's dishonest, and it's not journalism." Ken Auletta, a writer for the *New Yorker*, said, "[Reid is] wrong. It is commonly agreed that we shouldn't take shortcuts without telling the reader we're taking shortcuts, and by that I mean labeling it as fiction. We cover public officials, and we expect them to tell the truth. Journalists must abide by the same standards."[34]

In 2003, the *New York Times* discovered that one of its reporters, Jason Blair, had "fabricated or plagiarized portions of more than three dozen articles." He admitted to having "assembled many of his articles using such means as clippings from other newspapers, invented details and photographs he viewed in the *Times*'s computer system."[35] Two of the *Times*'s editors resigned over the disclosures. As part of its effort to ensure that the problem did not recur, the *Times* adopted a practice it had long opposed and created the role of reader's editor.

The problem was not limited to the *Times*. *USA Today* found that Jack Kelley had "fabricated" parts of stories. In March 2004 the media criticism site Romenesko "posted links to articles about the punishment or dismissal of reporters at the *Vancouver Sun* (over a sex and dating column that closely mirrored an article in the *Times*), the *Iowa State Daily* (a film review that was similar to one in the *Star Tribune* of Minneapolis), the *News Tribune* of Tacoma, Washington (a reporter who could not verify the existence of five sources in a column) and the *Macon Telegraph* of Georgia (a reporter's uncredited borrowings from the *San Diego Union-Tribune*.)[36]

Editors responded to such concerns, suggested a survey of 350 of them by the American Society of Newspaper Editors, by increasing their vigilance. "Fifty-one percent said they had addressed readers directly, publishing columns about their policies on such matters as news gathering or ethics; 21 percent said some of those policies were new; 7 percent said they had sent questionnaires to readers seeking feedback; and a number of others wrote that they had begun systematically reaching out to people quoted in the newspaper to ask if they thought they were treated fairly."[37]

As the line that separates news from entertainment continues to blur, questions about counterfeit coverage multiply. In a case in 1999, reporters from one television show, *Inside Edition,* caught those from another, *World's Wildest Police Videos,* in the act of fabricating footage. The *New York Times* reported that "producers of some of those shows' dramatic "caught on tape" segments were themselves caught on tape by sharp-eyed investigative reporters at the syndicated news magazine program *Inside Edition*. . . . *Inside Edition* showed how producers had staged re-creations of the police capturing criminals and of an elephant attacking a photographer in Kenya, and had passed off the re-creations as real."[38]

Inside Edition, which is syndicated by King World, aired an interview with one of the individuals in the chase scene who reported having been given a script. What tipped the producers of *Inside Edition* off about the faked footage was the implausibility of footage using multiple camera angles. A real police chase video would have been shot by a single camera.

One indicator that a norm is still operating is punishment of those who violate it. When in May 1999 a Kentucky reporter who had written a year-long series of stories about her struggles with brain cancer admitted that her illness was actually AIDS, she was fired for deceiving readers. Two *Boston Globe* columnists who fabricated stories experienced the same fate a year earlier. The first, Patricia Smith, made up both characters and quotations for her column. The second, Mike Barnacle, published accounts he had heard from others but had not verified. The accounts proved false.

Readers' Advocates

Newspaper readers' advocates represent efforts by media outlets to prevent and expose questionable journalistic practices. (The *Columbia Journalism Review* and the *Washington Journalism Review* provide forums for peer review of the profession.) In June 1967

BOX 3-3   Hiding the Source: Pseudo-News

"The *Madison County Record*, an Illinois weekly newspaper launched in September that bills itself as the county's legal journal, reports on one subject: the state courts in southern Illinois. A recent front page carried an assortment of stories about lawsuits against businesses. In one, a woman sought $15,000 in damages for breaking her nose at a haunted house. In another, a woman sued a restaurant for $50,000 after she hurt her teeth on a chicken breast.

"Nowhere was it reported that the U.S. Chamber of Commerce created the record as a weapon in its multimillion–dollar campaign against lawyers who file those kinds of suits."[a]

[a]Jeffrey H. Birnbaum, "Advocacy Groups Blur Media Lines," *Washington Post*, 6 December 2004, p. 10.

---

the *Louisville Courier-Journal and Times* appointed an ombudsman to serve as readers' representative in adjudicating complaints about news coverage. Such major papers as the *Washington Post* and the *Los Angeles Times* added ombudsmen to their staffs in the following years.

The title of the person performing these functions varies from paper to paper. The *St. Louis Post-Dispatch*'s ombudsman is called the "reader's advocate." Other titles are "public affairs editor," "Mr. Go-Between," "editor of action-line," and "reader-contact editor."[39] Readers' advocates have regular access to space, and their unedited copy is printed in a prominent place, ranging from the op-ed (opinion editorial) page to the front page. To assure their independence, their contracts typically protect them from pressure and stipulate fixed terms of employment. A survey of eighteen ombudsmen revealed that they have significant reportorial experience, are well educated and professionally active, and did not apply but were sought out for the job by the newspapers' editors.[40] In 1995, thirty-six of the nation's newspapers had ombudsmen, said John V. R. Bull, the *Philadelphia Inquirer*'s ombudsman and associate editor.

Even after three dozen papers had created the role of ombudsman, the *New York Times* was a holdout. The *Times* explained that "monitoring of reader concerns about accuracy and fairness was part of their editorial duties."[41] In October 27, in the wake of the Jason Blair scandal, the *Times* named Daniel Okrent as public editor with ombudsman duties.

"In the recent past, too many in American journalism have been indifferent to—even contemptuous of—those who buy their newspapers. That doesn't serve anyone, in the newsroom or outside it," wrote Henry McNulty, former reader representative of the *Hartford Courant*. "As with so much else in this business, the trick is to walk a fine line. We must listen to our subscribers but not pander to them; understand their point of view but reject their prejudices; be apart from any one philosophy but not aloof from the common wisdom."[42]

The following excerpts from a column by reader representative Lou Gelfand in the Minneapolis *Star Tribune* illustrate the value of an ombudsman:[43]

BOX 3-4   Pseudo-News as Advertising

In 2003, the public spent $91 billion on products touted on infomercials.[a]

[a]Frank Ahrens, "TV's Hard Sells are a $256 Billion Business," *Washington Post*, 26 September 2004, p. F1.

Wednesday, B3: "Macalester grad gets 6½ years for child porn." The story said a graduate of Macalester College last spring had possessed thousands of child pornography images on his computer at the school. [Reader] Patricia Freeburg said the fact that he was a Macalester graduate was immaterial and an unfair, ugly rap on the school.

Comment [by Gelfand]: It was all of that and a lot more.

Thursday, A3: "Bush bans a late-term abortion procedure." Robert Keller wrote: "Under Article 1 of the Constitution, Congress has the power to legislate, not the president." [Reader] Charles Dare: "Bush signed the ban, he didn't ban it himself."

Comment: I [Gelfand] should have recommended a clarification.

Confidence in the print press stood at 30 percent in 2004. This was up slightly from a June 1998 Gallup poll on public confidence in institutions, which showed that 24 percent of the respondents said they had a "great deal" or "quite a lot" of confidence in newspapers, an all-time Gallup low for this question.[44] From 1973 to 1999, confidence in the press dropped from 23 to 15 percent. Other institutions also experienced a drop, with Congress falling from 24 to 12 percent. During this time, however, confidence in the U.S. military doing its job well rose from 32 to 52 percent. In 2004 confidence in Congress stood at 30 percent and confidence in the military at 75 percent.[45]

News Analysis

Television reporting is less likely than print reporting to provide in-depth analysis, establish historical context, or probe for causes. Specialized print media are more likely than daily newspapers to deal in detail with complex stories. Thus, for example, the *National Thrift News* carried reports of the brewing savings and loan crisis long before that story surfaced in the large dailies. Similarly, medical journals, such as the *New England Journal of Medicine*, carry detailed reports of studies of the impact of diet on health, which specify the limitations on conclusions to be drawn from them. In contrast, reports in newspapers are written by nonexperts, and they tend to simplify these results, omit the limitations, and confuse readers, who read reports of apparently contradictory studies and cannot decide what kinds of changes in their diets might really make a difference.[46]

Like print journalism, television news tries to present good stories. In many situations, television handles the breaking stories responsibly. The conventions of the

---

BOX 3-5   Who's the Press For?

In response to a Gallup Poll finding that 60 percent of respondents believed the news media to be "out of touch with average Americans," Mark Jurkowitz of the *Boston Globe* came up with six ways to get back in touch:

1. *Make politics relevant to the readers*— give information about the campaign matters related to their lives, in language they can understand.
2. *Cut down on the cynicism*—go beyond the negative and confrontational news only.
3. *Make newsrooms diverse*—this includes not only racial, ethnic, and religious but also political and geographical diversity.
4. *Avoid media celebrity*—the opinions reporters give freely at paid speaking engagements and on Sunday morning talk shows compromise their journalistic integrity in the eyes of the public.
5. *Open up the factory*—let the public know how the press works and why it is important. Admit mistakes. Allow more media criticism.
6. *Initiate news councils*—follow the lead of the Minnesota News Council, which "adjudicates disputes between citizens and the local media."

"The most crucial task facing the American press," says Jurkowitz, "is convincing the public that it's on their side."[a]

[a]Mark Jurkowitz, "Six Ways to Reform the Media," *The Boston Globe Magazine*, 9 July 1995, p. 18.

---

medium, however, make it difficult, if not impossible, for television news to analyze or probe the complex causes of events. When that kind of analysis appears, it is likely to be in print news.

Media Convergence

The impact of elite media outlets can also distort news coverage. For example, the sudden increase in media attention to drug use in summer 1986 was not merely a reflection of real-world happenings. Although drug use steadily increased during the 1970s, among high school seniors and young adults, it actually declined between 1981 and 1986. (Most of the decline was in usage of marijuana; cocaine use remained steady.)[47]

Using data from forty-three Gallup polls reporting what Americans considered the "most important problem facing America today," Pamela Shoemaker, Wayne Wanta, and Dawn Leggett correlated public concern about drugs with 15 years of drug coverage in three newspapers (*New York Times*, *Los Angeles Times*, and *Wall Street Journal*), on three networks (ABC, CBS, and NBC), and in three newsweeklies (*Time*, *Newsweek*, and *U.S. News & World Report*). Newspaper coverage, especially in the *New York Times* and the *Los Angeles Times*, turned out to be the best predictor of public opinion.[48]

In studying this question, researchers developed the concept of intermedia "convergence" to describe "a process whereby the media discover issues and respond to each other in a cycle of peaking coverage." Convergence occurs most frequently when elite media discover an issue or when the story comes from the nation's capital, especially if the issue is stressed by national leaders such as the president.[49]

UNBALANCED INTERPRETATION

For years, media scholars have studied the discrepancies between events as experienced live and events as presented on television. As early as 1953, for example, Gladys Engel Lang and Kurt Lang contrasted the Douglas MacArthur Day Parade as experienced by observers on the streets of Chicago with the parade as experienced via television.[50] Television dramatized the parade and exaggerated crowd responses, perhaps because television had created expectations for what the parade would be like.

The discrepancies persist. In July 1986, seventy-four evening news segments on drugs were broadcast by the three major news networks. Half of these dealt with the use of crack. In the fall of that year, the *CBS Evening News* earned the highest Nielsen ratings of any comparable show in five years by reaching 15 million viewers with a documentary entitled "48 Hours on Crack Street." Yet as sociologists Craig Reinarman and Henry Levine noted in 1989, "For every one cocaine-related death in the U.S. in 1987, there were approximately 300 tobacco-related deaths and 100 alcohol-related deaths."[51]

How then does one account for more than 15 hours of airtime and more than 1,000 print stories on crack that flooded the United States in the seven months before the 1986 elections? Analysts concluded that "the issue conveniently served the interests of the media and politicians because it was dramatic, it afforded many opportunities for political posturing, and it reinforced stereotypes that minority groups (scapegoats) engage in deviant activities because they are fundamentally weak, uneducated, or immoral."[52]

On July 17, 1995, MTV inaugurated *MTV News Unfiltered,* a program designed to let individuals tell their stories from their own points of view. "You shot it. We air it," said host Alison Stewart on the first show. "This time if it sucks, it's your fault." Potential contributors were invited to call or send a proposal by mail, e-mail, or fax. Those selected received a video camera and explanatory tape. Editors pared down and polished the usable stories. The first program included an account of a househusband who objected to the absence of changing tables in men's rooms. Their absence prompted him to change his son's diaper in places such as public benches. The program also included a story by a young woman with breast cancer, a student who graduated from college in drag, and skateboarders who reported being hassled by police. This was a kind of public access television on a commercial outlet.

Insinuation through Selection of Language

On May 6, 1990, *Washington Post* ombudsman Richard Harwood wrote that the *Post's* "shabby" coverage of an April 28 pro-life rally at the nation's capitol "has left a blot on this paper's professional reputation." The paper had extensively covered a pro-choice rally of approximately 125,000 the previous year. The pro-life rally of 200,000 (the crowd numbers are police estimates) was given only two short articles. The dozens of stories on the pro-choice rally had featured charts and maps and appeared on page 1. The pro-life rally received no comparable attention. How did the *Post* account for the lapse? Staffers were aware of one rally and not the other. Wrote Harwood of managing editor Leonard Downie, "Journalists here, he thinks, not only are not part of the anti-abortion movement but don't know anyone who is."[53] The conservative Center for Media and Public Affairs provided another possible explanation. Stories filed in the *New York Times* and the *Washington Post* by female reporters quoted nearly three times more pro-choice sources than pro-life ones.

Following the *Post's* lead, David Shaw of the *Los Angeles Times* wrote a four-part series arguing that Harwood was correct. Shaw's series pointed out that protesters are frequently described as militant or asked by television producers to "look angry" to fit the stereotypes of sound bites. The controversy also prompted an analysis of the biases of language. *U.S. News & World Report's* John Leo wrote,

> About a year ago, I noticed that one of our major metropolitan newspapers had taken to using "abortion provider" as a neutral term in reporting the abortion debate. It is not neutral. "Abortion practitioner" and "doctor who performs abortions" are neutral terms. "Provider," with its overtones of nurturance and protection, is a one-word argument in favor of abortion, just as "abortionist" with its overtones of back-alley sleaze, is a polemic against it.[54]

(In a later chapter we discuss the reality that all language choices are selective.)

Unbalanced interpretations also result from quite subtle inequities in press treatment. Coverage of the 1984 presidential campaign mentioned Democratic vice presidential nominee Geraldine Ferraro's dress size but not nominee Walter Mondale's suit size. In 1988, Barbara Bush was characterized as "grandmotherly," but George H. W. Bush was not described as grandfatherly; her white hair was noted, but his graying hair was not.

Former Kansas senator Nancy Landon Kassebaum Baker once expressed dismay at the way women politicians are described in the media. "Some day I'm going to hit someone over the head for calling me diminutive and soft-spoken."[55] Such insinuations may reflect prejudices in the society. Newsworthy women tend to be identified by their clothing, degree of attractiveness, size, and whether or not they are married and have children, whereas these factors are not mentioned in stories about newsworthy men. Similarly, African Americans are more likely than whites to be identified by race. Sensitive to charges by women's rights and civil rights groups, editors have begun to change these practices in recent years.

In these cases, unbalanced interpretations result from insinuations, from the choice of language, and from the ways in which stories are routinely covered. But a case can be made that news coverage is unbalanced precisely because it develops certain themes and perspectives and suppresses others.

Ideological Bias

A common criticism of the media, especially the East Coast–based, nationally circulated *New York Times* and *Washington Post*, is that their reporting has a definite slant left of center.

Feeling that this bias was reflected in his treatment by the press, Jesse Helms, who had recently become chairman of the Senate Foreign Relations Committee, wrote a response to written questions in 1995:

BOX 3-6   Women and Newspapers: Reading and Writing

According to a study by the Newspaper Association of America, a trade group in New York, the total percentage of women reading daily newspapers has dropped from 78 to 60 during the last 22 years, while the percentage of male readers went from 78 to 65.

Another study conducted by the Women, Men and Media Project may explain the drop in women readers. It found that of twenty national newspapers, only 34 percent of all bylines were women's, and that women were the subjects of only 13 percent of all news stories. An estimated 82 percent of all senior editorial jobs nationwide are held by men.[a]

Columnist Ellen Goodman argues that women

of all ages "are more likely than men to feel that the paper doesn't speak to them. Or about them." She quoted Nancy Woodhull, a founding editor of *USA Today* who now runs her own consulting firm, as saying, "Women around the country really notice when the press doesn't report their existence. It's like walking into a room where nobody knows you're there. If you have choices, you don't go into that room anymore."[b]

[a]Betsy Israel, "What Do Women Want (to Read)?" *New York Times,* 4 October 1993, p. B4.
[b]Ellen Goodman, "In Newspapers, a Women's Place Is Far From Page 1," *Boston Globe,* 5 April 1992, p. 7.

Q: Do you feel that you have been taken seriously as a lawmaker?

A: Absolutely—and primarily by the ultra-liberal newspapers such as the *Washington Post.* Otherwise the *Post* would not have gone to such pains to discredit me. . . .

Q: Because the chairmanship is such a high-profile position, will you be more conscious, if not restrained, about the public comments you make?

A: I'll be at least as restrained as a U.S. senator as the *Washington Post* is as a newspaper. As a matter of fact, except for your exaggerated and unjustified criticism of those with whom you have disagreed down through the years, you would today have no basis for asking such a loaded question.[56]

The most controversial claims about distortions in news coverage are made by some contemporary sociologists and researchers who have studied the mass media intensively. They do not argue that there is a conspiracy or willful distortion in reporting and coverage. Instead, they argue that press coverage is ideological, that it reflects and promotes the interests of some groups and classes and not others, that it conceals the interrelationship between the public and the private sector, and that, in the words of former *New York Times* columnist Tom Wicker, "objective journalism always favors Establishment positions and exists not least to avoid offense of them."[57]

Instead of a laborious reconstruction of the social and political theory underlying these claims, one example may help explain them. The author is the former British journalist Henry Fairlie:

A few years ago I attended one of these pompous week-long seminars at the Aspen Institute to discuss "investigative reporting" with a number of celebrated American editors and newspapermen. I made my point that there was an economic system that needed inquiry, and at last burst out against the imperviousness of my American colleagues by saying that I would write without payment for them a series of articles to be entitled, "I Have an Enemy at Chase Manhattan." But there were no takers; and Walter Ridder, the owner of Ridder newspapers, made a very funny speech on the final morning of the seminar, saying that he had tossed and turned all night "wondering why we don't do what Henry asks, and attack the capitalists" and that as dawn had broken across the Rockies he had found the answer: "Because I am one of them."[58]

The conclusions of researchers are remarkably similar. Erik Barnouw, a distinguished media historian, contends that commercial sponsors control all facets of television content, from advertising itself to news and cultural programming on so-called public broadcasting.[59] Mark Fishman argues that the journalist's view of society is bureaucratically structured and that, by definition, bureaucracies reflect the establishment—government and private corporations.[60] The Glasgow University Media Group documents a bias in favor of the powerful. Michael Schudson, a social historian, argues "that the process of news gathering itself constructs an image of reality which reinforces official viewpoints."[61] Gaye Tuchman contends not only that the news reflects the interests of those in power but also that the news limits our knowledge of our own society.[62]

If these researchers and analysts are correct, then news coverage will be informed by certain perspectives with ideological significance. First, and most important, we should expect the news to tell us repeatedly that "the system works." This was a major theme, for example, of coverage of Watergate and of the Iran-Contra arms scandal. There is evidence of such a perspective in newsgathering. Newscasts, for instance, underscore the legitimacy of the three branches of government by treating each as an identifiable entity engaged in proposing and disposing, as in the phrase "the Congress today . . . ," and television routinely covers the rituals of government, such as swearing-in ceremonies, inaugurals, welcoming addresses, and press conferences, that reinforce our sense of governmental process.

We are told not only that the system works but also that those who disrupt it in strikes or social protest are wrong or deviant—a bias that will always favor the status quo over change. Coverage of the problems of the homeless is illustrative. Researchers have found that the homeless are consistently portrayed as psychotic, disordered, and "not like us." This perspective carries the corollary that "we could not be like them." As one sociologist explains,

> The notion that the homeless are largely psychotics who belong in institutions, rather than victims of displacement at the hands of enterprising realtors, spares us from the need to offer realistic solutions to the fact of deep and widening extremes of wealth and poverty in the United States. It also enables us to tell ourselves that the despair of homeless people bears no intimate connection to the privileged existence we enjoy—when, for example, we rent or purchase one of those restored townhouses that once provided shelter for people now huddled in the street.[63]

One difficulty with the view that the homeless are psychotic is that it is not consistent with what surveys tell us about that population: "[M]ost current studies consider the mentally ill to account only for 20 to 25 percent of the total homeless population, with some estimates as low as 16 percent."[64]

Some researchers argue that news coverage systematically supports the powers that be. We have summarized their conclusions and some of the supporting evidence, but they also claim there is systematic self-censorship within the media, a form of internal regulation that denies the audience access to certain types of information and that mirrors the tastes of mass audiences and advertisers.

Self-Censorship

In the face of almost nightly reports of high oil company profits in 1980, Mobil sponsored an ad arguing that the profits of the networks exceeded the profits of the oil industry. All three networks refused to air it. This sort of censorship of material about media issues accompanies the self-censoring suppression of coverage of media issues on newscasts.[65] In fact, corporate struggles to air advocacy advertising on television confront the most pervasive form of self-censorship in the medium.[66]

The Fairness Doctrine In 1987, the Federal Communications Commission (FCC) repealed the 40-year-old Fairness Doctrine on the grounds that it was no longer needed. In an era in which there were numerous voices in broadcasting, the public interest no longer required the doctrine, argued the Reagan-appointed commissioners. A federal appeals court subsequently ruled that the FCC had the right to eliminate the doctrine. Since then, there have been several unsuccessful attempts in Congress to revive it.

The Fairness Doctrine required radio and television stations to air material on issues of public concern and to air opposing views on them. If opposing views were not broadcast, a person representing the ignored view could request time for a response.

Beats Self-censorship also occurs as a result of the symbiotic relationship between reporters and the sources that provide information on their beats. This may result in the suppression of stories with political implications. Reporters "can make news out of inside information that aids an agency in its competition with other agencies or helps it get its message into the White House, but they cannot so easily propose stories that can hurt the agency. Consequently, beat reporters must often practice self-censorship, keeping their most sensational stories to themselves in order to protect their beat."[67]

Reporter Seymour Hersh won a Pulitzer Prize in 1970 for his stories on the My Lai massacre. When he was asked to account for the reasons that editors missed one of the biggest stories of the year, he responded, "I honestly believe that a major problem in newspapers today is not censorship on the part of editors and publishers, but something more odious: self-censorship by the reporters."[68] Because Hersh was able to write the story only with the help of U.S. Army sources who leaked crucial information, it is possible that reporters who had to maintain good relations with army sources felt unable to report this damaging story.

Government Support Some self-censorship involves a predisposition to support the government line. For example, the press accepted the White House explanation that the U-2 shot down over Russia in 1959 was really a weather plane and later accepted the Johnson administration's claim that a U.S. ship had been attacked in the Gulf of Tonkin. In both instances, administration officials were lying. The press also accepted the U.S. government's claims that during the Gulf War PATRIOT missiles had intercepted most of Saddam Hussein's SCUD missiles. That claim too was false.

The press is particularly vulnerable to government claims that revealing certain information would not be in the national interest. As former White House correspondent David Wise explains, "When the flag is attacked, or reporters are told it has been attacked, their reaction is not likely to be very different from that of any other citizen. Besides, it is vaguely unpatriotic to dispute the official version of events."[69]

Even unusual opportunities for newsgathering may be rejected on such grounds. As media historian Michael Schudson reports, "In 1956 American newspapers refused a Chinese government invitation to send correspondents to China because, as *New York Times* editor Clifton Daniel recalled, 'We did not want to embarrass our government.'"[70] Stories from China at that time would have been highly newsworthy, but this was at the height of the cold war.

The 1986 trial of a U.S. government worker charged with spying illustrates the ways in which government encourages self-censorship by the media. Ronald Pelton worked in a computer job at the National Security Agency (NSA) for 14 years. His job gave him access to secret government information. After Pelton left the NSA in 1979, he began selling secrets to the Soviets. He was caught and brought to trial in 1986.

Then-CIA director William Casey was alarmed to hear on NBC's *Today* show that the spy had apparently given "away one of the NSA's most sensitive secrets—a project with the code name Ivy Bells, believed to be a top-secret underwater eavesdropping operation by American submarines inside Soviet harbors." Casey asked the Justice Department to consider prosecuting NBC under Section 798 of Title 18 of the U.S. Code, which forbids the revelation of classified information about secret codes and other communications intelligence. Meanwhile, the *Washington Post* began its own coverage of the trial.

The *Post*'s coverage was the product of self-censorship. Casey had met with the editors to warn of possible prosecution. The meeting resulted in delaying a major article. President Ronald Reagan called Katherine Graham, owner of the *Post,* to stress the sensitive nature of the trial and to warn that he would back prosecution of the *Post* if the material Pelton had transmitted to the Soviets was revealed. The *Post* responded by withholding the controversial details. *Post* editor Benjamin Bradlee explained that the paper had been "unable fully to judge the validity of the national security objections of senior officials." He added, "In my heart, I think the Russians already know what we kept out of the story. But I'm not absolutely sure."[71]

Support for government policies can emerge in more subtle forms. During the crisis that followed Iraq's invasion of Kuwait and the deployment of U.S. troops in Saudi Arabia, for example, some commentators pointed out that far more of those interviewed by journalists supported the government's policy than raised questions about its rationales or costs. On August 21, 1990, for example, Ted Koppel's primary guest on *Nightline* was Undersecretary of Defense Paul Wolfowitz, who was followed by John Lehman, secretary of the Navy in the Reagan administration, and Edward Luttwak, a military analyst. After describing the discussion that followed, which ignored Iraq's insistence that it has a historic claim to Kuwait—a nation created by the British as its protectorate—and which touted U.S. military strength and described Iraqi leader Saddam Hussein as insane, television analyst Noel Holston commented,

> What happened, or didn't happen, on *Nightline* is a perfect example of what watchdog groups such as Fairness and Accuracy in Reporting (FAIR) have complained about for years. On TV news and issue programs, debate and discussion too often begin at an official level where the range of options has already been decided. And they stay within narrow parameters because journalists such as Koppel allow it. They shouldn't, however, even if they run the risk of alienating their sources or some members of their audience by asking hard questions and appearing skeptical or unpatriotic (as if asking elected public officials to be forthright and accountable is unpatriotic).[72]

Holston was referring to a report released early in 1989 in which FAIR alleged a bias on ABC's *Nightline*; it made this judgment on the basis of who was and who was not invited as an expert participant on the central 20-minute discussion each night. As reported by its executive director, Jeff Cohen, FAIR studied 865 programs with 2,498 guests and concluded that one's likelihood of appearing as a guest was enhanced by being a white male member of conservative government, military, or corporate elites. *Nightline* spokespeople responded that conservatives dominated the guest list because they had been in power lately, and that if a liberal administration were elected, the bias would shift in the other direction, a defense that FAIR saw as self-incriminating because it presented the news program as a forum for those currently in power.[73]

In some cases, journalists also are hampered by formal types of governmental censorship. The examination reports of bank regulators, for example, are not available under the Freedom of Information Act because Congress fears that making such data available to the press and public could cause runs on banks. The inaccessibility of such data made it more difficult for reporters to document the existence of banks whose loans were undercapitalized. This made the early stages of the savings and loan crisis more difficult to cover.

Journalistic self-censorship can reflect audience tastes as well as prevailing political views.

Audience Taste The success of recent efforts by the Coalition for Better Television and the Moral Majority to pressure advertisers and the networks to eliminate sex and violence from television programming reflects the desire of television producers not to offend audience tastes. (See Chapter 9 for more extended treatment of how groups and individuals can influence the media.) The pressure of the audience is illustrated by coverage of racial matters. Paul Good, an experienced television and print journalist known for his coverage of the civil rights movement, argues that "television found it both spiritually rewarding and financially profitable to cover racism so long as it was treated as a southern, not a national phenomenon."[74] His statement shows that the civil rights confrontations of the 1960s were dramatic and exciting news that, when confined to the South, were not perceived as an attack on the system.

Some contend, however, that current coverage of racism, or lack of it, reflects a desire to avoid offending the white-majority audience. Media analyst Edwin Diamond describes the conditions of African Americans as "a story that many white Americans in the audience may not want to dwell upon too long, out of fear, or doubt, or guilt, or a combination of largely unexamined emotions."[75] The racially divided reactions to the not-guilty verdict in the O. J. Simpson murder trial in 1995 reflected wide disparities in the ways that whites and African Americans see the world. Poll results also suggest many whites are mistaken about basic facts about African Americans, believing they are a larger percentage of the population than they are (they constitute only 12 percent) and believing they have made economic gains such that they have reached near parity with whites (they earn on average only 60 percent of what whites earn).[76]

The same pattern occurs in network coverage of gay rights. Once this identified audience was demonstrated to be large enough to have economic clout, networks began to respond to its sensitivities. So, for example, on February 8, 1990, CBS News suspended *60 Minutes* commentator Andy Rooney for three months without pay. The action followed complaints by the 10,000-member Gay and Lesbian Alliance Against Defamation. The alliance charged that in his syndicated columns, on air, and in a letter to the *Advocate*, a gay rights publication, Rooney had made insensitive remarks about gays. After Rooney's suspension, however, counterpressure arose from viewers and columnists. Under the counterpressure, CBS reduced the suspension from three months to three weeks.[77]

It is, of course, very difficult to demonstrate the existence of self-censorship because much of the evidence involves the absence or omission of coverage. In addition, much of the evidence consists of anecdotal reports of examples from which it is difficult to generalize. Nevertheless, as we indicate, there are powerful pressures for self-censorship and some evidence that news media organizations respond to them.

DIRECT INTERVENTION

In this final section, we detail the most extreme examples of persuasion by the news media, which involve direct intervention by journalists in news events. With few exceptions, these examples reflect audience acceptance of journalistic participation in the events that are covered.

Breaches of Neutrality

One of the more outrageous examples of direct journalistic intervention was reported in a series of articles in the *Toronto Globe*. As other news sources have verified, a 1981 invasion of the Caribbean island of Dominica was planned by U.S. and Canadian mercenaries and members of the Ku Klux Klan and neo-Nazi groups. According to the *Globe*'s investigative reporter Peter Moon, details of the operation had been known for months by the Toronto radio station CFTR, which had taped interviews with participants and planned to be on the island for the invasion. The articles quoted Robert Halliday, CFTR's news director, as saying, "If we'd gone to the police, we'd have had to work alongside them, and then we wouldn't have had the story."[78]

The viewing public is not prepared to accept such breaches of journalistic neutrality in the effort to get a good story. However, viewers are prepared to tolerate considerable intervention when they approve of the goals the journalist is promoting.

Producing Social Change

In recent decades, we have witnessed instances in which reporters were instrumental in producing social change. Bob Woodward and Carl Bernstein of the *Washington Post* uncovered many of the abuses that ultimately led to the resignation of President Richard Nixon, for example.

Not all influential investigative reporting, however, is done by major newspapers or the networks. Lea Thompson, a consumer reporter for the Washington, DC, affiliate of NBC, WRC-TV, was responsible for legislation mandating standards for infant formulas. Two infant formulas, Mul-Soy and Cho-Free, were missing a necessary dietary supplement, so infants fed this formula became seriously ill. The Food and Drug Administration recalled these formulas, but Thompson discovered that they were still stocked in Washington-area stores.

From October 1979 to March 1980, WRC pursued the story, which was eventually carried on *NBC Nightly News* (access was made easier by WRC's status as an NBC affiliate). Members of Congress and President Carter thanked Thompson for bringing the need for stricter standards in the production of infant formula to the attention of Congress, and Thompson was an invited guest at the ceremony at which Carter signed the standards bill into law.

In summer 1990, news coverage was responsible for action by law enforcement agencies against puppy farms. After the television shows *20/20* and *Geraldo* broadcast indictments of the pet-breeding industry, and the Humane Society of the United States called for a national boycott of puppies bred in six midwestern states, enforcement agents in those states began cracking down. The Kansas attorney general led a raid on a Topeka kennel, seized ninety dogs, and charged their breeders with cruelty to animals. Local newspapers took up the call, opposing the abuse because of its potential to hurt the state's image and economy. "Puppy breeding should be an ideal industry for Kansas," said the *Wichita Eagle.* "This state's image for Midwestern wholesomeness could be an invaluable marketing tool. Imagine the lines at pet stores in California and other states for puppies 'raised where Toto comes from.' "[79]

Journalists as Direct Participants

In some instances, journalists have become direct participants, not merely participant observers, in news stories. It was CBS News anchor Walter Cronkite, for example, not a U.S. State Department official, who made the 1977 visit of Egyptian premier Anwar Sadat to Israel possible by broaching the possibility in on-air interviews with the heads of state.

On September 6, 1990, CBS News moved explicitly into an advocacy posture in a 2-hour prime-time documentary titled "America's Toughest Assignment," a report on U.S. education. The program was complemented that week by special segments on all of CBS's regular news broadcasts, including *Sunday Morning, 60 Minutes, CBS This Morning,* and *The CBS Evening News with Dan Rather.* On September 6, at 11:30 P.M. eastern time, a live 1-hour national exchange among parents, teachers, and education experts was aired. Said CBS correspondent Charles Kuralt, the documentary's anchor, "We're actually going to be advocates for certain changes. We are going to tell America what needs to be done."[80] The proposed changes were rooted in the recommendations of Dr. Ernest Boyer, president of the Carnegie Foundation for the Advancement of Teaching and an adviser to CBS News's Project Education. The proposals included transforming kindergarten through fourth grade into a concentrated 4-year program focused on basic reading, writing, and math skills.

Neither the CBS educational initiative nor Cronkite's efforts to mediate in the Middle East drew criticism because both were consistent with bipartisan national goals and with ends approved by the U.S. public. Who, after all, opposes peace or excellence in education?

When their actions are not in agreement with such broad public and political consensus, however, journalists are criticized for becoming advocates. During coverage of the TWA hostage crisis in Lebanon in 1985, Dan Rather's pointed on-air questioning of Nabih Berri, the Islamic leader ostensibly trying to negotiate release of the hostages, prompted criticism that Rather had crossed the dividing line between journalism and personal diplomacy.

Journalists also draw criticism when they appear to be channels of propaganda for those whose views are widely condemned by the public and the politicians in the United States. "Checkbook journalism," the practice of paying for an interview, is frowned on by most reputable news organizations. In spring 1986, a related practice generated controversy in the news community. On May 5, *NBC Nightly News* featured an interview with Mohammed Abul Abbas, the terrorist suspected of planning the hijacking of the cruise ship *Achille Lauro* in October 1985. During that hijacking, a wheelchair-ridden American, Leon Klinghoffer, was killed and his body dumped overboard. Abbas had offered NBC an exclusive interview with the condition that the correspondent and crew not identify the location of the interview. During the meeting, Abbas stated that the United States was now the target of his efforts because "America is now conducting the war against us on behalf of Israel."

NBC News was careful to announce that it was not paying O. J. Simpson for a planned exclusive 1-hour interview on *Dateline NBC* on October 11, 1995. Hostile audience reaction to the interview, protests by the National Organization for Women and other groups, and withdrawal of advertising by advertisers reflected the controversy aroused by this news coup. Because of advertiser resistance, NBC expected to lose $2 million in the short run from airing the interview, but the very high ratings that the interview would probably have garnered would have offset these losses. By not paying Simpson, NBC treated the planned interview as a news event.[81] On the advice of his lawyers on the day of the scheduled interview, Simpson backed out.

Intervention by the media becomes even more controversial when the media intervention benefits one person but, in the process, harms another. When officials at the Loma Linda (California) University Medical Center refused to consider an infant for a heart transplant on the grounds that his unwed parents could not provide adequate postoperative care, the couple took their case to the media. "Baby Jesse" appeared in stories on the three major networks and in the nation's newspapers. While the couple was being interviewed on *Donahue,* a Michigan couple, whose son was brain dead at birth, agreed to donate their infant's heart to Jesse, whose story they had seen on television.

What the television coverage failed to reveal was that another infant had been waiting even longer for a heart transplant, but his parents had worked quietly through organ procurement channels instead of turning to the press for sympathy and help. After learning that Jesse had received the heart, the disappointed couple appealed through the media to Congress to "do everything possible to see that an improved system is set up to identify donors of organs." They added, "[I]t almost seems like publicity is the only method that's working." *Time* magazine commented, "Another ethical issue was brought to light by the baby Jesse case: the growing role of the media in determining who gets organs."[82]

The Civic Journalism Movement

In 1990, the *Wichita Eagle* introduced an election project titled "Your Vote Counts." It was, in the words of editor Davis Merritt, "an unabashed and activist effort to restore some role for citizens in the election process." The *Eagle* continued its effort in 1992, when it was joined by the *Charlotte Observer* and the *Minneapolis Star Tribune*, among others. Instead of covering the horse race and in the process accounting for the tactics used by the candidates to win, civic journalism focuses on the agenda of citizens. Their agenda is determined by polls, focus groups, and discussions with citizens. "That first Voter Project, in Kansas's 1990 gubernatorial election, produced some tantalizing signs of hope," wrote Merritt. "Voter turnout in areas we reached was measurably higher than in other areas of the state. Voters within the *Eagle*'s reach felt that they understood the issues at a measurably higher level than did voters outside our area."[83]

In 1999, a doctoral dissertation by Sean Aday of the Annenberg School for Communication at the University of Pennsylvania evaluated the impact of civic journalism with a series of controlled field experiments. Aday found that reporting that abandons the "objectivist" frame and the traditional journalistic norm of balance for solution-oriented reporting decreases the audience's ability to generate alternative options to the problem being discussed in the articles.[84]

TO SUM UP

All news coverage shapes events. In this chapter we have examined elements of news presentation that not only shape but also sensationalize, distort, modify, and create events.

Media technology is used to dramatize and sensationalize news stories and to increase the authority and credibility of anchors and correspondents. The pressures of deadlines, competition, and breaking news, along with the structure of news stories, all contribute to inaccurate and incomplete reporting. News coverage becomes persuasion when language is used to create insinuations, when news coverage supports or opposes governmental policies, and when self-censorship suppresses certain kinds of news stories. Finally, on occasion newspeople become participants in the events they are covering. Such direct intervention is accepted by viewers and readers when it supports widely approved goals but rejected when reporters' actions are controversial.

In all these instances, members of the news media influence us, not simply by selecting what events they will cover, but by deciding how these events should be treated and interpreted. In the next chapter, we examine countervailing forces that, in turn, influence the news media.

ANALYSIS: ANALYZING A NEWS ITEM

Our analysis of news has illustrated principles with historical examples. Here we include questions that can be used to analyze a current news item.

Newsworthiness

Why was the item considered newsworthy? To what event, if any, was it tied? Was drama, conflict, or violence incorporated into it? Was it personalized? Was it an extension of a continuing issue? Did it incorporate novelty or deviance?

How was its newsworthiness established in the report? Did it affect large numbers of people? a wide area? A celebrity? Did it have important consequences?

Was this a local, state, regional, or national story? What determined whether it would be reported in local, state, regional, or national media?

Did this story lend itself to coverage by one medium and not others—for example, a ballet on television but not on radio? If so, why?

Did the story appear in one newspaper or many? If it appeared in many, was the source of the story the same or different in different newspapers? (Did all carry it from the Associated Press? United Press International? the *New York Times* syndicate? Or did some carry one and some another?) Did any of the accounts combine sources of information (a story based on AP and UPI accounts, for example)? If there were differences, were they significant, and if so, how do you account for them? (Was there a local angle on a national story? Was there reaction to a story event from a prominent local person? Was the story informed by different political points of view?) Did the story appear on any of the network newscasts? If it appeared on some but not others, how do you account for that? How did the reports on different networks differ from one another? If it appeared in some media and not others, how do you account for that? How did national coverage differ from local coverage?

What was the angle on the story? What other angles could have been chosen? How would the story have changed if it had been framed by each of these other angles? Was the story pegged to some other event? If so, what, how, and why? How newsworthy was this other event? What other pegs could have been used (piggybacking)? If another peg had been used, how would the story have changed?

Reporter

Who reported the story? Was the person given a byline? If not, why not? Why did this reporter, not another, cover this story? (Regular beat? special expertise? special interest in this topic?) What are the stylistic, structural, evidentiary, and substantive predispositions of this reporter? If the story had been reported by some other specific reporter—say, Lesley Stahl (CBS) rather than Bruce Morton (CNN)—how would the story have differed, if at all? How did the reporter establish her or his credibility? What devices, if any, were used to suggest the reporter's "objectivity"?

The News Story

What sorts of claims were made in the story? What sort of evidence was marshaled to support the claims? Was the evidence accurate? Did the evidence warrant the claims? How was the evidence made credible? Was the source of the evidence identified? (Was it a highly placed source?) If not, who do you think the source was? Were eyewitnesses used? Were they interviewed willingly? Did the interviews seem to be an invasion of their privacy? Was expert testimony used? If so, was the authority quoted, paraphrased, or interviewed? What determined whether the authority was quoted, paraphrased, or interviewed? Why was this authority selected rather than some other? How was the credibility of the authority established? If the story was covered on television, did the authority look credible? sound credible? Were other authorities cited? If so, what was the relationship among the authorities (pro–con, accusation–defense)?

Was a concrete example used? Were statistics used? Were governmental sources used? If so, how and why?

If the story involved an interview, what was the relationship between the reporter and the person interviewed (friendly, hostile, distant)? Were the questions asked by the reporter included in the story? If not, could you determine what the questions were from the answers? If the reporter paraphrased the questions, did the paraphrases seem consistent with the answers? Did the person interviewed seem to be facilitating coverage of the story or attempting to limit coverage? Was access to the person interviewed limited in any way? Were questions submitted in advance? Were some topics off-limits? Did the reporter agree to print or air certain parts of the interview in exchange for it? Did anyone refuse to be interviewed for this story? If so, was that fact reported? How? Was the impression created that the person who refused was guilty of something? hiding something?

Was the event reported a pseudo-event? If so, did it accomplish the purposes of the persons who staged it? If so, did the reporter note that it was a pseudo-event?

Was the story part of a series? If so, what was its function as part of the series?

Constraints

Did people outside the media shape or try to shape the story? If so, why did they succeed or fail?

How did constraints in the media shape the story? Were media deadlines used strategically? Could the event be filmed or photographed? What were the costs of coverage? How did limitations of time and space affect coverage? How could these constraints have been overcome? (What would you have had to have argued to claim an exception?)

Did the elite media set the agenda for this story? If so, when and how? How was coverage by the elite media reflected in the story?

Framing

How was the news item introduced? (Headline? prefatory statement by reporter or anchor?) What expectations did the introduction create about the story?

What other introduction could appropriately have been used? How would other introductions have reframed the report? Was there a summary statement at the end of the report? What interpretation, if any, did it impose on the report?

What values does the story support? (Problems can be solved? The system works? Legitimate authorities should solve problems? Hard work pays off? Our system of government is the best?)

Inclusion/Exclusion

What of importance about the story is not reported? Why? Were apparently trivial pieces of information included in the story? If so, why?

Setting

Where was the report situated? (Dateline London? On location in Newark?) Is the setting readily accessible to the news outlet? How costly is it to cover and, if the medium is television, to send a camera crew? How did cost affect likelihood of coverage? Was the reporter actually at the scene of the event reported? If so, is that fact established in the story? If so, how? If not, is that fact evident in the report? If not, what is the reporter's source of firsthand information? Is the setting used to make the report more credible (for example, a televised report about politics from the steps of the Capitol)? How, if at all, did the setting dramatize the story?

Timing

When (what time of day) did the reported event occur? Did the time of occurrence mean that it was reported by some media and not others? Was the event deliberately timed to maximize or minimize coverage? On what day of the week did the event occur? Did occurrence on that day increase the likelihood that the event would be covered (slow news day), decrease the likelihood that it would be covered, or not make much difference? Did the event occur at a time of year in which there is little competition for access to the news? (Fourth of July weekend? post-Christmas, pre–New Year's? Thanksgiving weekend?)

If the event had not been reported in a brief span of time, would it have lost its news value (for example, a presidential press conference), or could the story be stored for another day if it couldn't be fit into today's broadcast or paper (for example, a report on some ongoing struggle)?

Placement

Was it treated as hard news or soft news? Could it have been transformed from hard to soft, or soft to hard? If so, how? Where was it placed in the news broadcast, newspaper, or newsmagazine? What items were placed in a more prominent space or time? What accounts for the placement of this item in relation to other items? How much space or time was this report allotted? Was that more or less than the other reports? Account for the differences. What sorts of news stories would bump this story from the lineup?

BOX 3-7 Terrorism and the Press

Terrorists often seek publicity, and to that end they try to use the press. Few have been as successful as the mail bomb terrorist called the "Unabomber," who was able to induce the *New York Times* and the *Washington Post*, two of the more prestigious newspapers in the country, to publish his 35,000-word manifesto calling for a world revolution against modern technology. The eight-page insert was published in the *Post* on September 19, 1995, with both papers sharing the estimated $30,000 to $40,000 cost.

In 1978 the Unabomber began his campaign against modern industrial society by mailing bombs to university faculty associated with computer sciences or genetics. In sixteen attacks, twenty-three were injured and three killed. The writer of the manifesto promised to stop killing if the papers cooperated by publishing his work (and additional annual manifestos for the next 3 years).[a]

In a joint statement on their decision to publish, Donald Graham, publisher of the *Washington Post*, and Arthur Sulzberger, publisher of the *New York Times*, said that they had for three months pondered the problem of publishing "under the threat of violence," and, on the recommendation of the U.S. attorney general and the director of the FBI, had decided to accede to the Unabomber's demands for "public safety reasons."[b]

Not everyone thought the right decision had been made. The chairman of NYU's Department of Journalism and Mass Communication called it a "shameful episode" on two counts. Not only had the publishers given in to the demands of a terrorist, but they had also let the press be directed by the government.[c] However, the decision to publish was vindicated when the Unabomber's brother recognized some stylistic similarities between the manifesto and letters from his sibling and called the FBI. The call led to the arrest and conviction of Ted Kaczynski.

[a]Howard Kurtz, *Washington Post*, 19 September 1995, p. A1.
[b]Donald E. Graham and Arthur Sulzberger, Jr., *New York Times*, 19 September 1995, p. B7.
[c]William Serrin, *Washington Post*, 24 September 1995, p. C3.

Patterns

Are authorities appearing on this broadcast familiar faces? Have they served as authorities on this channel before? Often? If so, why? What is the apparent bias of the authority, if any? Is the authority identified as being partisan? If so, is another point of view represented? What are the similarities among authorities used in this type of media outlet? How often and in what kinds of stories do women function as authorities? African Americans? Latinos? Older people? How often are professors used as authorities? With what schools are they associated? Are the schools located near the media outlet? Are they Ivy League schools? Are authorities from regions of the country other than that in which the media outlet is located represented?

Who is likely to cover what kind of story? Are female reporters more likely to be assigned to cover the women's movement? Wives of candidates? Socially significant weddings (Prince Charles's or Caroline Kennedy's)? When do African Americans, Latinos, and older reporters appear? Are stories about some foreign countries more likely to appear than stories about other foreign countries?

Manipulation

Did those outside the media capitalize on any preexisting patterns to manipulate media coverage? Did those outside the media capitalize on extrinsic or intrinsic constraints to manipulate the story? Did the efforts succeed? Were the efforts reported in the story?

How much of the report, if any, was based on press reports, actualities, or news reports provided by outsiders? How, if at all, would the report have differed if it had been prepared in its entirety by the reporter, without press releases and so forth?

How much, if any, of the story simply recycled information from some other news source? Which source was used, and how do you account for the recycling?

Impact

Who, if anyone, benefited from the coverage? Who, if anyone, was damaged by the coverage? How? If someone or some organization was likely to seek news coverage to counter an impression created by the story, who would it be? What would you expect that person or organization to do? What media outlets would you expect him or her to use? (Op-eds? Letters to the editor? Press conferences? Ads?) If the Fairness Doctrine were still in force, would they be entitled to equal time?

 Use InfoTrac College Edition to access information on topics in this chapter from hundreds of periodicals and scholarly journals. Enter keyword and subject searches: *persuasion and news, inaccurate reporting, The Fairness Doctrine, civic journalism.*

SELECTED READINGS

Bybee, Carl. "Constructing Women as Authorities: Local Journalism and the Microphysics of Power." *Critical Studies in Mass Communication* 7 (September 1990): 197–214.

Gans, Herbert. *Deciding What's News: A Study of* CBS Evening News, NBC Evening News, Newsweek, *and* Time. New York: Pantheon, 1979.

Glasgow University Media Group. *Bad News.* London: Routledge and Kegan Paul, 1976.

———. *More Bad News.* London: Routledge and Kegan Paul, 1980.

———. *Getting the Message: News, Truth, and Power.* Ed. John Eldridge. London: Routledge, 1993.

Herman, Edward S., and Noam Chomsky. *Manufacturing Consent.* New York: Pantheon, 1989.

Hess, Stephen. *International News and Foreign Correspondents.* Washington, DC: Brookings Institution, 1996.

Jensen, Carl. *Censored—The News That Didn't Make the News and Why.* New York: Four Walls Eight Windows, 1995.

Mann, Thomas E., and Norman J. Ornstein, eds. *Congress, the Press, and the Public.* Washington, DC: American Enterprise Institute and Brookings Institution, 1994.

Merritt, Davis. *Public Journalism and Public Life: Why Telling the News Is Not Enough.* Hillsdale, NJ: Erlbaum, 1995.

Smith, Joel. *Understanding the Media: A Sociology of Mass Communication.* Cresskill, NJ: Hampton Press, 1995.

Tuchman, Gaye. *Making News: A Study in the Construction of Reality.* New York: Free Press, 1978.

Wicker, Tom. *On Press.* New York: Viking, 1978.

4

Influencing the News Media

The power of the news media results from their capacity to select what is reported and to shape the content of news stories. The news media are pervasive and forceful persuaders with the ability to shape our perceptions and to influence our beliefs and attitudes. But there are limits to their power—countervailing forces that, in turn, manipulate the news media. These include people, like us, and groups, like those we belong to, who capitalize on journalistic norms and routines to create newsworthy events and to shape their coverage. The commercial pressures of profits and competition, and direct pressures from the political establishment, also limit the power of the media.

INFLUENCING JOURNALISTIC NORMS AND ROUTINES

"Manipulated journalism presupposes routine journalism."[1] The ability to influence news coverage is directly related to an understanding of the journalistic norms and routines described in the preceding chapters; hence, many successful public relations consultants are former newspeople. The news media are vulnerable precisely because reporters have deadlines and beats, because they are generalists who rely on sources, and because of demands for brevity and for dramatic, visual coverage. The media's criteria for what is newsworthy and the external and internal constraints and conventions influencing what is covered and published contribute to their susceptibility.

Manipulating Deadlines

Because the news media face deadlines and are induced by competition to favor the latest details and the freshest facts, information released shortly before a deadline by an important person about an important matter is likely to be reported uncritically. In such cases, the event is newsworthy, and the source is known and familiar. If reporters take time to investigate the veracity and accuracy of the information, they risk having a competitor break the story first. As a result, press secretaries or news managers release controversial information as close to deadlines as possible, to minimize critical scrutiny of it. This became the standard procedure of the Nixon administration in the final months of the Watergate investigation.

Once a medium has broadcast or published the story, a second constraint comes into play, which minimizes the chance that the released information will get the scrutiny it deserves. By tomorrow, today's news is stale. Fresh information is competing for space. Rehashing yesterday's news is taboo.

The news media can also be manipulated by groups and individuals who time the release of potentially damaging information when deadlines have passed or when the audience is harder to reach. Before the advent of 24-hour-a-day cable news, once the Sunday morning papers were on the newsstands and on the breakfast tables of the U.S. public, it was difficult to reach a mass audience until the regular Monday morning channels of news began—Monday morning drive-time radio, talk shows such as *Good Morning America,* and the Monday morning paper. Sunday evening network news is still often preempted by special programming or not aired by affiliates. Consequently, President Gerald Ford's controversial decision to pardon former president Richard Nixon was announced at 11 A.M., eastern time, on Sunday morning. The timing assured that even if the broadcast media, understaffed on weekends, turned their full attention to the pardon, few people would be reached by media news coverage.

David R. Gergen, former assistant to the president for communications, said, "If you've got some news that you don't want to be noticed, put it out Friday afternoon at 4 P.M."[2] The Reagan administration announced the formal end of U.S. participation in the international peacekeeping force in Lebanon on a Friday at 4 P.M. Other decisions announced at that hour included restoration of tax breaks to private schools that discriminate on the basis of race; a directive, later suspended, imposing lifetime secrecy agreements on more than 100,000 government officials; and the discovery of clinically benign polyps during a routine colonoscopy on President Reagan, conducted as part of a follow-up to his rectal colon cancer surgery.

Similarly, when President George H. W. Bush decided to break his campaign pledge of "No New Taxes," he did so in a memo released to coincide with Nelson Mandela's headline-stealing speech to a joint meeting of Congress. Whereas Bush spoke in first person in making the election pledge, his memo shifted to third person. Passive voice replaced active. The simple, straightforward word *taxes* became *tax revenue increases.* At the convention he had said, "The Congress will push me to raise taxes, and I'll say no, and they'll push, and I'll say no, and they'll push again, and I'll say to them, 'Read my lips, No new taxes.'"[3] By contrast, his memo stated, "It is clear to me that both the size of the deficit problem and the need for a package that can be enacted require all of the following: entitlement and mandatory program reform; tax revenue increases; growth incentives; discretionary spending reductions." Bush's efforts to minimize media scrutiny, however, did not stop with issuing a written statement on a news-filled day. Throughout the day, Bush avoided talking to reporters, noted the *New York Times,* and "when he was asked during one brief Rose Garden appearance to expand on his written words, he replied, 'I'll let the statement speak for itself.'"[4]

Under assault by critics for withholding a presidential daily briefing memo that had been the focus of concern by the 9/11 commission, the George W. Bush administration released the document on Saturday afternoon April 10, 2004.

Late Friday releases draw reporters' suspicions that those releasing the information have something to hide. So, for example, in February 2004, Elisabeth Bumiller reported that

When the White House released hundreds of pages of President Bush's National Guard records on Friday night [February13], the immediate conclusion from

Washington political analysts was that there had to be something incriminating buried in the two-inch stack. For most modern administrations, Friday night has been a favored time for unloading bad news aimed for the relative dead air of the weekend.

By Saturday morning, when it became clear that there was nothing significantly new in the repetitive, disorganized stack, however, the real reason for the release appeared to be a combination of the president's impatience and White House officials' eagerness to defuse the damage from decade-old charges that they say the Democrats are using more aggressively this year than ever before."[5]

Twenty-four-hour-a-day cable news increased the likelihood that a story released late Friday would receive immediate coverage, but that did not simultaneously change the public's media-watching habits. The tactics of the Clinton White House in this regard don't look very different from those of its predecessors. Reviewing Lanny Davis's book *Truth to Tell: Tell it Early, Tell It All, Tell It Yourself,* Mimi Hall of *USA Today* commented that the book offered a "fresh look at how Clinton's aides manipulated the news media—sometimes with great success." Their tactics were varied: "They released information about damaging stories on Friday nights, when fewer people are paying attention to the news. They leaked bad stories to newspapers they knew wouldn't run them on the front page. And they withheld key information, such as the dates that donors stayed in the Lincoln Bedroom."[6]

If the media can be manipulated by strategic timing of bad news, they are also susceptible to the release of good news when most of the audience is watching. For example, during prime time in the opening week of the fall 1978 television season, President Jimmy Carter announced unexpectedly that he had just secured an agreement between Prime Minister Menachem Begin of Israel and President Anwar Sadat of Egypt on an Egyptian–Israeli peace accord. As a result of timing, Carter reached an unprecedented number of viewers. The announcement found most audience members tuned to the first television showing of a remake of the movie *King Kong* or to a new program, *Battlestar Galactica* (mistakenly heralded as the hottest new show of the season).

Even an audience member uninterested in foreign affairs was likely to stay tuned through the peace accord announcement to see the rest of the prime-time program. Those who were more interested in public affairs could stay tuned for network news updates, read about the accord in the morning papers, hear about it on drive-time radio, or listen to it discussed on Monday morning talk shows. Once again, manipulation required a highly newsworthy event and a reliable source, but timing was used to influence coverage to reach the largest possible audience. Similarly, Boris Yeltsin guaranteed a huge international audience for his resignation announcement by delivering it on New Year's Eve as international coverage of the turn of the millennium was building.

Timing and speed affect the press's power to manipulate a public figure. The press manipulates the public figure if coverage of a gaffe or a problem is prolonged; the public figure manipulates the press if she or he can quash extended coverage with a quick explanation or confession. For example, President Gerald Ford made a significant error in a debate with Jimmy Carter during the 1976 campaign, asserting that Poland was free. After the debate, Ford did not admit immediately that he had made a mistake. The news media covered the fact that his aides were trying to persuade him to make such a statement, and played documentary footage showing the lack of freedom in the Soviet-controlled Poland. The Carter campaign treated the remark as a major policy error, and Carter, speaking before a Polish group, assured them that he knew how terrible things were in Poland. Ford finally acknowledged his error, and the topic quickly disappeared from the news, but the damage had been done. Ford's momentum in the polls leveled off, and his ratings began to rise again only at the end of that week. Some Ford strategists credit that error and its handling with the loss of the election.[7]

Republican strategists learned their lesson. When in a fall 1988 debate with Democratic contender Michael Dukakis, Republican nominee George H. W. Bush stated that he favored making abortion a crime, by the early hours of the next morning aides were on the air saying that after considering the issue carefully overnight, Bush wanted to clarify his position: Only the person performing the abortion, not the woman having the abortion, should be subject to criminal prosecution.

Similarly, after Vice President Albert Gore stated in a 2000 Democratic primary debate in New Hampshire that he would require that those he nominated to serve on the Joint Chiefs of Staff agree with his policy of allowing gays to serve openly in the military, the response of current and former military officers prompted Gore to hold a press conference at which he issued a "clarification." "I did not mean to imply," he said, "that there should ever be any kind of inquiry into the personal political opinions of officers of the U.S. military, nor would I ever tolerate such inquiries. . . . What I meant to convey was I would not tolerate, nor would any commander in chief, nor would any president tolerate orders not being followed."[8]

Prompt response by a vulnerable person can shift the questions being asked by the press. When British movie star Hugh Grant was charged in summer 1995 with committing a lewd act with 23-year-old prostitute Divine Brown, he promptly issued an apology, saying, "Last night I did something completely insane. I have hurt people I love and embarrassed people I work with. For both things I am more sorry than I can possibly say."[9] The apology shifted news coverage from such questions as, Did he do it? Will he be convicted? and Is he sorry? to What effect will the act and apology have on his acting career? This was an important question, because Grant had been arrested while in the United States promoting a new film, *Nine Months.*

Deadlines can also be used to insert questionable material into news stories, such as surveys done by interested parties using dubious methods. Michael R. Gordon, a staff correspondent for the *National Journal,* a Washington weekly on federal policy and politics, reports such successful manipulation. A public relations firm that was fighting trucking deregulation arranged simultaneous press conferences in five cities to publicize the results of a poll by the Group Attitudes Company, a subsidiary of the same public relations firm. The survey, said the press handout, showed "virtually no public support for the move in Congress to deregulate the nation's trucking industry." It was cited in a number of regional papers and wire service reports. None of these reports mentioned that the company that conducted the survey was owned by the public relations firm fighting deregulation, information not included in the press releases. Facing a deadline with limited knowledge of polling and statistics, reporters did not bother to question how the poll was conducted or whether its findings really supported the claim in the press release.[10]

The pressure of deadlines also makes it possible to manipulate coverage by releasing information in advance to reporters. Reporters are eager to predigest the news. This enables them to write much or all of a story in advance. Consequently, news managers delay official public release of information while making it available to the news media generally or to selected outlets or reporters. For example, in advance of a Senate committee hearing, the communications director for the committee might release the text of the chairperson's introductory statement and the testimony that witnesses will give before the committee. Reporters can then compose their stories in advance and attend the hearing to insert an update into the story or to report the unexpected. Those who provide such advance information to reporters influence the perspective that reporters will take in their news stories.

Manipulating Access

There is constant tension between those assigned to ferret out the news and those assigned to control press access to news sources. Press secretaries, public information officers, and public relations firms are hired to encourage press access to favorable information and to minimize or block access to unfavorable information. When negative information seeps out, it is the function of news managers to prevent or lessen its spread through the media and to cast it in the best possible light.

News managers control the press by controlling press access to those who have information—for example, by limiting the number of presidential press conferences or by communicating through press releases. Control can also be exerted by providing easy access to those likely to cover an issue or program favorably and limiting the access of those thought to be opposed to the interests of the news source.

Exclusive interviews with reporters function this way. The third highest-rated program of the spring 1995 season was Diane Sawyer's exclusive *Prime Time Live* interview with music star Michael Jackson and his then-wife, Lisa Marie Presley, daughter of deceased rock icon Elvis Presley. The interview was Jackson's first after his settlement of charges that he had sexually molested a young boy and after his marriage to Presley. Only the Super Bowl and the Academy Awards drew larger audiences. The agreement for the interview coincided with ABC's decision to trade ad time worth about $1 million for rights to the star's future videos. Those in ABC's news division denied that they had known of the entertainment division's talks with Jackson's managers when they scheduled the exclusive interview.

Jackson's goal was promoting his new album, "HIStory—Past, Present and Future, Book I," which was released shortly after the interview. News stories reported that "in return for the rights to Jackson's videos, according to an ABC executive, ABC Entertainment aired ten, 30-second advertisements promoting the album between Diane Sawyer's interview on June 14 and the release of the album on June 21."[11] The timing led some to surmise that Jackson's managers had, in effect, given ABC the exclusive interview in return for promotional time for Jackson's new album. By airing the spots between segments of the interview, the news show became, in effect, an extended promotion for the new album.

It is also possible to manipulate coverage by leaking information favorable to one position or damaging to an opponent's position. Finally, government officials control access by refusing to respond to a specific question on the grounds that the requested information would breach national security, by asserting that the person being questioned is not empowered to reveal the information, or by answering that the matter is still under study or in litigation.

The press's desire for access is generally expressed as "the public's right to know." Problems emerge when this right conflicts with an individual's right to privacy (should a rape victim's name be included in a news story about a rape?), the right to a fair trial (does publicity minimize a defendant's ability to get a fair trial?), and national security (should the media voluntarily suppress information that may damage the nation's interests at home or abroad?).

Manipulation through control of access is best illustrated by relationships between reporters and government officials. The reporter wants information, and the official expects something in exchange—a friendly hearing, a neutral report, or muted criticism, for example. Concealing the actual source of information is often a condition of access.

Bill Green, former *Washington Post* ombudsman, explains the "rough categories of attribution" this way. When a source speaks or holds a briefing "on the record," reporters can and do "quote the source by name." When a reporter attends a "backgrounder," he or she "can use the material but not the source." A "deep backgrounder," according to Green, "calls on the reader for an act of faith, and it produces some familiar phrases: 'it is known that' or 'it is believed that.' In other words, the fact that it came from a source cannot be revealed." When a statement is given "off the record," the reporter knows he or she "can't use it after all." Green acknowledges that this system of code phrases is necessary to elicit information that would otherwise be inaccessible but also notes that "the code and its vocabulary call credibility into question."[12] (See Figure 4-1.)

Under such circumstances, readers and viewers are asked to trust reporters and to take their news judgments on faith, a situation that makes reporters extremely vulnerable not only to manipulation but also to backlash from the audience. Some news outlets now have a policy of trying to help readers understand who the source is, or where his or her sympathies are, by the wording of the attribution: "sources opposed to the plan," "Democratic sources in Congress," or "a political consultant not affiliated with either campaign."

Access also can be limited by denying reporters the ability to get to the scene of a news story. By expelling reporters from a country, its government ensures that internal unrest will not be transmitted, at least not by them, around the world. In 1983, during the U.S. government's invasion of Grenada, the press was kept out. A blue-ribbon com-

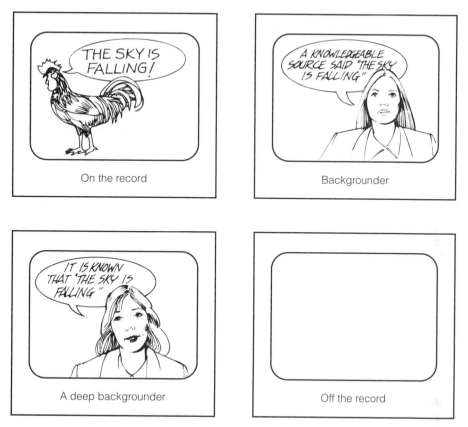

FIGURE 4-1 Identifying the source

mission headed by a retired major general, Winant Sidle, concluded that this action had been improper. In the future, the report stated, military commanders should make provision for at least a pool of reporters to witness such military operations. The Pentagon adopted the Sidle recommendations as its official policy.

In December 1989, the procedure was put to the test. Reporters selected to form the pool concluded that the policy was ignored during the invasion of Panama. Pool television correspondent Fred Francis noted, "The pool was repeatedly denied or ignored when it asked for access to front-line troops, wounded soldiers—simple interviews." When pool reporters asked to observe the securing of Panama strongman Manuel Noriega's headquarters, they were told that it was "too dangerous." The army major general whose paratroops had taken the international airport informed journalists, "Sorry, my operational orders are that I cannot let you talk with any of my men. I can't speak with you."[13] By denying reporters access to the invasion itself and by permitting them in only after the territory was presumably secured, the Bush administration minimized the likelihood that news stories would focus on bureaucratic inefficiency, needless civilian deaths, or confused soldiers who did not know the reasons why they were fighting and dying. In 1991, only a select pool of reporters was allowed access to information

---

BOX 4-2   What's a Source?

Mommy, what's a source?
A thing where something comes from; the beginning of a stream.

When is a source a person?
When the person talks to a reporter.

Why do reporters always talk to a source instead of a person?
Because they think it sounds better to quote a "source" than a "person."

Can you tell the difference between a source and a person?
No. As soon as a source is finished talking with a reporter, it turns right back into a person.

Why don't source-persons use their names?
Because they're afraid or ashamed.

Why afraid?
Because they're telling the truth and that will make someone very angry—or because they're not telling the truth and that will make someone very angry.

And why would they be ashamed?
Because they may be saying something unfair, or accusing somebody without a good reason.

Why would a reporter want information that isn't true or fair?
A good reporter will quote a source only if the information is true or provable.

How does the reporter know it's true?
Because the same person told the truth before or because another dependable person agrees that it's true.

If it's true, why does a reporter have to say a source said it's true?
Because if it turns out not to be true, the reporter can blame someone else.

Someone who is just a person?
Yes.

Isn't there something else they could call a source?
Well, many reporters call them "reliable sources" or "well-informed sources," but not in our favorite newspaper.

Why not?
Because readers might wonder why they would be going to unreliable or uninformed sources.

So what else do they call them?
Well, let's look at our favorite newspaper. Here it says: "A senior White House official," and "law-enforcement officials," and "a Clinton Administration official," and "a senior State Department official," and "a Vatican official," and "a Japanese Embassy official," and "a Housing Department official," and. . . .

But what if someone's not an official?
Well, in our favorite paper and very often the *Washington Post*, the *Boston Globe*, the *Los Angeles Times*, *Newsday*, and other newspapers, they write about sources "familiar with" the situation. Or they quote someone "close to" the case.

Is that good?
Not if the readers get to think that some sources are not close to the case or are unfamiliar with the situation.

---

about the Persian Gulf War, and even those reports were censored. In the Iraq War that began in 2003, the administration of President George W. Bush reversed the course set by his father and "embedded" journalists with the troops moving into Iraq.

Setting Up a Controlled Channel

The rise of the Internet created a way for those with resources to create their own spin site. Charged with securities fraud and obstructing a federal investigation, Martha Stewart launched www.marthatalks.com in June 2003. Her staff then took out an ad in

Why don't they just say "someone told me"?
Because "someone told me" makes it sound as if they're spreading a rumor.

What's wrong with that?
Good reporters don't spread rumors.

But how would a reporter know whether the sources or officials or people close to the case want to spread rumors?
Well, they don't. They just write that the sources who aren't named "insist on anonymity."

What does that mean?
It means the source said, "Please don't print my name," or "Don't quote me."

Why do they trust the reporter to hide their name?
Because they know the reporter is eager to get a colorful quote or fact—and may want to get information from them some other time.

Doesn't the reporter ever insist on printing their names?
I guess it happens, but you never read about it.

What would happen if reporters always insisted?
They should insist a lot more than they do. But they can't do it always. If a person—a source—can't speak with anonymity, the person might not speak at all. That means we wouldn't hear about things that could save lives or prevent bad decisions.

Like what?
Well, what if a factory is making an unsafe toy. A woman working there might want to tell about that, but not if her boss could find out and fire her. Or what if a committee chairman in Congress wanted to cut back school lunches real quick

before people found out about it? Some legislative assistant might tell about that, but not if that risked being fired. And we might never hear from all those courageous students in China that the police are putting in jail just for asking too many questions.

They go to jail for asking questions?
Yes. And sometimes in our country reporters have to go to jail for not answering questions.

What kind of questions?
About the names of their sources.

The reporters won't say who told them about the unsafe toy?
That's right, to protect that troubled woman in the toy factory.

I get it. But if a source's name has to be secret, why even mention a source?
I told you: when reporters talk to someone who doesn't want his name in the paper, they just say a source told them. The readers are supposed to know that the reporter would never repeat what the sources said unless the reporter thought it was true.

But what if it turns out to be untrue?
Then the reporter can always say the source was wrong, not the reporter.

Oh. But if the information turns out to be right, the reporter gets the credit?
Yes. And sometimes a prize.[a]

[a]Max Frankel, "Don't Quote Me," *New York Times Magazine,* 26 March 1995, pp. 38, 40. © 1995 by The *New York Times* Co. Reprinted by permission.

USA Today to draw viewers to the site. On it one could find favorable news reports and e-mails from those supporting her case. When he was charged with child molestation, Michael Jackson set up www.mjnews.us with a disclaimer about that charge and stating that only information about Jackson found on the site was trustworthy.

Manipulating News Assignments

Although presidents have tried, it is difficult to manipulate reporters by attempting to change their beats, but it is possible to manipulate newspeople who are on general assignment. For example, the Associated Press Calendar lists important events occurring in Washington. Virtually every news bureau in Washington uses it as a guide for what to cover on any given day. If an event is listed, it gets covered, whether it deserves it or not; if it's not listed, it probably won't get covered. When an event is listed, fears of competition prod the news outlets to cover it. This is also cost-efficient in the case of television, as some pooling of crews is possible under such circumstances. Arranging to have an event listed in the AP Calendar is one way to manipulate media news coverage.

Reporters on beats are vulnerable to manipulation. An example can be drawn from coverage of the Reagan presidential campaign. Joel Swerdlow reports some clever manipulation by Reagan news managers:

> Raw footage of a typical Reagan campaign day, for example, revealed that the crowds always seemed much larger than they actually were. To a large degree, this resulted from clever advance work by the media-sophisticated Reagan staff. At almost every stop, it was the same: they positioned a raised camera platform close to the speaker's platform, and roped off a huge "press area," designated off-limits to the public. This forced the crowd to pack tightly into the space between the candidate and the camera, ensuring that Reagan always spoke to an impressive-looking mass of humanity.[14]

In the 1950s and 1960s, some reporters acted as informants for and as channels of information from the Central Intelligence Agency. Stories initiated by the CIA found their way into major newspapers and onto the wire services. Before the revelations about the Vietnam War and Watergate cast doubt on the truthfulness of such government agencies, newspeople considered the CIA a trusted source of information. The CIA was able to provide reporters with access to information that they could not otherwise secure, a situation that gave those reporters a competitive edge. This information came easily and inexpensively; reporters did not have to invest time in ferreting it out, following false leads, or fighting for access to sources. The CIA also provided an angle by pegging its stories to local and international events, and most important, it provided stories based on beliefs and attitudes consistent with the reporters' views of the world: "us" versus "them," patriotism, the dangers of communism, the threat of communist infiltration. A variety of factors contributed to the association of the CIA with the media, and access to information was an important one.[15]

Media Competition

In Chapter 3 we discussed the ways that competition and deadlines contribute to incomplete and inaccurate reporting. Competition also influences coverage, particularly competition to keep up with the elite media. Consequently, in many cases news managers focus their attention on manipulating the elite media. If a news manager gains access to an elite medium, coverage in other media follows.

In some instances, access to an elite medium works to the advantage of both the medium and the newsworthy person. In the 2000 presidential campaign, for example, as rumors spread that the time Republican presidential hopeful John McCain had spent as a prisoner of war in North Vietnam had shaken his mental stability, McCain released his medical records, which confirmed that he had withstood the stress of that time well. He also made himself available for network interviews. In the process, the McCain campaign transformed a story about potential instability into an opportunity to remind voters of his heroism. Coverage by one medium influences coverage in other media. This is particularly true of the elite media, and news managers make special efforts to influence elite media coverage.

Using Access to Media to Manipulate the Agenda

The power of nationally televised speeches as well as the ability to shape the media agenda led President Bill Clinton to observe that "even a President without a majority mandate coming in, if the President has a disciplined, aggressive agenda that is clearly in the interest of the majority of the American people—I think you can create new political capital all the time, because you have access to the people through the communications network."[16] An examination of the major presidential addresses to the nation from those of Harry Truman through those of Ronald Reagan justified Clinton's conclusion. On average, the occurrence of such a speech coincided with a six-point increase in the president's approval rating.[17]

Expanded Opportunities for Direct Address

Satellites Technology has increased the ability of a leader to speak directly to the public. Access to satellites makes it possible for a leader to bypass the national media. Thus, for example, in 1992, 1996, and 2000, both Democrats and Republicans made their presidential hopefuls available for satellite interviews with local newscasters. In the primaries of 2000, a study by the Annenberg School of Communication found that every major news station in New Hampshire, South Carolina, and Michigan conducted satellite interviews with Gore, Bradley, Bush, and McCain during the primary season.[18]

The Internet The Internet allows politicians to circumvent journalists by creating a direct line of communication to their constituents that is unfiltered and unrestricted by the norms and structural constraints of traditional print and broadcast journalism. Although in the 24-hour news climate events are more heavily defined by journalists in their never-exhausted quest to get the story, on the Internet politicians can communicate with citizens outside the journalistic environment. Politicians now have at their disposal websites, e-mail, and online forums to generate a direct line of communication to citizens.

The Internet thus has the potential to be a direct channel of contact between leaders and the led. *Washington Post* reporter Howard Kurtz writes, "The new venues will give ordinary folks the ability to search voting records, election returns, exit polls, speech and position papers, enabling them to cut through the political fog by downloading the facts for themselves."[19] A citizen can express her or his views in the form of e-mail, in discussion groups, in chat rooms, or on electronic bulletin boards. (For a discussion of the political impact of the Internet, see Chapter 11.)

Language and Symbols

The print and electronic news media can be manipulated through the effective use of language and visual symbols. Because of its reliance on the visual, television news is particularly vulnerable to the strategic use of visual symbols. Thus for example, when early in his papacy Pope John Paul II knelt with two former concentration-camp captives at an execution wall in Auschwitz, the visual that resulted constituted a nonverbal Vatican repudiation of the view that the Jews killed Christ. John Paul II was uniquely suited to this scene. Because he had been a member of the Polish underground that acted to save Jews, the scene was an extension of his personal commitment. In addition, Auschwitz is in Poland, and his presence was a reminder of Polish Catholics' suffering at the hands of the Nazis and, implicitly, at the hands of the Soviets. Such events rivet photographic attention because little or no commentary is required—the picture is the story. If these kinds of scenes were routine, they would not be newsworthy. It is both the freshness of the symbols and their ability to stand for more than themselves that make them attractive to news photographers. Nonverbal symbolic acts that require verbal commentary are less effective.

Similarly, in spring 1990 Imelda Marcos, the wife of former Philippines president Ferdinand Marcos, shaped national network coverage of her acquittal on charges of misuse of state funds and at the same time secured front-page newspaper access. Marcos accomplished this by inching her way up the aisle of a church on her knees in a black mourning dress to "thank God" for the trial's outcome. The black dress reminded viewers of her widowhood, kneeling suggested that she was religious, and movement up the aisle in the posture of a penitent suggested her humility and the injustice of seeking to convict her. How, after all, could one assume the guilt of a humble, religious widow, kneeling in church?

Aware of the power of such symbols, political candidates search for locations that will visually reinforce sympathetic parts of their biographies. For 1996 Republican presidential hopeful Bob Dole, that backdrop was Russell, Kansas, his hometown. The town is filled with places linked to Dole's humble origins, including Dawson's drugstore, where the Kansan worked as a soda jerk. As reporters noted, Russell, Kansas, is "an irresistible symbol of the small-town virtues that helped Dole overcome a debilitating war injury and climb the ladder of electoral success."[20] When Democratic presidential hopeful Bill Bradley announced his candidacy, he followed the same sort of script, bringing reporters to the small town in Missouri where he was raised.

Nonverbal symbols are risky because sometimes they are open to more than one interpretation. At the close of the dedication ceremonies at the Nixon Library, for instance, former president Nixon raised his arms while shaping V's with the fingers of each hand. The gesture was one characteristic of Nixon the campaigner and Nixon the president. Parodists of the former president frequently used it to cue audiences that they were about to begin their impressions of Nixon. In the context of the library ceremony, the symbol could have indicated a final victory over those who forced his resignation from office. Alternatively, it could have suggested that this, too, was a campaign event, and as such a bid for a legitimacy not yet accorded him by history. In politics, a similar problem can arise when a campaign slogan is open to more than one interpretation or when it lends itself to easy parody (see Chapter 11).

The news media can also be manipulated by the language of a statement that is artfully constructed and skillfully delivered. Ideally, such a statement should be uneditable, dramatic, concise, and synoptic. It should be capable of being delivered in less than 35 seconds by a skilled speaker. If delivered by a credible person, about an important topic, and on an occasion accessible to the news media, it is virtually irresistible to

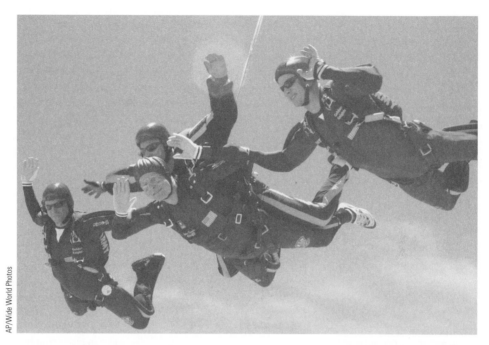

AP/Wide World Photos

Would this photo be newsworthy if President George Herbert Walker Bush were not the father of President George W. Bush? Suppose, for example, that former President Bill Clinton celebrated one of his birthdays by parachuting out of a plane.

the press. An example of such a statement was George H. W. Bush's 1988 promise, "Read my lips, No new taxes." But as subsequent use of that phrase illustrates, such digestive statements can also be turned against their creator. In 1992 Republican challenger Pat Buchanan reminded New Hampshire voters that Bush had broken that promise. No new taxes became, for Buchanan, No old Bush.

A similar problem affected President George W. Bush in the 2004 campaign. "On July 2 [2003]," recalled William Safire, "President Bush warned terrorists and Baathist diehards: 'There are some that feel like—if they attack us—that we may decide to leave prematurely. . . . My answer is, bring 'em on.' On top of a much-publicized landing by the president on an aircraft carrier in front of a 'Mission Accomplished' sign, this impromptu remark was promptly criticized as overconfident, even as inviting trouble." Recognizing that Bush's use of it could be turned into an indictment of the Bush's conduct of the war in Iraq and National Guard service, John Kerry modified the phrase by a word and added to his stump speech the statement "If George Bush wants to make national security an issue in this campaign, I have three words for him that I know he'll understand. Bring it on!" [21]

Carefully crafted synoptic statements can also create a context for viewing political information. Thus, for example, year 2000 Republican presidential hopeful John McCain indicted the tax proposal of his primary opponent Texas Governor George W. Bush and touted his own in a sound bite that focused press attention not on the amount of the proposed tax cuts (McCain proposed a much smaller amount) but on

---

**BOX 4-3   A Checklist for Creating Newsworthy Statements Likely
to Be Covered and Published**

To Be	Or . . . Not to Be
A single coherent statement	A rambling statement
clearly summarizing the issue	skirting the issue
in jargon-free English,	in gobbledygook,
written to be understood on	written to be figured out
first hearing or reading,	by a cryptographer,
which can be delivered	which could not be delivered
clearly and dramatically	effectively by Liam Neeson
in less than 14 seconds,	in less than 35 minutes,
requiring no additional	requiring at least a paragraph of
information,	clarification,
available before deadline	available at midnight
at a convenient place for newsgatherers,	at the North Pole,
delivered in a symbolic	delivered in a setting with no
setting	apparent relationship to the statement
or by a person who	or by a nondescript person who
dramatizes the issue	mumbles
in a manner not subject to	in a manner that brings joy to the
parody.	hearts of Art Buchwald and
	Garry Trudeau, who hope the
	speaker will seek the presidency.

---

who would benefit. "Sixty percent of [Bush's] tax cuts are for the wealthiest 10 percent of America," noted the Arizona senator. "I don't think that's necessary. I want the tax cuts for lower and middle income Americans."[22]

Because more Americans read newspaper headlines than read the articles they describe, a candidate gains an advantage when a charge he or she has made is translated into a headline. Accordingly, Gore is given an advantage when *USA Today*'s above-the-fold headline reads "Gore: Bradley could 'blunder' into recession."[23]

Because television is a visual medium whose ordinary form is the narrative, a visually evocative narrative has special power. Because news employs a story structure, narratives are particularly attractive to reporters. In summer 1995, the Democratic minority in the House of Representatives used these conventions to create a favorable context in hearings on the 1993 clash between federal officers and people inside the Branch Davidian compound in Waco, Texas, that led to the deaths of many of those within the compound.

The clash began on February 28, 1993, when seventy-five federal officers, who suspected that the Branch Davidians were making illegal drugs and stockpiling illegal weapons, tried to execute a search warrant at the compound. A shootout resulted, leaving four government officers and six cult members dead. Who shot first is contested. Despite repeated requests, their leader, David Koresh, refused to surrender to the agents. On April 19, the agents launched a tear gas attack, and eighty-one people

---

BOX 4-4   Memorable Sound Bites

In a section called "Verbatim" *Time* magazine lists the more memorable sound bites of the past week. Why are these sound bites, which appeared in the February 23, 2004, issue, newsworthy?

- "They're enemy combatants and terrorists who are being detained for acts of war against our country. That is why different rules have to apply." —Donald Rumsfeld, Defense Secretary "explaining the indefinite detention of foreign terrorism suspects in Guantanamo Bay."
- "I won't dignify your comments about the President because you don't know what you're talking about. . . . Let's not go there." —Colin Powell, Secretary of State, "responding testily during a congressional hearing when Democratic Representative Sherrod Brown of Ohio referred to allegations that Bush may not have fulfilled his National Guard duty in 1972."
- "I'm just deeply disappointed that once again we may have to settle for the lesser of two evils." —Howard Dean, "Democratic candidate for President, on a possible matchup of John Kerry and George W. Bush."

---

within the compound died in a fire. Branch Davidian supporters argued that the fire resulted from the ignition of the tear gas; the Clinton administration claimed that it might have been set from within the compound. On the grounds that the search warrant was unjustified and the deaths needless, Republicans set up hearings in spring 1995.

When Clinton supporters argued that the hearings had been set up and witnesses scheduled to show the administration in an unfavorable light, the Republicans agreed to permit the Democrats to choose one of the early witnesses. They chose 14-year-old Kiri Jewell, who graphically testified that she had been sexually abused by Koresh. Front-page pictures and headlines and prominent broadcast coverage were the result. Her testimony corroborated the claim of Attorney General Janet Reno that one reason for the assault was the belief by federal officials that children were being sexually abused. It also shifted the attention of the hearing and the public from questions about administration decisions to Koresh. The effectiveness of the strategy led the *New York Times* to headline a summary story on the hearings, "Role Reversal: Expecting Waco Hearings' Triumph, Republicans Were Instead Surprised."[24]

Language can be used to deter news coverage as well. For instance, the difficulties involved in covering highly technical, abstract material are exploited by those who want to minimize news coverage of their activities. *Politics and the Oval Office,* a report by the conservative Institute for Contemporary Studies, argues that the presidency has suffered from too much uncontrolled coverage by the media. To curb what it views as excessive coverage, the report urges the president to overwhelm media representatives with technical data: "This tactic should defuse complaints about total accessibility. It could reduce the total volume of reporting, because dry data are often defined as unnewsworthy."[25]

Adaptation to the style and perspective of specific news channels and to the interests, biases, and experiences of individual reporters is a means of manipulating the press. For example, news managers can tailor a story for the *Wall Street Journal* by filling it with technical and economic data or for *Time* magazine by providing anecdotal material and clever language.

Every reporter has special interests, biases, and experiences. For this reason, if news coverage is to be balanced, it is important to have men and women covering the news who are from different socioeconomic, ethnic, religious, and cultural backgrounds and who bring varied perspectives to reporting stories.

Language and symbols can be used to influence news coverage. Of particular force is the dramatic visual symbol, but dramatic or dull language can be used to attract or deter coverage as well. It is also possible to attract coverage by tailoring statements and events to the predispositions of the reporter or media outlet.

The Perils of Live Coverage

A special, limited opportunity to manipulate access arises with live coverage, where little or no editing occurs. The opportunities for manipulation are limited to people who are newsworthy for some other reason—winners of awards or of major sports events, for example. In such circumstances, people can use live television coverage to make a statement they could not otherwise make; in the process they have access to an audience they could not reach if the statement were made under other circumstances and had to compete for regular news coverage. One example occurred in 1990, when profanities uttered by the heavy-metal band Guns 'N' Roses were heard by millions of television viewers tuned in to Monday night's American Music Awards ceremony. The profanities brought a barrage of complaints, and an apology from ABC. On September 6, 1989, comedian Andrew Dice Clay was banned for life from MTV after making sexist remarks and using profanity on a live nationwide broadcast, the MTV Video Music Awards.[26] In February 2004, Janet Jackson and Justin Timberlake provoked a public outcry when in their half-time performance at Super Bowl XXXVIII, Timberlake ripped off a portion of Jackson's costume, exposing her breast. Television networks responded by instituting 5-second delays in live broadcasts of awards shows and half-time performances.

In November 2004, 66 ABC affiliates refused to carry the award-winning film *Saving Private Ryan.* The American Family Association had protested the airing of the film because, the group said, it contained profanity and "graphic violence." The film had been broadcast on these same stations on Veterans Day in both 2000 and 2001. The difference between then and 2004? Concerns that the FCC would fine stations for the profanity in the film.

Remarks in a print interview can have comparable effects. In late December 1999 the Atlanta Braves' relief pitcher, John Rocker, told *Sports Illustrated* that a black teammate was "a fat monkey," said the thing he didn't like about New York was "the foreigners," and described riding the subway to Shea Stadium as akin to a ride through Beirut. Baseball Commissioner Bud Selig demanded that the pitcher undergo psychological testing. A reporter for the *New York Times* explained, "His mental health aside, Mr. Rocker's diatribe has not been good for baseball's image, which is not good for business."[27]

Other instances have been more calculated. For example, a Native American woman was able to read a statement on Indian rights when she appeared on Marlon Brando's behalf to refuse an Oscar he had won, and Vanessa Redgrave was able to make a controversial statement about Palestinian rights during her Oscar acceptance speech. Early in the 1988 primaries, presidential candidate George H. W. Bush agreed to an interview with CBS anchor Dan Rather on the condition that the interview be broadcast live. This move guaranteed that his remarks could not be edited. His success in controlling the agenda of the interview helped Bush dispel reporters' image of him as indecisive, an impression that they had referred to as "the wimp factor." Admittedly, such opportunities are rare and special, but live coverage provides opportunities to air highly controversial messages and to reach exceptionally large and captive audiences.

Prepackaged News

Pseudo-events, news feeds, news conferences, and prepared, or "canned," editorials are examples of news prepackaged for the convenience of reporters. News managers are well aware of reporters' weaknesses and endeavor to exploit them through prepackaged news. As one public relations and political consultant wrote, "It is much easier for a reporter to be spoon-fed than to go on a scavenger hunt in government or industry to find his next story."[28]

Reliance on prepackaged news is one reason that most reporters missed the emergence of the savings and loan crisis. "We usually depend on governmental institutions or groups like Common Cause or Ralph Nader or General Motors or somebody to make sense out of all this data for us," explained Brooks Jackson, an award-winning CNN reporter.[29]

It is legal to buy news shows off the shelf. For example, the program *Hard Copy* began airing on Channel 2 in New York in fall 1989. It was purchased from an outside vendor, Paramount, which produced it as a package for stations around the country that were affiliated or owned by the three largest networks. Nobody at CBS or at Channel 2 had anything to do with what the packagers put in the program, including the topics covered. Everything was decided and manufactured by the packager. Such packaged news programs are appealing because the station splits the ad revenue with the packager, making a lot more money than if the station's staff puts the program together. Owing to the lack of a disclaimer, viewers were led to believe that reporters for the station had prepared the stories and were responsible for their content, even though they were not.[30] In such instances, the packager has a wide latitude for influence.

There are hazards in airing other people's work, however. In January 2000, ABC News decided not to air a BBC documentary accusing an executive at a modeling agency of having sex with underage models. Because ABC had already agreed to pay for the rights to the story, the decision not to run it entailed a "kill fee." The decision not to air the documentary on ABC's *20/20* was made after the executive charged that his remarks had been selectively edited to incriminate him.[31]

In a process almost too bizarre to be believed, a self-confessed murderer argued in summer 1995 that he had killed and would continue to do so to attract sufficient media attention to ensure that a prominent media outlet would publish his 56-page, 35,000-word treatise on the ills of contemporary society. In June, the man, tagged the Unabomber by the press, wrote both the *New York Times* and the *Washington Post*, giving the papers until September 29 to print the tract and three annual follow-ups, in return for his guarantee that he would stop trying to kill. If neither paper took up his offer, said the bomber, he would resume the killings. On August 2, both papers ran 3,000-word excerpts on page 16 as part of a report on FBI efforts to identify the bomber through analysis of his style and philosophy.

At the time that he made the original request, the killer had been blamed for sixteen bombings since 1978, which had resulted in the deaths of three and the injury of twenty-three more. His rationale suggested that he was deliberately manipulating media norms:

> To make an impression on society with words is . . . almost impossible for most individuals and small groups. Take us (FC [Freedom Club]), for example. If we had never done anything violent and had submitted the present writings to a publisher, they probably would not have been accepted. If they had been accepted and published, they probably would not have attracted many readers, because it's more fun to watch the entertainment put out by the media than to read a sober essay. Even if these writings had had many readers, most of those readers would have soon forgotten what they had read as their minds were flooded by the mass of material to which the media expose them. In order to get our message before the public with some chance of making a lasting impression, we've had to kill people.[32]

Through a joint agreement between the *Times* and the *Post*, the *Post* published the terrorist's entire text in September 1995. The alleged Unabomber was apprehended when his brother read the text on the Internet and recognized the themes and the style.

Pseudo-Events A pseudo-event is an arranged event, not an occurrence that happens of its own accord. An example is a Kansas City antiabortion group appearing with tiny white caskets at a local hospital. A pseudo-event, which takes account of newsgatherers' concepts of what is newsworthy, is arranged to exploit internal and external constraints on newsgathering and the conventions of news presentation. An ideal pseudo-event is therefore dramatic (in the example, the angry encounter between shocked hospital staff and the antiabortion group), personalized (abortion was reduced to individual fetuses symbolized by tiny white caskets), novel (this event got coverage because it was original; if many antiabortion groups imitated it, coverage would end), an event (there was a specific encounter between hospital staff and the antiabortion group), and part of an ongoing theme in the news (national efforts to have personhood defined as beginning at the moment of conception had been getting considerable news coverage).

In addition, the encounter took place at a convenient urban location, close to most local television stations, and at a convenient time (early afternoon) well before deadlines. The event was staged by a local group at a local setting (the hospital), making it attractive to local coverage. The event was visual (the encounter occurred just outside the hospital doors in good light and was easy to tape) and made use of highly charged, poignant symbols of sorrow and death. Taped with brief statements from both sides (the antiabortion group and the hospital administrators) and with a reporter's wrap-up, the event fit neatly into a 99-second news segment. As a result, its appearance on the local evening news could have been predicted.

Pseudo-events are designed to transform an issue, process, person, or the like into a newsworthy event that will be covered by the mass media. Many news events are partially staged to surmount the problems described in Chapter 2—scheduling, deadlines, access, and so forth. In a letter to the networks evaluating charges that coverage of the 1968 Democratic Convention in Chicago had involved "staged news," officials of the Federal Communications Commission wrote,

> In a sense, every televised press conference may be said to be staged to some extent; depictions of scenes in a television documentary—on how the poor live on a typical day in the ghetto, for example—also necessarily involve camera directions, lights, action instructions, etc. The term "pseudo-event" describes a whole class of such activities that constitute much of what journalists treat as "news."[33]

In other words, a wide range of staged events is routinely treated as news. The news media can be manipulated into coverage of these pseudo-events because of what they define as news and because of the constraints under which they operate. Because cost and the need to meet deadlines with fresh stories are important to those who produce the news, there is pressure to cover events that have the dramatic, visual, concise characteristics the media crave. Congressional hearings, news conferences, and pseudo-events have these characteristics. In covering such events, the reporter minimizes the amount of background information needed and the amount of time it takes to assemble a story, and has the news peg for the story—the event itself. The problem, of course, is that by covering such an event, the reporter often accepts the assumptions of those managing it. The well-staged event invites coverage from a particular point of view.

An important adjunct to the press conference and to other staged events is the press release. The press release attempts to create a context for viewing a specific event. Written to include basic information (who, what, when, where, how, why) required by editors, it is filled with dramatic, synthetic statements related to the emerging news item.

Attracting media attention carries risks if the attention has been obtained under false pretenses. A candidate's opponents are eager to bring such discrepancies to the attention of the media. For example, when Marc Holtzman, a Republican congressional candidate in Pennsylvania, announced in a news release in 1986 that he had facilitated the homecoming of a Vietnamese mother of a naturalized U.S. citizen in his district, the local press carried the heartwarming story. To Holtzman's embarrassment, the press reported days later that Holtzman's role had consisted of writing a letter to Vice President George Bush inquiring about the status of the case. Bush received Holtzman's letter a week after the State Department had issued the visa. The follow-up stories hurt Holtzman's chances for reelection.[34]

News Feeds   News managers attempt to exercise even greater control by offering radio stations news feeds containing audio "bites" of a politician's speech complete with "wrapped around" context narrated by someone on the politician's staff. Statements recorded specifically for "feeding" are also distributed. Such news feeds are common on Capitol Hill, in political campaigns, and in the executive branch. They are being used increasingly by business as well. A. Kent MacDougall of the *Los Angeles Times* reports,

> Business is supplying pre-recorded interviews with business advocates to television and radio stations which slip them into their newscasts, usually without reference to their source. And business is flooding small newspapers

with ready-to-use canned editorials, columns, and cartoons that carry hidden corporate messages.[35]

By accepting such feeds, the broadcast producer or editor is spared the cost of gathering the material or sending a reporter to the event but sacrifices the ability to make editorial judgments. Small stations and small papers are more likely to accept such feeds than larger ones. Most large stations and newspapers refuse as a matter of policy to accept such prepared materials, with the exception of opinion editorials and paid advocacy advertising.

Cost prevents small radio and television stations from having their own correspondents in Washington or following the major campaigns, yet an interview with an important government official or candidate is a news coup. If the staff at small stations can make it appear that they have such desirable access, they may be tempted to suppress details about how information was obtained. The Federal Communications Commission Code (Section 73.1212.d) requires that at both the beginning and end of a segment, broadcasters disclose the source of any such prepackaged news other than mimeographed or printed press releases. This restriction applies to feeds obtained when the station calls a predesignated number as well as materials sent or delivered to the station. This rule applies to political candidates and to anyone dealing with political subjects or controversial issues.

Video news releases (VNRs) were inefficient as long as they relied on videocassettes as their means of transport. Cassettes began to clutter newsrooms, unwatched and unaired. In the mid-1980s, public relations firms began switching to satellite transmission of news feeds. Medialink, a firm specializing in the production, distribution, and tracking of video, audio, Internet, print, and photographic material on behalf of public relations clients, reports that it has distributed more than 1,000 VNRs per year since 1994. Estimates place the number of VNRs distributed each year at between 5,000 and 15,000. When Nielsen Media Research surveyed 200 stations in 1988, it found that 93 percent had the capacity to downlink VNRs from satellite and that almost three quarters reported that they were willing to use such releases.[36] In 1999, both of those numbers stood at 100 percent.[37]

To increase the likelihood that VNRs will be used, their producers included a 90-second B-roll tape of visuals accompanied only by natural sound. Local announcers can then "voice" the narration, making it appear that the station itself produced the material.

Use of VNRs has enabled advertisers to circumvent bans on the advertisement of certain products. "In 1987, for example, the James B. Beam Distilling Company took to heart the admonition to hook an item to a news trend, and made a video news release that affirmed the patriotic preference of American distillers for domestic, instead of Canadian, grain. Television viewers in some 40 cities saw the report, illustrated with footage of workers packing crates with Jim Beam bourbon, on their local newscasts."[38]

Electronic press kits, the video equivalent of the written press release, now air routinely on hundreds of local television stations, as coverage of entertainment news increases. Frequently, this material is neither labeled nor described as film studio publicity. No one knows how often local reporters insert themselves into these publicity kits, but the videotapes are carefully created to allow local reporters to do so.

Major studios have produced dozens of these kits. Producing the kits is expensive but far less costly than comparable advertising. George Armstrong, who developed the electronic press kit at Universal Pictures as vice president in charge of advertising, noted that the kit for *E. T.* cost $125,000 but that it "brought in the equivalent of $700,000 worth of air time if we had [had] to buy it."[39]

On August 8, 1995, Sony released "Spirit of '73: Rock for Choice," a compilation featuring fourteen female music artists supporting abortion rights. One of the major marketing vehicles, said the director of marketing of the product, was a 10-minute electronic press kit featuring interviews with the artists and a behind-the-scenes look at the process of making the recording.[40]

Public relations firms attest that their materials often are used by television and radio stations. For example, following a Food and Drug Administration ruling favorable to a client's product, one public relations firm made a videotape for the client in the form of a news report on the FDA ruling, which was distributed to hundreds of television stations, most of whom used it. Similarly, those advising clients on how to obtain news coverage suggest that if the news media do not cover the event, you should do it yourself—audiotape or videotape the event, edit it into a 90-second package, attach a script for announcers, and ship it to radio or television stations in time for the evening news. In the 1990s, pharmaceutical companies raised these moves to an art form. VNRs' appeal for local stations increased in that decade as news budgets dropped.

The federal government has made use of video news releases as well. Many, such as those opposing youth smoking or warning of the dangers of steroids, provoked little discussion, because the cause advocated was uncontroversial. Not so in March 2004 when VNR-based news segments began to appear in local news markets touting the Medicare prescription drug benefits passed by the Republican Congress in December 2003. In this case, the local anchors were encouraged to read a script leading into the news segment. It said, "In December, President Bush signed into law the first-ever prescription drug benefit for people with Medicare. Since then, there have been a lot of questions about how the law will help older Americans and people with disabilities. Reporter Karen Ryan helps sort through the details." That video release ended with Ryan saying, "In Washington. I'm Karen Ryan reporting." But as federal investigators learned, Ryan was not a reporter but a person paid by the Bush administration to pose as one. The source of the videos was not revealed in the releases.

In the VNR, those with questions were encouraged to call 1-800-MEDICARE. Those who did so were told that they could obtain information by reciting the prompt "Medicare improvement." Because most Democrats in Congress opposed passage of the bill and its value was at issue in the Kerry–Bush 2004 presidential contest, this prompt was as controversial as the existence of the VNRs. Persuasion studies show that getting a person to state a position increases the likelihood that their attitudes will shift toward that point of view.

A person defending the releases noted, "The use of video news releases is a common, routine practice in government and the private sector. . . . Anyone who has questions about this practice needs to do some research on modern public information tools." But a representative of the Committee of Concerned Journalists disagreed, expressing "disbelief that any television stations would represent the Medicare videos as real news segments, considering the current debate about the merits of the new law. . . . 'It's running a paid advertisement in the heart of a news program.'"[41]

Prepared Editorials Another kind of influence results from distributing prepared editorials and feature stories to newspapers, particularly to small, news-hungry weeklies. E. Hofer and Sons, a public relations firm, has been among the most successful in getting its prepared editorials printed in newspapers. Once again, newspapers cooperate in their own manipulation. As one commentator writes, "To publish editorials prepared by Hofer while crediting the editorial to *Industrial News Review* [through which Hofer distributes prepared editorials], of course, would not constitute publication of 'canned' editorials. It is when newspapers publish editorials from such sources as their own views [and hundreds do] that an ethical problem arises."[42] Editorial writing is difficult and time consuming. As a result, it is tempting to use prepared editorials and pretend that they were composed by the newspaper staff.

Success in attracting advertising can make newspapers more vulnerable to the manipulations of news managers and public relations consultants. This is the case because, as advertising linage increases, the size of the space to be filled by news (the "news hole") also increases. Because their news staffs are small, newspapers tend to "rely on filler and fluff supplied by business publicists to supplement their own coverage."[43]

In other words, those who are knowledgeable about journalistic norms and routines have the ability to manipulate news coverage. By strategic use of the media's needs and constraints, public relations consultants and news managers, as well as individuals and groups, help determine what is covered and how news stories are presented.

COMMERCIAL PRESSURES

The news media are influenced not only by those who understand journalistic norms and routines but also by their own desire for profit, by their desire to beat the competition in the ratings, and by pressures created by advertisers. News programming has become one of the most lucrative sources of revenue for both the local stations and the networks. That is true in part because of its low production costs and because stations and networks own and produce the news, whereas in most cases they do not own and produce entertainment programming. For example, *World News Tonight* has become one of ABC's biggest revenue producers, bigger than many of its highly rated entertainment programs. The CBS news program *60 Minutes,* among the top ten in the Nielsen ratings for 13 consecutive years, has been the biggest moneymaker in network history, according to Don Hewitt, the program's creator: "My records tell me that we've had a net profit for CBS of over $1 billion."[44] Local news generates between 30 and 50 percent of the profits of individual television stations. As a result, there is intense pressure to achieve and maintain high ratings. Such pressures contribute to the tendencies to dramatize and sensationalize news content, as were described in the last chapter.

What competitive pressures do not produce is an alternative news agenda. So similar is the content of most competing newspapers, for example, that one scholar dubbed them "rivals in conformity."[45] That conclusion has weathered the tests of four decades of research.[46]

BOX 4-5　News Feeds

In December 2003 the Pentagon began "beaming a satellite feed from Iraq that can be picked up by television news organizations in the United States. The idea, says the Pentagon, is simply to give TV stations and networks access to press briefings from Baghdad and allow reporters in the U.S. to question the briefers.

　"Potentially, however—and the military spokespeople decline to rule it out—the new service also could become a full-fledged newsgathering and reporting entity with the mission of putting a 'good news' spin on the bad news coming out of Iraq—casualties, insurrections, political upheaval, civil dissent."[a]

[a]Neil Hickey, "Big Brother News?" *Columbia Journalism Review*, March–April 2004, p. 62.

Commercial pressures on newspapers have increased as the newspaper business has become controlled by an ever-shrinking number of large corporations. In the early 1980s, media critic Ben Bagdikian estimated that just forty-six companies in the world controlled most of the global business in daily newspapers, magazines, television, books, and movies. By 1990, he said that number was twenty-three. In 2004, he said that number was six. According to William Glaberson, "the effects of that change are pervasive." He argues that one effect is that journalists think about their work differently; it makes them more flexible in response to management demands. He writes, "It is now common for publishing executives to press journalists to cooperate with their newspapers' 'business side,' breaching separation that was said in the past to be essential for journalistic integrity." Editors have become more concerned about serving the needs of advertisers. Mary Jo Meisner, editor of the *Milwaukee Journal Sentinel,* created eight new neighborhood sections by examining advertisers' requirements, and Glaberson quotes her as saying, "You have to look at it from their perspective."[47]

Costs of Preempting Programming

When the news division of a network preempts regular programming for special news—such as the funerals of Ronald Reagan and Pope John Paul II, a space shuttle launch, or the efforts to locate survivors after September 11—advertisers who have paid to sponsor the regular programming are not given what they paid for and either have their money refunded or are offered alternate times to air their ads. Networks are corporations governed by boards accountable to stockholders who expect to receive dividends. The decision to preempt regular programming is a costly one. If the news interrupts or preempts a program that attracts a small audience, the network loses less money than if a popular program is interrupted. Consequently, a network whose programs are unpopular risks less by interrupting them with breaking news.

　The cost of preempting entertainment programming to cover government activities was documented by a government study, which concluded that there was one major reason for the "decline in network interest in matters of government—the enormous increase in network earnings and the huge loss of profits that would result from any preemption."[48]

Yet a network's prestige is, in part, a function of the quality of its news programming, and viewers are comforted by the assurance that if something important happens, the networks will interrupt regular programming to bring them that information. Therefore, whatever the cost, a network cannot afford to ignore important news. When President John Kennedy was assassinated, for example, there was no question that the networks would preempt whatever was on the air to bring that event and ensuing developments to the audience. Similarly on September 11, 2001, the networks stopped their regularly programming and suspended airing commercials to carry the breaking news to the nation. But most news is not as important as a presidential assassination or a terrorist attack. In such cases, profit and loss must be weighed against the gain in prestige that might result from the coverage or the loss in prestige if the event is not covered. A network is particularly vulnerable when one of its competitors covers an event.

Television networks occasionally agree to rotate coverage of an important event to minimize loss of advertising revenue. Accordingly, the networks rotated coverage of the Iran-Contra hearings. This gave the audience a chance to choose between regular programming and coverage of the hearings. Audience members know what they have missed, or that television should have aired an event and didn't, because newspaper television critics tell them. Caught in this bind, television has sought ways to ensure audience awareness of the news without interrupting regularly scheduled programming except in extraordinary circumstances.

The "news break," sponsored by an advertiser, represents one such avenue. News breaks occur during commercial breaks in programming and are brief summaries of the day's headlines. This format creates an association between news and advertising, which advertisers desire. With news breaks or news updates, advertisers, not the network, bear the cost of underwriting the time, and programming goes on as expected.

To bring important information to the viewer, television also runs print information across the lower third of the screen during regular programming. This device is used more often to tell the viewer that the local news will follow a program that is running overtime than to convey important breaking news, but it is also used to keep audiences posted on the status of hurricanes or tornadoes and to indicate disaster warnings and watches.

Not everyone agrees that live news coverage is a blessing. In 1986, for example, the ABC and NBC television networks were flooded with calls from angry viewers who tuned in to watch their favorite soap operas only to find them preempted by live coverage of congressional hearings on the Iran arms sale. All three networks preempted regular daytime programming for coverage of the hearings. ABC News spokesperson Thomas Goodman said the network received 1,330 calls. "All objected to preemption of soap operas," he said. NBC reported receiving 1,100 complaints. CBS received fewer than three dozen calls.[49] Some coverage, such as network coverage of Nixon's trip to the Soviet Union, was criticized as political propaganda. This charge was given credence when two of Nixon's reelection campaign commercials in 1972 consisted of edited news footage of his trips to Russia and China.

Commercial pressures for high ratings and the revenues they assure affect judgments about what news will be covered, particularly if coverage involves the costly preemption of other lucrative programming. As a result, in 1988, 1992, 1996, and 2000 all three major networks cut their coverage of the Republican and Democratic National conventions. The extensive coverage provided by CNN and MSNBC and the gavel-to-gavel coverage by C-SPAN, however, enabled viewers with cable television to see both the Democratic and Republican conventions firsthand.

Pressures from Advertisers

The price of subscriptions does not pay the total cost of producing a newspaper or magazine. Both are underwritten by advertising revenue, and commercial television and radio are almost completely financed by advertising. Their dependence on these external sources of funding renders them vulnerable to boycotts by advertisers. For example, in spring 1986, some Detroit car dealers canceled their ads in the *Detroit Free Press* after the newspaper published an exposé detailing antitrust charges against local dealerships. The Federal Trade Commission (FTC) had charged 105 dealers and 115 individuals with conspiracy for trying to limit showroom hours and for trying to limit competition by fixing prices.[50]

In August 1995, the *Columbia Journalism Review* awarded a "Dart" (for poor journalistic performance) to the *Gloucester County Times* of Woodbury, New Jersey, when the paper ran a front-page story on the twentieth anniversary of the John Wanamaker store. The paper had just acquired Wanamaker as an advertiser. When the news department told the ad department that it wouldn't run the story, the editor dispatched a reporter and ordered that the story run, complete with a photo spread.

For the first time, in early August 1995 the FTC acted against a group of advertisers that were boycotting a newspaper over coverage of their product. On May 22, 1994, a reporter for the *San Jose Mercury News* had written an article titled "A Car Buyer's Guide to Sanity," telling readers how to get a better buy on a car. Dealers responded by pulling about a million dollars' worth of advertising. The FTC initiated an antitrust investigation that resulted in a cease-and-desist agreement by the Santa Clara County Motor Car Dealers Association.[51] The dealers' boycott raised two concerns, said the FTC official who handled the investigation. The absence of advertising deprived readers of price information, and the boycott might chill the publication of similar articles.

Television, too, is subject to pressure from advertisers. Before the accident at the Three Mile Island nuclear plant in 1979, Jane Fonda appeared on a Barbara Walters ABC special to discuss her film *The China Syndrome* and its antinuclear message. General Electric, one of the four biggest builders of nuclear reactors in the world, promptly withdrew its sponsorship of the program.[52] During the health care reform debate of 1993–94, a number of stations refused to air an issue advocacy ad that attacked a pizza company for not providing health insurance for its employees in the United States although it does for those abroad. In addition, corporations whose environmental practices are portrayed unflatteringly on the news are striking back at the press with angry letters, point-by-point rebuttals, news releases, and paid ads. These include Hooker Chemicals and General Motors, among others.[53]

Still another example was action in early 1989 by the Washington State Fruit Commission, a growers' trade association that withdrew $71,300 worth of television advertising for northwest cherries from CBS affiliates in St. Louis, Atlanta, and Tampa to protest a news report on CBS's *60 Minutes*. The account dealt with a study by the Natural

Resources Defense Council on pesticides in foods that affect children and concluded that eating apples treated with Alar, a chemical used to control ripening, increased cancer risks for children. The report was disputed by the apple industry, and federal regulators had declared apples safe to eat, but the report sent apple sales into a steep decline. Growers contended that they lost millions of dollars as a result. "Our association wanted to voice its displeasure over the way the CBS broadcast of the *60 Minutes* program sensationalized the Alar story," said Pat Dunlop, a spokesperson for the Fruit Commission. Alar is not used on cherries, but many of the group's members grow both crops. The money budgeted for advertising was diverted to other stations in the three markets.[54]

As these examples demonstrate, advertisers actively attempt to affect news coverage.

Threat of Lawsuits

The costs of defending against a lawsuit are high. Coverage of controversial subjects, hard-hitting editorials, and investigative reporting are particularly likely to attract libel suits. Consequently, local television stations, particularly those in small markets, tend to shy away from such reporting, according to a survey by the National Association of Broadcasters. Who threatens to sue? Businesspeople threaten to sue over consumer reporting on pollution, car defects, and the like. Politicians threaten to sue over politically damaging material.[55]

In recent years, the U.S. Supreme Court has let stand awards of more than $2 million each in punitive damages made to individuals who sued a daily newspaper and a network-owned television station. Punitive damages are now awarded in 60 percent of the cases won by plaintiffs against the media. Average awards exceed $2.8 million.[56] In early 1990, in *Sprague v. Walter,* a jury in Pennsylvania awarded $31.5 million in punitive damages against the *Philadelphia Inquirer* for a story written in the early 1970s questioning a local prosecutor's handling of a homicide case. In 1988, in *Brown and Williamson Tobacco Corp. v. CBS Inc.* (485 U.S.993), the tobacco company sued a Chicago-owned CBS affiliate for libel, arguing that its advertisements had been misrepresented. CBS countered that the piece in question was commentary and as such protected by the First Amendment. The court held that the station had falsely accused the tobacco firm of soliciting young smokers as customers.[57]

Private individuals and corporations are not the only ones able to bring legal pressure to bear on the media. As we mentioned in Chapter 3, in May 1986, then-CIA director William Casey suggested that the Justice Department consider prosecuting NBC News for violation of a 1950 law prohibiting disclosure of "communications intelligence." The NBC News report to which Casey objected concerned the trial of accused spy Ronald Pelton.

Another example of the power of lawsuits came in August 1995, when ABC News agreed to apologize twice in prime time—during half-time of the broadcast of *Monday Night Football* and on *Day One*—for a report broadcast on the latter program that contended that Philip Morris and R.J. Reynolds controlled and manipulated nicotine levels in cigarettes to addict smokers. The apology was the settlement of two lawsuits by the tobacco companies charging ABC News with libel. The case against ABC News turned on a single word, "spike." In its report on how Philip Morris makes cigarettes, ABC contended that the company "spiked" cigarettes by adding nicotine in the manufacturing process. Because the production process removes nicotine from tobacco leaves used for filler, Philip Morris contended that it was "recombining" the ingredients, not spiking. The settlement aroused fears among employees that ABC might no longer be as vigilant in protecting news, particularly because Capital Cities, ABC's parent company, had been acquired by the Walt Disney Company. Both the correspondent on the *Day One* segment and its producer refused to sign the settlement.

John P. Coale, one of a consortium of lawyers that has mounted the largest class action suit in history against the tobacco companies, said that ABC was intimidated by the huge amount of damages, $10 billion, that Philip Morris was seeking in its suit. Richard A. Daynard, a professor at the Northeastern University School of Law and chair of the Tobacco Products Liability Project, a nonprofit antismoking group, said, "Philip Morris has bullied a major television network into apologizing for what was essentially a true story."[58] Cliff Douglas, executive director of Tobacco Control, Law and Policy Consulting, an antismoking research group, said, "There is no question that the documents ABC obtained from Philip Morris [as part of the libel suit] directly contradict ABC's apology." He and other critics cite this as proof that ABC's decision to settle was made by Capital Cities/ABC Inc. for purely financial reasons.[59] Reuven Frank, a former television news producer and former president of NBC News, which is owned by General Electric, put the decision in a slightly different light. "This is called the pay-the-$5-fine syndrome. Philip Morris could have tied up ABC in court for months."[60] Philip Morris took out full-page ads in many newspapers (including, for example, the *Washington Post*, the *New York Times*, the *Wall Street Journal*, and the *Minneapolis Star Tribune*), trumpeting its success in forcing ABC to apologize. By obtaining an apology, particularly in a period when tobacco companies are under attack, Philip Morris achieved what no amount of ordinary advertising could have done. Moreover, the company's success will make other news outlets more cautious in their coverage of these issues.

The limited amount of editorializing on radio and television stations also reflects fears of legal reprisals. When broadcasters do editorialize, they tend to take noncontroversial stands, such as "Support your local blood bank" or "Welcome the former hostages home." In many cases, the positions taken are vague and ambiguous. Threats of lawsuits contribute to such neutrality.

In June 1986, the U.S. Supreme Court made it easier for the news media to gain dismissal of libel suits without the high costs of trials. In a 6–3 ruling, the Court held in favor of columnist Jack Anderson and against the conservative Liberty Lobby. A magazine edited by Anderson had called the group neo-Nazi, anti-Semitic, racist, and fascist. The Court held that judges should dismiss cases unless evidence of "actual malice" by the media was "clear and convincing." To establish actual malice, a complainant must show that the media source knew the material was false or published it with reckless disregard for whether it was true or false.

POLITICAL PRESSURE

Anthony Smith reports that "during the Carter Administration, government was spending $1 billion a year on its own information services (the Pentagon alone had 1,500 press officers, spending $25 million a year)."[61] That expenditure reflects the magnitude of the government effort to influence what and how information is disseminated. But the government has resources far more important than money.

The president is always newsworthy and has great power to influence press coverage through such means as leaks, exclusive interviews, pseudo-events (such as White House Rose Garden activities), and appeals to national security. Some of the ways that campaigners manipulate the press are treated in later chapters. Here we consider the political pressure created by the federal government, particularly the executive branch.

Presidential Newsworthiness

The president is always able to make news, by calling a press conference, announcing a forthcoming event (an agreement or future summit meeting), or scheduling a ritual (awarding a medal, for instance). So, for example, when President George W. Bush held a prime-time press conference in mid-April 2004 to discuss the U.S. response to an uprising in Iraq, the major broadcast and cable news networks carried it live. The *New York Times'* former White House correspondent John Herbers notes,

> No other institution can demand space and attention throughout the media when there is no news there. The White House does every day. The President can demand front-page coverage by holding a press conference in which he says nothing that has not been said before. He can command prime television time by granting an exclusive interview to one of the networks, and newspapers feel compelled to write about it at length because millions saw it on television.[62]

Facts that would not be newsworthy about anyone else become newsworthy when tied to the president. For example, network television as well as newspapers carried major stories on George H. W. Bush's declaration, "I do not like broccoli and I haven't liked it since I was a little kid and my mother made me eat it and I'm president of the United States and I'm not going to eat any more broccoli." By providing a moment of comic relief in an otherwise serious day, the comment humanized Bush. To laughter, he then added, "Wait a minute. For the broccoli vote out there, Barbara loves broccoli. She's tried to make me eat it; she eats it all the time herself. So she can go out and meet the caravan of [trucks bringing] broccoli." With that as a tease, the story continued. On March 26, 1990, Barbara Bush's picture appeared in newspapers. In front of her was a table covered with broccoli.

A focus on "the human side" of the White House can displace other forms of coverage. Inviting such coverage is itself a form of manipulation of the news agenda. By early 1990, the Bushes' dog, Millie, had entered the annals of U.S. history, joining Franklin Roosevelt's Fala and Richard Nixon's Checkers. When Millie delivered puppies, network stories followed. A survey for the Center for the Media and Public Affairs concluded that from Bush's first day as president until November 30, 1989, Millie had appeared more frequently on network news than Bush's education secretary, his agricultural secretary, or his secretary for veterans' affairs. "Let me give you a little serious, political, inside advice," Bush told a Republican fundraiser. "One single word. 'Puppies.' Worth ten points [in the polls], believe me."[63] Although the subject of much coverage, the Clinton's kitten-less cat, Socks, and neutered dog, Buddy, did not garner the level of attention devoted to Millie's litter.

The Reagan administration proved highly adept at managing presidential press contacts. As one reporter noted, "The President delivers the good news, usually in situations that insulate him from questions, while aides deal with controversial matters. . . .

Few White House teams have exhibited such expertise in associating an executive only with the popular decisions and dramatic moments of his Presidency."[64]

Such control maintains the president's personal popularity, reduces situations in which gaffes might be made, and allows the anger generated by unpopular decisions to be deflected onto presidential assistants. Given such control of access, press coverage is inevitably limited and manipulated. More readily than any other politician or citizen, the president also can take to the airwaves to speak directly to the American people.

When the networks judge a topic to be newsworthy, the president is granted what amounts to automatic access. After former House Democratic leader Tip O'Neill denied Ronald Reagan's June 1986 request to address the House on the issue of aid to the Contras in Nicaragua, Reagan asked for network time to speak directly to the American people. The three major networks declined on the grounds that the president's speech would not make news. CNN, which carries news 24 hours a day, aired the speech.

When the White House indicated that President Clinton wished to address the nation about his relationship with Monica Lewinsky at 10 P.M. on Monday, August 17, 1998, however, ABC, NBC, and CBS all provided access.

National Security

Because information about foreign relations is more difficult to corroborate than information about domestic policy and because members of the press are citizens as well as reporters, reporters are susceptible to the administration's line on foreign policy. David Halberstam's book *The Powers That Be* documents the way that the government sustained press support for Vietnam policy. Appeals to support presidential policies are made in the name of "national security" and "protection of vital interests." Such appeals usually prove irresistible.

Appeals to national security are complicated by competition among news outlets. In some cases, journalists keep a story off the air or out of the papers only to see it broken by someone else. For example, for nearly a year the Carter and Reagan administrations tried to prevent publication of information about the existence of two secret listening posts operating in China with American equipment and Chinese personnel. The story was finally reported in June 1981 on *NBC Nightly News*. Earlier, when two *New York Times* reporters had learned of the posts' existence, they were talked out of publishing the story—first by Carter's national security adviser, Zbigniew Brzezinski, and later by Reagan's CIA director, William Casey. NBC News, last in the ratings, had a strong incentive to break the story. However, the existence of the listening posts had been hinted at in the *Washington Post* several days earlier, and China's offer to replace posts lost in Iran after the revolution there had been reported as early as April 1979. What gave the story such impact was the recent Reagan administration decision to authorize the first sale of "lethal" U.S. military equipment to China.[65]

Government Manipulation

Strategic leaks of classified material are also used to manipulate the press. Just how common this practice is became clear during lawsuits over publication of the Pentagon Papers during the Nixon administration. In answer to claims by the Nixon administration, the *New York Times* responded with 15 affidavits which laid out some of the ways in which government officials had selectively leaked classified material to the *Times* in the past to achieve their ends. . . . The *Post* also argued . . . that government officials had for years leaked classified material for their own purposes and introduced affidavits from staff members including Ben Bradlee, the newspaper's editor, and its foreign affairs specialist Chalmers Roberts.[66]

Stephen Hess, an analyst at the Brookings Institution, has identified six types of leaks. Each is based on a different motive:

1. *Policy leaks* are "a straightforward pitch for or against a proposal using some document or insider's information."
2. *Trial balloon leaks* are an attempt to assess a proposal's strengths and weaknesses, assets and liabilities.
3. *Ego leaks* satisfy the source's sense of self-importance.
4. *Goodwill leaks* attempt to cultivate credit with a reporter.
5. *Animus leaks* are designed to embarrass someone else.
6. *Whistle-blower leaks* are the last resort of a frustrated civil servant who feels that he or she has exhausted remedies within the government.[67]

The political use of strategic leaks illustrates the symbiotic relationship between the press and the government. The government needs the press to distribute information and to support its policies. The press needs the government as a major source of information.

This close relationship was illustrated by the Reagan administration's use of the press during trade talks held to persuade the Japanese to limit voluntarily their automobile exports to the United States. The situation arose because the administration did not want to make any overt effort to restrict Japanese exports. However, the press was used to put pressure on the Japanese through a news release from "sources close to U.S. trade officials" indicating that talks were going badly and that it was hoped that other proposals would be forthcoming from the Japanese. Reporters who were induced to print that story "later concluded that they had been gulled in a U.S. scheme to put overnight pressure on the Japanese." In effect, the Reagan administration used the press as a conduit for its negotiations while maintaining the fiction that it was making no attempt to restrict Japanese exports.[68]

In August 1995, when human rights activist Harry Wu was being held by the Chinese government on charges of spying, no formal offer of a quid pro quo for his release was made. But informal contacts through the media suggested that if Wu were released, First Lady Hillary Rodham Clinton would attend the U.N.-sponsored Decade of Women Conference being held in Beijing. Wu was convicted but sentenced to exile to the United States and released, and the First Lady announced that she would attend the conference.

Similarly there was widespread suspicion that the memo by Defense Secretary Donald Rumsfeld that was given to *USA Today* in October 2003 (approximately a week after it was written) had been leaked with Rumsfeld's consent. That memo observed that the U.S. forces in Iraq were faced with "a long, hard slog," an assessment markedly difficult from the rosier scenarios painted publicly by the administration. Observed

---

BOX 4-6   Military Pressure

For two weeks CBS News delayed reporting about U.S. soldiers' alleged abuse of Iraqi prisoners in Abu Ghraib, following a personal request of the joint chiefs of staff. Gen. Richard Myers called CBS anchor Dan Rather eight days before the report was to air, asking for extra time, said Jeff Fager, executive producer of *60 Minutes II*.[a]

Fager said he felt "terrible" being asked to delay the broadcast. "News is a delicate thing," he said. "It's hard to just make these kinds of decisions. It's not natural for us; the natural thing is to put it on the air. But the circumstances were quite unusual, and I think you have to consider that."

Bob Steele, a journalism values scholar at the Poynter Institute for Media Studies, said there should be an "exceptional principle and argument to justify withholding news of such magnitude. . . . I would want to have a very specific and short time period [to withhold the news]. If CBS believes it was justified, to hold back two weeks seems like an awful long time. Perhaps a day or two. But two weeks is a long time, particularly with the nature of the allegations in the video."[b]

[a]News Services, "CBS News Delayed Iraqi Prisoner Story," *Minneapolis Star Tribune,* 8 May 2004, p. E8.
[b]Ibid.

David Johnston writing in the *New York Times*, "In the hands of a skilled practitioner, a private memorandum, leaked immediately or strategically placed in a file for later use, is a device that can be used to criticize, deflect, settle scores, temporize, obfuscate, discredit, claim credit or deny without having to do it in public—or asking permission from a superior."[69]

Cooperation between press and government is increased by movements from press jobs to government jobs and vice versa. For example, NBC reporter Ron Nessen, who had covered Ford as vice president, became President Ford's press secretary. Eileen Shanahan, economic reporter for the *New York Times*, took a position in the Department of Education during the Carter administration and then became a reporter for the *Washington Star*. Leslie Gelb first worked in government for Secretary of Defense Robert McNamara and then became a reporter at the *New York Times* after a breather at the Brookings Institution. After 4 years at the *Times*, Gelb moved to the State Department as Cyrus Vance's assistant secretary for politicomilitary affairs. Two and a half years later, he left the State Department, paused at the Brookings Institution, and returned to the *Times*. Meanwhile, Richard Burt, who had taken Gelb's job at the *Times*, left his position to take Gelb's former job in the State Department under Alexander Haig. NBC legal reporter Carl Stern left his position to become spokesperson for the Clinton Justice Department. After leaving service in the White House, Clinton's press secretary Dee Dee Meyers was a regular network commentator, as were former Clinton aides George Stephanopolous and David Gergen. Such musical chairs between government and press raise questions of journalistic integrity. Can a reporter write objectively about a person now doing her or his former job or about policies or programs that she or he once defended? Can a reporter write without bias about those who have the power to advance his or her prospects for a government job?[70]

There is considerable evidence of the power of government to manipulate press coverage. Government agencies spend huge sums of money to disseminate their messages through the mass media. Recently those efforts have made news:

- The Department of Health and Human Services confirmed that it had paid $10,000 to Michael McManus, who writes a weekly syndicated column and is director of a nonprofit group called Marriage Savers, to help train marriage counselors.
- Another conservative writer, Maggie Gallagher, admitted having a $21,500 deal with the Department of Health and Human Services.
- In an interview, Wade Horn, the assistant secretary for children and families of the Department of Health and Human Services, said the line between journalism, commentary, and consulting had blurred. "Thirty years ago, if you were a columnist, you were employed full time by a newspaper most likely, and it was very clear," he said. "With the explosion of media outlets today, there are a lot of people who wear a lot of hats. Where's the line? What if you have your own blog? Are you a journalist?"[71]

Armstrong Williams, a conservative commentator who was a protégé of Senator Strom Thurmond and Supreme Court Justice Clarence Thomas, acknowledged that he was paid $240,000 by the Department of Education to promote its initiatives on his syndicated television program and to other African Americans in the news media during the 2004 election campaign. According to a copy of the contract provided by the department to the *New York Times*, Williams was required to broadcast two 1-minute advertisements in which Education Secretary Rod Paige extolled the merits of its national standards program, "No Child Left Behind." The arrangement also stipulated that a PR firm hired by the department would arrange for Mr. Williams regularly to comment on the initiative during his broadcasts, that Secretary Paige and other department officials would appear as studio guests, and that "Mr. Williams shall utilize his long-term working relations with 'America's Black Forum'—an African-American news program—"to encourage the producers to periodically address the No Child Left Behind Act."[72]

The power of the presidency also is used manipulatively. By managing the president's ability to make news, to control access to information, to plead national security, to schedule staged news events, and to leak material strategically, the executive branch can gain implicit news media endorsement for administration policies. For example, when asked how the administration would respond to Soviet leader Mikhail Gorbachev's televised speech on the Chernobyl nuclear accident, former White House spokesperson Larry Speakes responded, "If it's something really big, the President would say it. . . . If it was semi-big, I'd come out and say something. If it was teeny-tiny, we'd give out a piece of paper. And if it was teeny-tinier than that, we'd let the State Department do it."[73]

Allegations of blatant press manipulation by the Reagan administration reached a climax with the resignation of Bernard Kalb as chief spokesperson for the State Department. Kalb described his resignation as a protest against the deception and disinformation campaign launched in August 1986 against Libyan leader Muammar Qaddafi. "You face a choice—as an American, as a spokesman, as a journalist—whether to allow oneself to be absorbed in the ranks of silence, whether to vanish into unopposed acquiescence or to enter a modest dissent." He added, "Faith in the word of America is the pulse beat of our democracy. Anything that hurts America's credibility hurts America."[74] Before accepting the post of assistant secretary of state for public affairs, Kalb had been a correspondent for the *New York Times*, CBS, and NBC for almost 40 years.

Charges that the Reagan administration had engaged in a disinformation campaign about Libya and its leader arose after a story by Bob Woodward appeared in the *Washington Post*. The story disclosed details of a memorandum by Vice Admiral John M. Poindexter, then White House national security adviser, reportedly urging a campaign against Qaddafi involving "real and illusory events—through a disinformation program."

The White House denied that the administration had planted false reports with news organizations in the United States, but former presidential spokesperson Larry Speakes had no comment on whether the administration had tried to conduct such a disinformation campaign against Libya in foreign news organizations.

According to the *Post* story, major newspapers had carried erroneous news reports generated by this plan. A front-page article appeared on August 25, 1986, in the *Wall Street Journal*, saying that Libya was planning new terrorist attacks. Citing unidentified "U.S. and West European intelligence officials," the story said that the United States was on a "collision course" with Libya, that "growing evidence suggests" that new Libyan terrorist attacks were being planned, and that "the Pentagon is completing plans for a new and larger bombing of Libya in case the President orders it." All three network television evening news programs repeated the substance of the *Journal*'s report the night after it appeared, and on August 26, many major newspapers quoted identified and unidentified officials who seemed to confirm the *Journal* article. Some newspapers, including the conservative *Washington Times,* began to question the reports and to suggest that a disinformation campaign was under way.

In a news conference, Secretary of State George Shultz refused to comment on whether or not such a campaign of disinformation had been undertaken, but he seemed to confirm the report through his answers, which praised the use of deception if it would cause problems for the Libyan leader. An unidentified White House official was quoted making similar statements:

> We think for domestic consumption there will be no problems. It's Qaddafi.
> After all, whatever it takes to get rid of him is all right with us—that's the
> feeling, we think, in the country. On the foreign scene it will cause problems,
> though. We're constantly talking about the Soviets doing disinformation. It's
> going to cause difficulties for us. We don't think it's a major, lasting firestorm,
> but there will be some ripples.[75]

As these comments suggest, public attitudes about the proper roles of the press and the government are an important factor in setting the parameters of government manipulation of the press and press interference in political events.

It may seem peculiar that this chapter contains no extended discussion of influence exerted by the Federal Communications Commission. In our judgment, that influence in the past has ranged from minuscule to nonexistent. Network executives frequently express fears of licensing nonrenewal, but no such fears are warranted by past FCC action, at least in regard to news programming. Barry Cole and Mal Oettinger report, "A renewal application has never been denied solely because of a failure to meet community needs and problems, an excess of commercials, a lack of public service

---

**CASE STUDY 4-1   Pressure from Advocacy Groups: National Guidelines
for Coverage of Suicide**

The Centers for Disease Control, the Office of the Surgeon General, the National Institute of Mental Health, the Substance Abuse and Mental Health Services Administration, and the two major foundations working to prevent suicide partnered with the Annenberg Public Policy Center to persuade reporters to cover suicide more responsibly. The report the groups distributed cited twenty-seven scholarly studies documenting "suicide contagion."

Suicide Contagion Is Real
Between 1984 and 1987, journalists in Vienna covered the deaths of individuals who jumped in front of trains in the subway system. The coverage was extensive and dramatic. In 1987, a campaign alerted reporters to the possible negative effects of such reporting, and suggested alternate strategies for coverage. In the first six months after the campaign began, subway suicides and non-fatal attempts dropped by more than 80 percent. The total number of suicides in Vienna declined as well.

Research finds an increase in suicide by readers or viewers when

- The number of stories about individual suicides increases
- A particular death is reported at length or in many stories
- The story of an individual death by suicide is placed on the front page or at the beginning of a broadcast
- The headlines about specific suicide deaths are dramatic (A recent example: "Boy, 10, Kills Himself over Poor Grades")

Recommendations
The media can play a powerful role in educating the public about suicide prevention. Stories about suicide can inform readers and viewers about the likely causes of suicide, its warning signs, trends in suicide rates, and recent treatment advances. They can also highlight opportunities to prevent suicide. Media stories about individual deaths by suicide may be newsworthy and need to be cov-

ered, but they also have the potential to do harm. Implementation of recommendations for media coverage of suicide has been shown to decrease suicide rates.

- Certain ways of describing suicide in the news contribute to what behavioral scientists call "suicide contagion" or "copycat" suicides.
- Research suggests that inadvertently romanticizing suicide or idealizing those who take their own lives by portraying suicide as a heroic or romantic act may encourage others to identify with the victim.
- Exposure to suicide method through media reports can encourage vulnerable individuals to imitate it. Clinicians believe the danger is even greater if there is a detailed description of the method. Research indicates that detailed descriptions or pictures of the location or site of a suicide encourage imitation.
- Presenting suicide as the inexplicable act of an otherwise healthy or high-achieving person may encourage identification with the victim.

Suicide and Mental Illness
Did you know?

- Over 90 percent of suicide victims have a significant psychiatric illness at the time of their death. These are often undiagnosed, untreated, or both. Mood disorders and substance abuse are the two most common.
- When both mood disorders and substance abuse are present, the risk for suicide is much greater, particularly for adolescents and young adults.
- Research has shown that when open aggression, anxiety or agitation is present in individuals who are depressed, the risk for suicide increases significantly.

The cause of an individual suicide is invariably more complicated than a recent painful event such as the break-up of a relationship or the loss of a job. An individual suicide cannot be adequately explained as the understandable response to an individual's stressful occupation, or an individual's membership in a group encountering discrimination. Social conditions alone do not explain a suicide. People who appear to become suicidal in response to such events, or in response to a physical illness, generally have significant underlying mental problems, though they may be well-hidden.

Questions to ask:

- Had the victim ever received treatment for depression or any other mental disorder?
- Did the victim have a problem with substance abuse?

Angles to pursue:

- Conveying that effective treatments for most of these conditions are available (but underutilized) may encourage those with such problems to seek help.
- Acknowledging the deceased person's problems and struggles as well as the positive aspects of his/her life or character contributes to a more balanced picture.

Interviewing Surviving Relatives and Friends

Research shows that, during the period immediately after a death by suicide, grieving family members or friends have difficulty understanding what happened. Responses may be extreme, problems may be minimized, and motives may be complicated.

Studies of suicide based on in-depth interviews with those close to the victim indicate that, in their first, shocked reaction, friends and family members may find a loved one's death by suicide inexplicable or they may deny that there were warning signs. Accounts based on these initial reactions are often unreliable.

Angles to pursue:

- Thorough investigation generally reveals underlying problems unrecognized even

by close friends and family members. Most victims do however give warning signs of their risk for suicide.

- Some informants are inclined to suggest that a particular individual, for instance a family member, a school, or a health service provider, in some way played a role in the victim's death by suicide. Thorough investigation almost always finds multiple causes for suicide and fails to corroborate a simple attribution of responsibility.

Concerns:

- Dramatizing the impact of suicide through descriptions and pictures of grieving relatives, teachers or classmates or community expressions of grief may encourage potential victims to see suicide as a way of getting attention or as a form of retaliation against others.
- Using adolescents on TV or in print media to tell the stories of their suicide attempts may be harmful to the adolescents themselves or may encourage other vulnerable young people to seek attention in this way.

Language

Referring to a "rise" in suicide rates is usually more accurate than calling such a rise an "epidemic," which implies a more dramatic and sudden increase than what we generally find in suicide rates.

Research has shown that the use in headlines of the word *suicide* or referring to the cause of death as self-inflicted increases the likelihood of contagion.

Recommendations for language:

- Whenever possible, it is preferable to avoid referring to suicide in the headline. Unless the suicide death took place in public, the cause of death should be reported in the body of the story and not in the headline.

(continued on next page)

CASE STUDY 4-1 *(continued)*

- In deaths that will be covered nationally, such as of celebrities, or those apt to be covered locally, such as people living in small towns, consider phrasing for headlines such as: "Marilyn Monroe dead at 36," or "John Smith dead at 48." Consideration of how they died could be reported in the body of the article.
- In the body of the story, it is preferable to describe the deceased as "having died by suicide," rather than as "a suicide," or having "committed suicide." The latter two expressions reduce the person to the mode of death or connote criminal or sinful behavior.
- Contrasting "suicide deaths" with "nonfatal attempts" is preferable to using terms such as "successful," "unsuccessful," or "failed."

Special Situations

CELEBRITY DEATHS
Celebrity deaths by suicide are more likely than noncelebrity deaths to produce imitation. Although suicides by celebrities will receive prominent coverage, it is important not to let the glamour of the individual obscure any mental health problems or use of drugs.

HOMICIDE-SUICIDES
In covering murder-suicides, be aware that the tragedy of the homicide can mask the suicidal aspect of the act. Feelings of depression and hopelessness present before the homicide and suicide are often the impetus for both.

SUICIDE PACTS
Suicide pacts are mutual arrangements between two people who kill themselves at the same time, and are rare. They are not simply the act of loving individuals who do not wish to be separated. Research shows that most pacts involve an individual who is coercive and another who is extremely dependent.

Stories to Consider Covering
- Trends in suicide rates
- Recent treatment advances
- Individual stories of how treatment was life-saving
- Stories of people who overcame despair without attempting suicide
- Myths about suicide
- Warning signs of suicide
- Actions that individuals can take to prevent suicide by others

Source: Reprinted with permission of the Annenberg Public Policy Center. http://www.afsp.org/education/newrecommendations.htm (accessed 11 April 2005).

announcements, or an inadequate amount of news, public affairs, or other nonentertainment material."[76] That statement remains true today.

The FCC has taken other actions of significance, however. The 1996 Telecommunications Act turned issues of media ownership over to the FCC, requiring it to evaluate all of its media ownership rules every 2 years and change them if conditions had changed sufficiently to warrant such action. The act also eliminated the cap on the number of radio stations a company could own nationally, which had been 40. The vast majority of radio stations were sold after 1996. Clear Channel soon owned 1,200 stations.

The key remaining rules were those limiting the number of TV stations a single firm could own in a single market or nationally, the limit on the number of cable TV stations and broadcast outlets in the same community or newspaper and broadcast outlets in the same community. Broadcast ownership regulation has been one of the few areas of media control with teeth, in part because these rules were popular with the public and because politically influential small media companies knew that without them they would be unable to survive.

TO SUM UP

The news media influence and are in turn influenced. The most effective manipulators of media news are those who understand journalistic norms and routines and who use them to gain media access and to influence the nature of coverage. The news media are influenced by highly paid news managers and their clients and by other individuals and groups. The media are also affected by commercial pressures for ratings and revenues and by the protests of those offended by news coverage. Finally, they respond to pressures from those in positions of political power.

 Use InfoTrac College Edition to access information on topics in this chapter from hundreds of periodicals and scholarly journals. Enter keyword and subject searches: *influence of news, news management, political news.*

SELECTED READINGS

Cole, Barry, and Mal Oettinger. *Reluctant Regulators: The FCC and the Broadcast Audience.* Reading, MA: Addison-Wesley, 1978.

Gitlin, Todd. *The Whole World Is Watching: Mass Media in the Making and Unmaking of the New Left.* Berkeley: University of California Press, 1980.

Glasser, Theodore L., and Charles T. Salmon. *Public Opinion and the Communication of Consent.* New York: Guilford, 1995.

Goldenberg, Edie N. *Making the Papers.* Lexington, MA: Lexington Books, 1975.

Hess, Stephen. *The Government/Press Connection: Press Officers and Their Offices.* Washington, DC: Brookings Institution, 1984.

———. *The Rise of the Professional Specialist in Washington Journalism.* Washington, DC: Brookings Institution, 1986.

———. *News and Newsmaking.* Washington, DC: Brookings Institution, 1995.

McChesney, Robert. *The Problem of the Media: U.S. Communication Politics in the 21st Century.* New York: Monthly Review Press, 2004.

Pearce, David D. *Wary Partners: Diplomats and the Media.* Washington, DC: Congressional Quarterly, 1995.

Ranney, Austin. *Channels of Power.* New York: Basic Books, 1983.

Schmidt, Benno C. Jr. *Freedom of the Press vs. Public Access.* New York: Praeger, 1976.

Schwartz, Bernard. *Freedom of the Press.* New York: Facts on File, 1992.

Starr, Paul. *The Creation of the Media: Political Origins of Modern Communications.* New York: Perseus, 2004.

5   How Corporate Power Influences What We See

When you go to Blockbuster for a video or DVD, buy a book published by Simon & Schuster, watch the *Daily Show with Jon Stewart* on Comedy Central, tune in to MTV, watch Nickelodeon, BET, Showtime, or CBS, you are part of a world overseen by a parent company called Viacom.[1] Pick up a *TV Guide* or buy the *New York Post*, purchase a book published by HarperCollins, see a movie made by 20th Century Fox, or tune in to Fox News and you contribute to Rupert Murdoch's bottom line because all these outlets ultimately belong to his News Corporation. The same patterns are appearing online, with major portals backed by media companies. For example, the Tribune Company owns Blackvoices.com, America On Line owns 20 percent of Net-Noir, and Blackfamilies.com is operated by Cox Communications.[2]

This chapter is about power. Specifically, it is about how corporate power influences what we see, read, and enjoy. As we noted in Chapter 1, the primary function of the mass media is to attract and hold large audiences for advertisers. Here we examine the ways that the corporate and commercial character of mass media affect news, advertising, and politics. Specifically we suggest that media consolidation produces a focus on the bottom line that reduces news staff, minimizes some forms of local content, drives news and programming away from substantive content that would attract small audiences and toward a focus on human interest stories, and relentlessly cross-promotes the other content owned by the parent company. Consolidation also increases the impact of a pro-corporation point of view while minimizing the coverage of corporate self-interest. Finally, we argue that consolidation narrows the range of voices available through the most read, heard, and viewed channels of communication in the mass culture.

A BRIEF HISTORY OF MEDIA CONSOLIDATION

The 1980s produced a new trend: media consolidation. Time Inc. and Warner Communications merged to form the world's largest media organization, worth $18 billion. Gulf & Western, owners of Simon & Schuster books and Paramount Pictures, divested itself of its nonmedia industries and changed its name to Paramount Communications Inc. Analyst Ben Bagdikian observed in 1990, "A handful of mammoth private organizations have begun to dominate the world's mass media. Most of them confidently announce that by the mid-1990s they—five to ten corporate giants—will control most of the world's important newspapers, magazines, books, broadcast stations, movies, recordings, and videocassettes."[3]

The trend continued in the 1990s, when the Westinghouse Electric Corporation offered $5.4 billion to purchase CBS Inc., and the Walt Disney Company agreed to purchase Capital Cities/ABC Inc. for $19 million. The ABC/Disney alliance created the world's largest entertainment company.[4] At the time of the acquisition, Capital Cities/ABC owned the ABC Television Network with its top-rated prime-time comedy *Home Improvement* and its number-one newscast *World News Tonight with Peter Jennings*, as well as ten television stations; twenty-one radio stations; a controlling interest in the cable channels ESPN and ESPN2; Fairchild Publications, the publisher of *Women's Wear Daily*; newspapers, including the *Kansas City Star*; and partial interests in cable programming in Japan, Germany, and Scandinavia. Disney owned the Disney Channel, Walt Disney Pictures, Hollywood Records, Buena Vista Distribution, Touchstone Television, and Disney Interactive.[5]

"Once GE, owner of NBC, has the content-production power of Universal under its belt, an important industry-wide process of consolidation will be completed. All six broadcast networks will be tied directly to film and TV production studios, thereby completing the vertical integration of their industry," noted Margaret M. Smyth, a senior partner in Deloitte's Global Technology, Media & Telecommunications Practice. "Most of the broadcast, cable, and movie audience will be owned by five companies: Viacom, Time Warner, Disney (or Comcast), News Corp., and GE. With their working parts in place, these firms will have no compelling short-term business reasons to expand."[6]

Today, five conglomerates own and control most U.S. mass media (see Tables 5-1 and 5-2). The interests of those corporations and their owners play an increasing role in our political culture. At present, the big five—Time Warner, Disney, Murdoch's News Corporation, Viacom, and General Electric—own much of the media in the United States, and they are vertically and horizontally integrated to such an extent that, for all realistic purposes, they now control much of what the American public learns, or does not learn, about its own world.[7]

TABLE 5-1   Top 10 Television Broadcast Companies (by 2004 revenue)

RANK	COMPANY	STATIONS	REVENUE
1.	News Corporation Limited (Fox Entertainment Group Inc.)	37	$2,435,850,000
2.	CBS Television Network (Viacom Inc.)	41	$2,000,550,000
3.	NBC Universal Inc. (General Electric Co.)	44	$1,944,450,000
4.	Tribune Co.	30	$1,328,900,000
5.	ABC Inc. (Walt Disney Co.)	10	$1,247,925,000
6.	Gannett Company, Inc.	21	$918,800,000
7.	Hearst-Argyle Television, Inc. (Hearst Corp.)	36	$827,225,000
8.	Belo Corp.	20	$731,950,000
9.	Univision	62	$670,100,000
10.	Cox Enterprises Inc.	16	$649,400,000

Source: BIA Financial Network Inc., 2004 Estimated Revenues, 4/2005. Table reprinted by permission of The Center for Public Integrity. Online at http://www.publicintegrity.org/telecom/industry.aspx?act=broadcast.

TABLE 5-2   Top 10 Radio Broadcast Companies (by 2004 revenue)

RANK	COMPANY	STATIONS	REVENUE
1.	Clear Channel Communications, Inc.	1,195	$3,570,650,000
2.	Infinity Broadcasting Corp. (Viacom Inc.)	179	$2,223,700,000
3.	Entercom Communications Corp.	106	$487,775,000
4.	Cox Radio Inc. (Cox Enterprises Inc.)	78	$485,800,000
5.	ABC Radio Networks (Walt Disney Co.)	73	$454,850,000
6.	Citadel Broadcasting Corp.	224	$412,782,000
7.	Radio One Inc.	68	$377,200,000
8.	Univision Communications Inc.	70	$338,875,000
9.	Cumulus Media Inc.	303	$325,700,000
10.	Emmis Communications Corp.	25	$311,175,000

Source: BIA Financial Network Inc., 2004 Estimated Revenues, 4/2005. Table reprinted by permission of The Center for Public Integrity. Online at http://www.publicintegrity.org/telecom/industry.aspx?act=broadcast.

A Focus on Profits

Corporations owe their allegiance to their shareholders. Their purpose is not serving the public good unless doing so ensures profits. "Today, the business of news is business, not news. . . . [N]ews has become secondary, even incidental, to markets and revenues and margins and advertisers and consumer preferences," concluded a recent study of publicly owned newspapers.[8] Reporters agree. A 2004 survey of journalists conducted by the Pew Research Center for the People and the Press found that 66 percent of national newspeople and 57 percent of local journalists believe that "increased bottom line pressure is 'seriously hurting' the quality of news coverage."

"Journalists at national news organizations generally take a dimmer view of the state of the profession than do local journalists," said the report. "But both groups express considerably more concern over the deleterious impact of bottom-line pressures than they did in polls taken by the Center in 1995 and 1999. Further, both print and broadcast journalists voice high levels of concern about this problem, as do majorities working at nearly all levels of news organizations."[9]

Staff Cuts

The first effect of consolidation is a reduction in the number of news people. Staff cuts translate into fewer voices and perspectives in the news process. The Project for Excellence in Journalism's report on the state of journalism in 2004 found, for example,

- 2,200 fewer full-time editorial employees at newspapers since 1990
- A third fewer correspondents at the networks than in the 1980s, and a 30 percent increase in workload for those remaining correspondents; half as many foreign bureaus
- Budget or staff cuts reported by nearly 60 percent of local television news directors in 2002
- *Time* magazine's staff shrank by 15 percent, *Newsweek*'s by 50 percent, in the last 20 years; roughly a third fewer foreign bureaus for both

CASE STUDY 5-1   Thwarting Additional Consolidation

In June 2003 the Federal Communication Commission promulgated regulations that permitted a single corporation in the largest cities in this country to own three television stations, eight radio stations, the dominant newspaper, and the cable company itself. In mid-sized cities, a single company would have been able to own a major newspaper, two television stations, eight radio stations and several cable channels. The Poynter Institute created a chart of the changes:

Old rule	*What's changed*
Companies may not own broadcast and print organizations in the same market.	Cross ownership rules restrictions lifted in areas with nine or more television stations, which are the largest markets; other markets would face some limits; cross ownership banned in markets with three or fewer TV stations.
No broadcast company can own stations that reach more than 35 percent of the national audience.	The plan would allow the nation's four national television networks and other group owners to buy enough television stations to reach 45 percent of the national audience. The networks had sought total repeal, but the change at the very least ensures that News Corp. Inc.'s (NWS) Fox network and Viacom Inc.'s (VIA) CBS network, which currently reach nearly 40 percent of the audience, won't have to sell stations.
Companies can only own two stations in one market if they are not large stations, and there are eight other competitors.	Broadcasters will be allowed to own three stations in the biggest markets where there are 18 stations, such as Los Angeles, up from two; companies could add a second channel in smaller markets where there are at least five stations, as long as one is not in the top four, based on ratings.
A company may not own two of the top four broadcast stations in a market.	No change. The FCC bars a broadcaster from owning two of the top four rated stations in any market. Those four are usually the affiliates of the major networks—Fox, CBS, NBC, and ABC.
Companies are limited in radio station ownership.	No change to current rule; new constraints as the agency imposes new market definitions to avoid monopolies that have sprung up in some markets. But these monopoly clusters won't be broken up unless the clusters are sold.
No mergers between the top four networks.	No change; mergers prohibited among top four networks: ABC, CBS, NBC, and Fox[a]

(continued on next page)

CASE STUDY 5-1   *(continued)*

Consistent with the notion that the news industry fails to cover its own corporate interests an *American Journalism Review* study of reporting on the FCC change found that

> For the first five months of this year, leading up to June 2, when the FCC formally voted to relax the ownership rules, we found virtually no coverage on ABC, CBS, NBC, MSNBC, Fox, and CNN. While some newspapers produced a respectable flurry of stories in the weeks prior to the FCC's action, the major networks—where most people get their news—acknowledged the issue only after protests in Washington had grown impossible to ignore.
>
> Specifically, we found that NBC (owned by General Electric) ran nothing prior to the FCC's action except for a single three-minute segment on May 28—just five days before the FCC was due to act. CBS (owned by Viacom) ran nothing until May 13, when it broadcast a 50-word piece on its morning news program. It ran nothing in prime time until May 29. CNN (owned by Time Warner) didn't cover the issue until May 27, although there were a few segments in mid-May on its business news programs on CNN. Fox News (owned by Rupert Murdoch's News Corporation) ran nothing until May 30.[b]

The media industry's place at the table in the development of the regulations was confirmed by the Center for Public Integrity project that found that media companies and their lobbyists had met behind closed doors with FCC officials more than 70 times. FCC officials had been the beneficiaries of almost $450,000 of industry-sponsored travel and entertainment in 8 years. "The problem for me is the access and the personal face time the industry gets with these top officials they bring out to their events," said Andrew Schwartzman, president and CEO of the Media Access Project, a consumer advocacy group that works on telecommunications issues. "It's impossible for the public to get the same kind of access with those officials."[c] An October 28, 2004, report by the center revealed that "the broadcast industry spent more than $222 million lobbying the federal government from 1998 through June 2004—a period of increasingly intense battles over ownership rules."[d]

But that's not all. "In addition, television and radio companies contributed more than $26.5 million to federal candidates and lawmakers during the same period. The companies and their principal representative organization—the National Association of Broadcasters—also sponsored 84 trips for lawmakers and regulators at a cost of $165,474, bringing total spending to affect policy and elections by the industry to $248.9 million."[e]

According to the report, "The top spenders [were]

- General Electric Co., which owns 80 percent of NBC Universal in addition to a number of cable networks, topped the lobby spending list for broadcasters at $105 million. The total includes all lobbying. The giant conglomerate draws only a portion of its revenue from broadcast operations, but broadcast-related lobbying numbers are not reported separately.
- Second in broadcast lobbying is the National Association of Broadcasters, an influential trade group that represents the interests of free, over-the-air radio and television broadcasters. The NAB spent $43.2 million lobbying, according to records.
- Walt Disney Co., owner of the ABC television network, is a distant third at $24.2 million."[f]

In June 2004 a Federal Appeals Court, the Third Circuit Court of Appeals, blocked implementation of the rules after an unprecedented outpouring of protest from U.S. consumers and a formal legal challenge by groups that included the Media Access Project, a nonprofit telecommunication law firm. The project argued that increasing permissible market share would prevent small, local organizations from entering the media industry.

In its case before the court, those opposing the regulations argued dominance of the public sphere by large corporations while those favoring them argued that the media environment is more diverse than ever before. "'There is truly potential here for one company to have significant dominance of public discourse,' said Angela Campbell, a lawyer representing the groups, which include San Francisco's Media Alliance, the Consumer Federation of America and Prometheus Radio Project, a nonprofit group born from the ashes of a pirate station shut down in 1998."[g]

The FCC countered that "its new media rules would advance both industry competition and the diversity of local news. Powell has said the new rules 'take proper account of the explosion of new media outlets for news, information and entertainment, rather than perpetuate the graying rules of a bygone black-and-white era.'"[h] The Third Circuit held that the FCC had not provided reasoned analysis to justify its local ownership limits and therefore sent those rules back to the FCC for additional review.

Prior to the FCC rule change, no corporation could own television stations that together reached more than 35 percent of all U.S. households. Both Fox and Viacom had received temporary waivers to own more, but if the 35 percent cap held would have to sell off some of their stations. The FCC raised that limit to 45 percent. Facing a public outcry, Congress voted a 39 percent cap. Why 39 percent? A 2004 editorial in *Broadcasting and Cable* asked, "How big can a station group get? That is a question that occupied the FCC, broadcasters, Congress, and even consumers through much of 2003. It even became a political football." The outcome? "One group can own stations that cover 39% of the nation. Why that odd number? It happens to benefit two media giants: Viacom's holdings cover 38." News Corp., the owner of Fox, reaches 38 percent. Neither had to sell stations to satisfy the new ownership cap."[i]

The Media Access Project explains the state of media ownership rules in the following chart:

Local Radio Ownership Rule	Allows ownership of up to 8 radio stations (on a sliding scale) in a local market, depending on total number of stations in market. (Under review by FCC as of Feb. 2002)
Local Television Ownership Rule	Allows ownership of two TV stations in same market so long as that market has 8 independent voices and one station is not among the top four stations in that market. Sometimes called the "duopoly" rule. (Court remanded to FCC April 2002)
Local Radio–Television Cross-Ownership Rule	Permits up to 2 TV and 6 radio stations (or 1 TV and 7 radio) so long as there are at least the 20 independent voices in the market (TV, radio, daily newspapers, cable service).
Local Broadcast–Newspaper Ownership Rule	Prohibits ownership of a local radio or television station and a major local daily newspaper. (Under review by FCC as of Sept. 2001)

(continued on next page)

CASE STUDY 5-1 *(continued)*

Local Cable–Television Ownership Rule	Prohibits ownership of a cable system and a TV station in the same area. (Vacated in court Feb. 2002)
National Television Ownership Rule	Prohibits owning stations that reach more than 35 percent of the total audience. (Court remanded to FCC Feb. 2002)
National Cable Ownership Rule	Prohibits owning stations that pass more than 30 percent of total US households. (Court remanded to FCC and FCC suspended rule March 2001)[j]

The future? In an article in *Broadcasting & Cable,* Bill McConnell notes, "Media giants Comcast, News Corp., Viacom and other conglomerates will seek to strike new deals to grow their empires in a more relaxed regulatory environment. Media companies see consolidation as a means to economies of scale, whereby they can theoretically deliver superior services at a lower cost. A second Bush administration will resurrect deregulation to make it so."[k]

[a]Poynter Institute, compiled from various news sources, 2 June 2003. Online at http://www.poynter.org/column.asp?id=56&aid=36005.
[b]Charles Layton, "News Blackout," *American Journalism Review* (December–January 2004): 18.
[c]Center for Public Integrity, "Captive Audience Where Available?" 22 May 2003. Online at http://www.publicintegrity.org/telecom/report.aspx?aid=16.
[d]Robert Morlino, "Broadcast Lobbying Tops $222 Million," The Center for Public Integrity, 28 October 2004. Reprinted

with permission of The Center for Public Integrity. Online at http://www.publicintegrity.org/telecom/report.aspx?aid=406.
[e]Ibid.
[f]Ibid.
[g]Dan Fost, "Fewer moguls, bigger empires: Congress wrestles with media ownership," *San Francisco Chronicle,* 12 February 2004, p. B1.
[h]Ibid.
[i]Editorial, "Why 39%," *Broadcasting and Cable,* 19 April 2004, p. 54.
[j]Media Access Project, "Issues: Media Consolidation/Encouraging Diversity of the Electronic Media." Copyright 2004 Media Access Project. Reprinted with permission of Media Access Project. Online at http://www.mediaaccess.org/programs/diversity/index.html.
[k]Bill McConnell, "Fat Cats Get Fatter; and Four More Changes in the Next Four Years under George W. Bush," *Broadcasting & Cable* 134 (8 November 2004): 14.

Those defending consolidation argue that economies of scale increase the money available to produce a high-quality product. Those opposed to it see fewer voices producing news, a corporate perspective dictating what the public sees, hears, and reads, and relentless cross-promotion. But both sides agree that one clear effect is a focus on the bottom line.

Reduction in Serious Political Content That Draws Low Audiences

The emphasis on the bottom line affects coverage of political candidates and events. So-called free media, such as debates in the primary season, compete with paid media or political advertising. Moreover, preempting regular programming to air political

---

BOX 5-1   How Does Who Owns the Media Affect the Media?

The Annenberg Public Policy Center survey "Journalists and the Public, 2005" was conducted by Princeton Survey Research Associates International between March 7 and May 2, 2005, among 673 journalists, including owners and executives, editors and producers, and staff journalists, and representing both print and broadcast media and local and national organizations. Interviews were conducted online and by telephone. For results based on the total sample, one can say with 95% confidence that the error attributable to sampling is plus or minus 4 percentage points.

The public survey conducted between March 3 and April 5, 2005, is based on a nationwide representative sample of 1,500 adults 18 years of age and older. For results based on the total sample, one can say with 95 percent confidence that the error attributable to sampling is plus or minus 3 percentage points.

Concentrated ownership cuts voices and views to public. Fueling these concerns is the journalists' view that concentration of media ownership leads to a centralization of the voices and sources Americans hear. More than seven in 10 (72%) journalists believe these ownership changes reduce, not increase, the number of different voices and views the American people can hear each day.

Journalists say corporate ownership hurts news quality. The fact that most newspapers, radio stations, and television stations are owned by large corporations has a negative impact on the news, according to a sizable majority of journalists. Two in three (65%) journalists say the quality of the news suffers because most news organizations are owned by large corporations, while substantially fewer (21%) say it has no effect and a small percentage (11%) say it has a positive effect on the quality of news coverage. Print journalists (68%) are sightly more likely than broadcast journalists

(56%) to say large corporate ownership has a negative impact on the news the American people get.

Number of stories reduced. A majority of journalists (53%) say the push to make a profit has resulted in cuts in the number of stories covered each day. More of those who actually produce the stories each day—editors and producers (56%) and staff journalists (56%)—believe this is the case compared with the executives who set financial targets (33%).

Reduction in coverage type. A solid majority (64%) say the profit motive has led to a reduction in the types of stories covered overall. Again, more editors and producers (64%) and staff journalists (68%) than executives (44%) say there has been a reduction in the types of stories covered.

Nearly eight in 10 journalists (77%) say they have seen reductions in the number of stories that take extra time and money to report, such as investigative reports and in-depth features. Staff journalists are particularly sensitive to these cuts—a large majority (82%) say this is the case, compared to fewer executives (59%).

And most journalists (85%) say the pressure to make a profit has caused cutbacks in travel budgets. Staff journalists (88%) are more likely than executives (68%) to see the impact of travel budget limitations.

But there are areas where journalists clearly feel limited to some degree. Nearly half (47%) say news organizations shy away—intentionally or unintentionally—from stories that could be negative about the company's owners. Somewhat fewer journalists feel the pressure to go easy on major advertisers. One in three (33%) say news organizations avoid, to a great or moderate extent, negative stories about major advertisers. In a similar fashion, 29 percent of journalists say the media ducks unfavorable stories about friends of the company's owners.

---

debates results in lost revenue. In other words, more coverage on newscasts reduces the need for paid political advertising, which has come to be an increasingly significant share of the revenue of television stations.[10] According to projections by the Campaign Media Analysis Group, in the presidential race this year, the campaigns, the parties, and outside groups will have spent about $500 million on television ads by election day, more than twice the amount in 2000.[11] The Center for Public Integrity describes the

---

BOX 5-2   Does Ownership Matter?

The Project for Excellence in Journalism analyzed "172 distinct news programs, some 23,000 stories, over five years." Their findings suggest that ownership type did make a difference.

Among the findings were the following:

- Smaller station groups overall tended to produce higher quality newscasts than stations owned by larger companies—by a significant margin.
- Network affiliated stations tended to produce higher quality newscasts than network owned and operated stations—also by a large margin.

- Stations with cross-ownership—in which the parent company also owns a newspaper in the same market—tended to produce higher quality newscasts.

Local ownership offered little protection against newscasts being very poor, and did not produce superior quality.[a]

[a]The Project for Excellence in Journalism, 29 April 2003. Online at Journalism.org.

---

relationship between news coverage, paid political advertising, and campaign finance this way:

> At a time when television networks and local TV stations keep decreasing the amount of air time on actual political news, they keep getting richer from paid political ads. According to the Alliance for Better Campaigns, candidates, parties, and issue groups spent . . . more than $1 billion in 2002—so much, in fact, that they are now one of television's leading sources of revenue. Candidates can no longer depend on free media news coverage to get their word out, which means they must have sufficient funding to purchase campaign commercials.[12]

Because they did not think the opening nights of the party conventions would draw large audiences, in summer 2004 the networks did not cover the first night of the Democratic and Republican conventions. This meant that only viewers with cable were able to watch the keynote addresses of Illinois senatorial candidate Barack Obama and Georgia Senator Zell Miller or even the speech of former President Jimmy Carter. Keynote addresses express the convention theme, and they are moments when each party reaches out to all citizens for support. Recall that some 35 million Americans do not have cable, often because of its cost. Coverage of the conventions was limited to one hour per night, featuring the nomination acceptance speeches of the major candidates. That is unfortunate, because conventions remain one of the few venues in which there is extended talk about the welfare of the nation and the kinds of policies that political leaders believe are required, and such talk prompts discussion of public policy and exposes viewers to the diverse voices of those in both parties. Accordingly, as FCC Commissioner Michael Copps argues, airing them is an important way for stations "to serve the public interest."[13]

BOX 5-3   Can You Create a Media System That Would Have Produced a More Informed Public?

In October 2003 the University of Maryland's Program on International Policy Attitudes (PIPA) released its study of Americans' attitudes toward the war in Iraq, their knowledge of the issues, and the media they consumed. It revealed that the more commercial television news coverage of the war that Americans consumed, the greater were their misperceptions about it and the more likely they were to support the Bush administration's position. This was especially true of viewers of the Fox News Channel, but it applied to all commercial television viewers.[a] This study of misperceptions about the Iraq war and their relationship to the media, which are the primary sources of information for most Americans, is deeply disturbing. Given the quantity and quality of coverage by the commercial media, McChesney argues, "We have

a population ripe for manipulation by powerful public relations firms and consultants who are expert in sound bites and seductive imagery."[b]

[a]Steven Kull, Clay Ramsay, and Evan Lewis, "Misperceptions, the Media, and the Iraq War," Program on International Policy Attitudes (PIPA) and Knowledge Networks, October 3, 2003, University of Maryland, College Park, pp. 1–21. The issues on which the large sample were polled over time were whether Iraq had played an important role in 9/11; whether Iraq had provided substantial support to al Qaeda, whether weapons of mass destruction had been found in Iraq, and whether world opinion supported the Iraq war. Online at http://www.pipa.org/OnlineReports/Iraq/Media_10_02_03_Report.pdf.
[b]Robert McChesney. *The Problem of the Media: U.S. Communication Politics in the 21st Century* (New York: Monthly Review Press, 2004), p. 127.

To Attract Audiences, Definition of News Shifts toward Human Interest

In the world of U.S. television, what is entertaining and, thus, attracts advertisers is defined by the norms and conventions of prime-time programming. To remain profitable, newscasts are expected to attract audiences with items that feature conflict and human interest. Human interest stories generally are compelling, but such stories have a particularly powerful impact on news stories about military actions. Once the lives of U.S. soldiers are at risk, for example, television news and the public identify with them and their families, critical distance collapses, and media and public opinion are integrated into support for the war effort. That happened during the earlier Gulf War, and it is happening now through coverage of the war in Iraq. In Eric Alterman's blunt words: "Network news is getting it from all sides. Their corporate owners are squeezing them at every opportunity to increase profits by simultaneously skimping on costs, pushing for 'tabloid' stories, and dumbing down what's left."[14]

Loss of News That Is of Local but Not Regional or National Interest

In the world of consolidated media, some forms of news are going by the wayside as regional media replace local ones. The Farm Bureau reports, for example, that large ownership groups that have acquired multiple radio licenses are eliminating "timely weather information, local news, up-to-the-minute market reports and so on, affecting production of agriculture."[15]

Those who see consolidation as unthreatening argue that the new media will move in to capture these abandoned niches. If there is a local audience, an Internet service will emerge, they argue, to address its needs.

Magnified Pro-Business Message While Minimizing Scrutiny of Parent Corporations

Fewer voices and lost content are not the only concerns raised by consolidation. There is fear as well that a voice friendly to corporate interests will dominate those critical of them and that when a corporation owns a news outlet, the last thing that will be covered is corporate profit-taking, self-interested regulatory moves or financial interests.

The *New York Post*, for example, is owned by Rupert Murdoch's News Corporation. One result? "An article in the *New York Post* on Dec. 11 [2004] . . . reported that someone had agreed to pay $44 million for a fabulous Fifth Avenue penthouse being sold by the estate of the late Laurence S. Rockefeller. The buyer was identified only as 'a prominent New Yorker.'" Asked to explain, an editor at the *Post* said, "Generally, we don't want to write about our boss."[16]

Consistent with their self-interest, corporate owners prefer programming reaffirming their beliefs and values, programming with a pro-business, free-market message. So, for example, a study conducted for the *American Journalism Review* concluded that, in the first five months of 2003, commercial television and the cable networks offered "virtually no coverage" of the FCC deliberations on allowing expanded media ownership, and these are the outlets that would benefit most from changes allowing newspaper–broadcast cross-ownership.[17]

Such power is troubling in a democracy, but it is magnified by the dominance of corporate money in electoral campaigns. In spite of reforms, the contributions of "corporations, including media corporations, constitute 75 percent of all political contributions" and in amounts that are "many multiples larger" than those of labor unions.[18] In *The Buying of the President 2004* Charles Lewis and the Center for Public Integrity identify the top contributors to the campaigns of President Bush and Vice President Dick Cheney and all their Democratic challengers, among whom are many media corporations. Media corporations also figure prominently among the top 50 donors to both the Republican and Democratic parties. The Center for Public Integrity report also notes that all major presidential candidates and most national political reporters recognize that the top money raiser of the year before the election will become the party nominee; in effect, then, "the wealthiest interests essentially hold a private referendum the year before the election, . . . which effectively predetermines whom the nondonor public gets to vote on."[19]

Even those who recognize advantages in consolidation concede that the values of the corporate parent influence the owned outlet. "[M]edia giants wanting to turn a profit also can influence the material and perspective presented in media," notes a study conducted by Latteier and Gamson. "[A] television show owned by a company that also owned a tobacco company presented a pro-tobacco bias, and a news program owned by the Walt Disney Company devoted a two-hour show to the Orlando theme park's anniversary."

BOX 5-4   Corporate Control over Content

Fox News Channel, the highest-rated cable news network in the country, rejected a 60-second ad for *The Nation* during the 2004 Republican National Convention. The ad read: "Nobody owns *The Nation.* Not Time Warner, not Murdoch. So there's no corporate slant, no White House spin. Just the straight dope." According to a *New York Times* report, "A spokesman for Fox News, which has always rejected the charge that it brings a partisan bias to news coverage, said, 'We reject ads all the time,' and refused further comment."[a]

During the fall 2004 presidential campaign, Sinclair Broadcasting Group ordered its stations to suspend normal programming in prime time for one evening before the presidential election to air a documentary, "Stolen Honor: Wounds That Never Heal," written by an ex-Marine and former reporter for the *Washington Times.* Sinclair is owner of 62 U.S. television stations, more than any other single company; its stations are affiliates of most networks, reaching a quarter of U.S. households, fourteen of which aired in crucial swing states in the 2004 election. Allegedly, the film argues that John Kerry's antiwar activities in 1971 prolonged the war. What is noteworthy is that Sinclair intended to broadcast it as "news," which means that its costs would have been borne by SBG, as a kind of campaign contribution. Andrew Jay Schwartzman, head of the Media Access Project, responded, "What this shows is the dangers of media concentration. These are the problems that

arise when one company controls 62 channels."[b] Timothy Karr, executive director of Media for Democracy, adds, "We maintain that it is a business play.... [By airing the film, Sinclair is] looking for further relaxation of regulations that will allow them to own more stations."[c] Public protest produced changes in the content of the program to present divergent views, but the power to control what Americans see and when they see it during an election campaign and whether contrasting views are presented is an example of corporate power.

Leland Westerfield, a media analyst for Harris Nesbitt Gerard, said Sinclair deserved credit for . . . its aggressive techniques in finding ways to expand despite F.C.C. hindrances, which have resulted in the company owning or managing two stations in 21 of 39 markets (so-called duopolies). "I fully credit them for that pioneering spirit," Mr. Westerfield said, "but not for journalistic integrity."[d]

[a]David Carr, "The Left Asked to Speak to the Right, But a Gatekeeper Wouldn't Hear of It," *New York Times*, 30 August 04, p. C8; the ad aired on CNN, MSNBC, and Bravo.
[b]Julian Borger in Washington, "TV Channels to Rubbish Kerry on Eve of Poll," *The Guardian,* 12 October 2004. Online at guardian.co.uk.
[c]Quoted in John Reinan, "It's Prime Time for Sinclair Affiliate," *Minneapolis Star Tribune,* 19 October 2004, p. D4.
[d]In Bill Carter, "Risks Seen for TV Chain Showing Film about Kerry," *New York Times*, 18 October 2004, p. C1.

"With more media conglomerations, the fear is that the values presented will be consistent with the values of big business, that a capitalistic sensibility will come through," says Latteier. "This is definitely happening. But beyond this kind of self-interested spin, it's not clear that ownership concentration has a big effect on the diversity of ideas presented."[20]

Cross-Promotion: Synergy

The business page of the *Washington Post* described the new media world by giving the example of the production and marketing of a popular movie: "Viacom's *Forrest Gump* blitz exemplifies the cross-marketing 'synergies' that companies are trying to achieve by

---

BOX 5-5   Synergy

"ABC is taking aggressive marketing to a whole new level. Marrying Disney's corporate muscle to the net's reach, publicity for the 76th Academy Awards will span theme parks to soap operas. . . . Most of our comedies are tying into the Academy Awards with plotlines or stunt casting that involves a former Oscar winner or someone associated with the Oscars," says Judith Tukich, who carries the unusual title "director of synergy and special projects" at ABC.

"The network values its in-house promotional effort at a whopping $40 million—astronomical by any account. . . . Daytime dramas *One Life to Live, General Hospital,* and *All My Children* are incorporating Oscar storylines that will run Friday Feb. 27. Chat-fests *Good Morning America* and *The View* will focus many segments on the Oscars, with GMA hosting a weeklong celebration before the show.

"The Disney-owned cable channels are getting into the act, too. Even ESPN's new morning show,

Cold Pizza, discussed the Oscar nominations the day they were announced. A&E, Lifetime, and Disney Channel are all sponsoring Oscar-related events or promotions."[a]

Synergy explains why some shows land high-profile interviews with major book authors. For example, counterterrorism expert Richard Clarke and *Washington Post* reporter Bob Woodward published their spring 2004 books with units of Simon & Schuster Inc. Viacom Corporation owns both that publisher and CBS. So which network garnered large audiences with their interviews of these men? Unsurprisingly, Clarke and Woodward were first interviewed in broadcasts on their books on CBS's *60 Minutes.*

[a]All quotes cited in Paige Albiniak, "All Oscar, All the Time," *Broadcast & Cable Magazine,* February 16, 2004, p. 26. Republished with permission from Broadcasting & Cable, 2/16/04, a Reed Business Publication.

---

owning the movie studio that makes the hit, the video stores that rent it and the TV networks that advertise it."[21] "Synergy is defined as a situation where the whole equals more than the sum of the parts. With respect to conglomerates, it typically relates to a belief that components of the conglomerate (usually a company that's part of it) work together to create value over and above the value that any one of the firms could create," says professor Joseph Turow of the Annenberg School for Communication (personal communication, March 8, 2005).

Fewer Voices Providing News

Control over what we see and read in news, television, books, and movies has brought steadily increasing political power to these media conglomerates. As monopolies, broadcasters have enormous resources for lobbying, and control of the airwaves has made local television, especially local newscasts, a powerful threat to politicians who oppose them on important issues. Politicians and candidates know that reelection and the success of policies they support will be influenced by coverage in the outlets controlled by major media corporations. In its report the *State of the News Media 2004,* the Project for Excellence in Journalism (see Journalism.org) noted that 22 companies account for 70 percent of the country's newspaper circulation, the top twenty radio companies operate more than 20 percent of the radio stations and "in local television, the 10 biggest companies own 30 percent of all television stations reaching 85 percent of all television households."[22]

Economic forces have created a situation in which 97 percent of the nation's daily newspapers enjoy a local newspaper monopoly, and nearly half are owned by some group or national chain.[23] Competition among alternative media has taken the place of competition among newspapers. *Time* and *Newsweek* are both owned by large corporations or conglomerates. By contrast, *U.S. News & World Report* is employee owned. *Newsweek* is owned by the Washington Post Company, which also owns several television stations and ranks among the Fortune 500, with sales of nearly a half billion dollars a year. Time Warner Inc. has revenues of more than $1 billion a year, but only a small part of its revenues come from sales of *Time*. Robert Sherrill indicates some of the implications of *Time*'s conglomerate ownership: "A majority of its income is from the sale of corrugated containers and lumber; its forest products company, Temple-Eastex, is the biggest private landowner in Texas, with a million acres of timberland—which readers might want to bear in mind when they judge *Time*'s position on environmental legislation and housing prices."[24]

Should we worry when another outlet is controlled by one of the big five? In December 2004 Murdoch's News Corporation announced that it had closed an all-cash deal to enable Fox News radio news service, which to that point had provided news "for 275 stations nationwide" to program news for more than "100 Clear Channel news and talk stations, with a five-minute top-of-the-hour newscast and a nightly news broadcast." As such Fox would be "Clear Channel's primary source for breaking national news." The deal prompted Josh Silver, executive director of Free Press, an advocacy group focused on media policy, to observe, "You have the largest radio giant now running the news provided by one of the largest media empires, Exhibit A of what's wrong with media consolidation." He added, "Now what Rupert Murdoch decides is news suddenly becomes news."[25]

TO SUM UP

In this chapter we examined the ways that the corporate and commercial character of mass media affect news, advertising, and politics. Specifically, we suggested that consolidation produces a focus on the bottom line that reduces news staff, minimizes some forms of local content, drives news and programming away from substantive content that would attract small audiences and toward a focus on human interest stories, and relentlessly cross-promotes the other content owned by the parent company. It also increases the impact of a pro-corporation point of view while minimizing the coverage of corporate self-interest. Finally, we argued that consolidation narrows the voices available through the most read, heard, and viewed channels of communication in the mass culture.

Use InfoTrac College Edition to access information on topics in this chapter from hundreds of periodicals and scholarly journals. Enter keyword and subject searches: *synergy, media consolidation, media cross-ownership, Rupert Murdoch, bottom line.*

SELECTED READINGS

Ben H. Bagdikian. *The New Media Monopoly.* Boston: Beacon Press, 2004.

Charles Lewis and the Center for Public Integrity. *The Buying of the President 2004.* New York: Perennial/ Harper Collins, 2004.

Robert McChesney. *The Problem of the Media*: *U.S. Communication Politics in the 21st Century.* New York: Monthly Review Press, 2004.

6

What Is Advertising?

A nonstop coast-to-coast trip on United Airlines from Philadelphia to San Francisco takes about 6 hours. If a passenger chooses to eat a meal during that time, it arrives on a tray that obscures most of the tray table she has pulled down from the back of the seat in front of her. Reading material on one's laptop must be set aside to make way for the meal tray. In February 2004 the meal includes two breadsticks, a small salad, salad dressing, a choice of lasagna or chicken, and a 2- by- 3-inch folded ad not for air travel but for Celebrity Cruises. "What's in your destination?" asks the ad. "Caribbean in Spring? Europe in Summer? Panama Canal in Fall? Let Celebrity take you there." Inset into the appeals is a picture of a large cruise ship afloat on glass-smooth water off an island. If the passenger is interested, she can put the small ad card in her purse or pocket. The moment she reads it, Celebrity Cruises has reached an upper-income traveler with an image of travel more idyllic than that in a crowded plane. "From the moment you step on board," notes the second page of the folding card, "outstanding service awaits you. With one staff member for every two guests, savor a taste of luxury that makes you feel like the only guest onboard. Media Dynamics Inc. estimates that on an average day, an adult in the United States is exposed to 306 radio, television, newspaper and magazine, and Internet ads.[1]

In 2003 $18.35 billion was spent on magazine ads, $1,117.2 billion on television, $12.3 billion on cable; ad revenue on Spanish-language network television was $2.2 billion.[2] In 2003, total ad spending in the United States rose 6.1% to $128.3 billion.[3] The average cost of a 30-second ad in the broadcast of the 2005 Super Bowl was 2.4 million.[4]

When the woman who edits this book for Wadsworth sits down at her nationally advertised computer, she wears clothes advertised both by local retailers and through national ad campaigns. We have never seen her office, but we would bet that the paint on the walls, the desk on which the computer rests, the lamp on the desk, and the pens in the drawer are as familiar to us as they are to you, although we may live thousands of miles apart. All these products probably have been nationally advertised. This form of standardization in our lives is in part the by-product of global advertising.

In a sense, advertising has given us a world in common. You are familiar with the products we purchase, we are familiar with the products you purchase, and that familiarity transcends large geographic distances. In other words, we live in a world filled with advertised products; often the presence of one of these products rather than another in our lives is determined by the effectiveness of the ad campaigns for competing products.

In this chapter we examine what advertising is and what advertising through the mass media does.

DEFINING ADVERTISING

The ancient Romans identified three goals of rhetoric: to teach, to delight, and to move to action. Of course, these goals rarely occur in complete isolation from one another. As we argued in our discussion of news, the process of choosing a topic, narrowing it, and selecting evidence in its support gives all messages a persuasive component. Taken at face value, news professes to inform or teach, and ads profess to move to action, to advocate one purchasing decision rather than another. By contrast, most prime-time programming (sitcoms, crime shows) professes to delight.

In contrast to news or other types of programming, advertising is more likely to have a goal of explicit action. Here ads are more akin to editorials, which urge active response, than to the other sorts of content surrounding them. An ad asks us to go somewhere, do something, try something, buy something, accept some single idea, add a new word—generally a product's trade name—to our vocabulary, and associate positive images with that word. To accomplish any of these objectives, the ad contains a simple, highly repetitious message. In the past, we could sort the ad from its surrounding content by its simplicity, by its redundancy, and by the clarity with which it urges adoption, choice, or action.

A broadcast commercial is still to some extent a unit of content that appears in 10-, 15-, 20-, 30-, 60-, or 120-second time units and breaks unapologetically into the narrative line of some other broadcast content. Televised programming usually consists of larger units of 30, 60, or 120 minutes, interrupted by commercials. The smaller, 10- to 120-second units of information appear at regular and predictable intervals within the 30- to 120-minute units of content.

Because, unlike the shows broadcast in the early days of radio and television, television programs today are rarely sponsored by just one advertiser, the subjects discussed in the 30- to 120-minute units may differ drastically from those discussed in the adjacent 10- to 120-second blocks. For example, the evening news may report on the president's trip to Europe and cut to commercials for a shampoo, a laxative, or an automobile, then to a promotional ad for a prime-time program on the same network that evening, and then back to the news, where the anchor introduces a report about a hearing on organized crime. But as we will note in a minute, making ads look like programming is increasingly common.

This segmentation and aggregation of discrete, often incompatible thematic units violates all the rules by which we normally judge communicated content. Suppose you heard a speech discussing the president's trip, an upcoming prime-time program, a hearing on organized crime, the merits of a shampoo, a laxative, and a car. Such a potpourri of topics could not be blended into a coherent speech. As an audience member, you would doubt the speaker's grasp of the rules governing public communication and possibly would question the speaker's sanity as well. After all, the ability to address a subject coherently is one sign of a person's command of the speaking environment.

Yet we do not react negatively when television and radio break our train of thought, disrupt the story line, and introduce a series of unrelated messages. Indeed, we expect it. Consequently, *Sesame Street* built "commercials" into the program: "This part of *Sesame Street* is brought to you by the letter *A*."

BOX 6-1   On-Demand Media

"From TiVo to iPods, an estimated 27 million U.S. citizens own one or more on-demand media devices, according to a study by Arbitron and Edison Media Research released this week. The study, based on January telephone interviews with 1,855 participants, found that 10 percent of consumers watched video-on-demand via cable or satellite in the prior 30 days; 11 percent accessed news online; and 37 million consumers listened to Web radio.

"Additionally, Arbitron and Edison determined that 27 percent of 12- to-17-year-olds own an iPod or other portable MP3 player; an estimated 43 million Americans choose to record TV programming to watch at a different time, either with a VCR or TiVo/DVR; 76 percent of consumers own at least one DVD; and 39 percent own 20 or more DVDs in their personal collection. The study also found that awareness of XM Satellite and Radio has tripled since 2002, from 17 to 50 percent, while awareness of Sirius Satellite Radio has rise from 8 to 54 percent."[a]

[a]Gavin O'Malley, "Study Concludes—Surprise!—Consumers Taking Control of Media," *Online Media Daily*, 25 March 2005. Reprinted with permission of MediaPost Communications.

SHIFTING AD PLACEMENT

Traditionally the broadcast media provided programming at no direct cost to viewers. Advertisers paid for the programs by buying ads on them. The medium in effect sold eyeballs. Cable and satellite changed this equation somewhat by requiring pay for access to the channel itself while also drawing revenue from advertisers. For a higher subscription fee, premium channels such as HBO and Showtime offer commercial-free entertainment.

The remote control and then digital video recorders undercut the tie between exposure to programming and viewing ads. DVRs are like VCRs, but instead of storing the content on a tape, a DVR stores it on a computer disk drive. Advertisers responded by increasing their focus on product placement within programming, by identifying ways to ensure that customers would not block their ads in other venues, and by increasing their ability to identify people who might want their services or products.

Product Placement

The dilemma for advertisers is simple. The cost of advertising is rising on shows whose viewership is falling. Viewers' ability to block ads on shows they watch is increasing with access to DVRs. As a result, advertisers are making deals to include their products in the shows themselves. So, for example, it is no accident that Kieffer Sutherland's character in Fox's *24* races around exclusively in Fords. When products become integral to the plot, time on screen increases, as it did in an episode of *Everybody Loves Raymond* in which he knocks down a display of Ragu Express, a pasta meal, while stalking his wife in a supermarket.

Blurring Program and Ad Content

Some viewers resent product placement in programming. Concern that product placement may backfire, advertisers are also exploring "situ-mercials." By mimicking the look, format, and structure of the programming into which it is set, these ads increase the likelihood that viewers will think the program is still on and as a result pay attention to the ad. Political ads have mimicked news formats for decades, but this is a new phenomenon in product advertising.

In Fox's *24*, Kieffer Sutherland plays agent Jack Bauer. Ford Motors blurred the distinction between that program and its ads by bookending the drama with two long, action-packed ads, shot in the split-screen style that is the hallmark of *24*. Although these ads did not feature Sutherland, their lead character was called "Mr. Bauer." The mini-programs touted Ford Motor's cars.[5]

Incentives to View Ads

With blocking software, Internet users have fought against pop-up ads. In 2002 AOL, for example, added blocking capacity to its software. Google, Yahoo!, and Microsoft MSN followed suit

In March 2004 Google, the most used search engine on the Web, announced that it planned to offer free Web-based e-mail service, called Gmail, with a gigabyte of storage. Because most of us only have 50-megabyte e-mailboxes, those who accepted this free large-capacity service would receive ads tied to the content of their e-mail. Although representatives from Google argued that computers, not people, would search the e-mails and slot the ads, privacy advocates raised concerns. "The proposal is little different from asking people to let their phone companies listen in on their calls and butt in at any time to say, 'This call is brought to you by. . . ,'" argued one critic.[6] Others questioned the limits of such a contract between Google and consumers. Would a person who expressed condolences at the death of a friend receive ads for funeral homes? Would the preferences expressed in e-mail be aggregated and stored in a way that linked the owner of the computer to the preferences? "We have no immediate plans to do so in the future," said a spokesperson for Google.[7]

Unless we plan to spend our lives in a darkened room, wearing earmuffs to block the sound of radio and shunning television, the Internet, magazines, and newspapers, we will be exposed to advertisers' efforts to persuade us. Even those who do not subscribe to a newspaper pass newsstands as they move from place to place and see discarded newspapers and magazines on buses, subways, and planes, in cabs, or on coffee tables in homes they are visiting. Bus shelters, buses, the back seats of taxis, kiosks, public toilets, trash cans, and even sidewalks contain ads. Television viewers trying to watch a game glimpse ads in the background. Log onto the Internet and risk assault by banner ads, as well as pop-ups. Close a file and there is a pop-under.

People who want to avoid radio commercials have to ignore the ads being played over the portable radios carried down the street or at the beach, over car radios when they are carpooling, over the computer of the person at the next desk, or over the public address system at the supermarket or shopping mall. Online, 28 percent report avoiding some sites to duck ads; 15 percent have downloaded ad-blocking software.[8]

> ### BOX 6-2   Yahoo! Has Nearly 40 Million E-Mail Subscribers
>
> In spring 2004, according to Nielsen Net Ratings, "Yahoo! has nearly 40 million e-mail subscribers, Microsoft has 34.4 million, and AOL has 32 million."[a]
>
> [a]Katie Hafner, "In Google We Trust?" *New York Times*, 8 April 2004, p. E1.

People who want to ignore Internet ads have to shun e-mail and stay off-line. So obnoxious was the flood of unwanted solicitations from spammers touting penile extensions and Viagra that Congress took action in fall 2003. In December of that year, President Bush signed legislation restricting commercial e-mail. Violators face fines of $250 per violation with a cap of $2 million and could serve prison time.

Nor can we escape advertising by taking to the air. Because those who fly are affluent, they are a prime target for upscale products. So peruse the magazine in the seat pocket and you find ads, plug in the ear phone to listen to music, and you find the channels sponsored, watch the in-flight entertainment and find promos for television programs, and on some flights look down at your tray table and you'll find advertising there as well. "With an average domestic flight time of 2.5 hours," says SkyMedia's president, "our advertisers will be able to achieve a level of penetration, impact and recall unmatched by virtually any other medium." [9]

The mass media pervade our environment, and with the mass media come the advertisements that underwrite them. A message tailored to persuade an audience to accept a product is not, in itself, advertising. When the people selling the product pay for time or space to enable them to *bring the message in a specific unalterable form to that audience,* however, we call the message *advertising.* An advertiser, within the bounds of taste and the law, controls what the message says, how it says it, and where and how frequently it appears.

The mass media have rules of conduct guaranteeing that the advertisers can communicate what they want at the time or in the space purchased. For example, when a television ad is cut short by a technical malfunction or the programming in which the ad is embedded fails to reach an audience of the size guaranteed by the network, the advertiser is entitled to a "make-good," a rebroadcast of the commercial at a comparable time at no additional charge. Similarly, when a newspaper transposes two prices in an ad, the newspaper will, at no cost to the advertiser, run a correction in the next edition or in the next day's paper.

Some forms of advertising do not fit neatly into this definition, because they reach their audiences without the purchase of time or space. The dividing bar that separates your groceries from the next customer's at the checkout counter of the supermarket, for example, may carry a message from a cigarette manufacturer: "For a light smoke—

try X." The cigarette manufacturer has given the dividers to the store free of charge, in the hope or with the agreement that they will be used. Their use functions as advertising. When your groceries are bagged, you may notice a message about the store on the bag. When you carry the groceries away from the store or use the bag as a garbage bag in your home, you have become the carrier of an ad for the store, just as you have become a walking ad for Calvin Klein when you wear jeans with his name stitched onto the hip pocket.

A movie hero may drink a certain soft drink—a form of advertising purchased by the soft drink manufacturer in exchange for supplying cast and crew with the product, or in exchange for what is called a "promotional consideration." Whether promotional considerations were at play or not we do not know, but in the 2003 best-seller *By the Light of the Moon,* by Dean Koontz, the characters drink Sierra Nevada, like Cheez-Its but not Goldfish, and approve of the upscale Peninsula hotel in Beverly Hills. And in *Something's Gotta Give,* the writer played by Diane Keaton types through sorrow and glee on a laptop prominently displaying the Apple logo.

The ability to add images digitally that did not occur in the picture in the first place has enhanced moviemakers' ability to generate special effects such as the balletic fights in the *Matrix* trinity. It has also augmented the advertiser's ability to place products and the ability of those with a digital camera to alter photographs of family and friends. Jamieson did this at the University of Pennsylvania's Annenberg School for Communication, by taking a digital picture of the other deans and digitizing Winston Churchill into it. Of course, no one believed that Churchill had risen from the dead to administer at Penn. But who will know that the can of Coke shown for a second or so on the coffee table in the sitcom wasn't there when the show aired on network television but appeared only in syndication?

"Tie-in" campaigns are now big business. To enhance one another's markets, in December 2003, MasterCard engaged in cross-promotion of the holiday film *The Cat in the Hat.* Although his face is obscured, Dr. Seuss's famous cat is evident in the print ad showing his white-gloved paws and red- and white-striped hat. The identification is increased by ad lines that mimic the Seuss style: "travel book for friend, Nanook: $29." "bathtub ship for Cousin Chipo: $18." The point of the ad: remind readers to see the film, use MasterCard, and enter the MasterCard Trip-A-Day Giveaway to win a trip to the Universal Orlando Resort. Universal, of course, produced the film. Similarly the third movie in the *Lord of the Rings* trilogy was launched along with merchandise that included a *Lord of the Rings* chess set and a *Shards of Narsil* sword.

The assumption of such tie-ins is that those who like the movie will be disposed toward the products and vice versa. The corollary, of course, is also true. When the producers of *Bad Santa,* the story of a department store Santa who drinks, steals, and despises children, approached the ad agency with the Stolichnaya account about having the lead character drink that brand of vodka in the film, the liquor representatives turned them down on the grounds that the company's marketing principles ban "association with any situation involving abuse of our products."[10]

Sometimes, of course, advertisers have no control over the identification of their product with an undesirable individual. When U.S. troops captured former Iraqi dictator Saddam Hussein in December 2003, they found the canned meat Spam in his hideout. An article in the *New York Times* labeled the result "the product placement from

---

BOX 6-3   Guilt by Association

An ad for People for the Ethical Treatment of Animals (PETA) was, according to an editorial in *Advertising Age*, a clunker.

"It does a takeoff on the 'Milk, what a surprise' campaign. In it, PETA put a yellow mustache on comedian Sandra Bernhard above the line, 'Urine, what a surprise.' PETA's beef is that Wyeth-Ayerst Labs uses urine from pregnant horses in its post-menopause drug, to the detriment of the horses and their foals.

"The milk industry becomes an innocent by-stander here. It's not the object of PETA's wrath, unless milking machines are on their hate list. Yet PETA makes the association of milk with urine, surely not a milk marketer's dream."[a]

[a]"Lebow Sends a Reminder; End Ad Hijacks," *Advertising Age*, 25 March 1996, p. 18.

---

hell." "How do you respond to an unsolicited endorsement from the Butcher of Baghdad?" asked the story. "'It's not the most positive association,' conceded Julie Craven, a spokeswoman for Hormel Foods. But she pointed to the upside: 'It's further evidence of the worldwide appeal of Spam.'"[11]

Rental videos and DVDs have also become carriers of advertising, often for other movies by the same company or for movies trying to reach the same target audience. Rent a movie with French subtitles, and you are likely to see previews for other foreign language films, for example.

Realizing that movie cassettes and DVDs reach a predictable local audience—those living within a specifiable distance of the rental store—an inventive local marketer began placing local ads on video rentals. People in Wichita, Kansas, who rented *She's Having a Baby* saw ads for a local tire service. Because Paramount had released the film, it sued, charging copyright infringement. A Kansas circuit court judge dismissed the suit, saying, "This court is frankly skeptical that viewers actually care whether Paramount is the source or sponsor of the advertisements." Despite the judge's dismissal, the local marketer lost anyway. Fearful of being taken to court by Paramount, the tire service returned to more traditional advertising channels.[12]

Ads are also included in faxed newspapers, which usually are two- or three-page summaries of the day's top stories sent to businesses that cannot get same-day delivery. The *Hartford Courant,* the first newspaper to provide a fax service, started in April 1989. The *Courant* continues to produce its fax paper, which now has a readership of several thousand but has discontinued the sale of its bottom-of-the-page $100 ads. The *New York Times'* "TimesFax," however, which is sent all over the world, to seventy-eight Caribbean resorts and sixty-four cruise ships, considers advertising a big part of its publication and offers various special editions as vehicles for its advertisers.

Some advertising is faxed directly and without invitation to the fax machines of those owning them. Junk mail imposes costs on the recipient and the community in terms of disposal costs and opportunity costs. But the costs of junk mail are largely borne by the sendee. Junk faxes, however, impose involuntary costs on the receiver in a number of costly and direct ways. Not only does the receiver have to pay for the paper and toner costs, incur the costs of wear and tear on the fax machine, but also expend time and energy on printing, sorting, and reading the multitude of often unwanted messages. In December 1991, President Bush signed legislation to permit those who do not wish to receive junk faxes to enter their names on a list. Advertisers who transmitted to the fax machines on that list would be violating the law.

Telephones have also become conduits of unwanted advertising. We assume that most of our readers have at one time or another rushed to their phone expecting a call from a friend, only to hear a recorded voice telling them that they have won a trip or prize or were eligible to receive a deep discount on magazines. Such intrusive use of the telephone can be life-endangering when the numbers reached are those of the fire station, the police department, or a hospital's emergency line. By tying up the line, the advertiser blocks the access of those who need to reach the hospital or the fire or police station.

Some people contended that these calls are an invasion of personal privacy, particularly when, through random-digit dialing, such calls reach individuals who had paid to have their phone numbers unlisted. A 1990 U.S. Congress Energy and Commerce Committee report revealed that "more than 180,000 solicitors call[ed] more than 7 million Americans every day with recorded messages sent by automatic dialers, and more than 2 million businesses send more than 30 billion pages of information by fax each year."[13] Legislation in 1992 required telephone solicitors to provide their name, business, and business phone or address. These regulations were applicable to both live and recorded messages.[14] As direct marketers moved toward fully automated systems; the percentage of all telemarketing solicitations that were automated rose 10 percent between 1994 and 1997, reaching 41 percent in 1997.[15] In response to these intrusions, Congress authorized a federal Do Not Call Registry in October 2003.

In other words, television, radio, and newspapers are not the only conduits of advertising, and many forms of advertising do not appear in purchased time or space. This chapter focuses on advertising found in the mass media, however, because without this advertising the mass media as we know them in the United States would not exist.

MEDIATED ADVERTISING

Before the advent of the mass media, salespeople were often the bearers of their own advertising, repeating the same message and carrying the same products from door to door. With the rise of mass media, such door-to-door advertising has become prohibitively expensive for most nationally sold products. Even with products like Avon cosmetics that are still sold door to door and person to person, television ads are used to predispose residents to open their doors and purchase the product.

When the door-to-door salesperson was replaced by a mediated one, the ability of the salesperson to tailor the message to each individual receiver or adapt the message in response to audience reaction was reduced. The producer of an ad carried by the mass media, rather than in person, must create a message that speaks to what a mass audience shares rather than to the individual differences of the millions who will hear or see the message.

A second major shift occurred when television, radio, and print became the conduits of advertising. None of these media could bring a real product into your home. Instead,

BOX 6-4 Prime Time Cable Rankings and Ratings (May 2005)		
Channel	*People Ages 18–49* *(thousands)*	*Rating*
TNT	2,299	2.1
Disney	1,638	1.5
USA	1,527	1.4
Nick at Nite	1,517	1.4
Lifetime	1,227	1.1
Cartoon Network	1,200	1.1
Fox News	1,133	1.0

Source: Naomi Worrell, *The TV Ratings Wizard*, 2 May 2005, 8 May 2005.

each carried a representation of the product. So, although the traveling salesperson could show you that the product worked and could actually sell you the product, the mass-mediated ad was forced to add another step in the persuasive process. The ad needed to persuade you to go where the product could be found and to buy the product. First, the ad often attempted to give you a vicarious experience of using the product satisfactorily, so the next time you had the option to buy the product, it would already seem comfortable and familiar. Thus, the seller who would throw dirt onto a cloth stretched out on your carpet to demonstrate that the vacuum cleaner would efficiently pick it up was replaced with a mediated salesperson in an ad who showed you something the producer hoped would be comparable. But in your home you could see the dirt, see the vacuum, and testify that there were no tricks. The door-to-door salesperson offered firsthand experience of the performance of the product. In the ad, all sorts of tricks could be employed to make it appear that the vacuum was more effective than it really was. Consequently, a need arose for rules governing what an advertiser could and could not do in ads.

A third shift occurred with the arrival of Internet advertising. According to Nielsen/Netratings, nearly three quarters or 204.3 million homes had access to the Internet in February 2004, up 9 percent from 2003. Websites with the largest numbers of users were: Microsoft's MSN (95.2 million), Yahoo! (92.2 million), and Time Warner (71.9 million).[16] In 1998, $2 billion was spent advertising on the Internet.[17]

Internet ad spending peaked during the dot.com boom in 2000 at $8.1 billion.[18] Online ads dropped 12 percent from 2000 to 2001 and another 15 percent in the following year. In 2003 the revival began.

The convergence between the television and the personal computer is opening new opportunities for advertisers. WebTV, ACTV, Source Media, and World Gate are interactive software firms that enable people watching an ad in a television program to click on a link and be sent to the relevant website for additional information. A viewer can also link to a chat room to talk about the product. Although the advertiser isn't physically in your living room, you and he or she are now closer to the relationship of salesperson and client that characterized house-to-house selling. Meanwhile, of course, you are not watching the program that has returned to the screen after the ads. And you are paying no attention to any of the ads that followed the one that enticed you into hyperspace.

Early in the history of the Internet, programmers foresaw "some real problems with the prospect of giving television viewers one more reason to leave the tube and surf the Web," notes an article in *Electronic Media*.[19] Evidence that the decline in television viewing was accompanied by a rise in web use justified those fears.

KINDS OF TRADITIONAL MASS MEDIA ADVERTISING

All advertising identifies a product, service, or idea; differentiates it from related products, services, or ideas; associates it with things we value; induces us to participate in the creation of its claims; and repeats its key concepts. Most ads also are part of a campaign, and all employ slogans in some form. Yet despite these similarities, ads can be divided by type.

The regulations governing some ads (for example, political) differ from others (commercial and PSAs—public service announcements); the space or time to air some ads must be purchased (commercial, political, and advocacy or issue ads), but others (PSAs) are aired at no cost to the producer; and the objectives of different types of ads range from marketing a corporate image to electing a candidate. Therefore, we differentiate here in general terms the different kinds of advertising.

Obviously, some of these types overlap. Some ads sell both a product and a service, for example, and some PSAs urge us to vote, an appeal that may benefit one candidate or party more than another. Distinctions are also complicated by advertisers' deliberate blurring of image-building ads and PSAs. Similarly, product ads occasionally incorporate actors playing politicians whose reelection is ensured by judicious use of a certain brand of toothpaste or mouthwash. In general, however, categories are a useful way of understanding the special forms an ad can take.

Ads can be classified by the product they sell (service, goodwill, or special product ads); whether the time or space in which they run is purchased (commercials) or provided by the outlet as a community service (public service announcements); or the type of information they provide, the types of appeals they make, and the types of regulations that govern them (advocacy and political ads).

Product Ads

Some ads market a product or a product line. Ads for Dairy Queen, for example, create a world filled with Dairy Queen products and their ingredients. Mountains of chocolate and fields of fresh strawberries, pineapple, and bananas are all part of this world. Some of the ads argue that we ought to participate in this world without identifying specific products. Others tell us about a special kind of sundae or a banana split.

The televised ads for Dairy Queen illustrate well the purpose of an ad for a product or product line. By showing us the texture of the fresh fruit, the vibrant colors of the strawberries, and the rich "rivers" of chocolate, the ads preview the product, familiarize us with the product's name, and induce us to experience the sensations of eating the product. Although the world is a miniature one, the close-up shots create the illusion that there is actually a tropical retreat with larger-than-life fruit and mountains of chocolate. The world in close-up is the size of our television screen.

A food is a consumable commodity with which we've all had experience. The function of food is clear. Consequently, the strategy of an ad for food is generally to make the food appear as delectable as possible. But what is the function of a camera? Ads for digital cameras sell us the capacity to preserve the moment. They tell us that we can relive the best of now, unlike the ancient world of film; we can see what we will relive in time to correct the memory. Were Mom's eyes closed in the shot? Erase and reshoot.

The Product as Ad

When a small box of cereal, deodorant, or laundry detergent appears in your mailbox along with a coupon toward purchasing more of the product, the product itself is functioning as an ad. The product also becomes its own ad when a person behind a small table at the supermarket offers shoppers a free taste of a product and a discount coupon. The free sample has been a staple of product advertising since the inception of the profession.

When the product can be hazardous, such promotions provoke controversy. Under threat of government action barring advertising to children, a major cigarette advertiser in summer 1995 announced an end to the sample as ad. Philip Morris "said it will no longer send out 4 million to 5 million packs of cigarettes by mail nor will it give away 15 million to 20 million at events annually." The company indicated, however, that it would continue distributing coupons that could be redeemed for free packs.[20] Because nicotine is potentially addictive, providing the pack of cigarettes as a sample is a particularly insidious practice.

Service Ads

An ad for First Bank positions a bank official on camera looking at us, the banking customers. As the bank officer entangles himself in the esoteric jargon of his profession, his image is blurred on the screen, and his voice is muted. Everyone in the audience who has experienced institutional double-talk has a frame of reference for this type of institutional officer. The camera is reacting for us; we make little sense of such presentations. The audio track becomes our ears as we tune the message out. The ad has induced us to re-create a familiar experience. The announcer now can tell us that First Bank has simplified the banking process; the simplification brings the bank official back into focus. The ad has told us that this bank provides a service. Our past experience is used to help us make that service seem desirable.

Ads for a service often show us what it is like without, and then with, the service. An ad for an airline, for example, shows a large person crammed into a small seat being elbowed by the passengers on either side. The service? Wider seats, fewer people per row. In the second scene the same person is in an uncrowded seat with ample room.

Goodwill Ads

The ads we have described are clearly intent on selling something—a product, a product line, or a service. One type of ad is noteworthy for the absence of a specific sales pitch for a tangible profit-making item. This is the goodwill ad.

In the late 1970s, it was difficult to find an ad for a gas company that was selling gasoline or the services a gas station provides. Instead, oil companies were selling their concern for the environment, their conviction that we ought to conserve energy, or their safe driving tips. These goodwill ads were an attempt to alter the public image of the oil companies in the wake of rising gasoline prices, the long lines at the pumps, the oil spills that had endangered wildlife in the United States and abroad, and accusations of influence peddling that had pervaded the political climate during the Watergate investigations.

This type of ad falls under the general heading of "image advertising." Related forms are more specific in connecting their appeals to a product. IBM, for example, does not want to be associated with the notion that computers are dehumanizing and threatening. Consequently, ads for IBM show the humane uses of computers. IBM computers are instrumental in saving lives, argues one ad. Weyerhauser Lumber Company, "the tree-growing people," shows planned tree planting that, the ads argue, will make it possible for today's children to build houses tomorrow.

Such image advertising can produce substantial results. After sponsoring the 1984 coast-to-coast Olympic torch relay, AT&T conducted a survey to assess the relay's results. Every potential long-distance customer in this crucial time of divestiture was aware of the relay. Half were aware of AT&T's sponsorship. More important for the phone company, those who recognized that AT&T had sponsored the event were, by a statistically significant margin, more disposed to choose AT&T as their long-distance phone company.[21] In 1986, the growing awareness of such potential rewards prompted major companies, from Eastman Kodak to American Express, to tie their corporate identities to the reconstruction of the Statue of Liberty.

At the turn of the century, the images with which products tended to be identified were environmental. Crest toothpaste's print ad read, "Turn this page back into a tree. Simply send in this certificate with proofs-of-purchase from two Crest cartons. And, together with The National Arbor Day Foundation, we'll plant a seedling in a Yellowstone-area National Forest on your behalf." An IBM spot emphasized the ways that the corporation was working with the United Nations to solve environmental problems. The spot contrasted gridlocked traffic with a swarm of beetles. Pictures of nature were intercut with topographic maps on computer screens. We saw nature, then nature through the computer. IBM and nature were conjoined.

The causes to which goodwill advertising are tied are noncontroversial. No one opposes use of a designated driver to reduce traffic fatalities. Accordingly, Coca-Cola distributes free products to those identified as designated drivers who attend the home games of the Milwaukee Brewers. And because beer companies do not want to be associated with traffic fatalities, it is not surprising that one of the corporate sponsors of the baseball team's designated driver program is the Miller Brewing Company of Milwaukee. Image advertising is designed to identify a company and its products with a positive image and to dissociate them from any negative images that may have been created in news channels.

BOX 6-5   What Is the Image of ExxonMobil?

What is the image of ExxonMobil conveyed in a print ad showing an enlarged drawing of a mosquito under the heading "Help against anopheles"? The heading is a play on words. As the first line of the ad says, "In Greek, *anopheles* can be translated 'no help,' which is an appropriate name for the mosquito that transmits the parasites that cause malaria." Without explicitly saying so, the ad invites the reader to conclude that ExxonMobil is the help against "no help." The only words in bold in the ad are "Help against anopheles" at the top of the ad and "ExxonMobil: Taking on the world's toughest energy challenges" at the bottom. The text of the ad explains that ExxonMobil is donating the polyethylene to make bed nets to protect children from the mosquito that carries malaria.[a]

[a]*New York Times*, 15 April 2004, p. A33.

Companies that sponsor programming on Public Broadcasting Service stations are also engaging in image advertising. Instead of linking the company's name with some socially approved idea (conservation, for example), sponsorship links the company with bringing culture or quality programming at no direct cost to U.S. homes. Such sponsorship argues that the company is a good citizen of the community. We are less likely to believe evil of a good citizen. Consequently, such sponsorship insulates the company from criticism and creates positive associations for the company's products.

The benefits of event sponsorship were dramatically illustrated by the results of a survey conducted in summer 1995 on the 1996 Summer Olympics, held in Atlanta. The surveyors found that "23% of consumers would definitely or probably switch from their current brand to a brand offered by an Olympic Sponsor. And of the 64% who will be following the Olympic Games, 29% said they would definitely or probably switch to an Olympic-sponsored brand."[22]

Advocacy Ads

When the company as good citizen takes a position on a public policy in an ad, the ad becomes an advocacy ad. Many stations refuse advocacy ads out of fear that they will then be bound to air the other side's position as well. Determining what is and is not an advocacy ad is difficult. In 1981, ABC became the first of the networks to agree to air advocacy ads, but the network stipulated that the ads could run only on late-night television, a less than desirable time for most advertisers and a time when advertising space is more difficult to sell. By October 1990, stations owned and operated by NBC, CBS, and ABC were all being permitted to determine whether or not to accept such ads. The change in policy was prompted by the willingness of the stations' cable competitors to accept advocacy ads and by the demise of the Fairness Doctrine. Airing such an ad no longer carries an obligation to provide free airtime for opposing points of view.

In summer 1990, Anheuser-Busch aired a 30-second advocacy ad that opened by showing workers at lunch and farmers in their fields. The announcer said that America was built by individuals willing to give their fair share. The ad then said that Congress now wanted Americans (note, not Anheuser-Busch), who already were paying about

$3 billion in excise taxes on beer, to pay more than their fair share. As a foaming stein of beer appeared on the screen, the tag said, "Can the Beer Tax. 1-800-33-Taxes." When viewers called, they were asked if they would like to have a letter protesting a proposed hike in the excise tax sent for them to their congressional representative. In the campaign's first month, 110,000 callers asked to have the letters sent.

To magnify the power of the campaign, beer industry officials hinted that if the tax were increased, their companies might reduce sponsorship of sporting events and decrease spending on television advertising. Increasing the economic impact should have increased the number of groups supporting the beer industry's position. However, critics noted that reduction of advertising was unlikely because that was the industry's major means of sustaining sales and introducing such new products as ice beer.[23]

There have been occasional controversies over advocacy ads. In spring 1986, J. Peter Grace, chairman of W.R. Grace and Company, protested to the press and public that one of his ads had been rejected by the networks. Set in the year 2017, the ad showed an elderly man in a witness cage. The man is being cross-examined by a child who wants to know how the man could have let federal deficits reach $2 trillion. The networks refused to show the ad. In so doing, they were within their rights. In *Democratic National Committee v. CBS,* the U.S. Supreme Court held that the editorial judgment about what to air and what not to air belongs to the broadcaster.

Maintaining their ban on advocacy ads, in the 1993–94 season, the three major broadcast networks all rejected advocacy ads on health care reform. As a result, the only "national" ads that aired for and against the Clinton reform plan appeared on CNN, an outlet available in 1995 in about two out of three homes in the United States. During the health care reform debate of 1993–94, more money was spent on advocacy ads than had been spent to elect Bill Clinton president in 1992. We will discuss issue advocacy at greater length in the chapter on political ads.

Direct-Response Ads (Infomercials)

Infomercials, also known as direct response ads, ask you to call in to order the product. In form they resemble a program but are instead selling a product. Throughout the program, a toll-free number appears. By calling it, viewers can order the product. On January 1, 1990, when the Federal Communications Commission's regulation called Syndex (for "syndication exclusivity") went into effect, use of infomercials by cable stations rose. Syndex stipulates that cable stations cannot show syndicated programs if the same programs are being shown on local television in the same market. During the time that is now blocked out by Syndex, cable stations can, if they choose, pick up infomercials beamed to them 24 hours a day at no charge via satellite. In 2003, $154.1 billion in revenue was produced by direct-response television, up from $85.3 billion in 1997.[24]

Infomercials selling music often assume the look of a rock 'n' roll or country special. For one, a producer gathered the rights to 150 past hits and packaged them on twenty cassettes. He then paid disc jockey Wolfman Jack to endorse the product as "Wolfman Jack's favorite all time hits"; $200,000 in production costs later, the infomercial offering the cassettes was ready to air. Another infomercial featuring chef Arnold Morris resembles a Julia Child cooking show. Its title is "Arnold's Gourmet Kitchen."[25]

In April 2004, the Electronic Retailing Association, to which many infomercial makers belong, announced "a new self-regulatory program . . . to throw out companies that make false claims and send their names to the Federal Trade Commission for investigation." Under the new process "complaints about misleading infomercials, online ads and other direct response vehicles will be referred to an independent review board of the National Advertising Review Council, a partnership of advertising trade associations and the Council of Better Business Bureaus." The announcement came after a series of large settlements against direct response marketers. These included Fast Abs, which promised "six-pack" abs without exercise. Other products that didn't deliver as promised included the Rio Hair Naturalizer System, which caused hair loss and scalp irritation.[26]

Public Service Announcements

Unlike the advertising we have discussed so far, public service announcements (PSAs) are not aired in purchased time or space. Television stations meet part of their FCC-stipulated obligation to be responsive to the needs of the community by airing public service ads. A public service ad is generally created and sponsored by a nonprofit organization to convey noncontroversial information to the public.

Ads for charities such as United Way and the Children's Hospital of Washington are PSAs. The National Institutes of Health sponsors PSAs to remind people with hypertension to take their medicine, to warn us to watch for cancer's early warning signals, and to discourage us from smoking. During election years, the League of Women Voters, the networks themselves, and specially created committees use PSAs to urge us to register and vote.

The PSAs most likely to be aired are sponsored either by an agency of the government or by the Advertising Council. The Advertising Council, which accepts a limited number of campaign assignments each year, is sponsored by ad agencies. It costs a nonprofit agency upward from $100,000 to pay the production costs for an Ad Council campaign. Ad Council campaigns have been criticized for their pro-industry bias. In one often-run ad, for example, a Native American man is shown paddling his canoe down a polluted stream. As he steps to the shore, someone throws a bag of garbage from a passing car, and a tear runs down his cheek. Critics of this ad argue that littering is a minor form of pollution. Significant air and water pollution is caused by industry. Littering could be reduced by banning nonreturnable bottles—a proposal industries have fought bitterly. This Ad Council campaign provides some support for the contention that the council deflects criticism from industry and shifts blame and responsibility to individuals, who are often powerless to correct the problems isolated in the ads.

The major advantage of an Ad Council campaign is the ability of the ad industry to place its PSAs in desirable free time. Not all effective PSAs are sponsored by the Ad Council. A Clio award–winning ad for the Humane Society shows in slow motion the violence that occurs at rodeos, while a Strauss waltz plays in the background. The ad focuses our attention on an often-ignored facet of the rodeo. The ad argues persuasively that rodeos are inhumane. Similarly, Mothers Against Drunk Driving (MADD) sponsored a series of PSAs encouraging youths and the public at large to consider the cost in human life that is exacted by people who drive while intoxicated.

One $2-million PSA radio campaign was privately funded. Martin Himmel, former president of Jeffrey Martin Inc., commissioned media guru Tony Schwartz to produce an antismoking campaign. In one of Schwartz's spots, Patrick Reynolds, grandson of the founder of the R.J. Reynolds Tobacco Company, reveals that his grandfather, a tobacco chewer, died of cancer, as did his heavy-smoking father. His mother and three brothers all have emphysema, says Reynolds. "Now tell me," the ad concludes, "do you think the cigarette companies are truthful when they tell you that smoking isn't harmful? What do you think?"

Because its producers do not pay for the time in which the PSA is aired, they cannot control its placement. Stations tend to place PSAs in times no one has purchased. Consequently, PSAs often air early in the morning or late at night, when few viewers are watching, or in documentaries for which the network could not find enough sponsors.

In 1999 a federally sponsored antidrug campaign blurred the traditional distinction between the PSA and the paid ad. Concerned that antidrug PSAs produced by such nonprofit groups as the Partnership for a Drug Free America were not being given the airtime that would reach the targeted adolescent audience, Congress appropriated $170 million dollars for a televised advertising campaign based on purchased time.

The Internet increased the ability of PSAs to deliver audiences to messages. The "Face the Issue" campaign, which focuses on domestic violence, eating disorders and drug abuse, illustrates the way in which PSAs can drive viewers to help sites. Created by Jane Semel and Melanie Hall, who head a nonprofit production company, the campaign ties visually riveting ads to the www.facetheissue.com site. In one ad a young woman kneels on the floor over the toilet. "Sound familiar?" asks a female voice. "If so, you may have bulimia. You cannot flush away your problems. It won't go away until you stop gagging your pain and give it a voice." Run on channels such as MTV, the ads direct viewers to the website where they can discuss their problems. In its first two months of operation, the site generated two million hits.[27]

Political Ads

Some ads argue that we should elect one person rather than another or urge us to vote a specific way on a resolution or referendum. These ads, which differ in some important ways from other types of ads, will be discussed in Chapter 10.

Issue Advocacy Ads

Some ads argue for or against a piece of legislation, while others make a case that a politician is or is not doing a good job without using such terms as "vote for" or "vote against." These issue advocacy ads are discussed in Chapter 10 as well.

NONTRADITIONAL ADVERTISING

In-store advertising and adaptive billboards are among the areas in which technology has increased the capacity of advertisers to bring their ads to receptive audiences.

BOX 6-6 The Cost of Billboards	
Location	*Cost per Month*
Times Square, New York City	$50,000–$150,000
Sunset Strip, Los Angeles	$30,000–$100,000
Lincoln Tunnel, New York	$25,000–$60,000

Source: Advertising Age, 19 April 1999, p. 52.

In-Store Advertising

In-store televised advertising is increasing because the fragmentation of mass media has made it more difficult for advertisers to reach the mass audience. A customer in the "health and beauty" aisle is more likely to buy a deodorant than if he or she is wandering the electronics aisle. Advertisers customize ads for play in specific sections of stores: Health ads in the health aisle, ads for DVRs in the electronics aisle. This sort of placement tries to increase impulse buying. The executive vice president of sales for Premier Retail Networks, which places ads in stores, reports that "ads that communicate specific information about a product or an offer work better than the more emotional, slice-of-life advertising that dominates regular television."[28]

Digital Billboards

Digital technology now exists to permit advertisers to change the messages on billboards as often as they'd like. If a supermarket chain brings in a truckload of great peaches, the billboards on the routes to the store can tout the special on very short notice. Digital billboards also can adjust digital billboards according to the radio stations playing inside passenger cars. "Based on survey data of station demographics, Smart Sign calculates the average income of passersby based on what they are listening to, and then changes the message to target the biggest cluster of people driving by. The company [Smart Sign Media] operates 10 digital billboards in California."[29]

Search Advertising

Search a product, concept or service on sites such as Yahoo! and Google, and you receive a search-result page complete with links to an enterprise offering the product. The process works by using an algorithmic engine to scan the text of web pages and match the search to the keywords on which advertisers have bid. Companies bid to ensure that their ads are placed high on the search results page and then pay when a user clicks to their site. At up to $100 per lead, the highest-paying keyword in spring 2004,

---

BOX 6-7   Contextual Ads

"In addition to Overture and Google, other companies such as Kanoodle, Industry Brains and Vibrant Media offer variations of contextual ad programs. Vibrant Media's IntelliTXT technology, for instance, double-underlines keywords that advertisers have bid on within editorial news stories; when a user mouses over the highlighted word, a small ad pops up."[a]

[a]Ann M. Mack, "Meet the New Black: Contextual Advertising," *Adweek*, 12 April 2004, p. 9.

---

is *mesothelioma,* a rare asbestos-related cancer. This word ties victims to lawyers who advance cases that produce average settlements of about $6 million.

As the *Wall Street Journal* explains, "These Web searches by patients provide fertile advertising ground for lawyers. Paid-search ads typically run at the top of the side of main search results, so if people search for mesothelioma, they get nonpaid results framed by the ads. . . . When viewers click on the ads, they are sent to lawyer sites with a mixture of information, links to other cancer Websites—and a phone number, online form or e-mail address to contact an attorney."[30] The search, in other words, provides leads for attorneys in a high-yield area of litigation.

Complicating the search advertising process is the fact that ads can attach a product to a negative context. This occurred when an ad for luggage stores was placed on a news website about a murderer who "carried away his victims in a suitcase."[31] Nor was the sponsor pleased when an ad for steroids was tied to a news report on steroid abuse.[32]

Sponsored Links Three services that are in effect media buyers on the web, place ads on websites, and tally and track the results are DoubleClick Inc, Advertising.com Inc, and Google. Called *contextual advertising,* this process automatically tags a client's ads to pages likely to attract the prospective purchaser of the client's product. The owners of the site receive a payment for placement on the site. The service scans websites for words that indicate relevance to a client. As the *Wall Street Journal* explains, "Google uses an auction system of selling key words and placement to the highest-bidding advertiser—much as it auctions off the nicest spots on search results through i.s own Website, though 'relevance,' or the click-through rate of the ad, is also factored into placement. Google charges advertisers a wide range of prices for such placements, starting at five cents and going up. Its technology can deliver advertisers' promotions on both search Web pages and content Web sites."[33]

Spam In December 2003 Congress passed the Can-SPAM Act, a law that took effect January 2004 regulating unsolicited commercial e-mail. Under that law, there must be an existing relationship between sender and receiver; senders must have a valid U.S. postal address, and there must be a way for receivers to block future mailings from the sender. Until February 2004, spam made up 62% of e-mail traffic, up from 58% in December. In March 2004 a Pew Center for the People and the Press survey found that 53 percent of adult e-mail users hadn't noticed a change in the amount of spam since January 1; 24 percent said the percentage had increased at home and 19 percent reported an increase at work. Five percent reported ordering a product or service as a result of an unsolicited e-mail.[34] In the first major legal action under the act, four large Internet providers filed civil suits against hundreds of alleged spam producers in March 2004.

HOW TO DETERMINE WHETHER IT'S AN AD

Advertising can also be defined by distinguishing it from the content that surrounds it. In the mass media, advertisers pay for access to the audiences attracted by programming. How does the ad itself differ from that programming?

How Ads Reveal the Advertiser

What distinguishes a televised soft news story about Jamaica, presented from a human interest angle, from a televised commercial brought to you by the Tourist Bureau of Jamaica? The commercial will identify itself as a commercial by disclosing its source. This disclosure, called a "tag," generally takes a visual form and usually is placed at the end of the commercial.

What distinguishes a televised view of a candidate's day, broadcast as a news segment on the evening news, from a slice-of-life commercial paid for by the candidate's campaign committee? The commercial is required to contain a tag identifying the committee paying for the ad. Again, the tag generally occurs at the end.

Because we are less likely to be manipulated by a message that warns us that it is manipulating us, as a commercial warns us by identifying itself as a commercial, producers of commercials try to incorporate the identifying tag in an inconspicuous way. Political committees, for example, are often legally incorporated under such titles as "Friends of Reuben Spellman," precisely because the commercial can then legally be tagged thus: "and that's why this message was paid for by Friends of Reuben Spellman." Such a tag is called a "no-tag."

How Ads Reveal the Intended Audience

The biblical injunction "Seek and you shall find" takes on a new meaning when we are in the market for a product or have a problem that could potentially be remedied by a product. Have you ever noticed that when you have a cold, television and radio are filled with ads for cold remedies? And when you are trying to determine which car to buy, the number of automobile ads seems to increase? When we are troubled by a problem or an unmet need, we become information seekers about that problem or need. Communication that was always in our environment suddenly becomes relevant, and we recognize it and attend to it. We seek information to help us make a decision. At the same time, the presence of the information assures us that our problem is not an imaginary one and that the problem is important. Ads about our problem tell us it is a real one, it is significant, and we are justified in being concerned about it.

We also seek information once the decision to purchase has been made. After the decision, however, the reasons for seeking the information change. Before the decision, we seek information comparing products, arguing the unique benefits of one over the other. After we have purchased the product, we seek information to assure ourselves that the decision was a wise one. In these two instances, we function as active communication participants: We seek information.

Often, however, we are passive receivers of information. We are frequently receptive to information and willing to become involved in the creation of messages about products when we are not deliberately seeking certain types of information. How do advertisers alert the passive receivers that a product is designed for them?

In some cases, the identification is visual. In 1995, Domino's tried to increase its share of the $18.6-billion-a-year pizza market with ads featuring three 30-ish male football fanatics. At the center of the ads is Gus, his baseball cap turned backward on his head, who is both a wiseguy football expert and an expert at ordering and eating pizza. The ad indicates not only that it is seeking 30-something male customers but that it is trying to increase the number of orders it gets during football games. The ads were slated as part of the chain's sponsorship of the *NFL Live* "Halftime Report."[35]

Other ads telegraph their audience both visually and verbally. If an ad says, "Trabo, the fun game for the whole family," and shows a mother, a father, a boy, and a girl playing a board game, that ad is not soliciting the attention of single adults. Although single adults might buy the product, the ad is picturing youngsters and their parents as its prime audience. The tone of the ad—the laughter, the upbeat music, the good-natured comments among participants—may also be speaking to those in the audience who view recreation as a social rather than solitary activity, whether they identify themselves with the family in the ad or not. But the ad is clearly not speaking to the single adult whose idea of an enjoyable evening is dancing into the wee hours of the morning at the hottest nightspot.

By showing the game being played by children with adults, the advertiser is also establishing that this is a game better suited for both children and adults than for adults alone. It is not a game too difficult for children; moreover, it is not X-rated. Yet it can be played with satisfaction by adults and children. Many products, from toothpaste to breakfast cereal, can be used both by children and adults.

A major sports figure, such as basketball star Michael Jordan, appeals to sports fans in general and the market of young males in particular. The products endorsed by Jordan have included those manufactured by Gatorade, Nike, McDonald's Corporation, Rayovac, and Sara Lee Corporation. These products, unsurprisingly, were featured in Jordan's first film, titled *Space Jam,* released in 1996.

When Pepsi-Cola signed Grammy winner M. C. Hammer to promote its "cool cans" in rap's rhythmic chants, it was targeting the younger market. Similarly, Coca-Cola hired Heavy D & the Boyz to turn Sprite's "I like the Sprite in you" into rap ads for radio and television. In addition to its clear attraction to younger viewers and listeners, rap has a number of persuasive advantages. Rhyme is memorable. Moreover, as the senior vice president group creative director of J. Walter Thompson USA notes, "You can, without being untrue to the form of rap, get more lyrics per 30 seconds than with any other form of music."[36] In summer 1990, four of the country's top albums were by rap groups, and one of MTV's top-rated shows was *Yo! MTV Raps.*

Comparatively few products dictate use exclusively by either adults or children, as diapers and aftershave do. Yet many products are marketed to the whole family with the argument that the product is good for the children. One toothpaste, for example, is advertised with the appeal that if this product is used, the children will brush longer because they will like the taste of the toothpaste. The assumption, of course, is that Mom or Dad will buy the same brand for the whole family. Another toothpaste promises that it gives your mouth sex appeal—a claim that reveals that its target audience is very different from the audience for the ad featuring 6-year-old Johnny, who brushes longer with the better-tasting toothpaste.

Indeed, if the advertiser used children as spokespeople to claim that the toothpaste gives your mouth sex appeal, the ad would be offensive. Both of these ads identify an intended audience implicitly. An explicit identification of intended audience is made in ads for Ma Jolie that show a 20-something woman over the tag "Ma Jolie clothes for women."

Ads reveal not only the likely age of those targeted by the advertiser but also whether the ad is designed to reach men or women or both. Again, some ads do this explicitly. One deodorant ad, for example, tells us that the product was specially formulated for women. In another ad for a deodorant soap, a male character tells us that the product is strong enough for a man. Then an attractive woman adds that she likes it, too.

The ways in which ads signal the gender of the intended purchaser can be seen by turning off the sound on the television set and comparing the visual texts of ads for aftershaves and for perfumes. Without hearing the verbal pitch, we can tell whether the product is being sold to men or women by determining whether a man or a woman is the visual focus of the ad. Is she turning to look at him, or is he turning to look at her? Are several men in pursuit of one woman, or several women in pursuit of one man?

An ad can also solicit the attention of the intended audience by re-creating the lifestyle that the audience member either has or desires. Why do ads for beer show groups of people rather than individuals? Why are men rather than women shown in most beer ads? In what sorts of environments are the people in beer ads shown? How are the people in ads for beer dressed—formally or casually? Are the people in beer ads middle class or upper class?

Now consider the same questions about an expensive scotch (Chivas Regal) or gin. The lifestyle created in beer ads is different from the lifestyle portrayed in ads for more expensive hard liquor. The ads tell us that beer is an outdoor as well as an indoor drink, that beer drinkers are active, often in sports, and that beer is a drink for people who are comfortable in casual clothes with groups of friends; it is not a drink for the solitary drinker or for the man in the tuxedo. The advertisers single out their market by customers' preference for certain sorts of activities. One beer urges us to grab all the gusto we can get; the appeal is assertive and rugged. Another beer tells us that it is the beer for "when it's time to relax."

The mood of the two ads will be different, because the basic appeal is different. One is more active than the other, and one is more individualistic than the other. Beer ads also single out their audience by the types of environments in which the ad situates the product. Some ads place the beer drinkers in a bar; others place the beer drinkers outdoors. One beer's advertising tactic has been to show appropriate and inappropriate times for enjoying a beer, with the slogan "It's the right beer now."

Many beer ads appeal to sports enthusiasts by including famous hockey, baseball, or football professionals in the ads. Some beer advertisers set themselves apart by appealing to an upper-class market. They do this by adopting an exotic name (Michelob rather than Pabst, Schlitz, or Budweiser), by packaging the beer in a bottle with foil wrap, by implying that the beer is made by more expensive processes than other beers, by charging more for the product, by labeling the product "premium" beer, and by stressing that the beer or its recipe is imported. Thus, ads themselves provide some of the clues about the identity of the intended audience.

The place in which we find the ad also provides clues. Ads targeted to children appear during certain types of television programming, such as children's specials or cartoons, and at the hours when children's programming occurs—early morning, especially Saturday. They also appear in magazines such as *Ranger Rick*. Ads designed for homemakers are seen at all hours, particularly during soap operas in the afternoon and during morning talk shows; they appear in so-called women's magazines such as *Better Homes and Gardens*. Ads for older people appear more often during news and public affairs programming, the types of programming older adults are most likely to watch. Ads for men appear during sports events or in so-called men's magazines; ads for adults appear during prime time. An image-building ad for a corporation will appear adjacent to a prestigious public affairs program such as *Meet the Press* because highly educated people, opinion leaders, and those who control the other media are more likely to attend to such programs.

Some targeting is controversial. When R.J. Reynolds announced that it was introducing a new cigarette called Uptown, directed primarily at African Americans, protests from the African American community and from Louis Sullivan, then U.S. Health and Human Services secretary, followed. The cigarette, which was to have been test-marketed in Philadelphia in December 1989, was withdrawn.

ADVERTISING AND REALITY: STEREOTYPES

Stereotypes are simplified, inaccurate conceptions or images that have become standardized and are widely held. A stereotype can idealize or demean the group it types. If a depiction of a group reflects reality, we do not consider that depiction a stereotype.

Stereotypes make it possible for us to form generalizations about a person or advertised character without requiring a great deal of information or evidence. The less time we have to process information, the more likely we are to rely on stereotypes in drawing conclusions. The less time television producers have to communicate a message, the more likely they are to rely on stereotypes.

For example, in a 30-second commercial a writer cannot create three-dimensional characters but must instead deal in the shorthand of stereotypes. The Harried Housewife, the Bumbling Husband in the Kitchen, the Archetypal Grandmother, and the Nosy Neighbor are stock characters in commercials whose type we recognize immediately. Consequently, the writer can introduce a limited number of cues about them in a few seconds and proceed to deliver the message through them because we fill in the appropriate characteristics for this type of character.

Often the stereotypes found in commercials are so ridiculous or so harmless that they provoke no protest. Mr. Whipple, the storekeeper who lurked behind the display cases waiting to ensnare shoppers for squeezing the Charmin, and Aunt Bluebell, who arrived at the homes of relatives with toilet paper hidden in her purse, were two such eccentrics. These characters were so implausible that if we identified with them at all, it was as comic foils.

By contrast, when a lazy, greasy, conniving thief in a sombrero and gun belt speaking in a parody of a Mexican dialect was chosen as the trade character for Frito's corn chips, Latino groups protested. The Frito Bandito embodied and consequently reinforced negative stereotypes about Latin Americans in general and Mexicans in particular. By drawing public attention to the stereotypes on which the Frito Bandito was based, the protest made it more difficult for the ads to use the stereotype to convey a commercial message. The protests also demonstrated that the Bandito offended a large, vocal group of potential customers, a result no advertiser desires. Consequently, the Frito Bandito disappeared from ads.

Stereotypes that are nearly universally held rarely draw protests because we are unable to see them as stereotypes. For decades the public tolerated ads in which older people were portrayed as fools or comic foils. When the gray rights movement focused attention on these ads, the number of ads decreased in which older characters' seeming inability to hear, understand, or recall a product's name provided an excuse for repetition of that name.

Stereotypes are powerful means of reinforcing societal attitudes about groups of people because the process of stereotyping involves the receiver in creating the message. When the negative attitude that is reinforced is about a large, politically and economically important group such as Latinos, African Americans, women, or elders and is recognized by spokespeople for that group as destructive (messages, for example, that a woman's life is fulfilled if her floors shine, that older people are senile, or that Latinos are lazy and dishonest), then protest will follow because representatives of the stereotyped group fear that the stereotype will reinforce undesirable role models and will perpetuate discrimination against the group. Some groups have used the media to change the way in which they are portrayed by the media, as we will show in Chapter 9.

ADVERTISING VALUES

Often we are unaware that advertising embeds assumptions not directly related to the products being advertised. These assumptions are depicted in Figure 6-1.

Television transports people to a middle-, upper-middle-, and upper-class world. In the process it creates expectations in us all, expectations based on the assumption that the norm or standard in this country is a middle-class existence—or better. People in ads have spacious kitchens, large lawns, expensive appliances, and cars; they travel worldwide. Ads take for granted that the audience routinely buys soaps, deodorants, makeup, and cologne and that the audience is not making a decision about whether to buy the product but rather is deciding *which* brand to buy. The Television Bureau of Advertising reports that in 2001, 4,901 brands were advertised on network television.

The World According to Commercials

In the process of being urged to purchase the multitude of products that ads advocate, we are also being persuaded to a certain style of living. Contrast, for example, our standards of personal hygiene with those of our great-grandparents at the turn of the twentieth century. Underarm deodorants, in the forms we know them, did not exist,

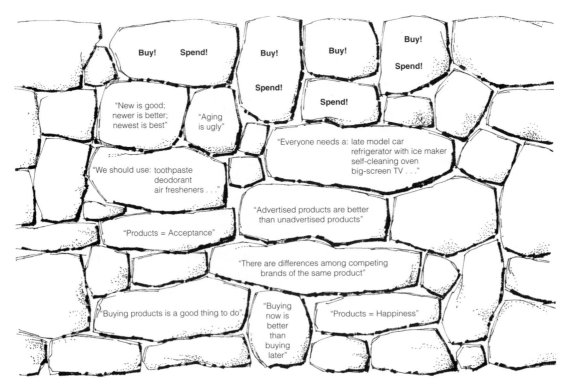

FIGURE 6-1 Assumptions embedded in advertising

and no one seemed to mind. Advertising and changing expectations about personal hygiene have persuaded us that certain types of body odors are offensive and ought to be camouflaged or altered. Embedded in the argument that we ought to use a specific mouthwash is the assumption that we ought to use a mouthwash.

Similarly, the argument that we ought to use a specific floor wax assumes that we ought to wax our floors. Embedded in the argument that we ought to use a specific room deodorant is the assumption that we ought to use one.

Reliance on packaged products has contributed to the growing problem of waste disposal in the United States. If we didn't use so many packaged products and such heavily packaged products, the problem would be smaller. Because advertisers want us to continue to use their products, they reassure us that doing so is environmentally responsible. This notion of responsibility was newly found in a climate in which the public began expressing concerns about the vulnerabilities of the planet.

Accordingly, in 1990, a number of companies began using and touting their use of recycled materials in their packaging. Lever Brothers announced in July 1990 that the plastic bottles containing Wisk, All, and Snuggle would contain "up to" (note the careful use of language) 35 percent recycled resins. Procter & Gamble announced that it would include at least 25 percent recycled high-density polyethylene in bottles of Tide, Cheer, Era, Dash, and Downy. Bottles containing Spic and Span liquid cleaner would be made entirely of recycled materials. The scope of the industry's contribution to the landfill problem is evident in its claim that "in the first year of P&G's bottle recycling program, the company will produce 110 million containers that use the recycled plastics, keeping about 80 million bottles out of the nation's waste stream."[37] By Earth Day in April 1995, Procter & Gamble could claim to have reduced the amount of waste it produced by 1 billion pounds.[38] However, in 2002 *OnEarth* magazine reported, "After several years of post-Earth Day '90 progress, P&G's efforts are flagging. Its use of recycled material in its products has fallen by more than half, and, in its annual sustainability report, the company has stopped reporting the recycled content of its packaging altogether." [39]

In the process of embedding assumptions about the kinds of products we should use, advertising has created norms governing our sense of the acceptable home: a home in which the faucets, floors, furniture, mirrors, and dishes (but not the faces of the women) shine; a home that is odor-free (no smell of cat, fish, cigars, feet) and filled with artificial, chemically created outdoor scents (lilac, rose, herbs, evergreen). This home is filled with subtle deceptions. Spouses marvel at the cleanliness, unaware of how little effort it took with the new product to achieve that effect; and they assume that foods created from chemically enhanced mixes are homemade.

In the world of commercials, avenging guardians of the social order exist to ferret out those who fail to use the sanctioned products. Nosy neighbors and socially superior guests are ever alert to spot the smell of a cat or a cigar, or to comment snidely about spots on glasses, dull dishes, or dust on the furniture.

The characters who live out their lives in the 30- to 60-second world of the broadcast ads and in the pages of print ads seek and obtain almost instant gratification. Problems arise and are met. Promises of product performance are made and kept. All this occurs in a very brief time span. The answer to all the problems, needs, and expectations in the ads is ultimately found in the purchase of some product. The link between problem and solution is clear and unequivocal. Not only is the gratification instant, but it also occurs as a result of the product advertised. In contrast, our lives are more complicated and more ambiguous than the lives of advertising's population.

Characters in ads are also what psychologists would describe as "other-directed." Characters seek the approval of others in ads. When that approval is withheld, crises ensue. Neighbors detect odors in the house, and a crisis erupts; an air freshener is the answer. Parents detect spots on drinking glasses, and a crisis occurs; a new dishwashing product eases the tension. Acquaintances spot "ring around the collar," and the family is thrown into turmoil. A clothes-washing product resolves the crisis. In each of these instances, the others disapprove not only of the condition (the ring, the odor, the spots) but also implicitly, if not explicitly, of the ad's protagonist *because* of the condition. It is not only the product that ultimately wins approval in the ad but also the person who uses the product.

The need for social approval is strongly felt by all of us. It is a need that advertising exploits. In the process of exploiting the need, advertising reinforces, legitimizes, and enhances it.

In one sense, advertising is powerfully conservative—it is loath to offend; it reinforces institutional values. In another sense, advertising is radical because it holds out a world full of products and promises the good life to those who buy them. Yet the mass media reach many who lack the money to buy the products. Ads are materialistic. Purchase and consumption of material goods are glorified in commercial ads. Our assumptions that ads are created to sell products are so deeply ingrained that we distrust ads created to enhance the image of a corporation, which claim that "this corporation is a good citizen of the community." The notion that a manufacturer might pay to bring us a noncommercial message is suspect because until recently we had seen few such ads. In fact, the manufacturer is still selling a product. The product here is the company's good name, and when we respect it, the advertiser can link it to the product line and urge us to buy.

The acquisition of material goods brings happiness in the ads; material goods are satisfying. Because the ads simplify, we do not see other factors that make a happy ending possible; we do not see those factors that make the happy ending impossible even with the product or see the unhappiness that may be caused by the product.

Seeing the Other Side

Although it is generally true that ads reinforce the assumption that consumption of products is good, there is at least one major exception. In the name of fairness, the Federal Communications Commission required stations that broadcast cigarette ads also to run a certain number of antismoking ads free of charge. During the period in which both pro-cigarette and anticigarette ads were aired, audiences were exposed to messages arguing that consumption of a product (cigarettes) was not only not good (as the pro-cigarette ads claimed) but also harmful and that it should be avoided or stopped. The antismoking campaign challenged an unspoken premise in commercial advertising—the premise that consumption of products is good. By challenging the premise, the antismoking ads made us aware of it. In a sense, the counterads were not merely countering smoking but also countering advertising.

THE INTERPLAY OF NEWS AND ADVERTISING

We live in a complex world in which messages interact with one another to form impressions. Because people pay attention to information on topics of importance to them, public recall of news about health is high. When scientific studies seemed to confirm that oat bran had the potential to lower cholesterol, advertisers hurried to capitalize on this finding, introducing new products such as Ralston Purina's Oat Bran Option, and making new claims for old products, such as General Mills's Cheerios and Quaker Oats.

The legitimacy that news can endow, however, news also can take away. In mid-January 1990, the prestigious *New England Journal of Medicine* published a major study downplaying the ability of oat bran to reduce cholesterol. The study was carried in print and broadcast media reports. In March, Arbitron/SAMI scanner reports showed that oat bran cereals, which had peaked at 4.9 percent of the cereals market in January, had plunged to a 3.18 market share. Note the claims that survive on the boxes of Post Raisin Bran and General Mills' Cheerios in 2004:

- Raisin Bran: Studies show high-fiber foods like Post Raisin Bran may actually help lower your risk of heart disease.
- Cheerios: As part of a heart-healthy diet, the soluble fiber in Cheerios can reduce your cholesterol.

BOX 6-8   Interplay: News and Ads

News and advertising have been encroaching on each other's territory for years. Some memorable news photographs seem to belong to everyone; whole populations have the same mental-image files, which constitute a large part of our common culture. Thus, flashing key images in ads guarantees instant connection and social commentary. For example, in December 1989, Pepsi showed video clips of the Berlin Wall as it came down, with the words "Peace on Earth" and the Pepsi company logo.

Advertising feeds on news photography because news imagery is so strong it does not entirely lose its meaning when radically displaced. Manufacturers can turn the familiarity of dire images to their advantage by spoofing them. For example, Kenneth Cole, the shoe company, ran a picture of former Panamanian dictator General Manuel Noriega with the tag line, "One heel you definitely won't see at our semi-annual sale."

Most news is commercially sponsored. Unwritten rules decree that there should be a separation between news and ads, but the dividing line can be thin. Local newscasts sometimes include interviews with the condemned criminal whose story provides the plot for the docudrama to be shown later in prime time—a public relations campaign pretending to be news.

Source: Janet Whitman, "Magazine Trade Group Reviews How It Tallies Ad-Page Revenue," *Wall Street Journal,* 21 January 2004, p. B7.

TO SUM UP

It is common to see the premises underlying a given ad campaign challenged in news and public affairs programming. News programs carry word of recalls, of Federal Trade Commission investigations, and of court cases in which advertisers' claims are challenged; consumer advocates in newspapers and on television investigate harmful effects of products. These exposés constitute a form of counteradvertising. They make us aware that ads do not tell the "whole truth" about a product and that they ought to be evaluated critically. In the next chapter we focus on the critical evaluation of advertising's claims and evidence.

 Use InfoTrac College Edition to access information on topics in this chapter from hundreds of periodicals and scholarly journals. Enter keyword and subject searches: *advertising, mediated advertising, infomercials, public service announcements.*

SELECTED READING

Turow, Joseph. *Breaking Up America: Advertisers and the New Media World.* Chicago: University of Chicago Press, 1997.

Persuasion through Advertising

THE ADVERTISER'S AIMS

If we are to be persuaded to buy a product or service, we must be able to recognize it, distinguish it from its competitors, conclude that we want it or need it, and remember our desire for that product when the opportunity to obtain it arises or when we create that opportunity. To accomplish their persuasive goals, advertisers

1. Create *product recognition* through use of trademarks, packaging, and slogans
2. *Differentiate* the product from others by creating a unique selling proposition
3. Encourage us to want the product by enveloping it in a set of favorable *associations*
4. Commit us to the product and its associated promises by inducing our *participation* in the creation of the ad's meaning
5. Ensure that we recall the product and our need for it by encapsulating these means of identification and differentiation and these associations and acts of participation in *redundant* messages—messages that are repeated again and again

In this chapter we examine the function served by advertisers' messages and expose some of the ways in which ads can entice the unwary consumer into false conclusions about products.

CREATING PRODUCT RECOGNITION

Trademarks

A trademark identifies a company's product. A trademark is a symbol—sometimes verbal, sometimes visual, sometimes both—that tells the consumer who makes the product. Trademarks do not have to be words found in the language, although once a trademark has been widely advertised it may find its way into the dictionary. *Exxon* and *Xerox* are words created specifically to serve as trademarks.

Read the fine print on the bottom of ads carefully and you will sometimes find explicit claims that a word or image is trademarked. For example, the Cingular ad that we will discuss in a moment has in its fine print: "Sony is the trademark or registered trademark of Sony Corporation. Ericsson is the trademark or registered trademark of Telefonaktiebolaget LM Ericsson. The Sony Ericsson logo is the trademark or registered trademark of Sony Ericsson Mobile Communications AB. Samsung is a registered trademark of Samsung Electronics America, Inc. and its related entities."

BOX 7-1   A Noun? A Verb? TiVo Says It's Neither

TiVo, the digital recording device and service, recently has stepped up efforts to police just how its trademark is used in a sentence. Using TiVo as a verb, for instance, as in "to TiVo" or "I TiVoed *The Apprentice* last night"—is forbidden. . . . Running a close second among uses the company frowns on is "TiVo-like." "We do aggressively protect our trademark," Kathryn Kelly, a TiVo spokeswoman

said, adding that with competing digital video recorders entering the market, TiVo wants to keep its name from going the way of Xerox or Kleenex.[a]

[a]Tom Zeller, "A Noun? A Verb? TiVo Says It's Neither," *New York Times*, December 13, 2004, p. C9. Copyright © 2004 by The New York Times Co. Reprinted with permission.

Sometimes advertisers are so successful in identifying the trademark with the product that the trademark becomes a common equivalent for the product. *Cellophane, aspirin, escalator, trampoline, nylon, linoleum,* and *thermos* were once trademarks held by individual companies. Because the manufacturers of these products and their advertisers did not protect these names adequately, the trademarks slipped into the public vocabulary and the public domain. To protect a trademark, manufacturers insist that it be used with the term for the generic product. So, for example, ads do not promote Kleenex but Kleenex *tissues.* In addition, the trademark is always capitalized.

A product may also be identified by a trade character that personifies the product's important characteristics. Often the trade character speaks for the product and functions visually as a substitute for the product: the Pillsbury Doughboy, for example, personifies and speaks for Pillsbury biscuits. The Doughboy resembles the biscuits—he's white in color, responds to touch by bouncing back (as freshly baked biscuits do), and is immaculately clean (he wears a white baker's hat). He's called Poppin' Fresh, suggesting that the biscuits rise, bake quickly, and taste fresh.

The value of a trade character was illustrated in 2003 when the Colombian Coffee Federation, the group that represents more than a half million Colombian coffee growers, announced that it would open its own coffee shops in the United States under the name Juan Valdez. Created in the 1960s, the Juan Valdez trademark is associated in the public mind with high-quality Colombian coffee. Ads in the 1990s showed the character standing in supermarket aisles. Juan Valdez would take on such coffee specialty shops as Starbucks with a lower-cost cup of Colombian coffee set in a simpler shop. By reducing the markup that now stands between grower and customer, the shops would increase the profit for the grower.

A Valdez representative noted the difference between the experience Valdez and Starbucks would market. "Our stores are going to be much more down to earth—less opportunities for social interaction. It's not going to be a gathering place; it's going to be a place to get superior coffee, the best coffee in the world."[1] That niche is consistent with the image of the trade character. Valdez wears a serape and sombrero and stands next to a donkey.

Because trade characters carry the company's image, they should be untainted by controversy. Toys R Us stumbled in fall 2003 when one of its ads featured its trade character Geoffrey the Giraffe inhaling from a helium balloon. Inhaling helium can

---

BOX 7-2   Generic Murphy Bed

The U.S. Court of Appeals for the Second Circuit in Manhattan declared that anyone who might wish to manufacture a bed of the type that stumped the likes of Charlie Chaplin and Jackie Gleason can call it, if they want to, a Murphy bed. The judges, reversing a lower-court decision, said that many people had come to use the term *Murphy bed* "to designate generally a type of bed." The dictionary says a Murphy is "a bed that may be folded or swung into a closet." Thus, the judges said, "Murphy bed" has become a generic part of the language that cannot be owned by anyone.[a]

[a]William Glaverson, "Open and Shut Case? Generic Murphy Bed," *New York Times*, 2 May 1989, p. 13Y.

---

produce unconsciousness by displacing oxygen in the lungs. Antidrug groups were among those who complained to the company and the media. The toy chain announced that the ad had run its rotation and would not be re-aired.

The vigilance with which companies protect their trademarks was evident in summer 1995, when the Hormel Foods Corporation, the producer of the pork-based luncheon meat Spam, sued the makers of the movie *Muppet Treasure Island* over the presence in the film of an evil boar named "Spa'am." "Hormel officials," reported the *New York Times*, "also objected in the lawsuit to plans by the movie makers to feature the Spa'am character in Happy Meals at McDonald's restaurant and on boxes of Cheerios cereal boxes."[2]

Some trade characters are a clear and simple extension of the name of the company. The greyhound of Greyhound buses symbolized the company's name and at the same time suggested that the buses were fast, sleek, and efficient.

In March 1995, the U.S. Supreme Court held that a color, such as the pink of fiberglass insulation or the blue identified with a sugar substitute, can have trademark protection. Before that ruling, companies could obtain federal protection only for "words, names, symbols, or devices" that distinguish their products. More than fifty companies claimed trademarked colors. At issue in the court case was whether Qualitex Company, which had trademark protection for its gold-green Sun Glow pads used in dry cleaning, could claim unfair competition from the Jacobson Products Company, which had begun selling a competing pad in green-gold. Color is among the characteristics consistently associated with products. For example, we recognize Campbell soups in part by the use of red and white on the can, and we identify Dr. Pepper in part by its maroon labels.

Naming

Those who name new products employ "phonologics" to translate our association with sounds and letters into a product identity. So, for example, Serafem is a pill designed for women experiencing premenstrual tension. The name was derived from "angelic seraphim, 'but with *-fem* from *feminine* and a very soothing prefix." The names of drugs require FDA approval. "The agency rejects about a third of all applications, weeding out dangerous sound-alikes. It frowns on syllables like 'ultra,' 'max' or 'new.'"[3]

> ### BOX 7-3 Packaging
>
> "Changes in packaging can increase an ad's effectiveness by more than 45 percent," Elliot Young, president, Perception Research Services, told a Cosmo/Expo packaging session. . . . "The new Diet Rite package . . . contributed to sales gains of more than 35 percent."[a]
>
> [a]"Packaging Linked to Ad's Effect," *Advertising Age*, 3 May 1982, p. 63.

Packaging

Packaging is another potent means of providing product identification. For example, we associate Quaker Oats with the smiling Quaker on a cylindrical box, and L'eggs pantyhose with their plastic egg-shaped containers. Ideally, the name of the product and the package reinforce each other, the way the picture of the Quaker underscores Quaker Oats and the egglike container is a reminder of the name L'eggs. Similarly, the Coca-Cola bottle is recognizable both by shape and by touch.

Study after study verifies the power of packaging. In one test, the same deodorant was packaged in three different color combinations. The participants were told that they were testing three different formulations. "In this case," notes Thomas Hine, author of *The Total Package*, color scheme B was the one considered "just right." Those tested praised its pleasant, yet unobtrusive fragrance and its ability to stop wetness and odor for as much as 12 hours. Color scheme C was found to have a strong aroma but not really very much effectiveness. And color scheme A was downright threatening. Several users developed skin rashes after using it, and three had severe enough problems to consult dermatologists.[4]

Selecting an appropriate name and appropriate packaging generally precedes selection of the slogan. The slogan describes either the product or the reasons people will want or need the product. Like the name and the package, it is usually repeated in all major forms of advertising for the product.

Slogans

An effective slogan summarizes the ad and provides a memory peg on which the name of the product is hung. So, for example, we associate the word "*pizza*" spoken by a cartoon Caesar with Little Caesar Pizza; the line "Sometimes you feel like a nut, sometimes you don't" with Almond Joy and Mounds candy bars; "Get a little taste of French culture" with the yogurt Yoplait; and "Can you hear me now?" with Verizon. If someone says, "When you care enough to send the very best," we think "Hallmark cards," because the trademark and the slogan are now fused in our minds. *AT&T* Wireless

---

BOX 7-4   A Cracker in Another Box

"When RJR Nabisco introduced a bite-size version of graham crackers last fall, the company was abuzz. . . . But to the company's dismay, sales were sluggish. As it turns out, looks—at least the looks of the box—were the problem. So, in a crash program, Nabisco's marketing people changed the logo and changed the name to Graham Bites from Honeycomb Graham Snacks. And perhaps most important, in their eyes, from a subdued blue to a bright yellow. As a result, sales of the six-sided snack . . . are strong and getting stronger."[a]

[a]Anthony Ramirez, "Lessons in the Cracker Market," *New York Times*, 5 July 1990, p. D1.

BOX 7-5   The Best Slogans According to the Admakers

In a special issue in 1999, *Advertising Age* listed its choices for the top ten slogans in the history of advertising. In order, they are

"Diamonds Are Forever" (DeBeers)
"Just Do It" (Nike)
"The Pause That Refreshes" (Coca-Cola)
"Tastes Great, Less Filling" (Miller Lite)
"We Try Harder" (Avis)

"Good to the Last Drop" (Maxwell House)
"Breakfast of Champions" (Wheaties)
"Does She . . . or Doesn't She?" (Clairol)
"When It Rains, It Pours" (Morton Salt)
"Where's the Beef?" (Wendy's)

Source: Advertising Age, 1999 special issue, p. 32.

---

capitalized on our memory of slogans past when in 2003 it resurrected AT&T's "Reach Out and Touch Someone" in the form of "Reach Out."

Long after a product's marketers have abandoned a slogan, the slogan may retain currency, because we tend to store highly redundant messages in our memories for later retrieval. Chicken producer Frank Perdue said in one of his ads that "golden yellow is the natural color of a chicken. . . . So don't wonder why my chickens are so yellow, wonder why some chickens are so white [lifting up a competitor's white chicken]. I wonder where the yellow went?" That last sentence becomes a barometer of the age of the listener. Those of us old enough to remember the Pepsodent toothpaste slogan "You'll wonder where the yellow went when you brush your teeth with Pepsodent" hear the line as a clever reconstruction of an old claim and also as a literal statement. People who were never exposed to the Pepsodent campaign hear only the literal statement.

A slogan can also be created to parody a product. Apple's iPod is a digital music player that holds hundreds of songs. Priced between $300 and $500 depending on capacity, the iPod's initials were transformed into a protest by an online critic who suggested that it was an acronym for "Idiots Price Our Devices."[5]

BOX 7-6   Differentiation

"'All the cosmetics companies use basically the same chemicals. It is all the same quality stuff,' says Heinz J. Eiermann, a former cosmetics chemist and industry executive who directs the Food and Drug Administration's division of cosmetics technology. 'The art of cosmetics is as much in marketing as in chemistry. Much of what you pay for is make-believe.'"[a]

"'I've never worked on a product that was better than another. They hardly . . . exist. So what I have to do is create an imagery about that product,' said George Lois, chairman of Lois Pitts Gershon Pon/GGK on *60 Minutes* in 1981."[b]

[a]Blaine Harden, "Vanity Fare," *Washington Post Magazine,* 30 May 1982, p. 10.
[b]Quoted by Roger Draper, "The Faithless Shepherd," *New York Review of Books,* 26 June 1986, p. 16.

As our discussion so far indicates, any trademark, package, or slogan that identifies a product also distinguishes that product from those employing a different trademark, package, and slogan. Indeed, the package may be all that distinguishes one product from another.

DIFFERENTIATION

Unique Selling Proposition

Rosser Reeves, one of the pioneers of advertising, coined the phrase "unique selling proposition." The unique selling proposition is a claim that differentiates one ad from another. In an era when advertising floods the environment, the unique selling proposition is even more important than it was when there were fewer products of the same kind and less advertising.

Unique selling propositions often include words such as "only" and "best." So, for example, in November 2003 Cingular urged readers of the *New York Times* to "Switch to the only company that lets you keep your number and keep your rollover minutes." Because federal regulations had just required that all phone companies permit customers to keep their numbers, that claim was not unique.[6]

Over-the-counter pain relievers are head-to-head competitors. The three major ones contain either aspirin, or ibuprofen, or acetaminophen. Taking a low-dose aspirin has long been touted as a way that older people can protect themselves from strokes. When a clinical study found that ibuprofen may block the heart-protecting effect of aspirin, Tylenol, which contains acetaminophen, not ibuprofen, began running a print ad suggesting: "Tylenol—a Better Choice." The ad noted, "Taking a low-dose aspirin a day for your heart can be a smart thing to do. Taking a pain reliever that won't interfere with it is even smarter."

Crest toothpaste, for example, contains fluoride. When it was introduced, Crest was distinguished from other toothpastes by the claim, certified by a major dental association, that it would reduce the number of new cavities. Once the other products were able to make the claim that they, too, could reduce the number of new cavities, Crest lost its unique selling proposition. Other competitors then entered the market claiming that they whitened teeth; some claimed to freshen breath. Once the unique selling propositions of a product such as toothpaste are well known and accepted, a competitor can combine the unique selling propositions of all the others. Thus, a toothpaste was marketed that promised fluoride and fresher breath: Double Protection AquaFresh.

Convenience can also be used to market difference. Crest did this for its Whitestrips in an ad that showed a young woman unable to talk to the camera because she has applied a competing product to her teeth and is now following its directions to keep lips from teeth as the product works.

It is also possible to adopt and extend a competitor's claim. A long-distance phone company, for example, urges you to use the phone to keep in touch. An airline extends the claim, arguing that flying there is the best way to keep in touch—an assertion that assumes you have granted the proposition that keeping in touch is a good thing.

A competitor can counter a unique selling proposition by co-opting it, as AquaFresh did in co-opting the claims of its rivals. Alternatively, it can undercut the selling proposition by granting that the product is unique but implying that that uniqueness is a disadvantage. Dove soap claimed as its unique advantage that it consists of one quarter cleansing cream. A competitor responded by claiming that its product didn't contain any greasy cream. The unique selling proposition had thus been recontextualized by a competitor and, in the new context, containing cream was a negative, rather than a positive, attribute of the product.

The package may be the product's major selling point. When a deodorant is advertised as "a convenient roll-on," when a frozen dinner is advertised as offering "oven-to-table service," it is the package, not the product being packaged, that we are being sold. *Once a mode of packaging has been widely adopted, it loses its utility as a unique selling point for any single product.* We now take for granted, for example, that rolls of waxed paper, foil, or plastic wrap will come in a box with a serrated edge so we can cleanly cut off the amount needed. By contrast, the use of plastic containers for products once bottled in glass is sufficiently new that the "unbreakable" or "squeezable" bottle is still advertised.

An advertiser also can use comparative data to bolster a claim of uniqueness. So, for example, Morgan Stanley notes in an ad that "Morningstar has identified our Special Value Fund as having less risk that 90% of other small blend funds." This claim distinguished this fund from 9 out of 10 others, a distinction that raises the question, Why wouldn't the investor want to invest in the funds in that top 10 percent?

Association

Advertisers attempt to associate their products with a slogan, a trademark or trade character, and a package; then they try to associate the product, slogan, package, trademark, and trade character with positive experiences. Ads create wants and transform wants into needs by associating products with desirable experiences. If the ad is to succeed, it must create a strong associative link between the experience portrayed in the ad and the product. That experience must be one we would like to share, and the experience portrayed must be different from and better than that promised by competitors.

When one product evokes more positive associations than competing products, the intended audience will tell surveyors that a brand name is an important factor in deter-

---

BOX 7-7   Antibrand as Brand

"Blackspot® sneakers. . . . A non-brand. An anti-brand. Its own brand. A shoe whose only advertising is the word of mouth of its owners, and the impact of the image of its wearers.

"But then I thought, why stop there? Why be an organization marketing an anti-brand, when one can become so much more than just that? Why not turn Blackspot sneakers into an anti-corporation? Fight fire with fire. Make the shoes' owners the company's owners. Whenever someone buys a pair of Blackspots, he or she is buying a share in Blackspot sneakers. A cooperative. An anti-corporation."[a]

[a]Adbusters, *Journal of the Mental Environment.* (May–June 2004): 53.

---

mining which product to buy. A study released in July 1995 by the International Mass Retail Association reflected the power of advertising when it reported that 60 percent of consumers aged 8 through 17 said that brand was important when buying sneakers; 58 percent said it was important when purchasing radios, CD players, and other electronic equipment; 54 percent indicated its centrality in choosing video games; and 37 percent identified it as important in purchasing jeans.[7] By 2003, the power of brand seemed to be declining. Whereas in 2000 "almost half of the 8,000 shoppers polled by America's Research in the week after Thanksgiving (48 percent) thought brand names were 'extremely important' for choosing holiday gifts. [In 2003] fewer than a third (32 percent) felt the same way."[8] Why the rise in popularity of off-brand products? Some people speculated that advertising was succeeding in selling a category of products but did not create sufficient distinctions within the category to permit one brand to stand out.

Leading the efforts to associate ads with a destructive consumer culture are groups such as Culture Jammers (culturejammers.org). Adbusters Media Foundation/Culture Jammers is a nonprofit organization that wants "to change the way we interact with the mass media and the way in which meaning is produced in our society." The Vancouver-based group made its name by releasing its own anticonsumerism magazine *Adbusters* with parodies of corporate fixtures replacing Joe Camel with Joe Chemo. Already famous for Buy Nothing Day, a day following Thanksgiving where a moratorium is placed on buying, TV Turnoff week slated for a week in April, Adbusters has recently launched a new campaign called Unbrand America. The group fashioned an American flag with corporate symbols replacing the stars. The movement calls for all culture-jammers to fly these flags on Independence Day in an effort to highlight the commercialization of America. The flag also makes an appearance in the documentary "Corporation" which opened on July 16, 2004.[9]

PARTICIPATION

By involving us in the creation of an ad's meaning, an advertiser can increase the likelihood that we will identify with the experience portrayed in the ad. At the same time, this involvement ensures that our experience of this product as portrayed through the experience in the ad will be different from and better than that portrayed in other ads.

Disentangling Meaning

Ads that succeed in prompting us to pause to make sense of them in effect highjack attention while increasing participation in the process of making meaning. An ad for CitiBank does this by playing on the double meaning of the word "quarters" when it markets its home equity loans with the appeal, change your living quarters into living dollars. At tax time, Tiffany & Co. did the same with an ad showing a sterling silver piggy bank peering down at the words "Tax shelter."

Other means of inducing participation by requiring the audience to disentangle meaning include the following:

1. Employing double entendres that prompt the audience to fill in a second meaning ("My men wear English Leather or they wear nothing at all"). Thus, for example, when Johns Hopkins Medicine took out an ad that said to *U.S. News & World Report,* "Thanks to you, our condition remains stable," it invited readers to ask what the five pictured issues of the newsmagazine could have to do with the stability of the medical complex in Baltimore. The answer is in the ad: "For the fifth straight year, *US News & World Report* ranked Johns Hopkins the #1 hospital in America."[10]

2. Employing a phrase outside its normal context to induce the audience to ask how, if at all, that phrase can be applied to the product. For example, automobile dealers appropriate a phrase from the film *The Godfather* to assert, "We'll make you an offer you can't refuse." And Crest headlines an ad "Years of Crest Cavity Protection and Nothing to Show for It." In smaller print, the reason is given: "No cavities: It's what every mom wants for her kids."

3. Creating a questionable grammatical construction such that, in the process of untangling the statement's meaning, the audience draws a new meaning from the words. For example, an automobile ad claims that "we" not only make the car "*well,* we make it *good.*"

Identification with Ad Characters

Ads establish commonality with us by creating characters and situations with which we identify. Some of the characters represent the sorts of people advertisers think we would like to be (rich, famous, glamorous); some represent the people advertisers think we think we are (unappreciated, overworked). Some ads represent people advertisers think we do *not* want to be. The purpose of such ads is to tell us that if we use the product, we will not become like that person (old, ugly, irritable, pain-ridden, covered with dandruff, disfigured by acne).

Thus, for example, when General Mills surpassed Kellogg in July 1999 as the "cereal sales leader in dollars," Kellogg responded with an ad campaign featuring supermodel Cindy Crawford representing Special K. "We've done extensive consumer research" on the campaign, noted a Kellogg executive, and concluded that "the key component missing was the aspirational aspect of wanting to look better, feel better, than you actually do. . . . Cindy Crawford embodies what the brand represents and adds back in the aspiration."[11]

Identification is a two-way street. Advertisers run the risk that the product will be tarnished by its association with a celebrity whose fame turns to notoriety. The risks of

---

BOX 7-8   Celebrity Endorsers

- *Nike:* tennis pros Serena Williams and Andre Agassi, cyclist Lance Armstrong, and football star Brian Urlacher
- *GAP:* actress Jamie Lee Curtis and model Claudia Schiffer
- *Lipton Sizzle & Stir dinners:* Loni Anderson and George Hamilton

What associations do these endorsers bring to the products they are touting? Who is the target audience implied by selection of these celebrities? If those endorsing GAP or Nike were instead to appear in the ads for Lipton's dinners, how, if at all, would the associations attached to the dinners change?

---

celebrity identification were on display in winter 2003 when tennis shoe endorser Laker basketball great Kobe Bryant stood trial for allegedly raping a young woman who worked at a resort at which he was staying. In fall 2003, CBS postponed a planned special featuring pop star Michael Jackson after he was booked on child molestation charges. CBS was concerned about being able to secure advertisers for the program. The chief global buyer for MediaCom told the *New York Times,* "There are certain things that even people who buy everything won't buy ads in, and child abuse has got to be at the top of that list."[12]

Celebrities whose public identity is positive, transnational, and unlikely to be tarnished by controversy are golden endorsers. In 2004 former heavyweight champion Muhammad Ali played this role for IBM and Adidas. "The awareness and recognizability of Muhammad Ali around the globe is a given, which is important if you're planning a global campaign" explained an Adidas executive. The theme of the Adidas campaign fits Ali's assertive image and record of accomplishment: "Impossible is nothing." "He's a great visualization and personalization of the attitude of our campaign," explains the executive.[13]

Significant Experiences

A 2003 print ad for Nissan Quest personifies the pictured vehicle with the words "It Remembers That Mothers and Fathers Are Lovers." Looking at the vehicle for signs of lovers or mothers and fathers, one notices that a man and a woman are standing out of view on the unseen side of the Nissan Quest. We know this because we can see two pairs of legs, one in open-toe dress heels, the other in wingtips. The seats in the vehicle "go from completely comfortable to completely hidden," says the text. Flexible seats have now been allied with two compatible roles, those of parents and lovers, major life experiences presumably facilitated by the car.

Some experiences, such as birth, are universal. Others, such as weddings, graduations, or anniversaries, are more culture-bound. But in this culture all these moments of change are important elements in our lives. Memorable, culturally significant moments are awaited expectantly—as a boy waits eagerly for the opportunity to shave (an activity greeted with less enthusiasm after years of shaving daily). Retirement is another such moment, although it is one more dreaded than embraced by many.

When advertisers re-create such important moments for us, they invite us to identify with their creation, to invest it with our own experience or the experience we hope to have. If an advertiser can induce us to invest the ad and, by implication, the product with our positive feelings and experiences, then we ought to emerge with a positive feeling about the product. It will not have the desired effect, of course, if we feel manipulated by the ad and believe it cheapens our memories or projections for the future.

Some moments in our lives are almost off-limits for advertisers, because the associations we bring to those events are not happy but sad. Death is one such moment. Consequently, life insurance ads seek to minimize the trauma. Indeed, one such ad features an escalator to the sky. The man being escorted up the escalator (presumably to heaven) is protesting that he's not ready to go yet. The ad reassures us that he is indeed ready because his life insurance is in order; he need not worry about the well-being of his survivors. Another ad for life insurance shows a man with his family and then simply removes him from the picture as the narrative tells what their lives will be like if he's not there.

Because we fear our own death and grieve when a person we love dies, death is almost taboo as a basis for ads. The indirect treatment of death in the ads for life insurance testifies to this. Yet an ad for the Catholic Church of Maryland fractures that taboo deliberately by showing a baptism and then making a transition to a funeral, with the narrator saying, "You only live once; shouldn't you go to church more than twice?" The ad is jarring, in part because it has encapsulated two moments, birth and death, that we all confront. In part it is jarring also because such bold, direct treatment of death in an ad shatters expectations about ads that we are not even aware we have until they are violated.

Making the Audience an Accomplice

Verbal and visual commonality forms the base from which the advertiser builds the ad's claims. If the advertiser then can lure us into the role of accomplice in endorsing the product, the ad will succeed. To do this, the advertiser determines what content we are willing to invest in the ad and then creates a structure that links that invested content to the product.

By eliciting action that reinforces an ad theme, an advertiser increases participation and retention of the message. So, for example, bourbon producer Jim Beam launched an ad campaign in 2004 showing its product stripped of the label to reinforce the theme "The stuff inside matters most." Print ads invite customers to peel the label off a pictured bottle. This is in effect advertising that says advertising doesn't matter; the product does. The campaign then builds identification with billboards saying, in New York, for example, "New Yorkers aren't about labels. Neither are we."

The Internet is being used to draw younger audiences to identification with products, as well. Burger King, for example, posted subservientchicken.com in April 2004 to turn around its declining sales. People were attracted to sites that permit the viewer to manipulate the image by, for example, requesting certain dance moves, which can make the person in a chicken suit set in a living room, jump, dance, do pushups, or watch television. The theme of the campaign was "Have It Your Way."

The site address flashed in Burger King television ads. The campaign also attracted media attention. "Burger King has come up with a feather-brained Internet scheme to get young adults talking about its chicken offerings," noted an article in the *Wall Street Journal*, "and in the process, it's showing how big-name advertisers are latching on to underground marketing methods to get the job done."[14]

The associations created by ads can be exploited in subsequent ads. Read an ad promising "Performance, Drive Power. Engineered for Maximum Efficiency," and you expect it to tout a car, truck, or perhaps a motorcycle. Instead, this ad leads with the phrase "High-Octane Litigation." It is a promotion for the law firm Arnold and Porter that appeared in the *Wall Street Journal*.[15] The ad uses the associations created by decades of ads for another product and invites the audience to ask how they could apply to a law firm. The untangling of meaning holds attention and invites the reader to create meaning of the message. The same process is at work when CitiBank places an ad at the teller's window that advertises a home equity loan with the statement "Change your living quarters into living dollars."

The ad may do this with such devices as a question, asking, for example, whether you deserve the luxury feel of a new car. Crate & Barrel used the question, "Could this be the perfect chair?" to invite readers to consider the case for the chair's perfection. "A size that's big enough to lounge in, small enough to tuck away in a corner. A fabric that looks like a gazillion dollars on a frame that feels like it could stop a truck. And a price that just might be the best economic news you've heard all year." Rather than answering the question, the ad then re-asks it: "Is 'Grace' the perfect chair? Could be, could be."

By using visual images, ads also can invite audience involvement in forging inferences. An ad for New York-Presbyterian, the University Hospitals of Columbia and Cornell, for example, does not show doctors in lab coats or high-tech diagnostic equipment. Instead it shows a closeup of a woman holding a sleeping child. Although the ad copy talks about "Academic excellence. Physician breadth and depth. Breakthrough research," the visual shows the presumed outcome, a contented woman, presumably a mother, and her healthy, sleeping child. She doesn't have to worry, suggests the ad. She knows that the answer to the question framed in the ad is "New York-Presbyterian." The question highlighted in red at the bottom of the printed page asks, "How do you find the best hospital care possible?"

In addition to the use of resonant symbols such as weddings and the construction of rhetorical questions for which the audience has a ready answer, advertisers also induce participation in the following ways:

1. *Using explicit content that triggers unarticulated audience predispositions.* In summer 1990, a black glossy insert in *Advertising Age* declared, "*Playboy* has put me in the hearts of 10 million men." The insert was designed to look like the *Playboy* centerfold foldout. Anticipating a nude female centerfold, readers opened the page to find a three-page pullout, similar to *Playboy*'s in form but showing a fully clothed businessman. The data sheet, also a carryover from *Playboy*, revealed that this was David Warren, president of Jordache. In the data sheet, Warren plugs *Playboy*. "Our previous print campaign didn't consist of major menswear publications. A big mistake. To correct it, we chose *Playboy* because it's got the largest readership among the men's magazines. And their reader is our customer: affluent, younger, contemporary with a disposable income. A perfect fit—pardon the pun."

2. *Using humor.* Since the beginning of theorizing about communication, rhetors have recognized that humor is a means of disarming an audience's defenses. The

person who laughs at a scenario sketched by an admaker has granted the assumptions underlying the script. The audience member and the creator of the ad are in effect laughing together. In an e-business television ad for Hewlett-Packard's HP NetServers, Kathleen Jamieson's son Rob, who writes ads for a living, used humor to invite viewers to conclude that using the Hewlett-Packard product would ensure that their companies would secure needed supplies on schedule (see Figure 7-1). In the ad a person trying to secure martial arts uniforms over the phone instead gets bunny suits, bellhop uniforms, and nuns' habits. The humor in the ad is drawn from the incongruity created by having martial artists execute their moves in uniforms unsuited to their sport. When the sensei learns from this experience and uses HP NetServers with Intel Pentium processors, he obtains the uniforms he needs.

KUNG FU

Open on an ancient Sensei sitting lotus position on a balcony overlooking a courtyard full of hundreds of martial arts students. A young master bows before him.

YOUNG MASTER: "Sensei, we need new uniforms."

[SCENARIO 1]

RECEPTIONIST: "Uniform Hut."

Cut to the Uniform Hut, a huge warehouse full of boxes and different uniforms on mannequins. An old lady is on the phone wearing reading glasses with the dangling chain and all.

Over the phone we hear the ancient Sensei, "We need two hundred your uniforms number DGB502."

Woman yells down the warehouse to an inventory guy with a clipboard, "We got any DGT502?"

Inventory guy, looking up at blank boxes that go up to the roof, "EGBG? Sure."

Wipe to a view of courtyard (a la *Enter the Dragon*), full of martial arts students doing drills in unison. They're wearing bunny suits.

Cut to angry Sensei on the phone, "No bunny suit. DGB502."

Cut to four martial arts students fighting with battle axes while wearing nun habits.

Cut back to Sensei on the phone, "DGB502!!!"

Cut to closeup of two martial arts students on a mat throwing kicks at each other. They're wearing bellhop uniforms.

FIGURE 7-1 This script and storyboard for an e-business television ad use humor to induce participation of the audience.

YOUNG MASTER: "Sensei, we need new uniforms."

Sensei on his computer. Clicks to Uniform Hut Web site. He actually sees a picture of the uniforms he's ordering. He enters "200" and submits the order.

Cut back to Uniform Hut. The inventory guy is holding up a karate uniform for the woman to see. She nods her approval.

AVO: "When HP NetServers with Intel Pentium processors power your e-business, you're in business."

Hewlett-Packard Expanding Possibilities
Intel logo and bong

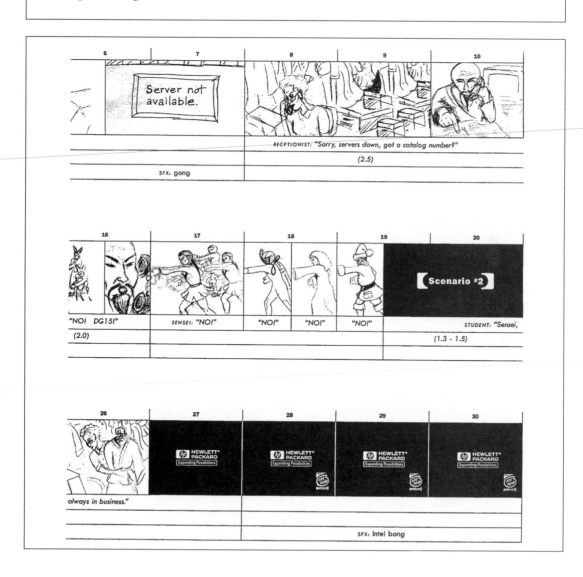

FIGURE 7-1 (continued)

By luring us into participating in the creation of the ad's meaning, the advertiser increases the persuasive power of the ad. But unless the message is repeated often, it is unlikely that we will either be exposed to or persuaded by it. The ad in Figure 7-2 is highly creative in its selection of means to induce participation. Because we are unaccustomed to slow-motion footage in television ads, this technique focuses our attention on the content of the shots. The ad also grabs attention by violating our expectations because it substitutes a Strauss waltz for the shouting crowds we expect to hear. But as the ad progresses, we sense that a tension is building between the grace and gentleness of the waltz and the wrenching, agonized animals we see on the screen. The visual message is not aesthetically pleasing, although the music tells us it ought to be. If we are accustomed to viewing rodeos as sport, as a spectacle to be appreciated and enjoyed, or as a form of relaxation and entertainment, the ad forces us to reevaluate our attitude. The jarring contrast between the music and the visual message forces that reevaluation. The ad induces participation by placing the viewer in the position of a judge who must determine whether the activities shown are "sport" or "cruelty." The claim that this is sport is offered by the announcer on behalf of "today's rodeos" is in the opening frame. The alternative claim is offered on behalf of the Humane Society of the United States in the fifth and sixth frames. The visual and audio content of the ad biases the viewer in favor of the second interpretation.

REDUNDANCY

Repeated Claims

We are more likely to remember a message we have heard often. Consequently, most ads are highly redundant: They repeat the same claim visually and verbally, underscoring the claim in the slogan and whenever possible in the packaging and in the name of the product as well. A radio ad for Sprite played on the notion that ads require repetition, by promising, "Here's a soda jingle that'll stick in your head. We'll play it day and night until you'll wish you were dead."

And note the number of times "free delivery" is repeated in the following ad:

There's 4 Shipping Days left
    Until Christmas
Keep on SHOPPING.
    We're still SHIPPING
    Outpost.com
    Is taking orders through
    Midnight December 23
    For delivery by Christmas Eve.
FREE DELIVERY, NEXT DAY
    It's our policy!
    Every product!
    Free delivery.
    Overnight.
    All Year.
    OUTPPOST.COM
    Free Delivery. Overnight.

The Humane Society of the United States

2100 L St., N.W. Washington, DC 20037

:30 TV P.S.A. "Rodeo"

16mm Color

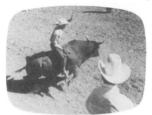

VO: The following "sport" is brought to you by today's rodeos.

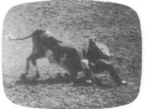

MUSIC UP (Strauss Waltz)

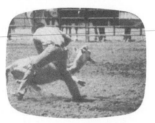

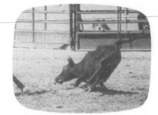

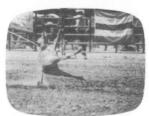

MUSIC UNDER
VO: The suggestion that this really isn't sport but cruelty

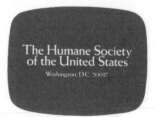

is brought to you by The Humane Society of the United States.

This commercial has won first place in both the 1980 Clio Awards and 1980 Andy Awards for BEST PUBLIC SERVICE TELEVISION.

FIGURE 7-2 This award-winning public service announcement, created for the Humane Society of the United States by the Earle Palmer Brown Advertising Agency, attracts attention by its use of slow-motion scenes of a calf-roping at a rodeo.

Once the product's name and slogan have been deeply embedded in the audience's memory, the advertiser can enlist the audience as an accomplice in filling one or the other into the ad, thus heightening audience participation and the persuasive impact of the message. In one ad for Coke, for example, the announcer did not utter the word *Coke*. Instead, the chorus sang, "It's the real thing," and where the ad ordinarily would have said "Coke" we heard instead the sound of the bottle being opened and the soda fizzing. Meanwhile, bottles of Coke were shown to encourage us to fill in our part of the slogan.

Repeated Exposure

Ads also are aired repeatedly, or printed again and again, in the hope that sooner or later we will be reading, listening, or watching when they occur, and we will pay attention. The likelihood that we will remember a part of the ad increases as exposure to the ad increases. For this reason, advertisers often create radio ads from their televised ads' audio tracks and use pictures from television ads in magazine ads. If the advertiser is successful, repetition ensures that the ad reaches the consumer with a message that creates *product recognition, differentiates* the product from its competitors, *associates* the product with favorable experiences, and *repeatedly* involves the audience in creating the ad's meaning. In this way ads create or underscore wants and transform them into needs to be satisfied by purchase of the advertised product.

Often, as a result of this process, we purchase products with which we are satisfied. Our experience with the product and the experience promised in the ad are comparable. But sometimes, after buying the product, we realize the ad led us astray. On examination, we realize the deception did not reside explicitly in the ad but in our eagerness to make faulty inferences, an eagerness abetted by the advertiser.

To review the functions served by name recognition, differentiation, association, participation, and redundancy, in the following case study we analyze an ad (Figure 7-3) created to market the Campaign for Tobacco-Free Kids.

ADVERTISERS' STRATEGIES FOR PERSUASION

People are culturally conditioned to recognize and respect certain forms of argumentation and to accept certain forms of evidence. Advertisers can exploit this training by couching their claims in forms of argument and evidence their audience is inclined to trust. Thus, for example, instead of simply urging you to use our product, we might adopt the language of social science research to claim that "four out of five professors surveyed recommended that you read this book." We are hoping, of course, that our use of social scientific language will lull you into uncritical acceptance of the claim. The four professors in question actually are close friends who recommended it after we bought them an expensive dinner. Because you might be suspicious if we said that 100 percent of those surveyed supported one side, we didn't pressure the fifth professor. If she had endorsed the book, we would have found a hostile sixth professor, ensuring that the claim would be phrased in a familiar manner. We used exactly five, but implied that "four out of *every* five" professors in a large-scale survey recommended our book.

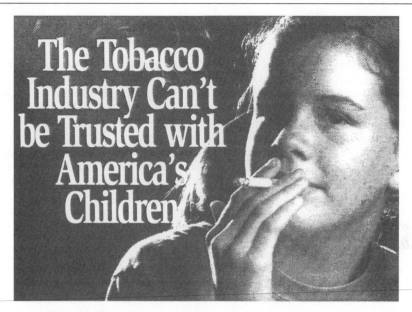

They say there is no proof that smoking and smokeless tobacco cause disease and death.

They claim nicotine isn't addictive.

They swear they don't market to kids.

They claim to be taking care of the problem of underage tobacco use.

Do you believe them? 3,000 children begin smoking every day, and the rate is increasing, especially among younger kids. Almost all of them smoke one of the three most heavily advertised brands. One third will eventually die of their addiction.

President Clinton and the Food & Drug Administration, joined by many members of Congress—Republicans and Democrats—have proposed new limits on sales and marketing of tobacco to children.

Please give your support. Write to the FDA, Dockets Management Branch, Docket 95N-0253, Room 1-23, 12420 Parklawn Drive, Rockville, MD 20857. Don't trust the tobacco industry to do the right thing. They never have. They never will.

This ad is sponsored by the American Cancer Society, the American Academy of Pediatrics, the American Heart Association, the American Lung Association, the American Medical Association and over 100 other organizations that support the *Campaign for Tobacco-Free Kids.*

For additional information, or to contribute to more ads like this: **1-800-284-KIDS.**

CAMPAIGN for TOBACCO-FREE Kids

FIGURE 7-3 This advertisement for the Campaign for Tobacco-Free Kids is analyzed in the case study. The advertisement was created in-house by the campaign staff.

CASE STUDY 7-1   Analysis of "Tobacco-Free Kids"

The Campaign for Tobacco-Free Kids is a privately funded, national organization designed to reduce tobacco use among children. The campaign's mandate is changing the social climate as well as public policies to decrease youth tobacco use, to limit the marketing and sales of tobacco to children, and to serve as a counterforce to the tobacco industry and its special interests.

Identification

Both the picture and the text communicate that the key ideas in this ad are kids and tobacco. The closely cropped picture focuses attention on the girl's youth and on the cigarette she holds. She looks innocent, the cigarette menacing. Whereas her face is shaded, the cigarette is a bright white matching the white of the words in the headline and in the process making the connection between picture and words.

Differentiation

The product the ad is advancing is the tobacco-free child. The enemy: the tobacco industry. One presumably wants the child to be tobacco free; the tobacco industry, implies the ad, has a vested interest in addicting her. One tells the truth—captured in claims to be taken as fact. "3,000 children begin smoking every day, and the rate is increasing, especially among younger kids. Almost all of them smoke one of the three most heavily advertised brands." The tobacco industry makes implausible claims. "They claim nicotine isn't addictive."

Association

The sight of a child awkwardly holding a cigarette to her lips is startling. It also evokes immediate associations—with the children in our lives as well as children in general. By suggesting that the girl is being threatened both by the cigarette and by the tobacco industry, the headline "The Tobacco Industry Can't Be Trusted with America's Children"

increases readers' identification with the young girl. The ad then invites the reader to identify with the bipartisan political forces and respected associations that support the campaign.

Participation

The ad does not say, "The tobacco industry is lying about the dangers of tobacco and about its marketing strategies." Instead it invites the reader to draw that conclusion on his or her own. "They say there is no proof. . . . They claim nicotine. . . . They swear. . . . They claim to be taking care of the problem of underage tobacco use."

Are the claims true or false? The indirect relation between the verb asserting their position (*claim, swear, say*) and the verb that suggests direct action ("there is no proof . . . nicotine isn't addictive . . . they don't market to kids") implies that the saying, claiming, and swearing are untrustworthy. The ad explicitly invites that inference with the question "Do you believe them?"

To help answer that question, the ad offers evidence on tobacco use and an indication that there is political sentiment to legislate against the tobacco industry. Assuming the audience has agreed that the tobacco industry is lying, the ad then reinforces that conclusion by saying, "Don't trust the tobacco industry to do the right thing. They never have. They never will."

The ad invites participation at another level. By including a 1-800 number, the ad makes it possible for the reader to call to get additional information or to contribute to the publication of more ads.

Redundancy

The ad repeats the refrain, "don't trust the tobacco industry." It also uses alliteration to increase the memorability of its message. The *tobacco industry* cannot be *trusted.* Tobacco causes *disease* and *death.* "They never have" forecasts "They never will."

> ### BOX 7-9   Calvin Klein—Owner of Sex
>
> Sam Shahid, who was [Calvin] Klein's advertising director in the 80s, recalls some advice the advertising legend Jay Chiat gave Klein: "He said to Calvin, 'Ralph owns romance. You own sex. Never lose it.'"[a]
>
> [a]Cathy Horyn, "Style: The Calvinist Ethic," *New York Times Magazine,* 14 September 2003, p. 68.

Similarly, in visual ads we might show glamorous, wise media moguls holding the book, in the hope that potential consumers would assume a necessary connection between the juxtaposed images.

In this section, we examine some of the ways in which advertisers use claims and evidence to prompt us to make desired inferences about a product, the maker's competitors, and distributor's promises.

Naming the Product

Note the associations conjured up by the following names and tag lines for two perfumes:

- *Sicily:* "Feel the Passion."
- *Estée Lauder:* "Beyond Paradise: an intoxication of the senses."

Each promises to transport the user to a state out of the ordinary. Each promises a sensual experience. Each takes the user out of the place in which the product is worn to a place filled with exotic associations. Sicily promises a place; Beyond Paradise promises an experience beyond place. Inclusion of Estée Lauder also assumes that that name suggests quality, elegance, a name associated with other products the purchaser has used with satisfaction. Naming matters.

In the 1990s low-fare air services such as Southwest took market share from more expensive, larger airlines. JetBlue defined better food, roomier seating, and lower cost as its unique selling proposition. Major carriers responded with competitors of their own, lower cost spinoffs. In the process they wanted to communicate that they were different from their large, established parent companies. They accomplished this with unconventional names. Delta called its spinoff Song. United took part of its own name to personify its spinoff as Ted.

Still, the name of a product may be misleading. Butterball turkeys, for example, contain no butter. Similarly, McDonald's Quarter Pounder, as served, does not weigh a quarter of a pound. McDonald's ads now reveal that the meat weighed a quarter of a pound before it was cooked. This disclosure appeared only after consumer groups protested that the name was misleading.

Best Western is the name of a motel chain. By what criterion or standard are these motels the best? Who says so? Easy-Off is an oven cleaner. The name implies that the product makes cleaning your oven easy. The ads carry through this theme: "Don't put it off, use Easy-Off. Easy-Off makes oven cleaning easier." Easier than what? Some other product? If so, which one? Who found that Easy-Off made the job easier? When? Where? Or is it easier than using no oven cleaner at all? The ad has not disclosed the criteria for assessing its claim. If the claim means that it is easier to clean your oven using this cleaner than using no cleaner at all, then it is a weak claim. But if it means that cleaning with Easy-Off is easier than cleaning with other products, then the claim is considerably stronger, and the burden of proof on the advertiser is correspondingly heavier. Without specifics, we must assume only the weaker claim. Of course, that is not what the advertisers hope we will do. They hope we will interpret this ad as a statement from some unseen authority about the comparative efficiency of Easy-Off.

Differentiating Products

In his book *Confessions of an Advertising Man,* David Ogilvy, founder of one of the most successful advertising agencies in the United States, admits that he is "continuously guilty of *suppressio veri*" (suppression of truth). "Surely," he notes, "it is asking too much to expect the advertiser to describe the shortcomings of his product: One must be forgiven for putting one's best foot forward."[16] Yet advertisers are often guilty not only of suppressing a product's shortcomings but also of concealing the criteria and the evidence on which their claims are based. Such suppression makes it difficult to use advertising as a basis for comparing one product with another.

Pseudo-Claims The problems in interpreting misleading slogans often involve ambiguous meaning. What does it mean, for example, to say that product X "fights" bad breath or product Y "fights" dandruff? A promise to control is stronger than a promise to fight, but neither claim promises to eliminate the problem. What is a consumer supposed to hear when an advertiser says that a certain shampoo "controls" dandruff with regular use?

Another word used to weaken claims subtly is *helps*. What does it mean to say, "Vaseline Intensive Care *helps* heal roughness, dryness"? Take "helps" out, and the statement claims that this lotion, acting alone, heals. Its action is direct, not indirect. The claim to "control" or "help" suggests that using the product will produce positive results. The promise to "fight" is a promise that the product will try to produce results, that it will oppose the negative condition (the dryness, the dandruff) but may not overcome it.

"And Texaco's coal gasification process could mean you won't have to worry about how it affects the environment." What does that mean? The word *could* suggests possibility without making a specific promise that any given outcome will occur.

Comparison with an Unidentified Other Ad Comparison with an unidentified other ad often promise "more" cleaning power, "better" cleaning action, or "stronger" whitening power, or they promise that a product has more or better ingredients. But more, better, whiter, stronger than what? No product at all? Some specific product? When an advertiser says that product X is better than product Y, a comparative claim has been made. Of course, advertisers often do not tell us what product the advertised product exceeds and on what grounds the performance of one is superior to another. Nonetheless, *better* implies comparison. The rules of grammar suggest that a product that is the "best" has no superiors. But what if all the products in a class are essentially equal? Then all are both "the best" and "the worst" because there is no basis for distinguishing one from another. (Such virtually identical products are called "parity" products.) However, we incorrectly interpret a claim that a product is the "best" to mean that it is better than all others. Similarly, we hear the claim that "Crest is unsurpassed in reducing new cavities" to mean that Crest is the best, when instead the claim literally means that no products are better at reducing new cavities. And we hear the assertion that "Nothing works better than Aleve" as a claim that the pain reliever is better than its peers when, instead, the claim keeps open the possibility that all produce identical results.

A related strategy implies but does not explicitly say that the product is the best. Tiffany and Company, for example, says in an ad, "Only Tiffany Diamonds. Diamonds of exceptional cut, color, clarity, and brilliance." Do only Tiffany diamonds have "exceptional cut, color, clarity, and brilliance"? What is being excepted by the word "exceptional"?

Comparing Their Product with an Unnamed Other Product "This trash bag is stronger than the cheap bargain bag." It probably *is* stronger than *some* cheaper bargain bag, but which one, and is the comparison a fair one? One ad claims that wine experts (which experts, and by what standards are they experts?) prefer one brand of wine to another, but the ad does not reveal that the price of the advertised brand is higher than that of its competitor. In effect, a top-of-the-line product has been compared with a middle-of-the-line product, and the middle product has been found wanting. What would the results have been if similar products had been compared?

In 1971, the Federal Trade Commission began encouraging comparative advertising. In 1972, the television networks lifted their bans on mentioning a competitive product by name.

Comparison of the Product with Its Earlier Form "Introducing the Touareg," says an ad in winter 2003. "The Volkswagen that does what other Volkswagens don't." "Lysol deodorizing cleanser has a great new fresh scent," reports an ad for the cleanser. New improved product X has 50 percent more cleaning power. To maintain their share of the market against competitors, who are continually introducing new products with new additives, advertisers adjust the familiar image of a comfortable product to include something new or improved. In the process, they hope that they will not undercut our reasons for buying the product in the first place. The promise that a familiar product is now new or better—a claim that must be backed by an actual change in the product—aims to reinforce the buying habits of those who already use the product and to insulate them from the claims of more recent market entries. At the same time, it aims to attract new customers.

Irrelevant Comparisons We tend to assume that the best seller is the best product. Instead, the best seller may be inferior to another product but have better distribution, a big early lead in the market, or better advertising than its competitors. Yet advertisers capitalize on our best-seller-is-best assumption by telling us when a product is out-selling others of its type. Claims of this sort invite the audience to infer that the product's high quality accounts for its status as the best seller.

Irrelevant criteria are often applied to establish uniqueness. Because we have been taught that you get what you pay for, advertisers can persuade us that what is costlier is better. Of course, cost may reflect factors other than quality, including inefficient production techniques, high tariffs, high profit taking, or even a large advertising budget. Nonetheless, a product can be made to seem unique by having a higher price than its competitors. Thus, for example, Boodles gin is advertised as "the ultra-refined British gin that only the world's costliest methods could produce. Boodles. The world's costliest *British gin.*" Note the qualifier. It is not the world's costliest gin but the costliest *British gin.* If we accept the assumption that costliness is next to godliness, perhaps we should scan the liquor store shelves to see whether there is a more expensive gin, British or not.

The Pseudo-Survey We live in a society impressed by the natural and social sciences and accustomed to trusting their authoritative, quantitative claims. Surveys appear regularly in the news media telling us how we plan to vote, what we think about specific issues, and whom we trust. By wrapping marketing claims in scientific language, by expressing claims in the style of valid surveys, and by placing actors in the settings we associate with the medical and scientific professions, advertisers increase the chance that we will mistakenly attach scientific validity to the claims they make.

When an ad claims that "four out of five dentists surveyed recommend sugarless gum for their patients who chew gum," it is using the familiar language of a survey report. A legitimate survey will disclose the population sampled (from what group were the dentists drawn—all dentists in the United States, dentists in a single state, dentists in a certain association or at a certain meeting?), how the survey population was chosen (random sample?), the total number of dentists asked, and the error we can expect in generalizing from this sample to the whole population. But the ad tells us *only* that four out of five dentists surveyed recommended a certain product for patients likely to engage in a certain activity. Conceivably, only five dentists were asked the question. Alternatively, the question may have been asked only of dentists already predisposed to the product. From the evidence offered in the ad, we simply don't know.

In addition, there is an important qualifier in the ad. Do the dentists who recommend sugarless gum for their gum-chewing patients recommend gum chewing? Perhaps the dentists would say, if asked, that gum chewing is unhealthy. Because the claim carries the qualifier "for their patients who chew gum," the dentists may not have recommended gum chewing at all. So we don't know how representative these dentists' views are, and we don't know whether they endorse gum chewing.

Use It: It's Been Tested by Disinterested Experts None of us has the time to test every product we buy. So many of us rely on others we trust to do the testing for us. The success of *Consumer Reports* is a tribute to our confidence in disinterested experts. Marketers who want us to buy their product use our trust of such experts when in their ads they claim that tests beyond those we would apply to a product certify its utility. For example, the corkscrew called the Rabbit is shown in an ad above the copy: "The

Rabbit pictured was selected at random and subjected to the equivalent of 20,000 cork pulls in an independent lab test. Its stunning performance has encouraged us to extend the Rabbit Warranty to 10 years from the date of purchase (even if there's a 2-year Warranty in the box. . . . If you opened a wine bottle every day, It would take 54 years to make 20,000 cork pulls. Maybe we should consider a 54-year Warranty."

CREATING ASSOCIATIONS

In this section, we examine the promises implied by the associations created in ads and the sources on which ads draw to build associations.

Associations with Celebrities and Authorities

Use It: Be Like Me When celebrities appear in commercials, they are often there to testify to the worth of a product. Sometimes they function as pseudo-authorities. At best, celebrities speaking outside their field of achievement give testimony about their ordinary experience, experience no more authoritative than yours and mine, about how coffee tastes or how well a detergent works. Often the celebrity not only tells us why he or she uses the product but also hints that if we want to be like him or her, we ought to use this product.

Actors also attempt to transfer the trust we have in their characters to the products they endorse. Tiger Woods is a champion golfer. "Is it enough for you to improve your game?" asks an ad for the consulting firm Accenture. "Or is it your goal to change the game itself? Go on. Be a Tiger." The words are overlaid on an image of Woods walking from a hole to a crowd at a championship game. At one level the ad works by analogy. Just as Woods changed the game of golf, so, too, suggests the ad, does this company. At another, the ad assimilates the positive feelings the reader has for Woods to the product.

In 2003 actress Catherine Zeta-Jones was tied to T-Mobile, comedian Jerry Seinfeld to American Express, Justin Timberlake to McDonald's, and Penelope Cruz, Courteney Cox, and David Arquette to Coke. Not all the associations created by celebrity endorsements are problem-free, however. Monica Lewinsky's weight was the focus of commentary and a great deal of cruel humor in the year-long period in which the Clinton–Lewinsky relationship was the subject of national and finally congressional scrutiny. After seven months of denying an inappropriate relationship with the young White House aide, Clinton admitted that one had existed. In the aftermath of the scandal, Jenny Craig, a weight-loss company, engaged Lewinsky's services as a spokesperson. In televised ads that noted that she had lost more than thirty pounds on the Jenny Craig regimen, Lewinsky spoke for the product. Some Jenny Craig franchises refused to pay for the ads. "As a person who has been successful on our program, she'd done great," said a franchise owner. "But, as a person to look up to, there are certainly some issues there . . . I wouldn't be pleased if my daughter came home and said 'I want to be just like Monica Lewinsky.' "[17]

Use It: I'm an Authority Advertisers associate their products with people we are likely to trust. We are culturally conditioned to trust older white males, for example, and this

---

BOX 7-10   Bush and Gorbachev for Drixoral

CBS and ABC announced that they would not broadcast a cold remedy commercial using pictures of President Bush and Soviet President Mikhail S. Gorbachev unless the drug company got permission from the two heads of state.

Schering-Plough Corporation was promoting Drixoral, its own weapon against the "cold war," which included shipping boxes of Drixoral to the heads of state of East Germany, Poland, Hungary, Czechoslovakia, Romania, and Bulgaria "to ease the effects of their treacherous winter," the pharmaceutical company said in its news release. NBC planned to run the ads, and Schering was considering placing them on cable television channels.

In the past, the White House has sent stiff cease-and-desist warnings to companies using the president's picture to endorse a product. Schering said it had not asked Bush's permission before making the ads. Matthew Margo, a vice president for program practices at CBS, said that it is "not appropriate" to use the presidency to sell products.[a]

[a]Marcy Gordon, "Two Networks Reject Cold-Medicine Ads Featuring Bush, Gorbachev," Associated Press, 28 December 1989.

---

cultural predisposition is reinforced by the leadership positions held by older white males in government and in the major religions. Consequently, it is not surprising that older white males appear more often as authority figures in ads than do older women. We are also conditioned to respect the advice and information provided by certain types of professionals, such as doctors, nurses, and pharmacists, who are also common figures in ads.

Cannibalizing the Past for Associations

The pervasive presence of claims that this or that product is "new" or, in the advertising cliché, "new and improved," tells us that advertisers regard *new* as a positive term. Indeed, they must. If we repaired small appliances rather than replacing them, if we faithfully repaired our cars instead of changing models, if we wore clothes until they became unpatchable, then sales of new appliances, cars, and clothes would drop precipitately—and so would the advertising budgets of their manufacturers. Advertisers must persuade us that new is better if they are to survive in the manner to which they have become accustomed.

To wed us to the new, advertisers adopt the commercial equivalent of social Darwinism: Change is improvement. Because we hold the distant past in nostalgic reverence, advertisers often argue for change in the name of recapturing something we have never experienced firsthand. This reverence for the mythic past is consistent with the cult of the new insofar as what is old-fashioned is identified not with our experienced past (if the new product isn't better, we stay with the old) but with a past that predates us. For example, Country Time, which is not lemonade, claims that it tastes just like good old-fashioned lemonade. The key characters in the Country Time ad are old and speak of real lemonade—the kind made by squeezing lemons—as a memory from their youth, a time clearly beyond the recall of anyone under 80. The ad implies that Country Time is better than anything else available now. Of course, we can still buy and squeeze fresh lemons, but in the world created by the ad that activity ceased at about the time the first Model T approached a highway.

In an ad for Xerox copiers, a monk miraculously made multiple copies of a rare manuscript faster than his superior imagined possible. The contrast between the ancient manuscript and the modern copies underlined our contentions that advertisers venerate newness and change and that they are committed to the sale of large quantities of mass-produced, identical products.

Before the advent of the printing press and its cousin the photocopying machine, monks and others copied books by hand. Treasured texts were beautifully written and ornamented by gold or illuminated letters, borders, and delicate illustrations. The process took years, but the result was often a magnificent work of art. Each manuscript was unique. Because the manuscripts were usually sacred texts, the monk's work was a labor of love and service to God. The painstaking labor of such monks made possible the transmission of learning during the Dark Ages; many classic texts survived because they were copied and hidden in cloisters. The monk, laboring by candlelight, quill in hand, evokes images of the quality and artistic value of the hand-lettered manuscript.

The ad for Xerox copiers would have us believe that the copier increased the speed with which the monk could produce manuscripts but did not diminish their quality. In place of a unique product, we now have a standardized product in as many units as we want. But the copier cannot produce the gold leaf of the original, the colors of the illuminated letters, or the intricate patterns drawn into the margins.

The copier can produce a readable copy of the text itself. Is this better? The ad implied that it is. By the end of the ad, the monk was no longer hand-copying manuscripts. Xerox copiers had made obsolete the monk who could produce a beautiful manuscript. The subtext of this ad told us that new is better than old, change brings improvement, uniqueness is neither necessary nor desirable, faster and more are better. Here, as in the ad for Country Time, the commercial identified the product with the kind of quality that you and I have not experienced directly. Such quality presumably existed only in the distant past.

Because our memory of the distant past is based on historical reconstruction, we have no primary experience with which to test claims about it. Yet the distant past is the source of powerful and evocative symbols. Advertisers cannibalize the past to link their products with those symbols. In the process, they desacralize the sacred and trivialize the historically significant.

Appropriating Historical People and Events The only widely accepted ritual employed to commemorate Presidents' Day, honoring the birthdays of Washington and Lincoln, is the Presidents' Day Sale. To draw us into stores, advertisers reduce George and Martha Washington to cartoonlike hucksters. Actors in white "Washington" wigs hector us about unbelievable bargains and swear that, like George Washington, they would never tell a lie. Similarly, ads for Fourth of July sales urge us to "declare our independence" from everything—from an old car to a malfunctioning air conditioner—and Thanksgiving Day sales imply that what we have to be thankful for are the "fantastic buys."

Another version of this tactic is employed in televised ads for Calvin Klein's perfume "Obsession." In the ads the fragrance is associated with passages from the world's great

---

BOX 7-11   Philip Morris Sponsors the Bill of Rights

The Philip Morris Company paid $600,000 for the right to link itself in televised and printed promotions with the National Archives, the official custodian of the United States' historic documents. The ad read, "Join Philip Morris and the National Archives in celebrating the 200th anniversary of the Bill of Rights. For a free copy of this historic document, call [an 800 number] or write Bill of Rights, Philip Morris Companies Inc. [followed by a Washington, DC, address]."

The law forbids Philip Morris from selling cigarettes on television. The company insisted that it was selling its diversified corporate image, not cigarettes. The association with the National Archives lent the company great prestige, but spokespeople for the archives insisted that the deal was a good way "to stretch the taxpayers' dollars." Congress made the National Archives an independent agency in 1984 and authorized the agency to solicit and receive gifts to enhance its role as "keeper of the nation's history."[a]

[a] "The Bill of Rights, for Rent," *New York Times*, 19 November 1989, p. 22E.

---

love stories, including Hemingway's *The Sun Also Rises,* D. H. Lawrence's *Women in Love,* and Gustave Flaubert's *Madame Bovary.* In one of the spots, a young woman is shown running her fingers over a man's face as the announcer reads from D. H. Lawrence, "How perfect and foreign he was, how dangerous. . . . This was the glistening forbidden apple."

Just as advertisers are eager to associate their products with positive moments in the past and present, so they are loath to develop associations with traumatic ones. During network coverage of the Persian Gulf War in 1991, Procter & Gamble, Sears, Pizza Hut, and major airlines refused to place spots. As a result, NBC reported a loss of $45 million in ad revenue[18]

Trading on Someone's Good Name   Companies appropriate the names of respected historical figures, such as Lincoln and Jefferson, to trade on the authenticity associated with those names. Service companies are more likely to adopt such names than manufacturers of more tangible products. Life insurance companies and banks are called Lincoln Life or Jefferson Trust, not because they were founded by Lincoln or Jefferson, but because the names themselves have residual credibility. Customers take the name, whether consciously or not, as a promise of the honesty and reliability associated with the historical person. Although the company may be only 20 or 30 years old, a name from the past suggests that it has been providing that reliable, trustworthy service for a long time.

Appropriating a Famous Phrase   We carry about with us a repertoire of phrases identified with important people or occasions from the past. For example, when someone says "of the people, by the people, for the people," we call up an image of Abraham Lincoln. Such phrases gain our attention by drawing from that common repertoire and proceed to make us accomplices in creating the ad's meaning.

Each of the strategies we have identified, however, will backfire if the audience is offended by the linking of the product and the phrase, person, or event. The following two instances, in our opinion, overstep the bounds of acceptable use of the past and become tasteless. An ad for a light beer included a photograph identified as that of Goethe—the German poet, scientist, and novelist—on his deathbed. In the ad, Goethe is calling—as he actually did just before he died—for "more light!" By twisting the last words of a great man into an appeal for a beer, the advertisers have trivialized his death and reduced an important historical figure to a huckster.

The strategy in a print ad for a motel is similar. That ad rephrased the invitation on the Statue of Liberty ("Give me your tired, your poor, your huddled masses yearning to breathe free. . . . Send these the homeless, tempest-tossed to me") to a come-on for the motel: "Give us your tired, your homeless, your weary, your thirsty." The motel did not invite "your poor." By reducing Emma Lazarus's stirring words to an invitation to choose one motel over another, the ad misappropriated a phrase we respect, a phrase that forms part of our cultural heritage.

Creating a Memorable Phrase "Where's the beef?" asked Clara Peller in a Wendy's commercial that added the phrase to the nation's vocabulary in the early 1980s. Bud Light ads created a comparable catchphrase in the early 1990s. A nervy young man (Eddie Jemison) talked his way into places well stocked with Bud Light by pretending to be someone he obviously was not. In the first ad of the series, after determining that a reserved limousine was well stocked with Bud Light, Eddie worked his way into it by claiming to be the man for whom it was being held—Dr. Galazkiewicz. When asked if he was indeed the intended person, Eddie replied, "Yes . . . I AM!"

Public service announcements have also carried phrases that moved beyond the ad into the culture at large; for example, the U.S. National Highway Traffic Safety Administration developed the phrase "Drinking and Driving Can Kill a Friendship" and the United Negro College Fund provided the slogan "A mind is a terrible thing to waste."

Exploiting Social Movements We learn the meaning of words from their use. Many words and phrases have gained especially rich meanings for some segments of an audience because they have been identified with an important social movement.

Because advertisements face severe time and space constraints, they tend to use symbols rich with cultural meaning. Using symbols drawn from social movements with which members of the audience still identify, however, is risky. A cookware manufacturer created the message "Black is Beautiful; White is Beautiful" to accompany a print ad showing a black and a white pot. Remove the pots from the ad, and the statement "Black is beautiful" reflects the ideology of the civil rights movement. Add the pots to the ad, and the ideological statement is trivialized. People who hear the statement "Black is beautiful" as a commitment to civil rights are likely to respond to this ad with anger. A statement used to express an ideological position can no longer express that position if it gains currency as a slogan to sell kettles.

Feminist reaction to the slogan for Virginia Slims cigarettes is similar. "You've come a long way, baby" combines affirmation of progress for women with a complete denial of that progress. If those of us in the audience who are women have come such a long way, then why are you still calling us "baby"? By using "you" rather than "we" in the slogan, the advertiser dissociates himself from the woman in the ad and assumes a superior position to her. At the same time, the photographs occupying the upper third of the

---

BOX 7-12   Advertisers' Influence on Women's Magazines

"Advertisers' control over the editorial content of women's magazines has become so institutionalized that it is . . . dictated to ad salespeople as official policy," writes Gloria Steinem. She gives these examples:

- Dow's Cleaning Products stipulates that ads for its Vivid and Spray 'n' Wash products should be adjacent to "children or fashion editorial"; ads for Bathroom Cleaner should be next to "home furnishing/family" features.
- The De Beers diamond company, a big seller of engagement rings, prohibits magazines from placing its ads with "adjacencies to hard news or anti-love/romance theme editorial."
- Procter & Gamble products were not to be placed in any issue that included any material on gun control, abortion, the occult, cults, or the disparagement of religion.

Steinem picked random issues of women's magazines and counted the number of pages, including letters to the editors and the like, that were not ads and/or copy complementary to ads. Some examples were as follows:

Magazine and Issue	Total Pages	Non-Ad or Non–Ad-Related
Glamour, April 1990	339	65
Vogue, May 1990	319	38
Redbook, April 1990	173	44
Family Circle, 13 March 1990	180	33
Elle, May 1990	326	39
Lear's, November 1989	173	65

Steinem quotes Sey Chassler, former editor-in-chief of *Redbook,* as saying, "I also think advertisers do this to women's magazines especially because of the general disrespect they have for women."[a]

EXERCISE: Has advertisers' influence changed since 1990? Why or why not?

[a]Gloria Steinem, "Sex, Lies and Advertising," *Ms.* (July–August 1990): 20, 21, 25, 27.

---

print ads reduce women's struggle for equality to a fight with some man over the right to smoke. This trivializes women's demands for the vote, for equal pay, for equal access to job opportunity, for equal access to housing and credit. If equal access to lung cancer is all the women's movement has accomplished, then the "you" in the ad hasn't come very far. However, by identifying itself with independent women and by implying that smoking this product controls weight (Virginia *Slims*), this brand has captured a sizable share of the women's market. This suggests that the campaign has not alienated its target audience.

Ad campaigns that celebrate the accomplishments of specific women who are shown in the ad wearing the product invite us to associate their accomplishments with a style of dress at the same time as we honor their achievements. The ads showing female stars wearing fur while celebrating them as legends fall into this category, as do the 2003 ads for the clothing line Eileen Fisher. "Women change the world every day," says the tagline. One print ad shows a young woman Rani Arbo, identified as "fiddler, singer, closet poet in silk mohair cardigan, cap and scarf." Another with the same tagline shows a distinguished gray-haired women identified as "Gail Koff, groundbreaking attorney, yoga enthusiast, mother of three in doubleface wool cashmere coat." Whereas it is unlikely that we believe that we will become a legend, identification with the women in the Eileen Fisher ads is more plausible. The ads imply that these women "change the world every day" in part because they dress well.

In the 1990s, the social cause most exploited by advertising was environmental. Advertising has capitalized on a powerful public sentiment. As concerns about pollution of the water and air spread around the globe, they took political form. The green movement was launched in Europe. Environmental summits of world leaders were held. Within a society saturated with claims that one package was environmentally better than the other, one detergent more biodegradable than the next, *National Geographic* set itself apart with an ad campaign claiming, "Only one magazine covered the environment before it was an issue." The process of associating products with a cleaner environment remained a mainstay of ads in 2003. "Introducing high performance technology that's also good for the environment," says a 2003 ad for Toyota's Hybrid Synergy Drive. "Earth Day, every day. From the cleanest car company on the planet," says an ad for Honda.

No sector of marketing was left untouched by environmental claims. In summer 1990, Estée Lauder announced that it would "become the first major U.S. beauty company to bring natural, non–animal-tested products packaged in recyclable containers into department stores."[1]

Why pay for a product and in the process donate part of the cost to a worthy cause when you could donate the full purchase price and forgo the purchase? In the cases of the bear and the watch (see the box on breast cancer advertising), one is purchasing a symbol crafted to communicate caring about the cause.

Nationalistic Associations Some nations are associated with certain products, often as the product's place of birth or most notable manufacturer. So when I say "whiskey" and ask for a high-quality nationality, you might say "Irish," "Scotch," or "Canadian," but probably not "French." An advertiser can capitalize on these associations by creating an image consistent with them. To exploit the national identification of some products, advertisers give a name evoking the original country to a product of that type made elsewhere. Consequently, perfumes are often given French or French-sounding names, and beers are often given German or German-sounding names.

One campaign allies the age of a whiskey recipe with the U.S. Constitution. The Constitution was written in 1787 and revised 17 times, notes the ad. "Jim Beam's recipe was written in 1795."

Sponsorship of the Olympics creates international associations and implicitly suggests that the sponsoring product has helped produce international harmony in a spirit of friendly competition. The 2002 Winter Olympics in Atlanta had an official courier (UPS), an official soft drink (Coke), an official beer (Budweiser), an official credit card (Visa), an official fast-food purveyor (McDonald's), an official film (Kodak), and an official watch (Swatch).

When an ad is mistranslated into another language, the national identification of the sponsor becomes an issue. "You are not one of us," says the mistranslation. "You do not understand our culture. How can we trust your product?" The examples are legendary. In the 1920s the Chinese translation of Coke was understood by native speakers as "Bite the wax tadpole" or "female horse stuffed with wax." More recently, an ad for the cheese- and meat-filled concoction known as *calzones* was heard as an appeal to

---

BOX 7-13   Associating Products for Women with the Fight against Breast Cancer

Breast cancer is the second largest killer of women in the United States. One in eight women will develop breast cancer in her lifetime. October is National Breast Cancer Awareness Month. In a full-page ad run in the nation's newspapers October 1, 2003, Macy's, DKNY, and the cosmetics brands Clinique, Donna Karan, Origins, and Prescriptives allied themselves with the American Cancer Society while appealing to customers to buy their products to fight breast cancer. The pink and white ad featured a pink-sweatered bear with the breast cancer symbol—a pink folded ribbon on its sweater. Above it the statement "for the love of her life." Below it, "Macy's."

"Join our 'For the Love of Her Life' Campaign to fight breast cancer," said the ad. "This cute $10 bear can get you started—the American Cancer Society will receive $6." Near the bottom of the page, the ad explains that "The pink-ribbon patch on the bear's sweater stands for the love of anyone who'd been diagnosed with breast cancer and for the determination to find a cure." The ad then transforms the act of purchasing a product into a symbol of caring about fighting breast cancer. "The DKNY Pink Watch: This limited-edition watch shows you care about fighting breast cancer and makes a bold fashion statement. A portion of the proceeds goes to The Breast Cancer Research Foundation. $150." A percent of the purchase price of the other products will go to the foundation as well. The ad targets women and anyone who cares about women. It translates consumerism into altruism and social concern.

---

buy underwear when marketed to Spanish speakers. When TransPerfect Translations surveyed 513 people in 2003, it found that 57% recalled an ad incorrectly translated from English to some other language.[20]

Associating Media Outlets to Products

When viewers tuned in to watch the Republican convention nominate George W. Bush president in 2000, they saw an ongoing promotion for one of the nation's larger cable companies. Comcast owns and named the center at which the convention was held. Similarly, you can now eat at ESPN or Fox Sports restaurants. In December 2003 the radio giant Clear Channel joined the mix with a restaurant in Minnesota that included "60 plasma-screen televisions, banquet space and private 'skyboxes' . . . [offering] patrons sports and a music programming from Clear Channel's seven area radio stations."[21] Companies also have branded cable channels. The Hallmark channel, which in 2003 promised "24 original, world premiere television events in 24 months," is an example.

Exploiting Argumentative Forms to Create Associations and Participation

Implying Causality Many ads imply a cause-and-effect relationship: Use this product, get that desirable effect. Critics of advertising ask if the effect occurs at all, if the effect is a result of using the product, if the effect is a necessary result of using the product, and if the effect is a result of using the product in conjunction with other factors or of the other factors alone. A toothpaste advertisement may claim, for example, that brushing regularly with that specific toothpaste will give you brighter teeth, fresher breath, and fewer cavities. Are these good things the result of the brushing or of the toothpaste? If you substitute baking soda for the toothpaste, would you achieve the same result? When an ad for a breakfast cereal, bar, or drink claims that when the product is served with milk, toast, and juice, you get a completely balanced and nutritionally sound breakfast, you might wonder whether the milk, toast, and juice alone would have the same result. What does the advertised product contribute to the total nutrition of the breakfast?

Juxtaposition   Juxtaposing images that have no necessary relation to one another can through association lead the audience to infer a relationship: "Have a Coke and a smile." Ads commonly juxtapose products and smiling people. Are the people smiling because they are using the product? (They're probably smiling because they are being paid to smile and will earn a lot of money in residuals when the ad is repeatedly aired.) Juxtaposed images encourage us to infer a relationship between the images, in this case between the smile and the product. Often we assume a causal relationship. Scenes that would not otherwise be juxtaposed can be edited together for television, and we accept such editing as part of the grammar of television and are comparatively uncritical of it. Televised ads can therefore create arguments by association more readily than print ads or speeches. The relationships between the juxtaposed images imply arguments. When an ad says, "Gimme sunshine . . . gimme a Dew" (Mountain Dew, a soft drink), as scenes of young people are intercut with pictures of the soft drink, we need to ask what the relationship is between the product and the other scene. The relationship is not inherent; the ad has simply juxtaposed two images. The audience fills in the relationship. If we assume a causal relationship, then the ad comes to mean either that drinking Mountain Dew gives the drinker sunshine, friends, and fun, or that having sunshine, friends, and fun gives us Mountain Dew. Because the last relationship makes no sense, we will probably conclude that those who drink Mountain Dew are more likely to have the fun shown in the ad than those who do not.

We may also see the relationship as one of identity. In this case sunshine and Mountain Dew would function as synonyms, and the relationship we read into the ad is described with the simile "drinking Mountain Dew is like experiencing sunshine." The ad may also be expressing a list of things important to us: Give us friends, sunshine, fun, Mountain Dew.

Exploiting Coincidental Relationships   There is no necessary relationship between use of a product and status, taste, or love. If these characteristics are related to the product at all, the relationship is coincidental. Advertisers would like us to believe that the relationship is a necessary one and to infer causality where none exists.

Did Mom make the Skippy Peanut Butter sandwich "because she knew peanut butter is more nutritious than salami or ham or liverwurst and has no cholesterol?" "No," responds the child in the ad, "she made it because she loves me." For years Pillsbury's ads claimed that "nothin' says lovin' like somethin' from the oven, and Pillsbury says it best." Some ads are indirect in their claim that purchase or use of a product is a sign of love. If we accept the Hallmark slogan "When you care enough to send the very best," then sending the card becomes a sign of caring.

Producing but not preparing a meal is taken as a sign of love in the world of ads. "The gift of time this holiday season from Cub Deli," says an ad promising that Mom can express love by producing a deli-prepared Thanksgiving. But if cooking equals love, the ad must explain to Mom that not cooking and instead purchasing a prepared meal will suffice. The ad shows a happy family of four seated in front of a Thanksgiving feast. Everyone is smiling.

Why does Mom purchase a complete holiday meal from Cub? Because the cranberry relish "tastes just like homemade," the stuffing is "homestyle," and "You won't have to get up at 5:00 on Thanksgiving morning unless you want to spend a little extra time with your family!" Buying the prepared meal is consistent with time with family, but making it is not. Alternatively, buying it is consistent with sleeping in and still showing that you love your family by producing a meal from Cub that tastes homemade. The value has now shifted from the value in making to the value in tasting.

Although Dad is featured in the picture with Mom and two kids, in the world of this ad mothers, not fathers or families, prepare holiday meals. Nonetheless, families value the taste of homemade. But Mom wouldn't get up at 5 A.M. unless she wanted to spend extra time with her family. If her family is up at 5 A.M., one might wonder why they aren't making the meal and letting Mom sleep. Interestingly, in its eagerness to make the preparation of Thanksgiving dinner seem arduous, the adwriter has misunderstood something very important about baking a turkey. The bird pictured weighs about 12 pounds. At 25 minutes a pound, the bird would cook in 5 hours. If Mom gets up at 5 A.M. and puts the bird in at 5:30, the family would eat Thanksgiving dinner at 10:30 A.M.

Feeling good about the homestyle meal tasting homemade that is "conveniently packaged," time-saving, and likely to produce a smiling family seated in front of a feast? Then don't read the fine print, which says, "All dinners are frozen solid. Simply heat and serve."

Because ads have allied products with status and taste, and because we are aware that this is a manipulative ploy, some advertisers capitalize on our awareness of the ploy by inverting it: "This product is for people who don't need to establish that they have taste or for people who don't need to demonstrate to the world that they have high status." One manufacturer of small cars, for example, employed the stock setting for an ad making a claim of status or taste (an estate with a mansion and circular drive in the background, with an elegantly dressed couple in the foreground). This manufacturer, however, claimed instead that the advertised car was the automobile for people who don't need to prove that they have status. Of course, the claim is the same as the claims in the other ads, that a car *is* a sign of status. But here the car is more: It is also a sign that the buyer does not have to prove that he or she has status. By implication, then, the other cars, whose advertisers make the status claim, are for insecure people, but this car is for the truly secure (in itself, a kind of status claim).

Implying "If . . . Then" Ads make promises visually as well as verbally. This is possible because we invest juxtaposed visuals with an "if . . . then" link. A beautiful woman uses a certain brand of lipstick in an ad, and men follow her everywhere. Without making the argument explicit, the ad implies that if you use this product you will be beautiful, and if you are beautiful (or if you use this product), then you will be more attractive to men. One could as readily take the visuals to mean that if you are already beautiful, why bother?

The "before and after" ad is the advertiser's way of countering this interpretation. In its classic form, a person or place is shown before using the product and then after: eyelashes before application of mascara, eyelashes after application of mascara. Argument: If you use this mascara, then you will obtain this difference. But look carefully at the before and after pictures. Is the mascara the only thing about the model that has changed? Has other makeup, a new hairstyle or clothing, a more pleasant expression, more dynamic action, or different lighting been added to the after segment? In other words, the critic asks, is the "if" necessary and sufficient to produce the promised "then"?

Implying "If Not . . . Then Not" Ads often imply that if you buy and use the product, you will be happier, more likable, and so forth. The converse of this strategy is used in ads designed to make us feel guilty if we don't buy the product. For example, the Hallmark slogan "When you care enough to send the very best" uses *when* to imply that there are times when you don't care enough. Sometimes you don't. Sometimes you care but not enough, and this is a very personal indictment when the person you care about is someone you ought to care about a great deal. In case you are having trouble envisioning someone you care enough about, the visual portion of the ad will fill in a son or daughter, mother or father, grandparent, or best friend in an environment or on an occasion (festival, birthday, graduation) at which remembering is expected social behavior.

Now that the ad has encouraged you to conclude that this is one of those times when you do care enough, it needs to legitimize sending a card as the appropriate expression of caring. By contrast, AT&T wants you to believe that phoning is the best expression of caring; the FTD floral delivery company wants you to think that sending flowers is the best expression of caring. So "sending" is slipped into the Hallmark slogan, and the joy the recipient experiences in the ad at "receiving" provides reinforcement for the claim that sending was the correct choice. But in case AT&T and FTD have made equally plausible claims, the ad will probably show the loved person enjoying the card again and again (its unique selling point). Unlike phone calls, which are brief and fleeting, and flowers, which wilt and die, a card, if you believe the ad, will be saved and cherished forever. Indeed, one ad shows an older person going through a trunk filled with loving cards.

Now that the slogan has us sending, it must differentiate its card from its competitors. It does this with the claim that you are sending not just the best, but the very best. Why not send a letter instead? It would be more personal, equally permanent, and more thoughtful. To counter this option, the ads also show people whose exact feelings are better expressed by the card than by their own words, people too shy or too inarticulate about their feelings to be willing or able to write a letter. So, the slogan has positioned the product against its competitors, one of which is the personal letter, and has done so memorably.

But the real genius of the slogan is its implied "if not . . . then not." If you don't send Hallmark, and you accept the assumptions inherent in the slogan, then you don't care enough to send the very best. Within the terms of this slogan, not sending Hallmark cards is a sign of not caring.

BUT DOES ADVERTISING WORK?

By the time the 1999 graduating class of college students finished senior finals, the typical student had seen an average of half a million commercials. What this generation finds persuasive differs from that which moves its parents. The 18- to-25-year-old market differs from the older markets, advertisers argue. Psychodemographic research reveals that the old hard sell doesn't work with those reared on television. Accordingly, in an ad for Pepsi featuring baseball player Alex Rodriguez, the word *Pepsi* was never spoken by the star.

The appeals that do work are discernibly different as well. Surveys show this group to be more preoccupied with making money, more willing to take risks, and more eager to venture into starting businesses. Therefore, a Pepsi ad showed a young person establishing his own vending operation on a beach.

The generation raised on television and attuned to the fast-paced visuals and music of MTV expects rapid cuts and edits in ads. Peter Kim of the J. Walter Thompson advertising agency believes that this younger generation's attention span is decreasing while its ability to grasp many bits of information simultaneously is increasing.[22]

Still, in this generation as in others, ads seldom create needs. Instead, they guide our selection from among competing products. As Michael Schudson argues in *Advertising: The Uneasy Persuasion,* those selections often are not based on legitimate differences among products. From the essential comparability of competing products and from advertisers' need to differentiate one from the other come a marketplace full of claims that are less than fully informative. Nonetheless, advertising not only cannot save a bad product; it can also hurry its demise. When a product fails to deliver on its advertisers' promises, customers don't buy it a second time.

Audience aversion to advertising may be on the rise. A 2004 survey by Yankelovich Partners reported that "54 percent . . . said they 'avoid buying products that overwhelm them with advertising and marketing; 60 percent said their opinion of advertising 'is much more negative than just a few years ago'; 61 percent said they agreed that the amount of advertising and marketing to which they are exposed 'is out of control.'"[23]

Advertisers respond with anti-ads that manipulate by suggesting that, unlike other ads, this one isn't manipulative. "We considered showing an NBA star drinking our soda," says a print ad for Sprite, "but we figured basketball players should stick to what they do best—endorsing sneakers." A television ad shows a glass of cod liver oil that looks like a glass of a caramel cola, as the announcer urges viewers to "drink what tastes good because television can make anything look delicious." The theme of the Sprite campaign asks the audience to reject ad claims and simply "Obey Your Thirst."

TO SUM UP

In this chapter we have examined some of the ways advertisers use claims and evidence to persuade us to purchase one product rather than another. This persuasive end is particularly difficult to attain when, as is often the case, the advertisers' product differs little if at all from several others on the market. In addition, advertisers operate in extremely limited time and space. Many of the complaints registered against advertising arise from these limitations. Unless checked by regulation, advertisers tend to tell us what is good but not what is bad about their products, relying on our willingness to invest messages with meaning to induce us to hear stronger claims than those actually being made.

 Use InfoTrac College Edition to access information on topics in this chapter from hundreds of periodicals and scholarly journals. Enter keyword and subject searches: *product recognition, advertising slogans, advertising strategies.*

SELECTED READINGS

Arlen, Michael J. *Thirty Seconds.* New York: Farrar, Straus and Giroux, 1980.

Barnouw, Erik. *The Sponsor: Notes on a Modern Potentate.* London: Oxford University Press, 1978.

Clark, Eric. *The Want Makers: The World Advertising Industry—How They Make You Buy.* New York: Viking, 1989.

Dillard, James P., and Michael Pfau. *The Persuasion Handbook.* Thousand Oaks, CA: Sage, 2002.

Ewen, Stuart. *All-Consuming Images: The Politics of Style in Contemporary Culture.* New York: Basic Books, 1989.

———. *Captains of Consciousness: Advertising and the Social Roots of the Consumer Culture.* New York: McGraw-Hill, 1976.

Hine, Thomas. *The Total Package.* New York: Little, Brown, 1995.

Knowles, Eric S., and Jay A. Linn (Eds.). *Resistance and Persuasion.* Mahwah, NJ: Lawrence Erlbaum, 2004.

Levine, Robert. *The Power of Persuasion.* New York: John Wiley, 2003.

Messaris, Paul. *Visual "Literacy": Image, Mind, and Reality.* Boulder, CO: Westview Press, 1994.

———. *Visual Persuasion: The Role of Images in Advertising.* Thousand Oaks, CA: Sage Publications, 1997.

Ogilvy, David. *Confessions of an Advertising Man.* New York: Atheneum, 1980.

Roman, Kenneth, and Jane Maas. *How to Advertise*, 3rd ed. New York: St. Martin's Press, 2003.

Schudson, Michael. *Advertising: The Uneasy Persuasion.* New York: Basic Books, 1984.

Schwartz, Tony. *The Responsive Chord.* New York: Doubleday, 1974.

Sethi, S. Prakash. *Advocacy Advertising and Large Corporations.* Lexington, MA: Lexington Books, 1977.

Twitchell, James. *Twenty Ads That Shook the World: The Century's Most Groundbreaking Advertising and How It Changed Us All.* New York: Three Rivers Press, 2000.

8

Influencing Advertisers

Listerine was compelled to confess in its ads that it will not help prevent colds or sore throats.

Producers of a diet product were told that they could not show a thin Santa Claus who stated that he lost his job because he lost weight.

The appearance of an elderly schoolteacher was changed in an ad before it was permitted to air.

Under a consent agreement with the Federal Trade Commission, R.J. Reynolds Tobacco Company agreed to state in future ads for Winston, "No additives in our tobacco does NOT mean a safer cigarette."

In this chapter we examine the regulatory and self-regulatory mechanisms that produced these changes. Chapter 9 shows how consumers can use these channels to influence news and advertising practices.

REGULATION AND SELF-REGULATION

Advertisers are influenced by formal regulation from government agencies and by agencies created by industry to preempt and forestall government regulation.

The Federal Trade Commission

The Federal Trade Commission (FTC) regulates "unfair methods of competition" (Section 5 of the Federal Trade Commission Act), "unfair or deceptive acts or practices" (Section 5), and "false advertising" (Section 12). The FTC's Bureau of Consumer Protection has issued a handful of guides to aid advertisers and the public in determining how certain types of products should be advertised and what techniques may be used. One guide discusses use of testimonials, for example. These guides are advisory, as are the FTC's opinions about the applicability of federal laws to specific cases.

The Trade Regulation Rules issued by the Bureau of Consumer Protection are, by contrast, legally binding. These rules govern what is and is not considered an illegal practice. The Advertising Evaluation Section of the Bureau of Consumer Protection was set up in 1973 to oversee advertising and to review the substantiation of advertising

BOX 8-1   Ad Complaints

To complain to the Better Business Bureau about a local ad, send a letter to Ad Review Program, Better Business Bureau, 257 Park Avenue South, New York, NY 10010.

To file a complaint about a national ad, write the Director, National Advertising Division, Council of Better Business Bureaus, 835 Third Avenue, New York, NY 10022.

claims. The staff of the Advertising Evaluation Section draws samples of televised and print ads for evaluation and also reviews complaints filed by the public.

When the FTC concludes that a complaint is worth pursuing, staff members determine whether, in their judgment, the ad has violated the law. If they find it has, they may seek voluntary assurance that the practice will be discontinued. Such an agreement is not legally binding, but if it is violated, the FTC may reopen the case against the advertiser. When the case is serious or the advertiser stubborn, the FTC institutes formal proceedings. To halt these proceedings, the advertiser may sign a consent order stipulating the facts in the case, the findings of the commission, and the conditions accepted by the advertiser, and indicating that the practice will not be repeated. This order is legally binding.

If, instead, the advertiser wishes to contest the findings, a hearing is held before an administrative law judge, who may dismiss all or some of the charges, issue a legally binding cease-and-desist order, or order corrective advertising. Either the FTC staff or the advertiser may appeal this decision to the five FTC commissioners. An advertiser who loses at this level may appeal to the federal court of appeals and, losing there, may appeal to the U.S. Supreme Court.

The appeal process may go on for years, during which the contested advertising practice may continue. For example, in 1965 the FTC told the producers of Geritol to eliminate the claim that the product combatted "tired blood." Being tired is not a reliable indicator of iron deficiency. Nonetheless, Geritol reintroduced the claim in subsequent ads. The FTC sued and finally won in 1976. Geritol's maker, which had since switched advertising strategies, was fined $125,000 for noncompliance.

The use of corrective advertising to counter false impressions is a relatively new phenomenon. In 1971, the FTC demanded that the producers of Profile Bread devote one quarter of one year's media budget to countering the impression that eating their product would produce weight loss. The corrective ad asked, in part, "Does Profile have fewer calories than other breads? No. Profile has about the same calories per ounce as other breads. To be exact, Profile has seven fewer calories per slice. That's because it's sliced thinner. But eating Profile will not cause you to lose weight."[1] Similarly, the producers of Domino Sugar were required to spend one quarter of a year's budget to correct the impression that their sugar was a better source of energy than other brands were.

In the first court test of the FTC's right to require corrective advertising, the U.S. Supreme Court in 1977 let stand the order by the U.S. Court of Appeals for the Second Circuit that the makers of Listerine mouthwash state in their next $10 million worth of

---

BOX 8-2   Listerine Once Again in the News for False Advertising

"Harold Weinberger can't fill a cavity or replace a broken cap. But in the battle to prevent tooth decay, he's definitely done his part. Thanks to Weinberger, a partner at Kramer Levin Naftalis & Frankel, Listerine was recently forced to yank an ad campaign that put its mouthwash on par with dental floss in fighting plaque and gingivitis. If the ads left any doubts about the absolute superiority of flossing, Weinberger has set the record straight. 'My periodontist was happy,' says Weinberger, who heads the New York–based Kramer Levin's false advertising group. 'It makes his life more difficult if people think they don't have to floss.' " [a]

[a]Susan Hansen, "Lord of the Floss," *IP Law and Business*, 20 May 2005, vol. 28, no. 5.

---

advertising that "Listerine will not help prevent colds or sore throats or lessen their severity." On August 18, 2000, the U.S. Court of Appeals for the District of Columbia upheld the FTC's right to require corrective advertising. The FTC demanded that Novartis Corporation issue corrective advertising to remedy false advertising alleging that the pain reliever Doan's is superior to other over-the-counter analgesics in treating back pain. The commission ordered Novartis to include in all of its ads in their next $8 million worth of advertising, except for television or radio ads lasting 15 seconds or less, the following words: "Although Doan's is an effective pain reliever, there is no evidence that Doan's is more effective than other pain relievers for back pain."[2]

A consent agreement was the basis for the March 3, 1999, resolution of the charge that Winston cigarettes had deceptively been advertised as a brand that contained "no additives." R.J. Reynolds, which produces Winston cigarettes, had, according to the FTC, "represented that because they contain no additives, Winston cigarettes are less hazardous than otherwise comparable cigarettes that contain additives. The complaint alleges that Reynolds did not have a reasonable basis for the representations at the time they were made. Among other reasons, the agency alleged, the smoke from Winston cigarettes, like the smoke from all cigarettes, contains numerous carcinogens and toxins."[3]

The settlement would, according to the FTC, "require Reynolds to include a disclosure in most advertising for Winston or any other tobacco products Reynolds advertises as having no additives." The order requires that "the disclosure must be included in all advertising for Winston no-additive cigarettes, regardless of whether that advertising contains a 'no additives' claim, for a period of one year beginning no later than July 15, 1999. Thereafter, the disclosure must be included in all Winston advertising that represents (through such phrases as 'no additives' or '100% tobacco') that the product has no additives." The FTC agreement has an important additional specification. "The disclosure is not required if Reynolds has scientific evidence demonstrating that its 'no additives' cigarette poses materially lower health risks than other cigarettes."[4]

In the corrective advertising agreements, the FTC can indicate the type of corrective language that is necessary, the dollar amount or percentage of the advertising budget to be spent on correcting the false impressions, and even the size of the ads and the outlets in which they will appear. Thus, for example, the settlement over the Winston claim of no additives includes the requirement that "the disclosure must be placed in a rectangular box 40 percent of the size of the Surgeon General's warning, in a clear and prominent location."[5] Such FTC specifications tax the ingenuity of copywriters to incorporate the required disclosure without undercutting the ability of the ad to sell the product.

Appointees of the Reagan administration made three changes in FTC operations. Rather than focusing on abuses in an entire industry (such as funeral operations and used car sales), the FTC started to work on a case-by-case basis. Second, the conditions required to establish deception were circumscribed. Whereas formerly the potential to mislead was considered deceptive, now a consumer acting reasonably in the circumstances must prove that an ad's representation, omission, or practice affected the actual buying decision. The FTC policy articulated in 1984 stated that "any representation, omission, or other practice that is likely to mislead the consumer acting reasonably under the circumstances to the consumer's detriment" was deceptive. Under the earlier definition, "any representation, omission, or other practice that has the capacity to mislead the consumer who is not sophisticated, wary, or cautious" constituted deception. Finally, the ground rules for substantiation of advertising claims were reframed. Inquiries are no longer conducted in public. Substantiation investigations are now revealed only on completion. These changes shifted the burden of proof from the advertiser to the consumer.[6]

This shift indicated the power of regulatory agencies to set their own course. Reagan's FTC chair, James Miller, tried unsuccessfully to get Congress to redefine "deceptive acts or practices." Miller then offered the FTC, controlled by like-minded appointees, a statement of policy that supposedly analyzed the law of deception but actually narrowed FTC jurisdiction in ways consistent with his failed congressional initiative.

Deception is one of two practices over which the FTC has jurisdiction. The other is unfairness. In August 1994, Congress ended a decade-and-a-half dispute about what constituted unfair advertising by defining unfairness as "acts or practices that cause or are likely to cause substantial injury to consumers, which is not reasonably avoidable by consumers themselves and not outweighed by countervailing benefits to consumers or competition."[7] From 1980 to 1994, Congress had not approved legislation reauthorizing the FTC because the House and Senate could not agree on the extent of FTC authority.[8] The impasse between the House and Senate originated in 1976, when an FTC inquiry seemed to be moving toward arguing that all television advertising aimed at children is unfair. The House took the position of the consumer groups, the Senate that of the advertising industry.

The FTC's Division of Advertising Practices focuses on

- Tobacco and alcohol advertising, including monitoring for unfair practices or deceptive claims and reporting to Congress on cigarette and smokeless tobacco labeling, advertising, and promotion
- Advertising claims for food and over-the-counter drugs, particularly those relating to nutritional or health benefits of foods and safety and effectiveness of drugs or medical devices
- Performance and energy-saving claims made for energy-related household and automotive products
- Environmental performance claims made for consumer products, including claims that products are environmentally safe, ozone-friendly, or biodegradable

---

BOX 8-3   Splenda Charged with False Advertising

"A federal court in Los Angeles has ruled on April 15 that the makers of the artificial chemical sweetener Splenda will face allegations that their marketing and advertising campaign is both false and misleading. The Sugar Association filed the lawsuit in December 2004, to force McNeil Nutritionals and parent company Johnson & Johnson to change their deceptive advertising practices.

"McNeil has spent millions on a marketing and advertising campaign which has misled many Americans into believing that their product Splenda is as natural as sugar. Splenda is a hydrocarbon containing chlorine; it is not sugar; and it is not natural. It is in fact an artificial chemical sweetener.

" 'The most important issue the federal court decided last week was that the Sugar Association can represent its members in charging McNeil with false advertising under the federal Lanham Act,' said Andy Briscoe, President and CEO of the Sugar Association. 'We are pleased that the court has ruled in our favor on that issue.' "[a]

[a]Splenda to Face California Courts on 'False Advertising' Claims." *PR Newswire US*, 19 April 2005.

- Infomercials, long-form (30-minute) broadcast advertising, to ensure that both the format and content of programs are not deceptive
- General advertising at the national and regional level, particularly advertising making objective claims that are difficult for consumers to evaluate

In November 2003, the FTC responded to a letter of complaint filed by the Center for Science in the Public Interest, by opening an investigation of ads for KFC, formerly Kentucky Fried Chicken. In one of the challenged ads a young man encounters a friend who has apparently lost weight. "Is that you? Man, you look fantastic! What the heck you been doin'?" he asks. As he munches on chicken, the friend reports "Eatin' chicken." The announcer touts the 11 grams of carbs and 40 of protein in one chicken breast. The spot closes, "For a fresh way to eat better, you've gotta KFC What's Cookin." The fine print reveals that KFC is "not a low fat, low sodium, low cholesterol food." The small print is difficult to read. At issue for the FTC is whether the "net impression" given consumers is both complete and accurate.[9]

For more information on the FTC's Bureau of Consumer Protection, you can visit its website at http://www.ftc.gov/bcp/menu-ads.html.

The Powers of Other State and Federal Agencies

When advertising for a product makes a "drug claim," that claim falls into the jurisdiction of the Food and Drug Administration. For example, if an ad claims that a product affects the structure or function of the skin, it is making a drug claim and subject to the FDA. In January 2004 the FDA sent "a warning letter to University Medical Products USA Inc., notifying the . . . cosmetics concern that its labeling for 11 different products marketed under the names Face Lift and Body Lift violated FDA rules against drug claims by cosmetics firms. 'Objectionable claims' singled out by the FDA included promises that the company's Face Lift Cell Regeneration Cream 'reduces deep wrinkles up to 70%' and that its Face Lift Intensive Lifting Complex 'enhances collagen production.' "

BOX 8-4   How Much Grain in Whole Grain

"A product that says it is 'made with whole grains' can contain just a tiny bit of whole grain and lots of refined flour. Even products labeled as 'a good source of whole grains' may be made largely with less-healthy refined grains, [nutritionists] point out.

"'Promoting . . . sugared breakfast cereals as a source of whole grains, to me, is ridiculous,' said

Bob Golden of Technomic. 'It's about as prudent as saying fruit rollups are a good source of fruit.'"[a]

[a]Margaret Webb Pressler, "Says Who? Food Companies Know What's Best. Just Ask Them," *Washington Post*, 22 May 2005, p. F1.

The Food and Drug Administration (FDA) has the authority to recall products that it determines pose hazards to public health. The U.S. Postal Service can also obtain court injunctions barring companies from receiving mail orders. In addition, states can sue corporations for consumer fraud. Outcomes of such suits include agreements not to market some products in some states. The case of Cal-Ban 3000, a so-called miracle diet product, is illustrative.

In ads in the pages of beauty magazines and tabloids, Cal-Ban 3000 was touted as a means of losing "up to 30 pounds in 30 days or your money back!" In July 1990, after documenting one death and numerous injuries from the product, the FDA asked the company to recall it. But the FDA was not the first agency to act. In 1987, the U.S. Postal Service had obtained a court injunction barring the company from receiving mail orders for the diet product. The manufacturers responded by substituting a toll-free telephone number. In 1989, the state of Iowa went to court against the product. The result was the company's agreement not to sell Cal-Ban 3000 in Iowa. Florida also moved to ban the sale. The company that produced the product, Health Care Products of Tampa, settled the civil suit in Florida by agreeing that it would never again sell the product in the United States. The company also paid a $1.3 million fine. In early July 1990, federal officials obtained a court order of their own, barring both mail and telephone sales of the product. This last action effectively ended the company.

Cal-Ban used guar gum, a commercial thickening agent found in some beverages and diet products. When combined with moisture, guar gum swells. The swelling inside the stomach was supposed to make the dieter feel full. In its uncoated form, Cal-Ban could swell while in the throat, causing life-threatening obstructions. One Florida user died of complications from surgery to remove the swollen gum from his throat. A postal inspector estimated that before the company's demise, between $20 and $30 million worth of Cal-Ban had been sold.[10]

In August 1999, the FDA announced that it had launched a computer system designed to track websites engaged in the illegal sale of prescription drugs. Of prime concern to the FDA are foreign websites that ship medications, from steroids to antibiotics. Such packages sometimes slip past customs officials. To help protect U.S. consumers from receiving inappropriate or dangerous medications, the National

Association of Boards of Pharmacy has begun offering its seal of approval to online pharmacies that are properly licensed and meet its other standards. This practice is designed to help the Internet surfer avoid counterfeit, counterproductive, and potentially dangerous medications. The reason for the concern is clear. Earlier in 1999, a man who was at risk for heart disease and as a result should not have taken Viagra ordered it through an online pharmacy. Use of the pill purchased over the Internet cost him his life.

Newspapers are cooperating in spreading the word that self-medication and self-prescription through the Internet can be problematic. "If you recently bought an at-home AIDS test called EZ Med over the Internet," noted an article in the *Philadelphia Inquirer* in August 1999, "expect a letter from the government urging you not to use it. The AIDS test is illegal, and worse, studies show it cannot detect the deadly virus as it claims."[11]

Like the FTC, the FDA can require corrective advertising. In March 2004, for example, an ad headed "Important Correction of Information about Pravachol (pravastin sodium) tablets" appeared in U.S. newsweeklies. "Bristol-Myers Squibb Company, maker of Pravachol, ran ads for Pravachol," said the corrective ad, "that the FDA determined were misleading. The statement they determined misleading was 'Pravachol is the only cholesterol-lowering drug proven to help prevent first and second heart attack and stroke in people with high cholesterol or heart disease.' This statement suggested that Pravachol has been proven to help prevent stroke in people without heart disease. Please note, Pravachol has <u>not</u> been proven to help prevent stroke in people <u>without</u> heart disease. Pravachol is proven to help prevent stroke only in people with coronary heart disease (CHD). Pravachol is no longer the only cholesterol-lowering drug approved to help prevent first and second heart attack. In April 2003, another drug was approved."[12]

The National Advertising Division

The National Advertising Division (NAD) of the Better Business Bureau is industry's main mechanism for policing its own advertising. The self-regulatory program of the NAD was established in 1971 "to help sustain high standards of truth and accuracy in national advertising." In 1974, the Council of Better Business Bureaus added the Children's Advertising Review Unit (CARU) to address ads targeted at kids.

The NAD reviews all charges of deception in advertising brought by consumers and manufacturers or submitted by local Better Business Bureaus. The NAD also monitors advertising on its own. The NAD's own monitoring is one source of complaints. The organization reports that it "conducts systematic monitoring of national broadcast and cable television and print advertising, and begins certain cases on its own initiative based on this in-house review. In recent years, approximately 20 percent of cases have originated from consumers and BBBs, 50 percent from competing advertisers and 30 percent from NAD's monitoring program." Information released by the NAD indicates that 96 of the 100 leading advertisers have participated voluntarily in the NAD review process—as either advertisers or complainants.

The NAD evaluates all complaints received. If it concludes that an ad violates good advertising practices or contains falsehoods or inaccuracies, the NAD tries to persuade the advertiser to change or drop the ad. If the advertiser and the NAD cannot reach agreement at this level, either may appeal the case to the National Advertising Review Board (NARB). A panel drawn from the seventy-member NARB serves as a court of appeal at this stage, and a public member sits on each review panel.

The NARB members employed by a company that manufactures or sells the product being evaluated or a competing product may not serve on a review panel. Similarly, advertisers who represent a competing product are disqualified from serving on such review panels.

Figure 8-1 details the review and appeals process. Note that if the matter cannot be resolved by the NARB panel and the advertiser, the case can be referred to the FTC for further action. The industry would clearly prefer to resolve its own differences and respond to consumer dissatisfaction without government intervention. Indeed, the NAD and the NARB were created to forestall restrictive legislation. Only 3 percent of the 3,200 cases reviewed in this process since the NAD's founding in 1971 have been forwarded to the FTC.[13]

The case against Slim America illustrates this process at work. In 1996, the NAD and the NARB both concluded that Slim America could not substantiate the weight-loss claims it made for its product. The NARB recommended discontinuation of the advertising. Slim America refused. The NARB referred the case to the FTC. At the trial, the NAD served as an expert witness. On July 19, 1999, the U.S. District Court for the Southern District of Florida ordered the president of Slim America to discontinue the company's deceptive ads, pay $8.3 million in penalties, and post a $5 million performance bond before the company engaged in "any business related to weight-loss products or services." After the judgment was announced, the Better Business Bureau put out a press release on 30 July with the headline "FTC Victory Confirms NAD and NARB Decisions in Judgment Against Slim America."[14]

In summer 1995, the NAD announced that it would begin monitoring advertising that appears online. NAD asked online services to provide it with cost-free access to the television networks and the Internet. Consumers and competitors can contact the NAD directly with complaints about net or non-net ads. In a twist that acknowledges the growing importance of computer sites, the NAD now will also take complaints through e-mail or through the Better Business Bureau's website (http://www.cbbb. org/cbbb).[15]

Like many self-regulatory moves, this one was inspired by discussions in Congress about regulating what appears online. "NAD will be better than the government at regulating the Internet," said American Advertising Federation president Wally Snyder, "because they [NAD] can offer a service that is quicker, less costly, and voluntary."[16]

Critics of this self-regulatory procedure point out that it is a post hoc mechanism: No action can be taken until a violation occurs. Industry defenders respond that the outcomes of previous cases clearly show advertisers what sorts of tactics to avoid. One side argues that asking the industry to police itself is like asking the fox to guard the chicken coop; the other side responds that a member of the public now sits on all the NARB review panels and that the number of findings against advertisers attests that this procedure is not a sham. Critics charge that the NAD/NARB procedure has no mechanism for meting out punishment or for correcting false impressions already created. Defenders concede this point but argue that U.S. antitrust laws make it difficult for the board or the panels to levy punishments.

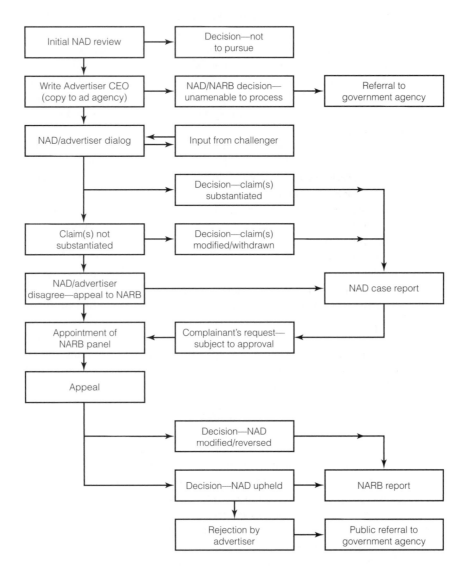

FIGURE 8-1 Steps in the NAD/NARB process

Copyright © 1981 Better Business Bureau. Reprinted by permission of the National Advertising Division of the Better Business Bureau.

The National Association of Broadcasters

The National Association of Broadcasters (NAB) adopted a radio code in 1929 and a television code in the early 1950s. Positions for code authority directors and a limited staff were established in 1952. In the early 1960s, when the payola and quiz-game scandals such as the rigged *$64,000 Question* triggered fears of stringent new regulations, the staff was enlarged, and the function of overseeing the two codes was combined under a single code-authority director.

In March 1982, U.S. District Court judge Harold Greene ruled that the section of the NAB code barring a sponsor from advertising more than one product in an ad shorter than 60 seconds violated antitrust laws. The NAB responded by suspending enforcement of the advertising standards of the code. The code has not been reinstated. Under pressure to clean up the broadcast airwaves, however, the NAB's board adopted voluntary guidelines in June 1990. The guidelines urged that depictions of "physical or psychological" violence be responsible, that the details of violence not be "excessive, gratuitous, or instructional," and that violence for its own sake be avoided. The guidelines also recommended that "the use of illegal drugs or other substance abuse should not be encouraged or shown as socially desirable." The NAB statement reiterated that the guidelines were purely advisory and carried no enforcement mechanism.[17]

That stations and networks did not rush to air ads for contraceptives and hard liquor and did not solicit ads for palm readers and phrenologists in 1983 revealed the extent to which the NAB norms had been adopted by the industry. Indeed, in many instances the networks, whose screening of ads remains, impose more stringent criteria than the NAB. Also, the restraining power of public sentiment continues to operate.

The print media also have policies governing acceptance of advertised material, although these policies are less uniform than those governing broadcast ads.

Network Standards

Public sentiment acts as a powerful constraint on broadcast advertising. As a *TV Guide* editorial noted, "It doesn't take a fortune-teller to predict the result if broadcasters opted for making an easy buck: viewers would be up in arms."[18]

The extent to which broadcasters fear offending the viewing community was evident in February 1987, when the U.S. surgeon general requested that the three commercial television networks air ads for condoms. Use of condoms could protect sexually active people from transmitting the AIDS virus, argued the surgeon general; accordingly, broadcasters should air them. Arguing that such ads would offend a significant part of the viewing audience, the networks initially refused.[19] Fifteen years later the climate had changed. Lovers in bed discussing condom use and an animated condom were features of the campaign sponsored by the Centers for Disease Control to reduce the spread of HIV infection. All four commercial networks and many cable networks and radio stations carried at least some of the spots. The network airtime donated was estimated to be worth $2 million.[20]

Each network is responsible for determining that its commercials meet its own standards. ABC, CBS, and NBC estimate that each receives 18,000 to 25,000 tapes a year. Only 1 to 2 percent are rejected outright.[21]

Because FCC regulations apply to the airwaves, which are publicly owned, but not to cable networks, some ads that have been rejected by the networks air instead on cable. USA Network estimates that it refuses about half as many commercials as do ABC, CBS, and NBC. Thus, for example, when the major networks rejected or required disclaimers on a Yoplait ad depicting supposed "news reporters" reporting on the heist of frozen yogurt, Vroman Foods simply took the ad and its $5 to $6 million account to cable television.[22]

The competition from cable is a factor in network standards. "In the past, it was easier to say no [to such ads]," notes Matthew Margo, vice president for program standards at CBS in New York. "But in a more complex media world today, it's critical that

---

BOX 8-5   What Do They Air, and When Do They Air It?

In January 2004, CBS rejected two Super Bowl ads. "The ad prepared by People for the Ethical Treatment of Animals asserts that meat-eating causes impotence, using two attractive women and an unlucky pizza deliveryman to make its point. Meanwhile, the liberal online advocacy website MoveOn. Org sought to place an ad that uses images of children working at adult jobs to criticize the federal deficit. . . . 'We do not accept advertising on one side or the other of controversial public issues, partly because we don't think the debate ought to be controlled by people with deep pockets,' said Martin Franks, CBS executive vice president. 'CBS also covers these issues in a balanced way with its news department, Franks said.'"[a]

[a]Associated Press, "CBS Rejects Two Ads for Super Bowl," *Palo Alto Daily News,* 17 January 2004, p. 12.

---

people come up with solutions to get [the commercials] on the air. There is a lot at stake to turn down an ad today. That's millions of dollars in revenue down the drain."[23]

To insulate the reviewers from economic pressures, each network has separated its broadcast standards division from its sales and programming divisions. If the staff in the broadcast standards division reported to the sales division, for example, it might conceivably be subject to pressures from major sponsors. Instead, the broadcast standards division reports directly to top management.

Typically, an advertiser will submit the storyboards or shooting scripts for a set of commercials to all television networks at the same time. If the commercial involves a demonstration, many advertisers will not wait for the network to ask for an affidavit from the producer testifying to the authenticity of the action in the commercial; they will supply this documentation and substantiation for any questionable claims when the storyboard is submitted.

The internal standards set by the national broadcast networks differ. For example, in December 2001 NBC broke with the policies of ABC, CBS, and Fox and began accepting ads for distilled beverages. Faced with strong opposition from public health groups, however, in March 2002 NBC stopped accepting those ads.

Occasionally, a commercial will be accepted by one network, rejected by a second, and sent back for changes by a third. It is not unusual for ads to run on local cable and broadcast and national cable but not the national broadcast networks. Although CBS, NBC, ABC, and Fox voluntarily reject distilled spirits ads, for example, ads for these products "now appear on two dozen national cable networks from AMC to WE, more than 140 local cable systems and 420 local broadcast stations."[24]

OBSTACLES TO REGULATION

The likelihood that the Congress will regulate is in part a function of the ideological disposition of the majority and of whether a person of like mind sits in the Oval Office. So, for example, one would expect a move to de-regulate when Republicans are in control and a greater disposition to regulate when the Democrats hold power.

Once in place, regulations can be difficult to consistently enforce. Here we treat some of the challenges to regulation of ads.

Problems Faced by Regulators

By acknowledging that audiences cooperate in acts of influence, we raise an important and troublesome problem for regulators. Once regulators admit that an ad may induce the audience to draw a false conclusion even though the ad itself is explicitly truthful, the regulators must examine the ad's implied content. Because that content resides not in the ad but in audience interaction with it, a regulator concerned with monitoring any implied deception is forced to study the audience.

> The audience of concern to regulators is the general public. The courts have characterized the general public as that vast multitude which includes the ignorant, and the unthinking, and the credulous, who, in making purchases, do not stop to analyze but too often are governed by appearances and general impressions. . . . The ordinary purchaser . . . is not an "expert in grammatical construction" or an "educated analytical reader" and, therefore, he does not normally subject every word in the advertisement to careful study.[25]

Because the law was established to protect "the trusting as well as the suspicious,"[26] an ad can be deceptive if it deceives people who are naive, uncritical, or even careless. Consequently, when a claim has two possible interpretations—one accurate, the other misleading—the advertiser can be found guilty of deceptive advertising. To determine what an ad promises, officials of the FTC and the courts must rely on the testimony of experts such as scholars who have studied certain types of advertising, consult surveys of consumers to determine whether or not they were deceived, and trust their own common sense.

In its review of a claim against the makers of the pain reliever Anacin, the court dismissed the testimony of two experts in marketing research and relied instead on tests of consumer reactions that the court called "the best evidence of what meaning consumers take from advertising." Customers had concluded from a television commercial for Anacin that the product was a superior analgesic. The ad claimed that "for pain other than headache, Anacin reduces the inflammation that comes with pain. These [Tylenol and Datril] do not. Specifically, inflammation of tooth extraction, muscle strain, backache, or if your doctor diagnoses tendinitis, neuritis." The court concluded that the makers of Anacin had misrepresented its properties by claiming that their product was an analgesic superior to Tylenol. A permanent injunction was issued restraining the makers of Anacin from making such claims in other ads.[27]

Determining Deception

The FTC's own sense of what constitutes deception is sometimes so strong that the commission relies on its own judgment to determine that an ad is deceptive, rather than on expert testimony or survey data.[28] The courts have acknowledged that the FTC is often better able than the judicial system to determine what is and is not deceptive.[29]

When a claim is implied but not explicitly stated, the NAD, the FTC, and the courts try to determine what is implied and whether that implication is deceptive. In 1992, for example, an ad for Eggland's Best claimed that clinical trials showed that eating a dozen of the firm's eggs each week as part of a low-fat diet would not increase serum cholesterol. "You can eat the eggs . . . and not increase your serum cholesterol," said the television ad. "They're special eggs from specially fed hens." The NARB agreed with the NAD that the ad "implied that the advertiser's eggs were uniquely capable of reaching the result found by [a University of Pennsylvania] study, when in fact the study . . . did not make any comparison between different brands of eggs." The panel recommended that the ad be pulled, and no claims about cholesterol effects "be made without the advertiser first assuring through appropriate testing that unintended claims were not heard by the audience." When the advertiser refused to comply with the recommendations, the case was forwarded to the FTC.[30]

An interesting situation arises when a deceptive claim is implied not by the ads currently on the air but by advertising that the audience remembers. Here the audience invests new ads with an old claim, and if the old claim was a powerful one, its residual power gives the maker of the product an unfair advantage in the marketplace.

For example, for almost 100 years ads for the popular mouthwash Listerine claimed that the product prevented colds and sore throats. It does not, and its new ads do not claim that it does. But in 1977, the U.S. Supreme Court upheld the FTC requirement that the next $10 million worth of Listerine's regular advertising include the corrective statement "Listerine will not help prevent colds or sore throats or lessen their severity." To justify its decision, the Court cited evidence that six months after the challenged claim had been removed from the ads, 64 percent of those responding to a survey cited as the main theme of Listerine ads the declaration that Listerine was "effective for colds and sore throats." Sixty percent of respondents concluded that Listerine was one of the best mouthwashes because of its effectiveness against colds and sore throats.[31] Some claims are not in the current ad; they reside wholly in the audience's memory.

Effects of Stricter Regulation

Our discussion to this point may have created the impression that advertisers make any claims they think the audience will find persuasive, and they continue to make these claims until challenged. Indeed, before 1971, the government regulatory system was reactive, not proactive, and corrective, not preventive. In 1971, however, the FTC began requiring that advertisers be able to prove claims about a product's performance, characteristics, quality, safety, effectiveness, or comparative cost. If the FTC challenges a claim, the advertiser has 30 days in which to provide proof.

Two unfortunate by-products of this stricter regulation of advertising have been claims that are more meaningless and information that is less specific. Fewer than half of the commercials sampled in one study were found to contain useful consumer information.[32] Although no one need bemoan the loss of misleading claims, the new ads are not exceptional either. Excedrin's makers used to contend that Excedrin was an "antidepressant." Now they claim it is more effective for pain "other than headache." Anacin's makers used to claim that it relieved pain faster than any other analgesic available; instead, the ads now claim that it is "better" and "stronger." Profile Bread used to claim that it promoted weight loss. Now it isn't advertised on television anymore. Ivan Preston identified the logic underlying this shift when he wrote,

> The effort to obtain information of greater quality and quantity has spurred
> tighter laws against false advertising, but the ad industry's response to them

has brought something other than hoped-for improvements. . . . Why not discontinue using information, they asked themselves, and substitute a type of content not subject to being called deceptive. . . . The law may have achieved its goal of making more information nondeceptive, but only in conjunction with the sad yet perfectly legal fact that a lesser proportion of message content now is informative.[33]

WHAT ADVERTISERS MAY NOT SAY AND DO

The mass media can be used to invest products with characteristics they do not possess, and the potential consumer has no immediate way to test many of the claims in ads. Therefore, in the United States a number of rules and laws have been developed to combat deceptive advertising.

Limitations on Distortion

In 1914, Congress passed the Federal Trade Commission Act. Section 5 declares "unfair or deceptive acts or practices in or affecting commerce" to be unlawful. In Section 12 the act forbids false advertisements for "food, drugs, devices or cosmetics." False advertisements are defined in Section 15 not only as those containing "material" misrepresentations but also as those failing to reveal material facts about the consequences that may result from use of the advertised product.

In June 1986, the FTC charged the R.J. Reynolds Tobacco Company with violating the law banning false and deceptive advertising. At issue was a print ad titled "Of Cigarettes and Science" that ran in twenty-five newspapers and magazines from February through June 1985. The ad, cast as an editorial, alleged that the results of a major, federally funded, national health study (the Multiple Risk Factor Intervention Trial) called into question the link between smoking and heart disease. The ad argued, "The controversy over smoking and health remains an open one."

Administrative law judge Montgomery K. Hyun ruled against the FTC, noting that the advertisement did not name any of the Reynolds brands or discuss their attributes. Rather, Hyun said, it expressed the company's view on smoking and health. The ad did not lose its status as constitutionally protected speech, he went on, merely because it coincided with the company's economic interest. The FTC indicated that it would appeal the ruling. Matthew L. Myers, director of the Coalition on Smoking or Health (a private organization that had asked the commission to file the complaint), said that the ruling "amounts to a license to lie to the American public."[34]

In June 1990, the issue was resolved. Under the settlement, R.J. Reynolds agreed in future ads not to misrepresent the results of the government study. During the four years of the controversy, however, the distorting information had stood. The tobacco company, in effect, had gained a four-year reprieve.

Some claims about a product are straightforward and easily confirmed or disconfirmed. That was the case with the Rock Creek Products dietary supplement called "Vitamin O", whose ads in *USA Today* and on the Internet suggested that "administered orally [it] allows oxygen molecules to be absorbed through the gastrointestinal system; [it] prevents and is an effective treatment for life-threatening diseases, including cancer and pulmonary disease." Not so, said the FTC. Calling these claims "blatantly false and unsubstantiated," on March 11, 1999, the FTC filed a complaint against Rock Creek Products in the U.S. District Court for the Eastern District of Washington in Spokane. "This case brings home the message that unsubstantiated and outlandish claims for dietary supplements will not be tolerated," said Jodie Bernstein, director of FTC's Bureau of Consumer Protection. "It also should remind the media that they can do their readers an important service by screening ads and refusing to run those that are clearly false."[35]

Determining whether an ad distorts is not as simple as it may at first seem, however. An examination of a number of advertising claims can illustrate when an ad is materially deceptive and when it is not, as follows.

Product Characteristics The product seen in the ad must look and act like the real product that the consumer buys. The color of the product as shown in the ad must approximate the actual color; the advertiser cannot recolor the grape juice to make it look a deeper purple than it actually is, or retouch the milk to make it look whiter or the lipstick to make it look rosier. Color can be enhanced in products *other* than the one being sold, however. Thus, for example, if the display in the ad shows chicken, the product being sold, on a plate with green beans, the advertiser can add color to the beans but not to the chicken.

The size of the product also must be represented accurately in the ad. An advertiser may not use a small soup bowl to make the amount of soup in a can seem more than it actually is. When the product is enlarged or visually distorted by camera angle, that fact must be disclosed. Often a product must be enlarged visually if the consumer is to appreciate its fine points, as with small articles of jewelry. In such ads, the product's actual size will be noted, the fact that the picture is an enlargement will be made clear, and a picture of the jewelry at its actual size will probably be included somewhere in the ad.

Advertisers are not permitted to construct a special instance of the product for the sake of the commercial. The product shown in the ad must be comparable to the typical product being produced, and it must be sold under the same name advertised.

Product Performance In a classic case of the deceptive use of a mock-up, the Colgate-Palmolive Company showed its Rapid Shave shaving cream softening sandpaper to the extent that the sandpaper could actually be shaved. The FTC received complaints from consumers who had tried to shave sandpaper with the product and had failed.

An investigation established that it was not actually sandpaper that was being shaved in the ad, but glass lightly covered with bits of sand. The FTC challenged the ad. Colgate countered by arguing that sandpaper covered with Rapid Shave could indeed be shaved, but that sandpaper was of such a fine quality that the television viewer would not be able to see that it could be. Hence, Colgate argued, shaving glass was a simulation of what the product could actually do.

Could the product enable a razor to shave coarse sandpaper, the kind of sandpaper suggested by the demonstration? No, Colgate conceded. Colgate said, however, that it had tested its claim on fine sandpaper but had to use a mock-up suggesting coarse sandpaper because on television the fine sandpaper would simply look like flat paper.

BOX 8-6   What's the Difference between "May," "Can," and "Will"?

Note the use of the word "may" in this claim in an ad appearing in the December 29, 2003, issue of *Newsweek* for the cigarette Eclipse: "Discover the difference. A cigarette that may present less risk of cancer, chronic bronchitis and possibly emphysema."* The asterisk directs the reader's attention to small print saying, "Eclipse is not perfect. For instance, we do not claim that Eclipse presents smokers with less risk of cardiovascular disease or complications with pregnancy. As everyone knows, all cigarettes present some health risk, including Eclipse."

The nature of television makes the accurate representation of some products, such as ice cream, difficult. When captured by the television camera, for example, coffee looks muddy. Because coffee advertisers have legitimate reasons for wanting to show coffee in their commercials, advertisers are permitted to substitute something that looks more like coffee than coffee does. Ironically, use of the actual product instead of a substitute would in this instance distort and be deceptive. But the FTC

has banned the substitution of oil for coffee because it looks both darker and richer than actual coffee.

To differentiate their product from others, advertisers often offer demonstrations supposedly showing their product's comparative superiority. As a general rule, both the FTC and the NAD require that such comparisons employ comparable products. Thus, for example, the NAD concluded that an advertiser could not compare its bias-belted tire with a competitor's lower-grade tire. Bias-belted tires must be compared with other bias-belteds, not with the lesser-grade bias-ply tires.

Similarly, the NAD ruled that an extra-thick spaghetti sauce must be compared with the extra-thick sauce manufactured by a competitor, not with the competitor's regular sauce. In the ad in question, the advertiser's extra-thick sauce and the regular sauce of the competitor were poured through kitchen strainers, creating an obvious but irrelevant demonstration of superiority for the advertised product.

In the course of the investigation, the FTC also learned that even fine sandpaper could not be shaved as quickly as the mock-up implied, but could be shaved only after being soaked for a long time. In the commercial, Rapid Shave was applied, and almost immediately the razor shaved the glass clean. The commercial did not indicate that it was taking place in a time span longer than that actually shown. Had it indicated that the elapsed time was ten or fifteen minutes, the FTC probably would not have challenged the ease and speed with which the shaving took place. The contest between the FTC and Colgate ultimately reached the U.S. Supreme Court, which ruled that when the point of the ad is to establish the reality of what is being demonstrated, the audience must be informed that a mock-up is being used.

This does not mean that viewers always see actual demonstrations on television. But when more time has elapsed in the course of a demonstration than that shown, that fact will be indicated in the ad. When a demonstration is a re-creation of what happened, the commercial is likely to disclose that fact. And when substitutions are made for products—when, for example, whipped potatoes are substituted for ice cream because ice cream would melt under the lights—the ad will not draw attention to any characteristic of the ice cream that might be misrepresented by the potatoes.

Puffery Advertising copy creates a world in which superlatives are commonplace. Products are "the very best," "the finest"; they produce "the cleanest, freshest washes," the "most beautiful," "softest" faces and hands. The systematic, habitual use of hyperbole has diluted the power of the advertiser's vocabulary. If everything is "the best," how is a genuinely superior product to be described?

In keeping with this penchant for exaggeration, advertisers tend to place adjectives before nouns and adverbs before adjectives. For example, a wine isn't simply "fine," it is "really fine wine." The tar in a cigarette is not "low" but "ultra low," and Hallmark and Nestlé make not the "best" but "the very best." This tendency conflicts with the need to make short, memorable claims. When adjectives and adverbs are pared from ad copy, it is often because the need for brevity has overcome the tendency toward hyperbole.

Most hyperbole is legally acceptable because it consists of subjective, undocumentable, nonfactual opinions. Although I may taste a product touted for its fine taste and find the taste disagreeable, my opinion does not invalidate the claim in the ad. Taste is a matter of—taste. For legal purposes, aesthetic and value judgments generally fall under the label "puffery." Thus I can claim that a paper napkin is "beautiful," that the soft drink on which you are gagging "tastes great," and that cookies as hard as cement are as good as Mother used to make; although you may disagree on all counts, I have made legally acceptable claims.

A hyperbolic claim is not protected as mere puffery, however, when it claims an attribute the product does not have. An ad cannot claim that a candy bar is the finest chocolate if it contains no chocolate. An ad cannot claim that margarine is a dairy product. A puffed statement in an ad is in effect a nonfalsifiable claim. But if falsity cannot be proved, then neither can truth.

So what value does puffery have for the advertiser? The advertiser benefits when we take the subjective claim to have objective validity, when we assume that there are criteria governing the determination of the quality claimed and that someone is assuring us that the quality as claimed exists. Puffed statements, however, should be treated as bald assertions of superiority with no evidence to back them up.

For example, the NAD concluded that the claim "Europeans . . . love Kronenbourg" was an expression of the opinion of the manufacturer and "not subject to substantiation by objective research data" but that the claim "Europeans drink more Kronenbourg than any other bottled beer" was a factual claim requiring proof. When the advertiser provided sales figures from the European brewers' association confirming that Kronenbourg was the best-selling bottled beer in Europe, the NAD concluded that the claim had been substantiated and closed the case.[36]

An ad may not promise something a product cannot do, and the FTC now has the power to require advertisers to include statements remedying past deceptions in current advertising. That is why Hawaiian Punch told us in one series of ads what percentage of its product is fruit juice, and Listerine conceded in its ads that it does not prevent colds.

Fantasy   No reasonable person believes that a cleaning product comes with a giant who will clean your sink, or that its competitor releases a white tornado. The rationale for permitting such claims is the same as that permitting puffery: Reasonable people do not believe such claims. The difficulty arises when some consumer believes the claims. If you believe that a support shoe will really enable you to walk on air, and you buy the product expecting to be transported above the crowd, the ad has deceived you. Nonetheless, the law assumes that you should not have been deceived by the fantasy in the ad, because its claim is patently ludicrous.

The NARB's treatment of the Chicken of the Sea claim that it was the "best" tuna illustrates the bounds of a claim based in fantasy. When Chicken of the Sea made the claim "in a whimsical jingle involving a mermaid," it was acceptable. When the mermaid was eliminated or deemphasized, "thereby diluting the whimsical quality of the claim," and the claim "What's the best tuna?—Chicken of the Sea" was juxtaposed with a visual image of a government seal, the NARB concluded that the ad had the capacity to deceive. The ad's use of the seal, available to any seafood manufacturer who maintains the required quality, implied that Chicken of the Sea had government endorsement as the "best" tuna.[37]

Limitations Imposed by the Audience

The mass media are available to people of all ages, and they address the whole public, not some specialized segment. Therefore, most ads accepted by the media (with the exception of political ads, to be discussed later) will not overstep what the media consider to be the standards of decency and taste of the audience. The *Washington Post*, for example, rejects sexually explicit ads for X-rated films.

Advertisers also will avoid association with content potentially offensive to any large segment of its buying public. The controversy over sponsorship of the Lingerie Bowl in December 2003 is illustrative. The pay-per-view 20-minute tackle football game scheduled to take place during the half time of the Super Bowl on February 1, 2004, features two teams of seven female models clad in bras and panties. The intended beneficiary of the event, the American Foundation for AIDS Research, disassociated itself from the event. A dealer council urged Dodge to drop its sponsorship, saying the event was sexist.[38]

Children in Audiences The presence of children in the audience also imposes special requirements on advertisers. In 1974, a NARB consulting panel concluded, for example, that "all product advertising must be 'child-proofed,' reviewed and evaluated from the standpoint of a child's interpretation of what he sees and hears."[39] So, for example, the Children's Unit of the NAD recommended that an ad showing a woman inside a dishwasher be discontinued, because the Dallas Better Business Bureau reported that a 3-year-old child had allegedly climbed into an automatic dishwasher after viewing the ad. The realization that children watch television at all hours of the day and night led the NAD to its conclusion that all ads should be child-proofed.

Advertisers are conscious that ads shape children's attitudes by the environments shown in the ads as well as by the appeals made on products' behalf. In response to the concern of the Children's Unit of the NAD, Dial-a-Story ads were changed to include the caution "And kids, be sure to ask your parents before you call," to ensure that children would not be encouraged to use the telephone without parental supervision or consent.

The language in advertising directed to children is also subject to special scrutiny. When research indicated that children do not understand the phrase "Assembly required," the NAD recommended that advertisers simplify such language. A recommended alternative was "You have to put it together before you can play with it."

Critics remain dissatisfied with advertising to children. Whittle Communications was widely criticized for making satellite dishes and playback equipment available to elementary and secondary schools that agreed to air its newscast, which carried advertising. In summer 1990, Consumers Union singled out a number of major advertisers

---

BOX 8-7 What Would a Visitor from Outer Space Think?

Because of the absence of the word *vagina* in ads, interplanetary guests might mistakenly conclude that a "feminine hygiene deodorant spray" is a room deodorizer.

Because of the absence of the word *anus* in ads, they might conclude that we line, wrap, clean, or write about our toilets on toilet paper.

And what would they make of the oblique references in ads to "disposable, absorbent protection" offered by older actress June Allyson?

And what would Emily Post say when she found them setting dinner forks on our sanitary napkins?

---

for criticism, among them Nike and Reebok International for using "emotional sells" in television spots featuring celebrities; Hershey Foods Corporation and Colgate-Palmolive Company and Procter & Gamble for candy and toothpaste ads, respectively, that resemble editorial matter; Campbell for giving schools sports equipment in exchange for soup labels; and PepsiCo for donating free products or sports equipment in exchange for vending machine placements.[40]

Taboos If visitors from another planet were to analyze all our commercials to determine what Americans are like as a people, they would conclude that we habitually speak in superlatives and view the purchasing of products as a solution to all our problems. Our visitors would also note that, despite our preoccupation with beauty, youth, sex, security, and social acceptability, we are also a remarkably prudish people. This prudery would be documented by ads that suggest a decided discomfort with speaking directly on the mass medium of television about the human body and its functions, and about the specific functions of products designed for use on taboo areas of the body. For example, ads for brassieres don't usually mention breasts. Similarly, ads for douches speak in a veiled fashion of "freshness" without indicating what is going to be made "fresher." "I don't know what 'freshness' is," notes ad critic Bob Garfield, "but it has to do with surf washing up on the beach."[41] Nor do ads discuss the actual contents of diapers. Instead, advertisers show their absorbency by pouring blue liquid into them.

There are taboos in print as well. The *Wall Street Journal* was among the publications refusing an ad for a device to correct impotence, and in early 1999 the paper also rejected a version of an ad promoting Victoria's Secret cyber-fashion show for Wall Street. In the rejected version, Tyra Banks is shown in bikini-like underwear with a flowing floor-length cape draped over her shoulders. The version that was carried in the *Journal* instead showed the model in lingerie more closely approximating a swimsuit. Because newspapers set their own standards, what is unacceptable to one may be acceptable to another. In this case, both *USA Today* and the *New York Times* carried the version that the *Wall Street Journal* had declined.[42]

Some products are advertised seldom, if at all, on television. For example, there are no nationally televised ads for birth control pills, but such ads appear in print.

If televised ads were their only source of information, our interplanetary travelers could make a strong case for a claim that Americans are uncomfortable discussing bodily functions or specific portions of the anatomy. What would the visitors say when

---

BOX 8-8   Why Euphemism?

On Sunday, December 28, 2003, the *New York Times* carried a full-page ad for KY Warming Liquid. A man's hand embraces that of a woman in the ad. On the woman's third finger is a wedding band. "How couples are staying warm this winter," says the copy. "Nothing enhances an intimate moment like KY Brand Warming Liquid. It's the personal lubricant that creates a gentle, warming sensation on contact." A white bottle of the "personal lubricant" is shown in the bottom left of the ad. Nowhere in the ad does the word "vaginal" appear. Perhaps KY warming liquid is a product that softens hands?

---

they heard the characters in a soap opera agonizing over whether one of the protagonists should have an abortion? Discussion of abortion in programming, but no ads for contraceptives? No ads for abortion clinics? No ads for Planned Parenthood? They would wonder why programmers are more liberal than advertisers, or network censors more liberal about program content than ad content. The executive creative director at the New York ad agency Kirschenbaum and Bond remarked, "TV commercials have always been subject to far more scrutiny than programming," and continued, "I remember one commercial of mine being pulled off the air because it used the word *hernia*."[43] (An episode of a sitcom, with Delta Burke as a U.S. representative, that showed and discussed condoms, was not aired.)

One answer to this conundrum is that there is a difference between deliberate exposure to a program and inadvertent exposure to a commercial. A person who tunes in to watch *Sex and the City* or *The Sopranos* presumably knows what to expect. We don't anticipate commercials and commercial content in the same way. Also, although many people find it hard to believe, advertisers are loath to offend any segment of the consuming public. Because television is a public mass medium, children are watching it at all hours. Advertisers do not want to create ads that will make consuming adults feel awkward about the product. If a child sees an ad for a douche or a contraceptive and asks the adult questions the adult would prefer not to answer, that adult is not going to respond with great affection toward the product or its sponsor.

Why, then, are such topics as abortion, incest, homosexuality, and rape treated on prime-time and afternoon television? In part, these topics are not taboo in programming because the sponsor is somewhat insulated from that content. It takes a sophisticated consumer to blame the advertiser for the content of the sponsored program. Also, because such content increases audience size, it performs a useful service for the advertiser. In short, the advertiser has more to gain than to lose by such discussion in programming, but more to lose than to gain by treatment of taboo parts of the body in ads.

The sensibilities of news outlets are not etched in marble but are instead responsive to shifts in public taste and opinion. The willingness of major newspapers to accept cigarette ads is a case in point. The *New York Times* announced that as of May 1, 1999, it would no longer accept cigarette ads. The *Honolulu Star Bulletin* was among the papers that appeared to follow suit. The explanation of the publisher of the Honolulu paper indicates instead that he was responding to complaints by readers, although not in the way they had intended. Publisher John Flanagan says the decision to ban tobacco ads was not made in response to the *Times'* action, but was an issue that had recently been debated. What prompted this debate was a reaction by readers, many of whom support the right to bear arms, challenging the newspaper's advocacy of gun restrictions. They argued that, when properly used, guns are safe, but that tobacco products, when used as intended, cause illness.[44]

By refusing to accept cigarette ads, Flanagan undercut the argument that his paper's championship of gun control was inconsistent with the acceptance policy.

Finally, creating ads that force the knowledgeable audience to invest them with meaning is strategically wise; making the audience an accomplice in the process of persuasion increases the likelihood that persuasion will occur. To decode euphemistic ads, the auditor or viewer is drawn into a participatory process highly advantageous to the advertiser. The viewer cannot resent the implied request to fill in explicit content, because the viewer probably is willing to acknowledge that discussion of the taboo subjects—in at least some of the environments in which people watch television and with at least some of the people with whom one watches television—could prove awkward. So euphemistic ads exist because it is to the advertiser's advantage that they do.

When a broadcast ad campaign speaks directly, the very fact of direct address, free of conventional euphemisms, gains our attention. The radio campaign for OXY 5 and OXY 10 facial cleansers, for example, included the word *zits* in the copy; the ad asked, "Which would you rather have, a few extra cents or a few more zits?" The contrast between the announcer's precise diction and the harsh slang word riveted the audience's attention.

Similarly, ads that violate advertising's unwritten rules about what may or may not be the visual focus of an ad may attract attention precisely because of that violation. The ad campaign for Calvin Klein jeans featuring then-teenage movie star Brooke Shields was rejected by some stations and one of the networks. The ad prompted negative columns in newspapers, negative editorials, and hostile letters to the networks not because of the double entendre in the verbal message—after all, the double entendre with sexual nuances is a staple in "beauty product advertising"—but because the use of a teenage model delivering such lines ("nothing comes between me and my Calvins") and the camera angle focusing on her pelvis bluntly acknowledged teenage sexuality. By breaking the rules, the ad campaign gained quick visibility and became the topic of public discussion.

In August 1995, Calvin Klein's ads again created a stir and drew press attention, this time for "crotch shots" of young models with their underwear exposed under their Calvin Klein One jeans. "The ads' appearance last week on the sides of New York City buses prompted an outcry," reported the *Philadelphia Inquirer*. "Iona Seigel, director of a rape crisis center . . . told the New York *Daily News,* 'I've never seen anything as disgusting as this. It's unbelievable.'"[45] Among the ads triggering the controversy was one showing a blond girl on her back, her miniskirt raised to reveal a section of her panties. Responding to the protests, Calvin Klein withdrew the ads.

In 2001 Abercrombie & Fitch "drew protest . . . when it sold thong underwear for girls with words such as 'eye candy' on the front. [In 2002] it sold t-shirts with Asian caricatures and the slogan: 'Two Wongs Can Make It White.' It pulled the shirts from stores and apologized, after complaints."[46] In 2003 Abercrombie & Fitch published its

Christmas Field Guide with the line "280 pages of moose, ice hockey, and group sex " on the front cover. After protest from a wide range of groups, the company withdrew the issue. An ad by a protesting group targeted investors in the publicly held company. The ad in the *Wall Street Journal* of 10 December 2003, showed a young woman under the headline "If you're investing in Abercrombie & Fitch, are you fully aware what you are invested in?"

TO SUM UP

In this chapter we have examined the complex relationships among government, industry, consumers, and advertising. We have demonstrated the eagerness of industry to regulate itself when faced with the threat of government regulation. Government and industry regulators often are faced with difficulties dealing with claims that exist in the minds of the audience members but do not reside explicitly in the advertising content.

Existing regulation of advertising provides a sense of what advertisers may and may not do, but unfortunately, efforts to minimize deception have produced an unintended result. Instead of producing ads with accurate but challengeable information, the regulations have prompted many advertisers to minimize informational content and instead emphasize unprovable puffery.

Audiences, however, are made up of potential consumers; the individuals and groups making up these audiences have the power to influence advertising and other media practices.

ANALYSIS: ANALYZING AN AD

In the brief space of three chapters on advertising, we have been able to touch on only a few of the questions that could be asked in a thorough analysis of an ad. Here we provide some of the other questions a person intent on critically analyzing an ad might ask.

What Type of Ad Is It?

1. Public service announcement (PSA)?
2. Advertising an idea?
3. Advertising a service?
4. Ad designed to engender goodwill?
5. Political ad?
6. Ad for a product?

If the Ad Is a PSA

1. Did it appear in a space or time when it was likely to reach its intended audience?
2. Was it sponsored by a nonpartisan source?
3. Why was it aired or printed? What distinguishes it from PSAs rejected by this media outlet?

If the Ad Is an Idea Ad (pro-life or pro-choice, for example)

1. Who is the sponsor?
2. Did the sponsor incorporate for the purpose of sponsoring this campaign or have an identity independent of the campaign?
3. Why sponsor this ad? How does this ad serve the sponsor's self-interest?
4. Did the sponsor pay to air or place the ad?
5. How is the idea particularized or made concrete in the ad?
6. What is the intended audience of the ad? What cues in the copy or visuals reveal the identity of this audience? What does the ad want the audience to do? to think?
7. Does this ad exist to counter other ads or unpaid coverage about opposing ideas? If so, how successful is it in accomplishing this objective?

If the Ad Advertises a Service Rather Than a Product (for example, travel on a certain airline)

1. How is the service made concrete in the ad?
2. What is the intended audience for the service? How did the ad reveal the identity of its intended audience? What techniques did the ad use to increase the audience's desire for its service? What attempts were made to convert this want into a need?

If the Ad Is a Goodwill Ad

1. Is there a problem with the image or product that the ad is trying to overcome? If so, what techniques are used to overcome the problem?
2. By what channels did the problem come to public attention?
3. Does the ad explicitly identify the problem it is trying to overcome? If so, did the ad inadvertently make you aware of a problem you were not aware of before?
4. What if anything is the relationship between the product manufactured by the sponsor and the content of this ad (such as an ecology ad sponsored by an oil company)? If the relationship is nonexistent or minimal, does the sponsor provide a rationale for the existence of the ad in the ad itself?

If the Ad Is a Political Ad

1. Is it sponsored by a committee associated with or dissociated from a candidate? By a political party?
2. Is it an attack ad or an affirming ad (attacking an opponent or supporting the candidate)?
3. Does the ad identify the party of the candidate? Why or why not?
4. Does the ad make explicit appeals to get you to register? to vote?
5. How long is the ad? Is it a "lift" taken from a longer ad? If so, what, if anything, is lost in the shorter version?
6. Is the ad consistent with unpaid coverage of the candidate? Has the ad incorporated newslike material about the candidate? Actual news footage of the candidate?

7. Did the ad appear adjacent to content with which it was compatible?
8. Did the ad employ a no-tag tag? If so, what was the tag and how effective was it? If not, what form of disclosure was employed to reveal the sponsorship of the ad?
9. What is the audience for which the ad is intended? How is the audience mirrored in the ad?

If the Ad Is a Product Ad

1. Who manufactures the product? Can you learn the identity of the manufacturer from the ad? If so, how? If not, what strategic purpose is served by the absence of an identifiable manufacturer in the ad?
2. Is the trademark for the product used in the ad? Is it central to the ad? What does the trademark tell you about the product? How is the trademark integrated into the ad?
3. What is the unique selling point in this ad?
4. What are the redundant elements in the ad? Is this redundancy productive?
5. Is the product shown in the ad? Is it focal to the ad? What is being done with or to the product in the ad? What is this attempting to tell you about the product?

Audience

1. What is the intended audience: Age? Sex? Ethnic background? Religion? Political Affiliation? Advertisers? Elites? Suppliers? Distributors?
2. Did the ad appear in a time or place likely to reach the intended audience?
3. How does the ad mirror the intended audience? Does the ad imply special knowledge about wants and needs of this audience?

Ad Content (not all points apply to PSAs)

1. What is the central claim in the ad? Is this claim believable?
2. What evidence is marshaled in support of the claim? Example? Lay testimony? Statistics? Figurative analogy? Literal analogy? Expert testimony? Does the explicit evidence in the ad warrant the claim? What associations are used to prompt inferences about the sponsor or product? What are some of these possible inferences? Are they legitimate?
3. Does the ad position the product (or service, idea, candidate) in relation to others? If so, how?
4. What specific strategies are used to personalize the product (service, idea, candidate)? to adapt the message to the audience?
5. Does the visual content of the ad support, underscore, or echo the verbal content? If not, what is the relationship between the visual and the verbal? Is it a productive relationship?
6. Is the ad trying to reach a new audience (persuade people to buy or support), or is it trying to reinforce belief in those who already own the product or support the candidate?

7. Is anyone likely to be offended by this ad? If so, on what grounds? Does the ad offend publicly accepted standards of decency or taste? If so, why was it aired or printed?

8. How does the ad create recognition, differentiation, association, participation, and repetition?

Assumptions (values presumed in the ad)

1. What assumptions about society—about progress, consumption, political participation, racial harmony, multigenerational families, and so forth—are embedded in the ad?

2. What assumptions about the role appropriate to various types of people—older people, children, women, men, African Americans, Hispanics, Native Americans—are inherent in the ad?

3. What assumptions about work or occupation—about blue-collar workers, professionals, professors, doctors, lawyers, working women as a class—are in the ad?

4. What assumptions about societal structures inhere in the ad?

   a. *Households:* What constitutes the normal family according to the ad? How many people? How many children? Number of boys? Girls? Significant others? Mrs. Olsen? Milkman? Tony the Tiger? What is their relationship to other characters in the ad? Who gives advice? Who takes advice? Who extends approval? Disapproval? What are the norms for appropriate behavior for different characters in the ad? What types of behavior can be initiated by some characters and not by others?

   b. *Medical establishment:* Is the doctor ever anything other than an authority? Are health care and healing ever separate from consumption of a product? When the physician is female, will she be found in different circumstances and in different relationships than when the physician is male? Is the female doctor ever seen treating a male patient?

   c. *Religious establishment:* If there is a rabbi, priest, or minister, what kind of a role does he or she play? How are religious symbols (or roles) used (nuns, monks, altar, candles, icon, and so forth)?

5. What assumptions are made about bodily processes—aging, euphemistic terms for parts of the body, body functions that are not identified?

6. What types of communication are legitimized in ads? What sorts of problems are revealed or concealed from other characters in ads? Are there things concealed from adults by children or from children by adults? Is duplicity sanctioned (for example, any pretext that a product made from a mix is really homemade)? Is one generation played off against another (Grandma tells Mother that if she bought the wrong thing, it is Granddaughter Susie's fault)? Does the product serve as a substitute for an expression of affection or some other form of communication? Does the ad advocate a particular type of communication—for example, preference for the telephone or writing a letter? If so, what are the special attributes of the preferred communication that are demonstrated in the ad?

7. How are politicians treated in nonpolitical ads?

Programming or Content Sponsored by an Ad

1. Is there a relationship between the content of the ad and the content of the sponsored program—for instance, an antidrug ad by a politician in an antidrug documentary or an ad for a beauty product in a women's magazine?
2. Is the content of the program potentially offensive to any organized interest group? If so, is the advertiser aware of this? If so, why is the advertiser sponsoring the program?

Content Surrounding (Contextualizing) an Ad

1. Do the programs or stories surrounding the ad provide a positive context for the ad? Do the ads surrounding this ad provide a positive context for the ad? Does the unpaid coverage of this product, idea, or candidate, if any, provide a favorable context for this ad? If not, how does the ad adapt?

Media Mix

1. How much money is being spent on purchases of advertising space and time? How many ads have been purchased? Where? When? To reach what total audience?
2. Does the ad appear in the same form in other media? What changes are made in the ad in other media? How do you account for the changes? Constraints in media? Audience adaptation?
3. Do different ads for this product appear in different media?
4. Is the ad one in a campaign? Is it related to others in a campaign? What is the relationship?
5. Why did the advertiser choose this medium? What are the advantages and disadvantages in this choice? Are there important claims about this product, idea, service, or candidate that cannot credibly be made in this medium?

Pressure on Advertiser

1. Has the advertiser or manufacturer been subject to pressure from groups that disapprove of the product or the program/content sponsored by the product's ads? Have ads or sponsorship been altered in response to this pressure?
2. Has the advertiser altered the ad in response to a consent agreement with the FTC?
3. Have the networks, stations, newspapers, or magazines in which the ad appears requested changes in the ad? Were the changes made? If so, how did the changes affect the ad's ability to convey its intended meaning?

Effect

1. Was this ad pretested? Was it altered as a result of pretesting?
2. Does evidence exist to document the effect of this ad or ad campaign on its intended audience? on an unintended audience? Was this effect positive or negative? Is the evidence of effect credible?
3. Can you construct a more effective version of this ad?

Use InfoTrac College Edition to access information on topics in this chapter from hundreds of periodicals and scholarly journals. Enter keyword and subject searches: *Federal Trade Commission, Better Business Bureau, National Association of Broadcasters.*

SELECTED READINGS

Preston, Ivan L. *The Great American Blow-Up.* Madison: University of Wisconsin Press, 1975.

U.S. Congress, Select Committee on Aging. *Hearings on Age Stereotyping and Television.* 99th Cong., 1st sess., 1977. Washington, DC: U.S. Government Printing Office.

9

How to Influence the Media

Short of running for political office or joining a congressional staff in order to change the laws, what can individuals or groups do to influence media practices? In this chapter we examine the means of persuasion available to individuals, groups, social movements, and nongovernmental organizations to change the content or form of ads or news. We assume that an individual who is aware of all the available means of influence is better able to select and skillfully employ effective means. We proceed from the simplest to the most complex, from the easiest to the most difficult, and from individual action to actions by established organizations.

INDIVIDUAL COMPLAINTS

The function of the media is to deliver an audience to advertisers, and advertisers want to persuade the audience to buy their products. Therefore, the media and advertisers cater to their audiences and spend large sums of money analyzing audience preferences. Chapter 5 considered the economic basis of the audience–media relationship; Chapters 2 to 4 on news, and Chapters 6 to 8 on advertising discussed the character of this relationship.

Until fairly recently, the relationship between audiences and the traditional media dictated that something as simple as writing a letter, sending a fax, or sending an e-mail could have an impact on a newspaper or a radio or television station. Because relatively few people contacted them, each communication to a media outlet had a disproportionate impact. Although media managers and advertisers knew that people who write letters are not typical of the entire audience, they tended to assume that each letter represented a large number of viewers or readers. As the number of letters protesting any single item, episode, or ad increased, the tendency to assume there was substantial dissatisfaction increased. When the offending medium or program had provided a mechanism for publishing or airing dissident views, a letter could also publicize one's grievance to the outlet's audience. For example, *60 Minutes* airs selected comments from viewers, as do the letters-to-the-editor columns in newspapers.

The interactivity and immediacy of the Internet have now simplified the process of expressing an opinion. Increasingly newspapers are posting the e-mail addresses of the authors of articles and columns. News outlets are scheduling online chats between readers and writers. Jonathan Dube, senior associate producer for ABC-NEWS.com, describes his interaction with readers during coverage of school shootings in Colorado:

BOX 9-1   Who Owns the Broadcast Spectrum?

Although the broadcast spectrum that television and radio broadcasts use is officially owned by the public, licensed by the federal government to radio and television stations, this would be news to most Americans. Only three in 10 Americans (29%) correctly say that the public owns the airwaves. An equal number (30%) say (incorrectly)

that the television and radio stations own the airwaves. A plurality (40%) acknowledge they do not know.

Source: "Annenberg Media Survey: Journalists and the Public, 2005," 24 May 2005.

"While covering the Littleton shooting, I answered questions from readers in two hour-long online chats, which together attracted more than 1,600 people." He adds, "This was draining but rewarding. Knowing what questions remained on readers' minds helped guide my future reporting. At the same time, I got to tell readers many of the details I had gathered that hadn't fit neatly into my stories. The chat transcripts became, in effect, another story about the shootings—one that the readers helped create."[1]

A new downloadable software tool called Third Voice Inc. (www.thirdvoice.com) makes it possible to produce what some are calling "electronic graffiti" and others are describing as a means of producing "a meta-Web composed of expert marginalia." After downloading the program, Third Voice permits users to read the annotations left on websites by other Third Voice users and to add annotations of their own. Third Voice also has a capacity to set up notes by experts. Internet lawyer David Johnson asks us to imagine the future: "Think about the possibilities that open up once you can read electronic marginalia on the Web written only by those you trust. A Federal Trade Commission expert could post warnings about false and deceptive offers. Commentators could attach their opinions to stories on a popular news site. Those quoted or described in a story could post corrections."[2]

Johnson also notes some of the complications associated with the advent of Third Voice. "What happens when obscene or harmful postings appear on a website designed for children? Will it be possible to locate the identity of a poster—and would that be a good thing? If postings can contain links to other sites, and if one company posts a comparative statement on a competitor's site (with an invitation to visit a competing store), would that constitute fair competition or unfair leveraging of the popularity of the competitor's trademark?"[3]

The era of interactivity is raising other questions as well. Some people are asking whether too much feedback from the supposed audience could reduce news outlets to panderers. Whereas focus groups were once a prime means by which editors received feedback about the interest value of specific stories, "[O]nline editors now have the ability to calculate, almost instantaneously, exactly how many readers look at each article on their site and how long they spend there. James Poniewozik, media columnist for *Salon,* wondered in a recent column whether, 'as we get better and better at giving readers exactly what they want, what will be the percentage in trying to give readers what we think they need?' "[4]

BOX 9-2   Viewers for Quality Television—How Many Letters Are Enough?

"Once upon a time viewers just sat quietly and watched," said one network executive who has been the recipient of tens of thousands of letters in the last few years and who asked, fearing more mail, that his name not be used. "Now they write. They write a lot." Dorothy Swanson, founder of the Virginia-based Viewers for Quality Television, which coordinates efforts to save television shows, commented, "They believe they can influence what's on their television set. Look at *Cagney & Lacey.*" She was referring to the first of the grass-roots campaigns to save a series. In 1984 CBS announced cancelation of the program about two women police detectives because of poor ratings. CBS received 20,000 letters over the next three months saying the program had fine writing and realistically portrayed working women; *Cagney & Lacey* was renewed.

But letters alone are not enough to return a show to the air. For instance, the ratings for *Cagney & Lacey* rose sharply during the summer between its cancelation and renewal, partly because it ran in a different time slot and partly because of publicity generated by the write-in campaign.

But Swanson and network executives say an avalanche of letters can influence a close call. In early 1987, CBS took *Designing Women,* a comedy about four partners in an Atlanta decorating firm, off the air indefinitely without actually canceling it. Harry Thomason, executive producer of the program, asked Swanson to ask the 1,500 members who receive her monthly newsletter to encourage their friends to write to CBS. The network received 50,000 letters, and *Designing Women* went on to become the highest-rated CBS comedy. It stayed on CBS through the 1992–93 season and then went into syndication. In 1994, Lifetime bought 162 episodes and exclusive rights to evening airing.[a]

"The more common these crusades become, the sooner they will kill the effect," Thomason said. "A mere 50,000 letters isn't as impressive anymore."[b]

[a]"Lifetime Acquires 162 Episodes of *Designing Women* Television Program," *Mediaweek*, 7 March 1994, p. 29.
[b]Lisa Belkin, "Viewers Pens Can Be Mightier Than the Ax," *New York Times*, 18 June 1987, p. 24Y.

As readers play a more active role in the shaping of media content, the whole notion of complaint may become obsolete at the same time as the need for audience vigilance will increase. This is because the proliferation of channels and websites is inevitable. An estimated 800 million pages existed on the Web as of summer 1999.[5] By 2006, every television station in the United States must become digital. In addition to adding hundreds of channels, this change will mean that television sets, like the computers of today, will be interactive. Lawrence Grossman, former president of NBC and PBS, prophesied, "In the digital era, amateur reporters as well as pros, 'real people' as well as certified pundits, outsiders as well as insiders, ordinary observers as well as authentic experts will be able to file their own videos and eyewitness reports to the world via Web sites and chat groups on the Internet."[6]

How will consumers know which site is trustworthy and which is not? And who is the object of complaint or suit when false material is posted on the Web? Those questions were raised in January 1999, when a story attributed to the *Montgomery County Ledger* was posted on the Web alleging that political consultant and pundit James Carville had been arrested for beating his wife, political consultant and pundit Mary Matalin. The report, which looked and read like a news story, carried the byline "Lee Canular" and the dateline "Rockville, Maryland." There is no *Montgomery County*

Ledger and no reporter named Canular. Carville and Matalin don't even live in Rockville. The story was an Internet hoax. Before it was discredited, however, it had been carried by American Family Radio to twenty-five states and had prompted thirty to thirty-five reporters from around the country to call the Rockville police station for confirmation.[7] Had the story been carried in a newspaper, Carville would have known which channels to employ to complain. Unless the perpetrator slips up and is identified, the Democratic pundit has little recourse in this case.

The structures that emerge to certify the trustworthiness of Internet information are likely to be the successors of today's networks, major papers, and magazines. The clearest evidence that structures that we trust will be institutionalized is the success of consumerreports.org, which has more subscribers—at $19 a month—than any of the other information-based websites, including *Wall Street Journal Interactive.* What accounts for its success? "*Consumer Reports'* powerful brand name is drawing online subscribers at a brisk clip even though they get pretty much the same content as print subscribers. There is almost no original content on the website, though there are message boards."[8] Even if you've saved your old issues of *Consumer Reports,* the Web is simply a more efficient way of getting the comparative information you need before making a major purchase. In other words, there will remain institutional sources of news with corresponding accountability. At the same time, the proliferation of information will heighten the need for consumers to be analytic and skeptical.

Even in this changing media world, it remains important to know to whom one should complain. One can complain directly to the advertiser. When in spring 2004 Abercrombie & Fitch attracted national publicity with its T-shirt saying "It's all relative in West Virginia" imprinted over an outline of the state, West Virginia Governor Bob Wise sent the retailer a letter urging that the put-down of his state be stopped. Because the shirt was a parody, he had little legal or regulatory recourse. By releasing his letter to the media, he established that he had stood up for his state, however.

Complaints about material appearing on network programs should be addressed to the network's audience services division in New York and to the community affairs director of the local station airing the material. This procedure pressures the people directly responsible for approving content at the network; at the same time, it magnifies the impact of the dissatisfaction by encouraging the local station, whose license depends on serving the local community, not to clear such material in the future. Because the network wants to keep its affiliates happy, expressions of dissatisfaction from local stations to the network are very persuasive.

Networks are responsible for what they air. Most of their programming and all of their advertising is internally prescreened and approved. When these internal checks work, they preempt objections. When they fail and protest is mounted by dissatisfied viewers, the existence of these checks assures the public that the network is conscientious. These checks also provide a bureaucratic structure through which complaints can be channeled. Although network news is not formally screened and approved by a separate division, any material that appears on news programs has been examined by various gatekeepers in the news bureau. Complaints about news content can be sent directly to the anchor or to the program's producer. A copy of each complaint should be sent to the president of the offending media outlet as well, to increase internal pressures for change within the system itself.

BOX 9-3   Where to Write to Comment or Complain

National Advertising Division
Council of Better Business Bureaus
845 Third Avenue
New York, NY 10022
(212) 754-1320

Federal Trade Commission
Pennsylvania Avenue at Sixth Street, NW
Washington, DC 20580
(202) 326-2180

Networks and Cable Companies
ABC
Capital Cities / ABC, Inc.
77 West 66th Street, 18th Floor
New York, NY 10023-6298
(212) 456-7777

CBS
CBS, Inc.
51 W. 52nd Street
New York, NY 10019
(212) 975-4321

NBC
General Electric Building
30 Rockefeller Plaza
New York, NY 10112
(212) 664-4444

Showtime, The Movie Channel
Showtime Networks, Inc.
1633 Broadway, 37th Floor
New York, NY 10019
(212) 708-1600

MTV, Nickelodeon, VH-1
1515 Broadway
New York, NY 10036
(212) 258-7800

Federal Communications Commission
Consumer Assistance Office
1919 M Street, NW
Washington, DC 20554
(202) 632-5050

HBO, Cinemax
1100 Avenue of the Americas
New York, NY 10036
(212) 512-1000

TBS, CNN
Turner Broadcasting System
P.O. Box 105366
Atlanta, GA 30328
(404) 827-1700

CBN
Christian Broadcasting Network
CBN Center
Virginia Beach, VA 23463
(804) 424-7777

ESPN
The Sports Network
ESPN Plaza
Bristol, CT 06010
(203) 585-2000

PBS
Corporation for Public Broadcasting
901 E Street, NW
Washington, DC 20004-2037
(202) 879-9702

Communication from an individual can also trigger industry-sponsored self-regulatory mechanisms. As we have indicated, self-regulatory agencies such as the National Advertising Division of the Better Business Bureau monitor advertising and initiate action against ads that seem deceptive. Similarly, readers' advocates for individual newspapers and the National News Council arbitrate complaints from dissatisfied readers and viewers. These individuals and organizations give the individual consumer the ability to initiate the investigation of a deceptive ad or an unfair news item.

An individual communication can also spur action by government regulatory agencies such as the Federal Trade Commission (FTC) and the Federal Communications Commission (FCC). The FTC monitors ads, calling for proof of questionable claims, and initiates formal proceedings against ads that seem deceptive. The FCC superintends the use of the airwaves.

An effective complaint presupposes a knowledge of the standards the self-regulatory agency or regulatory agency applies, an understanding of the sorts of complaints it is authorized to handle, and a comprehension of the avenues of redress it can exercise if a complaint is credible. In making a complaint, the audience member must clearly specify the time, location, date, and character of the offensive item.

In addition, a complaint should indicate either that the item violates the standards of the agency or that the standards ought to be broadened to include items of this nature. Three lines of argument are particularly effective when justifying a complaint: (1) the item or ad is inaccurate or deceptive; (2) the item or ad violates community standards or tastes; or (3) the news item is unbalanced or the ad is unfair (for example, it exploits negative stereotypes or capitalizes on the gullibility of children).

GROUP PRESSURE

What can a consumer do if the regulatory and self-regulatory mechanisms dismiss the complaint? If regulators and self regulators dismiss the consumer's complaint, the consumer's recourse is entering the public domain to try to persuade the legislature to change the regulatory rules. The consumer can also organize a boycott.

Boycotts

Because the relationships among the consumer, the advertiser, and the media outlet are economic ones, the consumer can threaten a boycott of the advertised product or the sponsored program or both if the desired change does not take place. To make this threat credible, the consumer must be able to marshal a large number of like-minded people willing to carry out the boycott. As you will see, the threat of a boycott often eliminates the need for an actual boycott.

Advertisers want to avoid boycotts for a number of reasons. First, negative publicity in the news is more believable than advertising and functions as negative advertising. In addition, if an advertising agency produces an ad that triggers a boycott, then it will lose the client's business—especially if sales begin to drop off or if the boycott seems so well organized and widespread that it will create negative associations in the public's mind with the manufacturer's other products. Consequently, the advertising agency is uniquely susceptible to pressure to change offensive ads. Groups of consumers can put pressure on the ad agency that produced the ad, the mass media outlet that carried the ad, or the manufacturer that produced the advertised product.

BOX 9-4   FCC Increases Fines

"The Federal Communications Commission has become more aggressive in fining broadcasters for showing too much flesh or allowing coarse language. Proposals to raise the penalties dramatically—as high as $500,000 per incident or $3 million per day—have majority support in Congress. Enforcement has become so erratic that 66 ABC stations were afraid to show the highly acclaimed war movie *Saving Private Ryan* because of its unsanitized battlefield dialogue. PBS stations even edited out the image of a nude lithograph from an episode of *Antiques Roadshow*." [a]

[a]"Cable Doesn't Need a Nanny," *USA Today*, 29 April 2005, p. 22A.

BOX 9-5   Canceled Subscriptions

What are the effects on the news outlet? Conservative talk radio hosts encouraged listeners to cancel their subscriptions when on the Thursday before the October 7, 2003, California gubernatorial recall, the *Los Angeles Times* carried an investigative report, headlined "Women Say Schwarzenegger Groped, Humiliated Them," that included interviews with six women who reported that they had been groped by Republican contender and actor Arnold Schwarzenegger. The story reported, "Six women who came into contact with Arnold Schwarzenegger on movie sets, in studio offices and in other settings over the last three decades say he touched them in a sexual manner without their consent." [a] More than a thousand canceled their subscriptions.

What are the effects on the organization? In late 2003 the AARP endorsed the Republican-championed prescription drug benefit plan that partially privatized the system and banned the import of low-cost medicine from Canada. Angry Democrats argued that the nation's largest organization representing seniors had sold out. Sixty thousand canceled their memberships. [b]

AARP responded with a print and television ad campaign: "What the new prescription drug benefit will do for you. No sound bites. No spin. No politics. Just the facts. Congress has just voted to add a prescription drug benefit to Medicare. While the benefit isn't perfect, it's an important step forward that we can build on in the future. . . . And we promise to keep fighting to make your prescription drugs more affordable."

[a]Gary Cohn, Carla Hall, and Robert W. Welkos, "Women Say Schwarzenegger Groped, Humiliated Them," *Los Angeles Times* 2 October 2003, p. 1.
[b]Bob Baker, "The Magazine That Won't Act Its Age," *Washington Post*, 11 April 2004, p. D6.

Similarly, groups can marshal members of the community to cancel subscriptions to an offending newspaper or turn off an offending news program. If this tactic works and the size of the audience declines, the media outlet's profits are threatened; it can no longer deliver the desired audience to the advertisers. Groups also can exert indirect

---

CASE STUDY 9-1 *Phil Sokolof v. McDonald's*

In 1966 Phil Sokolof had a heart attack. He was not overweight and considered himself physically fit. How had it happened? he wondered. The culprit turned out to be cholesterol. Sokolof vowed to wage a campaign against the cholesterol we ingest unmindful of its presence.

Sokolof had one asset the ordinary citizen lacks. As a building materials manufacturer, he had become a millionaire. By mid-1990, he had sunk $2.5 million of his own money into his campaign for change. In the process, he founded a group called the National Heart Savers Association.

In October 1988, Sokolof took out newspaper ads in more than a dozen daily newspapers indicting companies that created foods by using tropical vegetable oils such as palm oil and coconut oil, which are rich in *trans* fats, or monounsaturates. His targets included such corporate giants as Sunshine Biscuits, Quaker Oats, Nabisco Brands, Procter & Gamble, Keebler, Borden, General Foods, and Pepperidge Farms.

Media coverage followed. Public pressure mounted. Eleven of the companies substituted other oils for tropical oil. One company, Nabisco, held out. Sokolof turned his attention to that corporation in his second series of "Poisoning of America" ads. In June 1990, Nabisco too gave in.

By April 1990, Sokolof had settled on another target: the high-fat content of fast foods. His focus: McDonald's, the nation's leading fast-food marketer. His third phase of ads addressed McDonald's directly: "McDonald's, your hamburgers have too much fat!" The ads called on fast-food chains to lower the fat content of their hamburgers by 10 percent and urged readers, "If you agree, write or call now!" The ads listed McDonald's address and phone number.

Again he bought ads in the nation's major newspapers, including the *Wall Street Journal* and the *New York Times.* But $500,000 of his budget went unspent when the *Los Angeles Times,* the *Baltimore Sun,* and the *Chicago Sun-Times* rejected the ads. Because newspapers are privately owned, they may reject any ads they want. Presumably, these papers did not want to risk the wrath of one of the nation's larger advertisers.

By 1991, McDonald's was testing cooking french fries only in vegetable oil and noting that it had added bran muffins and low-fat yogurt and shakes to its menu.

In the course of his campaign, Sokolof's message was magnified by appearances on the major morning talk shows, the news, and in stories in the nation's newspapers. He explained his success this way, "I got the message to the people, and the people got the message to the food companies."[a]

[a]Judann Dagnoli, "Sokolof Keeps Thumping Away at Food Giants," *Advertising Age,* 9 April 1990, pp. 3, 63.

---

economic pressure by persuading advertisers not to buy space or time from the offending media.

The power of the threat of a boycott was illustrated dramatically in fall 2003 when news reports forecast that a forthcoming CBS made-for-television film would characterize former president Ronald Reagan as believing that those who died of AIDS were being punished for violating God's law and would focus on his wife's use of astrologers to set the date for national events at which he would appear. Prompted by calls from conservative talk radio and television hosts, 80,000 angry potential members of the CBS audience flooded the network with e-mail. The car and soft drink companies set to sponsor also were targeted for boycott. Rather than air *The Reagans* on CBS, the network shifted the program to Showtime, a pay-per-view cable outlet owned by the same company.

McDonald's,
Your Hamburgers Still
Have Too Much Fat!
and Your French Fries
Still are Cooked with Beef Tallow*

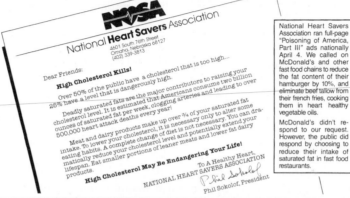

NHSA

National **Heart Savers** Association

4601 South 76th Street
Omaha, Nebraska 68127
(402) 339-3813

Dear Friends:

High Cholesterol Kills!

Over 50% of the public have a cholesterol that is too high...
25% have a level that is dangerously high.

Deadly saturated fats are the major contributors to raising your
cholesterol level. It is estimated that Americans consume two billion
ounces of saturated fat per week, clogging arteries and leading to over
500,000 heart attack deaths every year!

Meat and dairy products make up over ¾ of your saturated fat
intake. To lower your cholesterol, it is necessary only to alter some
eating habits. A complete change of diet is not necessary. You can dramatically reduce your cholesterol level and potentially extend your
lifespan. Eat smaller portions of leaner meats and lower fat dairy
products.

High Cholesterol May Be Endangering Your Life!

To A Healthy Heart,
NATIONAL HEART SAVERS ASSOCIATION

Phil Sokolof

Phil Sokolof, President

National Heart Savers Association ran full-page "Poisoning of America, Part III" ads nationally April 4. We called on McDonald's and other fast food chains to reduce the fat content of their hamburger by 10%, and eliminate beef tallow from their french fries, cooking them in heart healthy vegetable oils.

McDonald's didn't respond to our request. However, the public did respond by choosing to reduce their intake of saturated fat in fast food restaurants.

**A May Gallup Poll was commissioned by Advertising Age magazine.
It measured the impact of our Poisoning of America, Part III "McDonalds, Your Hamburgers
Have Too Much Fat!" ad, and other cholesterol awareness efforts.**
TWO QUESTIONS ASKED WERE:

In the last month, have you read, seen, or heard any claims that a fast-food hamburger restaurant cooks its products in animal fat, which has an impact on the cholesterol level of users of its products?

31% of adult Americans — 57 million people — responded YES.

Those who had responded yes were asked: Have these claims caused you to increase or decrease your usage of fast-food hamburger restaurants in general?

38% of those Americans — 21 million people — responded YES, they had decreased their usage.

Hamburger Fat

Our original ad stated that McDonald's hamburger contains 21.5% fat, precooked.

McDonald's claims their hamburger has 19.5% fat, precooked. Laboratory tests conducted for the New York Times after our ad ran showed McDonald's hamburger ranged from 20.28% to 22.50% fat, after cooking.

As the industry leader, Hardee's has introduced a new hamburger, The Lean 1, with 17.5% fat, precooked.

**McDonald's
Burger King
Wendy's
French Fries**

**All Cooked
With
Beef Tallow!**

Beef Tallow in French Fries

McDonald's, Burger King and Wendy's still cook their french fries with beef tallow!

Hardee's is the only big 4 hamburger chain to cook its french fries in heart healthy vegetable oils.

THIS ADVERTISEMENT IS A PUBLIC SERVICE OF NATIONAL HEART SAVERS ASSOCIATION.

*Both references are applicable to Burger King and Wendy's.

Courtesy of National Heart Savers Association.

BOX 9-6   National Association of Talk Show Hosts

Taxpayer Action Day was organized by the Council for Citizens Against Government Waste, a Washington lobby that claims 400,000 members.

The National Association of Talk Show Hosts mailed out flyers about the protest to 300 of its members. Some of them supported the protest on the air, such as Bob Grant, the host of *The Bob Grant Show* on WABC radio, New York City, which Arbitron says has 126,000 listeners, and Mary Beal, host of *The Morning Magazine* on WNSS, Wichita, with about 50,000 listeners.

Their reasons for supporting the protest are not entirely public spirited. Neil Myers, a host of NBC's Talknet shows, said, "Some of these people are in a numbers game. They are looking to grab headlines. . . . The campaign against giving Congress a raise was a perfect marriage between pub-

lic interest and the dramatization of hosts. It got covered in *Time* and *U.S. News & World Report* and seemed to galvanize everyone."

Talk-show–driven protests can be effective. A talk station, FM New Jersey 101.5, coalesced voter resentment against Jim Florio, the governor of New Jersey, because of a record tax increase that he pushed through the legislature in 1990. That protest generated 800,000 signatures on a petition seeking to provide a mechanism for recall of public officials and legislation by initiative and referendum.[a]

[a]Wayne King, "Tax Protest, Fueled by Talk Shows, Is Getting Steamed Voters Organized," *New York Times*, 26 October 1990, p. A12.

Legal Actions

Our ability to influence the media through legal action is constrained by the laws governing the agencies we seek to influence. Before 1966, only people who had a clear economic stake in a case could intervene in the FCC licensing of a station. This changed with a challenge to the renewal of the license of WLBT, a Jackson, Mississippi, television station. In this case, the court ruled that "civic associations, professional societies, unions, churches, and educational institutions or associations" may contest an application for a station's renewal of license. This decision gave such groups legal standing on the grounds that "the holders of broadcasting licenses [must] be responsive to the needs of the audience."[9]

Notice that not all individuals or groups have legal standing. To have legal standing, an individual must be a member of a group that represents a substantial portion of viewers or listeners and has a legitimate and genuine interest in the station's performance in the community. The challengers in the 1966 case, the Office of Communication of the United Church of Christ, argued that although the city of Jackson was 45 percent African American, the station was not sensitive to matters of concern to the African American population.

In response to this decision, a number of groups representing the interests of special segments of the audience focused their attention on the license renewal process. These included not only the pioneering Office of Communication of the United Church of Christ but also the National Association for the Advancement of Colored People (NAACP) Legal Defense Fund in New York, which seeks to increase minority involvement; Action for Children's Television in Newton Center, Massachusetts; and the Mexican American Legal Defense and Educational Fund in San Francisco.

BOX 9-7 Controlling Controversy

Networks appreciate controversy for its ability to attract viewers, but they like it best when the controversy is uncontroversial. When the system works, according to Kathryn C. Montgomery, an assistant professor of film and television at UCLA and author of *Target: Prime Time*, political and social issues are shaped "to conform to the institutional demands of network television. Important societal conflicts are extracted from the public sphere and injected into entertainment programs, where they are reduced to problems for individual characters." The result: "Controversial issues are consistently and carefully balanced within each program so that one clear argument cannot be discerned."[a]

But in spring 1989, in response to letters from angry television viewers, such major advertisers as Coca-Cola, McDonald's, Chrysler, General Mills, Campbell Soup, Ralston-Purina, and Sears canceled commercials on television programs because of material cited as offensive in viewer complaints. Typical of such grassroots protests was a campaign by Terry Rakolta of Michigan, who charged that the Fox Network series *Married . . . with Children* was offensively vulgar and shown at a time when children easily could watch it.

A number of factors contributed to a climate encouraging grassroots protest. Under economic pressure, all three networks cut back staff in their standards and practices divisions; the Hollywood writers' strike of spring 1989 shortened the time between program production and broadcasting, increasing the chances that potentially offensive material would air; technological improvements allowed viewers to tape broadcasts of offensive programming and cite specifics they found objectionable; and concern heightened about the vulnerability of U.S. children to violence and drugs.

Montgomery argues that corporate takeovers of all three networks in the preceding 5-year-period created a climate in which a new protest movement could flourish: "The reason the standards and practices divisions were working in the first place is because they were actively managing the advocacy groups. Then the ownership changed, the staffs were cut back, and all that institutional memory was lost. Of course, the advertisers have that institutional memory."[b]

[a]Walter Goodman, "How the Viewers Work Their Will on Commercial TV," *New York Times*, 24 April 1989, p. 18.
[b]Bill Carter, "Sponsors Heed Viewers Who Find Shows Too Racy," *New York Times*, 24 April 1989, p. 14.

Such groups are able to produce change not just by actual transfer of licenses but also by threatening to intervene in the licensing process if change does not occur. For example, in 1969, an African American coalition reached an agreement with KTAL-TV in Texarkana, Texas, under which news coverage, programming, and employment practices were altered. In return, the coalition withdrew its petition to deny the renewal of the station's license.

Group legal action also has produced important changes in advertising. A group of law students calling itself SOUP (Students Opposing Unfair Practices) deserves credit for paving the way for the FTC's use of corrective advertising. In 1969, the students tried to intervene in the FTC case against Campbell Soup. Campbell's advertisers had placed marbles in the bottom of soup bowls to accentuate the solid ingredients in the soup. The students argued that a consent order that would stop the practice was insufficient to remedy the impression created by the false ads. The students proposed corrective advertising instead.

Although the FTC did not impose corrective advertising to resolve the case, it did acknowledge that it had the right to do so if a case warranted such action. The impact of SOUP testifies to the power of groups that understand the regulatory process. SOUP's understanding of this process enabled it, a group otherwise powerless and underfinanced, to bring about a major change in advertising.

Group action often is more effective than individual action, but group action generally requires specialized legal expertise and the resources to support it. Groups with these advantages are better able to establish that they have standing before the FCC. In the case of the FTC, where standing is not a prerequisite for consideration of a complaint, individual action is possible. But even here the ability of a group to establish that it represents substantial sentiment in the community is more compelling than a comparable claim by an individual person.

Group legal action is not effective in influencing the press except in the area of advertising. The press is not licensed and has important First Amendment protections from government interference. Nongovernmental legal action against the print media is limited almost entirely to the enforcement of the libel laws. In extreme cases, such as the suit brought by Carol Burnett against the *National Enquirer,* this avenue can be very effective; the financial judgment against the tabloid in this case was large. The *National Enquirer* also lost a lawsuit filed by actor Clint Eastwood over a supposed "exclusive interview" with Eastwood that the court concluded had never taken place.

To the consternation of some, ABC News in 1995 agreed to an out-of-court settlement with Philip Morris and R.J. Reynolds in response to lawsuits brought by the tobacco companies over allegations made on ABC's *Day One* that cigarettes were "spiked" with added nicotine in the manufacturing process. In what the *New York Times* called "an extraordinary act of contrition," ABC News agreed to apologize twice during prime time as well as to pay legal expenses, estimated to be near $3 million. Said ABC senior vice president Patricia J. Matson, "There was a mistake. We corrected it."[10] The role of legal action in influencing the news is discussed in Chapter 4.

Those bringing action against a business or government make themselves vulnerable to the possibility of libel suits, however. In Suffolk County, New York, in 1986, several individuals and civic organizations ran an ad in a local paper objecting to the plans of a real estate developer. They also produced a leaflet and a flier telling citizens to attend a hearing at the town meeting. When the town board rejected the developer's plans, the real estate concern brought suit against nine civic organizations and sixteen individuals. University of Denver law professor George Pring notes that such suits are not usually brought with the aim of winning damages. Rather, they are intended to deter such actions in the future.[11]

Promoting Self-Regulation

Groups that understand the relationship between government and industry can also effect change by exploiting industry's desire to avoid government regulation. As we have noted, increased self-regulation of the broadcasting and the advertising industries is often prompted by industry fear of government regulation. By arousing industry fears that the government is about to regulate some facet of their operations, viewers or readers can prod industry to adopt its own preemptive regulations.

For example, the now defunct NAB Television Code allowed as much as 16 minutes of commercials per hour during children's Saturday morning programming, but permitted only 9.5 minutes during prime time. The Massachusetts-based organization Action for Children's Television (ACT) charged that this difference unfairly exploited children. The FCC responded to this charge by hinting broadly that if broadcasters did not limit the amount of children's advertising, the FCC would. Subsequently, the code was amended to set a ceiling of 9.5 minutes per hour on the commercials in children's shows.

Industry is aware of the power of self-regulation to forestall government regulation. Had the broadcasting or advertising industry regulated cigarette advertising, it might have been spared the anticigarette commercials and ultimately the ban on cigarette advertising on television. In 1971, the FCC cited the existence of the newly created National Advertising Review Board to justify dismissing arguments by TUBE (Termination of Unfair Broadcasting Exercises) for establishing an FCC Code of Advertising Standards for Television Advertising and an Advertising Advisory Board.[12]

As we re-write this chapter for this sixth edition, seventy consumer advocacy groups, including the National Consumers League and the Center for Science in the Public Interest, are seeing the first voluntary responses to their campaign to require producers of alcoholic beverages to follow the practice in place for packaged goods and to list the servings in each bottle, the calories per serving, the suggested serving size, the alcohol level, and the ingredients in the product. The coalition petitioned the U.S. Department of the Treasury to mandate that the group that regulates alcohol and tobacco require the labels.

In mid December 2003, Diageo, the maker of the brands Johnnie Walker, Guinness, and Smirnoff, indicated that it was willing voluntarily to list the quantity of alcohol, the calories, and the carbs in each bottle. The director of the alcohol practices project of the Center for Science in the Public Interest, George A. Hacker, responded, "Diageo's insistence on voluntary labeling approaches is not responsive. It doesn't provide the standardization and consistency that is required for consumers to actually compare Brand A to Brand B as well as liquor with beer, unless of course all producers provide the same kind of information voluntarily in the same format." Hacker's answer tells the industry how it can forestall regulation with voluntary compliance.[13]

As the low-carb Atkins and South Beach diets have risen in popularity, so too has the interest of the liquor industry in marketing low-carb drinks. One reason that Diageo may have announced a willingness voluntarily to label its products is that consumers overestimate the carbs in Guinness. With 10 grams of carbs and 125 calories in a 12-ounce drink, Guinness is lower in carbs than beers such as Budweiser and Coors. "The low-carb, high protein dieting trend should be terrific news for liquor makers," notes an article in the *Wall Street Journal*. "Rum, vodka, gin, whisky and tequila contain no carbs or fat at all, and never have. Still, 63% of consumers incorrectly believe wine and beer are lower in carbs than spirits, according to a study by Ipsos Public Affairs."[14] Diageo may see labeling as a way to increase the power of a unique selling proposition for Guinness.

Meanwhile the Alcohol, Tobacco, Tax and Trade Bureau of the U.S. Treasury weighed in with April 2004 with a ruling that a 12-ounce beer with under 7 grams of carbs could call itself low carb. By this standard most light beer is low carb. Miller Lite, for example, has 3.2 grams of carbs per 12 ounces, Bud Light has 6.6.[15]

BOX 9-8   The Process of Voluntary Compliance

In December 2003, the FTC put out an 18-page guide to help media outlets identify and reject false ads for weight-loss plans and diet pills. The guide focused on promises of weight loss without exercise or dieting and pledges that products would block the absorption of calories. Note how voluntary compliance forestalled legal action. The *New York Times* reports, "The guide has been under consideration for more than a year, as regulators evaluated how to enlist the support of media outlets in curtailing consumer spending on worth-less products. At issue was whether the government should look for voluntary cooperation from these outlets or threaten to sue if they run ads the commission deemed clearly false. . . . The decision to issue the guidelines came after several media companies voluntarily adopted policies to further screen the claims in weight-loss ads, which led to a recent decline in the amount of false advertising."[a]

[a]"FTC Offers Guide to Weight-Loss Ads," *New York Times,* 10 December 2003, p. C8.

PRESSURE FROM AN ESTABLISHED ORGANIZATION

Individuals may persuade advertisers and manufacturers that a sizable part of the audience opposes an ad or news practice by protesting through a respected, legitimate group recognized by the public, the media, and advertisers. The arguments of such an established organization will be widely aired and readily accepted even by people not affiliated with the organization.

The Parent Teacher Association (PTA) is one example. When the PTA takes a stand on advertising, particularly if the stand pertains to children's advertising or to the effects of ads on children, that stand is likely to bring about the desired change. The PTA is newsworthy under the criteria described in Chapter 2. It has a track record of being newsworthy and is perceived as speaking for a substantial segment of the news outlet's audience—parents, teachers, taxpayers, children, and other people interested in education.

In August 1976, the national PTA placed television programming on probation for the amount of violence shown and announced a national effort to monitor televised violence. If the level of violence did not decline significantly, the PTA indicated, it would consider sponsoring a boycott of those products advertised in the violent programs. Kodak, General Foods, General Motors, and Sears were among the companies that announced their support for the efforts to reduce violence in programming. This announcement piggybacked on the newsworthy PTA statement and garnered favorable national publicity for these manufacturers. By the end of 1977, a number of "violent" shows had been canceled "in a major concession to anti-violence crusaders."[16] Here it was not an actual boycott of products, but the threat of a boycott by a nationally respected organization, that produced results. In 1978, the PTA expanded its monitoring to include "offensively portrayed sexuality."

A group will be less effective if its economic self-interest is obvious to the audience. Although the PTA has a self-interest in the quality of education, changes in programming or advertising produce no direct economic benefit to its members. By contrast, efforts by ExxonMobil Oil Company to alter broadcast and print stereotypes of Arab

---

BOX 9-9   It's Not What You Know But Who You Know

Organized letter-writing campaigns are discounted by the journalists, but letters from officers of major national organizations are taken into account and are apt to be answered by an executive. If sent to a magazine, they may be published in the letters section.

Interest-group pressure appears to be effective when it obtains political support, in Congress or elsewhere; when it threatens advertisers and local television stations; and when it is persuasive to the journalists. However, pressure from powerless groups is ignored.[a]

[a]Herbert Gans, *Deciding What's News* (New York: Vintage Books, 1980), p. 265.

---

sheiks and efforts by the Tobacco Institute to alter the way the media cover the dangerous effects of smoking have been less effective, because their economic self-interest is apparent.

Financial resources are critical if a group plans to use paid channels (advertising) to influence unpaid channels (news coverage). When, for example, the Tobacco Institute took out ads reprinting news items that, in its judgment, were underplayed in the print press and placed them in elite media such as the *Columbia Journalism Review,* it was attempting to influence media decision makers directly by arguing that journalists had violated their own norms of balance and fair play. When such ads appear in the popular press, they suggest the audience should be more critical in its consumption of news items on such an issue. This strategic use of paid media is not available to resource-poor groups.

Resource-poor groups can gain media attention and with it adverse publicity for products or advertisers if they understand news norms well enough to make their protest newsworthy. For example, the Raging Grannies is an international group begun in Canada in the late 1980s as a pro-environment, antinuclear group. In December 2003, the *Palo Alto Daily News* carried the headline "Grannies Targeting Wal-Mart." The article noted that "Holiday shoppers at Mountain View's Wal-Mart today may be met with more than bargains, they'll be meeting the Peninsula Raging Grannies. The group of women, and some men, from Redwood City south to San Jose will be protesting violent toys for sale." Why Wal-Mart? Because, says a Palo Alto granny, "This is not a small mom-and-pop. This is global." Not only does the article specify that Wal-Mart sells the objectionable toys but it adds that the group has also protested outside Toys R Us in Redwood City. "If Hasbro was here, we'd be in front of them," says the Palo Alto granny. The article then notes "Hasbro is the Rhode Island-based toy giant that makes G.I. Joe military figures and Zoids Gun Sniper, among other things." [17]

The Peninsula Raging Grannies made news because their self-identification as "Peninsula Raging Grannies" invites attention. (We know that the author of the article took the label seriously, because she noted that men were part of the protest.) "Grannies" says that they are older (hence older protecting younger) and that they have grandchildren (hence a special interest in protecting the young). "Raging" defies the stereotypes of those who are grannies. Grannies is an edgy concept. Raging Grandmothers doesn't work as well. "Raging" invites us to ask, "What are they raging about?" or "What prompts their rage?"

The Raging Grannies used stock news themes well. The group added to its newsworthiness by providing a local angle on an international protest. All were from the peninsula and some, including the woman quoted, were from Palo Alto, and as such part of the audience for the Palo Alto paper. Grannies fighting to protect kids from large corporations is an appealing narrative. When the clipping services for Hasbro, Toys R Us, and Wal-Mart spot the article and transmit it to those in headquarters, the grannies will have reached one intended audience. When readers who have not seen the actual protest read the article, the grannies will have discouraged them from buying these toys and will have suggested that the corporations selling them are doing something inappropriate.[18]

The ways in which the fact of self-regulation can be used to respond to pressure from an established organization were illustrated when the American Psychological Association argued in February 2003 that television ads targeting children younger than 9 should either be banned or regulated. Of concern was evidence that young children don't understand that ads are designed to sell amid worries that children's characters selling junk food could be contributing to what some consider an epidemic of obesity among school age children. The response from advertisers? "A review panel of the Better Business Bureaus ensures responsible advertising to children through voluntary guidelines," says Dick O'Brien, head of the Washington office of the American Association of Advertising Agencies."[19]

PRESSURE FROM A SOCIAL MOVEMENT

Social movements are more loosely organized than groups such as the PTA. In their early stages, social movements lack the structure to distribute information efficiently; they often lack identified leaders whose opinions are accepted by the media as representative of the opinions of the movement as a whole.

Social movements seek to produce specific changes in society. They also attempt to create awareness of issues, generate audience identification with their cause, and have their leaders recognized as spokespeople for larger constituencies not formally identified with the movement. Social movements need to capitalize on journalistic norms and routines to accomplish these objectives. Ideally, they become part of someone's beat, their leaders are perceived as newsworthy by the media, their concerns become ongoing news themes, and their spokespeople are quoted on controversial issues affecting their constituencies.

As we indicated in our discussion of stereotyping in Chapter 6, the media are powerful purveyors of societal attitudes. African Americans and women, aware of this power of the media, have sought to increase their representation among newspeople. The civil rights and women's rights movements assume that female and African American reporters are more sensitive to sexism and racism and that their presence is a symbolic statement of support for these movements.

Changing the portrayal of women and minorities is also seen as a means of altering societal attitudes about these groups. In summer 1999, the NAACP and a coalition of Latino groups attracted widespread media attention with the complaint that the six broadcast networks were offering a fall 1999 season largely without African American

---

BOX 9-10   Neighbor to Neighbor versus Procter & Gamble

Neighbor to Neighbor is a citizen group organized to change the U.S. policy toward El Salvador. In 1989, the group began to focus its attention on coffee producers who use Salvadoran coffee beans.

Neighbor to Neighbor created an ad indicting Procter & Gamble for brewing "misery and death." Narrated by actor Ed Asner, the ad showed an overturned coffee mug spilling blood instead of coffee. Twenty-five stations in New Orleans, Kansas City (Missouri), Cincinnati, and New York rejected the ad. When the CBS affiliate in Boston aired the ad, Procter & Gamble responded by pulling $1 million in commercials from the station.

Neighbor to Neighbor countered by picketing N. W. Ayer, the advertising agency that holds the Procter & Gamble account. "Ayer, there's blood on your hands," read the picket signs.

Although most U.S. coffees use Salvadoran beans, the ad campaign targeted Folgers because it is the country's best seller. Neighbor to Neighbor next planned to picket stores that carry the coffee. By May 1990, the boycott begun in November had yielded minimal results. Stores in some college towns had dropped the brand. Red Apple markets in Manhattan agreed that it would not provide Folgers with end-of-the-aisle displays and would not feature Folgers in its ads.

"Boycotts are 'economic blackmail,'" says a Procter & Gamble spokesperson. "We can't buy time in New York because of the chilling effect of P & G and Ayer's action," said a Neighbor to Neighbor leader.[a]

[a]Judann Dagnoli and Lauri Freeman, "Coffee Boycott Boils," *Advertising Age*, 21 May 1990, p. 6.

---

or Latino actors. The evidence? Media critic Jonathan Storm noted, "Of the 38 new shows . . . only one-fourth feature even one African American character in a major role; half of those shows are on one network, UPN. The pilots of only three new shows had Latino characters: a police officer, an emergency medical technician, and a street-punk bully." The protest was effective. Five of the six networks responded by adding actors of color to the casts of prime-time shows.[20]

The NAACP followed up with the promise that it would issue a diversity report card on the cable industry.[21] If the results indicated a pervasive problem, Kweisi Mfume, then the head of the NAACP, did not rule out the possibility of a boycott. In January 2000 the NAACP and NBC agreed that the network had removed the threat of a boycott by promising to increase the number of minorities writing, producing, and directing its shows. ABC followed suit. As of January 10, 2000, deals with CBS and Fox were in the offing as well.

The potential impact of movements is seen in the dramatic changes in advertising that occurred as a result of the pressure of the women's rights movement, pressure that triggered industry self-regulation. The National Advertising Review Board, an industry-based board set up to monitor truth and accuracy in advertising, issued a report titled *Advertising and Women* in 1975. That report acknowledged that "the more vocal critics of advertising as 'sexist' are younger, better educated, more articulate women who often are opinion leaders. On the average, they have more discretionary income. As their numbers increase (with increasing educational and job opportunities), their challenge to advertising will probably become greater, unless constructive action is taken."[22]

Political pressure and economic self-interest allied to produce ads in which women no longer appeared simply as housewives and mothers but also in their roles in business, the professional world, and community affairs. The board offered a checklist of principles to be used by advertisers to determine whether their ads treated women in an appropriate fashion.

The power of respected institutions such as the PTA as well as large social movements such as the women's rights movement resides in their ability to speak for a large number of consumers who might be persuaded to boycott products or programming if the demands of the movement or institution are not met.

CREATING LEGISLATIVE PRESSURE

Legislative pressure can be exerted at both the state and federal level. Each level has different regulatory capacities.

State Level

Both the state and federal governments exercise considerable control over commerce, including advertising. Action by state governments often precedes federal action and, ironically, creates an incentive for industry to acquiesce to federal legislation. One instance occurred in July 1965, when Governor Nelson Rockefeller signed an act requiring a health warning on all cigarette packages sold in New York State. "If there was anything the cigarette companies wanted less than federal regulation," explains A. Lee Fritschler in *Smoking and Politics,* "it was state requirements that health warnings appear. This could have meant as many different labels as there are states, creating an obvious marketing problem."[23]

Federal Level

Congress can exercise enormous power over the government regulatory agencies, which were created by and can be modified by congressional legislation, are funded by congressional appropriations, and are overseen by congressional committees. In addition, high-level government appointments, including appointments of FCC commissioners, must be confirmed by the U.S. Senate.

Actual congressional action is not always necessary to produce change in the media. For example, on February 3, 1971, the FTC asked Congress to require that all print advertising for cigarettes carry a health warning. On April 15, seven of the nine largest cigarette companies began voluntarily including health warnings in all print ads.[24]

When Congress is affronted by the actions of a regulatory agency, however, it is capable of strong action. In the mid-1960s, for example, without consulting key members of Congress, the FTC bowed to pressure from anticigarette forces and issued a notice of rule making, requiring a health warning on all packages of cigarettes and in all cigarette advertising. Both houses of Congress held hearings on the FTC action. The resulting legislation removed the FTC's rule-making powers concerning cigarette advertising and negated the FTC rule.[25] In October 1995, R.J. Reynolds removed Joe Camel—the controversial cartoon icon—from billboards in response to pressure from those opposing advertising tobacco products to children.[26]

The interplay among the public, Congress, and the regulatory agencies was well illustrated when in April 2004 the FCC levied a $495,000 fine against Clear Channel Communication for an April 9, 2003, Howard Stern radio show that included three "indecency violations." Under federal law, graphic discussion of sexual or excretory activities cannot take place on the airwaves during the hours that children are most likely to be in the audience, from 6 A.M. to 10 P.M. Clear Channel responded by dropping the show from its six stations that had carried it. This wasn't Clear Channel's first run-in with the FCC over indecency. In January 2004, the company had paid three quarters of a $1-million fine over indecency in a show by Todd "Bubba the Love Sponge" Clem. After paying the fine, it canceled that show as well. Reasons for the firings included the cost of the fines and the prospect that neither Stern nor Clem would clean up their acts. In addition, Congress had put stations on notice that it was serious about indecency on air. Pending congressional legislation would revoke a station's license if, during the eight years of a license, the indecency rules were violated three times. In October 2004, shock-jock Howard Stern indicated that at the end of 2004 he would move from Infinity Broadcast to Sirius Satellite Radio. Sirius is commercial-free subscription radio that in late 2004 had approximately 600,000 subscribers and charged $12.95 a month.[27]

TO SUM UP

This brief consumer's guide to influencing the mass media describes how otherwise powerless individuals or groups can exploit the complex relationships among government, industry, and audience to influence advertising and news coverage. In some cases individual action is effective; in others, group action is necessary. Established organizations have a distinct advantage over social movements; resource-poor groups also operate at a significant disadvantage.

An understanding of journalistic norms and routines, regulatory and self-regulatory procedures, and the legal process enhances the likelihood that a rhetorically sophisticated but resource-poor group will succeed. In those instances when change can occur only through legislation, individuals may be forced to gain influence as members of congressional staffs or to run for office. Groups can support candidates for public office sympathetic to their points of view. Therefore, in the following chapters, we focus on the use of media to elect politicians.

ANALYSIS: CONSTRUCTING A STRATEGY FOR MESSAGE DISTRIBUTION

In Chapter 4 we spoke of the principles and processes involved in influencing news media. In the last chapter we noted avenues consumers can use to effect change in media practices. Here we combine the principles of these chapters in a checklist of steps useful in creating strategies to influence the media.

Following is an outline of steps in constructing a strategy for distributing a message through the mass media. These steps are appropriate for individuals, citizen groups, news managers, and political consultants.

Step 1: Isolating the Message

Distill the essential message to be communicated from the ocean of information, and draw together essential support material (forceful, dramatic evidence in support of your claim or position).

Step 2: Defining the Intended Audience

What the audience is expected to do with information often determines the target audience. Reach all the essential people but only the essential people with the message. (Prepare to answer the questions "Why is this on my desk and not on the desk of the assignment editor?" "Why is this on my desk when I don't write about this subject?") Determine whether the message will pass through more than one pair of hands if it accomplishes its objective.

Consider who the possible target audiences are for this message—employees of a cabinet department? Other government employees? Members of Congress? Scholars interested in this subject? Ordinary citizens affected by this policy? Residents of particular localities? Anyone else?

Step 3: Determining the Newsworthiness of the Message

Consider whether you will have to pay to distribute this message, and whether it can be communicated as soft news if it will not be used as hard news. Decide if it can be made newsworthy by piggybacking on other news, holding it for a slow news day or for dead news time, releasing it in a newsworthy setting, or releasing it through a newsworthy person.

Step 4: Determining Factors Constraining Release

Factors that may affect release of a news item include a congressional deadline, a public promise by a supervisor, someone wanting to see it buried, or someone wanting to see it released and heavily publicized.

Step 5: Selecting Appropriate Channels

In deciding the channels through which to release information, consider which channels best reach the target audience. Does your media list contain all relevant outlets (all publications reaching target audiences, all specialized publications that cover this subject, all outlets in a particular locality)? Have all possible channels been considered (press releases to county papers, radio feeds to the rural United States for use in predrive time)? Is the form of the message compatible with the selected channels? Different channels may require different forms. Is the language of the message compatible with the channel—popular language to popular channels, technical language to specialized channels? If the message is transmitted by phone or given in response to phoned inquiries, the information should be stored in a manner that lends itself to quick, clear retrieval. Responses to inquiries by phone or stories that must be transmitted by phone to meet deadlines should be written down.

Is the message to be released to selected outlets or mass-released? Decide if you should use the elite media such as the *New York Times* to draw the attention of the other media, and if you should use one medium (such as radio) to sensitize others (for example, print and television) to your message.

Determine whether your message is part of a larger message.

Step 6: Adapting the Message to the Channel

Each channel imposes constraints on the messages it relays: *format* (*The NewsHour with Jim Lehrer,* national network news, *Face the Nation,* or the *New York Times*); *deadlines* (morning or evening papers, drive-time radio); content (weeklies or dailies, audio, print, visual, or audiovisual content); and *cost* (costs in equipment and personnel to carry this message).

These constraints influence message construction. Television news is a visual medium (consider the talking head versus the visual aid; the effects of location), and it is an *audiovisual* medium (the brilliant statement might be mumbled, stumbled, and fumbled). Television news deals in 1- to 1.5-minute units, so try to write the quotable quote, the single synthetic sentence that digests the debate. It is also a medium favoring the dramatic, the confrontational; it often includes upbeat human interest stories at the end of a program. Also, what is not news today may be recast as news tomorrow (newsworthiness is a function of what else is newsworthy that day).

Television also includes interview shows (*Today, Face the Nation, The NewsHour with Jim Lehrer*) and televised documentaries. Other appropriate media might be radio news spots or all-news radio, newspapers (chains, national, or county), the wire services, and specialized publications.

Step 7: Monitoring Your Success or Failure

In reviewing the success or failure of your distribution effort, ask again what was covered and why. Future messages should be adjusted accordingly.

 Use InfoTrac College Edition to access information on topics in this chapter from hundreds of periodicals and scholarly journals. Enter keyword and subject searches: *National Advertising Division, consumer boycott.*

SELECTED READINGS

Fritschler, A. Lee. *Smoking and Politics: Policymaking and the Federal Bureaucracy.* Englewood Cliffs, NJ: Prentice Hall, 1975.

Krasnow, Erwin G., Lawrence D. Longley, and Herbert A. Terry. *The Politics of Broadcast Regulation,* 2nd ed. New York: St. Martin's Press, 1982.

Sethi, S. Prakash. *Up against the Corporate Wall: Modern Corporations and Social Issues of the Seventies.* Englewood Cliffs, NJ: Prentice-Hall, 1971.

Simons, Herbert W. *Persuasion: Understanding, Practice, and Analysis,* 2nd ed. New York: Random House, 1986.

10

Political versus Product Campaigns

Political advertising is a primary means through which candidates, parties, and issue advocacy groups communicate to the citizenry. In a typical presidential campaign, more than two thirds of the campaign budget will be spent for creating, testing, producing, and airing broadcast ads. Advertising is particularly effective when it is unanswered by those of opposing views. For example, in opposing the McCain tobacco settlement in spring and summer 1998 the tobacco companies outspent such opponents as the American Cancer Society and the Campaign for Tobacco-Free Kids by roughly forty to one. A survey conducted by the Annenberg Public Policy Center (APPC) at the University of Pennsylvania showed that the likelihood that the claims of the tobacco companies' ads would be believed was directly related to the amount of exposure purchased in service of their message. The McCain bill would have imposed substantial penalties on the tobacco industry if the rate of teen smoking did not drop, and it would have added a substantial tax—$1.10 to each pack of cigarettes. One reason why advertising does not appear to move votes dramatically in many election campaigns is that both sides are making cases and, in the process, canceling out each other's effect.

DEFINING ADS

In their treatment of advertising, reporters face other problems—among them a vocabulary that seriously confuses the electorate. Like pundits and many scholars, reporters tend to label any attack in an ad as "negative," a word that suggests the content is inaccurate or in some way illegitimate. Content analysis, however, shows that ads that attack and those that contrast—make a case for the sponsor and against the opponent—contain higher levels of policy claims and are, on average, more accurate than ads that simply make the case for the sponsor. By labeling attacks negative, we penalize what can be useful information that helps voters distinguish the records and proposals of the candidates. Reporters are also less likely to police so-called positive ads, even though research shows that such ads contain more distortion, on average, than ads that attack or ads that contrast.

To avoid this indiscriminate use of the word *negative,* we recommend separating ads into three categories: attack, advocacy, and contrast. An attack ad makes a case against the opponent but not for the sponsor; an advocacy ad makes a case for the sponsor without making a case against the opponent; a contrast ad makes a case for the sponsor and a case against the opponent. We consider contrast ads superior to attack ads because the presence of the sponsor's case increases candidate accountability and the case for the sponsor gives voters something to vote for, rather than simply reasons to vote against an opposing candidate.

CANDIDATE ACCESS: FREE TIME

For decades scholars and activists argued that candidates should be given free airtime, on the condition that they use it to speak directly to camera. The rationale for the proposal was straightforward. It would diminish the need to raise money and would increase candidate accountability, because, when speaking on camera rather than through an anonymous voiceover announcer, candidates would be credited or blamed for what they said.

In 1996, the FCC cleared the way for stations and networks to provide unpaid blocks of time, generally 1 to 2.5 minutes, free to major party candidates. This ruling opened another channel of access for the candidates offered the time. Free television airtime was made available to both major party presidential campaigns in 1996 by several networks in a variety of formats: Sometimes the time was included within news and magazine programs, sometimes as a stand-alone feature in programming. The candidates were invited to make short speeches, speaking directly to the camera, with few if any other production elements. In total, the Dole and Clinton campaigns each produced twenty-five free-time mini-speeches. These ranged from 1 to 2.5 minutes in length. In the final week of the 2000 election NBC offered Gore and Bush nightly interviews in the regular news broadcast by network anchor Tom Brokaw. Bush accepted for a single night. Gore appeared for five nights straight. The National Annenberg Election Survey (NAES) survey shows that among NBC viewers Gore gained by the exposure.

In some congressional and state races, airtime also was donated by local broadcasters. Proposals calling on broadcasters to give free airtime to candidates are part of current campaign reform legislation in Congress. Some believe that in return for being given the digitized spectrum at no cost, the networks (see Chapter 1) should provide candidates with free time.

WHAT PROTECTS VOTERS: RESPONSIBILITY OF JOURNALISTS

Campaign fundraising and advertising are a complex and integral aspect of the election process. Journalists who are knowledgeable about campaign finance and advertising can serve their audiences and positively affect political advertising. By understanding the laws governing the content and funding of political advertisements, discerning the differences among the three types of political ads, and learning how to analyze ads effectively, reporters can help their viewers and listeners dissect and digest the information they receive from candidates, parties, and issue advocacy groups. As a result, the public can make informed and educated decisions on election day. Adwatching also may help encourage accuracy and honesty in political advertising. When stations neglect these responsibilities, the public can be misled.

Products versus Candidates

Conventional wisdom says that candidates for political office are now sold to the electorate like cigarettes or soap. There is some truth to the claim. Both manufacturers and politicians develop mass media campaigns to persuade us to act as they wish. Both manufacturers and politicians seek to create name recognition and employ differentiation, association, audience participation, and repetition to communicate their messages. Both rely on campaigns that are centrally coordinated by people issuing many messages—or a single message to many media—across an extended period of time to accomplish a specific objective. Both condense their messages into slogans. And, as Michael Kinsley argues,

> a political name [such as Kennedy or Bush] . . . is the political equivalent of a commercial brand. "Brand extension," as it is called, means using the reputation of an established product to help peddle a new one. There is a certain logic to the notion that if Kleeneze is a good laundry detergent, then a dishwasher detergent named Kleeneze will be good too. . . . The notion that Jones Jr. will make a good senator because Jones Sr. did is less a rational assumption than a primitive instinct.[1]

The producers of product and political campaigns share a concern about the increasing capacity of their intended audiences to avoid televised ads. The Annenberg Public Policy Center's NAES survey of 1,845 respondents in New Hampshire from January 6 to 25, 2004, found that one third of those who said they had seen political ads on television in the previous week tried to avoid them. Fifteen percent switched channels. A paltry 1 percent reported using DVRs to avoid them.[2] But those numbers will probably rise soon. DVRs such as TiVo and ReplayTV are now in approximately 3 million homes.

Politicians are not soap or cigarettes, however, and the campaigns for products and politicians have contrasting functions, values, regulations, and financing. In this chapter we focus on these differences to indicate the peculiar limitations operating on those who would influence the outcome of a political campaign; we also examine the resources available to them. By contrasting political and product campaigns, we hope to increase understanding of both.

USING THE MEDIA

A political campaign's use of media is more short-lived and more intense than a campaign on behalf of a product. We may see the ads for a specific product, such as Ivory Soap, for decades. As long as the product holds a share of the market the manufacturer considers acceptable, the product will stay on the market. We use soap all year, so advertising for soap appears year-round. A political campaign is more akin to an ad campaign for a seasonal product, such as a brand of Christmas tree ornaments.

A political campaign is relatively short. Candidates for statewide office usually begin to air general election commercials in September before the election. The number of ads increases as the date of the election approaches. By contrast, a three-month campaign for a product would be a very short campaign. Often producers spend more than three months just testing the product and then spend additional time testing the commercials that will market the product. The short duration of the typical political campaign is one of the campaign's major liabilities, because it is difficult to create or change people's attitudes in a short period of time. Consequently, contenders are announcing their candidacy earlier than they once did, and speculation about likely presidential candidates begins the day after each inauguration. Long-lived intense campaigns for the presidency more closely match the patterns of product campaigns than they once did. In summer 1995, long before the Republicans had settled on Bob Dole as their nominee, the Clinton campaign for re-election had began airing ads sponsored by the Democratic National Committee. By March 2004, Republican presidential incumbent George W. Bush was airing ads at a level previously expected in general elections.

Creating an Image

The image for a product can be created more easily than the image for a politician because politicians bring to office a documentable past. Often the campaign seeks to capitalize on that past by stressing that experience has prepared the candidate in specific ways for the office sought. But the past can be a liability, too. A politician with no previous experience in an elected office can attempt to frame that lack of experience as an asset by creating an "outsider" image, but experience that isn't in the record cannot be fabricated. A politician—even a vice president—with a shady past may find that it returns to haunt him or her. By contrast, if a product doesn't taste the way potential consumers would like, the manufacturer will determine that fact in product testing and reformulate the product. The product can be repackaged more easily than the candidate can.

Targeting the Audience

The politician wants to reach potential voters. In most states, that audience includes unregistered voters until the registration books close. Once the deadline has passed, the politician can effectively discount people who are not registered to vote. In a primary election in which only registered Democrats can vote for a Democratic candidate, the various Democratic candidates focus their attention on reaching registered Democrats. The politician also focuses on voters who can be swayed to vote for him or her. When it is possible to separate one from the other, the politician is unlikely to target advertising to those committed to an opponent.

The politician often focuses attention on age groups different from those important to the commercial advertiser. For example, children and teenagers are prime audiences for the marketer of commercial products. For the politician, these audiences are comparatively insignificant, because they can't vote. By contrast, the politician focuses more attention on the older segment of the audience than will the commercial advertiser. As we age, the likelihood that we will vote increases. People over 65 cast proportionately more votes than their percentage of the population would suggest. The commercial advertiser is interested in people who are likely to spend money to purchase a product; the politician is interested in those who are likely to cast a vote.

Nonpolitical commercials are rarely broadcast to reach lower-income groups. Although people with lower incomes are less likely than their more affluent counterparts to vote, Democratic politicians, particularly liberal Democrats, routinely aim advertising at these groups. Often this advertising includes appeals to register and to vote as well as messages designed to persuade the audience to vote for the liberal Democrat. Voting power is a great equalizer in political advertising. It means that people who otherwise are not the focus of product advertising become the target audience in some sorts of campaigns.

Earlier we noted that the typical commercial was set in an upper-middle-class or upper-class environment. Nonpolitical ads do not show poverty, slums, or incorrigible despair. Product ads affirm the basic health of the economic system by creating a world in which people live comfortable, pleasant lives. The only discomforts the people in these ads experience easily can be remedied by purchase of a product.

By contrast, the politician out of power wants to indict the status quo and pin the blame for the ills of the system on the incumbent. These indictments are most effective when they are underscored visually. Consequently, the candidate tapes ads in slum housing to establish that the incumbent's promises of change have been unfulfilled. Political ads also feature testimony from the disenchanted—those who are unhappy at the way in which government is being run. Political ads can feature the poor, the unemployed, and those who are ill, and ads attacking incumbents are prone to do just that. Ads for liberal candidates, in particular, include the disadvantaged, who are otherwise seldom seen on television except on an occasional segment of the evening news.

Political ads are also more likely to include people with regional dialects, because their presence is a signal to the corresponding regional or ethnic group that the candidate has support from their peers. To reach the widest audience possible, commercial advertising, by contrast, tends to employ characters who speak standard American English with a general American accent.

Both candidates and manufacturers want to reach their target audiences in a cost-efficient fashion. It is generally easier for the manufacturer to meet this objective than it is for the politician, because the ways in which the electorate is segmented for electoral purposes do not always lend themselves to cost-efficient purchase of media space.

For example, a candidate who is running for governor in Connecticut can reach viewers in Fairfield County only if time is purchased on New York television stations; Fairfield County is part of the Greater New York Metropolitan Area for broadcasting purposes. But over 80 percent of the money spent on New York television advertising will reach New Yorkers who cannot vote in Connecticut. This means that, all other things being equal, a candidate who is well known in Fairfield County has an advantage. Such candidate can focus the media budget on buying television time in the central Connecticut cities of New Haven and Hartford, reaching primarily Connecticut voters. The candidate who is unknown in Fairfield County, however, must decide whether becoming known there is important enough to warrant spending 80 cents of every dollar reaching nonvoting out-of-staters (see Figure 10-1).

The competition for media time is particularly fierce in those markets that serve many states simultaneously. For example, Philadelphia stations reach voters in Pennsylvania, Delaware, and New Jersey; Washington, DC, stations reach the District of Columbia, Maryland, Virginia, and a slice of West Virginia. Because audiences are accustomed to being addressed by those who want them to purchase an accessible product, they run the risk of responding as did one Philadelphia, Pennsylvania, resident, who told a focus group that she planned to vote for Christine Todd Whitman—who was running for the governorship of New Jersey, another state entirely.

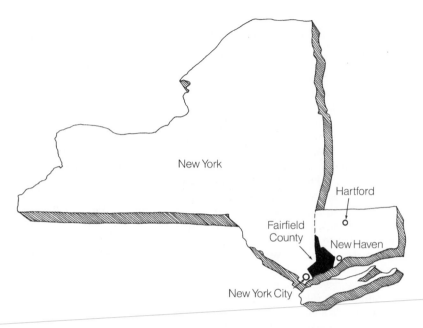

FIGURE 10-1 Outline of Fairfield County

Economic versus Political Values

Ads for products argue that buying is a good thing; ads for politicians argue that voting is good. Ads for products assume that purchasing products makes us as individuals happier. Ads for political candidates assume that involvement in the political process makes the world a better place. In the world of political ads, the system works. Ads do not argue for overthrow of people they oppose but for action within the system—voting. In political ads, problems exist but can be solved. Incumbents tell us that they have worked to solve the problems and have actually produced solutions. People out of office point to problems that remain unsolved and offer solutions. Both types of ads affirm that problems are manageable and ought to be addressed from within the system by voting for one candidate or another. In ads for products, problems exist, but these problems, too, are solvable. Here the solution is found not in voting but in purchasing.

Both political ads and ads for manufactured products affirm that we can be agents of change. We can buy the product that produces the whiter smile. We can vote for the politician who will turn the economy around. Consequently, both types of ads are fundamentally optimistic. Their outlook is positive.

Suppose, instead, that the world is filled with unsolvable problems. Suppose, for example, that wars are not winnable, that the federal deficit is intractable, that we are plagued by problems that do not lend themselves to political solutions within the system. If all this is true, then why should we worry about which candidate ought to be elected? All are equally powerless. Political ads must affirm that we can be agents of

---

BOX 10-1   From MTV to Product Ads to Political Ads

Since the advent of Music Television (MTV) and its popularity, the style of music videos has become standard in the advertising industry. These techniques began to be used in advertising on MTV that blurred the line between programming and commercials. Judith McGrath, MTV's senior vice president creative director, commented, "It's almost hard to tell one [video] from the other [commercials]."[a] Music videos used many techniques that originated in commercials (after all, videos are commercials), but commercials have adopted many of the techniques that were introduced in videos.

This new style soon found its way to other cable stations and networks, usually in an attempt to reach a younger audience. *Miami Vice*, originally conceptualized and sold as "MTV Cops," used music and MTV-style editing.[b] Harriet Seitler, MTV vice president of marketing, stated, "Just look at commercials on *Miami Vice* and you'll see we've changed the way people watch TV."[c]

The quick intercutting central to this style is not predictable; it requires the full attention of the viewer. Hence, it is more challenging because it requires viewer participation to be formed into a narrative, much like an enthymeme. Viewers read their own emotions and dramas into the intercuts. In this way, the dramas created become more emotionally binding than those advertisers concoct for viewers.

John Pettegrew views MTV and MTV-like commercials as a result of postmodernism. He believes that nonnarrative style is adapted to a generation of nonnarrative viewers (they watch many shows at once, do other things while watching television, randomly channel-surf, and so on). He also contends that replacing logical argument with a series of images creates an emotional connection to the product.[d]

By contrast, Alex Abrams, author of *Late Bloomers: Coming of Age in Today's America*, argues that advertising that is too much like MTV "doesn't reflect who this generation is, nor does it reach Generation X. . . . There's a significant number of older advertising people trying to do advertising for a generation that they don't understand."[e]

The impact of this style is recognized. In 1986, for example, the American Sewing Association won the Cable Television Advertising Bureau's $25,000 Grand Prize for a 90-second MTV-like music video aimed at increasing interest in sewing and achieved a "national presence that they never could have done traditionally for the same price."[f]

Similarly, automotive advertising has exploited many of the techniques of music videos in selling entry-level cars. In 1987, for instance, Pontiac used these techniques to sell the LeMans. Quick intercuts of a band in concert, cars, and "sultry scenes

---

change, that voting creates change, that politicians in office can make a difference, and that problems are solvable. In the process of affirming these premises, political ads reinforce our belief in our political system.

REGULATION

The laws governing political and product ads differ in important ways.

Censorship

Networks are free to recommend changes in product ads and often do so when, in the judgment of their staff the ads are inaccurate, are in poor taste, or embody negative stereotypes. In contrast, it is illegal to censor a candidate's political ad. Consequently,

such as a woman who shrugs off an oversize shirt to reveal her swimsuit as she runs past her LeMans at the beach" were seen as music played in the background.[g] Chevrolet claimed that these advertisements were copied almost directly from their own "Heartbeat of America" campaign.[h] Pontiac, however, added a 25-campus MTV tour to its campaign that included an expanded 210-second music video.[i]

MTV commercial director Stu Hagmann admits that MTV has influenced television commercials, but the use of these techniques concerns him: "The techniques become the message—and I think that's too bad."[j] Joe Saltzman, chairman of the Broadcasting School at the University of California, expressed concern about wider use of these techniques, particularly on political issues. He argues that when style and image replace substance, intelligent discussion and decisions become impossible:

Rational discussion becomes the first victim when these subjects are subverted to simple, one-dimensional images: a tasteless picture of someone's genitals, a drug-induced death, a twitching fetus, the American Flag. These powerful images overwhelm anyone's argument unless he or she can come up with equally gripping images to seduce the American public to another point of view. When public discussion of issues that go to the heart of a democracy is reduced to image and catchword, the very survival of the U.S. as a free society is in jeopardy. Citizens become conditioned to respond to the facial stereotype, to the symbols they trust or fear, and they become incapable of understanding and acting on real debate and questioning. They even grow to resent such discussion, wanting instead a quick fix, a fast image, an easy-to-grasp phrase.[k]

[a]Jennifer Pendleton, "Chalk Up Another Victory for Trend-Setting Rock 'n' Roll." *Advertising Age,* 9 November 1988, p. 160.
[b]Ibid, p. 160.
[c]Lenore Skenazy, "Explosive Promos Ignite MTV," *Adverztising Age,* 28 September 1987, p. 75.
[d]John Pettegrew, "A Post-Modernist Moment: 1980s Commercial Culture & the Founding of MTV." *Journal of American Culture,* 15 (Winter 1992): 60.
[e]Cited in Laurie Freeman, "Advertising Mirror Is Cracked: Generation X Sees Ad World's Projected Image, and Isn't Buying." *Advertising Age,* 6 February 1995, p. 30.
[f]Ronald B. Kaatz, "Creativity and Clutter," *Marketing & Media Decisions,* 22 (May 1987): 110.
[g]Raymond Serafin, "MTV Inspires Pontiac's Ad Effort in '88," *Advertising Age,* 21 September 1987, p. 84.
[h]"Chevrolet Exec Nips at Ads for Pontiac," *Advertising Age,* 21 September 1987, p. 84.
[i]Serafin, p. 84.
[j]Pendleton, p. 160.
[k]Joe Saltzman, "Style vs. Substance," *USA Today,* January 1989, p. 87.

material that would never be heard or seen in a commercial ad can be included in a candidate ad.

Similarly, candidate political ads may employ words found to be "obscene, indecent, or profane," although commercial ads and programming may not. In 1978, the U.S. Supreme Court upheld the FCC's right to impose sanctions on a radio station that broadcast George Carlin's monologue about words that cannot be used on radio and television.[3] In 1980, however, presidential candidate Barry Commoner was allowed to air a political radio commercial that included *bullshit,* one of the prohibited words in Carlin's monologue. "Bullshit" said the ad. "What? Reagan and Anderson—it's all bullshit."

What protects a station, then, from a libel suit claiming that a person or organization was defamed by a political commercial or statement made during broadcast time secured as a result of an equal-time request? In 1956, such a situation arose in Fargo, North Dakota. A candidate for the U.S. Senate requested and received equal time on

WDAY-TV. During the time secured by the equal-time request, the candidate charged that a prominent union, the North Dakota Farmers Union, was controlled by communists. The union responded by suing both the station and the candidate. In the landmark case *Farmers' Educational and Cooperative Union of America v. WDAY* (1959), the North Dakota Supreme Court held, and the U.S. Supreme Court affirmed, that stations could not be considered legally responsible for untrue or libelous statements made in such a circumstance. Because Section 315(a) of the Federal Communications Act forbids the censoring of remarks by candidates, the station could not be held accountable.

Occasionally the results offend. "This commercial is not suitable for small children because abortion is not suitable for America," said an ad broadcast on July 3, 1992, on the Atlanta superstation TBS. Pictures of three happy infants appeared with the label "Choice A." Next were bloody fetuses tagged "Choice B." Then Republican congressional candidate Jimmy Fisher stated, "When something is so horrifying that we can't stand to look at it, then why are we tolerating it? Pro-choice is a lie. This baby wouldn't have chosen to die. Vote Jimmy Fisher July 21 and stop the killing." In April 1992, another pro-lifer had won the Republican primary in Indiana's Ninth Congressional District with similar ads.

Within hours of the broadcast on TBS, the call-in lines at talk shows in Atlanta began ringing. Some expressed outrage. Others said that it was about time the effects of abortion were displayed. Still others asked, Why do they let pictures like that on television?

The simple answer is that the First Amendment guarantees freedom of speech. Initially the FCC responded to complaints about the ads aired in Indiana with a ruling that said that although the stations could not refuse such spots, they could "channel" or time-shift them to a time in which children were less likely to be in the audience. The ruling cautioned the stations to act in good faith. Channeling was not intended as a means of indicating the station's disapproval of the content. In 1996, however, the U.S. Court of Appeals overturned the FCC rule on the grounds that stations did not have the right "to deny a candidate access to adult audiences of his choice simply because significant numbers of children may also be watching television."[4]

The Federal Communications Commission has placed some limits on broadcast political speech, but not many. A station that has accepted ads from one candidate must accept them from the candidate's opponents. A station may refuse an ad for a bona fide candidate for federal office only if it is too long or too short for the time purchased, if it fails to indicate the name of the sponsor, if it has technical problems (for example, the sound breaks up in the middle of the ad), or if it is "obscene." A candidate cannot invoke free speech rights, for example, to show a copulating couple, even in the missionary position.

Even if a station manager knows that an ad by a federal candidate is unfair, factually inaccurate, or offensive to part of the community, the ad must be aired. The need for the protection was evident in the early days of radio, when station owners simply refused all ads by candidates they personally opposed. Whom would you trust to determine when political speech is fair and accurate? In essence, the FCC and the courts have answered, "In an open marketplace of ideas, we trust the public." That protection does not extend to PAC ads, however, or to issue advocacy advertising.

The results seem ironic to some. Whereas the stations and networks police product ads vigilantly, political ads by candidates are untouched. If an ad says that an aspirin

---

BOX 10-2   When the Demands of Business and Politics Collide

"To comply with federal campaign laws, the Coors Brewing Company has stopped broadcasts in Colorado of commercials that feature its chairman, Peter Coors. He announced yesterday that he would seek the Republican nomination for the Senate seat being vacated by Ben Nighthorse Campbell, also a Republican."[a]

[a]Stuart Elliott, "Coors Chairman Quits Commercials," *New York Times*, April 14, 2004, p. C8. Copyright © 2004 by The New York Times Co. Reprinted with permission.

---

reduces headache pain more quickly than its competitors, the viewer can fairly assume that the claim was not fabricated in a Madison Avenue back room. And if the accuracy of a product ad is questioned, the Federal Trade Commission can look into it, requiring corrective advertising if needed.

Not so with political ads. Thus, for example, a candidate's political ad can claim to be showing a "fetus" or "child" aborted in the third trimester when what is in fact being shown is a child stillborn during that period. How would a viewer know? If the press is doing its job, as newspapers around the country increasingly are, an "adwatch" will detail the facts. When the press is asleep at the switch, as it largely was until 1989, the voter must either turn investigative reporter or fall back on a lifetime's worth of judgment calls.

The courts have also held that candidates have a right to access. "It is the purpose of the First Amendment," wrote the U.S. Supreme Court in the famous Red Lion case decided June 9, 1969, "to preserve an uninhibited marketplace of ideas in which truth will ultimately prevail, rather than to countenance monopolization of that market, whether it be by the Government itself or a private licensee." Section 312(a)(7) of the Communications Act of 1934, added by Congress in 1972, states that "the Commission may revoke any station license or construction permit . . . for willful or repeated failure to allow reasonable access to or permit the purchase of reasonable amounts of time for the use of a broadcasting station by a legally qualified candidate for Federal elective office on behalf of his candidacy." It is important to note that this right to access applies only to candidates for federal office, that is, those running for the House and Senate of the United States and for the presidency. It does not ensure access for those running for governor, county commissioner, or mayor.

The access requirement has other exemptions as well. It applies to broadcast networks, not cable, and it does not bar stations from refusing to sell political ad time during newscasts. Candidates do have a right to access to time adjacent to news (news adjacencies) if advertising time is sold to product advertisers for placement there.

The protections afforded to broadcast political speech have broadened the latitude of discourse in ways that have variously offended liberals and conservatives. In 1972, the FCC protected the right of J. B. Stoner, a state office seeker in Georgia, to say in an ad that "[t]he main reason why niggers want integration is because niggers want our white women." Only a clear and present danger of imminent violence would justify tampering with political speech, reasoned the commission. The ruling was justified by the guarantee of free speech even for claims that are abhorrent.[5]

Equal Opportunity

If stations could effectively deny airwave access to candidates they opposed, or provide blocks of free time to candidates they supported with no responsibility to other candidates, the broadcast media would become dominant power brokers in the political arena. Section 315 of the Federal Communications Act guarantees that broadcasters who open their facilities to one legally qualified candidate must give equal opportunities to the other legally qualified candidates. To be legally qualified, a candidate must have announced for the office and must have met the legal requirements asked of those seeking the office. Thus, if one candidate is given five minutes of time at no charge, then other legally qualified candidates for the same office must also be given five minutes of equivalent time each. If one candidate has been permitted to buy time on a station, all other legally qualified candidates for the same office also must be permitted to buy time. The equal opportunity provision does not mean that a station must give all candidates free time if one candidate has purchased time; a purchase simply entitles other candidates to purchase equivalent time.

Right to Access

The U.S. Supreme Court has also held that candidates have "an affirmative right to access to the broadcast media." This ruling, handed down in July 1981, was the result of a challenge by the Jimmy Carter campaign to network denial of the right to purchase thirty minutes of prime time in December 1979. ABC and NBC had rejected the request outright. CBS had offered two 5-minute time slots instead. Under the new ruling, a broadcaster can deny access only if the requested purchase would substantially disrupt programming. The candidate may then appeal that decision to the FCC, which is empowered to determine whether or not to order that the ad run. If the station refuses an FCC request to air the ad, its license can be revoked.

Before this ruling, the FCC simply required stations to discuss controversial issues (the Fairness Doctrine) and to grant equal time to all qualified candidates if any one candidate was given or permitted to purchase time (Section 315). Writing for the U.S. Supreme Court in 1981, Chief Justice Warren Burger argued that "it is of particular importance that candidates have the opportunity to make their views known so that the electorate may intelligently evaluate the candidates' personal qualities and their position on vital public issues before choosing among them on election day."[6]

How, then, is it possible for presidential debates among two or three major contenders to take place? The debates between Richard Nixon and John Kennedy in 1960 occurred because Congress had suspended Section 315 to permit them to occur. Debates were held between Gerald Ford and Jimmy Carter in 1976, between Ronald Reagan and John Anderson and Reagan and Carter in 1980, between Reagan and Walter Mondale in 1984, between Michael Dukakis and George H. W. Bush in 1988, between Ross Perot, George H. W. Bush, and Bill Clinton in 1992, between Bob Dole and Clinton in 1996, between Al Gore and George W. Bush in 2000, and between George W. Bush and John Kerry in 2004. These debates were possible under a 1975 ruling of the FCC that held that such debates were bona fide news events and, as such, were exempt from the equal opportunity requirement.

To be considered a bona fide news event, the FCC's Aspen Institute ruling of 1975 held that the debates must be sponsored by an outside organization (in 1976, 1980, and 1984, it was the League of Women Voters; in 1988, 1992, 1996, 2000, and 2004, the Presidential Debate Commission), must be planned without the involvement of the broadcast media, must not occur in the broadcaster's facilities, and must be covered live and in their entirety.

Some other news formats are also exempt from the requirements of Section 315. Bona fide newscasts and interview shows, such as *Meet the Press,* are exempt. A news conference scheduled by the candidate and considered newsworthy by the broadcaster is also exempt if it is covered live and in its entirety.

In 1983, the FCC widened the scope of the Aspen ruling by exempting debates sponsored by broadcasters as on-the-spot news coverage. This cleared the way for the broadcast networks to sponsor debates in the presidential primaries, which they did for the first time in 1984. In the general elections, however, the debates have continued to be sponsored by an outside organization. Beginning in 1988, when the League of Women Voters objected to the level of candidate control demanded by Bush and Dukakis, the debates have been sponsored by the Presidential Debates Commission, a nonprofit organization headed by the past chairs of the two major parties.

Cost and Access

In 1970, the FCC added the Zapple Doctrine to its list of requirements for broadcasters. The Zapple Doctrine gives all legally qualified candidates the right to the same access to purchased time as any one political candidate. If a station sells time to one candidate, then comparable time must be made available to opposing candidates who want to purchase it and can afford to do so.

Many of the regulations we have discussed protect the public's access to political information. Because broadcasters are corporate entities whose existence is predicated on making a profit, they are inclined to limit the amount of time made available to candidates at a rate below the normal selling rate; they are reluctant to preempt a show such as *ER,* which produces high advertising revenues, for a political broadcast that produces minimal revenue. The Zapple Doctrine and the affirmative right-to-access rules are designed to ensure that the corporate desire to maximize profits will not significantly impede the public's right to political information.

CAMPAIGN SPENDING LIMITS

In 1971, Congress enacted the Federal Election Campaign Act, amended in 1974. The enactment of this law required that candidates running for the presidency or for Congress report campaign contributions and expenditures. It also "limited the amount of money that could be collected and spent, made public funds available for presidential contenders, and established the Federal Election Commission to administer and enforce the law."[7]

Subsequently, in *Buckley v. Valeo* the U.S. Supreme Court upheld limits on the campaign contributions of individuals and groups other than the candidate and upheld the limits on spending by candidates who accepted public funds.[8] In 1992, George H. W. Bush and Bill Clinton accepted public funds and the resulting spending ceilings. Independent candidate Ross Perot did not. As a result, in the general election, Clinton and Bush were limited to spending the $55.2 million each received in federal support, whereas Perot could spend as much as he wished.

The Court also permitted spending on a candidate's behalf by groups independent of the candidate. This provision gave rise in 1988 to such groups as Americans for Bush and the National Security Political Action Committee. The most famous ad of the campaign, the "Willie Horton" ad, was sponsored by a political action committee (PAC). PACs were less active in the presidential campaigns of 1992 and 1996 because of the rise of a new category of advertising, issue advocacy (discussed later). By contrast, there is no limit on the amount of money a manufacturer may spend on behalf of a product, and there are no limitations on the sources the manufacturer may tap to raise money—provided, of course, that the money is raised legally.

The Federal Election Campaign Act, as amended, was designed to minimize the influence of large anonymous contributors on government policy. The disclosure requirements were intended to ensure that the public would know to whom the candidates were indebted, personally and economically. The existence of these regulations made it possible for news reporters to determine which industries were contributing more heavily to one candidate than another and to correlate politicians' voting behavior with the sources of their campaign financing.

McCain-Feingold: Campaign Finance Reform

Passed by Congress in spring 2002 and upheld by the U.S. Supreme Court in fall 2003, the McCain-Feingold bill (passed as the Bipartisan Campaign Reform Act of 2002) banned unlimited contributions to political parties. These "soft money" donations had fallen outside the limits of *Buckley v. Valeo.* McCain-Feingold provided that

- A person could contribute up to $95,000 every two years to candidates for federal office or political committees, up from $50,000.
- A limit of $2,000 per candidate in a primary (up from $1,000) and another $2,000, up from $1,000, in each general election. A person can contribute to as many candidates as she would like up to a limit of $37,500 of these $2,000 contributions in a two-year election cycle.
- A donor can give a maximum of $5,000 a year to any political action committee. PACs can give a maximum of $10,000 in a two-year election cycle to any candidate. McCain-Feingold created a PAC-plus-party-committee cap of $57,500 in donations per person in a two-year election cycle. That cap will be adjusted for inflation.
- Individuals can give up to $25,000 to each of the party committees. Contributions to state and local parties are treated separately. The $57,500 cap applies to these contributions.
- Contributions are not counted by family but by individual. Husbands, wives, and children can each contribute.
- Consistent with *Buckley v. Valeo,* an individual can spend as much as she wants to buy her own ads promoting a candidate. However, if a person runs an ad that specifically identifies an individual, she must disclose that she paid for the ad—a

requirement that increases the chances that the person will become an issue in the campaign.

- Electioneering communication can be paid for only with regulated hard money. An ad is electioneering communication if it refers to a specific candidate, is broadcast within 30 days of a primary or 60 days of a general election, and reaches at least 50,000 adults.

527s

A 527 is so called because Section 527 of the Internal Revenue Code exempts such groups from taxation. A 527 cannot contribute to candidates and may not coordinate with a candidate's campaign. It can draw unlimited amounts of money from individuals, labor unions, and companies to be used to get out the vote and to air issue ads. The question before the Federal Election Commission in 2004 was whether 527s were legal and if so under what rules, if any, they must operate. The FEC decided not to decide until after the election. Whereas the Democrats had established 527s early, the Republicans had gambled that they would be held illegal. This gave the Democrats a fundraising advantage.

The Democratic 527s were able to raise the funds to ensure that the Democrat message got about as much play as the Republican one during critical periods in the 2004 election. The Democrats did this by drawing in large contributions from wealthy donors such as George Soros. Republicans funding 527s included Texas developer Bob Perry and Texas energy czar T. Boone Pickens. Between March and May 2004, when the Kerry campaign was busy raising money, the Democratic 527s stayed on the air with anti-Bush ads. These expenditures thwarted Republican efforts to knock the presumed Democratic nominee out of contention before his convention.

Overall, according to a December 16, 2004, report by the Center for Public Integrity, groups supporting Kerry's run for the presidency outspent those supporting the re-election of George W. Bush three to one. With $51 million in total outlays, the largest Democratic spender, The Media Fund, spent about the same amount as the SwiftVets and PFA combined. But comparable amounts of money for ads don't guarantee comparable rhetorical sophistication. Whereas the Democratic money was spent in service of a scattershot campaign, the Republican 527s relentlessly reinforced the Republican message. The so-called Swift Boat Veterans for Truth focused on undercutting the Democratic nominee's central argument that his military heroism in Vietnam better qualified him to pursue the "war" on terror and the war in Iraq. And a group calling itself Progress for America (PFA) argued that George Bush could be trusted to protect all Americans just as he had protected and comforted a young woman named Ashley whose mother had been killed on September 11, 2001. Campaign surveys showed that the SwiftVet ads and "Ashley" were the ones voters in battleground states remembered best. No Media Fund ad even made the list.[9]

According to the *New York Times,* "The field of presidential candidates raised about $851 million (including public financing), a 70 percent increase over 2000. National political parties raised more than $1 billion, 12 percent more than when they were able to gather six- and seven-figure soft-money checks."[10]

By the close of the election, reported the nonpartisan Center for Public Integrity, "So-called 527 committees raised and spent just over a half-billion dollars during the

2003–2004 election cycle—double the amount spent during the 2002 cycle." A Center for Public Integrity report issued December 16, 2004, concluded that "Although the 527 committees have been operating on the fringes of American politics for at least the past three election cycles, election 2004 was the first time they played a major role, perhaps a decisive role, in determining the outcome of a national election."[11]

Issue Advocacy

Exempted from the restrictions of *Buckley v. Valeo* was issue advocacy, advocacy that does not explicitly urge a vote for or against a candidate. This form of communication burst onto the national scene in 1993–94 during the debate over health care reform. Unlike candidate-sponsored ads, issue advocacy ads can be rejected by stations. Indeed, some stations rejected as unfair some AFL-CIO ads attacking Republican members of Congress in 1996.

Unlike candidates sponsoring ads, issue advocates do not have to disclose who is funding their operation or, indeed, who they are. The identity of some issue advocates is clear. We know who is behind an ad sponsored by the Chamber of Commerce, the Sierra Club, or the AFL-CIO. It is less clear who was behind an ad that asked, "Who is Bill Yellowtail? He preaches family values, but he took a swing at his wife. And Yellowtail's explanation? He 'only slapped her.' But her nose was broken." This ad, which ran in a Montana congressional election in 1996, was sponsored by a group self-identified as Citizens for Reform.

A national survey of 1,026 registered voters, commissioned by the APPC shortly after election day in 1996, showed that a majority of voters (57.6%) recalled seeing an issue advertisement during the campaign.[12] When issue ads were compared with other political communication, analysts found that viewership of issue advertisements ranked below that of presidential candidate-sponsored advertising and debates. More voters recalled seeing issue advertisements than recalled watching at least one of the short speeches delivered by Bill Clinton and Bob Dole using free airtime donated by broadcast networks. (See Figure 10-2.) The APPC compiled an archive of 107 issue advocacy advertisements that aired on television or radio during the 1996 election cycle. These ads were sponsored by twenty-seven separate organizations.[13]

Issue advertisements do not expressly advocate the election or defeat of a candidate. In many cases, the advertisement makes no call to action at all. An analysis by Deborah Beck, Jeffrey Stanger, and Doug Rivlin for the APPC found that 25.2 percent of the 1996 issue ads contained no action step. Of those issue ads produced in 1996 that solicited some action on the part of the audience, the greatest proportion asked voters to "call" a public official or candidate (37.4 percent). Some asked individuals to "tell" or "let a public official know" their support for or disapproval of particular policy positions (16.8%), whereas others asked that a call be placed directly to the advocacy organization sponsoring the ad (15.9%). A few of the advertisements called for support for or opposition to pending legislation (4.7%).

Consistent with prior APPC research on the discourse of political campaigns, the center categorized issue advertisements by their central arguments. Arguments were classified as *advocacy* (a case made only for the position supported by the ad's sponsor), *pure attack* (a case made only against the opposing position), and *comparison* (an argu-

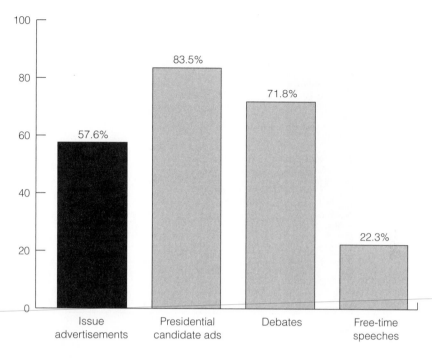

FIGURE 10-2 Audience sizes for political communication in 1996

ment that pairs a case against the opposition with a case for the sponsor's position).[14] Comparison is considered preferable to pure attack, because it allows evaluation of alternative positions. Pure attack contributes to the negative tone of political campaigns.

Compared with other discursive forms, including presidential candidate ads, debates, speeches in free time, and news coverage of the campaign (both television and print), issue advertisements aired in 1996 were the highest in pure attack.[15] Two in five arguments in issue ads were attacks. (See Figure 10-3.)

Arguments in issue ads were less likely to compare positions than were arguments in debates, free-time speeches, and ads sponsored by the presidential candidates. (See Figure 10-4.) Stations become involved in this political process and thereby assume responsibility when they air political ads. The 1996 and 1998 election cycles saw a dramatic increase in the number of candidate-sponsored and party-sponsored ads. Both elections also were marked by millions of new dollars of "soft money" raised and spent by third parties, such as PACs, individuals, and various interest groups. The size and scope of this new advertising raises two key issues for stations.

The first issue for stations is whether to air these ads. Nothing in the law requires that stations accept ads from PACs, independent expenditure ads, or issue advocacy ads. Whereas stations are protected from libel suits over ads for candidates for federal office—a protection extended in part because, with only a few exceptions, stations cannot interfere with the content of the candidate's ads—there is no such protection for stations choosing to air issue advocacy ads, independent expenditure ads, or ads by

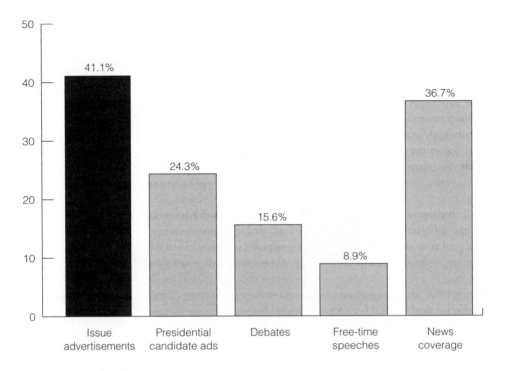

FIGURE 10-3   Pure attack in 1996 issue ads, presidential candidate ads, debates, free time, and news

PACs. There is, in other words, a small but discernible legal risk in accepting such ads when their claims are suspect, particularly when they misrepresent the views of an individual who can claim legal standing.

The second issue for stations is how to cover these ads. If one side is substantially outspending the other on broadcast ads, as the tobacco industry did in the campaign against the McCain bill, do the newscasters of the stations drawing revenue from the ads have an obligation to ensure that viewers are not misled? In other words, is this a circumstance that invites monitoring of ads in local news? Similarly, one might ask whether news reporters should help viewers make sense of the barrage of candidate ads in the fall of election years.

CAMPAIGN OBJECTIVES

For the politician, there is only one day that really counts; for the product advertiser, one day is as good as another, but sooner is better and often is best. A politician wants us to cast a vote on election day and to cast that vote for him or her. The politician also wants to mobilize that percentage of the electorate that occasionally works in a campaign, if that is possible, and to translate as much support as possible into money and volunteer time.

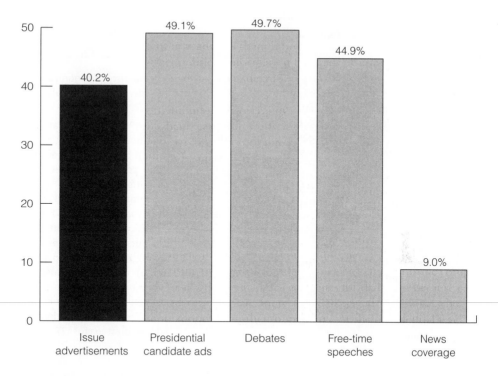

FIGURE 10-4   Comparison in 1996 issue ads, presidential candidate ads, debates, free time, and news

The manufacturer wants us to buy the product, sooner rather than later, and often—if that is possible. The manufacturer wants those of us who have purchased the product to recommend it to our friends and, when the occasion arises, to purchase it again. In that sense the manufacturer and the politician are alike: Both benefit if we become walking advertisements for them.

But "election day" for the manufacturer—the day on which we can vote to buy or not to buy the product—comes more frequently than it does for the politician. This poses a major problem for the politician; in a sense, he or she is trying to persuade us to take action, an important action that will benefit us, but to delay taking the action until a specified day and specified times within that day. It may rain that day. We may be ill. We may be out of town. We may forget to vote. The manufacturer is not plagued by rain, our illness, our business trips, or our forgetfulness in the same way the politician is, because we have repeated opportunities to buy the product.

Voting versus Buying

The manufacturer will make the product available to us in a convenient location, or by phone or mail whenever possible. Ideally, the product intrudes on our normal pattern of activity. We go to the supermarket, and there the product is, advertising itself to us from the shelf. But voting occurs in places most of us do not routinely visit—an elementary

BOX 10-3   Issue Advocacy in 2001–2002

The Annenberg Public Policy Center examined over 5,000 print and television ads that appeared in the Washington, DC, metropolitan area in 2001 and 2002 and focused on issues before the president, Congress, a regulatory agency, or that were a matter of public policy debate.

- The APPC estimates that over $105 million was spent on print and television issue advertising inside the beltway during the 107th Congress. These ads were sponsored by over 670 different organizations and coalitions.[a]
- Despite the large number of organizations and coalitions sponsoring issue ads, a few big spenders accounted for most of the dollars spent, with over half of all money coming from the twenty largest spenders.

- The majority of organizations that were top spenders in 2001 also made the list in 2002.
- The APPC found that organizations sometimes hid the nature of their sponsorship by omitting sponsorship tags or using pseudonyms that were vague or potentially deceptive.
- When the APPC looked at the organizations that spent over $1 million on issue advocacy, it found that business interests outspent other interests.
- About 72 percent of organizations (18 of 25) represented business interests. Spending on print advertising was much less concentrated than it was for television. The top 10 spenders on television ads accounted for 77 percent of the

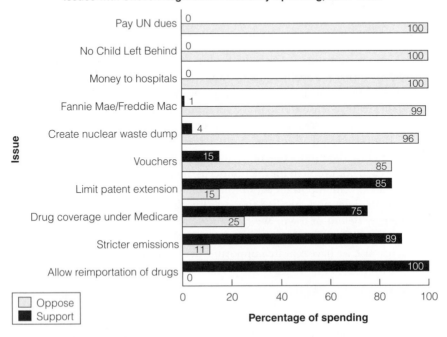

Issues with Uneven Legislative Advocacy Spending, 2001–2002

television total, whereas the top 10 organizations spending on print ads accounted for 31 percent of the print total.

- The organizations that sponsored print advertising were for the most part different from the ones that sponsored ads on television. The APPC documented only two organizations (Voices for Choices and Covering the Uninsured) that spent more than $1 million on print and $1 million on television.
- The APPC estimates that airtime for television legislative advertising in the Washington area in 2001 and 2002 cost over $41 million and was sponsored by 70 different organizations.
- The APPC estimates that spending for over 5,000 print ads purchased by over 600 organizations in Washington totaled about $64 million.
- The top 25 lobbies identified by *Fortune* magazine as having the most influence were not necessarily the highest advertising spenders. Only eight of those listed in the Fortune top 25 ranked in the APPC list of top 100 spenders. This

disparity in lists demonstrates that advertising spending is just one of the many ways organizations attempt to influence public policy.

- The top issues were energy and environment, health care, economy and business, and telecommunications. These four broad issues accounted for three out of every five dollars (61%) spent on inside-the-beltway legislative issue advertising.
- The APPC estimates that about $15.4 million was spent to advertise issues related to a National Energy Policy,[b] and that roughly 94 percent (about $14.5 million) of this spending was sponsored by energy/ business interests, with environmental interests spending the remaining 6 percent.
- Three subtopics accounted for 77 percent of the health care advertising. They were prescription drug benefits (42%), increased federal funding for hospitals and other providers (19%), and expanding coverage for the uninsured (17%).

(continued on next page)

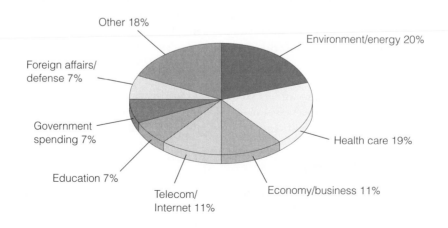

**Percentage of Spending on Top Issues
Legislative Issue Advertising
2001–2002**

Other 18%

Environment/energy 20%

Foreign affairs/ defense 7%

Government spending 7%

Health care 19%

Education 7%

Telecom/ Internet 11%

Economy/business 11%

BOX 10-3 *(continued)*

- Of the close to $20 million spent on health care advertising, almost three fifths (59%) of spending was from two types of groups that profit from health care. Industry groups (such as pharmaceutical manufacturers, insurance companies, and business associations) spent the most, close to $7 million (about 36% of the total health care spending). They were followed by health care providers, such as hospitals, nursing homes, and doctors ($4.7 million or 24%). Consumer groups, such as the AARP (formerly American Association Retired Persons) came in third, with about $3 million in spending (16%).

- Excluding the advertising that did not promote any specific plan for helping people afford prescription drugs, the APPC found that 75% of spending went to support plans outside of Medicare and 25% went to promote a prescription drug plan within Medicare.

- Overall spending was much more concentrated among a few issues in the tel-

evision ads. Spending on the top five issues in television ads accounted for 90 percent of broadcast/cable spending. Spending on the top five issues among print advertisements accounted for 71 percent of the ad spending.

- Of the 12 straightforward legislative issues the APPC looked at, all but two had greater spending on the prevailing side.

Source: From Erika Falk, *Legislative Issue Advertising in the 107th Congress.* Copyright © 2003 The Annenberg Public Policy Center of the University of Pennsylvania. Reprinted with permission.
[a]When three or more organizations sponsored an ad, they were counted as a distinct coalition. When two organizations sponsored an ad, all the spending was attributed to the organization with the larger logo or the first organization listed.
[b]Some ads were vague enough that the APPC did not know if they addressed a specific piece of legislation or regulation. They were classified together with ads on other environmental and energy issues and are not included in these totals. The APPC examined over 5,000 print and television ads that appeared in the Washington, DC, metropolitan area in 2001 and 2002 and focused on issues before the president, Congress, or a regulatory agency, or that were a matter of public policy debate.

---

school or a municipal building. The facts of a single election day and the special voting place complicate the job of the person who wants us to vote for a certain candidate.

Voting against a product is easier than voting against an elected official. If you buy a product and are dissatisfied, you can complain to the retailer, the manufacturer, and various consumer protection agencies. You can refuse to purchase another, attempt to get your money back, or discourage your friends from buying one. But what can you do when the politician you elect proves inept? The next chance you have to vote no will be the next election, unless you are governed by a charter that permits recalls; even then, the recall process is time-consuming, costly, and, with few exceptions, the recall of California Governor Gray Davis in fall 2003 notably among them, unsuccessful.

Criteria for Victory

The criteria for victory in elections are different from those in campaigns for products. If a manufacturer's product is fourth or fifth in the market compared with competing products, that level may be cause for rejoicing. A company can do very well financially by holding 5 or 6 percent of the market for a specific product. Many manufacturers earn a lot of money with a comparatively small share of the market, because the market is large enough to be shared profitably. Consequently, there are more winners in campaigns to sell products than in elections.

Dove, Dial, and Irish Spring can all make a profit, but Al Gore, Bill Bradley, Elizabeth Dole, and George W. Bush cannot all be president at the same time. Placing fifth in a field of candidates where the person with the most votes wins means you have lost. There is no consolation prize.

In most elections, the person who wins the majority of votes cast gets the office, and the rest are losers. An advertiser, on the other hand, can lose entire segments of the audience, can even alienate those who won't buy the product, yet the product may make a healthy profit. In contrast, the candidate needs 50 percent of the vote plus one in most instances and cannot, as a result, afford to write off as large a share of the audience as the manufacturer can.

We refer to "as large a share of the audience" because, like the manufacturer, the candidate does in effect write off a portion of the audience in most cases. It is unlikely that a voter who dislikes Candidate A, is committed to Candidate B, and has a high level of information about both candidates will be persuaded to vote for Candidate A. Such people are classed as "hostile" and written off in most campaigns. If that class of hostile voters makes up more than 51 percent of the electorate, Candidate A is usually advised to withdraw rather than to attempt the impossible.

UNPAID COVERAGE

A candidate is more likely than a product to obtain unpaid coverage unless the product is in trouble. Candidates both profit and suffer from the media coverage of political campaigns. There is no such thing as an election that is not newsworthy; some elections are simply more newsworthy than others. A mayoral contest in a small town is newsworthy to the town paper and may receive coverage in county papers as well. The mayoral contest in a large city such as Baltimore will receive coverage not only in the Baltimore media but also in Washington, DC, because the city is large and because the way it is governed affects the area surrounding it. In the nationwide presidential election, the nominees of the two major parties cannot avoid the attention of the media, and if they attempt to avoid it, their attempts at avoidance will be covered.

However, it is rare to see much news at all—or favorable coverage when coverage occurs—of a corporation, an industry, a manufacturer, or a product. For example, in 1990 we read a lot about savings and loans institutions. Most of the coverage focused on the need for the federal government to come up with billions of dollars to back Federal Deposit Insurance Corporation guarantees. The coverage started from the admitted premise that something was wrong. Overall, however, the news coverage of corporations and their products is almost nonexistent compared with the coverage of the typical political campaign.

Quality

Reporters are assigned to cover specific candidates and to become experts in matters pertaining to that candidate; reporters are not assigned to cover specific products unless there is a problem, such as a recall or malfunction. Consequently, there will be more routine investigative reporting about candidates and their campaigns than about products and their campaigns.

Endorsements

The endorsement of a powerful newspaper can save a candidacy. Campaigns typically translate endorsements by newspapers into paid advertisements by producing multiple copies of the endorsement and distributing them as fliers, paying to have the endorsement reprinted as a newspaper ad, reading it in a radio ad, or crawling it across the television screen in a commercial. There are few equivalents for products. When *Consumer Reports* ranks products, for example, it does so with the stipulation that the results may not be used in the products' ads.

Financing

A candidate must not only get you to buy the product—to vote—but must also raise money; a manufacturer has the money to create the product and does not advertise for contributions but rather urges you to buy the product. Presidential candidates who accept matching funds from the government must also accept a ceiling on expenditures. Manufacturers face no such limit.

TO SUM UP

In this chapter we have examined the ways in which the politician's use of media differs from the manufacturer's. We have touched on some of the unique constraints that govern the financing, creation, transmission, and reception of political messages. In Chapter 12 we examine the ways in which the political candidate manipulates the media.

 Use InfoTrac College Edition to access information on topics in this chapter from hundreds of periodicals and scholarly journals. Enter keyword and subject searches: *political campaigns, political censorship.*

SELECTED READINGS

Entman, Robert. "American Media and the Quality of Voter Information." Washington, DC: Aspen Institute, 2004.

Jamieson, Kathleen Hall. *Dirty Politics: Deception, Distraction, and Democracy.* New York: Oxford University Press, 1992.

———. *Packaging the Presidency.* New York: Oxford University Press, 1996.

———. *Everything You Think You Know about Politics— and Why You're Wrong.* New York: Basic Books, 2000.

Trippi, Joe. *The Revolution Will Not Be Televised: Democracy, the Internet, and the Overthrow of Everything.* New York: HarperCollins/Regan Books, 2004.

11　How Has the Internet Changed Politics?

The Internet has transformed politics today. It has enabled voters to locate candidate speeches, press releases, and position papers online. At the same time, citizens with computer access can locate press accounts from around the country, talk about politics with other citizens, and, on occasion, exchange messages with the candidates and officeholders themselves. Quick access to large bodies of information via the Internet makes it easier for reporters to check on the consistency of candidate messages. However, the information is not always of high caliber, and the difficulty of documenting all sources compounds the problem. Misinformation can be sent around the country and the world with the same dazzling speed as can solid information. At the same time, access makes opposition research less costly. By creating inexpensive web ads, campaigns invite news coverage of their content. And by e-mailing the link to the candidates' followers, campaigns secure cheap distribution of web ad content as followers relay the web ad page to their friends.

By 1992, candidates were already making use of the massive linking capacity of computers. For example, voters could directly query the Bill Clinton campaign for information. In 1996, voters also could gather information about President Clinton's policies as well as those of Republican nominee Senator Bob Dole by visiting their websites. Indeed, some people believe that use of the Internet made it possible for Reform Party candidate Jesse Ventura to win the Minnesota governorship in 1998. Limited by a shoestring budget, Ventura used the Internet to alert supporters about rallies and other activities. By 2004 the advent of Internet-arranged political meetings called "meetups," coupled with the Internet fundraising of MoveOn.org, powered the short-lived candidacy of former Vermont Governor Howard Dean, and broadcast his fall, as well as his subsequent steady return to power as chairman of the Democratic National Party.

HOW THE INTERACTIVITY OF THE INTERNET IS CHANGING POLITICS

The Internet is changing the electorate's access to political information, altering the way politicians raise money and mobilize supporters, increasing the communication between supporters and campaigns and audiences and reporters, and democratizing the production of political content. In addition, it is creating a new responsiveness—sometimes a hyperresponsiveness—among political candidates and leaders, who must respond

---

BOX 11-1   Blogs

Web logs, or *blogs,* are gaining momentum in the world of mass media. The phenomenon is characterized as follows:

■ "Veteran conservative activist Mark Krempasky, an expert on Internet Web logs (commonly known as blogs), has posted an online warning to political candidates everywhere: 'You cannot and will not hide anything anymore,' because some citizen sleuth, armed only with laptop and search engine, 'will ferret it out, just for fun.'"[a]

■ Some analysts attribute incumbent Tom Daschle's narrow defeat to John Thune in the 2004 South Dakota Senate race to blogging. Two bloggers, funded in part by the Thune campaign, launched independent sites titled South Dakota Politics and Daschle v. Thune attacking the incumbent.[b]

■ According to Joseph Epstein in the *Wall Street Journal,* "No big surprise, I suppose, in Merriam-Webster's recent announcement that 'blog' was the word most looked up on its Internet sites during the past year. Bloggers were much in the news; in fact, they often turned the direction of the news, and made a fair amount of news on their own. Bloggers caught up with many campaign lies during the past presidential election; by catching him out in shoddy journalistic practice, they cost Dan Rather an honorable departure from a long career."[c]

[a]Dick Polman, "Politics Spins a Web of Concerns," *Philadelphia Inquirer,* 13 March 2005, p. A01.
[b]Ibid.
[c]Joseph Epstein, "Blog, Blague, Blog," *Wall Street Journal,* 3 December 2004, p. A18.

---

to lightning-swift sharing of information around the country and the globe. The Internet exposes some of the inherent weaknesses of democracy, namely the ability of people to react quickly and thoughtlessly in great numbers. The Internet is the communications cement that permits multinational corporations to function seamlessly around the globe, producing an economic democracy that is truly worldwide—and extremely hard to control in the present, suddenly archaic state of global governance. It has linked up with satellite access and radio, as well as video and webcams, to produce a breathtaking immediacy of virtual experience and communication.

In less than 10 years China has gone from being a newcomer to the Internet to the country with the world's second-largest online population, but, in an effort to limit the impact of the Internet, the Chinese government uses a number of strategies to control what people see online, according to a report from the U.S. firm Dynamic Internet Technologies, which watches net use in the country. The Chinese government blocks net addresses that host web pages they do not want the Chinese people to visit. These include sites dealing with taboo subjects such as Tibet and Falun Gong as well as the BBC News website, the search engine Google, and sex sites such as Playboy as well as many blogs.[1]

Increasing Citizen Access to Information

When the presidential election of 2000 went into overtime, those with web access turned to it for the latest information on the recount just as they had rushed to it to read the Starr report on the investigation of President Clinton's conduct in the Clinton-

---

BOX 11-2   Are Bloggers Affecting the General Public?

Only one in four Americans are either familiar or somewhat familiar with blogs; more than half (56%) have no knowledge of them at all. Among Internet users only 32% are very or somewhat familiar with blogs and blogging.[a]

[a]Gallup Poll. See Lydia Saad, "Blogs Not Yet in the Media Big League," *The Gallup Organization,* 11 March 2005.

Lewinsky scandal. Readers pored over the rulings of the Florida Supreme Court and, ultimately, that of the U.S. Supreme Court. No one with Internet access had to wait for the newspapers of the following morning for the full texts. At the same time, 2000 was the first year in which both the candidates and news sites posted substantial amounts of issue information on line.

Mobilizing and Raising Money through the Web The Internet may or may not be changing the amount of political participation, but it is changing its character and channels of influence. Blogs, meetups, and organized action groups such as MoveOn.org are byproducts of the Internet. A meetup occurs when individuals from one geographic area use the Internet to post or register their interest in meeting and as a result learn that others share their interest in a topic and arrange to gather for a face-to-face mobilizing meeting. Campaign blogs replace direct mail as a means of communicating with supporters, and supporters create their own blogs to continue the conversation. Supporters talk with each other, creating communication and organization structure. The supporters of Howard Dean created identifying labels and sites (such as www.deaniacs.org). The rapid movement of organized support for Dean and his ideas has become the basis for his chairmanship of the Democratic Party, a bid to reverse the Democratic election losses of the recent years by taking advantage of grassroots sentiment as marshaled via the Internet.

In the primaries of 2000, the campaign of former New Jersey Senator Bill Bradley sought a Federal Election Commission advisory on whether the campaign could raise money through its website, accept credit card contributions, confirm contributions electronically, and use the funds raised this way toward federal matching requirements. In effect, the commission said yes, and in the process reversed its earlier decision and permitted credit card contributions. Bradley was the first presidential candidate to raise a million dollars on line. A similar fundraising effort was highly successful when the deadly tsunami struck Southeast Asia in the last days of 2004—the Internet was a crucial link in helping sympathetic citizens around the world immediately act on their feelings to send money to the devastated regions and to the primary helping organizations.

Online supporters contribute money whose cash value is enhanced because fundraising costs are all but nonexistent. These activated supporters talk back to

---

BOX 11-3 Dean and Internet Fundraising

Although Howard Dean didn't win the Democratic nomination, his campaign put Internet fundraising on the 2004 map. Before the 2004 presidential election, Howard Dean was a virtually unknown governor from Vermont. He entered the political race with a run-of-the-mill website including information of the campaign's positions. His campaign took off when volunteers transformed it into "the biggest and most active online campaign network."[a] The Dean campaign raised over $11 million online between April and September 2003.[b] In six months the Dean campaign registered more than 450,000 people to receive regular online campaign messages and sent 6.5 million emails to encourage engagement and financial support. In addition, thousands created their own, pro-Dean websites.

[a]Michael Cornfield, *Politics Moves Online* (New York: Century Foundation Press, 2004), p. xiv.
[b]Matthew J. Streb, *Law and Election Politics* (Colorado: Lynne Rienner, 2005), p. 100.

---

reporters as well as to the campaign. This process increases the efficiency of campaigns by identifying the likeminded and moving them from cyberspace to physical space. People meet others they would not meet. What does this movement from cyberworld to the noncyber political world look like, and what effect does it have on those in it?

Feedback In speeches and ads, candidates urge audiences to go to their websites for additional information and, as Democratic nominee John Kerry said in 2004, "to share your ideas." Supporters use the sites that let them talk back to the candidates. So, for example, one Kerry supporter posted a note in February 2004 saying, "Please stop repeating, after a short pause, the first few words of every other sentence in your speeches." Said another, "Since you asked. First, the wife has to look interested and engage the audience."[2]

New Forms of Attack If you searched for the phrase "miserable failure" on Google in December 2003, you would have been linked to the White House's official biography of President George W. Bush. The linking was an example of a kind of cybergraffiti known as "Google bombing." It works by individuals repeatedly linking a specific web page to a phrase, in effect teaching the Google search engine to make the association. How did this example link develop? The *New York Times* explained that a blogger tied

> the phrase to the Bush biography and began to send messages to the writers of other blogs with an anti-Bush tilt, telling them of his project. Many not only added the catchphrase to their own sites but urged readers to do the same. Craig Silverstein, Google's director for technology, says the company sees nothing wrong with the public using its search engine this way. No user is hurt, he said, because there is no clearly legitimate site for "miserable failure" being pushed aside.[3]

Websites also have become repositories of political parody. Want to see Secretary of Defense Donald Rumsfeld in his fighting poses? Cynical-C.com and paleblue.US have the pictures. For another example, take Jib-jab.com—released in July 2000—this political satire website began by featuring Bush, Kerry, and other political icons associated

---

BOX 11-4   The Rise of Google

- "To help decide if a word is ready to be entered into the lexicon, many lexicographers Google new terms. (So popular is the Internet search engine that its name has become a verb in general use—and will appear as such in the O.A.D. next month.)"[a]

- "In the past three years, Google has gone from processing 100 million searches per day to over 200 million searches per day. And get this: Only one-third come from inside the U.S. The rest are in 88 other languages."[b]

- "Google has so firmly staked out its place as the Internet search-engine leader that it has even earned a place as a verb in the English lexicon."[c]

- "In November, 47 percent of searches in the world were on sites owned by Google, up from 44 percent a year earlier. Yahoo's sites rose to 27 percent, from 25 percent a year ago."[d]

- Google has announced an ambitious new plan to create an online library: "Recently, the most popular Internet search service, Google, announced that it had concluded agreements with several leading research libraries—Harvard, the Bodleian at Oxford, Stanford, the New York Public Library—to make some of their books available online to researchers who won't have to travel to the libraries or dust their way through endless stacks of paper and ink."[e]

- "Less innocent is the industry dedicated to helping Web sites maximize their Google rankings—the racket known as 'search engine optimization.' Some American companies have armies of programmers toiling away in Bangalore solely to boost their Google rankings. Much of what the 'optimizers' do is reasonable, helping companies do a better job of presenting content, using keywords, and building pages to which others will want to link. (These are termed 'white hat' tactics.) But there are also plenty of black hats—known as 'index spammers'—who have simply adapted the methods and tricks of the old political machines."[f]

[a]Strawberry Saroyan, "In the Land of Lexicons, Having the Last Word," *New York Times,* 19 March 2005, p. 9.
[b]Thomas Friedman, "Is Google God?" *New York Times,* 29 June 2003, p. 13.
[c]Tim Gnatek, "Search Engines Build a Better Mousetrap," *New York Times,* 10 March 2005, p. G4.
[d]Saul Hansell, "Search Sites Play a Game of Constant Catch-Up," *New York Times,* 31 January 2005, p. C1.
[e]Alberto Manguel, "The Pursuit of Knowledge, From Genesis to Google," *New York Times,* 19 December 2004, Section 4, p. 5.
[f]James Surowiecki, "Search and Destroy," *New Yorker,* 31 May 2004, p. 31.

---

with the 2004 campaign, singing a parody of Woody Guthrie's "This Land is Your Land." Whitehouse.org is among the Web's most popular political satire sites. This website is a spoof of the Whitehouse's official site. It renames members of the administration; for example, Alberto Gonzalez was renamed Sec. of Genitorture, Karl Rove became Minister of Truth, and Donald Rumsfeld, Sec. Strangelove. On www.borowitz report.com, satirist Andy Borowitz writes columns satirizing politics, the economy, current events, and pop culture. You can register online and receive a free political parody delivered to your in-box every day.

These examples are not just amusing and interesting, they are extremely powerful political tools. Some present ideas in visual forms that are instantly available to shape opinion around the country; some provide instant rebuttal of positions earnestly held, some poke holes in argumentation and rationalization. The rapidity with which such parodies enter public discourse makes their creators and distributors political players to be reckoned with, for good or ill. A picture really *is* worth a thousand words.

Media consultant Tony Schwartz pioneered the use of mass communication to reach specific groups of individuals. The Internet enhances the capacity of those seeking influence to mimic Schwartz's moves. When a Bush announcement forecast his support for an amendment to the Constitution barring gay marriage, Dearmary.com was launched. This was a website launched by gay activists John Aravosis and Robin Tyler. The website urges Cheney's daughter Mary to speak out on gay rights and publicly oppose a constitutional amendment banning gay marriage The target? Vice president Dick Cheney's 34-year-old daughter Mary, a self-identified lesbian and director of Dick Cheney's vice presidential operations.

The www.prochoiceamerica.org invites you to sign up for e-mails with news. It also includes ways to take action, lets you sign the Freedom of Choice Act, facilitates contacting members of Congress, volunteering, and provides information on campus organizing. Lifenews.com is an independent news agency devoted to reporting news that interests the pro-life community. Topics covered include abortion, human cloning, and stem cell research, euthanasia and assisted suicide, campaigns and elections, and legal issues. This website invites visitors to sign up for daily or weekly emails with news. The website provides links to related websites, includes pertinent stories both national and international and editorials written by lifenews writers.

The Reader as Writer and Critic In this Internet-linked world, the reporter becomes an audience for the reader/viewer. Reporters covering the 2004 campaign and pundits who commented on it have been deluged with e-mail from outraged readers and viewers. Sometimes the channels are direct. Reader reads, listener listens, viewer watches and contacts reporter, anchor, or pundit. "Nearly every time there's a story about Dean in the paper, my e-mail in-box fills with complaints from his fans," writes *New York Times* public editor Daniel Okrent.[4]

E-mail offers a channel through which to launch an immediate critique. When U.S. Treasury Secretary John Snow appeared on CNBC's *MorningCall* and sidestepped questions on outsourcing, the controversial business practice of using relatively cheap foreign labor to do jobs that were formerly done by U.S. workers, his performance "sparked an hour-long torrent of e-mail to the show hosts. Most of it—by a ratio of five to one—was critical of the secretary. The most repeated description of his comments: 'Snow job.'" Conservative columnist and commentator Alan Murray noted, "Despite the quirks of this focus group, their strong reaction to Mr. Snow's comments is telling. The CNBC audience, after all, is more Republican than Democratic and more pro than anti-business. If the administration's message is failing here, imagine how it's playing with the broader public"[5] Murray then wrote a column offering the Bush administration some advice on how to handle the issue of outsourcing.

The Downside

Lurkers and Trolls The presence of lurkers and trolls makes cyberspace hospitable to the kind of political behavior that once took the form of midnight fliers left on windshields and, as a result, subject to subterfuge. In January 2003, for example, an e-mail was sent out from Dean campaign manager Joe Trippi, or so it seemed. In the message

---

BOX 11-5   Phishing: A New, Rapidly Expanding Type of Identity Theft

Phishing e-mails look as if they were urgent requests for personal information in the form of a reputable institution or company. The e-mails send you a link to a website requesting personal information that is later used to steal your identity. Physical disasters serve as the impetus for phishing. After the tsunami disaster, scammers sent e-mails with messages saying such things as "Please donate $100 to help give food and medical to two million forced immigrants, 500,000 homeless and 33,000 victims of South Asian tsunami." This e-mail provides a link to a website filled with pictures of tsunami victims and news accounts of relief efforts. When people respond to it and in the process provide a credit card number, they have turned information over to scam artists.[a]

[a]"Come into My Parlour," *Business Line,* 31 January 2005.

"he purportedly advised gay volunteers from out of state not to stay in the homes of Iowa supporters."[6] The e-mail was a fake. It took the campaign weeks to quell supporters' concerns about authenticity. Unlike midnight fliers, however, Internet traffic leaves an electronic trace. Under what circumstances would a campaign be able to gain access to that electronic trace? September 11 prompted a rush of fake Internet activity. For example, anonymous e-mails claimed that an Arab male had warned his wife not to fly on September 11 or visit any mall on October 31. The FBI dispelled the rumor, stating, "The FBI has conducted an inquiry into the source of this e-mail and determined that the alleged threat is not credible."[7]

Spreading Inaccurate Information   In other cases, talk radio or a blog encapsulates a report, sometimes with minimal accuracy. The communications take place outside public view. They burst into public sight when a mass outlet reports them, as Daniel Okrent, the public editor for the *New York Times,* did.[8] In that case, those complaining were not subscribers. They had been misinformed by a posting by "Doug from Upland" on FreeRepublic, which bills itself as the "premier Conservative News Forum." Doug had urged readers to call Richard Stevenson of the *New York Times* to insist that he "correct the record" contained in a *New York Times* story he had co-authored on reactions to new Bush ads. The appeal included Stevenson's phone number. "Soon," reports Okrent, "Stevenson's phone was ringing like an alarm clock, his voice mail filling up . . . 'with messages that impugned [his] professionalism and patriotism.' Only one person, he said, bothered to leave a name and a phone number."

The problem? An Australian paper had combined details from a number of news sources while leaving the *New York Times* byline in place. The material that offended Doug from Upland had not been in the original *Times* article. When informed of the fact, Doug posted an apology to Stevenson.

From an e-mail I received from Stevenson: "to those who read your post and called me to leave abusive messages that impugned my professionalism and patriotism, please pass along this response: We take criticism very seriously. When we mess up, we try to acknowledge it and correct it. But calling and swearing at me, making ugly personal statements and jumping to conclusions on the basis of sketchy information—which in this case turned out to be dead wrong—is no way to engage me or my newspaper in a dialog. And I would point out that not one caller other than Doug had the guts to provide a name or a phone number. . . ."

"Dick, this is to you. I hope you accept the apology, and I am sorry it ruined your Sunday. But I also want to challenge you. I hope you will write a follow-up story. 'Relatives of victims' was technically accurate, but it was incomplete. Please check out September 11 Families for Peaceful Tomorrows. Please investigate the source of a great deal of their funding. That is the next story that needs to be written. When that one is written, FReepers will send notes of congratulations to comments@nytimes.com."[9]

MAINSTREAM AS MONITOR OF THE NEW MEDIUM

The role of the Drudge Report in fueling news coverage of the Clinton-Lewinsky relationship has been well documented. Drudge pushed the Lewinsky allegations into the mainstream with a report that *Newsweek* was sitting on the story of incumbent President Bill Clinton's alleged involvement with a White House intern. The continuing pressure that Internet sources place on traditional news requires ongoing scrutiny. Among other things, mainstream news has begun to assume the role of policing the Internet. Important questions concern this new role: When, how, why, and with what effect are such policing efforts taking place? A 2004 move by the *New York Times* is illustrative. As Republican spokespeople, including former Republican House Speaker Newt Gingrich, argued that Kerry's "a Jane Fonda antiwar liberal,"[10] two images of Democratic presidential contender John Kerry began circulating through e-mail. In a controversial move, actress Jane Fonda had gone to North Vietnam at the height of the Vietnam War to protest the U.S. involvement in it. Those who opposed her move labeled her "Hanoi Jane" and denounced her as a traitor. Those who thought the war was unjust and futile were more disposed to applaud her protests. One picture accurately showed Kerry seated three rows behind Jane Fonda at an antiwar rally 35 years earlier. The second showed Kerry and Jane Fonda at the same podium, with Fonda at the mike. The *New York Times* ran a copy of the June 13, 1970, original showing Kerry alone at the podium and the doctored photo that included Fonda there, along with the observation that the second picture is a "hoax, according to the photo agency that owns the original."[11]

DEMOCRATIZING THE PRODUCTION OF CONTENT:

THE CITIZEN AS CONTENT PRODUCER

MoveOn.org's contest to find and air the best citizen-produced anti-Bush ad illustrates a new relationship between citizens and the media. The contest, which elicited over 1,500 entries, asked entrants to create a 20-second ad that "told the truth about the president and his policies." On line, viewers cast about 2.9 million votes to identify the "best" ad. The winner, which showed children working in low-wage jobs, asked, "Guess who's going to pay off President Bush's $1 trillion deficit?" The top-rated ad was given $15 million in air play by MoveOn.org in mid-January 2004. We don't ordinarily think of people with minicams as ad producers, because individuals can't afford airtime to bring content to a mass audience. By raising the funds and using the Internet to generate entries, however, MoveOn.org flipped on its head the traditional assumption about who produces political content for the masses.

MoveOn.org was founded in 1998. It drew its name from its mission: An effort to urge the U.S. Congress to move on and away from the impeachment process against President Clinton. It did the same with its March 2004 appeal to its e-mail list to help Al Franken, host of a new liberal talk radio show, find fodder for the show: "We're teaming up with Franken on a contest to find the stupidest or most clearly false (or preferably both) statement by a major right-wing figure or Bush administration official," said the e-mail appeal. "Over the next week, any stupid or misleading comment you hear on the radio or see on TV is fair game as an entry. If your comment is selected by Al Franken as the winner, you'll receive a personalized and autographed copy of Al Franken's book, *Lies and the Lying Liars That Tell Them,* and you'll be recognized on-air" (personal communication).

After a careful study of the effects of candidate web pages in 2000, Bruce Bimber and Richard Davis predicted that in the future

1. The Internet's supplemental role in U.S. electoral campaigns will solidify as a form of niche communication directed at specific audiences.
2. The Internet will offer campaigns a new and highly effective tool for mobilizing activists—a prediction since borne out by the Dean campaign and the success of MoveOn.org in the primaries of 2004. Democratic Party members are hoping that Howard Dean will employ his fundraising skills as new chairman of the Democratic National Committee (DNC). With Dean at the helm, the DNC raised $3.4 million in three weeks. This is more than twice the amount that organization raised in 2001 after George W.'s first presidential victory. So far, the money has been raised without a single Internet solicitation. Dean says he intends to begin Internet solicitation "sooner rather than later."[12]
3. Citizens who are politically interested and active increasingly will use the Internet as a vehicle for satisfying their need for information and support.
4. The Internet will *not* produce the mobilization of voters long predicted—a prediction called into question by the success of meetups in 2004. Meetup.com is the website that facilitates the meeting of likeminded people based on geographic location. "Meetups" is the term for the meeting that takes place as a result of the website.
5. The divide between those who are political activists interested in electoral campaigns and those who are not will expand.[13]

There is a great deal that those studying the Internet don't yet know about its effect on politics. Does the synergy of like-minded partisans affect their attitudes? Does it increase their willingness to contribute money and time, and their willingness to vote? Does it prompt them to overestimate the extent to which their candidate is supported by others? Push them to extreme opinions? Produce higher levels of partisan communication with nonpartisans than otherwise would occur? Are these the active communication participants who used to be the ones who wrote letters to the editor? Or a different group—newly energized by the capacities of the Internet? The large numbers that went on line in the 2004 election will make it possible for scholars to use the National Annenberg

---

BOX 11-6   Social Security: Discrepancy between SSA Website and Bush Plan

The Bush administration has been traveling the United States plugging the president's Social Security reform plan that would create individual investment accounts, but does the Social Security Administration's website agree? The agency's website includes a question-and-answer section with the following exchange:

"Question: I think I could do better if you let me invest the Social Security I pay into an individual retirement plan (I.R.A.) or some other investment plan. What do you think?

Answer: Maybe you could, but then again, maybe your investments wouldn't work out.

Remember these facts: Your Social Security taxes pay for potential disability and survivors benefits as well as for retirement benefits. Social Security incorporates social goals—such as giving more protection to families and to low-income workers—that are not part of private pension plans; and Social Security benefits are adjusted yearly for increases in cost of living—a feature not present in many private plans."

This exchange has been on the site for years.[a]

[a]David E. Rosenbaum, "Agency's Web Site Out of Sync with Bush Plan," *New York Times,* 25 March 2005, p. A12.

Election Survey's 85,000 individual interviews to answer these questions. According to a study conduced by the Pew Internet and American Life Project in 2004, 75 million Americans used the Internet to get political information.[14]

WEB ADS

By creating inexpensive web ads, campaigns invite news coverage of their content. By e-mailing the link to the candidates' followers, web ad content secures cheap distribution as followers relay the web ad page to their friends. In early April 2004, for example, the Kerry campaign posted an ad poking fun at the Bush budgeting process. In it the president is shown as a young man who can't figure out how to balance his budget. A voice pretending to be Bush interacts with his disapproving teacher. The teacher notes that he has forgotten to include his tax cut, prescription drug benefit, and Social Security plans in his numbers. "When I'm president," says the young voice, "I'm gonna spend as much money as I want." A voiceover closes the ad by intoning, "And that's exactly what George Bush did."

In mid-February the Kerry and Bush campaigns exchanged Internet ads, gaining free news time on "Meet the Press," "Hardball," and "Hannity and Colmes," among other outlets. The Bush-Cheney ad multiplied its impact when the campaign e-mailed it to 6 million supporters. Despite the rise in Internet activity, in the 2004 campaign more money was devoted to television commercials than web ads. The first study ever conducted on Internet ads, administered by the Pew Internet and American Life Project, found that the Bush and Kerry campaigns and associated independent groups spent $2.6 million on posted web ads from January to August 2004. An estimated $330 million was spent on television ads in the top 100 media markets during the same period of time.[15] The Democratic and Republican presidential candidates used different web strategies. The Bush campaign targeted ads at mothers and swing state voters.

BOX 11-7   The Future of the Internet

There exists speculation that we are still in the primitive stages of the Internet . . .

According to Joe Trippi . . . "Right now, we're in 1955, in terms of the Net's potential power in politics. We're at the three-channel, black and white stage. It will be explosive by 2008."[a]

The Pew Internet and American Life Project conducted a study regarding the future of the Internet.

- "This survey finds that there is a strong across-the-board consensus that the internet will become so important to users in the coming decade that the network itself will become an inviting target for attack. By a nearly 3–1 margin, the experts in this survey expressed worry about the vulnerability of the internet and the likelihood of an attack on the underlying infrastructure within the next 10 years."[b]
- "The internet will be more deeply integrated in our physical environments and

high-speed connections will proliferate—with mixed results."[c]

- "In the emerging era of the blog, experts believe the internet will bring yet more dramatic change to the news and publishing worlds. They predict the least amount of change to religion."[d]
- "Prediction: By 2014, most people will use the internet in a way that filters out information that challenges their viewpoints on political and social issues. This will further polarize political discourse and make it difficult or impossible to develop meaningful consensus on public problems." 32% agree, 37% disagree, 13% challenge and 18% did not respond.[e]

[a]Dick Polman, "Politics Spins a Web of Concerns," *Philadelphia Inquirer,* 13 March 2005, p. A01.
[b]Pew Internet and American Life, online at http://www.pewinternet.org/pdfs/PIP_Future_of_Internet.pdf.
[c]Ibid.
[d]Ibid.
[e]Ibid.

They spent most of their money at the beginning of the campaign on an ad featuring first lady Laura Bush. Parents.com, Ladies Home Journal Online, and Miami Herald's Spanish edition were among the sites used by the Bush campaign. The campaign then spent little money on web ads. The Kerry campaign focused its web ads on fundraising. It concentrated its websites on Democrats in metropolitan areas.

Probably the public's use of the web for political information and campaigns' use of it to reach the desired audience will continue to increase. Increased reliance will bring calls for regulation.

TO SUM UP

The Internet is a channel that affects news and politics and that offers an additional outlet for advertising. Its effects remain unclear. There is clear evidence of interaction between those using the Internet and those producing the news, and evidence that the Internet has influenced some dimensions of political campaigns. Pop-up and floating ads are everywhere on websites. At the same time, it is still difficult to assess the meaning and influence of interactions between news, advertising, and politics and the Internet.

BOX 11-8   Federal Election Commission Considers Web Politics

---

On March 24, 2005, the Federal Election Commission proposed new ways to apply the rules of campaign finance to online political activity. The rules address political advertising on the Internet, that such ads could not be bought using unlimited "soft money" contributions. At the same time, these rules would exempt political activity by individuals and web sites that carry news and editorial content.[a]

"We are almost certainly going to move from an environment in which the Internet was per se not regulated to where it is going to be regulated in some part," said FEC Commissioner David Mason, a Republican. "That shift has huge significance because it means that people who are conducting political activity on the Internet are suddenly going to have to worry about or at least be conscious of certain legal distinctions and lines they didn't used to have to worry about."[b]

Should bloggers who work for political campaigns be required to disclose that relationship? Should blogs include a disclaimer stating that they were paid for by a campaign? If a supporter links his website to a candidate's home page, is that a campaign contribution?

DailyKos.com, a popular liberal website, promotes political debate and participants attack conservative policies and discuss the future of the Democratic Party, lively free speech that the First Amendment was designed to protect. In the last election, however, DailyKos.com "urged readers to support the 'Kos Dozen,' a group of favored Democrats; raised more than $574,000 for candidates; provided online links to campaigns; and connected members to a PAC that supports progressive politicians. In June 2006, its readers are even holding their own political convention."[c]

Such activities show the challenge facing the Federal Election Commission in the wake of a court ruling forcing the commission to regulate political activity on the Internet. Although the First Amendment prohibits regulating most speech, a wide array of online activities arguably could be viewed as "contributing to" or "coordinating" with political campaigns, which falls under the FEC's domain.

[a]Glen Justice, "Election Commission Urges Finance Rules for Online Politics," *New York Times,* 25 March 2005, p. A10.
[b]Brian Faler, "FEC Considers Restricting Online Political Activities," *Washington Post,* 21 March 2005, p. A10.
[c]Dawn Withers, "Specter of Regulation Haunts Political Blogs Judge's Ruling Ordering New Federal Election Commission Rules on the Internet Provokes Uproar Among Civil Libertarians and on the Web," Washington Bureau, *Chicago Tribune,* 22 March 2005, online at chicago tribune.com.

 Use InfoTrac College Edition to access information on topics in this chapter from hundreds of periodicals and scholarly journals. Enter keyword and subject searches: *Google, blogs, meetups, Howard Dean, MoveOn.org.*

SELECTED READINGS

Bimber, Bruce, and Richard Davis. *Campaigning Online: The Internet in U.S. Elections.* New York: Oxford University Press, 2003.

Cornfield, Michael, *Politics Moves Online.* New York: Century Foundation Press, 2004.

Pew Internet and American Life, online at http://www.pewinternet.org/pdfs/PIP_Future_of_Internet.pdf.

Streb, Matthew J. *Law and Election Politics.* Colorado: Lynne Rienner, 2005.

12　News and Advertising in the Political Campaign

The U.S. political process has produced few candidates whose images when in office differed shockingly from their campaign images. A candidate knows that she or he cannot entirely control the news coverage of the campaign. Because differences between the image projected in commercials and the actual behavior of the candidate are likely to be exposed in campaign reporting, commercials cannot stray too far from the truth about the candidate without great risk. Indeed, major campaign goals are creating a positive, electable image of the candidate, ensuring that the image is communicated consistently throughout the campaign and that it is underscored by news coverage.

To accomplish these ends, the campaign staff seeks to

1. Control news coverage by controlling media access, setting the media's agenda, and creating credible pseudo-events
2. Blur the distinction between news and commercials to increase the credibility of the commercial's message
3. Exploit the linguistic categories reflecting criteria for newsworthiness and the conventions of news presentations through which journalists view campaigns
4. Insulate the candidate from attack.
5. Enlist the help of journalists in responding to attacks.

CONTROLLING NEWS COVERAGE

Particularly when a candidate seeks the U.S. presidency, it is unlikely that serious character flaws or past misdeeds will escape public scrutiny. If a candidate's commercials create the image of a quiet, reasonable individual but the politician hurls ashtrays when unhappy with staff work, a disgruntled or indiscreet staff member is likely to point out the disparity to journalists. If the candidate is a philanderer but the campaign stresses his image as a good family man, reporters are likely to find out and, in one way or another, convey the contrast to the public.

Journalists have always been aware of discrepancies between image and actuality. Until recently, however, an unwritten journalistic code said that private activities of politicians that did not affect their conduct in office, ought not be made public. During the 1982 centenary celebration of Franklin Delano Roosevelt's birth, reporters focused attention on this changed standard by telling us that during FDR's four terms as president, the news media hid the disabling effects of his polio from the public. An article in the *Washington Post*, for example, noted that in 1932 the press corps made no mention of FDR's fall when, during a speech in Georgia, the podium that was supposed to be bolted to the floor as a brace slid forward. The same article reminded readers that "although he spent most of his waking hours either in or near a wheelchair, no photograph of this chair ever appeared in the papers or magazines during his lifetime."[1] Nor did newspeople reveal FDR's prolonged involvement with Lucy Mercer. In Chapter 2 we examined the increasing encroachment of the press on what once was considered private space.

Candidates obviously want to minimize journalistic access to information that might contradict the image their campaigns are trying to convey. Strategies employed in this effort were explored in Chapter 4. Yet candidates are constantly being tripped up by news coverage of events they themselves supposedly controlled.

For example, on a cattle roundup, calculated to stress his masculine, Texas background, 1990 Republican gubernatorial candidate Clayton Williams commented to the assembled reporters that one should treat the advent of poor weather the way one should treat an inevitable rape—just lie back and enjoy it. The remark created a furor and raised questions about Williams's sensitivity to issues of special concern to women.

A candidate can also benefit from the image created by the media. Media focus on George (H. W.) and Barbara Bush's dog Millie, Bill and Hillary Clinton's dog Buddy and cat Socks, and George (W.) and Laura Bush's dog Barney added a dimension of humanity and warmth to their personas that would have been denied if the dogs and cat had not become media favorites. When Barney was featured in a holiday video on the White House website in December 2003, the video was played on television news shows and written up in newspapers.

To increase the probability that what people see and hear in the news will be consistent with the campaign theme, politicians employ all available strategies for manipulating the press. We next illustrate how these strategies have been used in past campaigns and demonstrate the incumbent's advantage in manipulating media.

Controlling Media Access

Public officials routinely control press access and media exposure as best they can. Control becomes particularly sensitive in times of international crisis or war. They also issue, at times less likely to reach large numbers of news viewers, material that they consider problematic. So, for example, in February 2004 in the face of ongoing press questioning whether Bush had fulfilled his obligations while serving in the Texas Air National Guard, his staff released his military records. The release occurred late on a Friday. Because the following Monday was a federal holiday and a long weekend for many reporters, the late Friday release decreased the likelihood that there would be critical coverage over the weekend.

Setting the Media's Agenda

Maxwell McCombs has argued persuasively that the news media do not tell us what to think as much as they tell us what to think about. From the thousands of events and people that satisfy basic news norms, some move to the top of the media agenda. For example, in 2004 the story that topped the news agenda, with a total of 1353 minutes of coverage on ABC, CBS, and NBC weekday evening news, was that the United States–led invasion forces combat continues in Iraq. Iraq postwar reconstruction, elections and new government placed second, with 710 minutes of coverage.[2]

Agenda-setting theory suggests that the public's sense of what problems need attention is affected as much by media coverage as by personal experience. Public opinion in turn influences political action. For example, in 1994, the U.S. crime rate was dropping. Violent crime was down as well. Yet polls reflected public concern about crime, so President Clinton expanded a section of his State of the Union address to respond to that concern. The concern may have been driven by overreporting of crime in local news.[3]

Because only a small number of issues can sustain public interest at any one time, the agenda-setting capacity of the media is limited. An issue, in other words, moves up the agenda at the expense of other issues. For example, news coverage of the federal deficit, the first Persian Gulf War, and the recession influenced how important the public thought each issue was, but the issues themselves competed for public attention. As an issue gained prominence, it drew converts from other issues. Agenda setting is a zero-sum game; as one issue gains coverage, other issues necessarily lose media attention.[4]

The more personal experience an individual has with an issue, however, the less likely it is that the media will set that person's agenda. On any given day, the president exercises more control over the news agenda than do most other public officials in the United States. An incumbent official, particularly an incumbent president, has more control over setting this agenda than does a challenger. An analysis of the period from 1986 to 1996 comparing *New York Times* coverage with the messages of presidents from Reagan through Clinton, found that when the president sets the national news agenda, public approval of his conduct in office rises.[5] The president's capacity to set the agenda is in part a function of the issues on which his party's credibility is high.

Media focus on one topic can displace others. For example, in 1998 a major U.S. corporation announced layoffs in a release timed to coincide with a significant break in the Clinton-Lewinsky scandal, and timing was rewarded by minimal news play. On a larger scale, the story that dominated the press in the weeks before September 11, 2001, the disappearance of Chandra Levi, House intern and friend of Congressman Gary Condit, became unnewsworthy after the terrorist attacks. In late 2003, the capture of Saddam Hussein prompted major newsweeklies to bump Democratic presidential frontrunner Howard Dean off their columns.

News focus can also drive policy. Policies such as laws against drunk driving were fueled in the 1980s in part by increased media attention to this issue between 1981 and 1984. When media attention faded, policy action continued, but at a slower rate.[6]

Creating Credible Pseudo-Events

Politicians routinely create pseudo-events, staged events designed for media coverage. In the last decade, reporters have become more skeptical of such events staged by or for politicians—particularly since Joe McGinniss's book *The Selling of the President, 1968* revealed the extent to which Richard Nixon had been packaged by media consultants in 1968. As a result, the artificial nature of such events and their explicit goal of media coverage are now pointed out by newspeople almost as a matter of journalistic honor.

CASE STUDY 12-1   Pseudo-Events

On February 8, 2004, the week before the Democratic primary in Tennessee in which retired General Wesley Clark was a contender, the *Los Angeles Times* reported (with no byline—a story headed "Surprise Supporter," p. A36) a story from Lebanon, Tennessee:

> Retired Army Gen. Wesley K. Clark received a welcome respite from the usual campaign grind during a Thursday stop at the military academy he attended as a sophomore. The surprise's name: Fitim Zeqiri.
>
> The 16-year-old ethnic Kosovar Albanian met the former NATO supreme commander in 1999 and reacquainted himself with the Democratic candidate here. Clark appeared touched and delighted when introduced to Zeqiri and his family, now settled in Gallatin, Tenn.
>
> Zeqiri said his family was living in a refugee camp in the Balkans when he first shook Clark's hand. Clark commanded the 78-day NATO bombing campaign that led to the end of the conflict in Kosovo and the downfall of Serbian leader Slobodan Milosevic. . . .
>
> "He's the one who really brought peace over there," a nervous Zeqiri told the audience. "Now 3 million people are living free over there, and having some rights that they never had and never even dreamed about."[a]

Zeqiri could have met privately with Clark. The public format ensured media coverage. To explain who Zeqiri is and why he is there, the reporter recaps Clark's role as NATO commander. Zeqiri's testimony says that Clark is responsible for the freedom of 3 million others like him, a claim that would sound self-aggrandizing had it been spoken by Clark.

Unanswered by the short piece is the question, Why Is Zeqiri in Tennessee and not Kosovo? What role, if any, did Clark's staff play in Zeqiri's appearance and statement? A pseudo-event is most effective when the audience assumes that is occurred on its own and was not contrived.

Pseudo-events also are used to rebut charges to which the candidate is vulnerable. So for example, a Democrat who favors the assault weapons ban (which came up for renewal in 2004) but also wants the votes of labor union members who are NRA members and gun owners might do as John Kerry did in October 2003 and go on a pheasant-hunting trip. The *New York Times* reported, "In duck boots from L.L. Bean, blue jeans, two flannel shirts and orange safety vest, Mr. Kerry tramped through the brush of an old cornfield with a local farmer's 9-year-old English pointer, Buck, trailing. Less than five minutes into his expedition, before journalists could get out of their cars and hurdle a barbed-wire fence to record the moment, Buck rousted a bird, Kerry took aim and fired, and the first blood of the Democratic presidential campaign was spilled . . . 'I believe in the Second Amendment in this country,' Mr. Kerry [said]. . . . 'But I don't believe that assault weapons ought to be sold in the streets of America.' "[b]

[a]"Surprise Supporter," from the article "Campaign 2004/Trail Mix," compiled from *L.A. Times* staff, wire, and web reports, *Los Angeles Times*, February 8, 2004, p. A36. Copyright 2004 Los Angeles Times. Reprinted with permission.
[b]David Halbfinger, "Shotgun in Hand, Kerry Defines His Gun-Control Stance," *New York Times*, November 1, 2003, p. A10. Copyright © 2003 by The New York Times Co. Reprinted with permission.

Using Ads to Contextualize News

A full-page ad in the *New York Times* on April 16, 2004 (p. A11) frames news that the reader will presumably see in the following days in the paper. "Will Bush and Cheney Break Their Promise to America's Police?" asks the headline. "Tomorrow," says the ad, "Vice President Dick Cheney speaks to the National Rifle Association convention in

Pittsburgh. What a golden opportunity to tell the NRA the President wants the federal assault weapons ban renewed!. . . The President says he supports renewing the assault weapons ban. But he's done absolutely nothing to make that happen. Here's his chance to do what he says—and confront the one special interest in America that's blocking renewal." Sponsored by stoptheNRA.com, and funded by the Brady Campaign to Prevent Gun Violence, the ad asks the reader to send Bush and Cheney a message. How? By signing a petition at the listed website, by joining the Million Mom March on Washington on Sunday, May 9, and by contributing money to the cause.[7]

This ad tries to set an agenda for reporters by setting up a conflict between the sponsoring group and Vice President Cheney. It reminds *Times* readers of President Bush's promise. And it seeks to turn the widespread support for the assault weapons ban, which was set to expire, into money to be used in the campaign against gun violence.

Blurring the Distinction between News and Commercials

Voters report that their voting decisions are more influenced by what they read, see, and hear in news, documentary, and public affairs programming than by what they gather from commercials. Such research is flawed by its reliance on self-report data. I am not likely to admit that I am influenced by something as crass and manipulative as a commercial when I can say instead that I was influenced by a more socially approved channel of information, such as the news. In addition, it is likely that most of us are unaware of the primary channels influencing our decisions. Channels also influence each other, making it impossible to distinguish the influence of one from that of the others. Nevertheless, the mandated disclosure statement, or tag, reminds us that the source of the message is self-interested.

As a result, campaign commercials often are made to look as much like news as possible. Commercials may use actual news footage, as San Francisco's former mayor Diane Feinstein did in the 1990 California gubernatorial race. Her ads included a news clip of her announcing the murder of her predecessor. The news clip underscored Feinstein's theme: "Tough and Caring."

Campaign commercials also use production techniques identified with news coverage. Cinéma vérité techniques such as handheld cameras and natural lighting give the commercials the look of documentaries, for example. Formats we identify as those of public affairs programs also invest commercials with the credibility of news.

Print ads can also capitalize on the credibility of news sources by reprinting and distributing favorable media coverage of the candidate or by reproducing newspaper editorials endorsing the candidate. Alternatively, attack ads feature negative news clips about the opponent. Throughout the fall of 2003, MoveOn.org sponsored print ads that quoted statements by the Bush administration about the existence of weapons of mass destruction in Iraq, in order to contrast them with the absence of postwar evidence of such weapons.

Slice-of-life commercials also resemble news clips. These commercials walk the viewer through part of the candidate's day, permitting voters to eavesdrop on exchanges with important people, overhear warm human exchanges with constituents or would-be supporters, and see the candidate with family. The difference between such a commercial and a comparable news item lies in who controls the editing process. The slice-of-life commercial will not show the candidate making a mistake, being manipulated by staff, or exhibiting characteristics inconsistent with the image being projected in the other paid media. The real news clip might well show all three.

To blur the distinction between news and commercials, the political ad often buries its mandated disclosure at the bottom of the last frames, thus minimizing the likelihood that we will recall that what we heard or saw was sponsored by the campaign. In addition, campaign managers encourage us to remember advertised content as news content by placing their ads adjacent to news and public affairs programming. In summary, then, politicians deliberately blur the distinction between news and ads by placing their ads near news and employing newslike formats and newslike or news content in the ads themselves.

Furthermore, a candidate can attempt to obtain news coverage that will serve as advertising as well as news by creating a pseudo-event that plays both in news and as advertising.

Exploiting Media Concepts of the Political Process

Like the rest of us, journalists see the world through language that limits what can be seen and how it will be interpreted. In the next sections, we discuss some terminology used to describe the political process; this terminology illustrates journalistic concepts of political campaigns and political candidates and also illustrates the criteria for newsworthiness discussed in Chapter 2.

The Campaign   The media tend to see political campaigns as contests. The contest is described in battle metaphors, sports metaphors, or a combination of the two. If the electoral process is viewed as a game, it has contending sides, rules, and a goal.[8] Sports metaphors enable reporters to describe vividly the stages of the process (early primaries are the first innings or the first quarter), the intensity of the struggle (two outs in the ninth with the runner at bat, third down in the last quarter), the stakes (Super Bowl Sunday, the World Series), and the outcome (touchdown, home run).

Battle metaphors enable reporters to describe the staff and volunteers as troops, the primary as a battleground, the strategy as a process of mapping out options, and the outcome as analogous to Armageddon or Waterloo. Strategic options include a holding action, a retreat, a withdrawal, a first strike, or a preemptive strike. The outcome can be defeat, victory, or a rout. Candidates can declare a truce, sign an armistice, sign a peace treaty, declare war, or continue hostilities. Reporters can also dip into the biblical past to resurrect images of David and Goliath or, in the case of feuding among ideological kin, Cain and Abel.

When candidates campaign by attacking rather than advocating, they invite the press to describe the campaign in military terms. However, the common assumption that candidates spend more of their time attacking is inaccurate. Jamieson's analysis of the speeches of presidential candidates during the 1996 general election campaign shows that candidate attack in speeches is rare. As the charts in Chapter 10 show, attack is not even the norm in political ads. Our belief that campaigns are saturated with attack is probably drawn from press accounts that feature attack and downplay advocacy.

The metaphors that the press and politicians use to discuss politics reflect and reinforce the view that "campaigning" is an extended battle. "Like heavyweight boxers," wrote Martin Kasindorf for *Newsday* in 1996, "they step into the ring tonight after days of seclusion in training camp. The titleholder, President Bill Clinton, has been alternately cramming and golfing. Republican Bob Dole had four sparring sessions last week in a ballroom below his Bal Harbour, Fla., condominium."[9]

The press casts politics as war by other means as well. In the 1992 presidential election, allegations about extramarital affairs were dubbed "bombshells." Clinton was described as organizing a "squadron" of defenders to respond. The attacks preceding Super Tuesday "shell-shocked" the Clinton campaign. Meanwhile, Senator Bob Kerrey "dive-bombed into the state with a strong attack." Jerry Brown was the "kamikaze" candidate with whom Clinton had to deal. Bush was engaged in an "anti-Perot blitz." Effective ads were labeled "killers" and "hand grenades." Political susceptibilities were termed "land mines."

The language of war invites us to see "campaigns" as a series of "tactical maneuvers," not as a discussion of the problems facing the country and the best means of addressing them. Winning, not finding the most practicable solutions, is the goal of the campaign as war. Such a framework invites public cynicism. At the same time, it obscures the relationship between the "campaign" and governance. The language of war traffics in the Manichean dualities of allies and enemies, the United States as savior against Saddam Hussein as Satan, the candidate of the rich versus the candidate of the rest, the champion of morality and middle-class values against the scoundrel bent on destroying everything we hold dear.

By conceiving of the candidates as adversaries without common ground, the language of war focuses on areas of conflict and ignores categories of consensus. Lost in the focus on the politics of maneuver and attack in 2000 was the fundamental difference between George W. Bush and Al Gore's positions on education reform, abortion rights, gun control, and the fundamental similarity of their positions on trade (both supported NAFTA, the North American Free Trade Agreement) and the death penalty (both favored it and opposed a moratorium).

Their areas of agreement forecast governance. Both favored a prescription drug benefit for seniors; both proposed voluntary, not mandatory, use of it; they differed on whether it should be administered solely through Medicare (a process Gore favored and Bush opposed). With some Democratic support, a prescription drug benefit passed and was signed into law by President Bush. Because the Republicans controlled both houses of Congress, private insurers had a bigger role in the final product than they would have had the Democrats controlled Congress with a Democrat in the White House. Yet it is precisely the areas of agreement that ultimately make governance possible. In a two-party system, lawmaking and other forms of collective action are the by-products of forms of compromise and conciliation that are not forecast by scorched-earth campaigns. The rhetoric of bullets and ballistics directs our attention to attacks and their effectiveness, not to expositions of the differences and similarities among the candidates' policy proposals. In the process, such rhetoric reduces press coverage of the campaign's most informative discourse to two meaningless questions: "Who won and lost the debate?" and "What was the debate's single decisive moment?"

The Candidates In the linguistic world of the news media, there are front-runners, contenders, minor candidates, and also-rans. "Could the race for the Democratic nomination turn into an expensive slugfest that could undercut chances of defeating President Bush?" ask John Harwood, Jeanne Cummings, and Jacob M. Schlesinger in

---

CASE STUDY 12-2   Campaigns as Seen through Their Slogans or Themes

---

The essence of a well-conceived political campaign is distilled in its advertising; the essence of its advertising is distilled in a slogan or theme reflecting the campaign's core by answering the questions "Why is this candidate running?" and "Why should I vote for this candidate?"

In the 1960 presidential campaign, for instance, Richard Nixon and his vice presidential running mate Henry Cabot Lodge summed up their campaign in the slogan, "Nixon–Lodge: They Understand What Peace Demands." The advertising slogan revealed that unlike Lyndon Johnson, John Kennedy's running mate, Lodge was a central part of the argument for the election of Nixon. Kennedy's slogan, "Leadership for the 60's," did not mention Johnson and, except for a milli-second glimpse of LBJ's picture on a placard in a televised ad designed both to build name recognition for Kennedy and to create a bandwagon for the Democratic ticket, LBJ was conspicuously absent from national televised advertising. By contrast, Lodge—his height dwarfing Nixon—not only was featured in the still photograph that closed each Republican ad but also starred in a series of ads. What the 1960 ads reflect is the respective functions of Lodge and Johnson in the campaign. Lodge appeared in nationally aired ads because he strengthened the ticket throughout the country. Johnson's value was primarily regional; consequently, as a campaigner he concentrated his time on rallying the South behind the Democratic ticket.

The Nixon–Lodge slogan also indicates that the campaign stressed the comparative advantage the Republican ticket offered in foreign policy from Lodge's U.N. ambassadorship and Nixon's vice presidential experience. Consistent with the campaign theme, televised ads for Nixon translated questions of domestic policy into questions of foreign policy. In one ad, for example, a disembodied voice asked, "Mr. Nixon, what is the truth? Is America lagging behind in economic growth?" Nixon, seated on a desk, assures the viewer that the U.S. economy is healthy and adds, "This is the kind of economic growth we must have to keep

the peace." Each ad closed with the tag "Nixon–Lodge: They Understand What Peace Demands."

Consistent with his theme, Kennedy's opening statement in the first Kennedy–Nixon debate focused the election on domestic questions:

In the election of 1860, Abraham Lincoln said the question was whether this nation could exist half-slave or half-free. In the election of 1960, and with the world around us, the question is whether the world will exist half-slave or half-free, whether it will move in the direction of freedom, in the direction of the road we are taking, or whether it will move in the direction of slavery. I think it will depend in great measure upon what we do here in the United States, on the kind of society that we build, on the kind of strength that we maintain.

Kennedy asked that we get the country moving again. By contrast, Nixon stressed that we were stronger than ever and that the Republicans had kept the peace:

> There is no question but that we cannot discuss our internal affairs in the United States without recognizing that they have a tremendous bearing on our international position. There is no question but that this nation cannot stand still; because we are in deadly competition, a competition not only with the men in the Kremlin, but the men in Peking. We're ahead in this competition, as Senator Kennedy, I think, has implied. But when you're in a race, the only way to stay ahead is to move ahead.

Each campaign had created a theme and a slogan consistent with the background and perceived strengths of its candidates. Kennedy's service in the Senate had provided no real foreign policy experience. Consequently, he stressed domestic affairs. Nixon could have stressed domestic affairs, but with the country in a recession, he had a stronger case if he stressed what was, for that ticket, a strength as well as Kennedy's weakness—foreign affairs. The theme chosen by Nixon explains Lodge's importance in the campaign and why he appeared in televised ads. Ads were created that recalled memorable moments from Lodge's U.N. service—his challenge to the Soviets over the bugging devices hidden in a U.S. office, for example.

An effective campaign slogan tells the audience what a vote for the candidate means, and it sums up the content of the candidate's advertising. In addition, an effective campaign slogan cannot be used to attack the candidate, and it is believable to voters.

Telling the Audience What a Vote Means

George Wallace, former governor of Alabama, was a potent force in the 1968 presidential election, where, running as a third-party candidate, he won almost 10 million votes. Wallace might have been a decisive factor in the 1972 presidential campaign had he not been shot and incapacitated during the Maryland primary campaign. His message in each of his tries for the presidency was simple and direct: "Send Them a Message."

A vote for Wallace was a message. But what was the message? In 1968 his commercials asked whether you were satisfied seeing your dollars sent to unsympathetic regimes, whether you were satisfied with crime-ridden neighborhoods, whether you were satisfied with seeing your children bused miles from home in order to attend school. If you were not, a vote for Wallace signaled your dissatisfaction.

Wallace's anti–big government, anti-intellectual, antibureaucratic appeals prefigured those that Jimmy Carter would successfully parlay into victory in 1976. In his speeches, Wallace wondered aloud what bureaucrats packed in those big black briefcases and speculated that if you opened one of them you'd probably find the *New York Times* and a peanut butter sandwich. According to Wallace, pointy-headed bureaucrats couldn't even park a bicycle straight, yet dared to meddle in the lives of working people. These statements revealed that the "them" of the slogan were the Washington establishment and federal bureaucrats. By framing the election as a contest of "us" (Wallace and his supporters) against "them" (the Washington establishment), the slogan provided a symbol consistent with the other rhetoric of the Wallace campaign.

Because the press labeled Wallace a spoiler and speculated on whether he would capture enough of the vote to send the 1968 election to the House of Representatives, Wallace needed to insulate himself against the suggestion that a vote for him would be wasted. The slogan accomplished this goal. The reason for supporting Wallace was not necessarily to get him elected but to send a message to the person elected and to other elected officials—that Wallace's constituency must be taken seriously and accommodated. A slogan like LBJ's in 1964, "The Stakes Are Too High for You to Stay Home," would not work for a candidate who was not regarded as having a serious chance of winning. LBJ's slogan is the sort useful only to a candidate who has a realistic chance of becoming president. "Send Them a Message" enabled Wallace to redefine the meaning of voting. A vote for Wallace might not elect him (although Wallace never discounted that possibility); rather, the message the vote carried would affect the behavior of those elected.

A campaign slogan can send a subtle, even unintended message. In his campaign for the position of mayor of Los Angeles, Tom Bradley, an African American former police officer, used the slogan "He'll Work as Hard for His Paycheck as You Do for Yours." The slogan was a message to whites that he would represent both whites and African Americans and a message to those who feared he would sell out the city to welfare recipients that he believed in the work ethic. According to Jeff Greenfield (one of David Garth's associates), what the media adviser in the Bradley campaign and his associates were trying to say with the slogan was "(a) Yorty [Bradley's opponent] wasn't working for his salary, (b) Bradley would earn the job of mayor, (c) Bradley understood the premises of the work ethic and was no permissive open-the-treasury welfare enthusiast, (d) Bradley understands how hard you, the typical voter, work for your paycheck because he is one of you."[a]

Bradley won in a landslide. The slogan was a prism through which the campaign could be viewed: It provided a reason to vote against Yorty and a

(continued on next page)

CASE STUDY 12-2   *(continued)*

---

number of reasons to vote for Bradley, it reassured voters who required assurance, and it identified Bradley with an important subsection of his audience—workers. The ads in the campaign were consistent with the slogan. They stressed Bradley's accomplishments and in the process demonstrated that in the past he had worked hard for his paycheck and had worked for things the voters supported.

Summarizing the Campaign's Advertising

The slogans used in the Kennedy and Nixon campaigns of 1960 offered reasons for voting for the ticket. Slogans can be directed against the opposing ticket as well. Lyndon Johnson's 1964 presidential campaign slogan was "Vote Johnson November 3. The Stakes Are Too High for You to Stay Home." The slogan implies a special urgency about the 1964 election. If "you" stay home and do not vote for Johnson, catastrophe may result. The slogan also reveals the campaign's concern that projections of a Johnson landslide would lull Johnson supporters into complacency. If all of Goldwater's supporters voted and most of Johnson's supporters stayed home, Goldwater could win the election. In a campaign with a slogan about the urgency of voting,

we would expect to find commercials advocating voting. In the Johnson campaign, for example, a commercial showed a man with an umbrella plunging through a downpour to get to the polls. The ad said, "If it rains on November 3, get wet. The Stakes Are Too High for You to Stay Home."

Just as the commercials run on behalf of Nixon and Kennedy in 1960 were summarized by the slogans of each campaign, so, too, the slogan used by the 1964 Johnson campaign previewed and summarized the thrust of the ads run for Johnson. In 5-minute commercials Johnson argued that, like other presidents before him, Republicans as well as Democrats, he was committed to keeping the peace. The implication, of course, was that Goldwater was not.

The famous daisy commercial made that implication explicit in the minds of auditors who read into an otherwise benign ad the conclusion that it was "trigger-happy," "shoot from the hip" Goldwater who would blow the little girl up. The ad did not explicitly make that claim, but simply showed a child in a field picking daisies as she counts from one to ten, slightly out of sequence, a sign of the genius of the ad's creator Tony Schwartz, who realized that children rarely count

---

the *Wall Street Journal*.[10] "That crucial question rose to the fore yesterday in the wake of a seven-state round of primaries and caucuses that left John Kerry the clear leader but also made John Edwards his leading challenger." With the labels come tactical analysis. "Having established himself as the Democratic front-runner, John Kerry now faces the double challenge of quickly forcing his rivals out of the race while better explaining to voters why he wants to be in it come November," notes David Rogers in an article in the *Journal* the same day.[11]

Front-runners and contenders receive more news coverage than do minor candidates and also-rans, and the type of coverage they receive differs. Although Representative Dennis Kucinich (D-Ohio) remained a contender and on the ballot in early February 2004, also-rans are treated as human interest oddities. Their stands on issues are not probed; their chances of winning are not pondered. It is assumed they are going to lose.

Once classified as a contender, a candidate is subject to comparison with past political figures. "He sometimes looks so Lincolnesque that all he lacks is the beard and the stovepipe hat," wrote Todd S. Purdum of the *New York Times* about Democratic presidential contender John Kerry.[12]

linearly. As the child reaches "ten," a voice from one of the satellite launch countdowns intones "Ten, nine, eight . . ." When the voice reaches "zero," the girl is replaced on the screen by an exploding bomb, and we hear Lyndon Johnson's voice saying that we must learn to love one another or we will surely perish. The tag then appears as the announcer's voice declares, "Vote Johnson November 3. The Stakes Are Too High for You to Stay Home." The tag prompted the audience to read Goldwater into the ad.

Other ads more explicitly provided the evidence that the daisy commercial left implicit. One ad for Johnson noted that Barry Goldwater had described the nuclear bomb as "merely another weapon." The announcer's incredulous voice then repeats, "Merely another weapon?" The ads for Johnson also argued that the stakes were too high domestically. One ad showed a Social Security card being torn apart as the announcer informed the audience that even William Miller, Goldwater's running mate, had claimed that electing Goldwater would mean the end of Social Security as we know it. A series of visually compelling production ads insinuated that Goldwater could not be trusted with the presidency. One of these ads purported to show the auction of the Tennessee Valley Authority, a dramatic illustration of Goldwater's suggestion that the TVA be

sold. Another showed a model of the map of the United States suspended over water. As a saw loudly severed the eastern seaboard off the map, the announcer reminded the audience of Goldwater's statement that perhaps "we ought to cut off the eastern seaboard and let it float out to sea." "Can a man who would say that really be trusted to serve all the people, justly and fairly?" the ad asked. The Johnson campaign aired ad after ad to reinforce the same claim—that a vote for Goldwater was a risky exercise in a high-stakes venture. The ads raised voters' anxiety about Goldwater's stands on issues and then reduced that anxiety by assuring viewers that a victory for Johnson would avert such catastrophes.

Some slogans are too imprecise to accomplish any of these purposes. In 1984, Democrats Mondale and Ferraro campaigned on the slogan "Mondale: Ferraro: Fighting for Your Future." Neither the slogan nor the advertising to which it was attached revealed the nature of that future. The same problem plagued the 1988 Democratic slogan "The Best America Is Yet to Come." Not only did that tag fail to define the future America but it also was a slogan equally applicable to the Republican ticket.

[a]Jeff Greenfield, *Playing to Win: An Insider's Guide to Politics* (New York: Simon & Schuster, 1980), p. 85.

Is this candidate glamorous, dynamic, wealthy? Or cold, sneaky, untrustworthy? Like Roosevelt, or Kennedy, or Reagan, or Nixon? Is this a common man, like Truman? Or an innovator, a communicator, like FDR? Is the candidate a philanderer, like Kennedy and Clinton, or a person who lusts only in his heart, like Carter? Is this a bookish, intellectual candidate like Wilson or Stevenson? Democrats compare Republicans with Hoover and Nixon; Republicans respond by tarring Democrats as Carteresque.

Candidates try to act so that journalists will associate their actions with those of admired historical figures such as Abraham Lincoln and Franklin Roosevelt. They also identify with those people, places, and actions that the intended voters stereotype positively, and divorce themselves from those we negatively stereotype. For example, in his successful 1990 campaign for the Democratic nomination for Cook County, Illinois, president of the Board of Commissioners Richard Phelan sat at a *Cheers*-like bar and told how his parents "sacrificed" to enable him to study at Notre Dame. He worked at "a one-lawyer firm," he said, and built it into one of the largest in the Midwest. "The boys in the backroom" carped about his success, he noted, but he added that that was because he planned to work for the taxpayers and not for the professional politicians. (He won.)

When a candidate succeeds in sculpting an image consistent with a stereotype, it begins to play out in press coverage. For example, a report in the *Washington Post* described the 1990 Republican Texas gubernatorial nominee this way:

> [Clayton] Williams, a West Texas millionaire oilman, is the most colorful political character to appear on the Lone Star scene in years. He brags about his fistfights, loves to drink beer, rides horses in his TV commercials, designs his swimming pools in the shape of cowboy boots, paints all his possessions, including two airplanes, in the maroon and white colors of his beloved Texas A & M Aggies, says he wants to double the state's prison capacity and get more criminals "pounding rocks," and talks wistfully about Texas the way it was when his daddy was around.[13]

Stereotypes, however, can cut two ways. When Williams refused to debate Democratic nominee Ann Richards, she told the press, "You can't pretend to be John Wayne and run from a girl."[14]

In fall 2003 the Democratic presidential contender for 2004, John Kerry, faced a similar problem. Frank Rich wrote in the *New York Times*,

> On November 11, 2003, Senator John Forbes Kerry . . . arrived [on the *Jay Leno Show*], via Harley Davidson, attired in a brown leather jacket, black boots, a denim shirt and jeans. [H]is entire performance reeked of phoniness. A dour Boston Brahmin was trying to pass himself off as a wisecracking biker. And he was doing so after having given an interview (to Julia Reed of *Vogue*) criticizing President Bush's handlers for identical theatrics: "They put him in a brown jacket and jeans and get him to move some hay or drive a truck, and all of a sudden he's the Marlboro Man."[15]

Note that Rich is indicting Kerry not only for appearing to be someone he is not (a wisecracking biker) but also for engaging in the sort of behavior he had condemned in his opponent.

Responding to or Preventing Attack

In summer 1999, Tipper Gore, wife of presidential hopeful Al Gore, revealed that she has struggled with depression. The revelation came on the eve of a White House Conference on Mental Health that Tipper Gore chaired. The conference provided a convenient justification for the disclosure. The revelation preempted possible press reports that could otherwise have come at a less opportune time. By making the disclosure herself, Tipper Gore shaped the press coverage of it. Had she waited for it to be revealed by an enterprising reporter, she would have been cast in the role of a respondent with something to hide. This was a classic use of preemption: Get the information that could be used to hurt you out on your own schedule and on your own terms.

In April 2004, a congressional candidate in New York used the same strategy. In the speech in which he declared his candidacy, John "Randy" Kuhl, Jr. noted that he had been arrested for drunk driving in 1997. "I brought it up simply to tell you I'm aware of it, and I don't want somebody out here taking potshots at me," he said.[16] In the final week of the 2000 election, reporters learned that as a young man, Republican nominee

George W. Bush had been arrested for driving while intoxicated. Some speculated that his campaign would have been well advised to have preempted by revealing the incident much earlier.

The sooner a candidate admits a mistake, the better. Republican presidential hopeful Elizabeth Dole illustrated this in mid-August 1999; she told both *Meet the Press* and the *Washington Post* that she favored a continued ban on federal funding for abortions. Then she was confronted by a reporter who informed her that federal funding was currently permitted in cases of rape, of incest, or to save the life of the mother. Dole responded, "I have been in favor of continuing what we are doing now." She then added, "I just want to be sure exactly what the situation is. Let's don't pursue that further now, because I need to check that." In the *New York Times*, Adam Clymer noted, "According to her spokesman, Ari Fleischer, she said, 'I made a mistake by not remembering what current law was.'" Added Clymer, "Such an admission, while not unprecedented, is truly rare among presidential candidates."[17]

Backlash

The prime function of an attack is to discredit an opponent. This is usually accomplished by casting suspicion on an opponent's campaign theme or by raising doubts about an opponent that can be corroborated by news channels. The danger in attacking an opponent is that the politician attacking, rather than the opponent, will be discredited.

Fear of backlash limits the attacks in a typical political campaign. A politician who violates our standards of fair play invites the judgment that she or he is not to be trusted with the office sought. But fear of backlash restrains behavior only when the person attacking is identified with the candidate running for office. The rise of independent political action committees removes this powerful constraint from the electoral process because, by law, PACs must function independently. Thus it is possible for a PAC to attack one candidate without creating a backlash against the candidate who benefits from the attack. Consequently, people attacked by an independent PAC seek to link the PAC to the opponent. If this can be done successfully, then any backlash resulting from the attack will hurt the opponent. If the reaction hurts only the PAC and not the politician who benefits from the attack, there is no restraining force controlling attacks because no one accountable to the electorate is held responsible for them. In general, candidates who are ahead in the polls and who anticipate winning by a comfortable margin do not attack their opponents. An attack invites reply and media coverage of the reply. This legitimizes the opponent and provides the opponent with media access. Counterattack is a legitimizing strategy that tacitly assumes comparable stature. Why would a politician waste time attacking someone who was inconsequential and no real threat to the politician's election?

In a multicandidate race, the consequences of attack and counterattack can benefit the candidate who stays above the fray. So for example, in the campaign preceding the Iowa caucuses in January 2004, Dick Gephardt and Howard Dean aggressively attacked each other in a barrage of ads. Both were hurt in the process, and the candidates who took a more low-key approach in their ads were helped. Senator John Kerry won the Iowa caucuses, and Senator John Edwards came in second, followed by the candidate earlier presumed to be the front runner, former Vermont Governor Howard Dean. After failing

---

**BOX 12-1   An APPC Adwatch—Treasury Tax Expert to Bush:
Clinton's Increase WASN'T the Biggest**

Study published by Bush's Treasury Department contradicts Bush's campaign.

Summary
In speeches and fundraising appeals the Bush campaign keeps making a distorted claim that Clinton's 1993 tax increase—supported by Kerry— was "the biggest in history." Republicans have been repeating this gross overstatement for more than a decade, but now there's less justification for it than ever. The GOP claim is contradicted by a study published last year by the Office of Tax Analysis of Bush's own Treasury Department.

Analysis
On Tax Day, April 15, the Bush campaign was still recycling this decade-old claim in an e-mail sent to supporters, asking for more campaign contributions:

Bush's E-Mail
   Subj: On Tax Day, another reason to
   support President Bush
   Sent: April 15, 2004

- Both Ted Kennedy and John Kerry Voted *Against* President Bush's Tax Relief in 2001 *and* 2003.
- Both Ted Kennedy and John Kerry Voted *For* Bill Clinton's 1993 Tax Increase—*the Largest Tax Increase in History.*

Bush himself said it in his first overtly political speech of the campaign on March 20:

- *Bush:* Over the years, he's (Kerry) voted over 350 times for higher taxes on the American people including the biggest tax increase in American history.

And Vice President Cheney told the US Chamber of Commerce March 29:

- *Cheney:* A career highlight was his (Kerry's) vote in favor of the largest tax increase in American history.

But that bit of political puffery has always been based on a simplistic tally of the number of dollars

---

to win in Iowa, Gephardt withdrew from the contest for the Democratic nomination. The ads in the New Hampshire primary the following week were notable for the absence of pointed attack.

Last-Minute Attacks

Not surprisingly, the sorts of attacks that have difficulty withstanding journalistic scrutiny tend to appear late in a campaign. In such circumstances the political system works for the attacker and against the candidate attacked. Because stations may not censor political ads, the burden of proof falls on the person attacked. If a lie is carefully worded, the burden of establishing its falsity can divert the time and attention of the attacked candidate's top-level campaign strategists, who, in the final days of a campaign, ought to be concentrating on getting out the vote. In such circumstances, a well-financed campaign with a skilled media consultant has at least the chance of placing responsive or counteractive ads on the air. A poorly financed campaign under attack must rely on the investigative tendencies of reporters and the sympathies of columnists.

When the Fair Campaign Practices Committee was still functioning, an injured candidate could appeal to it for a determination of whether an ad was fair. Newspeople

the Clinton tax bill yielded, without regard for population growth, rising incomes, or inflation.

Now comes a thorough study of every tax bill enacted since 1940, showing that the Clinton tax increase was indeed large, but not the largest.

A tax increase in 1942 boosted federal revenues by 71 percent, for example, as the U.S. geared up for war after the Japanese attack on Pearl Harbor. Measured in inflation-adjusted 1992 dollars, Roosevelt's wartime increase amounted to $73 billion a year, while Clinton's increase averaged $35 billion a year (average for the first two years).

The study said that inflation-adjusted "constant dollars" is probably only the second-best measure of the size of a tax increase. "The single best measure for most purposes is probably the revenue effect as a percentage of GDP." That's gross domestic product, the way we gauge the size of the economy. Clinton's tax increase isn't the biggest by that "best" measure, either. In the period since 1968, the study said, "the Tax Equity and Fiscal Responsibility Act of 1982 was the biggest increase." That was the tax increase signed by Ronald Reagan, rescinding some of the effects of his huge tax cut passed the year before.

That 1982 tax increase only slightly exceeded Clinton's in inflation-adjusted dollars ($37 billion a year vs. $32 billion) but it was much bigger in relation to the size of the economy. The '82 increase amounted to 4.6 percent of GDP (average for the first two years) while Clinton's was 2.7 percent.

Note: The study's author, Jerry Tempalski of the Office of Tax Analysis, put the following disclaimer on the cover page: "The views expressed in this paper are those of the author and do not necessarily represent the views of the U.S. Treasury Department." Apparently they are not the views of the President, either. Why let the facts get in the way of a campaign zinger?

Sources: Jerry Tempalski, "Revenue Effects of Major Tax Bills, "OTA Working Paper 81, Office of Tax Analysis, U.S. Treasury Department, July 2003. George W. Bush, "Remarks by the President at Florida Rally," Orange County Convention Center, Orlando, Florida, 20 March 2004. Vice President Richard Cheney, "Kerry's 350 Votes for Higher Taxes Make the Choice Clear," Remarks to US Chamber of Commerce, 29 March 2004. Office of Tax Analysis Working Paper 81: "Revenue Effects of Major Tax Bills."

then reported the complaint and the resolution. No functioning independent national group now exists to police the fairness of campaign tactics. In its absence, adwatches have emerged as the now-institutionalized response to deception in political ads. During the Nixon administration, the IRS pulled the committee's tax exemption status on the grounds that when the committee released information about a candidates unfair practices it in essence sided with a candidate making the committee an action group. The Carter administration reinstated its tax exempt status but the committee's funds were gone and it was never able to recover.

ADWATCHES

After the 1988 campaign, academic conferences around the country raised the question, Why did the press not point out the distortions and the false inferences invited by the 1988 presidential candidates' ads? Among these were the implications of a Michael Dukakis ad that George H. W. Bush would all but eliminate Social Security, and the implications of a Bush ad that as governor of Massachusetts Dukakis had released a large number of first-degree murderers and rapists to kill and rape again, including said Willie Horton.

CASE STUDY 12-3   The Adwatch

Those of us who study how politicians and the press communicate with voters are occasionally chided by our colleagues in the news media for being chronic complainers who haven't a clue about how to reform the practices we criticize. For reasons that I will explain in a moment, that diagnosis rings more true for one of us—Jamieson—than it once did.

Throughout the 1988 presidential campaign—the one that gave us the misleading ads featuring Willie Horton and the Boston Harbor—Jamieson expressed concern that reporters were focusing more on the political strategy behind the ads than on the accuracy of the claims presented. On *Meet the Press* and in an op-ed in the *Washington Post*, I suggested either the revival of the nonpartisan private watchdog group, the Fair Campaign Practices Commission, or alternatively that reporters themselves evaluate the fairness and accuracy of the ads.

Although I have been credited with prompting the adwatches that later characterized print coverage of the 1990 elections and print and broadcast reporting in 1992, the idea did not catch on until syndicated columnist David Broder embraced it in a column following the 1988 campaign. My actual contribution was different. Although I believed that adwatches were needed, as the presidential campaign progressed in fall 1988, I came to realize that they had to be done very carefully. A participant in a focus group had alerted me to this when what she recalled of a network newscast analyzing an ad was not the debunking words of the reporter but the ad itself. That ad showed Democratic nominee Michael Dukakis in an armored tank as words running across the image alleged

that he had opposed virtually every weapons system developed since World War II. Lost on the focus group member was reporter Richard Threlkeld's statement that Dukakis was on record favoring some of the weapons the ad said he opposed.

Subsequent testing confirmed that when network reporters showed ads on the full television screen, while verbally commenting on their distortions, viewers remembered the ads better than the corrections. The implication for the proposed adwatches was clear: They could amplify, rather than undercut, the influence of deceptive advertisements.

Because we believe that a first premise for scholars and doctors alike should be to do no harm, for the next two years, graduate students at the University of Pennsylvania's Annenberg School and I experimented with techniques for criticizing ads *without* magnifying their power. They finally came up with a formula that worked. In brief, when reporters showed the ad running on a television set rather than showing it full screen, when they identified it on the screen as an ad and superimposed print corrections over it, the ad's impact dropped and that of the reporter's commentary rose.

With help from the MacArthur Foundation and CNN, I and an Annenberg School team further tested the results and produced illustrated guidelines to show television producers how to put them into practice. In the primaries of 1992, CNN adopted the formula. The National Association of Broadcasters distributed the guidelines and an illustrative tape to its members at the group's annual convention in spring 1992, and in

---

Newspapers responded to the perceived problems in the 1988 campaign by printing the texts of 1990 ads in their entirety and then documenting the facts as the reporters knew them. For example, when an ad for Texas Democratic gubernatorial candidate Ann Richards claimed that her opponent Clayton Williams had "mountains of debt," the *Dallas Morning News* boxed the following information: "The Midland entrepreneur has borrowed extensively over the years to develop his oil, ranching, and long distance telephone enterprises. And he has seen his net worth fall by almost two-thirds since 1982, according to a review of his business dealings by the *Dallas Morning News*.

the general election of that year CNN, ABC, NBC, and CBS each used some version of the Annenberg formula.

Of course, the real utility of such strategies lies not in pointing out distortions to news audiences, whose numbers are comparatively small, but in preventing politicians from creating deceptive ads in the first place. Adwatches also help candidates who are the object of misleading ads because they can use the corrections of the adwatches in counteradvertising.

That's what happened in 1992. "George Bush is running attack ads," noted the unseen announcer in a 1992 Clinton ad. It went on to quote from news reports that outlined errors in the Republican attack ads.

Following the 1992 election, campaign consultants acknowledged that the adwatches had affected how they operated. "It was a terrible feeling when I used to open the [*New York*] *Times* and they used to take my commercial apart, or watch CNN and watch them take it apart. . . . I think these reality checks made our commercials less effective," observed Harold Kaplan, an adman for the Bush-Quayle campaign, during a conference at the Annenberg School after the election.

Noted Mandy Grunwald, advertising director for Bill Clinton's campaign, "I spent more time talking about economics and the latest statistics from the Bureau of Labor statistics and the Bureau of Census than I thought a creative person ever would in her lifetime." She said that she and the policy analysts in the campaign talked constantly about whether or not a particular statistic could legitimately be used in an ad.

Naively assuming that adwatches were here to stay, the research team at Annenberg muttered in self-congratulation, "Scholarship can make a difference." But as advertising on health reform flooded the airwaves in early 1994, the team learned that it was wrong.

Between September 8, 1993, and July 15, 1994, Joseph N. Cappella and I (Jamieson) studied news media coverage of $50 million in advertising designed to influence voters to urge specific legislators to vote for or against certain elements of health-care reform. Less than 10 percent of the reporting on these advertisements examined their fairness or accuracy. Instead press commentary focused on the political strategy behind them, analysis of little use to citizens trying to make sense of the controversy over access and choice in the health-care debate.

Moreover, two of the four networks that had faithfully followed some version of our formula for adwatches in 1992 were commenting on the strategy of the ads as they aired them full screen. Some of the other practices we had criticized were back as well. Several ads on health reform received more free exposure on news shows than they had when aired as ads in regular programming. The lapse wouldn't matter if the ads had been accurate, but an analysis of 73 of those broadcast and 125 printed during the period of our study revealed that more than half of those aired and more than a quarter of those printed were unfair, misleading, or deceptive.

In good soldierly fashion, we documented the demise of adwatching, the return of news coverage that focused primarily on strategy, and the escalating inaccuracy of the ads. Then in July he sat down with reporters at the National Press Club in Washington to talk about what we had found.

(continued on next page)

Still, the *News* puts Mr. Williams' net worth at about $116 million, concentrated in oil and gas properties."[18]

In 1992, for the first time, the advertising of a presidential campaign was monitored for fairness and accuracy by both print and broadcast reporters. The most systematic work was done by Brooks Jackson of CNN. On National Public Radio, Andy Bowers led analyses of radio advertising, an important move because the most serious distortions of the campaign were found in the final weeks on local radio. Eric Engberg of CBS and Brooks Jackson of CNN performed yeoman service in locating and analyzing the radio ads on television.

CASE STUDY 12-3   *(continued)*

We discovered that changes in press practice after the 1988 presidential campaign were driven by a pervasive belief that both reporters and the candidates had failed the electorate. No such sense filled discussions of the health reform debate. Just as important was that many who had done the adwatches in 1992 were now covering beats other than health care. And those who covered both no longer had adwatches as part of their explicit assignment. In other words, the practice of adwatching had not been institutionalized.

Reports of our findings in the *New York Times* and the *Washington Post* and an op-ed in the *Washington Post* didn't prompt a rush of adwatching either. Any effect that recent study has had on reporting about ads has occurred on the margins. National Public Radio and the *NewsHour with Jim Lehrer* have shifted from strategy-based discussions of health reform ads to coverage that includes analyses of accuracy. ABC did one news segment addressing the truthfulness of the ads. And when the Health Insurance Association of America (HIAA) released a new set of "Harry and Louise" ads the week after conference, the reporters who had attended ignored them.

Because earlier ads featuring this yuppy couple obsessing about weaknesses in the Clinton plan had garnered more than five minutes of free airtime on national newscasts and more than 700 press mentions in the previous eleven months, this silence did represent a change. As one of the reporters who attended the conference told me, a tree fell in the woods, and no one reported it.

Our six months of analyzing media coverage of the health reform debate made a difference only if impact is measured in millimeters rather than miles. In retrospect we made two major mistakes, focusing on reporters rather than on their bosses and failing to reinforce good adwatching with praise. Had we persuaded assignment editors of the utility of adwatches in 1992, these editors and producers could easily have reinstituted adwatches on health reform in 1994. And where we were quick to criticize reporters for inadequate treatment of ads in 1988, they were slower to praise the adwatches of 1992. Reward might have invited repetition or at least a discussion with editors about the merits of reviving the adwatch form. In short, as scholars of communication, we forgot the lessons of sociology and psychology.

Reporters approved of press coverage of ads. Of the reporters surveyed in a *Times Mirror* poll, 77 percent approved of these policing efforts. One television newsperson told *Times Mirror* that the debunking of the ads "is the primary reason why no Willie Horton ads or their cousins have appeared in this campaign. Our coverage is keeping the bastards honest." Another editor told the surveyors, "We'll need a Teddy White to come along later to see if those who planned commercials really sat around worrying about whether we'd criticize them or not."[19] Teddy White was a famous political journalist who wrote the *Making of the President* series, which chronicled presidential campaigns. In 1996, print adwatching continued, but network news all but abandoned the monitoring of ads. When asked why, news producers indicated that the presidential race was not close enough to justify the effort.

Responding to Last-Minute Attacks

The difficulty in dealing with last-minute attacks is compounded because an attack ad can run for a full day or more before the attacked candidate knows about it. Once alerted to its existence, the campaign staff must spend time securing a copy. Additional time is required to document its falsity. If the attack campaign includes many ads, the burden increases proportionately.

If the candidate decides to use a news conference to expose and reply to the attack ads, schedules must be cleared, an appropriate location must be secured, and the media must be alerted. All these activities take time. Meanwhile, the candidate's staff must develop a strategy to counter the ads. Under such pressure, strategic errors are likely to occur. Perhaps the candidate will panic and waste valuable time refuting ads that have reached few voters. Such a move enlarges the opponent's audience. Perhaps the candidate's rebuttal will seem histrionic and will discredit him or her. Finally, given the time pressure, there is a danger that even if the attack ads are exposed as false by journalists, they will have reached more people than the rebuttal. There may not be time for a backlash to build against the attacker, and the sight of two candidates battling it out over the truth of the ads may drive voters to a third candidate not contaminated by the controversy.

As polls repeatedly report, the public hates negative ads. But refine the question and the answer changes. An Annenberg Center for Public Policy survey suggests that voters accept accurate, issue-based, civil attack ads. Such ads both exist and work. For example, one of Reagan's effective ads in 1980 asked, "Can we afford four more years of broken promises? In 1976 Jimmy Carter promised to hold inflation to 4 percent. Today it is 14 percent. He promised to fight unemployment. But today there are 8½ million Americans out of work. . . . Can we afford four more years?"

Voters, however, report that they prefer contrastive ads that provide a reason to vote against one candidate while also justifying a vote for the ad's sponsor. Contrast not only differentiates but also anchors the winner's ability to govern. The ads of George H. W. Bush's 1988 campaign for president, for instance, cast him as preoccupied with prison furloughs in Massachusetts, the home of challenger Michael Dukakis; the Pledge of Allegiance, which he said Dukakis didn't want said in schools; and Boston Harbor, which the Republicans blamed the Democrats for despoiling. These ads provided little sense of what voters might expect from George Bush Sr. if they elected him, which they did. That vagueness made it more difficult for him to successfully govern.

Attack ads have a bad reputation because reporters and the public associate them with deception. Yet in past presidential elections, more distortions appeared in ads bragging about the sponsor than in those blasting the opponent. In 2004, cases of self-inflation included Kerry's advertised claim that he "cast a decisive vote that created 20 million new jobs" and Bush's suggestion that he (not Ronald Reagan) provided "the largest tax relief in history."

Money matters. Money backing attack works even more. The National Annenberg Election Survey (NAES) showed that in 2000, by outspending Vice President Gore on attack ads questioning his credibility, the campaign of Texas Governor Bush blunted the accurate Democratic charge that the Republican Social Security plan was $1 trillion short of keeping its promises to seniors, boomers, and the young. Had the Republicans not gained that final-week ad advantage in the battleground states, Gore would have won both the popular vote and the electoral college vote. The April 2004 NAES survey of those in the ad-saturated battleground states found that 61 percent had been gulled by the false claim that George W. Bush "favors sending American jobs overseas," 56 percent by the notion that Kerry "voted for higher taxes 350 times," and 72 percent by the assertion that "3 million jobs" had been lost in the Bush presidency. Who protects the

BOX 12-2   Detecting Deception in the Presidential Ads of 2004

The press slings the word *negative* at attack ads and complains about its high level even when the amount is low and the specifics in the ads largely accurate. But in the 2004 general election, the grousing reporters and pundits were on to something. The highly specific nature and sheer number of the incumbent President's attacks on the Democratic nominee's record increased the questionable claims in Republican ads. In addition, the barrage of attacks on President Bush from 527 groups and from the SwiftVets against Senator Kerry multiplied the suspect assertions. In 2004, as in the past, bogus blasts are most prevalent in ads sponsored not by candidates but by outside groups.

Political ads don't usually spread outright lies. In fact, many of their troubling statements contain an element of truth. Kerry had voted to raise taxes, but not as often or as much as the Republican ads would have had us believe. Jobs had been lost during the Bush administration, but not as many as the Democrats charged. Contrary to a Democratic ad, the war in Iraq had not yet cost $200 billion, although it would in the foreseeable future.

As is the case with product ads, political spots often sin by omission. As Republican ads noted, Kerry did oppose some weapons systems. Unmentioned was the fact that both the current president's father President George H. W. Bush and his Secretary of Defense Dick Cheney did as well. And comparisons to the Great Depression aside, the unemployment rate in fall 2004 was about where it was when Democratic incumbent Bill Clinton was campaigning for a second term in 1996. In

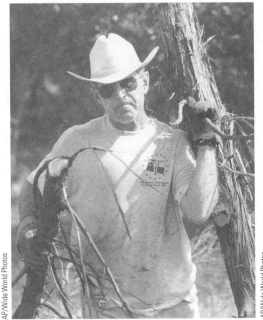 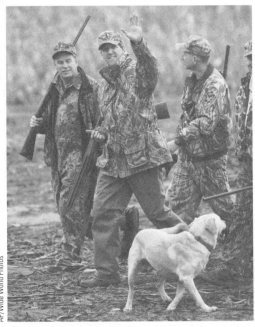

AP/Wide World Photos

AP/Wide World Photos

Politicians use pseudo-events to communicate who they are and what they stand for. What traits are the two political candidates communicating here? What issue positions are implied by the images?

addition, some of Kerry's tax-raising votes supported the deficit-reduction package of the president's father, whereas others (six to be exact) supported the McCain tobacco bill that in 1998 would have increased the cost of a pack of cigarettes to reduce the likelihood that teens would smoke. In other words, the Bush campaign was attacking Senator Kerry for voting for a tax championed by the Arizona senator who was campaigning at the president's side and for others supported by President George W. Bush's father.

Other deceptions existed not in the ads but in the meaning the audience made of them. In addition, admakers know that evocative images short-circuit our ability to analyze them critically. That's what was going on when an AK47 assault rifle was shown on the screen of a MoveOn PAC ad (the ad contains explicit advocacy; as a result, it has to be funded by a PAC and not by a 527) focusing on Kerry's support for extending the assault weapons ban whereas Bush "let the assault weapon ban expire."

"This is an assault weapon," says the announcer as the frightening weapon is pictured. True. "It can fire up to 300 rounds a minute." True, for the fully automatic version. "In the hands of terrorists it could kill hundreds." True. But contrary to the inference the ad invites, the fully automatic weapon shown and described was not banned by the assault weapons ban, which applied to semiautomatic weapons only. Access to fully automatic weapons has been restricted since 1934 by the National Firearms Act. Still, there is an element of truth in the ad. Kerry did support extending the ban, whereas Bush said he supported it but did not encourage the Republicans in Congress to send him a renewal.

public from all of this? Truth has an advantage only when a credible source makes it known. In the case of political ads, that source is the press.

Holding candidates accountable for the campaigning done in their name is a reporter's job. When done well, it works. Questioned by a reporter about whether he actually believed his ad's claim that his Republican primary opponent Senator John McCain opposed funding breast cancer research, candidate George Bush admitted "No, I don't believe that."[20]

When the candidate ducks questions, the journalistic fact check is another line of voter defense. Although media truth squads risk voter cynicism by implying that all ads lie, APPC's controlled laboratory experiments conducted with voters show that the process works. For example, in the Georgia primary of 1992, viewers penalized Republican hopeful Patrick Buchanan for a deceptive ad attack on incumbent President George H. W. Bush after it was widely criticized in national and local news. That ad condemned the Bush administration for investing "our tax dollars in pornographic and blasphemous art, too shocking to show." One APPC focus group member summarized what he had learned from news accounts by saying, "the film was funded . . . while Reagan [not Bush] was president, and what the agency (National Endowment for the Arts) does now is . . . symphonies and opera." A CNN-Gallup poll confirmed what APPC focus groups had revealed. Twenty-three percent reported that the ad had increased support not for the sponsor but for the target of the attack.

When presidential ads are bombarded with critiques from news outlets, their sponsors and "unaffiliated" supporters usually change the challenged claim. The Bush campaign did this in reducing its claim of 350 Kerry votes for tax increases to 98, and a Moveon.org Pac ad did the same in revising the cost of the war in Iraq from the $200 billion in a critiqued Kerry ad down to $150 billion.

When they see the argument as key to victory, however, campaigns persist in misleading even after being caught, because they gamble that partisans' belief in their candidate will insulate them from critical news and frequent airing will drown out corrections before they influence the undecideds. Reporters could thwart this second calculation by objecting every time exaggeration was passed off as exact fact. The *Post* did this when it reported Kerry claiming "1.6 million jobs lost (the actual number is 1.1 million)."[21] But that story is exceptional.

Although campaigns would prefer to be ignored by fact checkers, having numbers challenged has advantages of its own. Corrections inadvertently reinforce the ads' focus on the opponent's vulnerabilities and underscore as well the ads' assumptions, some of them true and others less so. Thus, people believed that under Bush a lot of jobs were lost, even if the figure wasn't 3 million; that the war in Iraq is very expensive, even if it hadn't yet cost $200 billion; and that even if he didn't vote that way 98 times and despite his statement that he will raise taxes on only those making over $200,000, Kerry has been chronically protax.

Television talk by pundits and partisans also reinforces the assumption that the discussed ad raises a legitimate issue—why else would they waste time on it? By obsessing about the Swift Boat Veterans for Truth ads, cable talk and repeated cable airing legitimized the assumption that there was something suspect about Kerry's medals. The National Annenberg Election Survey showed that 48 percent of heavy cable viewers saw the medals ad in its first 8 days of airing compared with only 22 percent of those who watched no cable in that period. People exposed to the ad or talk about the ad were more likely to doubt Kerry's story. Only 12 percent of those who reported no exposure to the ad doubted it, whereas 31 percent of those who saw the ad and 25 percent who heard about it did. News corrections mattered. After news investigations challenged the SwiftVet medals claims and an eyewitness account in the *Chicago Tribune* backed Kerry's account of a key event, public belief in the ad's charge, which had risen from 23 percent to 30 percent before the corrections aired, dropped back to 24 percent (NAES).

A focus on the distortions in ads and on the difficulties news organizations face in checking the ads' worst tendencies can obscure two facts: Political spots include useful information, and press reports fill in most of the holes they create in ads. In 2000, for example, the Bush ads forecast his first term with their promises of a prescription drug benefit, tax cuts, educational reforms, and private investment accounts for Social Security. As president, Bush kept the first three promises and has renewed the fourth. Those who mistakenly believed that they would get a tax cut even if they paid only payroll taxes didn't focus enough on the promises in the ads and the news accounts that reported that the taxes being reduced were "income" only.

Exploiting Blunders

At some point in their political lives, most public figures have said something they regret. These blunders are often newsworthy, not only because they reveal a previously unknown fact but also because they express a candidate's position succinctly. In 1976, presidential candidate Ronald Reagan made the mistake of attaching a specific figure to the amount of money that could be cut from the federal budget. The gaffe was a headline writer's dream: "The Ninety Billion Dollar Blunder." The statement was newsworthy not simply because Reagan was newsworthy as a candidate but also because it was brief, concise, specific, concrete, and dramatic. It haunted Reagan through the rest of the campaign. The same problem affected Democratic nominee John Kerry in 2004. When he responded to a question about his vote against funding for the Iraq war by saying, "I voted for the funding before I voted against the funding," the Bush campaign rushed an ad containing that clip onto the air.

When a prominent candidate makes this sort of slip, it receives news coverage. By incorporating reminders of the gaffe in attack commercials, the candidate's opponents can keep the charge alive and make it a focal factor in voting decisions. The "revolving-door prison furlough program" ad that the Republicans aired against Democratic nominee Michael Dukakis in 1988 drew its power from the furlough of Willie Horton during Dukakis's term as governor of Massachusetts and from Dukakis's resistance to public calls for change in the law and his refusal to meet with Horton's victims or to apologize to them. During the 1996 campaign, the Republican National Committee aired an ad showing Clinton agreeing that he might have raised taxes too much. Clinton's ads quoted Dole's initial opposition to the establishment of Medicare.

When an attack ad replays an opponent's blunder, the purpose is often to make the mistake concrete for the audiences. For example, in a 1976 commercial Gerald Ford reminded workers gathered around him that Carter had promised to lower taxes for those below the median income and raise taxes for those above the median income. But the median income in this country turned out to be lower than Carter had imagined. Ford then said he didn't think the people surrounding him needed to have their taxes raised.

When the blunder is not a concise synthetic statement but part of a long, rambling answer to a question, it cannot be used very effectively, either in news or in an ad. A commercial that opens in the middle of an opponent's sentence or cuts from the sentence before it is finished invites us to conclude that the statement has been taken out of context. This saved Ronald Reagan from hearing replays of his 1976 statement that he might order the use of troops in Rhodesia (now Zimbabwe). The statement came in the middle of a long, rambling, involved answer that did not lend itself to use in an opponent's commercial. Instead, the Ford campaign assumed audience familiarity with the statement and created an ad that warned, "Governor Reagan couldn't start a war. President Reagan could."

Attacks Legitimized by the Media

News and ads are not the only outlets for, or sources of, attacks in political campaigns. Editorial cartoons, political columns, and comic monologues are among the other sources of attacks over which a candidate exercises no direct control. These forms are especially difficult for a candidate to counter effectively.

A political attack in a comic strip is effective because it appears in a context that does not ordinarily provoke critical responses. We expect to be entertained, so we relax our guard. The same is true of the political humor in Jay Leno's monologues. Audiences laugh and, in the process, accept the premises underlying the jokes. Occasionally, when a comic strip becomes too blatantly political, the editors will move it from the comic section to the editorial page, as was done with Al Capp's "Li'l Abner" in the 1960s and with Garry Trudeau's "Doonesbury" in the 1980s. Occasionally newspapers drop "offending" cartoons altogether or selectively delete them when the message proves distasteful or controversial.

The nature of humor is such that a cartoonist or a comedian tends to reinforce existing attitudes rather than create new ones. When audiences fail to laugh at a certain type of joke, that joke is quickly dropped. This ensures that Jay Leno will underscore, not initiate, attacks.

Editorial cartoonists have more latitude than any other agent in the broadcast or print industry. Because their content is primarily visual, they are not readily subjected to tests for truth that are most suited to assessing verbal statements of factual propositions. Thus, for example, when one editorial cartoonist wanted to claim that Reagan's secretary of the interior was not interested in protecting wildlife, he showed James Watt at a desk with Bambi's stuffed head decorating the wall. The claim in the drawing, which can be comprehended in seconds, is stronger, clearer, and more damning than any of the columns of ponderous prose that defended a milder version of the same claim in deadly—and probably unread—detail.

Similarly, as reporters struggled to find the language to contrast the eagerness with which the Bush administration embraced and acted on questionable information about weapons of mass destruction in Iraq with the lags in connecting the dots about September 11, 2001, editorial cartoonist Matt Davies of *The Journal News* digested the message in a cartoon showing President Bush reading from a briefing memo titled "Iraq WMDs" and saying "Tsk . . . How could anyone have expected me to act on this lousy, vague, non-specific intelligence." At his side, an aide is offering a memo titled "Al Qaida Activities." "That's the wrong file, Sir," says the aide.[22]

The effectiveness of such cartoons poses problems for attacked candidates. If a candidate is attacked in an editorial, a newspaper column, or an opinion editorial (op-ed), he or she may appeal to the newspaper for space to respond. Unlike the broadcast media, newspapers are under no legal obligation to permit reply. Nonetheless, most newspapers give an aggrieved party who has been directly attacked space in an op-ed or in the letters-to-the-editor column. The controversy adds excitement to the paper and holds readership. Presenting both sides creates a sense that the newspaper is fair and responsive to the interests and needs of the community, so it is in the newspaper's self-interest to permit a person attacked in its pages the opportunity to respond. There is, however, no effective way to respond to an editorial cartoon.

The national syndication of cartoons and columns means that when an attack occurs or misinformation is published, the impact is widespread. A column by nationally syndicated *New York Times* columnist William Safire will reach an audience in every major city in the country. Someone attacked by Safire who wants to respond to a column and does not have access to the syndication service will have to deal directly with hundreds of op-ed page editors across the country.

Editors occasionally refuse to print a regular column when, in their judgment, it has overstepped professional boundaries. Jack Anderson's free-wheeling columns on occasion failed to appear in the *Washington Post*, for example. Columnists also police themselves. In 1972, when Anderson learned that vice presidential candidate Thomas Eagleton had not been convicted of drunken driving as Anderson had claimed, he admitted the error and apologized. It is difficult to determine what damage was done by the false charge.

Enlisting the Help of Journalists

The material used in attacks against a candidate is often culled from the public record. Among the channels that preserve the public record are often the print and broadcast media. Consequently, any political figure has a vested interest in accurate reporting about his or her activities. If uncorrected, misinterpretations by journalists can be resurrected for use against a candidate.

Reporters have access to those who have followed the careers of candidates and to the public record of candidates' activities, as reported by journalists in past stories and broadcasts. Thus, it is often a reporter or columnist who is in the best position to determine the accuracy of an attack. Because interpreting the meaning of a candidate's voting record is a complex process involving analysis of many substantively meaningless procedural votes, it is often the knowledgeable columnist, editorial page writer, or reporter who alerts the public that, although an attack is a technically accurate report of a procedural vote, it misrepresents the actual position of the attacked candidate. In 2003 the Annenberg Public Policy Center launched FactCheck.org to monitor accuracy in the presidential campaign ads of 2004.

When candidates believe they have been unfairly attacked, they often try to enlist the aid of the media in combatting the attack. Journalists can be drawn into the campaign as arbiters of the truth or falsity of attacks by the attacker, by the person attacked, or by the dynamics of the interchange itself.

Political commercials also reveal their creators' perception that material culled from news reports constitutes credible evidence. Hard-hitting attack spots quoting an opponent's stand are often insulated from journalistic censure by their use of actual quotations from newspaper articles or television coverage to document their claims.

Tests of Credibility Applied by Journalists

Journalists are uniquely sensitive to changes in the position a candidate takes.[23] Consistency is one of the categories reporters use to test a candidate and a campaign. If the candidate is a prominent one or if the election is an important one, the meaning of the change in a position will be probed. Throughout his 1988 presidential bid, George Bush repeated the promise, "Read my lips, No new taxes." When, in summer 1990, he concluded that new tax revenues were in fact needed, the switch in positions provided fodder for editorial cartoonists and dominated three days of broadcast and print coverage. In the 2000 campaign, candidate George W. Bush said that he opposed nation building. In 2004 reporters repeatedly asked whether the U.S. presence in Iraq was not in fact nation building. Journalists focus so tightly on consistency because it is easy to test and because it lends itself to the behind-the-scenes-of-the-campaign perspective with which reporters are comfortable. By focusing on inconsistency, newspeople provide credible evidence for opponents to use in attacking the inconsistent candidate.

Charges of inconsistency can be damaging for a reason implied in the closing statement of an ad that Democrats for Nixon ran in 1972 against George McGovern. The ad asked, "Last year . . . this year . . . what about next year?" The tactic is commonplace in races at all levels. In February 2004 for example, incumbent president George W. Bush attacked John Kerry by saying that the Democratic contenders have "diverse opinions: for tax cuts and against them, for NAFTA and against NAFTA, for the

Patriot Act and against the Patriot Act, in favor of liberating Iraq and opposed to it. And that's just one Senator from Massachusetts."[24]

Concentration on inconsistency is evident in a 1999 column by Maureen Dowd of the *New York Times*, which repeated an earlier analysis in the *Times* concerning Republican presidential hopeful George W. Bush: "If Bush did try cocaine, how does that square with his support of Texas legislation putting those caught with less than a gram of the drug in jail?"[25] Knowing that one is vulnerable to a charge means that it would be hypocritical to try to discredit an opponent on the same grounds. For example, the discovery by reporters near the end of the 1996 presidential campaign that before the formal end of his first marriage, Republican party nominee Dole had had an affair explained Dole's insistence in the campaign that he would not address Clinton's private life.

HOW HAS TELEVISION CHANGED POLITICS?

Television has changed politics by changing the way in which information is distributed, by altering the way politics happens, and by changing our patterns of response to politics. By giving the electorate direct access to the candidates, television diminished the role of the political party in the selection of the major party nominees. By centering politics on the person of the candidate, television accelerated the electorate's focus on character rather than issues.

Television has altered the forms of political communication as well. The messages on which most of us rely are briefer than they once were. The stump speech of one to two hours that characterized 19th-century political discourse has given way to the 30-second spot ad and the 10-second sound bite in broadcast news. Increasingly, the audience for a speech is not the one standing in front of the politician but the viewing audience that will hear and see a snippet of the speech on the news.

In these abbreviated forms, much of what constituted the traditional political discourse of earlier ages has been lost. In 15 or 30 seconds, a speaker cannot establish the historical context that shaped the issue in question, cannot detail the probable causes of the problem, cannot examine alternative proposals and argue that one is preferable to others. In snippets, politicians assert but do not argue.

Although rarely used by President George W. Bush, the prime-time press conference can attract large audiences. The size of the audience is in part a function of the carriage. On April 13, 2004, 41 million people watched part or all of his press conference (carried live on ABC, CBS, NBC, CNN, CNBC, Fox, and MSNBC) on the conduct of the war in Iraq; 73 million tuned in to hear his March 17, 2003, ultimatum to Iraq before the start of that engagement.[26]

Because television is an intimate medium, speaking through it required a changed political style that was more conversational, personal, and visual than that of old-style stump oratory. Reliance on television means that increasingly our political world contains memorable pictures rather than memorable words. And words increasingly have been spoken in places chosen to heighten their impact. "We have nothing to fear but fear itself" (FDR in his first inaugural address) has given way to "Let them come to Berlin" (JFK, delivered to crowd in front of the Berlin Wall) and "Mr. Gorbachev, tear down this wall"(Reagan, delivered to people of West Berlin). Schools traditionally

---

BOX 12-3   Substance and Shrinking Sound Bites

The average length of a candidate sound bite on NBC, CBS, and ABC nightly news fell from 9.8 seconds in 1988 to 8.4 in 1992, 8.2 in 1996, and 7.8 in 2000.[a] However, if citizens crave extended candidate speech, they can find it on the morning shows, The *NewsHour with Jim Lehrer, Nightline,* and the Sunday morning interview shows, all available on broadcast. Lichter reports that in 2000, "Total speaking time for the candidates on the *NewsHour* more than doubled the combined total of the three commercial networks (3 hours and 40 minutes vs. 1 hour and 42 minutes)."[b] The problem isn't availability but voter interest.

[a]Stephen J. Farnsworth, and S. Robert Lichter, *The Nightly News Nightmare: Network Television's Coverage of U.S. Presidential Elections, 1988–2000* (Lanham, MD: Rowman and Littlefield, 2003). p. 80.
[b]Robert Lichter, "A Plague on Both Parties: Substance and Fairness in TV Election News," *Press/Politics* 6 (2001): 24.

---

teach us to analyze words and print; in a world in which politics is increasingly visual, informed citizenship requires a new set of skills.

Recognizing the power of television's pictures, politicians craft televisual, staged events called pseudo-events designed to attract media coverage. Much of the political activity we see on television news has been crafted by politicians, their speechwriters, and their public relations advisers for televised consumption.

Because context contributes to the meaning of images, meaning can change in ways unintended by the manufacturers of the moment. For example, when President George W. Bush's staff staged his May 1, 2003, landing on aircraft carrier *USS Lincoln,* they did not envision that the photos of Bush in his flight suit or those of him delivering a speech beneath a banner saying "Mission Accomplished" would take the form of an October 6, 2003, cover of *Time* magazine showing the flight-suited president under the heading "Mission NOT Accomplished."

Political managers spend large amounts of time ensuring that their clients appear in visually compelling settings so that the pictures seen in the news will reinforce those seen in ads. In debates, candidates recall those staged pseudo-events. Sound bites in news and answers to questions in debates increasingly sound like ads.

By focusing on mainstream values, television mainstreams its viewers. Heavy viewers of television differ from light viewers in some politically relevant ways. The likelihood that a character in a prime-time program will be the victim of a crime is higher than victimization is in real life. Heavier viewers therefore come to believe that they are more likely to be victims of crime than they actually are. Heavy viewers are also more conservative in their views about the socially appropriate response to crime. They are, for example, more likely than light viewers to favor heavy sentences and use of the death penalty. Heavy-viewing conservatives and heavy-viewing liberals are more likely to agree on how to respond to crime than are heavy- and light-viewing liberals. Whereas heavy viewing makes liberals more conservative on crime, however, television's legitimization of government response to social problems draws conservatives closer to a more liberal view of the value of government solutions to social problems.

The quantity, quality, and audience for televised information about politics is changing. In the mid-1980s, a rise in the quality of political programming on the Public

Broadcasting Service and the rise of cable meant that the amount of substantive political information available on television multiplied. With the addition of Fox and MSNBC to CNN, the amount of political content on cable jumped as well.

The rise of cable meant that specialized audiences could now be addressed directly by candidates. What had been a broadcast medium, reaching a large, undifferentiated mass audience, was increasingly becoming a narrowcast medium, reaching smaller, more homogenous audiences. What was once true only of radio and direct mail became true of television in the mid-1980s. Spanish-language cable reached Hispanics in large numbers; MTV reached young voters. Whereas broadcasting dictated that political messages speak to concerns that transcended our differences, the narrowcasting of cable meant that the special concerns of special segments of the audience could now be addressed.

Whereas the limited number of broadcast channels meant that reporters could easily eavesdrop on and criticize candidate ads, however, the narrowcasting available on more than 100 cable channels and millions of Internet sites made this increasingly difficult.

Image versus Issues; Character versus Positions

Scholars have wasted a lot of time trying to distinguish between messages that relate to candidates' images and messages that relate to candidates' stands on issues. The problem, of course, is that almost every message says something that can be interpreted as an issue and tries to enhance the candidate's credibility and hence her or his image. It is more useful to recognize that stands on issues produce an image and that such "image" questions as trustworthiness and competence often are issues.

A more useful distinction separates the character, the natural temperament and disposition, and the relevant biography of the candidate from the specific legislative action that the candidate proposes. A candidate might demonstrate her compassion, a facet of character, by indicating her strong support for Aid for Dependent Children, a policy position, or stand on an issue. Since the early 1970s, voters have been telling pollsters that the character of the candidates is more important to them than the candidates' policy positions or stands on issues.

The Comparative Relevance of Character and Stands on Issues

In the second half of the 20th century, the electorate learned that judging a candidate on stands on issues was not a totally reliable predictor of his or her conduct in office. Some candidates acted against voter expectations: Lyndon Johnson, elected in 1964 as the peace candidate, escalated the war in Vietnam. Some presidents proved unable to meet their objectives. John Kennedy did not succeed in translating his campaign promises into law; only after his death did his successor secure passage of some of Kennedy's key initiatives. Jimmy Carter, elected to bring the budget into balance and lower inflation and unemployment, had not accomplished these goals by the end of his first term. Bill Clinton failed to make good on his campaign promise to deliver a health care reform plan that could be financed by cost savings in the existing system. Similarly, contrary to his campaign promise, in his first term George W. Bush did not aggressively push for legislation to permit individuals to invest part of their payroll tax in the market to increase the survivability of Social Security. It is important to note, however, that at the presidential level at least, more than two thirds of the time those elected make a substantial effort to keep their promises. From this perspective, one might note that Clinton tried to keep his promise to reform the health care system but was thwarted by the intransigence of his own party and the opposition of the Republican minority.

Meanwhile, the character of a candidate seemed increasingly important in judging performance in office. Whether a person was truthful and trustworthy was a focal concern of those probing the failures of Johnson's handling of the Vietnam War, Nixon's handling of Watergate, Clinton's handling of Whitewater and the Lewinsky affair, and (George W.) Bush's claim that the presence of weapons of mass destruction justified military intervention in Iraq; whether a person was competent was central to those probing the failures of the presidencies of Ford and Carter; whether a person was candid about his health was of concern to those who learned of Kennedy's Addison's disease only after his death. Therefore, we turn next to the question, What can and does television tell us about issues and the character of presidential candidates?

Determining Which Issues Are the Likely Focus of a Campaign In their own ads, in debates, and in news clips, candidates reveal their popular past positions and conceal their unpopular ones. At the same time, candidates reveal the unpopular past positions of their opponents. Public opinion polls and focus group tests (analysis of the response of small groups to various messages) help campaigns determine which issues will resonate with which voting group:

- When an issue is controversial but nonetheless beneficial to one side or the other, that issue is more likely to be raised in the ads and news coverage of a PAC, not in the candidate's own messages.
- When an issue hurts multiple candidates or both major parties, as the savings and loan crisis did in 1988, it will be not be raised by either side.
- In general, at the presidential level the party affiliation of the contenders has accurately predicted their likely positions on certain issues. Republicans will, for example, favor less government intervention and less taxation but will support greater defense spending than will Democrats.
- In general, the issues on which news, advertising, and debates focus are those advanced by major party nominees. Although in 1988 more than 100 citizens filed the appropriate papers to be considered bona fide presidential contenders, public discussion focused, with few exceptions, on the Democratic and Republican nominees and on the issues they considered important.
- Issues of general concern will receive treatment in the mass media; issues of less national concern or highly specialized issues will be treated in specialty publications and broadcasts. For example, those interested in a candidate's monetary philosophy are more likely to find such information on *Wall Street Week in Review* or in the *Wall Street Journal* than on the *NBC Nightly News* or in *USA Today*. Specific environmental policies are likely to be treated in magazines devoted to the subject.
- Because television is a visual medium, the messages produced for it are more likely to speak to issues that lend themselves to visualization. This means that crime and environmental pollution are more likely to be the subjects of political ads and of news coverage than is the national debt or international liquidity.

Nonpartisan fact-finding groups assist news organizations and campaigns in locating trustworthy information. One such group is the Center for Responsive Politics, which tracks money in politics. In an exchange of Internet ads in February 2004, the Bush campaign attacked Massachusetts Senator and Democratic presidential contender John Kerry for accepting more money from lobbyists than any other senator. Kerry responded that Bush had set new records and exceeded Kerry in money raised from such groups. Their reliance on data from the center prompted an editorial in the *New York Times* saying, "A valuable patch of common ground has unexpectedly surfaced in the first phase of the presidential election. In their early skirmishes over who's pandering most to special interests, both Democrats and Republicans have begun citing the same authority—the Center for Responsive Politics, a research group dedicatedly nonpartisan in publicizing the power of money in politics. Imagine, in lieu of mud, the slinging of accurate information."[27]

Determining Which Facets of Character Are the Likely Focus in a Campaign The character defects of the most recent president are likely to shape the criteria by which the character of the candidates is judged. After Nixon's resignation, Carter won his election campaigning as a candidate who would never lie and who would provide a government as good as its people.

Societal norms shape the criteria we set for candidate character. In the 1950s and 1960s, a candidate who was divorced was weakened by that fact. During their presidential runs, divorce was raised as an issue against Adlai Stevenson and Nelson Rockefeller. By the 1980s, being divorced no longer carried a social stigma, and the country elected its first divorced president, Ronald Reagan.

The press and public are continually in the process of determining which facets of character are relevant to governance. In the 1988 primaries, we learned that having smoked marijuana in one's youth was not a disqualifier. In the Texas gubernatorial campaign of 1990, we learned that the press and public considered it inappropriate for a candidate for governor to have purchased the services of prostitutes in his youth. In 1992, those who voted for Clinton seemed to say that a candidate's past infidelity was acceptable if it was not ongoing and his wife had remained with him in spite of it.

Any form of hypocrisy, any discrepancy between private behavior and public, political statement, is likely to be scrutinized by the press. As a result, during the primaries of 1992, two facets of Bill Clinton's past preoccupied the press: his failure to serve in Vietnam and his alleged affair with a nightclub singer. Similarly during the primaries of 2000, the press spent a lot of time chasing rumors that the Governor of Texas had used cocaine or been convicted of driving while intoxicated in his younger years. In the closing days of that election, the press learned that the Republican campaign had in fact failed to disclose a DUI arrest.

THE INTERPLAY OF INFLUENCE: ISSUES AND CHARACTER IN ADS, NEWS, AND DEBATES

Although separating issues from the character of the person advancing them is difficult if not impossible, scholars, pundits, and reporters talk as if the two are discrete. Here we examine the role of issues and image in ads, news, and debates.

Ads

There is more issue content in many ads than in broadcast news. The typical television viewer gets most of his or her political information from ads. A number of factors minimize the ability of ads to convey useful issue information.

Limitations   Conveying useful information is not the goal of the advertising. By stressing issues that will benefit them, candidates' ads attempt to set the issue agenda for the campaign. Because ads are partisan sources of information, they are poor sources of primary political information. Ads suppress information that would hurt their candidate, ads occasionally take evidence out of context, and ads occasionally invite false inferences.

Political ads for bona fide candidates for federal office are not subject to tests of fairness or accuracy by those broadcasting them. A political ad for a bona fide candidate for federal office must meet only four tests: (1) It must have a discernible disclaimer disclosing its sponsor, (2) it must fit the time purchased, (3) it must meet the technical standards of the broadcast outlet, and (4) it may not be obscene.

If a station has sold advertising time to one candidate in a race, it must make comparable time available for sale to all other bona fide candidates for that race. Because candidates must pay for most ad time, we are more likely to see ads for those who are wealthy or able to raise more money than their opponents. At the presidential level, in the general election, this advantage is muted by equal federal financing of both major party candidates.

Ways to Compensate for or to Counter These Limitations   Here are some of the major ways to compensate for or counter the kinds of limitations just described:

1. The best way to protect oneself against distortions in advertising is to seek out alternative forms of information. The best-informed voters are those who combine television viewing with newspaper and magazine reading. Because candidates often respond to the distortions of ads in press conferences, viewing news helps obtain the "other side."
2. In debates, candidates are directly accountable to a press panel and to their opponents. Some questions of accuracy can be resolved by attentive debate viewing.
3. Concern about the distortions in attack advertising has prompted calls for legislation. Opponents of these proposals argue that they violate the U.S. Constitution's protections of free speech. Proposals include requiring that attacks be made by a candidate speaking in person in an ad, requiring that free response time be provided for a candidate attacked by a PAC ad, and requiring that shortly after an ad begins airing, the sponsoring candidate hold a press conference to respond to questions about it.

News

Viewers tell pollsters that their voting choices are more influenced by print and broadcast news than by ads. This finding, however, may be the by-product of our human tendency to report that we are influenced by approved sources and uninfluenced by presumably manipulative sources. There is no dispute that when news coverage of a candidate is consistent with that candidate's ads and debate performance, the power of the candidate's message is magnified.

Limitations   Several factors may minimize the ability of news to communicate useful issue information. For over a decade, scholars have consistently found that broadcast and print journalism focuses not on the issue content of campaigns but on the strategic intent of the candidates, on the outcome of their strategies, and on who is winning or losing. This focus on the "horse race" and "game plan" displaces discussion of other matters.

In addition, candidates attempt to control the news agenda. When they succeed, the news agenda and their ads are similarly focused, employ similar pictures, and use much of the same language.

When network newscasts do focus on issues, some of their news norms minimize the impact of their discussion. For instance, news is only news once. Once a story on an issue has aired or been printed, it is unlikely to be re-aired. The problem occurs when an ad repeatedly makes a false claim that is corrected or put into context only a single time in news. A problem occurs as well when the attention of parts of the public has not yet focused on the campaign at the time at which the issue is covered.

Another news norm problem is that it is the job of reporters to cover the story, not to make it. Accordingly, reporters focus on the issues preselected by the candidates. However, reporters are willing to set the agenda for discussion of character and to probe any discrepancies between candidate character and accepted social norms.

Ways to Compensate for or to Counter These Limitations   Here are some of the major ways to compensate for or counter the kinds of limitations just described:

1. Gather information from multiple news sources and multiple media.
2. Determine what issues are relevant to you and seek out forms in which those issues are likely to be addressed.
3. Begin paying attention to news and debates in the early presidential primaries, when news coverage is likely to treat emerging issues in depth.
4. Use computers in libraries or at home to retrieve early news stories of importance in putting candidate claims into context. Early in the primaries newspapers often carry careful studies of the biography and record of a candidate.

Debates

In a national election, debates are the single most useful form of information available to voters. In debates, a large viewing audience has the opportunity to compare the candidates and their positions. Debates provide the only direct comparison available in most campaigns. The results are beneficial to every segment of the viewing audience from the least to the best educated. Surveys have shown that after each presidential debate, viewers could more accurately identify and report the candidates' positions on the major issues debated.

Limitations   Several factors minimize the ability of debates to communicate useful information on issues. First, the candidates' desire to protect themselves from gaffes leads them:

BOX 12-4   Wolf Blitzer Interviews Kucinich

The focus on horse race undercuts the candidacies of those doing poorly in the polls. The *Columbia Journalism Review* reported the first five questions CNN's reporter Wolf Blitzer asked Democratic contender Dennis Kucinich in a January 27, 2004, interview:

> *Blitzer:* How does it feel to be at the bottom of the polls, you and Al Sharpton? . . . What's the point?. . .
>
> *Blitzer:* . . . How frustrating does it get though,

that you are not registering really in any of these polls? . . .

> *Blitzer:* So . . . you're going to be in this until when? . . . At what point do you say, You know what, I can't go on? . . .
>
> *Blitzer:* What does that mean, you're in it all the way? At some point you're going to run out of money. . . .
>
> *Blitzer:* So you're going to keep on going?[a]

[a]March–April 2004, p. 8.

---

1. To seek a panel of reporters, on the expectation that reporters will ask predictable questions
2. To negotiate a format that includes only short answers, on the assumption that all possible questions can be anticipated and short answers prepared
3. To negotiate a format that denies reporters the ability to follow up their questions, on the assumption that inconsistencies and inaccuracies are less likely to be exposed if there are no follow-up questions.

Second, the press panelists tend to ask questions of more interest to a knowledgeable reporter than to an information-seeking voter. This flaw was remedied in the 1992 and 1996 campaigns, when in one of the candidate debates nonreporter citizens asked questions directly of the presidential candidates.

Third, press coverage tends to reduce debates to one decisive moment. This focus distracts attention from information in the debate about the candidates and their positions. These supposedly decisive moments include "There you go again," "Do you remember when you said, 'There you go again?'" (1980 Reagan/Carter debate, Reagan is the speaker), and "Senator, you are no Jack Kennedy" (Quayle/Bentsen 1988 debate, Bentsen is the speaker). They also include Clinton's claim in the first 1992 debate that George H. W. Bush's attacks on Clinton's patriotism betrayed Bush's father's memory: In the 1950s, Senator Prescott Bush had objected to the tactics of Senator Joseph McCarthy.

Fourth, the press focuses on the strategic intent of the candidates and on who won or lost the debate. There is no intelligent way to judge a win or loss. More important is that the focus on winning and losing displaces other more useful discussions of what could be and should be learned from debates.

Ways to Compensate for or to Counter These Limitations Here are some of the major ways to compensate for or counter the kinds of limitations just described:

1. The well-informed voter will be able to spot errors and inconsistencies.
2. The well-informed voter need not rely on commentators to determine what was and was not significant in the debate.

3. The well-informed viewer will not let debate coverage determine what is useful but will instead ask what issues and traits of character are important and will seek out that information systematically.

TO SUM UP

In this chapter we have examined the complex interactions among the candidates and the media in campaigns. One medium can be used to provide a context for the content carried by another; for example, a print reporter may determine the accuracy of charges contained in a broadcast ad. Alternatively, an ad such as the anti-Nixon Watergate ads run by George McGovern may take articles published in a print form and employ them in a televised ad.

We also noted the interplay of news and advertising across the various media. Ads become the subject of analysis in news, and items in the news become the content of ads. In the process, the well-financed candidate has the ability to take his or her case directly to the U.S. public in ads, but even as this right is exercised, it is subject to the scrutiny of the news media.

Finally, we have shown some of the ways in which politicians manipulate the news in their attempts to impose a consistent image of themselves and their campaigns on all media outlets. This chapter illustrates the systemic and commercial character of the U.S. mass media. Political communication includes both news and advertising. As news, political activities are shaped by the criteria for newsworthiness and the conventions of news presentation. In advertising, candidates, like products, must achieve name recognition; differentiate themselves from their competitors; create identification with and participation by target audiences; associate themselves with admired people, activities, and values; and use repetition to overcome audience resistance.

In political communication, news and advertising interact in an unusually significant way. News coverage can make a candidate credible, reinforce the messages in political ads, and protect the candidate against certain kinds of attacks. As a result, politicians seek to blur distinctions between news and advertising; campaign managers create pseudo-events to attract media coverage; and news footage or newslike content and formats are used in political advertising.

Journalists, with their special access to information and their credibility as investigators, evaluate the claims in political ads and serve as a corrective to deceptive and misleading advertising. Conversely, through ads candidates can respond to news coverage and influence the way that audiences react to news items.

National and state political candidates cannot be elected without the credibility conferred by news coverage or without the images created through advertising. As a result, the costs of political campaigning have increased. Political advertising is expensive, as are the services of professionals with the expertise to influence news coverage. In one sense, mass media have made political communication more efficient—the cost of reaching each voter has decreased—but they have also made politics a game successfully played primarily by the affluent and the media savvy.

ANALYSIS: POLITICAL ADS AND NEWS

Many of the questions found at the ends of the chapters on news and advertising can also be asked about the political use of ads and news. Here we include some additional questions that pertain specifically to advertising and news in political campaigns.

Determining Who Is Newsworthy

What criteria are governing which candidates are receiving news coverage? Are some candidates receiving more coverage than others? Are some candidates receiving more coverage in one medium than in others? If so, why? How are the candidates using the conventions and routines of news coverage to secure news coverage? Are some candidates doing this with greater skill than others? Are reporters reporting these efforts at manipulation?

Determining What Is Covered

Are the candidates' ads a subject of news reporting? If so, what is the focus of such stories? (Cost? Claims? Evidence? Fairness? Image? Media Consultants?) Is one candidate more clearly setting the agenda for the media than others? What agenda is being set for voters by the media? Are they focusing on issues that favor one candidate over the others? Are the media focusing on some primaries and not others? If so, why? Which candidates are benefiting from this focus? Has the nature of coverage changed during the campaign? Has the quantity of the coverage increased, decreased, or remained the same as the campaign has progressed? What interpretation has been placed on each announcement of candidacy and each statement of withdrawal? Are journalists acting to determine the truth or falsity of charges in the campaign? If so, to what effect? Has any candidate invoked libel laws, equal opportunity, or right to access? If so, to what effect? If this is a statewide campaign, a congressional or senatorial campaign, has it received coverage in the national media? If so, what of significance or interest to a national audience is being credited to this campaign?

Relationship of Candidates and Reporters

Compare the treatment of reporters by each campaign. Are they better fed and housed, more courteously treated, in one campaign than others? If so, what effect, if any, is this having on media coverage? Are some journalists being given preferential treatment? If so, to what effect? Are some reporters being punished by the campaign for unfavorable coverage? If so, what form of action is the punishment taking? (Restricted access? Undesirable Accommodations?) What are the ongoing themes in the coverage of this campaign? (Horse race? Appearance versus reality? Consistency?)

The Image of the Candidate

Is the image projected by the candidate consistent? If not, what are the discrepancies, and what accounts for them? Is the image projected in person consistent with the image in ads? In news? Are some of the candidates more visually appropriate for televising than others? If so, what impact is that having on the campaign? On reports about the campaign? Has the image of the candidate altered over time? If so, why and to what effect? Is the presence of a media consultant an issue in this campaign? If so, what is the consultant saying about his or her role in the campaign? Is the media consultant helping or hurting the candidate? What are the adjectives used most often by the media to describe this candidate? Is an independent PAC running ads to create a positive or negative image about one of the candidates? If so, to what effect? How are the candidates reacting to the PAC?

Candidates' Ads

Are candidates using ads to contextualize news? Are materials from news reports functioning as evidence in ads? Have ads been a subject of news reports? If so, did the coverage help or hurt the candidate? Is the candidate using attack ads? If so, are they truthful and fair? If so, are they airing throughout the campaign, at specific points in the campaign, or at the end of the campaign? How does the pattern of airing attack ads affect their impact in this campaign? Will these ads provoke a backlash? If so, why? If not, why not? Are these attack ads responding to other attacks? If so, is the response legitimizing the attack of the opponent? How are the ads creating recognition, differentiation, association, participation, and repetition?

Use InfoTrac College Edition to access information on topics in this chapter from hundreds of periodicals and scholarly journals. Enter keyword and subject searches: *agenda-setting theory, media access, Internet and campaign politics.*

SELECTED READINGS

Bimber, Bruce, and Richard Davis. *Campaigning Online: The Internet in U.S. Elections.* New York: Oxford University Press, 2003.

Crigler, Ann N., Marion R. Just, and Edward J. McCaffery, eds. *Rethinking the Vote: The Politics and Prospects of American Election Reform.* New York: Oxford University Press, 2004.

Farnsworth, Stephen J., and S. Robert Lichter. *The Nightly News Nightmare: Network Television's Coverage of U.S. Presidential Elections, 1988–2000.* Lanham, MD: Rowman and Littlefield, 2003.

Hart, Roderick P. *Political Talk.* Princeton, NJ: Princeton University Press, 2000.

———. *Seducing America: How Television Charms the Modern Voter.* Chicago: University of Chicago Press, 1994.

Hutchings, Vincent L. *Public Opinion and Democratic Accountability: How Citizens Learn about Politics.* Princeton, NJ: Princeton University Press, 2003.

Jamieson, Kathleen Hall, and Paul Waldman. *The Press Effect.* New York: Oxford University Press, 2003.

Patterson, Thomas E. *The Vanishing Voter: Public Involvement in an Age of Uncertainty* New York: Knopf, 2002.

Notes

Chapter 1 The Media: An Introduction

1. David Potter, *People of Plenty: Economic Abundance and the American Character* (Chicago: University of Chicago Press, 1954), pp. 172–173.
2. Robert Strauss, "On the Money," *Philadelphia Inquirer*, 11 August 1999, p. D2.
3. Survey of Americans by the Pew Center for the People and the Press, June 9, 2002. Online at http://people-press.org/report/print.Php3?page ID=618.
4. Online at www.newscorp.com, 14 November 2003.
5. "Tony Snow Heads to Fox Radio," NewsMax.com, 27 October 2003.
6. Brian C. Anderson, "Winning the Culture War," 3 November 2003, online at FrontPagemagazine.com.
7. Ken Auletta, *The New Yorker*, 26 May 2003, p. 9.
8. Staff, "Roger's Balancing Act; Fox's Ailes Shakes Up the News Status Quo," *Broadcasting and Cable*, 27 October 2003, p. 28.
9. Patricia Horn, "Oh, Television Watcher, You Ain't Seen Nothin' Yet," *Philadelphia Inquirer*, 18 July 1999, p. A21.
10. "Network Radio," *Marketer's Guide to the Media* (New York: BPI Communications, 1998), pp. 72–73.
11. Nat Ives, "On Public TV, Not Quite an Ad but Pretty Close," *New York Times*, 28 March 2005, p. C1.
12. "Consumer Ownership and Subscription Statistics," *International 36 Television and Video Almanac*, ed. Tracy Stevens (New York: Quigley Publishing, 1999), p. 9.
13. Richard Huff, "Titanic Might Not Make Big Waves on HBO," *New York Daily News*, 9 April 1999, p. 131.
14. Fall Cable Preview, *New York Times Magazine*, 28 September 2003, advertising supplement.
15. Thomas Tyrer, "Cable Gains, Broadcast Flat in This Season's NFL Ratings," *Electronic Media*, 11 December 1989, p. 6.
16. "ESPN," *Advertising Age*, 8 May 1995, p. C17.
17. "How the Network for Nerds Became a Hit," *Wall Street Journal*, 26 March 2004, p. W11.
18. Debra Aho Williamson, "Building a New Industry," *Advertising Age*, 13 March 1995, p. S3.
19. Scott Donaton, "The Battle for Online Content," *Advertising Age*, 15 May 1995, pp. 16–17.
20. "Pay-per-View," *TV Dimensions*, ed. Ed Parazian (New York: Media Dynamics, 1999), p. 160.
21. *Broadcasting & Cable*, 19 June 1995, p. 6; *Philadelphia Inquirer*, 2 February 1996, p. A6.
22. *The DBS Digest*, 4 April 1999, online at http://www.dbsdish.com/dbsdata.html.
23. *Broadcasting & Cable*, 27 March 1995, p. 54.
24. "Multichannel for Rural Areas," *Communications Daily*, 20 May 1994, p. 2.
25. Wireless Communications Association International, 23 May 1999, online at http://www.wcai.com/index.htm.
26. *Broadcasting & Cable*, 19 June 1995, p. 6; *Philadelphia Inquirer*, 2 February 1996, p. A6.
27. Edmund L. Andrews, "From Communications Chaos, Order?" *New York Times*, 17 June 1995, sec. 1, p. 1.
28. "AT&T's High-Stakes Gamble on Interactive Cable Television," *New York Times*, 3 January 2000, p. C3.
29. Patricia Horn, "Oh, Television Watcher, You Ain't Seen Nothin' Yet," *Philadelphia Inquirer*, 18 July 1999, p. A21.
30. Online at http://www.nielsenmedia.com/.

31. Jennifer Weiner, "When It Comes to All-Time Ratings, Clinton Apology Is a Poor Third," *Philadelphia Inquirer*, 20 August 1998, p. D10.

32. "Living Happily Ever After in Syndication," *Tampa Tribune,* 17 May 1998, p. 6.

33. Jeremy Gerard, "TV Networks Want Nielsen to Change Ratings Methods," *New York Times*, 14 December 1989, p. D1.

34. Bill Carter, "TV Viewing Cited Outside of Homes," *New York Times*, 10 May 1990, p. C15.

35. "Study Finds Many Viewers Not at Home," *Variety,* 17–23 July 1995, p. 26.

36. "Nielsen Will Change the Way It Gathers Ratings on Black TV Viewers," *Jet,* 7 November 1994, p. 40.

37. George Hunter, "Ads Often Miss for Minorities: In Touchy Industry, White- and Black-Owned Agencies Struggle to Overcome Stereotypes," *Detroit News,* 18 October 1998, p. B1.

38. *New York Times*, 15 April 2004, p. A7.

39. Online at http://www.nielsenmedia.com/.

40. Sam Diaz, "TiVo to Provide Viewing Breakdown," *Los Angeles Times*, 5 February 2004, p. C1.

41. "Network Radio, " *Marketer's Guide to the Media* (New York: BPI Communications, 1998), pp. 72–73.

42. R. Unmacht, ed., *The M Street Radio Directory* (Alexandria, VA: M Street Corp., 1994), p. 19. The 1998 statistics come from "U.S. Radio Formats by State and Possession," *Broadcasting & Cable Yearbook,* 1998, p. D616.

43. John von Rhein, "Bach, Beethoven and the Bottom Line: Classical Radio Is Imperiled, but Chicago's Two Stations Are Holding On," *Chicago Tribune,* 8 May 1994, Arts, p. 5.

44. "The National Public Radio Idea: Give Them What They Need, Maybe Not What They Want," *Nieman Reports,* Summer 1997, pp. 32–37.

45. Interview with Shelby Oros, National Public Radio, Washington, DC, 7 June 1999.

46. Donna Petrozzello, "Public Radio Groups Contemplate Merger," *Broadcasting & Cable,* 3 November 1997, p. 81.

47. R. Unmacht, ed., *The M Street Radio Directory* (Alexandria, VA: M Street Corp., 1994), p. 19.

48. Lorne Manly, "As Satellite Radio Takes Off, It Is Altering the Airwaves," *New York Times,* 5 April 2005, p. A01.

49. Daren Fonda, "The Revolution in Radio," *Time*, 19 April 2004, pp. 55–60.

50. Interview with Carol Nashe, Carol Nashe Group of Radio Talk Show Hosts Consultants, 8 June 1999.

51. David Shaw, "Heard the Local News? It May Soon Be Harder to Find," *Los Angeles Times*, 1 June 2003, p. 12.

52. These data come, respectively, from *Electronic Media,* 16 April 1990, p. 66; Newspaper Association of America, "Facts about Newspapers," May 1999, online at http://www.naa.org/info/irc/framquery.html); "National Newspapers," *Marketer's Guide to the Media* (New York: BPI Communications, 1998), p. 190.

53. Pew Center for the People and the Press survey, 9 June 2002.

54. *Philadelphia Inquirer*, 20 April 1995, p. C1.

55. Jacques Steinberg, "After Circulation Scandals, Newspapers Create New Safeguards," *New York Times*, 25 October 2004, p. C9. Copyright © 2004 by The New York Times Co. Reprinted with permission.

56. "Growth of Magazines in the U.S.," *Magazine Dimensions '99,* ed. Ed Parazian (New York: Media Dynamics, 1999), p. 11.

57. "Adult Readership of Newsweekly Magazines," *Magazine Dimensions '99,* ed. Ed Parazian (New York: Media Dynamics, 1999), p. 246.

58. Bob Tedeschi, "Digging up Low Web Fares," *New York Times*, 18 April 2004, p. 4Tr.

59. Pew Center for the People and the Press release, 11 June 2000.

60. Web Sites/News Organizations, *New York Times*, 29 March 2004, p. C7.

61. Pew Center, 11 June 2000.

62. Michael Totty, "Making Them Pay," *Wall Street Journal*, 22 March 2004, p. R4.

63. Totty, p. R4.

64. Bob Tedeschi, "E-Commerce Report," *New York Times*, 19 January 2004, p. C7.

65. *New York Times*, 22 November 2004, p. C7.

66. Erla Zwingle, "Goods Move. People Move. Ideas Move. And Cultures Change," *National Geographic,* August 1999, p. 30.

67. Neva Chonin, "Tuning in Online," *San Francisco Sunday Examiner and Chronicle,* 8 August 1999, p. 36.
68. Barbara Crossette, "The Internet Changes Dictatorship's Rules," *Philadelphia Inquirer,* 1 August 1999, sec. 4, p. 1.
69. Elizabeth Weise, "Around the World in a Click with Webcams," *USA Today,* 5 August 1999, p. D1.
70. Mary Beth Marklein, "Living Dorm Life in Camera's Eye," *USA Today,* 5 August 1999, p. D2.
71. Doug Bedell, "Webcams Could Doom Any Thought of Privacy," *Philadelphia Inquirer,* 5 August 1999, p. F3.
72. Lisa Ramirez, "Web Sites on Health: Use with Caution," *Philadelphia Inquirer,* 26 July 1999, p. C1.
73. Ingrid Volkmer, "Universalism and Particularism: The Problem of Cultural Sovereignty and Global Information Flow," *Borders in Cyberspace,* ed. Brian Kahin and Charles Nesson (Cambridge, MA: MIT Press, 1998), pp. 49–50.
74. James Naughton, "This Just In! and This!" *New York Times on the Web,* 1 February 1998.
75. David Halberstam, *The Powers That Be* (New York: Knopf, 1979), p. 514.
76. Michael Wolff, "Bad News for the Media Elite," *New York Times,* 23 November 1998, p. 34.
77. Wolff, pp. 32–34.
78. Pew Research Center for the People and the Press, 8 June 1998. For more details, go to http://people-press.org/reports/print.php3?PageID=568.

Chapter 2   What Is News?

1. In May 1994, Sean Aday, Christopher Ferris, and Michael Grant of the Annenberg School for Communication, University of Pennsylvania, presented an analysis of subjects covered by urban newspapers; they found that crime stories were prominent. Crime, and the related subjects of violence and the courts, made up 22.2 percent of Philadelphia daily newspaper stories in a one-month period.
2. Robert MacNeil, "The Flickering Images That May Drive Presidents," *Media Studies Journal* (Winter 1995): 124–125.
3. *The Abu Ghraib Investigations,* Ed. Steven Strasser (New York: Public Affairs, 2004).
4. Ben Bagdikian, *Double Vision: Reflections on My Heritage, Life, and Profession* (Boston: Beacon Press, 1995), p. 186.
5. John Woestendiek, "Camp Seeks, and Fears, City's Notice," *Philadelphia Inquirer,* 26 July 1995, pp. A1, A8.
6. Helen Benedict, *Virgin or Vamp: How the Press Covers Sex Crimes* (New York: Oxford University Press, 1992), p. 219; Don Terry, "In the Week of an Infamous Rape, 28 Other Victims Suffer," *Gender and Public Policy,* ed. Kenneth Winston and Mary Jo Bane (Boulder, CO: Westview, 1993), p. 160.
7. David Simon, "Cops, Killers, and Crispy Critters," *Media Studies Journal* (Winter 1992): 36.
8. On pseudo-events, see Daniel Boorstin, *The Image: A Guide to Pseudo-Events in America* (New York: Atheneum, 1962).
9. Mark Fishman, *Manufacturing the News* (Austin: University of Texas Press, 1980), pp. 63–70, 134.
10. David L. Altheide and Robert P. Snow, *Media Logic* (Beverly Hills, CA: Sage, 1979), p. 19.
11. Tony Schwartz, "Ratings Sweeps Boost Lurid Side of the News," *New York Times,* 25 November 1980, p. C17.
12. Tom Wicker, *On Press* (New York: Viking, 1978), p. 44.
13. "Actor and 71 Others Arrested at Nuclear Test Site," *New York Times,* 28 January 1987, p. Y13.
14. Edie N. Goldenberg, *Making the Papers* (Lexington, MA: Lexington Books, 1975), p. 28.
15. Edie N. Goldenberg, "An Overview of Access to the Media," *Women in the News,* ed. Laurily Keir Epstein (New York: Hastings House, 1978), pp. 55–56. Goldenberg also cites the work of William A. Gamson, *The Strategy of Social Protest* (Homewood, IL: Dorsey, 1975), in support of her claims.
16. Neil Hickey, "It Exposed TV's Failures—as Well as NASA's," *TV Guide,* 24 January 1987, p. 3.
17. Report of the Columbia Accident Investigation Board, vols. 1-4 (Washington, DC: GPO, 2003).
18. Leon V. Sigal, *Reporters and Officials: The Organization and Politics of Newsmaking* (Lexington, MA: Heath, 1973), p. 121, table 6–1.

19. See David Halberstam, *The Powers That Be* (New York: Knopf, 1979), especially p. 434, for numerous examples of the powers of President Lyndon Johnson to suppress news stories from correspondents in Saigon.

20. William E. Porter, *Assault on the Media: The Nixon Years* (Ann Arbor: University of Michigan Press, 1976), p. 227.

21. Quoted by Bonnie Anderson in *News Flash* (San Francisco: Jossey-Bass, 2004), p. 46.

22. *Face the Nation* (New York: Simon and Schuster, 2004), p. 158.

23. Michael M. Phillips, "Embedded Reporters Tell Campaign Tales," *Wall Street Journal,* 29 December 2003, p. A4.

24. Anderson, *News Flash*, p. 31.

25. Bob Schieffer, *Face the Nation* (New York: Simon and Schuster), p. 175.

26. Dan Rather, *The Camera Never Blinks* (New York: William Morrow, 1977), p. 234.

27. *New York Times*, 16 December 1984, p. 9.

28. Robert MacNeil, "The Flickering Images That May Drive Presidents," *Media Studies Journal* (Winter 1995): 123.

29. Tracey Thompson, "Buying Drugs for the President Was No Easy Task," report from the *Washington Post* carried in the *Philadelphia Inquirer*, 16 December 1989, p. A12.

30. Ellen Hume, "Why the Press Blew the S&L Scandal," *New York Times*, 24 May 1990, p. A19Y.

31. Stephen Labaton, "F.D.I.C. Sues Neil Bush and Others at Silverado," *New York Times*, 22 September 1990, p. Y17.

32. Kathleen Quinn, "As S&L's Sink, a Trade Weekly Is Soaring," *New York Times*, 27 August 1990, p. C8.

33. Tom Freedman, "While Journalists Chase 'Sexy' Issues," *New York Times*, 16 September 1990, p. E23.

34. David Bauder, "Tragedy Boosted Network and Cable Ratings," *Philadelphia Inquirer*, 22 July 1999, p. A14.

35. Anderson, *News Flash*, p. 155.

36. Diane Mermigas, "'*Today*' Airs Follow-up after GE Controversy," *Electronic Media,* 11 December 1989, p. 2.

37. Lou Cannon, *Reporting: An Inside View* (Sacramento: California Journal Press, 1977), pp. 134–135.

38. Lou Gelfand, "If You Ran the Paper?" *Minneapolis Star Tribune,* 1 February 1987, p. A25.

39. Walter Cronkite, *A Reporter's Life* (New York: Ballantine Books, 1996), p. 220.

40. Michael Kinsley, *Curse of the Giant Muffins* (New York: Summit Books, 1987).

41. E. J. Dionne, "The Elusive Front-Runner," *New York Times* Magazine, 3 May 1987, p. 83.

42. Kathleen Hall Jamieson, *Eloquence in an Electronic Age: The Transformation of Political Speechmaking* (New York: Oxford University Press, 1988), p. ix.

43. Albert R. Hunt, "L'Affaire Clinton: A Press Scandal, Not a Sex Scandal," *Wall Street Journal*, 27 January 1992, p. A12.

44. Richard Cohen, "A Judgment of Questions," *Washington Post*, 16 February 1999, p. A17.

45. Ibid.

46. George Condon Jr., Copley News Service dispatch, 19 December 1998.

47. James Toedtman, "Affair Disclosure under Fire," *Newsday,* 18 September 1998, p. A5.

48. Stephen Hess, in *The Washington Reporters* (Washington, DC: Brookings Institution, 1981), documents this situation for the DC press corps. According to his survey, most Washington journalists are generalists (p. 49). They use no documents in the presentation of nearly three fourths of their stories; when used, documents are likely to be newspaper articles (p. 18). Although 93 percent of Washington reporters in 1978 were college graduates and 33 percent had graduate degrees (p. 83), a beat was considered more desirable if no documents research was required (p. 52). Even on specialized beats such as economics or law, journalists tend to read popular rather than scholarly journals (p. 64).

49. On December 19, 2002, the convictions of four African American and one Latino juveniles were dismissed by a judge following the confession of a convicted rapist, which was confirmed by DNA evidence. For more details, see http://www.aaregistry.com/african_american_history/2059/Central_Park_Jogger_case_dismissed.

50. Helen Benedict, "Covering Rape without Feminism," *Women and Law in the Media,* ed.

Martha Fineman (New York: Routledge, in press), p. 2. Survey results on p. 7.

51. Mark Fishman, *Manufacturing the News* (Austin: University of Texas Press, 1980), pp. 92–93. Stephen Hess reports that Washington journalists in his survey conducted close to five interviews per story; Hess, *The Washington Reporters*, p. 17.

52. Barbara Gamarekian, "In Pursuit of the Clever Quotemaster," *New York Times*, 12 May 1989, p. Y10.

53. Stephen Hess, "New Phase Makes TV News Increasingly Dishonest," *Minneapolis Star Tribune,* 17 October 1989, p. A13.

54. Gertrude Joch Robinson, "Women, Media Access and Social Control," *Women in the News,* ed. Laurily Keir Epstein (New York: Hastings House, 1978), p. 89.

55. Cited in Timothy Crouse, *The Boys on the Bus: Riding with the Campaign Press Corps* (New York: Random House, 1972), p. 296.

56. Ray Richmond, "A Pioneering Show's Anniversary," *Philadelphia Inquirer*, 8 November 1989, pp. E1, E8.

57. Michael Schudson, *Discovering the News: A Social History of American Newspapers* (New York: Basic Books, 1978), p. 157.

58. James W. Carey, "The Communications Revolution and the Professional Communicator," *The Sociology of Mass Media Communicators,* Sociology Review Monograph, no. 13, ed. Paul Halmos (Keele, UK: University of Keele, 1969), p. 32.

59. Hillier Krieghbaum, *Pressures on the Press* (New York: Crowell, 1973), p. 11.

60. Daniel Patrick Moynihan, "The President and the Press," *The Presidency Reappraised,* ed. Rexford G. Tugwell and Thomas E. Cronin (New York: Praeger, 1974), p. 159.

61. Lou Cannon, *Reporting: An Inside View* (Sacramento: California Journal Press, 1977), pp. 46–47.

62. Paul Weaver, "Newspaper News and Television News," *Television as a Social Force* 87 (1975): 89.

63. James W. Carey, "The Communications Revolution and the Professional Communicator," *The Sociology of Mass Media Communicators,* Sociology Review Monograph, no. 13, ed. Paul Halmos (Keele, England: University of Keele, 1969), p. 36.

Chapter 3   News as Persuasion

1. Glasgow University Media Group, *More Bad News* (London: Routledge and Kegan Paul, 1980), p. 402.

2. D. Lachrenbruch, "HDTV," *TV Guide*, 5 June 1989, p. 19.

3. Gaye Tuchman, *Making News: A Study in the Construction of Reality* (New York: Free Press, 1978), pp. 112, 114.

4. William C. Adams, "Visual Analysis of Newscasts: Issues in Social Science Research," *Television Network News: Issues in Content Research,* ed. William C. Adams and Fay Schreibman (Washington, DC: Television and Politics Study Program, School of Public and International Affairs, George Washington University, 1978), p. 169.

5. Irving Kristol, "Crisis for Journalists: The Missing Elite," *Press, Politics and Popular Government,* ed. George Will (Washington, DC: American Enterprise Institute, 1972), p. 51.

6. John Carmody, *Washington Post*, 15 February 1994, p. E4.

7. "ABC Exposed by Pat Robertson," *Accuracy in Media, Electronic Media,* 4 December 1989, p. 6.

8. Harry Stein, "How *60 Minutes* Makes News," *New York Times Magazine,* 6 May 1979, p. 28.

9. Howard Kurtz, "Can Sam Donaldson Be Made to Look Sheepish?" *Washington Post,* 12 May 1995, p. B3.

10. Ibid.

11. *Time*, 28 April 1986, p. 55.

12. Caryn James, "Pictures Tell 2 Versions of the Story, as Planned," *New York Times*, 23 April 2000, p. 16.

13. Walter Goodman, "How the Networks Coped with Scant Information," *New York Times*, 19 October 1989, p. B16.

14. Adam Buckman, "NBC News Bans Using Re-Creations," *Electronic Media,* 27 November 1989, p. 3.

15. Walter Goodman, "Critic's Notebook," *New York Times*, 11 February 1993, p. B5.

16. Neil Hickey, "Have Hair Spray, Will Travel," *TV Guide*, 14 February 1981, p. 5.

17. "CBS Considers the Future of Evening News," *New York Times*, 27 September 2004, p. C11.

18. Desmond Smith, "The Wide World of Roone Arledge," *New York Times* Magazine, 28 February 1980, p. 66.

19. "Making of the Digital Press Corps, 2004," *New York Times*, 29 January 2004, p. E1.

20. Lou Cannon, *Reporting: An Inside View* (Sacramento: California Journal Press, 1977), p. 31.

21. Doug Halonen, "Barry Tape Gets Wide TV Play," *Electronic Media,* 2 July 1990, p. 2.

22. "The Hottest TV News Controversies," *TV Guide*, 13 January 1979, p. 10.

23. Bill Carter, "ABC Expects No Loss from Series Suspension," *New York Times*, 19 October 1989, p. B16.

24. John J. O'Connor, "How the Three Networks Treat Breaking News," *New York Times*, 12 April 1981, p. D29.

25. *TV Guide*, 17 April 1981, p. A1.

26. Tom Wicker, "TV's Tough Problem," *New York Times*, 7 April 1981, p. A19.

27. John Carmody, "The TV Column," *Washington Post*, 14 October 1996, p. D6.

28. Bill Green, "Stories in the *Washington Post*," *Washington Post,* 19 April 1981, pp. A12–15.

29. Michael Kramer, "Just the Facts, Please," *New York,* 25 May 1981, p. 19.

30. "News Watchdog Group Scores Voice Pulitzer Prize Winner," *Washington Post*, 12 June 1981, p. A2.

31. James M. Markham, "Writer Admits He Fabricated an Article in *Times Magazine*," *New York Times*, 22 February 1982, pp. Y1, Y4.

32. "A Lie in the *Times*," *New York Times*, 23 February 1982, p. Y26.

33. Bill Green, "The Story: First the Idea, and Finally the Presses Rolled," *Washington Post*, 19 April 1981, p. A12.

34. Maureen Dowd, "A Writer for the *New Yorker* Says He Created Composites in Reports," *New York Times*, 19 June 1984, pp. Y1, Y5.

35. Jacques Steinberg, "In Book, Ex-*Times* Reporter Admits to Series of Deceptions," *New York Times*, 27 February 2004, p. A18.

36. Ibid.

37. Ibid., p. C 4.

38. Lawrie Mifflin, "Truth in Packaging," *New York Times*, 5 May 1999, p. E10.

39. Suraj Kapoor and Ralph Smith, "The Newspaper Ombudsman—A Progress Report," *Journalism Quarterly* 56 (Autumn 1979): 629.

40. Ibid., pp. 629–630.

41. Jacques Steinberg, "The *Times* Chooses Veteran of Magazines and Publishing as Its First Public Editor," *New York Times*, 27 October 2003, p. A17.

42. Phil Record, "It's Not Just Me, I See; Other Ombudsmen Have Concerns, Too," *Fort Worth* [Texas] *Star-Telegram,* 7 May 1995, p. C6.

43. Lou Gelfand, "Readers Voice Objections to Headlines," *Minneapolis Star Tribune*, November 9, 2003, p. A13.

44. Gallup Organization, "Gallup, CNN, *USA Today* Poll," June 1998.

45. Gallup Organization, "Gallup, CNN, *USA Today* Poll," May 2004.

46. Lena Williams, "Studies on Diet Add to Confusion," *New York Times*, 11 October 1995, pp. B1, B7.

47. Peter Kerr, "Anatomy of the Drug Issue: How, after Years, It Erupted," *New York Times*, 17 November 1986, sec. A, pp. 1, 12.

48. Pamela Shoemaker, Wayne Wanta, and Dawn Leggett, "Drug Coverage and Public Opinion, 1972– 1986," *Communication Campaigns about Drugs: Government, Media, and the Public,* ed. Pamela J. Shoemaker (Hillsdale, NJ: Erlbaum, 1989), pp. 67–80.

49. Lucig H. Danielian and Stephen D. Reese, "A Closer Look at Intermedia Influences on Agenda Setting: The Cocaine Issue of 1986," *Communication Campaigns about Drugs: Government, Media, and the Public,* ed. Pamela J. Shoemaker (Hillsdale, NJ: Erlbaum, 1989), pp. 57–58.

50. Gladys Engel Lang and Kurt Lang, "MacArthur Day in Chicago," *Politics and Television* (Chicago: Quadrangle Books, 1968), pp. 36–77.

51. Craig Reinarman and Henry Levine, "Crack in Context; Politics and Media in the Making of a Drug Scare," *Contemporary Drug Problems,* vol. 16, no. 4 (Winter 1989): 535–577.

52. Charles T. Salmon, "God Understands When the Cause Is Noble," *Gannett Center Journal* (Spring 1990): 26.

53. Richard Harwood, " A Weekend in April," *Washington Post,* 6 May 1990, p. B6.

54. "Is the Press Straight on Abortion?" *U.S. News & World Report,* 16 July 1990, p. 17.

55. Bella Abzug, *Gender Gap* (Boston: Houghton Mifflin, 1984), p. 171.

56. John Monk, "Helms Lashes Out over Reporter's Questions," *Philadelphia Inquirer,* 22 January 1995, p. A7.

57. Tom Wicker, *On Press* (New York: Viking, 1978), pp. 36–37.

58. Henry Fairlie, "Profit without Honor," *New Republic,* 7 May 1977, pp. 17–18.

59. Erik Barnouw, *The Sponsor: Notes on a Modern Potentate* (New York: Oxford University Press, 1978).

60. Mark Fishman, *Manufacturing the News* (Austin: University of Texas Press, 1980).

61. Michael Schudson, *Discovering the News: A Social History of American Newspapers* (New York: Basic Books, 1978), p. 185.

62. Gaye Tuchman, *Making News: A Study in the Construction of Reality* (New York: Free Press, 1978), p. 210. Elsewhere she writes of "television programming that reflects and reinforces the economic and socio-political structure of the United States"; Gaye Tuchman, "Introduction," *The TV Establishment: Programming for Power and Profit,* ed. Gaye Tuchman (Englewood Cliffs, NJ: Prentice-Hall-Spectrum, 1974), p. 6.

63. J. Kozol, "Distancing the Homeless," *Yale Review* 77 (1986): 154–155.

64. Richard Campbell and Jimmie L. Reves, "Covering the Homeless: The Joyce Brown Story," *Critical Studies in Mass Communication* 6 (1989): 22.

65. Thomas R. Lindlof and William R. Canning, "Network News Coverage of the Broadcast Media," *Journalism Quarterly* 57 (Summer 1980): 333–338.

66. For information on issue or advocacy advertising by large corporations, see S. Prakash Sethi, *Up against the Corporate Wall: Modern Corporations and Social Issues of the Seventies* (Englewood Cliffs, NJ: Prentice Hall, 1971), and S. Prakash Sethi, *Advocacy Advertising and Large Corporations* (Lexington, MA: Lexington Books, 1977). In 1981, ABC accepted some issue advertising on *Nightline* on an experimental basis.

67. Herbert Gans, *Deciding What's News: A Study of* CBS Evening News, NBC Evening News, Newsweek, *and* Time (New York: Pantheon, 1979), p. 133.

68. Seymour Hersh, "The Story Everyone Ignored," *Columbia Journalism Review* 8 (Winter 1969–1970): 55.

69. David Wise, *The Politics of Lying* (New York: Random House, 1973), p. 311. See also David Halberstam, "A Letter to My Daughter," *Parade,* 2 May 1982, pp. 4–7.

70. Michael Schudson, *Discovering the News: A Social History of American Newspapers* (New York: Basic Books, 1978), p. 173.

71. *Time,* 2 June 1986, p. 67.

72. Noel Holston, "TV Ducking the Hard Questions on Mideast," *Minneapolis Star Tribune,* 24 August 1990, p. E7.

73. Jeff Cohen, "ABC's *Nightline* Serves as a Soapbox for Conservative Elite," *Minneapolis Star Tribune,* 28 February 1989, p. A11.

74. Paul Good, "Is Network News Slighting the Minorities?" *TV Guide,* 5 March 1977, p. 5.

75. Edwin Diamond, "Miami Riots: Did TV Get the Real Story?" *TV Guide,* 30 August 1980, p. 20.

76. Richard Moon, *Washington Post,* reprinted in *Minneapolis Star Tribune,* 9 October 1995, pp. A1, A9.

77. Jeremy Gerard, "Hurting Words, Fighting Words," *Columbia Journalism Review* (July–August 1990), p. 25.

78. Andrew H. Malcolm, "Toronto Paper Recounts Intrigue to Invade Dominica," *New York Times,* 17 May 1981, p. A4.

79. "Dogs from 'Puppy Mills' Jam Midwestern Shelters," *Philadelphia Inquirer,* 31 July 1990, p. A6.

80. Diane Mermigas, "CBS News Takes on 'Project Education,'" *Electronic Media,* 16 July 1990, p. 16.

81. Bill Carter, "Simpson Deal Causing Angst inside NBC and Out," *New York Times,* 11 October 1995, pp. A1, C19.

82. *Time,* 23 June 1986, p. 68.

83. Davis ("Buzz") Merritt, "Imagining Public Journalism: An Editor and Scholar Reflect on the Birth of an Idea," *Roy W. Howard Public Lecture,* no. 5, 13 April 1995, p. 4.

84. Sean Aday, *Public Journalism and the Power of the Press*, unpublished doctoral dissertation, University of Pennsylvania, 1999.

Chapter 4   Influencing the News Media

1. Mark Fishman, *Manufacturing the News* (Austin: University of Texas Press, 1980), p. 15.
2. Stephen Engelberg, "The Bad News Hour: 4 P.M. Friday," *New York Times*, 6 April 1984, p. Y10; *Washington Post*, 18 January 1986, p. A6.
3. George H. W. Bush, acceptance speech to the Republican National Convention, 18 August 1988.
4. Andrew Rosenthal, "Bush Now Concedes a Need for 'Tax Revenue Increases' to Reduce Deficit in Budget," *New York Times*, 27 June 1990, p. 1.
5. "Speedy Release of Files Came at Bush's Request," *New York Times*, 15 February 2004, 16.
6. Mimi Hall, "Nothing but the 'Truth' from Clinton Spinmeister," *USA Today*, 20 May 1999, p. D8.
7. Jules Witcover, *Marathon: The Pursuit of the Presidency, 1972–1976* (New York: Viking, 1977), pp. 606, 608.
8. Richard Benedetto, "After Getting Flak, Gore Adjusts His Position on Gays in the Military," *USA Today*, 10 January 2000, p. 6A.
9. Cindy Pearlman, "A New Hugh?" *Philadelphia Inquirer*, 4 July 1995, p. E1.
10. Michael R. Gordon, "The Profits and Perils of Progress in P.R.," *New York Times*, 3 August 1980, p. E19.
11. "ABC Cut Ad-Video Deal with Jackson Prior to Interview," *San Francisco Examiner*, 24 June 1995, p. C3.
12. Bill Green, "That 'Unnamed' Source," *Washington Post*, 29 May 1981, p. A12.
13. Arthur Lord, "Operation Just Cause—the Press in the Dark Again," *Nieman Reports* (Spring 1990): 7.
14. Joel Swerdlow, "The Decline of the Boys on the Bus," *Washington Journalism Review* (January–February 1981): 16.
15. "The CIA's 3-Decade Effort to Mold the World's Views," *New York Times*, 12 December 1977, p. A12; "CIA Established Many Links to Journalists in U.S. and Abroad," *New York Times*, 27 December 1977, pp. A1, A40.
16. Sidney Blumenthal, "The Education of a President," *The New Yorker*, 24 January 1994, p. 33.
17. Paul Brace and Barbara Hinckley, *Follow the Leader: Opinion Polls and Modern Presidents* (New York: Basic Books, 1992), pp. 53ff.
18. Annenberg School for Communication news release, March 15, 2000.
19. Howard Kurtz, "Webs of Political Intrigue: Candidates, Media Looking for Internet Constituents," *Washington Post*, 13 November 1995, p. B1.
20. Howard Kurtz, "The Press in Campaignland," *Washington Post Magazine*, 16 July 1995, p. 9.
21. "Bring It On! Whose Slogan Is This, Anyway?" *New York Times Magazine*, 29 February 2004, p. 34.
22. "Endorsed by Dole, Bush Steps Up Run in New Hampshire," *New York Times*, 5 January 2000, p. A16.
23. Susan Page, "Gore: Bradley Could 'Blunder' into Recession," *USA Today*, 4 January 2000, p. 1.
24. Neil A. Lewis, "Role Reversal," *New York Times*, 3 August 1995, p. A9.
25. "Reagan Advised to Reduce 'Imperial Media' Access," *Washington Post*, 2 February 1981, p. A2.
26. "ABC Apologizes for Rocker's Remarks," *Philadelphia Inquirer*, 24 January 1990, p. D4.
27. James C. McKinley Jr., "Weighing Therapy for a Narrow Mind," *New York Times*, 9 January 2000, p. 5.
28. J. Kyle Goddard, "Let's Abolish News Conferences," *New York Times*, 2 December 1979, p. E12.
29. Quoted in Ellen Hume, "Why the Press Blew the S & L Scandal," *New York Times*, 24 May 1990, p. A25.
30. Anthony Lewis, "TV: Selling Off Credibility," *New York Times*, 13 October 1989, p. Y23.
31. Peter Johnson, "ABC Kills BBC Report about Elite Executive," *USA Today*, 10 January 2000, p. 4D.
32. Ellen O'Brien, "Newspapers Publish Unabomber Manifesto," *Philadelphia Inquirer*, 3 August 1995, p. A2.
33. FCC Letter to the Networks (no. 69-19227767), 28 February 1969, p. 9, cited in Edward Epstein, *News from Nowhere* (New

York: Random House–Vintage, 1973), p. 159.

34. Maralee Schwartz, "Taking Too Much Credit," *Washington Post*, 27 May 1986, p. A4.

35. As quoted in "The Credibility Gap," *Washington Journalism Review* (July–August 1981): 21.

36. Randall Rothenberg, "The Journalist as Maytag Repairman," *Gannett Center Journal* (Spring 1990): 105.

37. "Results from a Nationwide Telephone Survey of 110 TV Newsroom Decision-makers by Nielsen Media Research on Behalf of Medialink," *Medialink Online,* June 1999 (online at http://www.media linkworldwide.com/sv0002.htm).

38. Randall Rothenberg, "The Journalist as Maytag Repairman," *Gannett Center Journal* (Spring 1990): 107.

39. Sally Bedell Smith, "Electronic Press Kits Pervade TV Newscasts," *New York Times*, 30 January 1984, p. Y18.

40. Chris Morris, "Sony's 'Spirit of '73' Rocks for Pro Choice," *Billboard,* 22 July 1995, pp.1, 88.

41. Robert Pear, "U.S. Videos, for TV News, Come under Scrutiny," *New York Times*, 15 March 2004, p. A16.

42. Harry W. Stonecipher, *Editorial and Persuasive Writing: Opinion Functions of the News Media* (New York: Hastings House, 1979), p. 67.

43. A. Kent MacDougall, "Business Puffery Costs Press Credibility, Short Changes Readers," *Los Angeles Times*, 3 November 1980, sec. IV, p. 1.

44. Bill Carter, "Success of 60 Minutes in Dollars and in Years," *New York Times*, 15 September 1990, p. Y13.

45. Stanley K. Bigman, "Rivals in Conformity: A Study of Two Competing Dailies," *Journalism Quarterly* 25 (Spring 1984): 127–131.

46. Stephen Lacy, "The Effects of Intracity Competition," *Journalism Quarterly* 64 (Summer–Autumn 1987): 281–290.

47. William Glaberson, "The Press: Bought and Sold and Gray All Over," *New York Times*, 30 July 1995, sec. 4, p. 1.

48. The Second Report with Recommendations of the Temporary Select Committee to Study the Senate Committee System, cited in Marvin Barrett, *Rich News, Poor News* (New York: Crowell, 1978), p. 136.

49. *New York Times*, 11 December 1986, p. Y10.

50. *Washington Post*, 28 May 1986, p. G1.

51. Anthony Ramirez, "Advertising," *New York Times*, 2 August 1995, p. D3.

52. Marvin Barrett and Zachary Sklar, *The Eye of the Storm* (New York: Lippincott and Crowell, 1980), pp. 130–131.

53. A. Kent MacDougall, "Reporting Environmental Hazards, Job Dangers Pose Risks for Media," *Los Angeles Times*, 23 November 1980, sec. V, pp. 1, 2.

54. "Fruit Growers Kill Ads in Protest to CBS," *New York Times*, 7 May 1989, p. Y15.

55. Steve Winberg, "New Coverage for TV News," *Panorama,* March 1981, p. 14.

56. J. Zirin, "In the Land of the Multimillion Libel," *London Times,* 20 May 1997.

57. Lee Levine and David L. Perry, "No Way to Celebrate the Bill of Rights," *Columbia Journalism Review* (July–August 1990): 38.

58. Mark Landler, "ABC News Settles Suits on Tobacco," *New York Times*, 22 August 1995, p. A1.

59. Mark Landler, "Critic Presses Tobacco Case Despite Settlement by ABC," *New York Times*, 24 August 1995, p. C2.

60. Mark Landler, "Philip Morris Revels in Rare ABC News Apology for Report on Nicotine," *New York Times*, 28 August 1995, p. C5.

61. Anthony Smith, *Goodbye Gutenberg: The Newspaper Revolution of the 1980's* (New York: Oxford University Press, 1980), p. 175.

62. John Herbers, *No Thank You, Mr. President* (New York: Norton, 1976), p. 41.

63. David Hoffman, "The Frictionless Presidency," *Gannett Center Journal* (Spring 1990): 92.

64. Howell Raines, "Reporter's Notebook: Insulating a President," *New York Times*, 5 August 1981, p. A12.

65. Murrey Marder, "Monitoring Not-So-Secret," *Washington Post*, 19 June 1981, p. A10.

66. William E. Porter, *Assault on the Media: The Nixon Years* (Ann Arbor: University of Michigan Press, 1976), pp. 97–98.

67. Stephen Hess, *The Government/Press Connection: Press Officers and Their Offices* (Washington, DC: Brookings Institution, 1984), pp. 75–94.

68. William Chapmen, "Reporters Gulled into Being a Channel for Auto-Imports Haggling," *Washington Post*, 7 May 1981, p. A31.

69. "This Memo Must Not Be Leaked: Wink, Wink," *New York Times*, 25 October 2003, p. A12.

70. Philip Nobile, "Covering Yourself: From Bureaucrat to Beat," *New York,* 30 March 1981, pp. 8–9.

71. Anne E. Kornblut, "Third Journalist Was Paid to Promote Bush Policies," *New York Times*, 29 January 2005, p. A13.

72. David D. Kirkpatrick, "TV Host Says U.S. Paid Him to Back Policy," *New York Times*, 8 January 2005, pp. A1-A10.

73. Marjorie Williams, "Talking Points," *Washington Post*, 15 May 1986, p. A19.

74. Minneapolis *Star Tribune,* 9 October 1986, p. A1.

75. Bernard Weinraub, "White House and Its News," *New York Times*, 3 October 1986, p. Y4.

76. Barry Cole and Mal Oettinger, *Reluctant Regulators: The FCC and the Broadcast Audience* (Reading, MA: Addison-Wesley, 1978), p. 134.

Chapter 5   How Corporate Power Influences What We See

1. See Ben H. Bagdikian, *The New Media Monopoly* (Boston: Beacon Press, 2004), pp. 3–4.

2. Saul Hansell, "Big Companies Back a New Web Site Aimed at Blacks," *New York Times*, 12 August 1999, p. C5.

3. Ben Bagdikian, "Global Media Corporations Control What We Watch (and Read)," *Utne Reader,* June–August 1990, p. 84.

4. Geraldine Fabrikant, "CBS Accepts Bid by Westinghouse; $5.4 Billion Deal," *New York Times*, 2 August 1995, p. 1.

5. "Who Owns What," *Philadelphia Inquirer*, 1 August 1995, p. A6.

6. Margaret M. Smyth, "What's Left to Merge?," *Broadcasting and Cable,* 16 February 2004, p. 46.

7. Ben H. Bagdikian, *The New Media Monopoly*, p. 36.

8. Gilbert Cranberg, Randall Bezanson, and John Soloski, *Taking Stock: Journalism and the Publicly Traded Newspaper Company* (Ames: Iowa State University Press, 2001), p. 2.

9. Pew Research Center for the People and the Press, "Bottom-Line Pressures Now Hurting Coverage, Say Journalists," 23 May 2004.

10. "Network News Cost-Cutting Spreads," *Electronic Media*, 9 April 1990, p. 46.

11. Jim Rutenberg, "Scary Ads Take Campaign to a Grim New Level," *New York Times*, 17 October 2004, Sec. 1:20. More recent figures show that over $600 million has been spent.

12. Charles Lewis and the Center for Public Integrity, *The Buying of the President 2004* (New York: Perennial/Harper Collins, 2004), p. 5.

13. See comments of FCC Commissioner Michael J. Copps, "Show Me the Convention," *New York Times*, 30 August 2004, p. A21.

14. Eric Alterman, "Anchors Aweigh: The Refs Are Worked," *The Nation,* 1 November 2004, p. 12.

15. Senator Byron Dorgan (D-North Dakota), September 28, 2004, Senate Commerce Committee.

16. Nat Ives, "Who Bought That Home? Oh, Never Mind," *New York Times*, December 20, 2004, p. C8. Copyright © 2004 by The New York Times Co. Reprinted with permission.

17. Charles Layton, "News Blackout," *American Journalism Review* (December–January 2004). Online at www.ajr.org.

18. Bagdikian, *The New Media Monopoly,* pp. 18, 151. The ratio is calculated at 10 to 1.

19. Lewis and the Center for Public Integrity, *The Buying of the President 2004*, p. 6.

20. Pearl Latteier, "Media Giants Don't Always Lead to Less Diverse Content," 9 August 2004, online at http://www.news.wisc.edu/releases/10027.html; also see Joshua Gamson and Pearl Latteier, "Do Media Monsters Devour Diversity?" *Contexts* 3 (Summer 2004): 26–32.

21. Paul Farhi, "Selling Is as Selling Does," *Washington Post*, 30 April 1995, p. H1. See also "The National Entertainment State" (centerfold), *The Nation,* 3 June 1996.

22. Project for Excellence in Journalism. *State of the News Media 2004*, online at Journalism.org.

23. Raymond B. Nixon, "Trends in U.S. Newspaper Ownership: Concentration with Competition," *Mass Media and Society,* 3rd ed., ed. Alan Wells (Palo Alto, CA: Mayfield, 1979), p. 35.

24. Robert Sherrill, *Why They Call It Politics* (New York: Harcourt Brace Jovanovich, 1979), pp. 273–274.

25. Lola Ogunnaike, "Fox News's Deal Will Make It a Radio Power, Analysts Say," *New York Times*, 9 December 2004, p. 3.

Chapter 6   What Is Advertising?

1. Media Dynamics Incorporated, "Ask the Experts," http://www.mediadynamicsinc.com/askexpert.htm.

2. Janet Whitman, "Magazine Trade Group Reviews How It Tallies Ad-Page Revenue," *Wall Street Journal*, 21 January 2004, p. B7.

3. Suzanne Vranica, "U.S. Ad Spending Rose 6.1% in 2003," *Wall Street Journal*, 9 March 2004, p. B6.

4. Stuart Elliott, "Ad Reaction Claims Superbowl Casualty," *New York Times,* 3 February 2005, p. C1.

5. Brian Steinberg, "Advertising," *Wall Street Journal*, March 2, 2004, p. B11.

6. "Senator Blasts Google Plan," *Palo Alto Daily News,* 10 April 2004, p. 4.

7. Katie Hafner, "In Google We Trust?" *New York Times*, 8 April 2004, p. E6.

8. "Trends (A Special Report): The Net—Safety, Blogs and Protocols," *Wall Street Journal*, 9 February 2004, p. R3.

9. Joe Sharkey, "High-Altitude Advertising for a Captive Audience," *New York Times*, 23 December 2003, p. C6.

10. John Lippman, "Hollywood Report," *Wall Street Journal*, 21 November 2003, p. W12.

11. John Tierney, "Political Points," *New York Times*, 21 December 2003, p. 30.

12. Joanne Lipman, "Local Video-Ad Business Goes on Blink," *Wall Street Journal*, 23 August 1990, p. B6.

13. "House Considers Restriction on Advertising by Telephone and Fax," *New York Times*, 31 July 1990, p. A13.

14. N. Paradis, "Reducing Telephone Solicitations," *St. Petersburg Times* (Florida), 15 March 1998, p. 2F.

15. "Degrees of Telemarketing Automation," *The Direct Marketing Association Statistical Fact Book* (New York: Direct Marketing Association, 1998), p. 152.

16. "Home Access to Web Rises to Nearly 75% in U.S.," *Wall Street Journal,* 18 March 2004, p. B5.

17. "Everything You Always Wanted to Know about Advertising," *Advertising Age*, 3 May 1999, p. 32.

18. Mylene Mangalindan. "Starting to Click: After Wave of Disappointments, The Web Lures Back Advertisers—New Generation of Pitches Nets Data on Consumer; Not a Mass Audience—Getting Drivers to Showroom," *Wall Street Journal,* 25 February 2004, p. A1.

19. Lee Hall, "Convergence," *Electronic Media*, 5 April 1999, p. 11.

20. Ira Teinowitz, "Philip Morris Hits Youth Smoking," *Advertising Age*, 10 July 1995, p. 31.

21. Martin Gottlieb, "Cashing in on Higher Cause," *New York Times,* 6 July 1996, p. E6.

22. Leah Rickard, "'96 Olympics Capture Consumer Awareness," *Advertising Age*, 10 July 1995, p. 21.

23. Kim Foltz, "Busch Spots Fight Rise in Beer Tax," *New York Times*, 30 July 1990, p. D11.

24. Nat Ives, "Infomercials Clean Up their Pitch (But Wait, There's More)," *New York Times,* 12 April 2004, p. C12.

25. Anthony Gnoffo Jr., "The Ad That Looks Like a Show," *Philadelphia Inquirer,* 27 November 1989, p. E1.

26. Ibid., p. 22.

27. Shaila K. Dewan, "The New Public Service Ad: Just Says 'Deal with It,'" *New York Times,* 11 January 2004, p. 4:5.

28. Erin White, "Advertising," *Wall Street Journal,* 23 March 2004, p. B11.

29. Kimberly Palmer, "Highway Ads Take High-Tech Turn," *Wall Street Journal,* 12 September 2003, p. B5.

30. Carl Bialik, "Lawyers Bid Up Value of Web-Search Ads," *Wall Street Journal,* 8 April 2004, pp. B1–B7.

31. Saul, Hansell, "Internet Advertising Thrives on Targeted Ads," *New York Times,* 29 December 2003, p. 6.

32. Ann M. Mack, "Meet the New Black: Contextual Advertising," *Adweek,* 12 April 2004, p. 9.

33. Mylene Mangalindan, "Seeking Growth, Search Engine Google Acts Like an Ad

Agency," *Wall Street Journal,* 16 October 2003, p. B2.

34. "No Spam Relief," *Wall Street Journal*, 18 March 2004, p. B4.

35. Melanie Wells, "Domino's Ads Play on Football," *USA Today,* 4 August 1995, p. 10B.

36. Patricia Winters, "A Trend, Friend: Is Rap 4 U, 2?" *Advertising Age*, 25 June 1990, p. 22.

37. Laurie Freeman, "Lever, P&G Green Plans Differ," *Advertising Age,* 23 July 1990. p. 46.

38. Don Hopey, "Earth Day Message Is Clear," *Pittsburgh Post-Gazette,* 22 April 1995, p. A3.

39. Jason Best, "Spin Machine: Briefings; Proctor & Gamble and Recycled Plastics," *OnEarth*, 2 September 2002, vol. 24, no. 3, p. 10.

Chapter 7   Persuasion through Advertising

1. Sherri Day, "Move over, Starbucks, Juan Valdez Is Coming," *New York Times*, 29 November 2003, pp. B1/B3.

2. James C. McKinley Jr., "Unamused, Hormel Sues over Spa'am the Muppet," *New York Times*, 26 July 1995, p. B3.

3. Donald G. McNeil Jr., "The Science of Naming Drugs," *New York Times*, 28 December 2003, p. 4:10.

4. Thomas Hine, "What You See Is What You Buy," *Philadelphia Inquirer Magazine,* 2 April 1995, p. 21.

5. Rob Walker, "The Guts of a New Machine," *New York Times Magazine*, 30 November 2003, p. 78.

6. *New York Times*, 30 November 2003, p. 32.

7. "USA Snapshots," *USA Today,* 21 July 1995, p. B1.

8. Tracie Rozhon, "Brand Names Are Paying the Price for a Change in Shopping Trends," *New York Times*, 10 December 2003, p. C1.

9. Tommy Nguyen, "Red, White and Golden Arches: The Star-Spangled Banner Ad," *Washington Post,* 4 July 2004, D01.

10. *New York Times*, 23 July 1995, p. 18.

11. Stuart Elliott, "Advertising," *New York Times*, 5 January 2000, p. C5.

12. Bill Carter, "Jackson Says Molestation Charges Are Untrue," *New York Times*, 27 December 2003, p. A15.

13. Stuart Elliott, "Advertising," *New York Times*, 23 February 2004, p. C8.

14. Brian Steinberg and Suzanne Vranica, "Burger King Seeks Some Web Heat," *Wall Street Journal*, 15 April 2004, p. B3.

15. *Wall Street Journal*, 15 October 2003, p. A12.

16. David Ogilvy, *Confessions of an Advertising Man* (New York: Atheneum, 1980), p. 140.

17. Associated Press, "Some Diet Franchises Refuse to Foot Bill for Lewinsky Ads," *Honolulu Advertiser,* 6 January 2000, p. A4.

18. "The 1990s Prices Go through the Stratosphere," *Advertising Age*, 28 February 1995, p. 53.

19. Pat Sloan, "Cosmetics: Color It Green," *Advertising Age*, 23 July 1990, p. 1.

20. Janet Whitman, "Translated Ads Can Miss the Point," *Wall Street Journal*, 18 September 2002, p. B8.

21. "Clear Channel to Begin Tie-In to Restaurant," *New York Times*, 29 September 2003, p.C8.

22. Margot Hornblower, "Madison Avenue Adapts to Generation of Skeptics," *Washington Post,* 29 May 1986, p. A1.

23. Stuart Elliott, "Advertising," *New York Times*, 14 April 2004, p. C8.

Chapter 8   Influencing Advertisers

1. "Profile Bread's Well-Buttered Correction," *Consumer Reports*, February 1972, p. 64.

2. Ira Teinowitz, "Doan's Decision Sets Precedent for Corrective Ads," *Advertising Age,* 4 September 2000, p. 57.

3. "US FTC," *M2 Presswire* from Nexis/Lexis, 4 March 1999.

4. Ibid.

5. Ibid.

6. Jeffrey Mills, "Deceptive Business Practices Definition Disputed," *Associated Press,* 27 March 1984.

7. FTC website, online at http://www.ftc.gov/reports/21cent/attach1.htm.

8. Christy Fisher, "How Congress Broke Unfair Ad Impasse," *Advertising Age*, 22 August 1994, p. 34.

9. Anna Wilde Mathews and Brian Steinberg, "FTC Examines Health Claims in KFC's Ads," *Wall Street Journal*, 19 November 2003, p. B1.

10. Barry Meier, "Diet-Pill Death Raises Questions on F.D.A. Role," *New York Times*, 4 August 1990, p. 48.

11. Lauran Neergaard, "For Prescription Drugs, Net Can Be a Web of Danger," *Philadelphia Inquirer*, 8 August 1999, p. C1.

12. Ad appeared in newsweeklies and in the *New York Times* on February 20.

13. Andrea Sachs, "NAD Turns Ad Monitor to Cyberspace," *Advertising Age*, 8 May 1995, p. 20.

14. www.ftc.gov.

15. Sachs, "NAD Turns Ad Monitor to Cyberspace," p. 20.

16. Ibid.

17. Doug Halonen, "NAB Sets Standards for Cleaning Up Airwaves," *Electronic Media*, 25 June 1990, p. 3.

18. "As We See It," *TV Guide*, 17 April 1982, p. A2.

19. "Surgeon General Urges Ads on TV for Condoms in Combating AIDS," *New York Times*, 11 February 1987, p. 1.

20. Jim Cooper, "Television Networks Air Condom PSAs," *Broadcasting & Cable*, 10 January 1994, p. 59.

21. Wayne Walley, "Network Ad Rejections: At What Cost?" *Advertising Age*, 9 April 1990, p. 22.

22. Ibid.

23. Ibid.

24. Stuart Elliott, "Thanks to Cable, Liquor Ads Find a TV Audience," *New York Times*, 15 December 2003, p. C1.

25. *FTC v. Sterling Drug Inc.,* 317 F. 2d 669, 674 (2d Cir. 1963).

26. *FTC v. Standard Education Society,* 302 U.S. 112, 116 (1937).

27. *American Home Products v. Johnson and Johnson, 3 Media Law Reporter,* 1097 (1977).

28. Ira M. Millstein, The Federal Trade Commission and False Advertising, 64 *Columbia Law Review,* 439, 469 (1964).

29. *FTC v. Colgate-Palmolive Co.,* 380 U.S. 375, 385 (1965).

30. Steven W. Colford, "Paper Tiger Litmus Test; FTC Gets Eggland's, Its First NARB Case," *Advertising Age*, 20 December 1993, p. 2.

31. *Warner-Lambert Co. v. FTC,* 562 F. 2d 762 (1977).

32. Alan Resnick and Bruce L. Stein, "An Analysis of Information Content of Television Adver-

tising," *Journal of Marketing* 41 (January 1977): 50–53.

33. Ivan L. Preston, *The Great American Blow-Up* (Madison: University of Wisconsin Press, 1975), p. 276.

34. Laura Mansnerus and Katherine Roberts, "Ideas and Trends: A Tobacco Ad Wins Protection," *New York Times*, 10 August 1986, p. E7.

35. "US FTC," *M2 Presswire* from Nexis/Lexis, 16 March 1999.

36. "News from NAD" (press release), 15 May 1981, p. 10.

37. NARB release, 30 January 1980.

38. Sholnn Freeman and Neil E. Boudette, "Chrysler's Dodge Brand Moves to Drop Out of Lingerie Bowl," *Wall Street Journal*, 17 December 2003, p. B4.

39. "News from NAD," National Advertising Division Council of Better Business Bureaus, 15 April 1981, p. 1.

40. Judann Dagnoli, "Consumers Union Hits Kids Advertising," *Advertising Age*, 23 July 1990, p. 4.

41. Jane M. Von Bergen, "Now Advertisers Discuss What Mom Wouldn't Tell You," *Philadelphia Inquirer*, 19 February 1995, p. D1.

42. David Noack, "While Sex May Sell, There Are Limits," *Editor & Publisher,* 13 February 1999, p. 10.

43. Stuart Elliott, "Madison Ave. Finds Courage to Ask: Want a Condom?" *New York Times*, 9 January 1994, p. 4.

44. David Noack, "Tobacco Ads Smoked," *Editor & Publisher,* 5 June 1999, p. 8.

45. Roy H. Campbell, "Is Calvin Klein over the Line?" *Philadelphia Inquirer*, 20 August 1995, p. H3.

46. Shelly Branch, "Abercrombie Learns Sex Isn't Sure Lure," *Wall Street Journal*, 12 December 2003, p. B2.

Chapter 9   How to Influence the Media

1. Jonathan Dube, "The Water's Fine," *Columbia Journalism Review* (July–August 1999): 37.

2. David Johnson, "Next: Notes on the Net," *Brill's Content,* September 1999, p. 62.

3. Ibid.

4. Nicholas Stein, "New Media, Old Values," *Columbia Journalism Review* (July–August 1999): 11.

5. Yahoo! *Internet Life,* September 1999, p. 38.

6. Lawrence Grossman, "In the Public Interest: From Marconia to Murrow to—Drudge," *Columbia Journalism Review* (July–August 1999): 18.

7. Joe Strupp, "Carville Targeted in Internet Hoax," *Editor & Publisher,* 30 January 1999, p. 12.

8. Joseph Gomes, "*Consumer Reports'* Online Push," *Brill's Content,* September 1999, p. 76.

9. *Office of Communication of the United Church of Christ v. F.C.C.,* 359 F. 2d 994, 1002 (D.C. Cir. 1966), 425 F. 2d 543 (D.C. Cir. 1969).

10. Mark Landler, "ABC News Settles Suits on Tobacco," *New York Times,* 22 August 1995, p. A1.

11. *Washington Post,* 19 July 1986, p. A23.

12. *Adoption of Standards Designed to Eliminate Deceptive Advertising from Television,* 32 F.C.C. 2d 360, 372–374.

13. Sherri Day, "Diageo to Put Nutrition Labels on Liquor," *New York Times*, 18 December 2003, p. C3.

14. Christopher Lawton, "Liquor Industry's New Pitch: How to Drink on a Diet," *Wall Street Journal,* 27 December 2003, p. D1.

15. Christopher Lawton, "Most Light Beer Is Low Carb, U.S. Decides," *Wall Street Journal,* 9 April 2004, p. B1.

16. "ABC: Laughing All the Way with Its New Schedule for Prime Time," *Broadcasting,* 2 May 1977, p. 23.

17. Christine Lias, "Grannies Targeting Wal-Mart," *Palo Alto Daily News,* 13 December 2003, p. 5.

18. Ibid.

19. Marilyn Elias, "Television Ads Aimed at Kids Must Change, Psychologists Say," *USA Today,* 24 February 2004, p. 9D.

20. Jonathan Storm, "The Color of Money," *Philadelphia Inquirer,* 3 August 1999, p. F1.

21. R. Thomas Umstead, "NAACP Targets Cable," *MultiChannel News,* 16 August 1999, p. 1.

22. National Advertising Review Board, *Advertising and Women,* Report of the National Advertising Review Board, 1975, p. 6.

23. A. Lee Fritschler, *Smoking and Politics: Policymaking and the Federal Bureaucracy* (Englewood Cliffs, NJ: Prentice Hall, 1975), p. 121.

24. Ibid., p. 165.

25. Ibid., pp. 118–120. The legislation is U.S.C. § 1331 (1965).

26. Melanie Wells, "RJR Pulls Star Joe Camel," *USA Today,* 27–29 October 1995, p. 1.

27. Nat Ives, "Advertising," *New York Times,* 7 October 2004, p. C4.

Chapter 10   Political versus Product Campaigns

1. Michael Kinsley, "Dad, Can I Borrow the Scepter?" *Time,* 11 November 2002.

2. Annenberg Public Policy Center, University of Pennsylvania, National Annenberg Election Survey, January 30, 2004. Online at www.naes04.org.

3. *FCC v. Pacifica Foundation et al.*, 3 July 1978, in 3 Med. L. Rptr. 2553 (Washington: Bureau of National Affairs, 1978).

4. *Becker et al. v. FCC,* 95 F. 3d 75 (D.C. Cir., 1996).

5. "FCC Won't Block Racist Ad in South," *New York Times,* 4 August 1972, p. 37.

6. Fred Barbash, "Court Eases Candidates' Access to TV," *Washington Post,* 2 July 1981, pp. A1, A4.

7. Herbert Alexander, "Rethinking Reform," in *Campaign Money,* ed. H. E. Alexander (New York: Free Press, 1976), pp. 1–2.

8. *Buckley v. Valeo,* 424 U.S. 1 (1976).

9. Center for Public Integrity, "527s in 2004 Shatter Previous Records for Political Fundraising," 16 December 2004. Online at http://www.publicintegrity.org.

10. Glen Justice, "Even With Campaign Finance Law, Money Talks Louder Than Ever," *New York Times,* 8 November 2004, A16.

11. See note 8.

12. Polling was conducted by Chilton Research Services of Radnor, Pennsylvania, on 9–12 November 1996. The 57.6 percent figure represents those who recalled seeing advertisements sponsored by major issue advertisers such as the AFL-CIO, business groups, the National Education Association (NEA), antiabortion advocates, or abortion rights groups.

13. Of the thirty-one groups catalogued in the report, only twenty-seven were included in this analysis. Some organizations engaged only in

express advocacy campaigns and thus were excluded; advertisements were unavailable from others.

14. See "Assessing the Quality of Campaign Discourse, 1960, 1980, 1988, and 1992," *Annenberg Public Policy Center Report Series,* no. 4, 22 July 1996. See also "Tracking the Quality of the 1996 Campaign," a series of eighteen releases published by the Annenberg Public Policy Center, and "Free Time for Presidential Candidates: The 1996 Experiment," *Annenberg Public Policy Center Report Series,* no. 11, March 1997, p. 9.

15. News coverage figures are based on a random sample. For a summary of pure attack and comparison in the 1996 campaign, see "Free Time for Presidential Candidates: The 1996 Experiment," *Annenberg Public Policy Center Report Series,* no. 11, March 1997, p. 9.

Chapter 11   How Has the Internet Changed Politics?

1. Mark Ward, "China's Tight Rein on Online Growth," 8 March 2005. Online at http://news.bbc.co.uk/2/hi/technology/4327067.stm/technology/4327067.stm.

2. Perry Bacon and Viveca Novak, "With Friends Like These," *Time,* 23 February 2004, p. 14.

3. Saul Hansell, "Foes of Bush Enlist Google to Make Point," *New York Times,* 8 December 2003, p. C8.

4. Daniel Okrent, "Dr. Dean Assumes His Place on the Examining Table," *New York Times,* 18 January 2004, p. 4:2.

5. Alan Murray, "Political Capital," *Wall Street Journal,* 9 March 2004, p. A4.

6. Howard Fineman and Michael Isikoff, "Grins and Grenades," *Newsweek,* 26 January 2004, p. 31.

7. Daniel Okrent, "Setting the Record Straight (But Who Can Find the Record?)," *New York Times,* 14 March 2004, p. 4:2.

8. "Malls Beef Up Security in Wake of Terrorist Rumors," *The Boston Business Journal,* 21(38), (26 October 2001): 6.

9. Online at FreeRepublic.com, 7 March 2004.

10. "Bush Campaign Will Soon Become More Aggressive," *New York Times,* 15 February 2004, p. 14.

11. Michael Janofsky, "McCain Fights Old Foe Who Now Fights Kerry," *New York Times,* 14 February 2004, p. A11.

12. Will Lester, "Dean: Democrats Raise $3.4 M in Three Weeks," *Associated Press,* 8 March 2005.

13. Bruce Bimber and Richard Davis, *Campaigning Online: The Internet in U.S. Elections* (New York: Oxford University Press, 2003).

14. Lee Rainie, John Horrigan, and Michael Cornfield, "Reports: E-Gov and E-Policy," Pew Internet and American Life Project, 6 March 2005.

15. Liz Sidoti, "Study: More Internet Ads in Presidential Race, But Still TV Dominates," *Associated Press,* 4 October 2004.

Chapter 12   News and Advertising in the Political Campaign

1. Hugh Gregory Gallagher, "FDR's Cover-Up: The Extent of His Handicap," *Washington Post,* 24 January 1982, p. D4.

2. *Tyndall Report,* May 2005, p. 3.

3. See Maxwell McCombs and Dixie Evatt, "Los Temas y los Aspectos: Explorando una Nueva Dimensión de la Agenda Setting" [The Themes and the Aspects: Exploring a New Dimension of Agenda Setting], *Comunicacion y Sociedad* 8(1) (1995): 7–32.

4. Jian-Hua Zhu, "Issue Competition and Attention Distraction: A Zero-Sum Theory of Agenda Setting," *Journalism Quarterly* 69 (1992): 825–836.

5. David B. Holian. "The Press the Presidency and the Public: Agenda Setting, Issue Ownership, and Presidential Approval from Reagan to Clinton," unpublished dissertation, Indiana University, 2000.

6. "News Coverage a Cost-Effective Way of Promoting Health Behavior Change; Drunk Driving," *The Brown University Digest of Addiction Theory and Application,* vol. 1, no. 2, 1 January 2003, p. 1

7. stoptheNRA.com, "Will Bush and Cheney Break Their Promise to America's Police?" [advertisement], *New York Times,* 16 April 2004, p. A11.

8. For an excellent analysis of the function of metaphors in press coverage of the 1972 Democratic presidential campaign, see Jane

Blankenship, "The Search for the 1972 Democratic Nomination: A Metaphoric Perspective," *Rhetoric and Communication,* ed. Jane Blankenship and Hermann G. Stelzner (Urbana: University of Illinois Press, 1976), pp. 236–260.

9. Martin Kasindorf, "For Many Americans, the Battle Is Joined Tonight," *Newsday,* 6 October 1996, p. A5.

10. John Harwood, Jeanne Cummings, and Jacob M. Schlesinger, "Democrats Weigh the Risks of a Long Fight for Nomination," *Wall Street Journal,* 5 February 2004, p. 1.

11. David Rogers, "Kerry Must Top Rivals, Tout Vision," *Wall Street Journal,* 5 February 2004, p. 1.

12. Todd S. Purdum, "Can the North Rise Again?" *New York Times,* 8 February 2004, p. 4:1.

13. David Maraniss, "In GOP Race, Money Takes Lead," *Washington Post,* 10 February 1990, p. A7.

14. Wayne Slater, "Richards Goes on Attack in New TV Ad," *Dallas Morning News,* 17 August 1990, p. 18A.

15. Frank Rich "Paar to Leno, J.F.K. to J.F.K.," *New York Times,* 8 February 2004, sect 2, p. 1.

16. Dana Milbank, "Preemptive Attack on Himself," *Washington Post,* 11 April 2004, p. A4.

17. Adam Clymer, "Summer Wind on the Campaign Trail," *New York Times,* 18 August 1999, p. A20.

18. *Dallas Morning News,* 17 August 1990, p. 18A.

19. "The Press and Campaign '92: A Self-Assessment," Times Mirror Center for the People and the Press, 20 December 1992, p. 7.

20. Terry Neal and Edward Walsh, "Bush Begins NY Swing Talking Breast Cancer," *Washington Post,* 5 March 2000, p. A6.

21. Jim VandeHei, "Kerry Accuses Bush of Dishonesty on Iraq," *Washington Post,* 16 September 2004, p. A4.

22. Reprinted in the *New York Times,* 18 April 2004, p. 4:3.

23. Donald R. Matthews, "The News Media and the 1976 Presidential Nominations," *Race for the Presidency: The Media and the Nominating Process,* ed. James D. Barber (Englewood Cliffs, NJ: Prentice Hall, 1978), p. 67.

24. Judy Keen and Richard Benedetto, "Bush Defends Record, Goes on the Attack," *USA Today,* 24 February 2004, p. 7A.

25. Maureen Dowd, "White Noise," *New York Times,* 18 August 1999, p. A25.

26. Mark Memmott, "Washington," *USA Today,* 15 April 2004, p. 6A.

27. "Resorting to Facts," *New York Times,* 23 February 2004, p. A20.

Index

AARP, 267
Abbas, Abul, 112
Abortion, 290
Abrams, Alex, 288
Abu Ghraib prison scandal, 149
Access to news
    beat system and, 54–55, 57
    manipulation of, 123–126
Action for Children's Television
    (ACT), 273
Action news approach, 74
Aday, Sean, 113
Adbusters magazine, 205
Advertisements
    advocacy, 183–184, 282, 296
    analysis of, 255–259
    associations created through,
        204–205, 221–231
    assumptions embedded in,
        193–196, 258
    audience participation in,
        205–212
    billboard, 187
    case study of, 215–216
    children as target of, 251–252,
        273, 274, 276
    differentiating products
        through, 203–205
    direct-response, 184–185
    disentangling meaning in, 206
    effectiveness of, 232, 259
    false or deceptive, 234–238,
        245–246, 247–251, 271
    faxed, 177–178
    goodwill, 182–183, 256

humor used in, 209–210
infomercials as, 101, 184–185
in-store, 187
intended audience for,
    189–192, 257
Internet, 174, 175, 179–180,
    187–189, 314–315
issue advocacy, 186, 296–298,
    300–302
magazine, 28, 29
name recognition through,
    198–202
placement of, 173–178
political, 21, 186, 256–257,
    282–304, 314–315,
    320–322, 347, 352
product, 180–181, 257
PSAs as, 185–186, 255
radio, 22
redundancy in, 212–214
search engines and, 187–189
service, 181, 256
stereotypes in, 192–193
telephone, 178
trade characters in, 199–200,
    206–207
types of, 180–189, 255
women as target of, 225–227,
    228, 277
Advertisers
    aims of, 198
    boycotts against, 266–269, 277
    commercial pressures from,
        143–144
    mass media system and, 5

persuasion strategies used by,
    214, 217–221
product placement by, 173–174
regulations imposed on, 184,
    185, 234–255, 259
revealed by advertisements, 189
video news releases produced by,
    138–139
Advertising
    contextual, 188
    corrective, 235–237, 240,
        271–272
    definition of, 175
    image, 182–183
    interplay of news and, 196–197,
        346–348
    mediated, 178–180
    nontraditional, 186–189
    overview of, 171–172
    prevalence of, 174–178
    programming vs., 189–192
    role of, 5–6
    taboos related to, 252–255
    targeting audiences for,
        285–286
    television, 243–244,
        251–255
    unfair, 237
    values and, 193–196
Advertising Age, 202, 209
Advertising agencies, 5
Advertising and Women report
    (NARB), 277
Advertising Council, 185

Advertising regulation/self-
     regulation
  audience-imposed limitations
     and, 251–255
  children and, 240, 251–252
  effects of, 246–247
  Federal Trade Commission and,
     234–238
  Food and Drug Administration
     and, 238–240
  individual complaints and,
     265, 266
  limitations on distortion,
     247–251
  methods of influencing,
     261–281
  National Advertising Division
     and, 240–242
  National Association of
     Broadcasters and, 242–243
  network standards and,
     243–244
  obstacles to, 244–247
Advertising revenues
  audience size and, 6
  political campaigns and, 293
Advertising: The Uneasy Persuasion
     (Schudson), 232
Advocacy ads, 183–184, 282, 296
  issue advocacy, 186, 296–298,
     300–302
Advocacy group pressures,
     152–154
Adwatches, 330, 331–342
African Americans
  group influence of, 270–271,
     276–277
  news coverage related to,
     109–110
  Nielsen ratings and, 18, 19–20
  radio broadcasts and, 23, 24
  television programming and,
     276–277
Agenda setting, 318–319
Ali, Muhammad, 207
All Things Considered, 22
Alterman, Eric, 165
American Banker, 62

American Cancer Society, 228
American Journalism Review,
     160, 166
American Psychological
     Association, 276
American Public Radio (APR), 23
American Society of Newspaper
     Editors, 99
America's Most Wanted, 91
Analysis
  of advertisements, 255–259
  of news, 101–102, 114–118
  of political campaigns,
     351–352
Anchors, news, 92–93
Anderson, Bonnie, 59, 64
Anderson, Jack, 145, 340
Animus leaks, 148
Annenberg Public Policy Center
     (APPC), 25, 282, 284, 296,
     300, 341
Anonymous sources, 97–99
Anti-ads, 232
Anti-brands, 205
Arbitron ratings, 23–24
Archived news footage, 61
Argumentative forms, 228–231
Arizona Republic, 66
Arledge, Roone, 92, 93, 95
Armstrong, George, 139
Arquette, David, 221
Arts and Entertainment (A&E)
     network, 9
Asner, Ed, 277
Associations
  argumentative forms for
     creating, 228–231
  cannibalizing the past for,
     222–228
  celebrity and authority,
     221–222
  media outlet to product, 228
  nationalistic, 227–228
  reasons for using, 204–205
Assumptions
  embedded in ads, 193–196, 258
  regarding mass media, 2–3
Atlanta Constitution, 55

Attack ads, 282, 330, 334–342
Audiences
  advertising regulations and, 245
  children in, 251–252
  intended for ads, 189–192, 257
  interest indicated by, 54, 56
  mass media, 5, 6
  participation by, 205–212, 216
  political campaigns and,
     285–286, 297
  share of, 17
  targeting, 285–286
  tastes of, 109–110
  upscale vs. downscale, 6
Auletta, Ken, 98
Authority figures, 221–222
Avarosis, John, 310

Backlash, political, 329–330
Bagdikian, Ben, 42, 141, 156
Baker, Nancy Landon
     Kassebaum, 104
Bakker, Jim, 88
Baltimore Sun, 47–48
Banisar, Dave, 32
Banks, Tyra, 252
Barnacle, Mike, 99
Barnouw, Erik, 106
Barr, Bob, 71
Barry, Marion, 94
Beal, Mary, 270
Beat system, 54–55, 57, 72, 107
Beck, Deborah, 296
"Before and after" ads, 231
Begin, Menachem, 121
Benedict, Helen, 72
Berg, Nick, 65
Bernstein, Carl, 75, 111
Bernstein, Jodie, 248
Berri, Nabih, 112
Bettag, Tom, 75
Better Business Bureau, 5, 235,
     240–241, 242
Bias, 104–107
Billboard advertising, 187
Bimber, Bruce, 313
Bipartisan Campaign Reform Act
     (2002), 294–295

Black Entertainment Television (BET), 18
Black Radio Network, 23
Black Radio Today, 24
Blair, Jason, 98, 100
Blitzer, Wolf, 349
Bloch, Felix, 91
Blogs, 306, 307, 316
Blunders, political, 338–339
Borowitz, Andy, 309
Boston Globe, 99, 102
Bowers, Andy, 333
Boycotts, 266–269, 277
Boyer, Ernest, 112
Bradlee, Benjamin, 108, 148
Bradley, Bill, 130, 307
Bradley, Tom, 325–326
Brady, Jim, 95
Bralnick, Jeff, 93
Branch Davidians, 132–133
Brando, Marlon, 134
Breaking news
    live coverage of, 95–96
    preempting programming for, 141–143
Breast cancer, 228
Britten, Nan, 66
Broadcast advertising
    audience participation in, 205–212
    children and, 251–252
    issue advocacy and, 296–298, 300–302
    network standards for, 243–244
    political campaigns and, 293, 296–298
    taboo subjects in, 252–255
Broadcasting & Cable, 162
Broadcast spectrum, 262
Brokaw, Tom, 91, 93, 283
Brown, Bill, 89
Brown, Jerry, 323
Brown and Williamson Tobacco Corp. v. CBS Inc. (1988), 144
Bryant, Kobe, 64, 207
Brzezinski, Zbigniew, 147
Buchanan, Pat, 131, 337

Buckley v. Valeo (1976), 293, 294, 296
Buddy, Mike, 87
Bumiller, Elizabeth, 120
Bureau of Consumer Protection, 234, 238
Burger, Warren, 292
Burke, Delta, 253
Burke, Kenneth, 3, 82
Burnett, Carol, 272
Burt, Richard, 149
Burton, Dan, 47, 71
Bush, Barbara, 104, 146, 318
Bush, George H. W., 61, 90, 104, 120, 122, 130–131, 135, 137, 146, 178, 292, 294, 331, 335, 337, 341, 349
Bush, George W., 62, 63, 120, 131, 146, 175, 228, 283, 285, 292, 295, 308, 314, 318, 323, 329, 335, 341, 342, 343, 344
Bush, Jenna, 36
Bush, Laura, 315, 318
Bush, Prescott, 349
Buying of the President, The (Lewis), 166

Cable Communications Act (1984), 10
Cable News Network. *See* CNN
Cable television
    diversified programming of, 9–12
    household demographics related to, 2
    increase in subscribers to, 8–9
    infomercials on, 184–185
    network contact information for, 265
    news and, 34–36
    ratings for, 179
Cabletelevision Advertising Bureau (CAB), 13
Cable TV Consumer Protection Act (1992), 12
Cagney & Lacey, 263
Camera usage, 85–87

Campaign for Tobacco-Free Kids, 215–216
Campaign Media Analysts Group, 163
Campaigns. *See* Political campaigns
Campbell, George, 3
Candidates. *See* Political candidates
Cannon, Lou, 64, 76, 94
Can-SPAM Act (2003), 188
Capital Cities, Inc. v. Crisp (1984), 10
Capp, Al, 339
Cappella, Joseph N., 333
Carey, James, 82
Carlin, George, 289
Carpenter, Teresa, 98
Carter, Jimmy, 74, 121, 122, 164, 292, 325, 335, 339, 344, 346
Cartoons, political, 339–340
Carville, James, 263–264
Casey, William, 108, 144, 147
Cash, Johnny, 64
Cause-and-effect relationships, 228–229
CBS Evening News, 35, 51, 75, 90, 92, 103
Celebrity endorsements, 207, 221
Censorship
    Internet, 31
    political ads and, 288–291
    product ads and, 288
    self- (by news media), 107–110
Center for Media and Public Affairs, 104
Center for Public Integrity, 163, 166, 295–296
Center for Responsive Politics, 345
Central Intelligence Agency (CIA), 128
Chafee, John, 47
Challenger disaster, 50–51
Chamberlain, Richard, 44
Chappelle, Dave, 18
Character issues, 344–346
Charities, ads for, 185
Chase, Rebecca, 88

Chassler, Sey, 226
Checkbook journalism, 112
Cheney, Dick, 166, 310, 321
Cheney, Mary, 310
Chenoweth, Helen, 70–71
Chiat, Jay, 217
Chicago Tribune, 55, 57, 338
Children
    advertising aimed at, 251–252,
        274, 276
    regulation of advertising to,
        240, 251–252, 273, 276
Children's Advertising Review
    Unit (CARU), 240
China, Internet regulation in, 306
Christian, George, 33
Chung, Connie, 92
Cigarette advertising, 196
Citizen regulators, 5
Civic journalism, 113
Clark, Wesley, 320
Clarke, Richard, 168
Clarke, Victoria, 60
Clay, Andrew Dice, 134
Clear Channel Communication,
    25, 154, 169, 228, 279
Clem, Todd, 279
Cleveland, Grover, 66, 69
Clinton, Bill, 17, 24, 33, 37,
    38–39, 46, 68–71, 129, 147,
    292, 294, 305, 312, 323,
    344, 346, 349
Clinton, Hillary Rodham, 70,
    148, 318
Close-up camera shots, 85
Clutter, 76
Clymer, Adam, 329
CNN (Cable News Network),
    34–36, 90
Coale, John P., 145
Cohen, Jeff, 109
Coincidental relationships,
    229–230
Cole, Barry, 151
Coll, Steve, 65
Columbia Journalism Review, 99,
    143, 275, 349
Columns, political, 339–340

Comedy news, 79
Commercial pressures
    advertisers and, 143–144
    competition and, 140–141
    legal threats and, 144–145
    preemption and, 141–143
Committee on National Television
    Audience Measurement, 19
Commoner, Barry, 289
Communications Act (1934), 291
Company names, 224
Comparisons
    political, 296–297
    product, 218–220
Competition
    accuracy of news coverage and,
        94–95
    commercial pressures and,
        140–141
    deadline manipulation and,
        119–123
    elite media and, 128–129
    government regulation of,
        234–238
Complaints
    address list for, 265
    boycotts and, 266–269, 277
    creating legislative pressure
        through, 277–279
    established organizations and,
        274–276
    individual actions and,
        261–266
    legal actions and, 270–272
    promoting self-regulation
        through, 272–273
    social movements and, 276–278
    strategies for creating change
        through, 279–281
Composite sources, 97–99
Condit, Gary, 319
Condon, George, Jr., 71
Confessions of an Advertising Man
    (Ogilvy), 218
Conflict, newsworthiness of,
    43–44, 45–47
Consolidation. *See* Media
    consolidation

Constraints
    analysis of, 115
    external, 54–60
    internal, 61–66
Consumer Reports, 220, 264, 304
Consumers Union, 251
Content of ads, 257–258, 259
Contextual ads, 188
Contrast ads, 282
Controversy, controlling, 271
Convergence, media, 102
Cooke, Janet, 97
Coors, Peter, 291
Copps, Michael, 164
Corporate power
    FCC regulation of, 159–162
    news media content and, 167
    political power and, 168–169
    pro-business bias and, 166–167
    profit motive and, 158
    synergy and, 167–168
    See also Media consolidation
Corrective advertising, 235–237,
    240, 271–272
Cosmopolitan, 28
Cost per thousand (CPT), 6
Cox, Courtney, 221
Craven, Julie, 177
Crawford, Cindy, 206
Crime stories, 47–48
Cronkite, Walter, 33, 67, 75,
    92, 111
Cross-promotion, 167–168
Cruz, Penelope, 221
C-SPAN, 10–12
Culture Jammers, 205
Cummings, Jeanne, 323
Cuomo, Mario, 69
Cutaway shots, 88

*Daily Show with Jon Stewart,
    The*, 79
Dallas Morning News, 38, 332
Daly, Michael, 97–98
Daniel, Clifton, 108
Daschle, Tom, 306
Dateline NBC, 92, 93, 112
Davies, Matt, 340

Davis, Gray, 302
Davis, Lanny, 121
Davis, Richard, 313
Daynard, Richard A., 145
Day One, 272
Deadlines
  impact of, 94–95
  manipulation of, 119–123
Dean, Howard, 133, 305, 307, 313, 319, 329
Death in ads, 208
Debates
  limitations of, 348–349
  presidential, 292–293, 296, 297, 298
Deceptive advertising
  corrective measures for, 235–237
  determination of, 245–246
  examples of, 248–251
  FTC definition of, 237
  group legal action against, 271–272
  limitations on, 247–251
  political campaigns and, 336–337
  regulation of, 234–240
Deep Dish Television Network, 10–11
Democratic National Committee (DNC), 313
Democratic National Committee v. CBS, 184
Demographics, 17, 20
Designing Women, 263
Des Moines Register, 55
Detroit Free Press, 143
Diamond, Edwin, 109
Differentiating products, 203–205, 218–221
Digital billboards, 187
Digital television, 14–15, 16
Digital video recorders (DVRs), 21
Direct Broadcast Satellite (DBS), 12–13
Direct-response ads, 184–185
Disentangling meaning, 206
Distortion. *See* Deceptive advertising

Dole, Bob, 46, 130, 285, 292, 305, 323, 339, 342
Dole, Elizabeth, 329
Donahue, 112
Donaldson, Sam, 89
Door-to-door advertising, 178
Douglas, Cliff, 145
Dowd, Maureen, 342
Downie, Leonard, Jr., 53, 103
Downscale audiences, 6
Drama
  news as, 45–48
  persuasion and, 84–93
Drudge, Matt, 38–39, 70
Drudge Report, The, 38, 312
Dube, Jonathan, 261
Ducat, Sue, 57
Dukakis, Michael, 122, 292, 331, 332, 335, 339
Dunlop, Pat, 144
DVDs, ads on, 177
Dwyer, R. Budd, 65

Eagleton, Thomas, 340
Eastwood, Clint, 272
Economic news, 62–63
Economics
  of news coverage, 57–59
  of political campaigns, 293–298, 304
Economy, Elizabeth, 30
Editing news footage, 88–90
Editorials, 140, 145
Edwards, John, 79, 326, 329
Ego leaks, 148
Eiermann, Heinz J., 203
Election news, 51
Electronic Media, 93, 180
Electronic Media Ratings Council, 5
Electronic press kits, 138–139
Electronic Retailing Association, 185
Elite media, 128–129
Elliott, Stuart, 17
Eloquence in an Electronic Age (Jamieson), 68

E-mail
  ads delivered via, 174, 175
  number of subscribers to, 175
  phishing scams via, 311
  political critiques via, 310
  spam as, 175, 188–189
Embedded journalists, 60
Endorsements
  political, 304
  product, 207, 221–222
Engberg, Eric, 333
Environmental issues, 227
Epstein, Joseph, 306
Equal Time, 39
ESPN, 9, 228
Ethics, 89
Event sponsorship, 183
Exner, Judith Campbell, 67
Experiences, significant, 207–208
External constraints, 54–60
ExxonMobile image ads, 183

"Face the Issue" campaign, 186
Face the Nation, 7, 57, 59
FactCheck.org, 341
Fager, Jeff, 149
Fair Campaign Practices Committee, 330, 332
Fairlie, Henry, 105
Fairness and Accuracy in Reporting (FAIR), 109
Fairness Doctrine, 107
False advertising. *See* Deceptive advertising
Fantasy in ads, 250–251
Farmers' Educational and Cooperative Union of America v. WDAY (1959), 290
Faxed advertisements, 177–178
FCC. *See* Federal Communications Commission
FDA. *See* Food and Drug Administration
Federal Communications Commission (FCC), 5, 107, 138, 151, 154, 159–162, 184, 196, 266, 290

Federal Election Campaign Act (1974), 293, 294
Federal Election Commission (FEC), 295, 316
Federal government
    advertising regulation by, 184, 185, 234–240
    antidrug campaign sponsored by, 186
    creating legislative pressure through, 278–279
    manipulation of news by, 147–151
    media's support of claims by, 107–109
    news leaks by, 147–149
    regulation of media by, 5, 151, 154–155, 159–162, 184, 234–240
    See also State government
Federal Trade Commission (FTC), 5, 32, 143, 219, 234–238, 265, 266, 278
Federal Trade Commission Act (1914), 247
Feinstein, Diane, 321
Ferraro, Geraldine, 104, 327
Filmed news coverage, 90–92
First Amendment, 290, 291, 316
Fisher, Jimmy, 290
Fishman, Mark, 49, 106
Fitzwater, Marlin, 35
527 committees, 295–296
Flanagan, John, 253–254
Fleischer, Ari, 329
Florio, Jim, 270
Flowers, Gennifer, 68–70
Flynt, Larry, 71
Fonda, Jane, 143, 312
Food and Drug Administration (FDA), 139, 203, 238–240
Forbes, Malcolm, 44
Ford, Gerald, 120, 122, 292, 339
Foreign correspondents, 55, 58–59
Fox Broadcasting Company, 7
Fox News Channel (FNC), 7, 167
Foxe, Fanne, 67
Framing, 115–116

Francis, Fred, 125
Frank, Reuven, 46, 145
Franken, Al, 313
Franks, Martin, 244
Freaks and Geeks, 22
Freedman, Tom, 63
Freedom Forum Media Studies Center, 55
Free Press, 169
Fricker, Mary, 62
Friday burial tactic, 121
Friedman, Paul, 48
Friendly, Fred, 98
Fritschler, A. Lee, 278
FTC. *See* Federal Trade Commission
Fund, John, 11

Gallagher, Maggie, 150
Gallup polls, 102
Garfield, Bob, 252
Garth, David, 325
Gartner, Michael, 62, 93
Gay rights, 45, 110
Gelb, Leslie, 149
Gelfand, Lou, 100–101
General Social Survey, 2
Gephardt, Dick, 329, 330
Geraldo, 111
Gerbrandt, Larry, 35
Gergen, David, 57, 120, 149
Gingrich, Newt, 312
Giuliani, Rudy, 52
Glaberson, William, 141
Gloucester County Times, 143
Godfather, The, 206
Goethe, 225
Goldenberg, Edie, 50
Goldwater, Barry, 326–327
Gonzalez, Elian, 90, 91
Good, Paul, 109
Good Housekeeping, 28
Goodman, Carl, 44
Goodman, Ellen, 105
Goodman, Thomas, 142
Goodman, Walter, 91, 92
Good Morning America, 120
Goodwill ads, 182–183, 256

Goodwill leaks, 148
Google, 30, 174, 188, 308, 309
Gorbachev, Mikhail, 150, 222
Gordon, Michael, 122
Gore, Al, 122, 132, 283, 292, 323, 335
Gore, Tipper, 328
Government. *See* Federal government; State government
Grace, J. Peter, 184
Graham, Donald, 117
Graham, Katherine, 108
Gramm, Phil, 47
Grant, Bob, 270
Grant, Hugh, 122
Green, Bill, 97, 124
Greene, Harold, 243
Greenfield, Jeff, 48, 325
Grossman, Lawrence, 263
Group pressure
    boycotts, 266–269, 277
    legal actions, 270–272
Grunwald, Mandy, 333

Hacker, George A., 273
Hagmann, Stu, 289
Haig, Alexander, 149
Halberstam, David, 33, 147
Hall, Melanie, 186
Halliday, Robert, 110
Hallmark Channel, 228
Hammer, M. C., 190
Hampton, Henry, 87
Hard Copy, 135
Harding, Warren G., 66
Hard news
    characteristics of, 42–53
    definition of, 41–42
Hardwood, Richard, 103
Hart, Gary, 68
Hartford Courant, 100, 177
Harwood, John, 323
Hatfield, Mark, 44
Hays, Wayne, 67
Health care reform debate (1994), 46–47

Health Insurance Association of America (HIAA), 334

Helms, Jesse, 104

Herbers, John, 146

Hernandez, Raymond, 17

Hersh, Seymour, 57, 107

Hess, Stephen, 73, 148

Hewitt, Don, 140

Heyward, Andrew, 96

High definition television (HDTV), 15, 16, 85

Hill, Lauryn, 32

Himmel, Martin, 186

Hine, Thomas, 201

Hispanics. *See* Latinos

Historical figures/events, 223–224

Holston, Noel, 109

Holtzman, Marc, 137

Home Box Office (HBO), 9

Homeless people, 43–44, 106–107

Home Shopping Network (HSN), 13

Honolulu Star Bulletin, 40, 253

Hope, Bob, 64

Horn, Wade, 150

Horton, Willie, 331, 332, 334, 339

Hoye, Rick, 80–82

Huffington, Arianna, 39

Hughes, Karen, 79

Humane Society, 185, 213

Human interest stories, 165

Hume, Ellen, 62

Humor, 209–210, 340

Hunger strike case study, 80–82

Hunt, Al, 69

Hussein, Saddam, 35, 36, 61, 109, 176, 319, 323

Hustler, 71

Hyde, Henry, 71

Hyperbole, 250

Hypocrisy, political, 67, 68, 70–71

Hyun, Montgomery K., 247

Idaho Statesman, 71

Identification, 4

with ad characters, 206–207

with advertisements, 190–192, 216

Ideological bias, 104–107

"If not...then not" ads, 231

"If...then" ads, 230–231

Image advertising, 182–183, 285

Imus in the Morning, 24

Inaccurate/incomplete reporting, 94–102

Industrial News Review, 140

Infomercials, 101, 184–185

InfoTrac College Edition, 37

Inside Edition, 89, 99

Inside Job: The Looting of America's Savings and Loans (Pizzo, Muolo, and Fricker), 62

Insinuation, 103–104

Institute for Contemporary Studies (ICS), 133

In-store ads, 187

Interactive technology, 12, 32–33, 262, 305–312

Interest groups, 275

Internal constraints, 61–66

Internet

advertising on, 174, 175, 179–180, 314–315

audience participation on, 208–209

blogs on, 306, 307, 316

censorship on, 31

citizen created ads on, 312–313

credibility of information on, 32, 264

downside of, 310–312

expressing opinions on, 261–264, 308

fundraising via, 307–308, 316

future of, 315

high-speed connections to, 30

illegal drug sales via, 239–240

inaccurate information on, 311

information access via, 306–310

interactivity and, 32–33

monitoring of ads on, 241

news sites on, 26, 29

overview of, 29–33

parody sites on, 308–310

political campaigns and, 129, 305–316

programming on, 30–32

regulation of, 316

search advertising on, 187–189

spam and, 175, 188–189

spin sites on, 126–127

sponsored links on, 188

television combined with, 179–180

traditional news media and, 312

transnational communication and, 30

webcams on, 31

Interpretation of news

discrepancies in, 103

ideological bias in, 104–107

language choices and, 103–104

self-censorship in, 107–110

unbalanced, 103–110

Interviews

advantages of, 42

editing of, 88–89

journalist use of, 72–73

Investigative reporting, 111

iPods, 202

Iraq War, 165

Isikoff, Michael, 38

Issue advocacy ads, 186, 296–298, 300–302

Jackson, Brooks, 135, 333

Jackson, Janet, 32, 134

Jackson, Michael, 123–124, 127, 207, 232

Jamieson, Rob, 210

Jennings, Peter, 93

Jewell, Kiri, 133

John Paul II, Pope, 130

Johnson, David, 262

Johnson, Lyndon, 33, 324, 325, 326–327, 344

Johnson, Robert L., 18

Johnston, David, 149

Jones, Christopher, 98

Jones, Paula, 38, 69, 70

Jordan, Michael, 190

Jordan, Vernon, 70

Journalists
  beat system for, 54–55, 57, 72,
    107
  breaches of neutrality by, 110
  checkbook journalism and, 112
  civic journalism and, 113
  credibility tests applied by,
    341–342
  direct intervention by, 110–113
  embedded, 60
  expertise of, 72–73
  objectivity of, 73–74, 78–79
  on-air, 92–93
  political campaigns and,
    283–284, 303–304,
    317–318, 341, 351
  social change influenced by, 111
  television appearances by, 57
Journal News, The, 340
Jump cuts, 88
Jurkowitz, Mark, 102
Juxtaposition, 229

Kaczynski, Ted, 117
Kalb, Bernard, 150–151
Kaplan, Harold, 333
Karl, Peter, 64
Karr, Timothy, 167
Kasindorf, Martin, 322
Kassirer, Jerome, 32
Keaton, Diane, 176
Kelley, Jack, 99
Kelly, Kathryn, 199
Kennedy, Caroline, 64
Kennedy, Edward, 64, 68
Kennedy, John, Jr., 64
Kennedy, John F., 67, 68, 142,
    292, 324, 344
Kerik, Bernard, 52–53
Kerrey, Bob, 323
Kerry, John, 12, 61, 63, 79, 131,
    167, 292, 295, 308, 312,
    320, 326, 328, 329, 335,
    338, 339, 346
Kim, Peter, 232
Kinsley, Michael, 68, 284
Klinghoffer, Leon, 112
Kondracke, Morton, 57

Koontz, Dean, 176
Koppel, Ted, 75, 91, 108
Koresh, David, 132
Kramer, Larry, 57
Krempasky, Mark, 306
Krieghbaum, Hillier, 76
Kristol, Irving, 86
Kucinich, Dennis, 326, 349
Kuhl, John "Randy", Jr., 328
Kuralt, Charles, 111
Kurtz, Howard, 129

Lang, Gladys Engel, 103
Lang, Kurt, 103
Language
  insinuation based on, 103–104
  media manipulation through,
    129–134
  political campaigns and,
    322–323, 326–328
  translation issues and, 227–228
Larry King Live, 6
*Late Bloomers: Coming of Age in
    Today's America* (Abrams), 288
Latinos
  Nielsen ratings and, 19–20
  television programming and,
    276–277
Lawrence, D. H., 224
Lazarus, Emma, 225
League of Women Voters, 293
Leaks, 147–149
Legal actions
  influencing media through,
    270–272
  news media as target of,
    144–145
Leggett, Dawn, 102
Lehman, John, 108
Lehrer, Jim, 8
Leno, Jay, 79, 339
Leo, John, 104
Letterman, David, 79
Letter-writing campaigns, 263, 275
Levi, Chandra, 319
Levine, Henry, 103
Lewinsky, Monica, 17, 33, 37,
    38–39, 147, 221, 312

Lewis, Charles, 166
Liberty Lobby, 145
Libya, 150–151
Lichter, S. Robert, 35, 93
*Lies and the Lying Liars That Tell
    Them* (Franken), 313
Limbaugh, Rush, 24
Lincoln, Abraham, 224, 324, 327
Liptak, Greg, 13
Live coverage
  breaking news and, 95–96
  manipulation of, 134–135
  preempted programming and,
    141–143
  taped coverage vs., 90
Livingston, Robert, 71
Local news, 165–166
Local people meters (LPMs), 20
Lodge, Henry Cabot, 324
Loftus, Jack, 21
Lois, George, 203
Los Angeles Times, 52, 55, 100,
    102, 104, 137, 267
*Louisville Courier-Journal and
    Times*, 100
Lowenstein, Allard K., 98
Low-power television (LPTV), 14
Lurkers, 310–311
Luttwak, Edward, 108
Lying, newsworthiness of, 69–71
Lynch, Jessica, 67

MacDougall, A. Kent, 137
MacNeil, Robert, 8, 42
MacNeil/Lehrer News Hour, 8, 42
Madison County Record, 100
Magazine Publishers of America, 29
Magazines
  advertising in, 28, 29
  foreign language versions of, 28
  overview of, 27–29
  ownership of, 27–28
  women's, 226
Making of the President series
    (White), 334
Malraux, André, 98
Mandela, Nelson, 120

Manipulation
  of access, 123–126
  of agendas, 129
  of deadlines, 119–123
  of language and visual symbols,
    129–134
  of live coverage, 134–135
  of news assignments, 127–128
  of prepackaged news, 135–140
Marcos, Ferdinand, 130
Marcos, Imelda, 130
Marcus, Ruth, 12
Margo, Matthew, 222, 243
Market-research organizations, 5
Mason, David, 316
Mass media
  advertising trends and, 178–180
  audience for, 6, 109–110
  consolidation trends in,
    156–169
  controlling controversy in, 271
  convergence of, 102
  fundamental assumptions
    about, 2–3
  government regulation of, 151,
    154–155, 159–162, 184,
    234–240
  group pressure on, 152–154,
    266–273
  history of, 4
  impact of, 118
  individual complaints against,
    261–266
  legislative pressure on, 277–279
  methods of influencing,
    261–281
  organizational pressures on,
    274–276
  political agendas and, 318–319
  presidential access to, 129
  prevalence of advertising in,
    174–175
  public opinion and, 102
  role of advertising in, 5–6
  social movements and,
    276–278
  social systems of, 5

  strategies for influencing,
    279–281
  See also News media
Masterpiece Theater, 8
Matalin, Mary, 263–264
Matson, Patricia, 272
Matthews, Chris, 57
McCain, John, 128, 131, 337
McCain-Feingold bill,
  294–295
McCarthy, Joseph, 76, 349
McChesney, Robert, 165
McCombs, Maxwell, 318
McConnell, Bill, 162
McGinniss, Joe, 319
McGovern, George, 341
McGrath, Judith, 288
McLuhan, Marshall, 3, 84
McManus, Michael, 150
McNamara, Robert, 149
McNulty, Henry, 100
McWethy, John, 96
Media
  elite, 128
  on-demand, 173
  See also Mass media
Media Access Project, 161, 167
Media consolidation, 156–169
  brief history of, 156–157
  corporate values and, 166–167
  FCC regulations on, 159–162
  free media content and,
    162–164
  human interest stories and, 165
  local news and, 165–166
  news media bias and, 167
  political power and, 168–169
  profit motive and, 158
  staff cuts and, 158, 162
  synergy and, 167–168
Media for Democracy, 167
Media outlet associations, 228
Mediated advertising, 178–180
Medicare news releases, 139
Meet the Press, 7, 39, 192,
  293, 329
Meetup.com, 313
Meisner, Mary Jo, 141

Mercer, Lucy, 318
Merritt, David, 113
Metaphors, campaign, 322–323
Meyers, Dee Dee, 149
Mfume, Kweisi, 277
Miami Herald, 26, 68
Michel, Bob, 47
Military pressure, 149
Miller, James, 237
Miller, William, 327
Miller, Zell, 164
Mills, Wilbur, 67
Milwaukee Journal Sentinel, 141
Minneapolis Star Tribune, 27, 100
Minorities
  group pressure from, 270–271,
    276–277
  Nielsen ratings and, 18, 19–20
  television programming and,
    276–278
Mitchell, George, 46
Mondale, Walter, 74, 104,
  292, 327
Moneyline, 6
Montgomery, Kathryn C., 271
Moon, Peter, 110
Moore, Rasheeda, 94
MorningCall, 310
Morton, Bruce, 79
Mothers Against Drunk Driving
  (MADD), 185
MoveOn.org, 244, 305,
  312–313, 321
Moynihan, Daniel Patrick, 76
MTV (Music Television), 9, 190,
  288–289
MTV News Unfiltered, 103
Multichannel, multipoint
  distribution service
  (MMDS), 14
Muolo, Paul, 62
Murdoch, Rupert, 7, 156,
  166, 169
Murphy bed, 200
Murray, Alan, 310
Myers, Matthew L., 247
Myers, Neil, 270
Myers, Richard, 149

Names
  for companies, 224
  for products, 200, 217–218
Narrative-dramatic structure, 76
Nashe, Carol, 24
Nation, The, 167
National Advertising Division
    (NAD), 240–241, 242,
    251, 265
National Advertising Review
    Board (NARB), 5, 241, 242,
    251, 265
National Annenberg Election
    Survey (NAES), 283, 284,
    313–314, 335, 338
National Association for the
    Advancement of Colored
    People (NAACP), 270,
    276–277
National Association of
    Broadcasters (NAB), 5,
    242–243, 332
National Association of Radio Talk
    Show Hosts, 24, 270
National Endowment for the Arts
    (NEA), 10
National Enquirer, 272
National Geographic, 227
National Heart Savers Association,
    268
Nationalistic associations,
    227–228
National Journal, 122
National Mortgage News, 62, 63
National News Council, 98
National Public Radio (NPR),
    22–23
National Rifle Association (NRA),
    320–321
National security, 147
National Security Agency
    (NSA), 108
National Thrift News, 101
Naughton, James, 33
NBC Nightly News, 61, 93, 111,
    112, 147
"Negative" ads, 282–283
Neighbor to Neighbor, 277

Nelson, Jack, 55, 73
Nessen, Ron, 149
Nestlé products boycott, 80–82
Network advertising standards,
    243–244
Network affiliation, 7
Neutrality, breaches of, 110
New Century Network, 26
New England Journal of Medicine,
    32, 101, 196
News
  access to, 54–55, 57, 123–126
  ads related to, 101, 196–197,
    320–321
  analysis of, 101–102, 114–118
  campaign commercials and,
    321–322
  characteristics of, 41–53
  concept of, 40–41
  controlled channels of, 126–127
  interpretation of, 103–110
  leaks of, 147–149
  personalization of, 42–45
  prepackaged, 135–140
  sources of, 124, 125, 126–127
  staged, 136–137
  themes in, 51–53
  twenty-four-hour, 33
  Web sites, 26, 29
News breaks/updates, 142
News Corporation, 156, 169
News coverage
  audience interest and, 54, 56
  breaking news and, 95–96,
    141–143
  CNN's influence on, 34–36
  competition for, 94–95,
    119–123, 128–129
  direct journalistic intervention
    in, 110–113
  dramatizing and sensationaliz-
    ing, 84–93
  economics of, 57–59
  embedded journalists and, 60
  external constraints on, 54–60
  fairness and balance in, 73–74
  government claims and,
    107–109

  inaccurate and incomplete,
    94–102
  internal constraints on, 61–66
  language and symbols used in,
    129–134
  live, 90, 134–135
  local news and, 165–166
  manipulation of, 65–66, 118
  objectivity in, 73–74, 76, 79
  offensive content and, 64–65
  persuasive quality of, 84–118
  political campaigns and,
    283–284, 317–331,
    347–348, 351
  pseudo-events and, 136–137,
    319, 320, 343
  public opinion and, 102
  reporter expertise in, 72–73
  tabloids and, 91
  technology and, 59
  time and space constraints on,
    59–60, 74–75
  unbalanced interpretation in,
    103–110
  visual events and, 61–63
  See also Television news coverage
Newsday, 52, 322
News feeds, 137–140, 141
News Flash (Anderson), 64
NewsHour with Jim Lehrer, 8, 75
News media
  agenda setting by, 318–319
  campaign attacks legitimized by,
    339–340
  changing influence of, 33–37
  characteristics of news in, 41–53
  commercial pressures on,
    140–145
  controlling access of, 318
  descriptions of political
    campaigns by, 322–323,
    326–328
  FCC's influence on, 151,
    154–155
  ideological bias in, 104–107
  Internet stories and, 312
  lawsuits against, 144–145
  manipulation of, 119–140

norms in, 66–71
political pressures on, 145–151
self-censorship of, 107–110
Newspaper Association of
    America, 105
Newspapers
    circulation figures for, 25,
        26–27
    commercial pressures on, 141
    competition among, 94
    fax services by, 177
    ombudsmen for, 100–101
    overview of, 25–27
    political cartoons and columns
        in, 339–340
    public opinion and, 102
    standards for advertising in, 252
    Web sites of, 26
    women as readers of, 105
News stories
    analysis of, 101–102, 114–118
    fiction and nonfiction in,
        76–77
    hiding the source of, 100
    length of, 74–75
    presentation of, 72–82
    structure of, 76, 96–97
Newsweek, 27, 38, 70, 169,
    249, 312
Newsworthiness
    of conflicts, 43–44, 45–47
    of currently prevalent issues,
        50–53
    of events or occurrences,
        48–49
    of news stories, 114
    of novel events, 49–50
    of people, 63–64
    of political statements, 132
    of the president, 146–147
    of violence, 47–48
New York Daily News, 97, 254
New Yorker, 98
New York Post, 38, 166
New York Times, 20, 40, 53, 54,
    55, 72, 99, 100, 102, 104,
    117, 135, 147–148,
    253–254, 311, 320

New York Times Magazine, 98
Nickelsburg, Robert, 36
Nielsen ratings, 15–21
    minority groups and, 18, 19–20
    people meters and, 17–18,
        20, 21
    share of audience and, 17
Nightline, 75, 84, 108–109
Nixon, Richard, 111, 120, 130,
    142, 292, 319, 324
Nontraditional advertising,
    186–189
Noriega, Manuel, 125, 197
Novel events, 49–50

Obama, Barack, 164
Objectivity in news coverage,
    73–74, 78–79
O'Brien, Conan, 79
O'Brien, Dick, 276
O'Connor, John J., 95
Oettinger, Mal, 151
Offensive news stories, 64–65
Ogilvy, David, 218
Oklahoma City bombing, 96
Okrent, Daniel, 100, 310, 311
Olympic Games, 183, 227
Ombudsmen, 100–101
On-demand media, 173
OnEarth magazine, 195
O'Neill, Tip, 57, 147
Online services. *See* Internet
Operation Cure.all, 32
Organizational pressures,
    274–276
Ortega, Daniel, 10
Outweek, 44
Ownership
    consolidation trends in,
        156–169
    magazine, 27–28
    quality issues and, 163, 164
    regulation of, 154–155,
        159–162

Packaging, product, 201
Paige, Rod, 150

Parent-Teacher Association
    (PTA), 274
Participation, 4
    argumentative forms for
        creating, 228–231
    of audiences in advertising,
        205–212, 216
Past associations, 222–228
Paxson Communications, 13
Pay-per-view (PPV), 12
PBS (Public Broadcasting Service),
    7–8, 183
Peller, Clara, 225
Pelton, Ronald, 108, 144
Pentagon Papers, 147
People for the Ethical Treatment of
    Animals (PETA), 177, 244
People magazine, 28
People meters, 17–18, 20, 21
Perdue, Frank, 202
Perot, Ross, 292, 294
Perry, Bob, 295
Persian Gulf War, 17, 35, 95
Personal Communications Service
    (PCS), 14
Personalization of news,
    42–48
Persuasion
    by advertising, 198, 214,
        217–221
    by direct journalistic
        intervention, 110–113
    by dramatizing and sensation-
        izing content, 84–93
    by inaccurate and incomplete
        reporting, 94–102
    by unbalanced interpretation,
        103–110
Petrelis, Michael, 44
Pettegrew, John, 288
Pew Center for the People and
    the Press, 7, 26, 28, 37, 56,
    158, 188
Pew Internet and American Life
    Project, 314, 315
Phelan, Richard, 327
Philadelphia Inquirer, 43, 45, 100,
    144, 240, 254

Phillip Morris Company, 144–145, 224, 272

Phishing, 311

Photo opportunities, 49

Phrases
appropriation of famous, 224–225
creation of memorable, 225
identified with social movements, 225–227

Pickens, T. Boone, 295

Pizzo, Stephen, 62

Playboy magazine, 209

Poindexter, John M., 151

Policy leaks, 148

Political action committees (PACs), 294, 329

Political campaigns
access to the media in, 283, 292–293
advertisements for, 21, 186, 256–257, 282–304, 314–315, 320–322, 347, 352
adwatches in, 330, 331–342
analysis of media in, 351–352
attack response/prevention in, 328–331, 334–342
blunders made in, 338–339
censorship of ads used in, 288–291
controlling the media in, 317–331
cost of air time in, 293
criteria for victory in, 302–303
debates in, 292–293, 296, 297, 298, 348–350
deceptive ads in, 336–337
endorsements in, 304
equal opportunity laws for, 292
financing of, 293–298, 304, 316
527 committees and, 295–296
free air time for, 283
image creation in, 285, 344, 351–352
Internet and, 129, 305–316
issue advocacy and, 186, 296–298, 300–302

journalist responsibility in, 283
language used for describing, 322–323
media use in, 284–288
news coverage of, 283, 317–331, 347–348, 351
objectives of, 298–299, 302
online fundraising for, 307–308
political parodies and, 308–310
product ads vs., 284, 287–288, 289, 299
pseudo-events in, 319, 320, 343
regulation of, 288–293, 316
slogans used in, 324–327
spending limits on, 293–298, 304
targeting the audience in, 285–286
television-based changes in, 342–346
unpaid coverage in, 303–304

Political candidates
image vs. issues of, 344
impact of television on, 342–346
judging the character of, 344–346
language used for describing, 323, 326–328
political attacks on, 328–342
selling of, 284, 319
sound bites of, 343

Political cartoons, 339–340

Political columns, 339–340

Political satire, 308–309

Politics
election news and, 51
hypocrisy and, 67, 68, 70–71
Internet and, 129, 305–316
media manipulation and, 119–129
news media pressures and, 145–151
sex scandals and, 38–39, 66–71
talk radio and, 24–25
technological advances and, 129

Politics and the Oval Office (ICS Report), 133

Poniewozik, James, 262

Pop-up ads, 174

Portable People Meters (PPMs), 21

Potter, David, 5–6

Powell, Colin, 133

Powers That Be, The (Halberstam), 147

Preemption
of entertainment programs, 141–143
of media attacks, 328

Prepackaged news, 135–140
news feeds as, 137–140, 141
prepared editorials as, 140
pseudo-events as, 136–137

Prepared editorials, 140

Presentation of news stories, 72–82

Presidency
candidate advertisements for, 296, 297, 298
debates for, 292–293, 296, 297, 298
media manipulation and, 120–121, 150, 319
newsworthiness of, 146–147
sex scandals and, 38–39, 66, 67, 69–71

Presidential Debates Commission, 293

Presley, Lisa Marie, 123

Press conference, 137

Press kits, 138–139

Press release, 137

Preston, Ivan, 246

Prime Time Live, 123

Print media. *See* Magazines; Newspapers

Producers, 5

Product advertisements
analysis of, 257
censorship of, 288
characteristics of, 180–181
creating associations in, 221–231
new styles in, 288–289
persuasion strategies used in, 214, 217–221

political advertisements vs., 284, 287–288, 289, 299
pseudo-claims and -surveys in, 218, 220
regulation of, 288
Product placement, 173–174
Product recognition, 198–202
naming and, 200
packaging and, 201
slogans and, 201–202
trademarks and, 198–200
Products
advertising regulations on, 247–251
comparison of, 218–220
differentiating, 203–205, 218–221
free samples of, 181
media outlets and, 228
naming, 200, 217–218
packaging for, 201
testing of, 220–221
Profit pressures, 158
Programming, 5, 259
Program on International Policy Attitudes (PIPA), 165
Project for Excellence in Journalism, 164, 168
PSAs. *See* Public service announcements
Pseudo-claims, 218
Pseudo-events
political campaigns and, 319, 320, 343
prepackaged news and, 136–137
Pseudo-news, 100
Pseudo-surveys, 220
Public Broadcasting Service. *See* PBS
Publicity, 117
Public opinion
news coverage and, 102
politics influenced by, 319, 345
Public Radio International (PRI), 23
Public service announcements (PSAs), 180, 185–186, 255

Public television, 7–8
Puffery in ads, 249–250
Pulitzer Prize, 97, 98, 107
Punitive damages, 144
Purdum, Todd S., 326
Pure attack ads, 296

Qaddafi, Muammar, 150, 151
Quayle, Dan, 24

Racial issues, 109–110
Radio
advertising on, 22, 174
audience ratings for, 23–24
broadcast companies for, 158
networks and stations, 22
overview of, 22–25
talk, 24–25
Raging Grannies, 275–276
Rather, Dan, 51, 58, 93, 112, 135, 149
Ratings
commercial pressures for, 142–143
radio, 23–24
television, 15–21, 179
Ray, Elizabeth, 67
Readers' advocates, 100–101
Reagan, Ronald, 74, 88, 90, 95, 108, 128, 146–147, 268, 292, 338–339, 346
Redgrave, Vanessa, 134
Redundancy in advertising, 212–214, 216
Reenactments, 91–92
Reeves, Rosser, 203
Regulations
advertising and, 184, 185, 234–255, 259
censorship and, 288–291
government agencies and, 5, 151, 154–155, 159–162, 184, 234–240
individual complaints and, 265, 266
Internet, 316
legal actions and, 270–272

mass media and, 5, 151, 184, 234–240
media consolidation and, 159–162
ownership rules and, 154–155, 159–162
political campaigns and, 288–293, 316
self-regulatory actions and, 5, 272–273
Reid, Alastair, 98
Reinarman, Craig, 103
Reno, Janet, 133
Repetition in advertising, 212–214, 216
Reporters. *See* Journalists
Reynolds, Patrick, 186
Rice, Donna, 68
Rich, Frank, 328
Richards, Ann, 328, 332
Ridder, Walter, 106
Rivlin, Doug, 296
R. J. Reynolds Company, 144, 192, 236, 247, 272, 278
Roberts, Chalmers, 148
Roberts, Cokie, 87
Robertson, Pat, 88
Rockefeller, Nelson, 278
Rocker, John, 134
Rogers, David, 326
Roll Call, 44
Rooney, Andy, 110
Rooney, Emily, 93
Roosevelt, Franklin Delano, 317–318, 327
Rosenthal, Abe, 98
Rumsfeld, Donald, 133, 148, 308
Rush Limbaugh Show, 22
Russert, Tim, 39
Ryan, Karen, 139

Sadat, Anwar, 111, 121
Safire, William, 131, 340
Salon, 71, 262
Saltzman, Joe, 289
Samples as ads, 181
San Francisco earthquake, 90–91
San Francisco Examiner, 57

San Jose Mercury News, 143
Satellite interviews, 129
Satellite radio, 23–24
Satellite television, 12–13
Saving Jessica Lynch, 67
Saving Private Ryan, 134
Sawyer, Diane, 123
Schaefer, Donald, 25
Schieffer, Bob, 59
Schiffman, Steve, 15
Schlesinger, Jacob M., 323
School violence, 48
Schudson, Michael, 76, 106, 108, 232
Schwartz, Tony, 186, 310
Schwartzman, Andrew Jay, 167
Schwarzenegger, Arnold, 267
Screen, television, 84–85
Search advertising, 187–189
Seelye, Katharine Q., 94
Seigel, Iona, 254
Seinfeld, Jerry, 221
Self-censorship, 107–110
Self-regulatory mechanisms, 5, 272–273
Selig, Bud, 134
Selling of the President, The (McGinniss), 319
Semel, Jane, 186
Sensationalizing news, 84–93
Service ads, 181, 256
700 Club, 88
Seventeen magazine, 28
Sex scandals, 38–39, 66–71
Shahid, Sam, 217
Shanahan, Eileen, 149
Share of audience, 17
Shaw, Bernard, 34
Shaw, David, 104
Sherrill, Robert, 169
Shoemaker, Pamela, 102
Shultz, George, 151
Sidle, Winant, 125
Silver, Josh, 169
Silverman, Peter, 64
Silverstein, Craig, 308
Simmons Market Research Bureau, 28, 29

Simon, David, 47
Simpson, O. J., 17, 110, 112
Sinclair Broadcasting Group (SBG), 7, 167
Sirius Satellite Radio, 23–24, 279
Situ-mercials, 174
60 Minutes, 69, 70, 78, 88–89, 110, 140, 143–144, 168, 261
Slice-of-life commercials, 321–322
Slogans
    political campaigns and, 324–327
    product recognition through, 201–202
    repetition of, 212, 214
Smith, Anthony, 145
Smith, Patricia, 99
Smith, Richard G., 51
Smoking and Politics (Fritschler), 278
Smyth, Margaret M., 157
Snow, John, 310
Social change, 111
Social movements
    phrases identified with, 225–227
    pressure on media from, 276–278
Social Security Administration (SSA), 314
Social systems, 5
Sokolof, Phil, 268
Soros, George, 295
Sound bites, 133, 343
SOUP (Students Opposing Unfair Practices), 271
Sources of news, 124, 125, 126–127
Space constraints, 59–60, 74, 75
Spam (Internet), 175, 188–189
Speakes, Larry, 150, 151
Spears, Britney, 64
Special effects, 87
Sponsored links, 188
Sports Illustrated, 28, 134
Sprague v. Walter (1990), 144
Staff cuts, 158, 162
Staged events, 136–137

Stanger, Jeffrey, 296
Starr, Kenneth, 38
State government
    creating legislative pressure through, 278–279
    media regulation and, 238–240
    See also Federal government
State of the News Media 2004 report, 168
Statute of limitations, 68–69
Steele, Bob, 149
Steinem, Gloria, 226
Stephanopolous, George, 149
Stereotypes in ads, 192–193
Stern, Carl, 149
Stern, Howard, 279
Stewart, Alison, 103
Stewart, Jim, 96
Stewart, Jon, 79
Stewart, Martha, 126–127
St. Louis Post Dispatch, 100
Stoner, J. B., 291
Stories. *See* News stories
Storm, Jonathan, 277
Strachan, Stan, 63
Subscription cancellations, 267
Sughrue, Karen, 57
Suicide coverage, 152–154
Sullivan, Louis, 192
Sulzberger, Arthur, 117
Surveys, 220
Sutherland, Kieffer, 173, 174
Swanson, Dorothy, 263
Sweeney, Dennis, 98
Swerdlow, Joel, 128
Swift Boat Veterans for Truth, 61, 295, 338
Syndex regulation, 184
Synergy, 167–168

Tabloid news programs, 91
Taboos, advertising, 252–255
Talk of the Nation, 23
Talk shows, radio, 24–25
Taped news coverage, 90–92
Target: Prime Time (Montgomery), 271

Target Market News, 20
Taxpayer Action Day, 270
Taylor, Paul, 68
Technology
  interactive, 12, 32–33, 262, 305–312
  news coverage and, 59
  politics and, 129, 305–316
  See also Internet
Telecommunications Act (1996), 25, 154
Telephone advertising, 178
Television
  advertising on, 243–244, 251–255
  clutter on, 76
  household demographics related to, 2
  Internet combined with, 179–180
  journalist credibility and, 57
  network contact information, 265
  overview of, 7–22
  political impact of, 342–346
  top broadcast companies, 157
Television audiences
  network shares of, 17
  Nielsen ratings of, 15–21
  targeting, 285–286
Television news coverage
  anchors and, 92–93
  archived footage used in, 61
  audience taste and, 109–110
  breaking news and, 95–96
  camera shots and, 85–87
  CNN's influence on, 34–36
  commercial pressures on, 140
  deadlines and, 94–95
  dramatizing and sensationalizing, 84–93
  economics of, 58
  editing material for, 88–90
  filmed and taped, 90–92
  inaccurate and incomplete, 94–102
  on-air reporters and, 92–93
  reenactments on, 91–92

screen size and, 84–85
special effects used in, 87
tabloids and, 91
unbalanced interpretation in, 103–110
visual events and, 61–63
Television stations
  advertising standards of, 243–244
  cable television and, 8–12
  government regulations on, 184
  low-power, 14
  network affiliation of, 7
  number in U.S., 7
Terrorism, 117
Tested products, 220–221
Themes
  campaign, 324–327
  news, 51–53
Third Voice software, 262
Thomas, Clarence, 150
Thomason, Harry, 263
Thompson, Lea, 111
Thune, John, 306
Thurmond, Strom, 150
Tiananmen Square demonstrations, 34
Tie-in ad campaigns, 176
Tillman, Pat, 65
Timberlake, Justin, 64, 134, 221
Time constraints, 59–60, 75, 94–95
Time magazine, 27, 28, 98, 113, 133, 134, 169
Times Mirror, 334
TiVo, 21, 32, 199
Tobacco company lawsuits, 144
Today show, 64, 108
Toffler, Alvin, 30
Toronto Globe, 110
Total Package, The (Hine), 201
Trade characters, 199–200, 206–207
Trademarks, 198–200
Translation issues, 227–228
Travolta, John, 44
Trial balloon leaks, 148

Tripp, Linda, 38
Trippi, Joe, 310, 315
Trolls, 310–311
Trudeau, Garry, 340
Truth to Tell: Tell It Early, Tell It All, Tell It Yourself (Davis), 121
TUBE (Termination of Unfair Broadcasting Exercises), 273
Tuchman, Gaye, 106
Tukich, Judith, 168
Turow, Joseph, 168
TV Guide, 93, 95, 243
Twenty-four-hour news, 33, 38–39
20/20, 66, 111, 135
Tyler, Robin, 310
Tyndall, Andrew, 48, 55

UHF television stations, 7
Unabomber, 117, 135–136
Unbalanced interpretation, 103–110
Unfair advertising, 237
Unique selling proposition, 203–204
United Paramount Network (UPN), 18
Unsolved Mysteries, 91
Upscale audiences, 6
U.S. News & World Report, 27, 28, 57, 104, 169, 206
U.S. Postal Service, 239
USA Today, 99, 148, 252

Valdez, Juan, 199
Values, advertising, 193–196
Vance, Cyrus, 149
Ventura, Jesse, 305
VHF television stations, 7
Videocassette recorders (VCRs), 2
Videocassettes, ads on, 177
Video news releases (VNRs), 138–139
Video-on-demand, 15
Viewers for Quality Television, 263
Village Voice, 98
Violent events, 47–48
Visual events, 61–63

Visual symbols, 129–134
Volkmer, Ingrid, 32
Voluntary compliance, 274
Voting, 299, 302

Wallace, Chris, 95
Wallace, George, 325
Wallace, Mike, 78, 88, 89
Wall Street Journal, 18, 29, 31, 38, 69, 133–134, 151, 188, 209, 252, 255, 306
Walters, Barbara, 96, 143
Wanamaker, John, 143
Wanta, Wayne, 102
War coverage, 60
Warner Brothers (WB), 18
Warren, David, 209
Washington, George, 223
Washingtonian magazine, 57
Washington Journalism Review, 99
Washington Post, 54, 62, 65, 67, 71, 89, 97, 100, 103, 104–105, 108, 117, 135, 151, 167
Washington Times, 151
Watergate investigation, 75

Watt, James, 340
Way Things Ought to Be, The (Limbaugh), 24
Webcams, 31
Web sites. *See* Internet
Weinberger, Harold, 236
Westerfield, Leland, 167
Whistle-blower leaks, 148
White, Teddy, 334
Whitman, Christine Todd, 25, 286
Wichita Eagle, 111, 113
Wicker, Tom, 49, 96, 105
Williams, Armstrong, 150
Williams, Clayton, 318, 328, 332
Wilson, Carnie, 31
Wilson, Steve, 89
Winfrey, Oprah, 64
Winter, Peter, 26
Wireless cable, 14
Wise, Bob, 264
Wise, David, 108
Wolff, Michael, 33
Wolfowitz, Paul, 108
Wolzien, Tom, 58
Women
    advertising directed at, 225–227, 228, 277

group pressure from, 277
    newspaper readers as, 105
Women's magazines, 226
Woodhull, Nancy, 105
Woods, Tiger, 221
Woodward, Bob, 74–75, 98, 111, 151, 168
Wooten, Jim, 84
World News Tonight, 87, 91, 93, 140
World's Wildest Police Videos, 99
World Wide Web. *See* Internet
Wu, Harry, 148

XM Satellite Radio, 23–24

Yahoo!, 175
Yeltsin, Boris, 122
Young, Elliot, 201
Young, Steve, 67

Zapple Doctrine, 293
Zeqiri, Fitim, 320
Zeta-Jones, Catherine, 221